INTERNATIONAL TRADE, DISTRIBUTION AND DEVELOPMENT

Empirical Studies of Trade Policies

World Scientific Studies in International Economics
(ISSN: 1793-3641)

Vol. 32 Asian Free Trade Agreements and WTO Compatibility: Goods, Services, Trade Facilitation and Economic Cooperation
by Shintaro Hamanaka (Asian Development Bank, Philippines)

Vol. 33 Economics and Politics of Trade Policy
by Douglas R Nelson (Tulane University, USA)

Vol. 34 Applied Trade Policy Modeling in 16 Countries: Insights and Impacts from World Bank CGE Based Projects
by David G Tarr (Consultant and Former Lead Economist, The World Bank, USA)

Vol. 35 The Floating World: Issues in International Trade Theory
by Wilfred J Ethier (University of Pennsylvania, USA)

Vol. 36 Trade Policy in Asia: Higher Education and Media Services
edited by Christopher Findlay (University of Adelaide, Australia), Hildegunn Kyvik Nordas (Organisation for Economic Co-operation and Development, France) & Gloria Pasadilla (APEC Secretariat, Singapore)

Vol. 37 The Path of World Trade Law in the 21st Century
by Steve Charnovitz (The George Washington University, USA)

Vol. 38 International Trade, Distribution and Development: Empirical Studies of Trade Policies
by Paul Brenton (The World Bank, USA)

Vol. 39 Evolving Patterns in Global Trade and Finance
by Sven W Arndt (Claremont McKenna College, USA)

Vol. 40 Shadow Banking Within and Across National Borders
edited by Stijn Claessens (International Monetary Fund, USA), Douglas Evanoff (Federal Reserve Bank of Chicago, USA), George Kaufman (Loyola University of Chicago, USA) & Luc Laeven (International Monetary Fund, USA)

The complete list of the published volumes in the series can be found at
http://www.worldscientific.com/series/wssie

38 World Scientific Studies in International Economics

INTERNATIONAL TRADE, DISTRIBUTION AND DEVELOPMENT

Empirical Studies of Trade Policies

Paul Brenton
The World Bank, USA

World Scientific

NEW JERSEY • LONDON • SINGAPORE • BEIJING • SHANGHAI • HONG KONG • TAIPEI • CHENNAI

Published by

World Scientific Publishing Co. Pte. Ltd.
5 Toh Tuck Link, Singapore 596224
USA office: 27 Warren Street, Suite 401-402, Hackensack, NJ 07601
UK office: 57 Shelton Street, Covent Garden, London WC2H 9HE

Library of Congress Cataloging-in-Publication Data
Brenton, Paul.
International trade, distribution and development : empirical studies of trade policies / Paul Brenton.
pages cm. -- (World Scientific studies in international economics ; 38)
Includes bibliographical references.
ISBN 978-9814603379 (hardcover : alk. paper)
1. Commercial policy. 2. International trade. I. Title.
HF1411.B743 2014
382'.3--dc23
2014020839

British Library Cataloguing-in-Publication Data
A catalogue record for this book is available from the British Library.

In-house Editor: Li Hongyan

Typeset by Stallion Press
Email: enquiries@stallionpress.com

To Rachel, Hannah and Jonathan

Acknowledgements

Several of the essays in this collection have also appeared in other publications in different versions. Below are the citations to the original sources with grateful acknowledgement of the publications and co-authors in each case.

Chapter 2. Quantifying the Economic Effects of Non-Tariff Barriers: The Case of UK Footwear (co-authored with Alan Winters), was originally published in *Kyklos*, Vol. 44, No. 1 (February 1991), pp. 71–92;

Chapter 3. Voluntary Export Restraints and Rationing: U.K. Leather Footwear Imports from Eastern Europe (co-authored with Alan Winters), was originally published in *Journal of International Economics*, Vol. 34, No. 3–4 (1993), pp. 289–308;

Chapter 4. Anti-Dumping Policies in the EU and Trade Diversion, was originally published in *European Journal of Political Economy*, Vol. 17 (2001), pp. 593–607;

Chapter 5. The Potential Trade Effects of an FTA between the EU and Russia (co-authored with Natalia Tourdyeva and John Whalley), was originally published in *Weltwirtschaftliches Archiv*, Vol. 133, No. 2 (June 1997), pp. 205–225;

Chapter 6. Technical Barriers to Trade in the European Union: Importance for Accession Countries (co-authored with John Sheehy and Marc Vancauteren), was originally published in *JCMS: Journal of Common Market Studies*, Vol. 39, No. 2 (June 2001), pp. 265–284;

Chapter 7. Economic Integration and FDI: An Empirical Analysis of Foreign Investment in the EU and in Central and Eastern Europe (co-authored with Francesca Di Mauro and Matthias Lücke), was originally published in *Empirica*, Vol. 26, No. 2 (1999), pp. 95–121;

Chapter 8. Assessing the Adjustment Implications of Trade Policy Changes Using the Tariff Reform Impact Simulation Tool (TRIST) (co-authored with Christian Saborowski, Cornelia Staritz, and Erik von Uexkull), was originally published in *World Trade Review*, Vol. 10, No. 2 (April 2011), pp. 249–276;

Chapter 9. Outsourcing and Low-Skilled Workers in the UK (co-authored with Robert Anderton), was originally published in *Bulletin of Economic Research*, Vol. 51, No. 4 (October 1999), pp. 267–286.

Chapter 10. What's Trade Got to Do with It? Relative Demand for Skills within Swedish Manufacturing (co-authored with Robert Anderton and Eva Oscarsson), was originally published in *Weltwirtschaftliches Archiv*, Vol. 138, No. 4 (December 2002), pp. 629–651;

Chapter 11. Trends in Disaggregated Import and Export Prices in Europe: Implications for the Trade and Wages Debate (co-authored with Anna Maria Pinna), was originally published in *Scottish Journal of Political Economy*, Vol. 49, No. 1 (February 2002), pp. 1–21;

Chapter 12. Adjustment to Globalisation: A Study of the Footwear Industry in Europe (co-authored with Anna Maria Pinna and Marc Vancauteren), was originally published in Robert Anderton, Paul Brenton, and John Whalley (eds.), *Globalisation and the Labour Market: Trade, Technology and Less-Skilled Workers in Europe and the United States*, London: Routledge, 2006, pp. 72–95;

Chapter 13. Integrating the Least Developed Countries into the World Trading System: The Current Impact of EU Preferences Under "Everything But Arms", was originally published in *Journal of World Trade*, Vol. 37, No. 3 (2003), pp. 623–646;

Chapter 14. Making EU Trade Agreements Work: The Role of Rules of Origin (co-authored with Miriam Manchin), was originally published in *The World Economy*, Vol. 26, No. 5 (May 2003), pp. 755–769;

Chapter 15. Watching More than the Discovery Channel to Diversify Exports (co-authored with Richard Newfarmer), was originally published in Richard Newfarmer, William Shaw, and Peter Walkenhorst (eds.), *Breaking into New Markets: Emerging Lessons for Export Diversification*, Washington, D.C.: World Bank, 2006, pp. 111–124;

Chapter 16. The Life and Death of Trade Flows: Understanding the Survival Rates of Developing-Country Exporters (co-authored with Martha Denisse Pierola and Erik von Uexkull), was originally published in Richard Newfarmer, William Shaw, and Peter Walkenhorst (eds.), *Breaking into New Markets: Emerging Lessons for Export Diversification*, Washington, D.C.: World Bank, 2006, pp. 127–144;

Chapter 17. What Explains the Low Survival Rate of Developing Country Export Flows? (co-authored with Christian Saborowski and Erik von Uexkull), was originally published in *The World Bank Economic Review*, Vol. 24, No. 3 (March 2010), pp. 474–499;

Chapter 18. Product specific technical assistance for exports — has it been effective? (co-authored with Erik von Uexkull), was originally published in *The Journal of International Trade & Economic Development: An International and Comparative Review*, Vol. 18, No. 2 (2009), pp. 235–254;

Chapter 19. Carbon Labelling and Low-Income Country Exports: Review of the Development Issues (co-authored with Gareth Edwards-Jones and Michael Friis Jensen), was originally published in *Development Policy Review*, Vol. 27, No. 3 (2009), pp. 243–267;

Contents

Chapter 1
Introduction and Overview

More than 25 years ago Robert Baldwin decried the "long-standing lack of interest by economists in trade policy matters". Has this changed? The assertion of this introductory chapter is that empirical analysis of international trade and trade policies is as important as ever. While the theoretical support for the benefits of open trade regimes has been strengthened over time, policymakers remain skeptical that trade liberalization is more than a zero sum game and fail to internalize that openness to trade brings significant benefits to an economy that exceed the costs of adjustment that may be incurred. The chapter then summarises the subsequent collection of papers which have sought to contribute to policy discussions around the impact of trade policies.

Sound empirical analysis is critical for informed and effective trade policy making. This is because trade policies typically have important distributional impacts; of particular concern is how they affect the poor and inequality. Trade policies fundamentally affect the incentives in an economy towards trade-related activities and the allocation of resources across sectors. They also affect long-term growth outcomes and hence the number of jobs in an economy as well as the capacity for certain groups within a country to participate in trade. But too often trade policy discussions and decisions are made by small groups within government using at best limited information on potential economic outcomes and overly influenced by politically well-connected interest groups.

It is important for policymakers and other trade policy stakeholders to have access to relevant and reliable information and analysis on the effects of different trade policies options. Empirical studies can be vital in bringing an important trade policy issue to the attention of policymakers. Certain stakeholders, especially the poor are often sorely under-represented in trade policy deliberations. This is particularly the case for women. In Africa and other regions, women are key participants in trade but their interests are rarely captured by trade officials and political leaders. Analysis that shows the constraints and harassment that women face in crossing borders and the costs these impose on their families can elevate discussion of this issue and lead to implementation of simple measures that can facilitate the activities for poor traders.[1]

The availability of data will typically frame the type of analysis that can be undertaken. Detailed and comprehensive data can be used to provide careful estimates of changes in welfare for the country as a whole and for key stakeholders. Nevertheless, policymakers can be confronted with important information even in the most challenging environments using rudimentary data. For example, Brulhart and Hoppe (2012) used simple survey methods to discover that if the residents of San Francisco faced the same charges pro rata in crossing the Bay Bridge to Oakland as do residents crossing the Congo River between Kinshasa and Brazzaville, a similar distance, they would pay more than $1200 for a return trip. As a result passenger traffic at this obvious focal point for cross-border trade between the two Congo's is around five times smaller than that between East and West Berlin in 1988 — well before the dismantling of the Wall!

Empirical trade analysis can provide some support to the process of policy formulation and to ensure that choices are based on better knowledge of underlying realities. Of course, politicians and officials may not act on this information. The assertion of Rodrik (1995) that "no other area of economics displays such a gap between what policymakers practice and what economists preach as does international trade", still has much relevance. This is leading to more emphasis on applied trade analysis that looks carefully at the political environment in which trade policy decisions are made and the incentives affecting the actions of officials. It is only by understanding the politics behind trade policy decisions that we will be able to ascertain why it is often very difficult politically to introduce trade measures that it is believed would raise national welfare and also why particular policies are implemented even though theory and empirical analysis suggest they will reduce national welfare.

The trade policy agenda has become much broader in recent decades reflecting key changes in the global economy and in regional trade and in the data and tools available to trade economists that can now be reflected in empirical trade analysis. First, we are no longer living in a bi-polar trading world dominated by trade between rich countries in Europe and North America and developing countries. The emergence of the BRICS and recent growth in Africa has led to a multi-polar trading world with expanding markets in different locations generating new trade opportunities. So the focus is no longer just on enhancing old established trading relationships but allowing new trade flows to new markets to flourish. In

[1] See for example, Brenton *et al.* (2012).

many countries in Africa, while important, the challenge is no longer how to add value to commodities and minerals being shipped to rich countries but also how to exploit new opportunities for trade in manufactures, in services as well as agriculture with neighbours and emerging countries in Asia and South America.

Second, the nature of global production and trade has changed throughout the latter part of the last century and has continued into this century. Production processes have been split up and different parts of production relocated around the world. This great unbundling (Baldwin, 2006) necessitates a reappraisal of the role of trade and investment policies and the need to look at competitiveness in a different way. No longer do countries just import and export finished products, for which all of the production stages were undertaken within a strict physical area. Countries now import to produce to be competitive in the domestic market and import to export to integrate into global value chains. At the same time this has exposed workers at all stages of the value-chain, sometimes in sectors or activities that were previously thought to be non-tradable, to competition from the global market. This, in turn, may entail important impacts on particular groups of workers, such as the low-skilled.

Third, is the increasing importance of trade in services. Services are key inputs into all other economic activities and access to a wide variety of efficiently produced services is critical to competitiveness and an additional important factor governing participation in global value chains. Just as one example, more than 83% of the selling price of fresh cut flowers exported from Ethiopia to Europe is accounted by services. Trade opening can be an effective mechanism for increasing competition in services sectors. Competition is essential in order to increase efficiency in the provision of services and improved access to lower priced and better quality services in the domestic market. Also exports of services offer new opportunities to diversify and create jobs. Tourism has been a traditional services export for many developing countries but new opportunities to export are being exploited in finance, telecommunications, and professional services as well as in IT-related services.

While the benefits of liberalizing trade in services are compelling, it can also bring risks and potential costs that may require appropriate government intervention. This arises because of the need to regulate many services sectors to overcome market failures giving rise to concerns about both efficiency and equity. For example, when imports of services through commercial presence are liberalized, it is important that foreign entry leads to more competition and improved service, not merely to a transfer of ownership from a state monopoly to a private one or from a national monopoly to a foreign one. Reforms to establish an appropriate regulatory framework may need to precede the opening up of a particular sector so as to set the rules of the game for new investors by establishing appropriate competition and pricing rules for foreign investors in services, defining service and access requirements when relevant, and ensuring adequate oversight and conflict resolution mechanisms. Hence, trade opening may need to be carefully coordinated with regulatory reform.

Fourth, is the changing climate for trade for developing countries, especially those in Africa. Many countries in Africa have grown strongly since 2000 and are enjoying a sustained period of economic growth. This has been driven by increasing exports of commodities and export diversification remains a key objective to drive job creation and more inclusive growth. It is being increasingly recognized that in addition to exploiting opportunities in global markets there is enormous potential to drive export diversification through regional trade integration (Brenton and Isik, 2012). Regional trade can bring staple foods from areas of surplus production across borders to growing urban markets and food deficit rural areas. With rising incomes in Africa there are emerging opportunities for cross-border trade in basic manufactures such as metal and plastic products that are costly to import from the global market. The potential for regional production chains to drive global exports of manufactures, such as those in East Asia, has yet to be exploited, and cross-border trade in services offers untapped opportunities for exports and better access for consumers and firms to services that are cheaper and provide a wider variety than those currently available.

However, Africa is not achieving its potential in regional trade as substantial barriers remain to the free movement of goods, services, people and capital across African borders with the consequence that it is often easier for Africa to trade with the rest of the world than it is with itself. Effective regional integration is of particular pertinence now. While uncertainty surrounds the global economy and stagnation is likely to continue in traditional markets in Europe and North America, enormous opportunities for cross-border trade within Africa in food products, basic manufactures and services remain unexploited. Regional integration in Africa could provide a much-needed source of export diversification away from minerals and hydrocarbons and a vital source of job creation.

But to deliver integrated regional markets that will attract investment in agro-processing, manufacturing and new services activities, policymakers have to move beyond simply signing agreements that reduce tariffs to drive a more holistic process to deeper regional integration. An approach is needed that: reforms policies that create non-tariff barriers; puts in place appropriate regulations that allow cross-border movement of services suppliers; delivers competitive regionally integrated services markets; and builds the institutions that are necessary to allow small producers and traders to access open regional markets. The appropriate metric for successful integration is not the extent of tariff preferences but rather reductions in the level of transaction costs that limit the capacity of Africans to move, invest in, and trade goods and services across their borders.

This is a different approach to one that proceeds within the straightjacket of specific sequential steps to integration: free trade area, customs union, common market, and economic and monetary union. For example, there are enormous opportunities from trade in services in Africa that are not dependent on a common external tariff being in place. Countries can work to improve trade facilitation at the border and to remove non-tariff barriers with neighbors while free trade agreements are being designed and implemented. Countries that are not members of the same free trade agreements can work to disseminate information on market prices to producers and traders.

Finally, it has become apparent that successful export growth and diversification require not only entry into exporting but survival and subsequent growth. Evidence suggests that developing countries have much lower survival rates for new exports than do rich countries. As a result, more attention needs to be given to the factors that undermine the survival of trade flows including uncertainty (of producers over costs, of buyers over the quality of product they will receive, of both buyers and sellers when contracts are weakly enforced) and lack of information that prevents effective matches between buyers and sellers in international markets. An interesting finding from initial analysis is the importance of learning-by-doing for export survival: experience with exporting the same product to other markets or different products to the same market are found to strongly increase the chance of export survival. A better understanding of such learning effects could substantially improve the effectiveness of export promotion strategies.

Section 1: Modelling the Impacts of Trade Barriers and FDI Flows

The first section of the volume contains a set of papers that have sought to apply appropriate empirical techniques to available data to contribute to dialogue around a range of trade policy issues. The first two chapters of this section focus on a detailed case study of trade policy barriers in the UK footwear sector undertaken under the leadership of Alan Winters in the late 1980s and early 1990s. At that time footwear was typical of a manufacturing sector in high income countries under pressure from imports from developing countries in East Asia for which policymakers granted additional protection beyond tariffs in the form of quantitative restrictions. The particular non-tariff barrier analysed in these papers is voluntary export restraints (VER), a quantitative restriction imposed by a government to limit the quantity of goods that can be exported to another country during a specified period of time. The reason governments impose VERs to limit their own exports is to appease the importing country and prevent the imposition of more draconian and less flexible trade barriers. VERs are typically implemented on a bilateral basis and became a popular form of protection during the 1980s, perhaps in part because they did not violate countries' agreements under the GATT at that time. However, during the Uruguay Round of trade negotiations members of the newly created WTO agreed not to implement any new VERs and to phase out any existing VERs over a four-year period.

These papers show the high economic costs for UK consumers of the quantitative trade barriers imposed on footwear imports. The papers address a key technical challenge with regard to a quantitative restriction (QR) on trade — it necessarily induces rationing. If suppliers raise their price in response to the restriction so that there is no excess demand then they are rationed, since they would like to sell more than they are permitted to at the new higher price. On the other hand, if prices do not rise fully to clear demand then it is consumers who are rationed, since at that price they would like to buy more than they are able to because of the restriction. Such rationing leads to additional welfare costs beyond those that will be normally estimated. These papers develop techniques for identifying when rationing of consumers was taking place.

Chapter 2 combines the analysis of demand side rationing with a simple supply side simulation model to assess the impact of the VERs on production and employment in the UK. The papers show clearly the high cost to UK consumers of quantitative restrictions on footwear imports in the 1970s and 1980s and the relatively small impacts on output and employment. It is concluded that the economic costs of these restrictions will have considerably exceeded the costs of adjustment that the sector would have borne in the absence of such trade protection.

The third chapter in this section looks at the impact of another controversial trade policy measure: anti-dumping duties. Empirical analysis is essential at all levels in the formulation and implementation of such measures to identify whether dumping has taken place and if so whether it is having a material impact on local firms and then whether anti-dumping measures are appropriate and, if applied, their impact.

The chapter starts from the fact that anti-dumping policies are discriminatory; not only do they discriminate against (some) firms in the targeted country in favour of domestic firms in the protecting country, they also discriminate between firms in countries named in the anti-dumping petition and firms in other exporting countries. In other words, anti-dumping measures may divert trade from named to non-named countries rather than create sales for domestic firms at the expense of the named countries. The chapter applies a simple trade model to detailed import data for products that have been subject to anti-dumping petitions in the EU. It allows for trade to be diverted away from named countries to both EU countries and non-EU countries. The analysis finds no evidence that anti-dumping measures applied in the EU led to a significant increase in imports from fellow EU members. There is however, evidence of a significant increase in the volume of imports from non-EU countries starting in the second year after the anti-dumping investigation is announced and coinciding with a substantial decline in imports from the countries subject to measures. This suggests that anti-dumping measures may not have been successful in protecting EU firms from imports from outside of the EU in products that have been subject to anti-dumping measures. The measures have primarily had the effect of diverting trade from one source in the rest of the world to another.

The next chapter, Chapter 5, written with Natalia Tourdyeva and John Whalley provides an analysis of the potential impacts of a free trade agreement between the EU and Russia. The analysis concentrates on the effects of the preferential removal of tariffs on mutual trade in a situation in which one of the countries has substantially higher tariffs than the other. Empirical analysis of preferential trade agreements plays a key role in their assessment because the standard theory shows the impact on economic welfare is ambiguous. There will be a positive impact if the removal of tariffs creates trade between the two countries as more efficient production from the partner is imported at the expense of less efficient domestic production. However, there will be a detrimental effect on welfare if trade is diverted from more efficient producers in the rest of the world (who still have to pay the tariff) to less efficient producers in the partner, but who benefit from duty-free access.

The chapter looks at the structure of imports in both the EU and the Russian markets to identify the potential for trade diversion. If imports from the potential partner are concentrated in the same products as imports from third countries then an agreement which gives preferential access to imports from the partner could lead to a shift in demand away from the other countries. The higher the external tariff (the larger the margin of preference) for the products which dominate imports from these countries the more likely significant trade diversion will occur. The analysis showed that in the EU market, products of particular interest to Russia, and which also form a large share of EU imports from other countries, tended to face very low duties. However, in the Russian market tariffs tend to be higher on the products that dominate imports from the EU and for which there are significant risks of diversion away from imports from countries selling similar products to Russia. As a general conclusion, countries with high tariffs should be wary of signing preferential trade agreements with countries that have very low tariffs.

The analysis in Chapter 5 focused solely on the economic impacts arising from the removal of tariffs. This remains very pertinent today for agreements such as those that the EU is negotiating with developing countries in Africa. Nevertheless, this collection of papers on trade reflects that regional integration is now quite different from that pursued in the 20th century. Old regionalism focused on the mutual exchange of tariff preferences and trade in goods. The new regionalism concerns a wide range of regulatory issues and is about the "trade-investment-services nexus" (Baldwin, 2011). In this context much greater attention is given to non-tariff barriers to trade (NTBs). One broad type of NTB is technical barriers to trade. These arise when an exporter has to alter their product to be able to access an overseas market due to differing requirements regarding issues such as health, safety, and consumer protection compared to home market or other export markets. Additional costs may also arise if a product has to undergo multiple testing to demonstrate compliance with regulations that differ across markets.

Removing technical barriers to trade (TBT) has become a key element of both global and regional trade negotiations. Chapter 6, written with John Sheehy and Marc Vancauteren, contains an analysis of the potential impacts of removing TBTs on Eastern European countries as part of their process of accession to the European Union. Many of the requirements are in place to achieve genuine public policy objectives and so cannot be removed like traditional trade policy instruments such as tariffs and quantitative restrictions. The chapter looks at the different mechanisms that can be used to remove the barriers caused by technical rules and regulations. In particular, it looks at mutual recognition and harmonization and how the application of these differs across sectors and products. It finds for example that TBTs are more important for certain accession countries than for others and that few showed a comparative advantage in sectors where detailed harmonization of regulations was required. Rather, these countries were specialized in exporting products subject to the so-called "new approach" whereby the common EU regulations specify minimum or essential requirements that are necessary to achieve the underlying public policy objective while allowing producers flexibility in designing their products to meet these requirements.

Chapter 7 develops the issue of deeper regional integration further by looking at the impact of trade agreements on foreign direct investment (FDI). Written with Francesca Di Mauro and Matthias Lücke, the chapter develops and applies a model similar to the established gravity model of bilateral trade flows to study bilateral stocks and flows of FDI in Europe. Specifically, the model is used to assess the extent to which deepening integration between the EU and the Central and Eastern

European countries would affect the existing stock of FDI. This is important since FDI can be an important source of capital but also of knowledge. The analysis also considers how flows of FDI from EU countries to Eastern European countries impact on the level of exports and imports between these countries. For the country which is providing the investment, growing FDI outflows can imply lower domestic output as exports to the partner country are replaced by local production ("horizontal" FDI). Such FDI may enable firms in the source country to produce overseas with lower labour costs and then substitute through imports goods that were previously produced at home ("vertical" FDI). This implies that FDI flows will lead to some structural changes in the source country with the attending adjustment costs. Finally, the model is used to assess whether regional integration and increasing flows of FDI to Eastern Europe affected the magnitude of FDI going to other European countries.

Careful analysis of the adjustment impacts of trade reform is essential to policymakers in developing countries as they seek to improve the structure of incentives within an outward looking trade and competitiveness strategy. The need to adjust will arise in a number of areas. An immediate concern, especially in low-income countries, is the impact on tax revenues. Tariffs are typically an important source of tax revenues in low-income countries, often reflecting the weakness of the domestic tax base and of other tax instruments. In addition, changes in output in different sectors and associated impacts on employment are likely to be an important aspect of the political economy driving support and opposition to trade reform. Further, trade reform entails changes in prices and an important consideration is how these will affect households, especially the poorest. A good understanding of the potential adjustment implications of trade reform can contribute to the design of better trade reform strategies and to the discussion and implementation of policies that can reduce the impact of adjustment, especially when the costs are concentrated upon particular groups in society. The latter is of particular importance in countries that lack social safety nets with broad coverage.

Chapter 8 written with Christian Saborowski, Cornelia Staritz and Erik von Uexkull describes a recently developed spreadsheet tool called TRIST (Tariff Reform Impact Simulation Tool) that has been designed to provide better estimates of the impact of changes in tariffs on government revenues, imports, protection and prices. The key features of the model are that it uses detailed data on actual revenues collected from trade whereas other tools use hypothetical revenues from applying duty rates on paper. It also includes all taxes levied on trade, not just tariffs, and so shows the change in trade tax revenues, which is more relevant than the change in tariff revenues alone. Unlike other tools it does not require any proprietary software, programming skills or internet access. It is free and easy to use, transparent, with a simple underlying trade model, and flexible, in that it can quickly address different trade policy scenarios. The model can be downloaded from http://go.worldbank.org/LWNQ4LUDF0. This chapter provides a description of the TRIST tool and provides some examples of its use.

Section 2: Trade, Wages and Adjustment

While more open trade brings significant economic benefits it can have important distributional consequences. An important concern has been the relative worsening of the economic fortunes of low-skilled workers in developed countries and the consequent increase in inequality in Western Europe and North America. Empirical studies based upon the traditional neoclassical trade theory, which identifies trade and technology as the potential causes of inequality have tended to conclude that the increase in imports from low-wage countries has played, at most, a relatively minor role in increasing inequality.

Traditional trade theories primarily explain movements in relative wages across industries, whereas industrialised countries have experienced a dramatic fall in the relative wages and employment of unskilled workers within sectors. Indeed, the observed shift away from the use of unskilled labour within all industries is in contradiction with trade being the principal cause of rising inequality in the traditional model. If trade with low-wage countries has reduced the relative wage of unskilled labour then firms within all sectors have an incentive to use relatively more of this now cheaper factor. Consequently, there should be an increase in the relative use of unskilled labour in all sectors. This has led a number of authors to conclude by deduction that factor-biased technological change must be the principal cause of the observed shift away from the use of unskilled labour.

However, as we noted above, a major change in the global economy over the past 40 years has been the splitting up of production chains and the relocation of parts of the overall process to different locations around the world. This 'outsourcing' of activities from developed to developing countries can provide an explanation of how globalization may push down the relative wages and employment of unskilled workers within industries in rich countries. Outsourcing occurs where firms take advantage of both low wage costs in relatively labour abundant countries and modern production techniques — whereby the process of manufacturing a product can be broken down, or fragmented, into a number of discrete activities — and move the low-skill-intensive parts of production abroad, but continue to carry out the high-skill-intensive activities themselves. Once the low-skill activities have been performed, the goods are then imported back from the low-wage countries and either used as intermediate inputs or sold as finished goods. Hence, trade with low-wage countries via this route will shift demand away from less-skilled towards skilled workers in advanced industrialized countries, and put downward pressure on the relative wages and employment of low-skilled workers within industries.

Empirical work on this issue is presented in Chapter 9 on the UK written with Bob Anderton and on Sweden in Chapter 10, written with Anderton and Eva Oscarsson. These studies econometrically estimate the wage bill and employment shares of low-skill workers at the industry level and includes a measure of imports from low wage countries as a proxy variable for outsourcing. Previous studies had used the share of imports in total consumption from all countries, which assumes outsourcing of production to advanced industrialized countries as well as to low-wage countries. It is unlikely firms in industrialized countries would outsource low-skill-intensive activities to other industrialized countries.

The study of the UK utilized data for eleven sectors within the textiles industry (usually defined as low-skill-intensive) and the non-electrical machinery industry (high-skill-intensive). The key finding of this research is that while total imports from all countries were not important, imports specifically from low-wage countries were found to have a statistically significant positive influence on the wage bill share of high skill workers within the sectors analysed. In other words, increasing import penetration from low-wage countries reduced the share of total wages going to low-skill workers and thereby increased inequality. Further analysis showed that the parameter with regard to import penetration from low-wage countries was much smaller for the higher-skill non-electrical machinery sectors relative to the low-skill-intensive textiles sectors, suggesting that the higher-skill-intensive UK industry has been far less prone to outsourcing.

Sweden is an interesting and contrasting case since it is a much smaller and more open economy than the UK and has fundamentally different labour market policies. Nevertheless, Sweden also experienced a shift away from unskilled towards skilled workers within the manufacturing sector. However, in Sweden there was a larger proportionate change in the employment share compared to the wage-bill share of skilled workers. This suggests that the increase in inequality between skilled and unskilled worker in Sweden was realized more through increasing disparities in employment opportunities than in greater differentials in wages. Structural labour market rigidities in Sweden may explain why most of the adjustment took place on the employment side, while relative wages remained stable. For example, the Swedish labour market is characterized by 'strong' trade unions and wage bargaining in Sweden was highly centralized during a considerable part of the sample period.

Accordingly, the econometric approach in Chapter 10 focused on the employment share of skilled workers. Import penetration, measured in volume terms or the relative price of imports, was found to have a significant and positive impact on the employment share of skilled workers but again only for imports from low-wage countries. Another interesting result was that the impact of trade with low-wage countries on Swedish inequality was larger for high-skill sectors than for low-skill sectors, in contrast to the analysis for the UK. This may reflect that when outsourcing requires foreign direct investment in low-wage countries — involving the production of specific components/products possibly requiring supervision and technical expertise from the investing company — then this may only be feasible for high-skill/high-profit firms. Also, the scope for outsourcing depends upon the degree to which production of the final product can be fragmented into discreet stages with substantially different factor intensity ratios. This will be determined by technological conditions in the industry, which may be more conducive to outsourcing in high-tech sectors. This may have been the case in Sweden.

Chapter 11, written with Anna Maria Pinna, contributes to the discussions over the impact of trade on wages by looking at movements in the prices of traded goods. It is changes in the price of low-skilled labour intensive goods relative to the price of skilled-labour intensive products that lie at the heart of traditional economic explanations of the impact of globalisation on domestic labour markets. Existing empirical price studies had found no clear evidence of a decline in the domestic prices of unskilled-labour intensive products relative to those of skilled intensive products (Slaughter, 1998). Producer prices of unskilled labour-intensive goods did not appear to fall by more than those of skilled-labour-intensive products in neither the '70s nor the '80s.

This chapter explores whether this reflects that sectoral producer price indices are unable to capture the impacts of trade because they are too aggregated. These indices will be biased if there is heterogeneity of goods within sectors and changes in quality over time, which could be correlated with the skill intensity of production. If sub-sectors within industries differ in their use of skilled and unskilled labour, then more open trade may reduce the prices of some goods but raise the prices of others, leaving the industry aggregate price unchanged.

To address these concerns the chapter looks directly at movements in import and export unit values, which are commonly used to proxy import and export prices, within two skilled-intensive sectors (electrical and non-electrical machinery) and three key unskilled-intensive sectors (textiles, clothing and footwear) using data at the most detailed (tariff-line) level for five European countries (UK, France, Germany, Belgium-Luxembourg and Italy). A key feature of the analysis is allowance for quality upgrading within sectors distinguishing pure changes in prices from changes in the bundle of goods imported within the sector.

The analysis finds evidence that during the 1980s, but not the 1970s, the price of unskilled intensive products fell relative to that of skilled intensive goods. Relative price declines were particularly strong for imports of textiles and clothing from Asia. The substantial movements in relative prices found in this chapter are consistent with trade having played a significant role in affecting the fortunes of unskilled workers in Europe.

What does the finding that trade with low-wage countries has had an adverse effect on the distribution of wages and employment within manufacturing sectors imply for economic policy? An impulsive reaction might aim at stopping those factors that are perceived as contributing to inequality and social exclusion by restricting imports. However, given the array of domestic policies available in modern industrial countries, it is clear that intervention that constrains trade will be one of the least effective mechanisms. In essence, trade brings benefits as well as difficulties and those benefits are expected to significantly exceed any costs that arise. Thus, more effective policies will be those which tackle the problems of inequality affecting unskilled workers without removing the gains from trade. In other words, policy should seek to address as directly as possible the problems of social exclusion without making matters worse elsewhere, as would happen if trade barriers were raised.

The final chapter in this section, written with Mark Vancauteren and Anna Maria Pinna, provides a specific case study example of the adjustment implications of globalization. The focus is on the footwear sector in Europe, a typical low skill-intensive manufacturing sector where comparative advantage decisively shifted to low-wage labour abundant countries in the 1980s. The study finds that adjustment to import competition varied across European countries. In Germany, production was relocated overseas through the outsourcing of parts of the production process. In Italy, on the other hand, domestic output and employment levels were maintained as export intensity increased at the same time as imports rose. Thus, while globalization leads to additional competition in the domestic market from imports it also provides increased opportunities for sales overseas.

The chapter also shows that unskilled or manual labour are often far from homogeneous with significant differences in wages paid to certain types of workers within this category. In the footwear sector, the study found that manual workers with the highest level of skills and the highest wages experienced longer periods of unemployment than the least skilled footwear workers. Hence, retraining schemes for unemployed manual workers may need to be better targeted to reflect that certain types of manual workers have less flexibility in adjusting to globalization and may incur higher costs of adjustment.

Section 3: Trade and Development

The papers in the section focus on trade and development and in particular the integration of African countries into regional markets and the global economy. Developing countries typically face substantial constraints in participating in trade due to weak infrastructure (including energy and transportation) and poor business climate. As a result exporters from developing countries are handicapped when competing in overseas markets. In response, developed countries have provided preferential access for products originating from developing countries. These preferences take the form of reduced tariffs relative to the most-favoured nation rate that is levied on imports from other countries. Trade preferences in OECD countries are expected to encourage the importation of products from developing countries, raising the export earnings of these countries, stimulating investment and growth. Initial preference schemes were introduced in the 1970s under the "Generalised System of Tariff Preferences" (GSP).

The first two papers in this section look at the impact of trade preferences offered by the EU including the enhanced preferences for least developed countries under the Everything but Arms program. Chapter 12 shows that for many developing countries, especially those in Africa, preferences in the EU are of little relevance since the products which dominate exports by these countries to the EU typically face a zero MFN tariff and so no preference can be granted. This reflects that exports of many African countries to the EU are dominated by a small number of minerals and raw agricultural products such as cocoa, coffee and tea. Export Diversification is crucial for sustained export growth in Africa. Developing countries that have grown strongly for sustained periods have used trade and the global economy as a driver of growth. Typically, export growth rates in excess of 10% are needed to propel GDP growth of 7%, the level necessary to double incomes in 10 years. At the same time few countries have been able to consistently grow exports at such rates without diversifying beyond a narrow range of commodity-based exports. The lack of export diversification reflects fundamental problems of competitiveness that require action in 3 key areas (i) getting domestic incentives right so that there is no bias against exports (ii) improving access to, and reducing the cost of, key backbone services, such as energy, transport, finance and telecommunication (iii) providing effective export support institutions, such as, export promotion agencies and market oriented standards bureaus.

The chapter discusses how the impact of trade preference schemes is determined by their design. This is developed further in the next chapter, Chapter 13, written with Miriam Manchin, which looks at a key factor that affects the nature of trade preference schemes: the rules of origin. On the one hand, these arcane aspects of trade agreements have received little attention. Indeed, one policymaker has argued that "Rules of Origin are very, very complex. You don't want to know about them. They are terrible things to deal with."[2] On the other hand, it is essential for analysis to bring light on the role of these rules in influencing the development impacts of trade preference schemes.

Rules of origin are necessary to ensure that only products from eligible countries receive trade preferences. Rules of origin are applied to prevent trade deflection, or simple transshipment, whereby products from non-participating countries are redirected through a free trade partner to avoid the payment of customs duties. However, rules of origin can be manipulated to achieve other objectives, such as protecting domestic producers of intermediate goods. In general, as rules of origin become more technical and more complex they offer scope for the participation of industries in setting restrictive rules of origin (Hoekman, 1993).

Restrictive rules of origin, those that go beyond what is necessary to prevent trade deflection, raise the costs of supplying the markets of preferential partners by requiring changes in production which lead to the use of higher cost inputs and through the expenses which are incurred in proving conformity with the rules. These costs will constrain market access relative to what is promised on paper in the trade agreement. The rules of origin are, therefore, a key element determining the magnitude of the economic benefits that accrue from preferential trade agreements and who gets them.

The chapter on rules of origin looks at information on the extent to which EU trade agreements deliver improved market access, in terms of the amount of a beneficiary country's exports to the EU which are actually granted favourable treatment. It shows that actual market access in practice is much less than on paper. Particular attention is given to clothing products, since these are often held to be a labour intensive manufacture into which developing countries can diversify. However, much of the preferences that appear on paper for these products have been going unrequested often because producers in exporting countries cannot satisfy the rule of origin, which typically precludes the use of imported fabrics. Since many developing countries do not have a competitive fabric producing sector this is binding constraint on the export of clothing products under trade preferences. One of the key features of AGOA, and of its initial success in facilitating exports of clothing products from Africa was the so-called 3rd country fabric rule of origin which allowed the competitive sourcing of fabrics from any supplier. This is

[2]Canadian Finance Minister, Hon. Michael H. Wilson, February 12, 1992, quoted in in Clark-Flavell (1995).

an approach that the EU has now moved towards in its Economic Partnership negotiations with Africa countries.

The subsequent three chapters in this section are also concerned with the issue of export diversification of developing countries. Chapter 14, written with Richard Newfarmer, builds on work by Hausmann and Rodrik (2003) which suggests that lack of export diversification and growth in developing countries is the result of under-investment in the discovery of new export products. They contend that this occurs because firms that would invest and move first into export markets fear that their initially high returns would be eroded by subsequent new entry. This ease of entry into exporting is seen as the key factor impeding diversification.

Chapter 14 starts by suggesting a broader approach to the development and growth of new exports comprised of four phases analogous to the product cycle: a discovery phase in which firms identify profitable activities in an overseas market or markets and launch a new export product; this is followed by a rapid growth phase in which successful firms expand into existing and new foreign markets; there is then a maturation phase in which products experience widespread competition and successful firms focus on maintaining market share by improving quality and productivity; finally there is a declining phase in which successful firms exploit existing products for rents that are invested in new activities.

This chapter examines the issue of whether the discovery process should be the primary concern of policymakers wishing to promote export diversification relative to other parts other parts of the export cycle? The chapter starts by decomposing the export performance of a wide range of developing countries into changes at the intensive (existing export flows) and extensive (new export flows) margins. It finds that overall export growth for developing countries was primarily driven by the growth of exports of existing products to existing markets in the 1995–2004 period under study. The main distinction between poorly and strongly performing countries was the higher death rate of products for the former leading to overall growth at the intensive margin being much slower. At the extensive margin the analysis finds that growth was driven primarily by selling into new geographic markets during the acceleration and maturation phases rather than by introduction of new products in the discovery phase. The conclusion from this is that governments should look for market failures that are constraining export growth beyond just the discovery phase.

The chapter also looks at the performance of countries in exploiting potential demand among importing countries for its current export portfolio by means of an index of export market penetration (IEXP). This suggests that low income countries are typically less effective in exploiting available opportunities to sell the products that they produce in overseas markets than are richer countries. As an example,

Kenya (income per head of $480 in 2004) exported 2148 products (about three-quarters of the number exported by Korea), which generated 6789 bilateral export flows. While Korea (income per head of $14135), exported 2930 products, but these generated almost 67000 bilateral flows. The IEXP shows that Kenya was exploiting less than 4 percent of the potential bilateral flows for the products that it exported compared to Korea which was exploiting almost 30 percent of the available export opportunities.

Thus, successful export growth and diversification require not only entry into exporting but survival and subsequent growth. Initial evidence suggests that developing countries have much lower survival rates for new exports than do rich countries. The next two chapters concentrate on seeking to understand factors that may explain the low export survival rate in developing countries. Chapter 15, written with Denisse Pierola and Erik von Uexkull, builds on the seminal paper on this issue by Besedes and Prusa (2006). The chapter starts by noting the preponderance of zeros in matrices of bilateral trade flows and suggests that this raises the need to understand the factors that encourage the initiation of trade flows (entry into the market) and the disappearance of flows (exit). Recent trade theory and empirical work has devoted considerable analysis to the determinants of entry, but less has been written on exit.

The chapter investigates a detailed set of bilateral trade data and confirms that survival rates for developing countries tend to be much lower than those of developed countries. It is also apparent that the longer the trade flow has existed the higher are the chances of survival to the next year. The chapter then digs a little deeper by exploring factors that undermine the survival of trade flows and in particular uncertainty (of producers over costs, of buyers over the quality of product they will receive, of both buyers and sellers when contracts are weakly enforced) and lack of information that prevents effective matches between buyers and sellers in international markets.

The chapter then discusses the estimates from a statistical analysis of the determinants of hazard rates, the probability that an existing trade flow will disappear in the next period. This analysis strongly suggests that the larger the initial export flow the lower the hazard rate. The results also suggest that survival is harder in more distant markets. Variables included to capture information and search costs and the ease of finding well matched buyers or sellers all appear to have a significant impact on the chances of survival. In addition, trading with a neighbor, having a common language and colonial ties all increase the chances of survival. It is also apparent that exchange rate volatility is important in explaining differences in survival of export flows and hence the importance of governments in maintaining stable and competitive exchange rates.

The statistical analysis of hazard rates of bilateral trade flows is developed further in Chapter 16, co-authored with Christian Saborwski and Erik von Uexkull. The chapter assesses the standard Cox continuous time proportional hazards model that has been the workhorse of empirical analysis of the determinants of the hazard rates of export flows. The analysis shows how this model is mis-specified in the presence of unobserved heterogeneity, a strong possibility in this context from the unobserved quality of the management of the underlying exporting firms. Using a broad dataset of bilateral export flows with a high level of product and exporter-country detail the chapter formally tests, and rejects, the assumption of proportional hazards that underlies the standard model. With unobserved individual heterogeneity the likely cause of the failure of the proportional hazards assumption, a different model is estimated, the Prentice–Gloeckler model augmented by a gamma mixture distribution, to summarize unobserved individual heterogeneity. The results show that allowing for unobserved heterogeneity is indeed important.

The empirical results confirm the significance of a range of product and country specific factors in determining the survival of export flows. From a policy perspective, an interesting finding is the importance of learning-by-doing for export survival: experience with exporting the same product to other markets or different products to the same market are found to strongly increase the chance of export survival. A better understanding of such learning effects could substantially improve the effectiveness of export promotion strategies.

Linked to this, the next chapter, Chapter 17, written with Erik von Uexkull, looks at the impact of donor-funded projects that have sought to increase exports from developing countries. In the context of the effectiveness of "aid for trade" the chapter provides a statistical analysis of the impact of product specific export development programs. Previous evaluations of aid for trade programs had looked for broad impacts and generally found disappointing results. By focusing on interventions that targeted a specific product, this study has the advantage of assessing a clear measurable outcome indicator: exports of that product.

As with all empirical studies of the impact of a specific policy change, the challenge is in defining the alternative situation or counterfactual to which actual performance can be compared. Simply comparing exports before and after the program is not sufficient. It is necessary to identify what would have happened to the exports of those receiving support in the absence of this technical assistance. A typical approach is to use a difference in differences approach and assume that if the policy intervention did not take place exports of the country would increase at the same rate as the average of a group of comparator countries. In other words, the assessment of impact is made by comparing the before and after performance (difference) of exports of the product from the country concerned with the average export performance (difference) of that product in the comparator countries.

A key issue is how to select the countries that have not received support for development of exports of the particular product — the "without treatment" control group. This study uses two approaches. First, it compares the country with the export development program to all other developing countries in the world that export the product concerned. However, there is a potential source of bias in the results. This arises because the decision to implement an export development program may be influenced by other factors that determine export performance. To address this, a second approach selects the countries of the control group by pairing the country which receives support for a specific export product with other countries that exhibit similar observable characteristics. The study estimates the probability of a country to export the good in question based on a set of general determinants of a country's export portfolio such as its level of development, its factor endowments and its climate conditions. Then, each country that has an export development program for the specific product is paired with the country that is closest to it in terms of the predicted likelihood to export that product.

The main results from applying the first standard differences in differences approach to a wide range of instances of support from OECD countries to export development programs of developing countries are that exports have on many occasions increased significantly under export development programs and that much stronger performance is found for programs delivered to industries with initially high export levels. However, the study finds substantial differences between the results from this approach and that based on the matching of exporters for each product. This suggests that the export growth observed after the implementation of an export program may often not be a direct result of the program, but rather reflect that sectors with strong prospects for future export growth have been selected. This raises the concern that technical assistance may be being channeled to sectors that would have prospered anyway and that the funds could have been better used to address constraints in sectors that lag behind. Overall, this chapter clearly demonstrates the importance of defining carefully the counterfactual situation when assessing the impact of specific policy intervention to support trade.

The final chapter in the book, written with Gareth Edwards-Jones and Michael Friis Jensen, looks at a policy response to climate change that would potentially have a substantial impact on the exports of developing countries: carbon labelling. This involves measuring greenhouse gas emissions from the production and transportation of products or services and conveying that information to consumers and those making sourcing decisions within companies. The chapter demonstrates the challenges that carbon-labelling schemes must successfully overcome to be able to reflect the complexity of carbon emissions along international supply chains. It also shows that that there will be opportunities to reduce carbon emissions at many points along the supply chain. However, the common perception is that transport is likely to be the most important source of carbon emissions which leads to simple but politically attractive schemes such as food miles and buy-local campaigns. The chapter shows how emissions from transport can be more than offset by efficiencies in other stages of production and distribution. Schemes that focus only on transport and the location of production therefore do not capture the complexity of carbon emissions, they will distort trade and may even increase emissions.

This is particularly important for low-income developing countries since in general they tend to have a more favourable climate and use technologies that are less carbon-intensive than richer countries. The chapter discusses issues that must be addressed in the design and implementation of carbon-labelling schemes if the interests of low-income countries are to be properly reflected. Low-income countries have many potential advantages as low emission sources of products but these exports will not be realized if they are unable to measure and verify their emissions in a cost-effective way. Effective participation in carbon-labelled trade will require the infrastructure and institutions that provide the necessary measurement and certification mechanisms that are often lacking in low-income countries.

References

Baldwin, Richard (2006). "Globalisation: The great unbundling(s)", Chapter 1, in Globalisation challenges for Europe, Secretariat of the Economic Council, Finnish Prime Minister's Office, Helsinki.

Baldwin, Richard (2011). "21st Century Regionalism: Filling the gap between 21st century trade and 20th century trade rules", Staff Working Paper ERSD-2011-08, WTO, Geneva.

Baldwin, Robert (1988). *Trade Policy Issues and Empirical Analysis*, NBER and University of Chicago Press, Chicago.

Besedes, T. and T. Prusa (2006). "Ins, Outs and the Duration of Trade", *Canadian Journal of Economics*, 104, 635–54.

Brenton, Paul; Celestin Bashinge Bucekuderhwa; Caroline Hossein; Shiho Nagaki and Jean Baptiste Ntagoma (2012). "Risky Business: Poor Women Cross-border Traders in the Great Lakes Region of Africa", in Brenton, Paul and Gozde Isik (eds.) *De-Fragmenting Africa*, World Bank, Washington, 25–32.

Brulhart, Marius and Mombert Hoppe (2012). "Economic integration in the Lower Congo Region Opening the Kinsahsa–Brazzaville Bottleneck", in Brenton, Paul and Gozde Isik (eds.) *De-Fragmenting Africa*, World Bank, Washington, 33–41.

Clark-Flavell (1995). "Canadian Rules of Origin", A Joint Study Prepared by Grey, Clark, Shih and Associates, and Flavell Kubrick LLP, Barristers & Solicitors for the Japan Machinery Exporters' Association.

Hoekman, Bernard (1993). "Rules of Origin for Goods and Services: Conceptual and Economic Considerations", *Journal of World Trade*, 27, 81–99.

Rodrik, Dani (1995). "Political Economy of Trade Policy" in G. Grossman and K. Rogoff (eds.), *Handbook of International Economics*, Vol. 3, North Holland.

Section 1:
Modelling the Impacts of Trade Barriers and FDI Flows

KYKLOS, Vol. 44, Fasc. 1, 71-92

Chapter 2

Quantifying the Economic Effects of Non-tariff Barriers: The Case of UK Footwear

L. ALAN WINTERS and P.A. BRENTON*

In the 1970s the British footwear industry experienced great pressure on its output and prices as a result of rising imports. In the non-leather footwear sector imports from the Far East boomed, while in leather footwear Comecon and Italy provided much of the growth. In view of the treaty of Rome, Italian footwear exports to the UK could not be restricted, but the other booming suppliers were subject to NTBs — mostly to voluntary export restraints (VERs).

This paper quantifies the economic costs of such restrictions. The usual analysis assumes that, following the imposition of an NTB, exporters raise their prices to a level which cuts demand back to the permitted level of supply. In this paper we adopt a more general approach. We estimate the extent to which the prices of constrained footwear were raised, but then allow for the possibility that even at these new prices consumers were rationed — that is, that prices did not rise far enough to clear excess demand. In this case there are costs to consumers additional to those normally estimated[1].

We analyse the four principal classes of footwear, (i) men's leather, (ii) women's and children's leather, (iii) textile and (iv) rubber and plastic. Initially the demand for these groups is modelled in isolation from each other; sub-

*University of Birmingham. We are grateful to the participants of seminars at the Universities of Surrey and Cambridge, the University of Wales, Bangor, the Institute for International Economic Studies, Stockholm, and the European Workshop on International Trade, and to our collaborator WENDY TAKACS for comments on earlier drafts, and to SUE JAMES for typing. This work was conducted at the University of Wales, Bangor, under the auspices of the Centre for Economic Policy Research, London, and was financed by The Ford Foundation, the Department of Trade and Industry and the World Bank (under project RP 672-40) to whom we are grateful.

1. The paper pulls together and extends the authors' previous work on footwear trade — WINTERS [1990], BRENTON and WINTERS [1990], and TAKACS and WINTERS [1990], from which further details may be found.

sequently however, they are integrated into one model together with details of the UK footwear sector to analyse the effects on UK output and employment. The results are of topical interest since increased import pressure in the mid and late 1980s has led to further calls for protection for the British footwear industry.

As well as its direct interest the analysis of restrictions on footwear imports provides a useful case-study of non-tariff barriers in general. Indeed footwear has almost unique attractions in that regard: it is typical of the labour-intensive goods in which comparative advantage has shifted from the industrial to the developing world; it has experienced several trade shocks and policies; it is fairly competitive, at least at the production level; and the NTBs are reasonably well documented and transparent.

I. THE IMPORT RESTRICTIONS

The NTBs which we analyse are the set of voluntary export restraints (VERs) on imports of leather footwear from Czechoslovakia and Poland, which were imposed in the mid-1970s, and the quota and VERs on non-leather footwear imports from Taiwan and South Korea dating from 1977. The periods in which the restrictions were in place are summarised in *Table 1* together with our estimates of the periods over which they were actually binding.

Table 1

The Nature and Timing of UK Restrictions on Imported Footwear 1971-1986

Type of Footwear	Constrained Suppliers	Type of Policy	Period Restriction in place	Period Restriction binding
Mens Leather	Poland	VER	1975 -	1977 - 1986
	Czechoslovakia	VER	1975 -	1977 - 1979
Womens and childrens leather	Poland	VER	1975 -	1977 - 1980
	Czechoslovakia	VER	1975 -	1977 - 1980
Textiles	Taiwan	Quota (all non-leather)	1977 - 1980	1977 - 1980
		VER	1981 - 1985	1981 - 1982
	Korea	VER	1979 -	1979 - 1980
Rubber and plastic	Taiwan	Quota (all non-leather)	1977 - 1980	1977 - 1980
		VER	1981 - 1985	1981 - 1985
	Korea	VER	1979 -	1979 - 1980

THE ECONOMIC EFFECTS OF NON-TARIFF BARRIERS

Undershipping of the VER level was apparent for imports of both leather types from Czechoslovakia, women's and children's leather from Poland, and both non-leather types from Korea. However, this does not necessarily imply that the restrictions were not binding: informational problems may have prevented the complete exhaustion of the quotas, and aggregation can result in binding constraints for the important trade flows coupled with under-supply in the rest. Industry sources (the British Footwear Manufacturers' Federation) reported that they feared a huge expansion of Comecon exports if the VERs were removed. That is, they felt that the VERs bound. However, when imports average less than 60% of quota we take this as a sign that the restriction is no longer binding.

In the case of Taiwan actual imports were almost identical to those permitted during the period of the quota but there was significant overshipping of the VER. Again this may not necessarily signify that the VER was not binding. Actual imports may exceed the agreed level but may still be less than what would have been supplied in the absence of the restriction. However, when actual levels greatly exceed the restriction we suspect that imports are no longer bound. This appears to be so in the case of textile footwear imports from Taiwan. A possible explanation for the overshipping in this instance is that much of this footwear was classified by the Taiwanese as being textile products[2].

The next question is at what level did the VERs bind; at the negotiated quota level or at the level of actual imports? This is a particularly pertinent issue when working with quarterly data but annual VERs, or with VERs permitting some virement between categories. We assume throughout that each VER binds at the actual level of imports: in the presence of a VER, exporters feel constrained from supplying units beyond those observed because they fear going over-quota, or because they wish to conserve some quota for subsequent sales. Either way, additional demand cannot bring forth extra supply, so the UK market is constrained[3].

2. This was suggested to us by discussions with a representative of the Taiwanese footwear producers, to whom we are grateful.

3. BRENTON and WINTERS [1990] discuss this assumption further.

II. THE MODEL OF NTBs

We consider the direct effects of the trade restrictions in two stages: first we estimate the degree to which the NTBs led exporters to raise their prices, and second, we allow for the possibility that these policy-induced price rises were insufficient to clear excess demand so that some demand was rationed[4]. The usual analysis of NTBs considers only the first step, assuming that the prices of the constrained goods rise to the market clearing level.

These points are illustrated in *Figure 1*. Following the imposition of quantitative trade restriction at q_A, the constrained exporters may raise their prices above the free trade level (P_F). If prices rise to the level P_V then excess demand will be cleared. However, a price anywhere between P_F and P_V, say P_A, will lead to consumers being rationed; that is, consumers will be off their demand curve. Coincidentally, any rise in price will cause suppliers to be rationed, since at the new higher price they would wish to supply more but are constrained from doing so by the VER. Hence the imposition of an NTB means that someone, somewhere must be rationed.

4. The need to consider rationing was suggested by simple inspection of the footwear data, where the increases in price following the imposition of the trade constraints were not as large as we had expected.

THE ECONOMIC EFFECTS OF NON-TARIFF BARRIERS

Figure 1

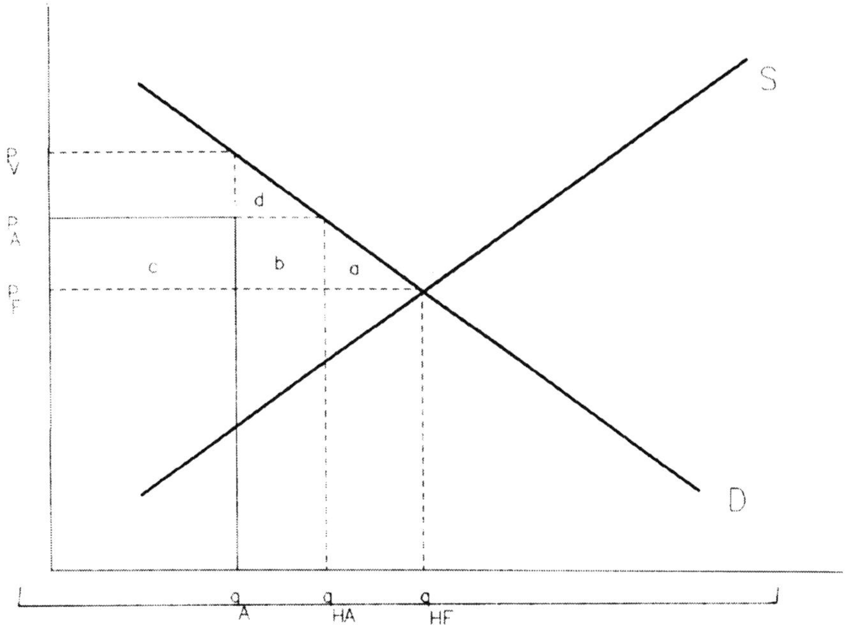

The method for estimating VER-induced price increases — the price wedges — is based upon WINTERS [1990]. It estimates the price of footwear that the constrained countries would have charged in the absence of the trade restriction by comparing the evolution of prices of imports from the constrained countries into the UK with the evolution of the prices of imports from the same countries into unconstrained markets.

If exports of footwear to different markets are highly substitutable in production, their nominal prices will be closely related, and the following equation may be used to estimate the policy price wedges arising from trade restrictions[5].

5. Provided that the elasticities of demand are constant, (1) refers equally well to firms with some market power as to those with none.

$$\ln P_u = \alpha_1 + \beta_1 \ln P_c + \gamma_1 D \quad (1)$$

where P_u is the price of UK imports of footwear from the constrained country, P_c is the price of such footwear imported by a country without restrictions and D is a dummy variable representing the UK restrictions. If footwear exports are highly substitutable then β_1 will be approximately unity. If the trade restrictions lead to a higher than normal price in the UK γ_1 will be significantly greater than zero: the trade constraint leads to a rise in price in the UK but prevents supplies from being diverted towards the UK market.

Alternatively, if supplies for different markets are imperfectly substitutable in production, prices in different markets may fluctuate relative to each other, especially in response to changes in real exchange rates. Then one might estimate the following equation

$$\ln\left(P_u/P_c\right) = \alpha_2 + \beta_2 \ln\left(\bar{P}_u/\bar{P}_c\right) + \gamma_2 D \quad (2)$$

where $\bar{P}_u$ and $\bar{P}_c$ are indices of the wholesale prices of manufactures or industrial products in the relevant countries, included to measure the effect of changes in real exchange rates, and the other variables are as before. If sales in different markets are heterogeneous then β_2 will be significantly positive. Again a significantly positive value of γ_2 would reflect the presence of policy-induced price rises. Thus equation (2) can be estimated to test the hypothesis of market segmentation and then, depending upon whether β_2 is significant and positive, either equation (1) or (2) can be used to estimate the policy price wedges.

The choice of comparator countries is an important issue. Ideally each country should have a similar economic structure to that of the UK, similar location (to minimise differences in transport costs), significant imports of footwear from the relevant countries and be free from trade restrictions. Based on HAMILTON [1989] five countries (W.Germany, Belgium-Luxembourg, Netherlands, Austria and Switzerland) were identified as allowing fairly liberal trade in footwear with Taiwan and Korea. No western European country appears to have entirely unfettered imports of footwear from Comecon countries. There is, however, no evidence that the above countries' restrictions changed during the periods relevant for identifying the effects of UK policy. Comparisons are made first with regard to W. Germany alone — W. Germany is a major importer of footwear and the principal alternative outlet to the UK for Polish footwear — and second, relative to the simple unweighted mean of the five comparator markets.

The approach described above attempts to capture the response of suppliers to the imposition of a quantitative restriction on sales to one of their markets.We now turn to the demand side and discuss how systems of demand equations can be estimated in the presence of NTBs.

We model the allocation of the (exogeneously given) UK expenditure on each type of footwear across different suppliers, including constrained, unconstrained and domestic suppliers[6]. BRENTON and WINTERS [1990] develop a methodology for considering non-price rationing using the constant elasticity of substitution (CES) model. This model meets our requirements of allowing quantity-constrained and quantity-endogeneous regimes to be estimated simultaneously, permits explicit welfare judgements to be made and admits the simple treatment of hierarchies to cope with groups of suppliers. Being separable and linear homogeneous the model allows only restricted substitutions between suppliers, but by imposing much structure upon the data it does allow us to make sense of the very noisy information sets available to us. The application of a more flexible functional form — the Rotterdam model — in WINTERS and BRENTON [1988] — proved difficult to fit, gave rather imprecise parameter estimates, and generated severe numerical difficulties when our desired geographical disaggregation was attempted.

Starting from the basic CES estimating equation — see ARMINGTON [1969] and HICKMAN and LAU [1973] — and taking a single type of footwear supplied in differentiated form by n sources, we have

$$s_{it} = \alpha_i \, p_{it}{}^{\sigma} \, p_t^{-1} + \varepsilon_{it} \qquad (3)$$

where subscripts t denote observations, α_i and σ are parameters to be estimated, σ being the elasticity of substitution, s_{it} is the quantity share of the ith supplier, ε_{it} is a stochastic error, p_i, q_i are the price and quantity respectively of footwear from i, and $p_t \equiv \sum_{j=1}^{n} \alpha_j \, p_{jt}{}^{\sigma}$ is a fixed weight price index. Adding up requires

6. Our data set initially identifies 14 country/country group suppliers of imports — the individual countries being the principal sources of imports. Suppliers are allocated to sub-groups of a hierarchy according to our a priori views as to the main substitutions that have occurred.

that $\sum_i s_{it} = 1$, all t, which in turn implies that $\sum_i \alpha_i = 1$ and that $\sum_i \varepsilon_{it} = 0$, all t.

Under unrestrained price-taking conditions, the prices, p_i, are exogenous, and (3) can be estimated as a system of equations, i = 1 ...n, in a perfectly straight-forward manner.

When a quota or a VER is imposed, the above system must be partially inverted with price as the endogenous variable for the constrained supplier(s). Assume that commodity i alone is subject to the QR; temporarily dropping the time subscript, we may rewrite the aggregate price index as $p = \left[\alpha_i p_i^{\sigma} + J\right]$, where $J \equiv \sum_{j \neq i} \alpha_j p_j^{\sigma}$ is the component of the price index referring to the exogenous prices. Substituting into (3) and manipulating we obtain

$$\alpha_i p_i^{\sigma} = J(s_i - \varepsilon_i)/(1 - s_i + \varepsilon_i) \tag{4}$$

Further, substituting (4) into (3) for the remaining unconstrained commodities, k, yields the conditional demand curve (conditional on s_i)

$$s_k = (1 - s_i)\, \alpha_k p_k^{\sigma} J^{-1} + \alpha_k p_k^{\sigma} J^{-1} \varepsilon_i + \varepsilon_k \tag{5}$$

Equation (5) shows that the share allocation among the unconstrained commodities depends on (a) their relative prices, $\beta_k \equiv \alpha_k p_k^{\sigma} J^{-1}$, in a way analogous to (3), (b) a scale factor, $(1-s_i)$, reflecting the fact that after commodity i has been bought only $(1-s_i)$ of the total remains to be allocated, and (c) a somewhat complex error term.

If, as is usual, it is assumed that the import restriction causes the price of commodity i to rise sufficiently to reduce demand to the constrained supply, i.e. to clear all markets perfectly, then equation (5) will faithfully reflect the demand surface and may be used to identify it. Equations (4) and (5) may then be used to estimate the parameters of the demand system, but only after transforming them to make their stochastic components well-behaved. Provided that the distributions of ε_i and ε_k are unaffected by the imposition of the import restriction, such a transformation will merely undo our previous manipulation and take us back to (3). Thus both constrained and unconstrained

THE ECONOMIC EFFECTS OF NON-TARIFF BARRIERS

observations may be used in equations (3) to estimate the demand surface[7]. This is the market-clearing model: imports of i are constrained, but not rationed, because their price has risen sufficiently to curtail demand.

If, on the other hand, commodity i is quantity-rationed — that is, if at the ruling price p_i, consumers are unable to obtain the share indicated by (3) — then the observed price-quantity pairs in the rationed market lie not on the demand surface but below it. Of course, we cannot observe directly by how much below, and so cannot use the observations to identify that surface, but following NEARY and ROBERTS [1980] we can express the demand for *un*rationed goods during the period of rationing as a function of the parameters of the demand system, observed prices, and the ration. This allows information from the rationed period to be used in the identification of some of the parameters affecting demand for the rationed good(s).

NEARY and ROBERTS' [1980] model of constrained allocation introduces the concept of virtual prices — that vector of prices which would cause the actual quantities observed to be chosen voluntarily, holding the level of utility constant. Virtual and actual prices are identical for unrationed commodities, while for rationed commodities the virtual price may be calculated by inverting the Hicksian demand curve. In the CES case, this is equivalent to inverting (3) to get (4). Equation (4) is not estimable under rationing, but using it do define the virtual price of i and applying this to the equations for other commodities yields (5), which *is* estimable. A complication arises, however, because we cannot even approximate the stochastic error ε_i, which occurs in every equation of (5). This is because the residual contains not only ε_i but also the degree of rationing, say r_i. We may assume, however, that the shocks to demand have the same distribution with rationing as without. Thus if the (nxn) error covariance matrix $E\left(\underline{\varepsilon}_t\,\underline{\varepsilon}'_t\right)$ is Σ, where $\underline{\varepsilon}_t$ is the vector of errors $\left[\varepsilon_{1t} .. \varepsilon_{it} .. \varepsilon_{kt} .. \varepsilon_{nt}\right]$ for the period t, the (n-1) x (n-1) matrix of error covariances for equations (5) will be

$$\tilde{\sum_t} = E\left(\underline{\tilde{\varepsilon}}_t\,\underline{\tilde{\varepsilon}}_t{}'\right) = G'_t \sum G_t \tag{6}$$

where $\underline{\tilde{\varepsilon}}_t$ is the vector of errors for the unconstrained commodities and

$$G'_t = \left(\tilde{\beta}_t\, I_{n-1}\right) \tag{7}$$

7. That is, given the stochastic component, ε_i, it is a matter of indifference how we normalise equation (3).

where $\tilde{\beta}_t$ is the (n-1) vector of $\beta_{jt} = \alpha_j p_{jt}{}^{\sigma} J_t{}^{-1}$ and where, without loss of generality, the constrained commodity has been given index i = 1. Thus observations from periods with no quantitative restrictions described by equations (3) may be combined in estimation with observations on the unrationed commodities from the periods of rationing as described by equations (5) - (7)[8].

Our extraneous information on the timing of the constraints allows us to avoid RICHARD's [1980] problems identifying changes in the exogeneity of prices and quantities. We do, however, still have to seek evidence on the incidence of rationing. Under market clearing the distributions of the residuals will be the same in periods both with and without quantity restrictions. If rationing occurs in the constrained period (T_2), however, then the residuals will include the effects of rationing, $\underline{r}_t$. With no information on $\underline{r}_t$ we cannot predict the precise nature of the differences between the distributions, but assuming that $\underline{\varepsilon}_t$ is distributed normally with zero mean, observations of $\hat{\underline{\varepsilon}}_t$, $t \in T_2$, which suggested non-centrality or strong differences in the variance-covariance ma-trix between periods T_1 and T_2 might reject H_0 (market-clearing). Several tests of the latter hypothesis are described in BRENTON and WINTERS [1990].

Prior to empirical application we extend the model in three ways: by introducing time trends into the share parameters, α_i; by allowing for two or more constrained suppliers; and by introducing simple dynamics. These extensions are described in detail in BRENTON and WINTERS [1990].

III. THE WELFARE EFFECTS OF NTBs

Figure 1 illustrates the losses to consumers arising from the imposition of a quantitative restriction. The policy price wedge is the difference between P_A, the price we observe, and P_F the price estimated to have ruled in the absence of the constraint. The virtual price, P_V, is the price at which the actual quantity, q_A, would have been bought voluntarily along the 'Hicksian' demand curve, while q_{HA} and q_{HF} are 'Hicksian' quantities, defined respectively as the quantity that would have been bought in the absence of rationing and the quantity demanded under free trade.

8. Fortunately, we do not need the endogeneous regime-switching techniques of, for example, QUANDT [1982], because we have a priori information about the nature and timing of disequilibrium. To have estimated our system of demand equations with endogeneous regimes would certainly have overstretched our data.

THE ECONOMIC EFFECTS OF NON-TARIFF BARRIERS

The loss to consumers resulting from the price wedges comprises a dead-weight loss (area a) as consumers switch away from the footwear whose price has risen, plus a transfer to exporters (area b + c) as the price of units still imported is driven up. NEARY and ROBERTS [1980] and JOHANSSON [1987] show that area d under the compensated demand curve represents the loss of welfare due to rationing. The compensated demand curve shows the marginal valuation of the rationed good, and over the range q_A to q_{HA} it exceeds the actual cost by area d. The net effect is as if sales had been made at P_V but with $(P_V - P_A)$ per unit being returned to consumers.

Given the estimated parameters from the CES demand system we can compute the loss to consumers of both the price wedges and rationing directly. Since the Hicksian demand functions are the derivatives of the cost function, the equivalent variation can be found from the difference in costs at the different price vectors. Hence the loss of consumers surplus due to rationing is given by $C(U, P_V) - C(U, P_A)$, from which must be deducted the area $q_A (P_V - P_A)$. The loss due to the policy price wedges is given by $C(U, P_A) - C(U, P_F)$, where the area $q_A (P_A - P_F)$ is distributed to the exporters and the residual is the deadweight loss[9].

IV. THE DATA

Unfortunately, because of data limitations, the two approaches described above are not entirely consistent in empirical application. The data used to estimate the demand system are more detailed than those available across markets for the price wedge exercise. The principal data series for the former are the volume and value (tariff inclusive) of UK imports disaggregated by supplier and domestic sales (domestic production minus exports) for each category of footwear. In the case of textile footwear domestic sales are negligible and are thus not considered in the analysis. Actual import prices are generally unavailable, and so in common with previous research, we have used unit values to approximate the prices of traded goods. To maintain conformity and to permit

9. The analysis above implicitly assumes that prices and quantities pertain directly to final consumers, but unfortunately our data refer only to imports measured cif plus tariffs and domestic supplies at the factory gate. This raises a number of conceptual problems, but for reasons given in BRENTON and WINTERS [1990] we believe that the present approach is the best of the alternatives. However, the presence of a single, foreign owned, importer of Polish footwear suggests that this firm may be able to gather the VER scarcity rents for itself. In this case the area $q_A(P_V - P_A)$ will accrue not to consumers but to foreigners.

finer disaggregation, unit values are also used as the measure of the prices of domestically produced footwear. The basic data are quarterly and cover the period 1971 quarter I to 1986 quarter IV[10].

For the price wedge exercise the need for fairly comprehensive and comparable series precluded direct collection from national sources. We were obliged to use annual trade data at the 5-digit level of the SITC[11], where SITC(R) 85101 covers footwear of rubber and plastic and SITC(R) 85102 covers footwear of leather and textiles.

The policy dummy variables (D) differ by exporter, according to the UK policies in place and their likely degree of effectiveness. For Czechoslovakia and Poland the variable was assigned zero value over 1970-76, one half in 1977 and unity thereafter. For Taiwan and Korea, two versions were used: first a dummy taking the value unity for all the full years in which the policy was formally in place — 1978-84 and 1979-86 respectively; second a dummy with unity during the periods when the restraints probably bound — 1977-82 for Taiwan (with values ½ in the first and last years) and 1979-80 respectively. These patterns of 'effective restriction' were derived on the basis of institutional details and movements in trade volumes.

V. THE RESULTS

The results of the market segmentation test, based on the coefficient β_2 in equation (2) suggested that the prices of Polish exports to the UK relative to exports to the comparators are strongly related to real exchange rates. The hypothesis of a single integrated export market is thus rejected. Taiwan on the other hand shows no signs of market heterogeneity, while the results for Czechoslovakia and Korea vary by footwear type and comparator group, see WINTERS [1990].

The estimated price wedges, based on the estimates of γ_i from whichever is the relevant equation of (1) or (2) are shown in *Table 2*. We report wedges only where they are statistically significant. While none were identified for Czechoslovakia, we find material and long-lived wedges for Poland (19%) and Taiwan (12% and 16%), and short but sharp wedges for Korea, (27% and 28%).

10. The original source of the trade data is HM Customs and Excise, whilst the domestic data are taken from Business Monitor PQ450. Many of the data were provided to us, however, by the British Footwear Manufacturers Federation, to whom we are most grateful

11. The data were obtained from the World Bank Trade System.

THE ECONOMIC EFFECTS OF NON-TARIFF BARRIERS

The first step in the rationing exercise was to estimate the demand systems under the assumption of market clearing behaviour and test for rationing over the periods in which we believe the trade restraints were binding. Using the test statistics from BRENTON and WINTERS [1990] in conjunction with our institutional information we identified the periods of rationing shown in *Table 2*. We found evidence of rationing for all suppliers except Korea, which is perhaps not surprising given the magnitude of the latter's price increases over 1979 and 1980. Following the identification of the periods of rationing the model was re-estimated taking its presence into account. The parameter estimates were not dramatically different from those under market-clearing, with only small changes in the elasticity of substitution and the trend effects; in other circumstances, however, the identification of rationing and allowance for it in estimation could be a significant aspect of the numerical analysis of NTBs[12].

Table 2

The Timing and Extent of the Price Wedges and the Period of Rationing

		Price Wedge Period	Extent	Rationing Period
Czechoslovakia	Leather			
	- Mens	-	-	1977QIII - 1979QII
	-Womens & Children	-	-	1977QIV - 1980QI
Poland	Leather			
	- Mens	1978-86	19%[(a)]	1977QIII - 1986QIV
	-Womens & Children			1977IV - 1980QI
Taiwan	Textile	1978-84	16%	1977QIII - 1982QIV
	Rubber and Plastic	1977-82	12%[(b)]	1977QIII - 1985QI
Korea	Textile	1979-80	27%	-
	Rubber and Plastic	1979-80	28%	-

Notes: (a) wedge half size in 1977
(b) wedge half size in 1977 and 1982

12. The parameter estimates are presented in detail in BRENTON and WINTERS [1990] together with a thorough discussion of the estimation. Some of the estimated elasticities of substitution are given below in *Table 5*.

Before discussing the costs of these restrictions to consumers we briefly consider their effect upon prices and the changes in sales they induced. The latter are measured by comparing actual quantities with the estimated Hicksian quantities at actual and estimated free trade prices, all calculated on the assumption that changes in demand are met at constant prices and that total demand is given. *Table 3* presents quantity shares for each of the constrained suppliers together with the domestic share and the share of unrestricted imports for 1979 — the year in which the number of binding trade restrictions was at a peak.

For men's leather and both the non-leather groups the trade restrictions led to large declines in the shares of the market for the restricted supplies (particularly Poland and Taiwan) relative to their positions under unfettered access. These losses are balanced by increases in sales for other suppliers which are distributed fairly evenly amongst producers in the UK and unrestricted imports. Thus these restrictions had significant trade diverting effects towards non-restricted import suppliers. The table shows that, for the leather groups, the principal beneficiary of this trade diversion was Italy, the UK's main foreign supplier of such footwear. With no domestic sales of textile footwear UK producers gained only indirectly from the restrictions on such footwear from Taiwan and Korea. *Table 3* also shows the virtual prices implied by these market shares. The differences between the actual and virtual prices are large, and particularly for mens' leather footwear from Poland, and Taiwanese textile footwear, suggest a severe degree of rationing.

THE ECONOMIC EFFECTS OF NON-TARIFF BARRIERS

Table 3

Differences in Market Shares and Prices as a Result of Trade Policy in 1979[a]

	S_{HF}	S_{HA}	S_A	P_V	P_A	P_F
				(£ per pair)		
Mens Leather						
Poland	0.23	0.16	0.07	6.15	3.64	3.06
Czechoslovakia	0.06	0.06	0.05	4.81	3.71	
UK	0.40	0.44	0.50			
Italy	0.15	0.18	0.20			
Other	0.16	0.16	0.18			
Womens and Childrens Leather						
Poland	0.04	0.03	0.02	4.99	3.58	3.01
Czechoslovakia	0.03	0.03	0.01	6.65	2.93	
UK	0.54	0.54	0.56			
Italy	0.23	0.24	0.25			
Other	0.16	0.16	0.16			
Rubber and Plastic						
Taiwan	0.18	0.15	0.05	3.21	1.93	1.66
Korea	0.03	0.02	0.02		2.51	1.96
UK	0.43	0.46	0.51			
EEC	0.07	0.07	0.09			
other	0.45	0.48	0.57			
Textile						
Taiwan	0.21	0.20	0.07	9.91	2.11	1.82
Korea	0.27	0.24	0.28		2.02	1.59
Other	0.52	0.56	0.66			

S_A - Actual quantity share
S_{HA} - quantity share computed at actual prices
S_{HF} - quantity share computed at free trade prices
P_A - Actual price
P_V - estimated virtual price
P_F - estimated 'free-trade' price
(a) Assuming no changes in supply prices except due to the policy price wedges

Table 4 shows the welfare costs of the trade restrictions assuming no change in the supply prices except for the policy price wedges. The deadweight loss to consumers from rationing ranges from £14.62m in 1978 (men's leather, women's and children's leather, rubber and plastic, textiles) to £32.49m in 1986 (men's leather only). The increasing costs of the VER on imports of men's leather footwear from Poland reflect the increasing burden implied by a roughly constant quota in the face of growing demand. Annual costs (in current prices) more than doubled between 1983 and 1986.

These deadweight losses from rationing are compounded if one allows for increases in price somewhere between the exporter and the final consumer. If, for the leather groups, foreign-owned import agents buy from the Polish suppliers at low prices and sell in the UK at the market-clearing price, the resulting transfer $(P_V - P_A)q_A$ will go abroad. In 1986 this adds an extra £20.2m to the welfare costs faced by consumers of men's leather footwear. Finally *Table 4* shows the deadweight losses and transfers associated with the estimated policy price wedges. These increase the welfare costs to consumers of the trade restrictions to £26m in 1978 and to £69m in 1986.

VI. UK PRODUCTION AND EMPLOYMENT

The analysis of the previous sections assumed that demand for each type of footwear is fixed and that UK supply of each type is perfectly elastic. We now relax these assumptions using a simple simulation model which translates the changes in prices estimated earlier into changes in quantities, allowing for substitutions between the different types of footwear.

In essence this is perfectly straightforward. The estimates of the demand systems for each footwear type from BRENTON and WINTERS [1990] are combined into a single system using a CES aggregator with an elasticity of substitution of -1.5 and a price elasticity of demand for all footwear of -0.75. This is then combined with a UK supply module describing own-price and cross-price elasticities of supply for each footwear type given exogenous factor and materials prices. The supply module is based on TAKACS and WINTERS [1990] which estimates a multi-input multi-output profit function for the UK footwear sector. The function — which takes the Generalised Leontief form — distinguishes leather and non-leather output, and labour, material and capital inputs, the last of which is assumed to be fixed over the medium term. Finally the combined model is solved at VER-distorted prices (including price policy wedges and the price equivalents of rationing) and at free-trade prices, to yield the quantities traded and sold domestically and the prices of UK supplies.The relevant elasticities are listed in *Table 5*.

Table 4

Estimated Consumption Costs of VERs and Quota on Footwear Imports (£m)

	Mens Leather				Womens and Childrens Leather			
	Price Wedge		Rationing		Price Wedge		Rationing	
	DW	T	DW	T	DW	T	DW	T
1977	0.04	0.35	0.15	0.53	0.01	0.10	0.34	0.56
1978	0.40	2.05	0.78	2.71	0.14	0.86	2.26	2.54
1979	0.58	3.11	2.04	4.14	0.18	1.04	2.26	2.88
1980	0.62	3.67	2.35	4.19	0.16	0.96	0.30	0.62
1981	0.62	3.93	3.37	4.78	0.18	1.11		
1982	0.69	5.25	7.01	6.73	0.20	1.21		
1983	0.74	7.07	12.20	9.15	0.21	1.29		
1984	0.72	9.29	18.13	12.72	0.24	1.47		
1985	0.82	11.00	22.99	15.14	0.22	1.32		
1986	0.81	13.88	32.49	20.18	0.23	1.39		

	Textiles			Rubber and Plastic			Total
	Price Wedge		Rationing	Price Wedge		Rationing	
	DW	T	DW	DW	T	DW	
1977			2.01	0.01	0.14	0.78	5.02
1978	0.05	1.08	10.13	0.12	1.25	1.45	25.82
1979	0.18	3.25	7.76	0.33	2.58	2.51	32.84
1980	0.21	3.79	5.30	0.30	2.48	2.33	27.28
1981	0.13	2.61	9.40	0.18	1.69	1.28	29.28
1982	0.14	2.75	6.16	0.22	2.10	1.39	33.85
1983	0.17	3.70				1.22	35.75
1984	0.22	5.13				0.72	48.64
1985							51.49
1986							68.98

DW - Deadweight Loss
T - Transfer

Table 5

Elasticities in the Simulation Model

Elasticities of substitution in demand between different suppliers of			
men's leather	-2.75		
women's and children's leather	-1.88		
rubber and plastic	-2.16		
textiles	-0.83		
between footwear types	-1.50		
Elasticity of demand for footwear	-0.75		
Elasticities of UK supply	**men's leather**	**women's leather**	**rubber and plastic**
men's leather	0.56	0	-0.2
women's and children's leather	0	0.56	-0.2
rubber and plastic	-0.75	-0.75	1.14

The solutions are most easily derived by a linear iterative procedure. Starting from the actual situation — the 'with-VERs' solution — we use ARMINGTON's [1969] linearisation of the CES hierarchy. Assuming aggregate demand for all footwear to be fixed, the percentage change in demand for footwear of type i from supplier j can be expressed as

$$\frac{dq_{ij}}{q_{ij}} = -\eta_{ij}\frac{dp_{ij}}{p_{ij}} + \sum_{k\neq j}\mu_{ik}\frac{dp_{ik}}{p_{ik}} + \sum_{k\neq l}\nu_{ikl}\frac{dp_{kl}}{p_{kl}} \qquad (8)$$

where

$\eta_{ij} = (1 - s_{ij})\,\sigma_i + s_{ij}\,\lambda_i$,
$\mu_{ik} = s_{ik}(\sigma_i - \lambda_i)$,
$\nu_{ikl} = \lambda_k^i\, s_{kl}$
$\lambda_i = (1 - s_i)\,\sigma + s_i\,\lambda$ is the direct price elasticity for i,
$\lambda_k^i = s_k\,(\sigma - \lambda)$ is the cross-price elasticity,
σ is the aggregate elasticity of substitution, and
λ is the elasticity of demand for footwear.

For convenience we rewrite (8) in matrix form and partition as

THE ECONOMIC EFFECTS OF NON-TARIFF BARRIERS

$$\begin{bmatrix} y_1 \\ y_2 \end{bmatrix} = \begin{bmatrix} A_{11} \, A_{12} \\ A_{21} \, A_{22} \end{bmatrix} \begin{bmatrix} r_1 \\ r_2 \end{bmatrix} \tag{9}$$

where 1 denotes the UK and 2 denotes imports, y and r are vectors of quantity and price changes respectively, and A is a matrix of parameters. Now, to allow for the endogeneity of UK supply we define

$$y_1 = Br_1 \tag{10}$$

where B is a matrix of price elasticities of supply. Rearranging we obtain

$$\begin{bmatrix} y_1 \\ y_2 \end{bmatrix} = A \begin{bmatrix} (B - A_{11})^{-1} A_{12} \\ I \end{bmatrix} \gamma_2 \tag{11}$$

To allow for the linearisation imposed by equation (8) we compute (11) iteratively breaking r_2 (the percentage changes between virtual and free trade prices) into steps and recomputing the levels of q_{ij}, p_{ij} (for the UK) and s_{ij} at each step. The step length is 0.1*dp, where dp is the difference between the free trade price (the ultimate destination) and the level of p_{ij} at each step.

We report here the results of applying the above model to assess the effects of the abolition of the various quantitative restrictions on UK footwear imports in 1979, the year in which constraints were most widespread. Removing all restrictions in 1979 would have led to a 4 per cent fall in the price of UK output of leather footwear and a 5.4 per cent decline in non-leather (rubber and plastic) output prices. The accompanying changes in quantities are relatively small; output of leather footwear declines by 1.2 per cent whilst there is a negligible change in output of non-leather footwear as supply switches from leather to non-leather forms.

Applying these price changes to the labour demand equation derived by TAKACS and WINTERS [1990] suggests that employment in footwear would have declined by 1064 workers (approximately 2 per cent of the total workforce). Taking all adjustments into account we estimate that consumer welfare would have increased by £79.2 million if all import restrictions had been abolished in 1979, whilst the loss of profits and tariff revenue would have amounted to £22.4 million.

Finally, TAKACS and WINTERS estimate the adjustment costs avoided by the trade restrictions under various scenarios regarding the rate at which trade-displaced labour is re-employed. The most pessimistic scenario (which assumes labour turn-over far below any observed rate in footwear) results in once-and-for-all adjustment costs of £9.6 million. The present value (discounted at a 10 per cent annual rate) of the net social costs of the restrictions estimated in this paper is £568 million.

These large net losses emanate from the relatively low substitutability of UK footwear for footwear from restricted importers, and the low degree of responsiveness of UK footwear output to changes in price; the low adjustment costs reflect additionally the insensitivity of the demand for labour to footwear prices. Thus the UK's NTBs on footwear imports raised the prices of imported and domestically supplied footwear, but had little effect on domestic output and employment.

VII. CONCLUSION

Non-tariff barriers lead to the rationing of either suppliers and/or demanders. This paper suggests that non-tariff barriers to UK footwear imports resulted in consumer-rationing in at least some cases. The welfare costs of rationing must be added to those associated with the import price rises induced by trade policy and are further supplemented by the rises in domestic prices that they induce. The paper shows the high consumer costs of UK restrictions on footwear imports, and the relatively small effects that such restrictions had on UK output and employment. Even allowing for increased UK profits from footwear, the economic costs of import restrictions far exceed any possible adjustment costs avoided by the introduction of protection.

REFERENCES

ARMINGTON, P.S.: 'A theory of demand for products distinguished by place of production', *IMF Staff Papers*, Vol. 16 (1969), pp. 159-176.

BRENTON, P.A. and WINTERS, L.A.:'Non-tariff barriers and rationing: UK footwear imports', Discussion Paper No. 365, Centre for Economic Policy Research, London, (1990).

HAMILTON, C.B.: 'The political economy of transient "new" protectionism', *Weltwirtschaftliches Archiv*, Vol. 125 (1989), pp. 522-546.

HICKMAN, B.G. and LAU, L.J.: 'Elasticities of substitution and export demands in a world trade model', *European Economic Review*, Vol. 4 (1973), pp. 347-380.

JOHANSSON, P-O.: *'The Economic Theory and Measurement of Environmental Benefits*, London: Cambridge University Press, 1987.

NEARY, J.P. and ROBERTS, K.W.S.: 'The theory of household behaviour under rationing', *European Economic Review*, Vol. 13 (1980), pp. 25-42.

QUANDT, R.E.: 'Economic disequilibrium models', *Econometric Reviews*, Vol. 1 (1982), pp. 1-63.

THE ECONOMIC EFFECTS OF NON-TARIFF BARRIERS

RICHARD, J.F.: 'Models with several regimes and changes in exogeneity', *Review of Economic Studies*, Vol. 47 (1980), pp. 1-20.

TAKACS, W.E. and WINTERS, L.A.: 'Labour adjustment costs and British footwear protection', Discussion Paper No. 376, Centre for Economic Policy Research, London, 1990, *forthcoming* in *Oxford Economic Papers* (1991).

WINTERS, L.A.: 'The effects of voluntary export restraints on the prices of UK imports of footwear', Discussion Paper No. 324, Centre for Economic Policy Research, London, 1989, *forthcoming* in *Weltwirtschaftliches Archiv* (1990).

WINTERS, L.A. and BRENTON, P.A.: 'Voluntary export restraints: UK restrictions on imports of leather footwear from Eastern Europe', Discussion Paper 283, Centre for Economic Policy Research, London, 1988.

SUMMARY

This paper quantifies the economic effects of NTBs on UK footwear imports. The extent to which the various VERs and a quota on imports from Eastern European countries and Taiwan and Korea led exporters to raise their prices is estimated. The paper then allows additionally for the possibility that the prices of constrained imports were not raised to the level which clears the market, so that consumers were quantity rationed. Finally, it examines the effects of the restrictions on UK footwear output and employment. The results suggest that the net social costs of the constraints greatly exceeded the estimated costs of adjustment to their abolition.

RÉSUMÉ

Cet article quantifie les effets économiques des NTB sur les importations anglaises de chaussures. Il évalue l'impact des différents VER et des quotas d'importations des Pays d'Europe de l'Est, de Taïwan et de Corée sur la tendance des exportateurs à augmenter leurs prix. Les auteurs estiment, en outre, possible que les prix des importations, ainsi limitées, n'aient pas été augmentés autant qu'il l'aura fallu pour assainir le marché. Ceci a amené, pour les consommateurs, une sorte de rationnement sur ces produits. L'article examine enfin les effets des restrictions sur la production et l'emploi dans le secteur anglais de la chaussure. Les auteurs en arrivent à conclure que les coûts sociaux nets des limitations d'importations ont largement excédé les coûts estimés des ajustements consécutifs à leur suppression.

ZUSAMMENFASSUNG

Der Artikel untersucht die ökonomischen Wirkungen von nichttarifären Handelshemmnissen auf die englischen Importe von Schuhwerk. Es wird das Ausmass geschätzt, in welchem die verschiedenen freiwilligen Exportbeschränkungen sowie eine Importquote für osteuropäische Länder, Taiwan und Korea die Exporteure zu einer Anhebung ihrer Preise veranlassten. Die Untersuchung wird auf den Fall ausgeweitet, in welchem die Preise nicht auf das erforderliche Marktniveau stiegen, was für die Konsumenten eine Art von Mengenrationierung zur Folge hatte. Schliesslich werden die Auswirkungen der Restriktionen auf Produktion und Beschäftigung in der englischen Industrie analysiert. Die Ergebnisse zeigen, dass die aus den Importrestriktionen resultierenden sozialen Nettokosten bei weitem die geschätzten Kosten überstiegen haben, die im Falle einer Anpassung an die neue Situation entstanden wären.

Journal of International Economics 34 (1993) 289–308. North-Holland

Chapter 3

Voluntary export restraints and rationing

U.K. leather footwear imports from Eastern Europe*

Paul A. Brenton and L. Alan Winters

Department of Economics, University of Birmingham, Edgbaston, Birmingham B15 2TT, UK

Received December 1989, revised version received May 1992

Following the imposition of a quantitative import restriction someone somewhere must be quantity rationed. Concentrating on demand we develop methods to test and allow for the presence of rationing in the estimation of demand equations and in the calculation of the welfare effects of quantitative restrictions. Using a CES model we analyse the voluntary export restraints on U.K. imports of two types of leather footwear from Comecon countries. The results suggest that, even if prices did not rise to clear the market, U.K. consumers could have lost up to £60 million in 1986 from these restrictions.

1. Introduction

An important feature of international trading relations since 1970 has been the increasing use of quantitative restrictions (QRs). Fundamental to the analysis of non-tariff barriers (NTBs) is the modelling of quantity constraints, and in this paper we develop a general approach to them by allowing for the possibility that they lead not only to a rise in import prices, but also to non-price rationing. The paper develops statistical methods of identifying rationing, given information of when a QR is in place, and of allowing for it in the estimation of demand systems and in making welfare calculations. We also place much more emphasis than previous studies of NTBs upon the *estimation* of the parameters of behaviour in the presence of binding quantitative restrictions.[1]

Although this paper concentrates on the demand side of the market, the techniques developed are of general relevance to the modelling of QRs.

Correspondence to: L.A. Winters, Department of Economics, University of Birmingham, Birmingham B15 2TT, UK.

*We are grateful to two anonymous referees, the participants of seminars at the Universities of Surrey and Cambridge, the University College of North Wales, the Institute for International Economic Studies, Stockholm, and the European Workshop on International Trade, and to our collaborator Wendy Takacs for comments, and to Sue James for typing. This work was conducted in the University of Wales, Bangor, in conjunction with the Centre for Economic Policy Research, London, and was financed by The Ford Foundation, the Department of Trade and Industry, and the World Bank (under project RP 672-40) to whom we are grateful.

[1]This paper is a condensation of some of the work described in Brenton and Winters (1990).

0022-1996/93/$06.00

When a QR is imposed, someone somewhere is rationed. If suppliers do not raise their prices sufficiently, demanders are rationed as we assume here. If, on the other hand, prices are raised to a level where there is no excess demand, then suppliers must be rationed in the sense that at the new higher price, they would wish to provide more than the quantity permitted. Thus a consistent treatment of rationing is a necessary part of the complete empirical analysis of QRs.

Having developed a model of non-price rationing we use it to assess the effects of the U.K.'s restrictions on two classes of leather footwear (men's, and women's and children's) imported from Poland and Czechoslovakia. The aim of the paper is as much methodological as substantive, but the latter aspect is significant. To our knowledge this is the most detailed study of European footwear protection and the first of imports from Eastern Europe. Given the recent liberalisation of such trade our conclusion that consumer rationing has occurred and is costly assumes considerable policy relevance.[2]

2. The basic model of demand[3]

To explore rationing resulting from geographically discriminatory quantitative import restrictions, we require a demand system that admits the simultaneous estimation of quantity-constrained as well as regular quantity-endogenous equations, permits explicit welfare judgements and allows the simple treatment of hierarchies to cope with groups of suppliers. In Winters and Brenton (1988) we developed a model of non-price rationing using the Rotterdam system. This met these criteria and, in principle, allowed a fairly general set of substitutions between different suppliers/product types. However, in empirical application it proved difficult to fit, gave imprecise parameter estimates and proved estimable only for Comecon as a whole. In the present paper, therefore, we try to obviate some of those problems by adopting a more constrained functional form – the constant elasticity of substitution (CES) model. CES functions have a long history in applied international trade; see, for example, Armington (1969) and Hickman and Lau (1973). Being separable and linear homogeneous they permit only restricted substitution possibilities between goods and frequently appear to impose too much structure on the data; see, for example, Winters (1984) or Brenton (1989). However, by concentrating all price responses into the estimation of a single parameter, they allow us to make sense of very noisy

[2] The policy implications of our work are spelt out more fully in Winters and Brenton (1991), which integrates the results of this study with similar research on Taiwan and Korea, an investigation of the price effects of the VERs [Winters (1990)] and a production/employment model [Takacs and Winters (1991)].

[3] Further details of the model may be found in Brenton and Winters (1990) and Winters and Brenton (1991).

data sets such as those presently available to us. Since our concern here is with rationing, we take the CES's separability and homotheticity as maintained hypotheses and exploit its greater focus to allow us to disaggregate our study by footwear type and supplier.

Taking a single type of footwear supplied in differentiated form by n sources, we assume that consumers maximise the sub-utility function

$$U = \left[\sum_{i=1}^{n} a_i q_i^{\delta} \right]^{1/\delta} \tag{1}$$

subject to the budget constraint

$$M = \sum_{i=1}^{n} p_i q_i,$$

where q_i and p_i are, respectively, the quantity and price of footwear from source i, U is the sub-utility level, M is expenditure on all footwear of the type under consideration, assumed to be determined by a previous higher-level budgeting decision, and a_i and δ are parameters.

The elasticity of substitution is $-1/(1+\delta) \equiv \sigma$, which must be negative in order that (1) constitute a proper sub-utility function. Standard manipulations – see Armington (1969) – produce the demand functions

$$q_i = a_i^{-\sigma} \left(\frac{p_i}{p^*} \right)^{\sigma} U, \tag{2}$$

where p^* is the CES dual price function, $p^* = [\sum_j a_j^{-\sigma} p_j^{(1+\sigma)}]^{1/(1+\sigma)}$.

This may be further transformed – see Hickman and Lau (1973) – into

$$s_i = \alpha_i p_i^{\sigma} p^{-1} + \varepsilon_i, \tag{3}$$

where

$\alpha_i \equiv a_i^{-\sigma}$,
$s_i \equiv q_i / \sum_{j=1}^{n} q_j$,
ε_i is a stochastic error, and
p is a fixed-weight price index $= \sum_{j=1}^{n} \alpha_j p_j^{\sigma}$.

Expressing (3) in share form helps to avoid the heteroskedasticity that frequently results from having quantities on the left-hand side, and emphasises the usual adding up constraints that $\sum_i \alpha_i = 1$ and that $\sum_i \varepsilon_i = 0$, for all observations.

Eq. (3) is usually estimated with exogenous prices, but it is equally applicable when a quota or a VER is imposed and prices become endogenous. Assume, without loss of generality, that commodity i alone is subject to the QR, we can 'partially invert' (3) to substitute p_i out of the equations for commodity k to get the conditional demand curves (conditional on s_i)

$$s_k = (1 - s_i)\alpha_k p_k^\sigma J^{-1} + \alpha_k p_k^\sigma J^{-1}\varepsilon_i + \varepsilon_k, \quad k \neq i, \tag{4}$$

where $J \equiv \sum_{j \neq i} \alpha_j p_j^\sigma$ is the component of the price index referring to the exogenous prices – see Winters and Brenton (1991). Thus allocation among the unconstrained commodities depends on the product of a term in the relative prices of the unconstrained products and a scale factor which reflects the fact that only $(1 - s_i)$ of total expenditure remains to be allocated; there is also a complex error term.

Although we have fixed the quantity (share) of good i in total consumption, nothing so far mentions rationing. The usual assumption in studies of protection is that the import restriction causes the price of imports of commodity i to rise sufficiently to reduce the demand for q_i to the constrained supply, i.e. to clear all markets perfectly. If so, the inverse of eq. (3) reflects demand for i, and it, plus eqs. (4), for $k \neq i$, may be used to estimate the parameters of the demand system. Assuming that the distribution of the basic errors is invariant with respect to which variable is exogenous, transformation of the demand equations to make their stochastic components well behaved merely takes us back to (3). We refer to this as the market-clearing model below: although imports of i are constrained, they are not rationed, since their price has increased sufficiently to curtail demand.

We do not face the problems discussed by Richard (1980). He showed (a) that statistics based on the residuals of equations normalised in different ways – i.e. $q = \theta(p) + \varepsilon$ and $p = \Psi(q) + \mu$ – cannot shed light on switches in the exogeneity of q and p, and (b) that estimates of the parameters of $\theta(p)$ and $\Psi(q)$ depend upon the parameters of the joint distribution of (q, p) and the distributions of ε and μ. But we have no need to test for switches in exogeneity, because prior information identifies the change from an endogenous quantity to an endogenous price regime, i.e. we know fairly accurately when the trade restrictions were in place. What we seek below by way of regime change is evidence that in the latter regime demanders are rationed. Second, our transformations of the observations for which $p = \Psi(q) + \mu$ would be the natural regression model back into the form $q = \theta(p) + \varepsilon$ are designed expressly to cope with Richard's point (b).

Richard also argues the implausibility of assuming that the distribution of ε is invariant with respect to changes in exogeneity; this view commands some respect, but in our problem the prices of other goods and changes in taste – probably the two major contributors to ε – are likely to be independent of exogeneity.

The remainder of this section explores the statistical implications of rationing and develops some tests for its presence. Suppose that, at the ruling price, p_i, consumers are unable to obtain the share indicated by (3) for q_i but are rationed to consume less. Clearly the observed pair (p_i, q_i) will lie below the demand surface, but because we cannot observe directly by how much below, we cannot use the pair to identify that surface other than directionally. This might appear to suggest that almost no information from the rationed period may be used to estimate the parameters of the demand function, but in fact this is too pessimistic. Neary and Roberts (1980) show that even while the ration binds, the demand for unrationed goods may be expressed as a function of the parameters of the demand systems, observed prices, and the ration; this in turn permits us to identify a sub-set of the parameters empirically even while the ration binds. This is done by inverting the Hicksian demand curves (2) for the rationed goods to estimate their 'virtual prices' and substituting these into the demand functions for unrationed goods. Since for homothetic systems such as the CES inverting (2) is equivalent to inverting (3), this amounts to no more than estimating (4) directly – see Winters and Brenton (1991) for details.

The error affecting commodity i, ε_i, cannot be separated empirically from the degree of rationing, but if we assume that the stochastic element of demand is unaffected by rationing we can write the $(n-1)\times(n-1)$ matrix of error covariances for eqs. (4) as

$$\tilde{\Sigma}_t = E(\tilde{\varepsilon}_t \tilde{\varepsilon}_t') = G_t' \Sigma G_t, \tag{5}$$

where $\tilde{\varepsilon}_t$ is the vector of errors for the unconstrained commodities for observation t, $G_t' = [\tilde{\beta}_t I_{n-1}]$, $\tilde{\beta}_t$ is the $(n-1)$ vector of $\beta_{jt} = \alpha_j p_{jt}^{\sigma} J_t^{-1}$, and where we have assumed that commodity 1 is constrained.

A common way of estimating the effects of a distortionary trade policy is to fit the demand system on pre-distortion data and then to use the estimates to define an anti-monde for the distorted period. Our approach is more efficient for we combine observations from periods with no quantitative restrictions, (3), with observations on the unrationed commodities from the periods of rationing, (4) and (5), in the same estimation. Making efficient use of the information to hand can be a very significant advantage when there are only a few unconstrained observations. In this crucial regard our work differs from Deaton's (1981). His Almost Ideal Demand System is not invertible analytically and hence precludes the combination of rationed and unrationed observations.[4]

As well as defining an estimation procedure, the previous analysis also

[4]It was to allow such combination that our earlier, more general, modelling used the Rotterdam System. Deaton is careful to note the lack of relation between the AIDS and his Rationed AIDS (RAIDS) model.

offers a means of distinguishing between market clearing and Neary–Roberts rationing through the distribution of the residuals. Assuming market clearing we may estimate (3) on all observations. Letting a caret (^) denote observed residuals, H_0 (market clearing) entails that

$$\text{distribution}\,(\hat{\varepsilon}_t, t \in T_2) = \text{distribution}\,(\hat{\varepsilon}_t, t \in T_1),$$

where T_1 is the period with no constraints and T_2 is the period of suspected rationing. The alternative hypothesis H_1 (Neary–Roberts) is that

$$\hat{\varepsilon}_t = \varepsilon_t + r_t, \quad t \in T_2, \tag{6}$$

where r_t is the vector of the effects of rationing. By comparing the distributions of $\hat{\varepsilon}_t$ in T_1 and T_2 we might identify whether rationing distorts observed behaviour. Several tests for this are described briefly in the appendix.

3. Extensions of the basic model

This section makes three extensions to the basic model: the introduction of time trends in the share parameters, the introduction of dynamics and the extension to two or more constrained commodities.

Following Hickman and Lau (1973) we permit the share parameters, α_j, to evolve through time according to

$$\alpha_{jt} = \alpha_j^0 \exp(\sigma\gamma_j t) \approx \alpha_j^0 (1 + \sigma\gamma_j t), \tag{7}$$

where t is centred to be zero in mid-sample. The adding-up constraint requires that ${}_j\sum \alpha_j^0 \gamma_j = 0$, which is imposed during estimation.

Experience in Winters and Brenton (1988) suggested the need for some form of dynamics. It is not practicable to estimate a full vector autoregressive scheme on the vector of shares, and so we are obliged to use the rather restrictive approach of adding the terms $\sum_{l=1}^{4} \lambda_l L^l s_i$ to each eq. (3), $i = 1 \ldots n$, where L^l is the lag operator and the λ_l are dynamic coefficients which are common to all suppliers. No position intermediate to full autoregression or this common parameter form preserves adding up – see Anderson and Blundell (1983). In practice our quarterly data needed only lags one and four. Similar manipulation as before yields

$$s_k = (\bar{s}_i - \lambda_1 L\bar{s}_i - \lambda_4 L^4 \bar{s}_i)\beta_k + \lambda_1 L s_k + \lambda_4 L^4 s_k + \beta_k \varepsilon_i + \varepsilon_k, \tag{4'}$$

where $\bar{s}_i \equiv 1 - s_i$ and $\beta_k \equiv \alpha_k p_k^{\sigma} J^{-1}$, see Brenton and Winters (1990). This is perfectly analogous to eq. (4), and may be estimated in exactly the same way. Simple manipulation shows that (4′) still adds up.

The extension of the model to two rationed commodities is also straightforward, if tedious. The final estimating equations with both i and j rationed are

$$s_k=(\tilde{s}-\lambda_1 L_1\tilde{s}-\lambda_4 L^4\tilde{s})\beta_k+\lambda_1 Ls_k+\lambda_4 L^4 s_k+\beta_k(\varepsilon_i+\varepsilon_j)+\varepsilon_k, \qquad (4'')$$

where $\tilde{s}\equiv 1-s_i-s_j$ and previous terms are defined as before.

4. Estimation

The equations above are all estimated by maximum likelihood methods using GAUSS. As is well known, allocation models are singular in their variance–covariance structure, which entails either omitting one commodity from the system or substituting $(\Sigma+ii')$ for Σ in the likelihhod functions. The present work entails three further complications.

First the demands on the data of estimating a full variance–covariance matrix, Σ, are fairly heavy, for it entails $n(n+1)/2$ freely estimated parameters. If n, the number of commodities included in the system is large, Σ can absorb considerable amounts of sample information, and even preclude convergence. In this paper, therefore, we adopt a restriction due to De Boer and Harkema (1984) and De Boer et al. (1987). They suggest the characterisation

$$\Sigma''=\hat{d}-(d'i)^{-1}d\,d', \qquad (8)$$

where d is a vector of parameters of dimension n, the number of commodities, and i is a unit vector also of dimension n. Harkema and de Boer show how maximum likelihood systems using Σ'' may be estimated iteratively from a concentrated likelihood function, but we preferred to treat the d as genuine parameters and use a full likelihood function.

The second complication in estimation involves the change in regime discussed above. In the absence of rationing we have an n-equation system with $\varepsilon_t\sim \mathrm{N}(0,\Sigma'')$, whereas with one rationed good we have an $(n-1)$ equation system (still subject to adding up) with $\tilde{\varepsilon}_t\sim \mathrm{N}(0,G_t'\Sigma''G_t)$. These must be combined into the log-likelihood function

$$\left(\frac{T_1 n_1}{2}+\frac{T_2 n_2}{2}\right)\log 2\pi-\frac{n_1}{2}\log|\Sigma''+ii'|-\frac{1}{2}\sum_{\tau\in T_1}\varepsilon_\tau'(\Sigma''+ii')^{-1}\varepsilon_\tau$$

$$-\frac{n_2}{2}\log|G_t\Sigma''G_t'+ii'|-\frac{1}{2}\sum_{\tau\in T_2}\tilde{\varepsilon}_\tau'(G_t\Sigma''G_t'+ii')^{-1}\tilde{\varepsilon}_\tau, \qquad (9)$$

where

T_1 and T_2 are the numbers of observations in the unconstrained and constrained periods,
n_1 and n_2 are the numbers of commodities which are never constrained and sometimes constrained,
$\boldsymbol{\varepsilon}_t$ are vectors of residuals in T_1 (of order n_1),
$\tilde{\boldsymbol{\varepsilon}}_t$ are vectors of residuals in T_2 (of order n_2).

This again requires us to use a full rather than a concentrated likelihood function, for no satisfactory concentration exists.

Clearly (9) may be generalised to cope with two constrained commodities, although in that case there are potentially four regimes to be combined: no rationing, i rationed, j rationed, and i and j rationed. When Σ is unconstrained – save, of course, for its usual adding-up and symmetry – (9) provides no interpretational difficulties. When Σ is constrained, however, as in (8), there is no reason other than convenience for believing that it is Σ, rather than $\tilde{\tilde{\Sigma}}$, that satisfies the particular constraints. In this case, however, convenience wins the day.

Finally, given our assumption that rationing occurs in particular periods the likelihood function should contain additional terms reflecting the likelihood that in the absence of rationing imports would exceed the actual level of imports. Writing $s_{\mathrm{H}i}$ for the 'Hicksian' share of imports of origin i – the level predicted by the estimated Hicksian demand curve at the observed vector of prices – and recognising that actual imports would differ from this by a stochastic component ε_i even in the absence of rationing, the probability of rationing is

$$\mathrm{prob}\,(s_i \leqq s_{\mathrm{H}i} + \varepsilon_i) = \mathrm{prob}\,(\varepsilon_i \geqq s_i - s_{\mathrm{H}i}). \tag{10}$$

Given our previous assumption that the vector $\boldsymbol{\varepsilon}$ has the multivariate normal distribution with covariance matrix Σ'', ε_i is $N(0, \Sigma''_{ii})$, where Σ''_{ii} is the (i,i)th element of Σ''. Thus, given $s_{\mathrm{H}i}$, the probability of rationing is

$$\int_{(s_i - s_{\mathrm{H}i})/\sqrt{\Sigma''_{ii}}}^{\infty} \mathrm{N}(0,1)\,\mathrm{d}t, \tag{10'}$$

the log of which for each rationed observation may be added to (9).[5]

5. The welfare effects of QRs

The previous section discussed the identification of different regimes and the methods of estimating demand appropriate to them. Once the parameters

[5]The additional factor required when both i and j are rationed is described in Brenton and Winters (1990).

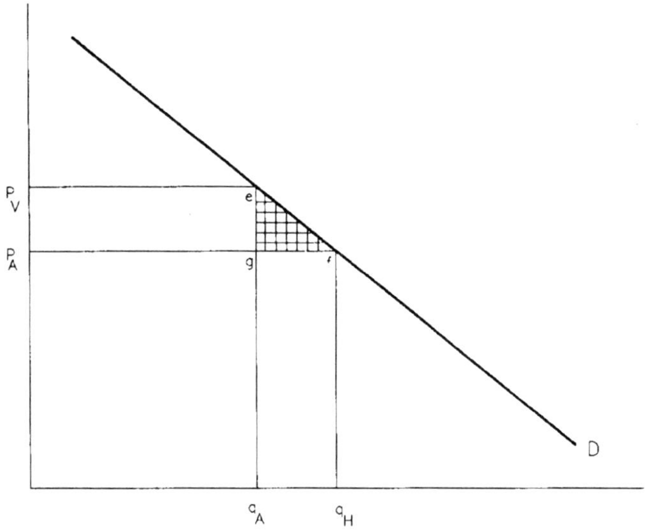

Fig. 1

of demand have been identified, we wish to use them to estimate the welfare effects of the NTBs under consideration. Here we concentrate on rationing, taking the actual price of the constrained imports as given and seeking evidence that, at that price, markets do not clear. The issue of post-QR price rises is discussed by Winters (1990).

The costs of rationing are illustrated in fig. 1. The actual price and quantity (p_A, q_A) lie off the compensated (Hicksian) demand curve. The virtual price, p_V, is the price at which quantity q_A would have been bought voluntarily at the given level of utility, while q_H, the 'Hicksian' quantity, is the quantity that would have been bought at p_A in the absence of rationing. Neary and Roberts (1980) and Johansson (1987) show that the area shaded under the compensated demand curve (*efg*) for the constrained goods represents the loss of welfare due to rationing. Intuitively, the loss of the units $(q_H - q_A)$ would reduce consumers' surplus by $p_V efp_A$ if it were achieved by an increase in price, but under rationing the expenditure $p_V egp_A$ remains with consumers, leaving a net loss of *efg*. We calculate the welfare effects on consumers directly from the cost functions underlying the CES demand system, holding utility constant at its level under rationing and subtracting the area $q_A(p_V - p_A)$.

All this implicitly supposes that observed prices and quantities pertain directly to final consumers, and that it is the latter who are rationed.

However, the price data available to us refer to imports measured cif plus tariffs and domestic supplies at the factory gate. If somewhere along the domestic distribution chain profit margins are raised as a result of the QR so that final prices reach the market-clearing level, consumers are no longer rationed, and they suffer the usual loss of welfare associated with a price rise $-p_V efp_A$. A model of quantity rationing is still required, however; someone's margins have risen and in an unfettered market, higher returns would surely cause this individual to increase his level of activity – i.e. to buy in more footwear – and the fact that the VER prevents this means that he is rationed. Whether the national welfare loss in this case included the transfer rectangle would, of course, depend on whether the enhanced price–cost margin accrued to residents or not.

6. Measurement issues: Imports and import restrictions

To estimate the demand system we require data of the volume and value of U.K. imports distinguished by supplier and domestic sales (domestic production minus exports) for both women's and children's, and men's leather footwear.[6] In common with previous research, the absence of actual import prices has led us to use unit values to approximate the prices of traded goods.[7] To maintain conformity and to permit our desired degree of disaggregation, unit values are also used as the measure of the prices of domestically produced footwear. The basic data are quarterly and cover the period 1971 quarter I to 1986 quarter IV.[8]

Here we concentrate on modelling separately the allocation of predetermined expenditure on the two types of leather footwear across suppliers. Initially there are 14 separate country/country group suppliers of imports which we treat in a hierarchical manner. The allocation of countries to subgroups of the hierarchy is determined by our a priori views as to the main substitutions that have occurred [see Brenton and Winters (1990)]. Prices and quantities are passed to higher levels of the hierarchy using the correct CES aggregators,

$$p_t = \left(\sum_j \alpha_{jt} p_{jt}^{(1+\sigma)} \right)^{1/(1+\sigma)} \quad \text{and} \quad q_t = \left(\sum_j \alpha_{jt} q_{jt}^{(1+\sigma)/\sigma} \right)^{\sigma/(1+\sigma)},$$

[6]Initially we had hoped to model the demand for women's and children's footwear separately, but major tariff classification changes in 1978 necessitated that the two groups be combined. These categories correspond to the groupings used to define the U.K. import restrictions.

[7]All import values are tariff inclusive.

[8]The original source of the trade data is HM Customs and Excise, whilst the domestic data are taken from Business Monitor PQ450. Many of the data were provided to us, however, by the British Footwear Manufacturers Federation, to whom we are most grateful.

except for the lowest levels of the hierarchies where, for numerical reasons, we used the simple sum of volumes and a current weighted index of unit values.

The QR which we analyse is the set of voluntary export restraints (VERs) on imports of leather footwear from Czechoslovakia, Poland and Romania, which were imposed in the mid-1970s. We treat imports from Poland and Czechoslovakia as separate goods, but combine the small and barely restrained imports from Romania into a rest of the world category.

There is a surprising degree of confusion in official sources about the timing and nature of the VERs in their early years, and their precise conditions are still confidential. Contemporary and current issues of *Hansard* and *British Business* conflict as to whether the restrictions on women's and children's and men's footwear were agreed from 1975, 1976 or 1977, while the Polish import agents, whom we interviewed, suggested that effective restraint did not occur unti mid-1977 or even 1978. We have, however, received official confirmation (on a private basis) of the existence of the VERs for years since 1978. Taking all this information into account, it seems clear that the VERs were not fully operative until 1977 at the earliest.

In the men's leather group actual imports from Czechoslovakia fell sharply in 1977 and 1978 and then fluctuated between 50 and 60 percent of permitted levels. The trend increase in imports from Poland was halted in 1977, and the volume of imports began to fall in 1978. However, actual quantities did not fall below the VER level until 1979 and then were stabilised at around 80 percent of the agreed volume. In the women's and children's group imports from Poland declined rapidly in 1977 and 1978 and then remained at about 50 percent of the quota level, while those from Czechoslovakia fell rapidly in 1978, rose during 1979 and 1980 (the VER level was increased in 1979) only to decline continuously thereafter. Simultaneously with the restrictions on Eastern Europe, home sales stabilized temporarily while Italian and other suppliers' sales in the United Kingdom increased.

The fact that actual imports fell below permissible levels raises the question of whether the VERs were actually binding after 1977. We believe so. The importers of Polish footwear – Skorimpex Rind plc, whom we interviewed – reported that they could easily have obtained at least 25 percent more orders and that their sales were immune to cyclical fluctuation. Their failure to fill their quota appeared to reflect two phenomena. First, informational and coordination problems. They felt an exaggerated concern not to overshoot their quotas (saying they feared penal reprisals), and since they arranged most of their sales at two major annual fairs could not readily replace cancelled orders. (This absence of aggressive marketing is perhaps further evidence of a perceived binding constraint.) Second, aggregation: Skorimpex reported that when the demand for sandals fell below the agreed

VER level, permission was refused to transfer this quota to other footwear types; unfortunately, data are not available to remove sandals from our exercise.[9] Finally, we note that British industry sources (The British Footwear Manufacturers Federation) reported that they feared a huge expansion of Comecon exports if the VERs were removed. That is, they felt that the VERs bound.

For modelling purposes we assume that each VER binds at the actual level of imports. This seems a natural procedure, but it has two possible dangers. First, because exporters have to allocate their annual quotas across quarters, they have some flexibility in most periods and thus the observed quantities are not wholly exogenous; see Anderson (1987). While this is clearly true in principle, we believe that the traditions of quantity targetting and rigid planning would make the required flexibility hard to achieve in the Eastern bloc.[10] Second, taking actual imports as the binding limit makes it necessary to be careful in identifying periods of rationing. As actual imports fall progressively below the quota level, the likelihood that the VER is actually binding falls, but the tightness of the constraint, if it does indeed bind, increases because the assumed bound level falls with the level of actual imports. Whenever imports persistently fall more than 30 percent below quota we consider it unrealistic even to contemplate the restrictions binding.

A related question is: If the VER binds, why do exporters not raise their prices to market-clearing levels? A plausible, if somewhat unsatisfying answer is that Eastern bloc economies operated entirely on quantity plans and at domestic prices; thus firms experienced no incentive to raise prices, and planning authorities were ill-prepared to exploit their market position. A second explanation could arise from the fact that the U.K. importers of Polish footwear were wholly owned by the single footwear exporting agency in Poland and that this agency was also charged with importing Western machinery back into Poland.[11] By keeping cif import prices down the exporters were able to reduce payments of the U.K.'s ad valorem tariff and yet still reap any scarcity rents by raising prices inside the United Kingdom. As we noted above, such behaviour entails the loss of rents to the U.K. economy just as if prices were at market-clearing levels, but it does not change the fact that someone is rationed and that the VER pushes us off the

[9]The VERs included 'inner limits' on various types of footwear, although it has not proved possible to identify one on Polish sandals in official source documents. Nevertheless, the basic difficulty over aggregation still stands.

[10]Moreover, given the particular form of our model, such endogeneity is not a major problem econometrically. In eq. (6), p_i, the price of constrained sales plays no direct role, while any shock in s_i affects all s_k proportionately and hence their shares in $(1-s_i)$ not at all. Indeed, the term $\alpha_k p_k^\sigma J^{-1}\varepsilon_i$ precisely counteracts any such effect. In a more sophisticated demand model endogeneity might be a potential difficulty.

[11]Such arrangements were common for state trading countries. Information made available to us by the licensing authorities suggests that during our sample period Czech footwear was also imported into the United Kingdom by a single agent.

Table 1

Estimates of market-clearing model.

	Italy	R.O.W.	Czechoslovakia	Poland	U.K.
(a) Men's leather					
α_i	0.1562[a]	0.0989[a]	0.0090	0.0086	0.7273
γ_i	0.0060	0.0041	−0.0073[a]	0.0041[a]	−0.0018
σ	2.7850[a]				
δ_1	0.4567[a]				
δ_4	0.2759[a]				
R^2	0.9690	0.8266	0.5150	0.3529	0.9600
LM(1–4)	9.3636	18.1086	25.8603	17.6438	18.4961
(b) Women's and children's leather					
α_i	0.1659[a]	0.1444[a]	0.0032[a]	0.0059[a]	0.6807
γ_i	0.0116[a]	0.0093[a]	−0.0168[a]	−0.0055	−0.0047
σ	1.7503[a]				
δ_1	0.3124[a]				
δ_4	0.3155[a]				
R^2	0.8901	0.9246	0.6024	0.4605	0.9438
LM(1–4)	9.5693	17.5178	7.0762	4.1762	3.8180

[a]Represents $t>2$; the parameter estimates for the United Kingdom were derived from the adding-up conditions and standard errors were not evaluated.

notional import demand schedule.[12] Even if there were no rationing, our model would provide a useful response to the problems posed by unobservable consumer prices.[13]

7. The results

One further extension of the basic model proved necessary. Footwear trade is highly seasonal, and ideally we would have treated this by adding seasonal dummies to the estimating equations. However, this was precluded because the additional 12 parameters would have over-stretched our data and estimation ability and so we were forced into using de-seasonalised data. The de-seasonalisation was applied to the regression data, i.e. s_{it} and p_{it}, by regressing them on seasonal dummies constrained to sum to zero over a year. The model is non-linear so this is not equivalent to including dummies in the estimating equations; however, we never detect signs of residual seasonality in the following results.

The estimates of the market-clearing model with trends and lagged dependent variables are reported in table 1. They use the De Boer and Harkema covariance matrix, although the unrestricted version produced

[12]Under these circumstances, however, interpreting the model is somewhat more complex than in this paper – see Brenton and Winters (1990).

[13]We are grateful to a referee for noting this.

similar results. To this model we apply the statistics discussed in the appendix to test our prior views about rationing over the period 1977–1986. Starting with the men's leather group and testing individual quarters for the start and finish of rationing by (T1) we found, as expected, no evidence of regime changes over 1975–1976. There was, however, a strong market disturbance in 1977 QIII, the χ^2 statistic of 15.5 being significant at 1 percent. Associated with this statistic was a large negative residual for Czechoslovakian imports (algebraically the lowest residual observed) followed by a string of negative residuals. The residual for the Polish share in this quarter was just positive,[14] although several large negative residuals were apparent immediately afterwards. These latter observations produced relatively high values of the test statistic (T1).

These results corroborate our institutional information, namely that imports from both Poland and Czechoslovakia were quantity rationed towards the end of 1977. As noted above, imports from Czechoslovakia fell away quickly after the imposition of the constraint and, as expected, in 1979 QIII a high positive residual for Czechoslovakia is accompanied by a relatively high, although not quite significant, value of the test statistic. No subsequent quarter appeared to reflect the removal of restrictions on Polish imports, which suggests, along with our institutional information and interview results, that the VER on Polish suppliers still bound in 1986. Thus these tests identify two periods of rationing, for Czechoslovakia and Poland together during 1977 QIII–1979 QII, and Poland alone over 1979 QIII–1986 QIV. The portmanteau tests for the whole period 1977 QIII to 1986 QIV broadly confirm this: the F-test on the difference in the constrained and unconstrained covariance matrix, (T3), was not significant, but the likelihood-ratio statistic (T4) was strongly so, taking the value 388.7 compared with a critical value of 15.5 at 5 percent.

With regard to the women's and children's leather group a strong disturbance, significant as 5 percent, was apparent in 1977 QIV. Its associated large negative residuals for Czechoslovakia and Poland followed by a further series of negative residuals (including algebraically the lowest residual observed for both suppliers) and fairly high test statistics seemed to confirm a switch in regime. Rationing of both sources of imports appeared to cease in 1980 QII with large positive residuals for both suppliers and a high, although not significant, value of the test statistic for this observation. Again this confirms our prior view that with falling imports rationing no longer applied. The portmanteau tests of rationing over the period 1977 QIV to 1980 QI provide much stronger evidence of a change in regime, with both the F-test (T3) and the likelihood-ratio test being overwhelmingly significant.

[14]However, when rationing was admitted, as the Czechoslovakian result required, this residual also became negative.

Table 2

Estimates of the Neary–Roberts model.

	Italy	R.O.W.	Czechoslovakia	Poland	U.K.
(a) Men's leather					
α_i	0.1602[a]	0.0998[a]	0.0114[a]	0.0193	0.7092
γ_i	0.0058	0.0040	−0.0079[a]	0.0242[a]	−0.0024
σ	2.7511[a]				
δ_1	0.5038[a]				
δ_4	0.2642[a]				
R^2	0.9674	0.8338			0.9657
LM(1–4)	9.9514	16.2677			19.0887
(b) Women's and children's leather					
α_i^0	0.1926[a]	0.1517[a]	0.0091[a]	0.0118[a]	0.6348
γ_i	0.0082	0.0094	−0.0089	−0.0034	−0.0046
σ	1.8793[a]				
δ_1	0.2412[a]				
δ_4	0.5377[a]				
R^2	0.8964	0.9284			0.9445
LM(1–4)	5.5257	17.4359			8.1930

[a]See table 1.

In response to these tests the model was re-estimated with rationing for Polish and Czech footwear over the periods detailed above. In the women's and children's case we experienced severe convergence difficulties, and hence turned to a more restrictive form of the covariance matrix [see Deaton (1975)] whereby $\Sigma = s^2(I_n - (1/n)i_n i_n')$, where s^2 is a parameter to be estimated.

Although the results, which are presented in table 2, appear at first glance to be similar to the previous set, in fact they differ in crucial respects. When we allow for rationing the estimated base year shares (α_i) for the constrained countries increase strongly as, in the case of men's leather, do the trend rates of growth. There are also large differences in the dynamic adjustment parameters. Hence, although the slopes of the demand curves for constrained footwear do not change greatly (see the elasticities of substitution) their positions shift markedly. Moreover, the coefficient estimates involved in identifying these shifts are generally well determined.

Turning to the economics of the results, we consider first the changes in sales induced by the VERs. These are calculated by comparing actual quantities under the ration with the corresponding Hicksian quantities calculated on the assumption that changes in demand are met at constant-prices and that total demand is given.[15] For men's leather the market share losses to Poland are considerable; our equations suggest that without the VER Poland would have supplied around 40 percent of the market rather

[15]That is, applying the parameters from table 2 to actual prices and total sales in eq. (3) modified for trends and lags.

than its actual 10 percent in 1986. These losses to Poland are balanced by increases in sales for other suppliers which are distributed fairly evenly amongst producers in Italy, the United Kingdom, and the rest of the world. For women's and children's leather the share of the market for both constrained suppliers under the VERs is less than half the share that would have occurred in their absence.[16]

It may seem surprising that trade restrictions could have had such strong effects on market shares, and we recognise the possibility that we have over-estimated the suppliers' ability to expand sales in Britain at constant costs. On the other hand, with relatively long-lived restrictions such as those imposed on Poland, and with the pattern of price movements that actually occurred, it is difficult to find convincing a priori reasons to reject the shifts in the patterns of demand that we have identified. Indeed, we suspect that the traditional insensitivity of demand patterns that colleagues implicitly use as a benchmark when they wonder at our results, stems from the existence or threat of restrictions of the sort that we have been analysing.

The concomitants of the strong effects of the VERs on relative market shares are their implications for virtual prices.[17] A small difference between the actual and virtual prices of men's leather imports from Poland emerges in the latter two quarters of 1977 and in 1978 and grows strongly thereafter. By 1986 the ratio of virtual to actual price exceeds 2.5.[18] The strength and duration of this effect reflects the tightness of the restriction whilst its growth shows the economic distortions that occur when a constant VER is confronted by expanding demand.

For women's and children's leather footwear the actual and virtual prices of both Poland and Czechoslovakia diverge sharply in the first quarter of rationing and the differences increase to a factor of over 3 for Czechoslovakia and 1.6 for Poland in the middle of the constrained period. There is a marked tendency for the virtual and actual prices to converge during 1979, however, as rationing becomes less important.

The final statistics of interest are the welfare costs of rationing. These are shown in table 3. The first column under each type of footwear shows the deadweight loss to the consumer corresponding to the shaded area of fig. 1. The losses to U.K. consumers range from £3.04 million in 1978 (both women's and children's, and men's) to £32 million in 1986 (men's only). The increasing costs of the VER on imports from Poland of men's leather footwear reflect the increasing burden implied by a roughly constant quota

[16]The size of these effects dwarfs any possible under-fulfilment of the quota. Hence even if we could somehow have modelled the VERs as binding at their nominal limits these results would still have suggested a strong degree of restriction.

[17]For reasons explained in Brenton and Winters (1990), we refer here to the 'equilibrium' virtual price not the 'dynamic' one.

[18]During the short period in which Czechoslovakian imports of men's leather footwear are bounded the Czechoslovakian virtual price exceeds the actual price by approximately 40 percent.

Table 3

Estimated welfare costs of VERs on men's and women's and children's, leather footwear (£million).

	Men's rationing		Women's and children's rationing		Men's, and women's and children's, price rise	
	Deadweight loss	Transfer	Deadweight loss	Transfer	Deadweight loss and transfer	Total
1977	0.15	0.53	0.34	0.56	1.84	3.42
1978	0.78	2.71	2.26	2.54	4.57	12.86
1979	2.04	4.14	2.26	2.88	5.78	17.10
1980	2.35	4.19	0.30	0.62	7.55	15.01
1981	3.37	4.78			5.62	13.77
1982	7.01	6.73			4.50	18.24
1983	12.20	9.15			4.36	25.71
1984	18.13	12.72			4.07	34.92
1985	22.99	15.14			4.50	42.63
1986	32.49	20.18			5.59	58.26

in the face of growing demand. Annual costs (in current prices) more than double between 1983 and 1986.

The deadweight losses to consumers are compounded if one allows for increases in price somewhere between the exporter and the final consumer. The second column under each type of footwear in table 3 is a measure of the rectangle $(p_V - p_A)\, q_A$. As noted above, this represents the transfer from consumers to domestic distributors if the latter raise their margins, or the transfer abroad if the foreign-owned importers sell at the market-clearing price and gather themselves the VER-scarcity rents. In 1986 this adds an extra £20.2 million to the welfare costs faced by consumers of men's leather footwear.

The estimates of the welfare costs of the VERs given here refer only to the effects of rationing at a given import price. Winters (1990) has estimated the extent to which exporters raised their prices in response to the VERs. On admittedly rather crude data he finds no evidence of increases in Czechoslovakian or Romanian prices, but suggests that the Poles raised their leather export prices by around 19 percent between 1977 and 1986. The additional welfare losses of these price rises are given in the fifth column of table 3.

Yet further losses of welfare from footwear protection are identified in Brenton and Winters (1991) which considers restrictions on imports of non-leather footwear from Korea and Taiwan. They show that while the VER on the relatively concentrated Korean industry never resulted in rationing – that is, prices rose to market-clearing levels – the U.K. administered import quota on the competitive Taiwanese industry did result in rationing. That is, competition between exporters appeared to prevent the Taiwanese from collecting the scarcity rents. Moreover, once the quota on Taiwan was converted into a VER in 1981 the rationing of textile footwear soon ceased.

8. Conclusion

The imposition of a quantitative trade restriction necessarily leads to either demanders or suppliers being rationed. This paper has made two contributions stemming from this observation. First, it has developed a means of identifying and modelling rationing: we have applied the approach to a system of demand equations, but it is of equal relevance ot supply relations, and, as noted above, any empirical work on quantitative restrictions must grapple with rationing somewhere in the market. Second, we have shown that for U.K. leather footwear imports from Eastern Europe there is a strong presumption that demand-side rationing occurred. Complete proof is, of course, impossible, but from institutional and interview data we identified periods when rationing was plausible and then with detailed data found that in those periods market clearing was rejected in exactly the fashion predicted by rationing theory. These results – the most detailed on European footwear markets and the first on Eastern Europe – suggest that even in the absence of price rises to the market-clearing level, British consumers have been materially penalised by the VERs which restricted their access to men's, and women's and children's footwear from Czechoslovakia and Poland.

Appendix: Tests for rationing

Under the null hypothesis that the model is perfectly specified the residuals ε from systems estimation of (3) are asymptotically normal with mean zero and variance σ^2, and

$$\frac{1}{T}\sum_{k=1}^{T} \varepsilon_k \varepsilon_k' \to \Sigma,$$

where ε_k is ε for observation k. Thus for period k

$$\varepsilon_k'(\hat{\Sigma} + ii')^{-1}\varepsilon_k \sim \chi^2_{n-1} \tag{T.1}$$

and for several periods (T' in all)

$$\sum_{k=1}^{T} \varepsilon_k'(\hat{\Sigma} + ii')\varepsilon_k \sim \chi^2_{T'(n-1)}, \tag{T.2}$$

where $\hat{\Sigma}$ is the estimate of Σ, and n the number of commodities.

Following Harvey (1981, p. 157) these tests might be more powerful if the estimate of Σ were based not on the whole sample but on only that part for which the market-clearing model was strongly believed to be correct. However, in our case this period is too short to give reliable estimates of Σ, and so the whole of the period is used.

Harvey also suggests an exact test for heteroskedasticity based on single equation recursive residuals. However, data limitations and the complexity of calculating recursive residuals for systems estimated by maximum likelihood require that an approximation be used. In vew of (T.1)

$$\frac{\sum_{t\in T_1}\varepsilon_t'(\hat{\Sigma}+ii')^{-1}\varepsilon_t}{\sum_{t\in T_2}\varepsilon_t'(\hat{\Sigma}+ii')^{-1}\varepsilon_t} \tag{T.3}$$

will be distributed approximately $F_{(n-1)T_1,(n-1)T_2}$, where T_1 and T_2 are sets of unconstrained and constrained observations.

Finally we consider maximum-likelihood tests of the variance–covariance structure. Under H_0, Σ is common to both regimes, whereas under H_1 the variances Σ_1 and Σ_2 vary between regimes. A rather crude approximation of a standard likelihood-ratio test is given by

$$2{*}LL \approx T\log|\hat{\Sigma}| - \sum_{i=1}^{2} T_i \log|\hat{\Sigma}_i|, \tag{T.4}$$

with $\hat{\Sigma}_i$ appproximated by the residuals of the estimation under H_0. This test essentially considers the first step of a maximum-likelihood search for the parameters under H_1 (different Σ_i) starting from the estimate of H_0 (identical Σ_i). If it suggests rejection of H_0 one can be sure that further steps towards convergence, all of which increase the likelihood, would not reverse that conclusion. The derivation of these tests are described in more detail in Brenton and Winters (1990).

References

Anderson, G. and R. Blundell, 1983, Testing restrictions in a flexible dynamic system: An application to consumers expenditure in Canada, Review of Economic Studies 12, 397–410.

Anderson, J.E., 1987, Quotas as options: Optimality and quota licence pricing under uncertainty, Journal of International Economics 22, 21–39.

Armington, P.S., 1969, A theory of demand for products distinguished by place of production, IMF Staff Papers 16, 159–176.

Brenton, P.A., 1989, The allocation approach to trade modelling: Some tests of separability between imports and domestic production and between different imported commodity groups, Weltwirtschaftliches Archiv 125, 230–251.

Brenton, P.A. and L.A. Winters, 1990, Non-tariff barriers and rationing: UK footwear imports, Discussion Paper No. 365, Centre for Economic Policy Research, London.

Deaton, A.S., 1975, Models and projections of demand in post-war Britain (Chapman and Hall, London).

Deaton, A.S., 1981, Theoretical and empirical approaches to consumer demand under rationing, in: A.S. Deaton, ed., Essays in the theory and measurement of consumer behaviour (Cambridge University Press, Cambridge) 55–72.

De Boer, P.M.C. and R. Harkema, 1984, Undersized samples and maximum likelihood estimation of sum-constrained linear models, Report 8331/E, Economic Institute, Erasmus University, Rotterdam.

De Boer, P.M.C., R. Harkema and B.J. van Heeswijk, 1987 Estimating foreign trade functions: A comment and a correction, Journal of International Economics 22, 369–373.

Greenaway, D., 1986, Estimating the welfare affects of voluntary export restraints and tariffs: An application to non-leather footwear in the UK, Applied Economics 18, 1065–1083.

Harvey, A.C., 1981, The econometric analysis of time series (Philip Allen, Oxford).

Hickman, B.G. and L.J. Lau, 1973, Elasticities of substitution and export demands in a world trade model, European Economic Review 4, 347–380.

Johansson, P.-O., 1987, The economic theory and measurement of environmental benefits (Cambridge University Press, London).

Neary, J.P. and K.W.S. Roberts, 1980, The theory of household behavior under rationing, European Economic Review 13, 25–42.

Quandt, R.E., 1982, Economic disequilibrium models, Econometric Reviews 1, 1–63.

Richard, J.F., 1980, Models with several regimes and changes in exogeneity, Review of Economic Studies 47, 1–20.

Takacs, W.E. and L.A. Winters, 1991, Labour adjustment costs and British footwear protection, Oxford Economic Papers 43, 479–501.

Winters, L.A., 1984, Separability and the specification of foreign trade functions, Journal of International Economics 17, 239–263.

Winters, L.A., 1990, Voluntary export restraints and the prices of UK imports of footwear, Weltwirtschaftliches Archiv 126, 523–542.

Winters, L.A. and P.A. Brenton, 1988, Voluntary export restraints: UK restrictions on imports of leather footwear from Eastern Europe, Discussion Paper 283, Centre for Economic Policy Research, London.

Winters, L.A. and P.A. Brenton, 1991, Quantifying the economic effects of non-tariff barriers: The case of UK footwear, Kyklos 44, 71–91.

ELSEVIER

European Journal of Political Economy
Vol. 17 (2001) 593–607

European Journal of
POLITICAL
ECONOMY

www.elsevier.com/locate/econbase

Chapter 4

Anti-dumping policies in the EU and trade diversion ☆

Paul Brenton *

Centre for European Policy Studies, Place Du Congrès 1, B-1000 Brussels, Belgium

Received 15 February 1999; received in revised form 29 February 2000; accepted 17 July 2000

Abstract

Anti-dumping actions are by nature discriminatory. Imports from targeted countries are discriminated against relative to domestic producers but also relative to imports from non-named countries in the rest of the world. This paper analyses the impact of anti-dumping actions in the EU, distinguishing between the impact upon named countries, non-named countries in the rest of the world and non-named countries in the EU. The results suggest that anti-dumping policies cause trade diversion and that this diversion is primarily to non-EU suppliers. © 2001 Elsevier Science B.V. All rights reserved.

JEL classification: F13; F15
Keywords: Anti-dumping; Trade diversion; EU

1. Introduction

The purpose of this paper is to investigate the effects of EU anti-dumping measures. Anti-dumping actions are by nature discriminatory. Imports from targeted countries are discriminated against relative to domestic producers in the EU,

☆ Information on anti-dumping cases are taken from various editions of *The Annual Report from the Commission to the European Parliament on the Community's Anti-Dumping and Anti-Subsidy Activities* and the relevant issues of the *Official Journal of the European Communities*. The trade data were obtained from the *Comext* database of Eurostat.

* Tel.: +32-2-229-3936; fax: +32-2-219-4151.
E-mail address: paul.brenton@ceps.be (P. Brenton).

PII: S0176-2680(01)00047-7

and also relative to non-named extra-EU countries.[1] It is therefore not necessarily the case that firms initiating anti-dumping procedures will be beneficiaries of restrictions on imports from the named countries. Trade can be diverted to other suppliers in the EU and to non-named suppliers in the rest of the world. In this case, the effect of the removal of the duties or the ending of price undertakings will be felt beyond the complainant firms.

The focus of this paper is to assess the extent of trade diversion associated with EU anti-dumping actions. Previous empirical studies suggest that trade diversion has been important in the EU in the 1980s (Messerlin, 1989) and in the US (Prusa, 1997). The first section of the paper provides a simple graphical analysis of the economic impact of EU anti-dumping actions on trade within the EU, imports from named countries and imports from other countries in the rest of the world. The paper then proceeds to an econometric analysis of trade diversion in EU anti-dumping policies. A final section provides conclusions.

2. The economic impact of EU anti-dumping actions

This section considers whether the trade restrictions (or undertakings) divert trade to non-named countries, either in the EU or in the rest of the world. I use data for a range of cases initiated between 1989 and 1994.[2] In total, there are 98 anti-dumping cases involving 47 products.[3] Of these, 31 cases resulted in no further action due to lack of dumping, lack of injury, or 'other reasons'. Overall, during this period 193 cases were initiated but some cases against countries of the former Soviet Union and Yugoslavia are excluded due to the absence of comparable trade data over time. Also excluded are investigations involving reviews of existing cases and cases where anti-dumping measures were currently or previously in force, since the pre-announcement data will be clouded by the earlier actions. Thus, here we look at first investigations of dumping and exclude cases where trade flows may be affected by existing or previous actions. A small number of regional investigations, that is, cases relating to a single member of the EU, are also excluded.[4]

[1] There are cases where all significant suppliers of a product are named in an anti-dumping petition.

[2] Cases prior to 1989 have previously been analysed by Messerlin (1989). Thus, our sample is completely different to that of Messerlin and so this study provides an assessment of the robustness of the results presented in that paper.

[3] We use trade data at the eight-digit level of the HS. When the anti-dumping action refers to a number of eight-digit codes we sum across these, rather than include them all individually, since the aggregate is the relevant market.

[4] More precise details of the products and suppliers covered by these cases are available from the author.

P. Brenton / European Journal of Political Economy 17 (2001) 593–607 595

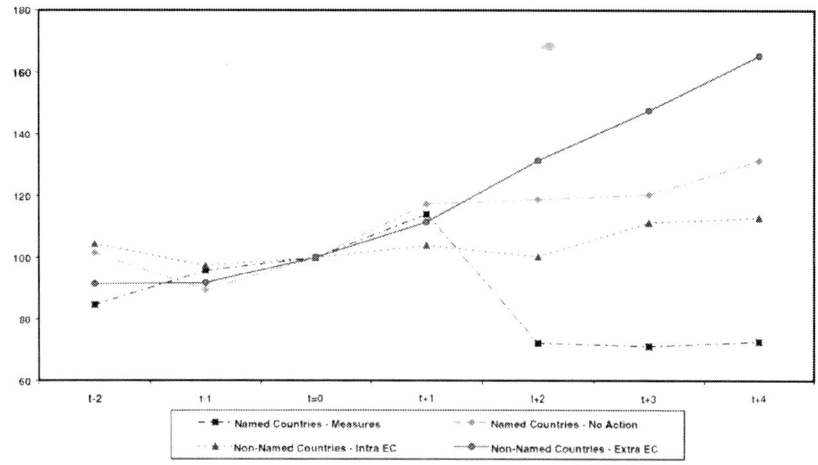

Fig. 1. Changes in import values and anti-dumping in the EU ($t_0 = 100$).e

Where measures (ad valorem duties, specific duties, minimum prices, or price undertakings) were applied, the average unweighted duty (including ad valorem equivalents of specific duties) exceeded 25%.[5] This suggests that anti-dumping measures are likely to have a major impact upon trade. The average duty is considerably higher than the level of tariff protection affecting most products, with the exception of agricultural goods and products such as tobacco and alcoholic drinks. The average tariff for industrial products entering the EU during this period was around 5% to 6%.

The products figuring most prominently in the anti-dumping cases were mineral products and chemicals (Sections 25 to 29 of the Harmonised System), primarily organic chemicals, and machinery and equipment (Sections 84 and 85), mainly electrical machinery and equipment. These products accounted for over half of the cases that are considered in this paper. Countries targeted in cases involving electrical machinery and equipment were typically in the Far East, with Japan and the NICs (Hong Kong, Singapore, South Korea, and Taiwan) being most commonly cited.

Fig. 1 shows the impact of anti-dumping cases on the value of EU(12) imports over a period beginning 2 years before the investigation is initiated and ending 4 years after this date. Provisional duties are typically applied in the first year after the investigation is initiated, with definitive duties or other measures, if sanctioned, normally being levied in the following year. We distinguish between (1)

[5] For price undertakings we use, where available, the duty determined in the investigation but not subsequently applied.

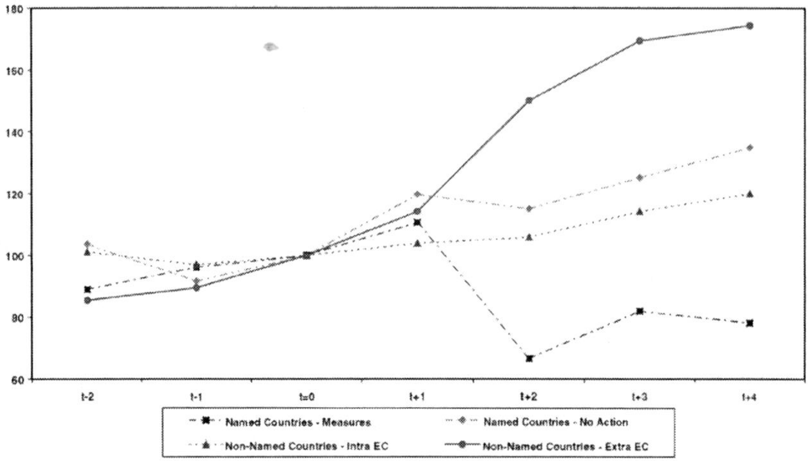

Fig. 2. Changes in import volumes and anti-dumping in the EU (t_0 = 100).

imports from countries that are named in an anti-dumping petition, and are subsequently subject to restrictive measures of some kind, (2) those countries that are named but where measures are not imposed, and (3) imports from other countries, firstly, in the EU and, secondly, in the rest of the world, which are not named in the petition. The figure shows the unweighted[6] average (across all of the cases considered) change in imports relative to the year in which the investigation is initiated (t_0). Figs. 2 and 3 show the average changes in import volumes and in import prices, as proxied by unit values (value per unit of volume).

These figures suggest a number of observations.

- There is no significant decline, on average, in the value or volume of intra-EU imports in the year preceding anti-dumping cases (Figs. 1 and 2). Thus, the observed increase in the value and volume of imports from named countries, in the year before the action is initiated, is not at the expense of a fall in the value of intra-EU imports. Of course, what matters in anti-dumping cases is the value of domestic sales by EU firms. Unfortunately, such data are not available but we return to discuss this issue later.
- Following a rise in the first year after the action is initiated,[7] there is a large decline (over 20%) in the value of imports from named countries as duties or other

[6] Weighting the value of imports for each case by the total of all imports subject to investigation made little difference to the averages that are presented.

[7] This could reflect issues of timing since our data, and so our analysis, is based upon calendar years. Hence, we cannot distinguish between actions initiated in January and those in December. The pattern of imports in the years after the initiation of the action may also reflect variations in the time taken before the imposition of first, provisional, and then definitive duties.

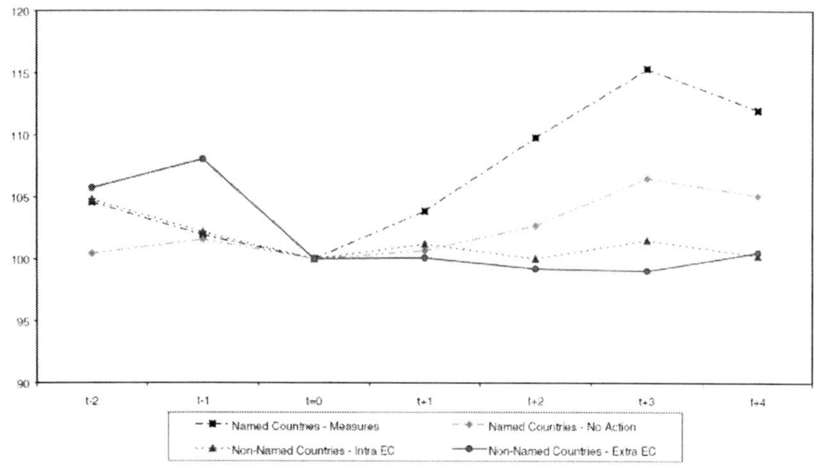

Fig. 3. Changes in import unit values and anti-dumping in the EU ($t_0 = 100$).

measures are imposed. The fall in the volume of imports is slightly more pronounced. This relatively low level of imports is then maintained in the subsequent 2 years (Figs. 1 and 2).

· As imports from named countries decline, there is a surge in the value of imports from non-named countries in the rest of the world. The value of intra-EU imports grows but at a much slower rate than imports from outside of the EU.[8] Thus, *trade diversion away from countries subject to anti-dumping measures appears to be primarily to non-EU countries.*

· Imports from countries that are named in an anti-dumping petition, but which are not subsequently subject to measures, also appear to be affected, with the value of imports remaining relatively constant in the 2 years following the announcement of the investigation. The value and the volume of such imports increase in the third year after the investigation is initiated (Figs. 1 and 2).

· The prices of imports from extra-EU sources (both named and non-named) fall in the year before the anti-dumping action is initiated, as does the price of intra-EU imports. It would therefore appear that movements in prices rather than in trade values and trade volumes trigger dumping complaints in the EU (Fig. 3).

· The initiation of the anti-dumping procedures appears to interfere with the trend movements in prices; the price of imports from named countries subject to measures increases substantially relative to the year of initiation, whilst the price of extra-EU imports from non-named countries and EU import prices stabilise. In

[8] In fact, the increase in intra-EU imports occurs in the year after the decline in imports from named countries.

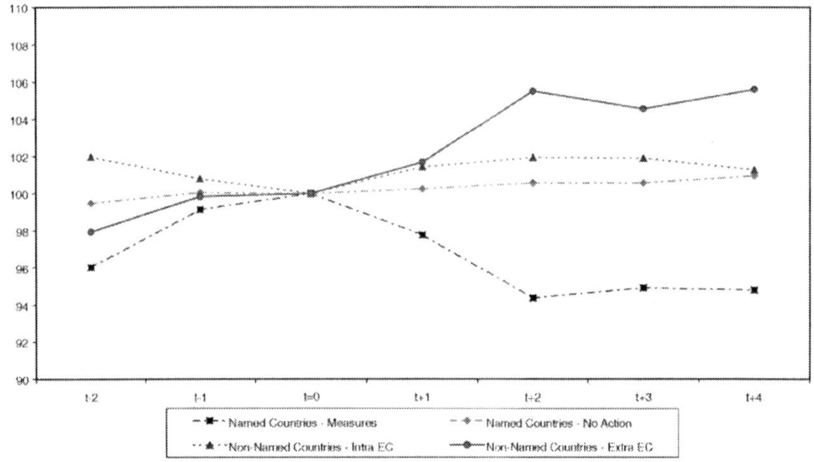

Fig. 4. Changes in import value shares and anti-dumping in the EU ($t_0 = 100$).

the fourth year after the action was initiated, prices fall back, with the price of intra-EU imports almost identical to that when the investigation was initiated (Fig. 3).

The averages presented in these first three figures typically have a very large associated standard error, reflecting in part the different magnitude of imports for the various anti-dumping cases. In Figs. 4 and 5, the data are normalised by

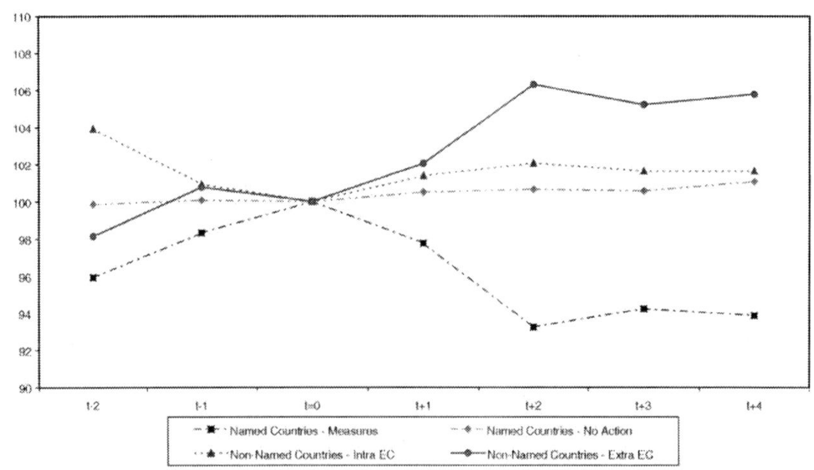

Fig. 5. Changes in import volume shares and anti-dumping in the EU ($t_0 = 100$).

looking at the average of changes in the share of the EU market for imports (intra-EU imports + extra-EU imports), in terms of both value and volume. These figures are likely to be less prone to the influence of extreme trade values or volumes. The figures show the difference in percentage points in market share relative to the base year in which the action was initiated. Both Fig. 4, for value shares, and Fig. 5, for the volume share, clearly show that the principal effect of anti-dumping actions is to raise the share of total EU imports of non-named countries in the rest of the world at the expense of suppliers subject to anti-dumping measures. There is a very slight rise in the share of intra-EU imports. It is also noticeable that, prior to the initiation of the anti-dumping action, the share of intra-EU suppliers declines, due mainly to the rising share of imports from countries that are subsequently named in anti-dumping petitions and are then subjected to measures. Anti-dumping actions appear to curtail the trend decline in the share of intra-EU imports in the EU market. The share of imports from countries that are named but are then not subjected to measures remains relatively constant both before and after the initiation of the anti-dumping proceeding.

What matters in anti-dumping cases is not just trends in EU imports but also changes in domestic sales by EU firms. However, it is likely that movements in intra-EU trade relative to imports from non-EU members are representative of the competitiveness of EU firms in general and of changes in comparative advantage. It is reasonable to expect that the elasticity of substitution between intra-EU imports and extra-EU imports is very similar to that between domestic sales by EU firms and extra-EU imports. It would be surprising if the ratio of extra-EU imports to domestic sales in the EU were to move in a different direction to the ratio of extra-EU imports to intra-EU imports.

Given this, our analysis would imply that, prior to a request for anti-dumping proceedings, the value of sales by domestic firms remains fairly constant. This then suggests that revenues are unlikely to be falling fast, and therefore begs the question of the extent to which domestic EU firms suffer (economic) injury from the specified imports. Morkre and Kelly (1994) show that, in the US, in most anti-dumping cases domestic firms incur no fall in revenue. If one accepts the link from the performance of EU firms selling in other EU countries to the performance of EU firms in their national domestic market, the results here lead to a similar conclusion for the EU.[9]

The above simple analysis suggests that anti-dumping actions are triggered not by absolute falls in the value or volume of sales by EU firms, but by declining market shares and/or by falling average and relative prices. However, the impact of remedies to the perceived dumping is primarily to increase imports from non-named import suppliers rather than EU suppliers. The discriminatory nature of

[9] Messerlin and Reed (1995) note that confidentiality concerning injury determination means that a specific investigation of this issue is not possible in the EU.

anti-dumping measures leads to trade diversion. The magnitude of this trade diversion is highlighted by the fact that, on average, the total value and volume of imports does not decline in the years after the initiation of an anti-dumping investigation. Trade diversion to other suppliers mitigates the decline in imports from named countries. Any beneficial impact upon complainant EU firms in terms of higher sales and higher prices is reduced, or even eliminated. This implies that the impact of the removal of anti-dumping measures on EU firms will also be dissipated; it will be firms in the rest of the world that will be most affected.

3. An econometric analysis

I now proceed to a more formal analysis of the impact of anti-dumping actions. I investigate import volumes, import prices and then import value shares using a simple model of the evolution of imports similar to that applied by Prusa (1997) to US data. More sophisticated models cannot be used because of the lack of a long time-series of data to provide sufficient variation in prices. The equation estimated is

$$\ln x_{i,t_j} = \alpha + \beta_1 \ln x_{i,t_{j-1}} + \beta_2(\ln x_{i,t-1} - \ln x_{i,t-2}) + \lambda_1 \ln \mathrm{Duty}_i$$
$$+ \lambda_2 \mathrm{Numnamed} + \delta_{1j}\mathrm{td}_j + \delta_{2j}\mathrm{td}_j \mathrm{Dec}_i + \eta_j \mathrm{Year}_{t_j} + \varepsilon_{i,t_j}$$

where $x_{i,t}$ is the volume (price or value share) of imports for case i at time t_j, and where t_0 is the year the action was initiated and $j = 0,\ldots,4$. Duty measures the size of the duty imposed (the ad valorem equivalent of specific duties and the difference between actual and minimum prices). Following Prusa (1997), we include a dummy variable, Numnamed, which takes a value of 1 if the number of named countries exceeds two and zero otherwise. This variable is included to allow for trade diversion to be greater when a larger number of countries are named in an anti-dumping petition. The variables td_j are time dummies taking a value of 1 in year j and 0 otherwise. They are included to capture the impact of anti-dumping investigations on named countries in the years after the investigation is initiated. These variables are then interacted with a decision variable, Dec, which takes a value of 1 if duties are levied. The parameters on these variables should indicate any additional impact upon imports from countries subject to measures. Finally, year dummies are included to control for changes in macroeconomic conditions.

This model is used to investigate the evolution of imports from named countries and imports from non-named countries in total. Separate equations are estimated for imports from countries in the rest of the world and imports from EU partners. For imports from named countries, each case is included. Since there are often a number of cases for the same product, when estimating equations for imports from non-named countries, we analyse trade for each product and include the average of the duties that are levied. Hence, there are fewer observations in the intra- and extra-EU trade regressions.

Results from estimating this equation on import volumes, import prices (unit values) and import value shares are reported in Tables 1–3, respectively (the coefficients on the year dummies are not presented). Since the data cover a wide range of products with vastly differing levels of imports, I first sought to identify potential outliers. This was done by selecting observations with a studentised residual exceeding two. In all the estimates, the number of observations identified as potential outliers was (surprisingly) relatively small. For example, in the import volume equations 13 out of 490 observations had a studentised residual in excess of two in the named-country regression, whilst 3 out of 235 observations were identified as outliers in the regression for non-named countries. The results presented below are based upon estimation without these observations. Given their small number and the similarity between the estimation with all observations and with the outliers removed, I did not proceed further to bounded influence estimation.

Starting first with the estimations for import volumes (Table 1), the results demonstrate a statistically significant decline in the volume of imports from named countries in the second and third years following the initiation of the action (shown by the coefficients on the dummy variables $t+2$ and $t+3$). For those countries subject to measures, there is a highly significant negative impact on the volume of imports in the EU in the second year after the investigation is announced (the parameter on the variable $t+2 \times$ decision), which is the year in which definitive measures are usually applied. The size of the duty is not a significant determinant of the volume of imports from named countries. I return to discuss this in more detail below.

For the results for import volumes from non-named countries in total, we see that there is a significant (but only at a level of 10%) increase in import volumes for products where a large number of countries (more than two) are named. There is, however, no significant increase in imports in the years following the initiation of the anti-dumping action. The next two columns report separately the results for imports from fellow EU members and for imports from non-named countries in the rest of the world. The results for imports from the EU provide no significant evidence that anti-dumping investigations or the imposition of anti-dumping measures increases import volumes. For non-EU countries, on the other hand, there is a strong and highly significant increase in the volume of imports in the second year after the investigation is announced, which is consistent with the strong fall in imports from named countries subject to measures. There is also evidence that trade diversion to these countries is greater when three or more countries are named in an anti-dumping investigation. This was also found by Prusa (1997) for the US. The results for extra-EU countries have to be treated with

Table 1

Dependent variable: import volumes				
Explanatory variable	Named countries	Non-named countries—Total	Non-named countries—Intra-EU	Non-named countries—Extra-EU
$\ln(x_{t-1})$	1.006 (0.157)***	1.018 (0.150)***	1.014 (0.011)***	1.046 (0.023)***
$\ln(x_{t-1}) - \ln(x_{t-2})$	0.034 (0.061)	−0.141 (0.196)	−0.164 (0.107)	−0.045 (0.150)
ln(Duty)	−0.024 (0.027)	0.010 (0.021)	0.016 (0.017)	−0.030 (0.030)
Dummy number named > 2	0.053 (0.068)	0.068 (0.037)*	0.031 (0.038)	0.145 (0.067)**
$t+1$	−0.122 (0.175)	−0.009 (0.084)	−0.091 (0.095)	−0.073 (0.148)
$t+2$	−0.266 (0.140)*	−0.026 (0.095)	0.040 (0.091)	−0.193 (0.129)
$t+3$	−0.380 (0.189)**	−0.065 (0.092)	0.056 (0.081)	−0.097 (0.159)
$t+4$	−0.198 (0.145)	−0.132 (0.097)	−0.099 (0.096)	−0.121 (0.155)
$t+1 \times$ decision	−0.117 (0.169)	0.001 (0.086)	0.058 (0.094)	0.218 (0.166)
$t+2 \times$ decision	−0.552 (0.154)***	0.009 (0.110)	−0.117 (0.113)	0.442 (0.144)***
$t+3 \times$ decision	0.023 (0.191)	0.051 (0.098)	−0.042 (0.081)	0.260 (0.190)
$t+4 \times$ decision	−0.080 (0.151)	0.112 (0.090)	0.084 (0.090)	0.042 (0.141)
Constant	0.278 (0.276)	−0.341 (0.276)	−0.115 (0.130)	−0.309 (0.270)
R^2	0.931	0.988	0.990	0.967
F	270.11	791.46	915.37	198.86
Observations	477	232	231	231
Reset test	1.85	1.59	1.39	5.50

Observations with a studentised residual greater than 2 (outliers) are excluded. Heteroskedastic consistent standard errors are in brackets. Year dummies included.

* Significant at 10%.

** Significant at 5%.

*** Significant at 1%.

a degree of caution given that this equation fails the Reset test. There are therefore doubts concerning the specification of this equation and there is the possibility of omitted variable bias.

The next set of results, in Table 2, is from regressions on import prices. All these equations satisfy the specification test. The results do not suggest a significant impact upon the (duty exclusive) price of imports from named countries, except for a negative effect for countries subject to measures in the third and fourth years after the investigation is started. There also appears to be no significant impact of anti-dumping actions on the price of imports from other EU countries. The results for non-named countries in the rest of the world, on the other hand, do suggest that anti-dumping investigations in the EU may have an important impact. There is a significant positive impact on prices in all 4 years following the initiation of an investigation, the effect being particularly large and significant in the second and third years.

The results therefore suggest the possibility that an important effect of anti-dumping investigations in the EU is to raise the price of imports from countries not named in the petition. This may reflect the potential threat of being named in subsequent investigations, which other suppliers seek to avoid by raising their prices. In cases where measures are applied, the price of imports from non-named countries in the rest of the world falls significantly in the third year after the investigation is announced, in concert with the price of imports from the named countries subject to measures.

The final set of results in Table 3 is for import value shares (the share of total imports (intra plus extra)). Here, all the equations fail the Reset test and so we should be more tentative in accepting these results. Bearing this in mind, these regressions suggest that anti-dumping investigations have a significant negative impact on the shares of named countries in the third year after the investigation commences and a very strong negative impact in the second year on the share of named countries subject to measures. There appears to be no significant impact of anti-dumping cases upon the share of imports from other EU countries, but a strong and highly statistically significant impact upon the share of non-named countries in the second year after the investigation is announced, for products where measures are applied.

A common feature from these results is the lack of significance of the parameter on the duty variable: variations in the size of the duty imposed apparently do not contribute to the explanation of the evolution of imports in cases subject to anti-dumping measures. The insignificance of the size of duty is not surprising if demand elasticities vary by product and if high duties tend to be concentrated on relatively price inelastic products, and low duties are applied to price elastic products. A small anti-dumping duty could have a significant impact upon market shares for a price-sensitive product. If anti-dumping actions are used primarily as a tool for preventing imports from causing injury to domestic firms (Eymann and Schuknecht, 1993), then the duty required to avoid a given degree of

Table 2

Dependent variable: import prices (unit values)

Explanatory variable	Named countries	Non-named countries—Total	Non-named countries—Intra-EU	Non-named countries—Extra-EU
LNG(x_{t-1})	0.994 (0.005)***	0.991 (0.007)***	0.984 (0.007)***	0.992 (0.005)***
$\ln(x_{t-1})-\ln(x_{t-2})$	−0.132 (0.053)**	−0.301 (0.143)**	−0.087 (0.109)	−0.333 (0.103)***
ln(Duty)	0.013 (0.009)	−0.006 (0.013)	−0.013 (0.016)	0.009 (0.011)
Dummy number named > 2	0.023 (0.022)	−0.026 (0.029)	−0.012 (0.030)	−0.014 (0.018)
$t+1$	0.012 (0.031)	0.051 (0.050)	0.058 (0.066)	0.070 (0.041)*
$t+2$	0.022 (0.038)	0.052 (0.050)	−0.029 (0.064)	0.126 (0.046)***
$t+3$	0.045 (0.033)	0.100 (0.060)*	0.022 (0.074)	0.182 (0.048)***
$t+4$	0.044 (0.035)	0.061 (0.061)	0.078 (0.071)	0.101 (0.055)*
$t+1\times$decision	−0.012 (0.038)	−0.010 (0.061)	−0.035 (0.075)	−0.033 (0.047)
$t+2\times$decision	0.011 (0.042)	−0.027 (0.054)	0.041 (0.070)	−0.077 (0.049)
$t+3\times$decision	−0.096 (0.050)*	−0.039 (0.064)	0.004 (0.074)	−0.163 (0.050)***
$t+4\times$decision	−0.097 (0.044)**	−0.022 (0.058)	−0.087 (0.060)	−0.087 (0.055)
Constant	−0.105 (0.060)*	0.101 (0.091)	0.049 (0.093)	−0.039 (0.066)
R^2	0.989	0.993	0.992	0.995
F	2912.94	2004.96	1745.78	2193.48
Observations	477	227	225	228
Reset test	0.65	0.24	0.13	0.93

Observations with a studentised residual greater than 2 (outliers) are excluded. Heteroskedastic consistent standard errors are in brackets. Year dummies included.

* Significant at 10%.

** Significant at 5%.

*** Significant at 1%.

Table 3

Dependent variable: import value shares

Explanatory variable	Named countries	Non-named countries—Intra-EU	Non-named countries—Extra-EU
$\ln(x_{t-1})$	1.018 (0.025)***	1.023 (0.039)***	1.057 (0.087)***
$\ln(x_{t-1})-\ln(x_{t-2})$	0.056 (0.046)	−0.069 (0.083)	−0.062 (0.140)
ln(Duty)	−0.021 (0.032)	0.003 (0.009)	−0.055 (0.032)*
Dummy number named > 2	0.058 (0.074)	0.015 (0.019)	0.062 (0.067)
$t+1$	−0.146 (0.148)	−0.076 (0.071)	−0.165 (0.128)
$t+2$	−0.173 (0.154)	−0.017 (0.044)	−0.201 (0.134)
$t+3$	−0.359 (0.162)**	0.068 (0.058)	0.114 (0.139)
$t+4$	−0.134 (0.163)	0.008 (0.055)	0.124 (0.169)
$t+1\times$decision	−0.061 (0.166)	0.080 (0.075)	0.302 (0.149)**
$t+2\times$decision	−0.472 (0.166)***	0.029 (0.049)	0.480 (0.151)***
$t+3\times$decision	0.043 (0.171)	−0.010 (0.053)	0.195 (0.156)
$t+4\times$decision	−0.072 (0.169)	−0.005 (0.046)	0.086 (0.141)
Constant	−0.008 (0.170)	−0.017 (0.051)	0.212 (0.178)
R^2	0.853	0.860	0.720
F	126.84	72.18	27.13
Observations	481	232	232
Reset test	2.39	3.07	4.73

Observations with a studentised residual greater than 2 (outliers) are excluded. Heteroskedastic consistent standard errors are in brackets. Year dummies included.

* Significant at 10%.

** Significant at 5%.

*** Significant at 1%.

market disruption (loss of share of domestic firms) will be inversely proportional to the price elasticity of demand.

In addition, EU anti-dumping cases are often characterised by a range of exceptions to the general duty that is levied. Certain firms, usually those that co-operate with the investigation, can be subject to lower duties. In certain cases, mixed measures are applied, with price undertakings being accepted for some firms and duties being applied to other suppliers. We apply the maximum duty relevant to each case, which may not reflect the average impact across firms in the named country. Finally, it may also be that our use of provisional duties for cases subsequently settled by undertakings is inadequate.

This statistical analysis, albeit crude, tends to confirm the impression given by simple analysis of the data. That is, trade diversion resulting from anti-dumping actions is primarily to non-EU countries. In addition, we find that anti-dumping actions can have a significant impact upon the prices of imports from non-named countries in the rest of the world. There are some problems with the chosen specification in certain applications. However, our results are consistent with those of the previous studies by Messerlin (1989) and Prusa (1997), who use different data sets. Ideally, in future research, a model more consistent with the theory of demand could be applied. This would, however, require data over a sufficiently long period.

4. Conclusions

An important feature of the application of anti-dumping measures in the EU appears to be the diversion of trade away from countries subject to measures to other countries exporting to the EU market. The trade diversion appears to be significant only for imports from non-EU countries. Imports from other EU members are not greatly affected. This conclusion, that anti-dumping actions in the EU cause trade diversion, is consistent with similar studies of the US and studies of the EU using data for a previous period.

Lack of data prevents an analysis of the impact of anti-dumping measures on the firms that petition for the action. However, developments in intra-EU trade may provide a proxy for the impact upon domestic suppliers. If so, then it would appear that these firms are unlikely to benefit from an increased volume of sales or an increase in market share following the levying of anti-dumping measures against particular external suppliers of the EU market. Anti-dumping investigations may curtail the trend decline in market share of domestic firms and appear to affect the price of imports from non-named countries in the rest of the world. Here, we have only been able to look at the (cif) price of imports as they enter the port. It would also be interesting to look at developments in the final selling price of products subject to anti-dumping measures.

Acknowledgements

This research is part of the research project 'Trade Between the European Union and the Associated States: Prospects for the Future' financed by the European Commission under the ACE Research Programme 1996 (Project Number P96-6148R). This paper has benefited from the comments of Daniel Gros, Jacques Pelkmans, and three anonymous referees. I am grateful to Anna Maria Pinna for excellent research assistance. The usual disclaimer applies.

References

Eymann, A., Schuknecht, L., 1993. Antidumping enforcement in the European Community. In: Finger, J. (Ed.), Antidumping: How it Works and Who Gets Hurt. University of Michigan Press, Ann Arbor, pp. 221–239.

Messerlin, P., 1989. The EC antidumping regulations: a first economic appraisal, 1980–1985. Weltwirtschaftliches Archiv 125, 563–587.

Messerlin, P., Reed, G., 1995. Antidumping policies in the United States and the European Community. Economic Journal 105, 1565–1575.
Morkre, M., Kelly, K., 1994. Effects of unfair imports on domestic industries: US antidumping and countervailing duty cases, 1980 to 1988. Bureau of Economics, Federal Trade Commission, Washington, DC.
Prusa, T., 1997. The trade effects of US anti-dumping actions. In: Feenstra, R. (Ed.), The Effects of US Trade Protection and Trade Promotion Policies. National Bureau of Economic Research, Cambridge, MA.

Chapter 5

The Potential Trade Effects of an FTA between the EU and Russia

By

Paul Brenton, Natalia Tourdyeva, and **John Whalley**

I. Introduction

The EU has recently signed Partnership and Cooperation Agreements with all of the republics comprising the Commonwealth of Independent States (CIS). The agreements with the European CIS countries (Belarus, Moldova, Russia, Ukraine) provide for an evaluation in 1998 of whether negotiations should commence to establish a free trade area between the EU and the respective CIS republic. The inclusion of an article explicitly mentioning the *possibility* of a free trade area reflects a compromise between the demand, at that time, for preferential trade from Russia and the other European CIS countries, and EU member states, which, with the exception of Germany perhaps, were less interested in the idea.

In this paper, we consider some of the basic economic implications of a free trade agreement between these CIS countries and the EU, and concentrate upon the case of Russia. This country is of particular interest because it is the largest trading partner with which the EU is contemplating a preferential trade agreement. The analysis is based upon the standard approach to economic integration and attempts to show the potential for such a free trade agreement to divert trade away from countries in the rest of the world. This is detrimental to the interests of third countries and is also welfare-reducing for those participating in the free trade area.

The paper confirms, what may be politically obvious, that preferential access to the EU market cannot be limited to Russia alone. Most, if not all, of the other CIS countries would also have to be

---

Remark: This paper has benefitted from the comments of Michael Emerson, Daniel Gros, Paul Luyten and an anonymous referee. The paper was prepared whilst the authors were working on TACIS project ED9301.

included.[1] For Russia it is shown that, if the currently high level of its external tariff were maintained, then a free trade agreement with the EU may cause significant amounts of trade to be diverted away from other suppliers of the Russian market. This, together with the potential adverse terms of trade effects that Russia could suffer due to the high level of its external protection compared with that of the EU, lead us to question the economic motivation of countries such as Russia in seeking a free trade agreement with the EU.

II. Basic Considerations

The standard approach to preferential trade agreements stresses the ambiguity of their impact upon economic welfare. There may be a beneficial impact from trade creation, the increase in trade between the participating countries as relatively inefficient domestic output is replaced by production by the partner. There may also be a detrimental effect upon welfare in the participating countries from trade diversion. This will occur for products which can be produced most efficiently in countries in the rest of the world. Trade diversion happens when sales by such countries in the markets of the participating countries are lost to less efficient producers within the free trade area. This arises because of the margin of preference provided towards producers within the participating countries by the tariff on imports from the rest of the world.

There has been some discussion of the usefulness of the concepts of trade creation and trade diversion in analyzing preferential trade agreements, see, for example Kowalczyk (1990). A key feature of recent work on regional trade arrangements is to explicitly incorporate endogeneity of trade barrier determination into the analysis. Thus, when countries form regional trade agreements, optimal policies both toward and by third parties may change. This is the theme of the widely cited paper by Krugman (1991), which stresses that any net gains from regional trade agreements have to be balanced against their effects in raising Nash tariffs, should a non-cooperative trade war occur. Perroni and Whalley (1994) stress how much of the new regionalism involves small countries negotiating safe-haven trade agreements with larger partners to provide insurance in the event of a trade war. Bagwell and Staiger (1993) evaluate multilateral tariff

[1] Gros and Steinherr (1995), using the gravity model of trade flows, recommend a European Free Trade Zone stretching from the Atlantic to the Urals.

cooperation during the formation of a customs union, again stressing the endogeneity of policy.

Thus, recent literature stresses that more is at stake in evaluating the impact of regional trade arrangements than simply Vinerian trade creation and trade diversion. The relative size of blocs changes, and with it optimal policy. There is, however, little evidence that policy-makers seek to set trade policies which maximize national welfare, as against narrower interest group welfare. For this reason, and for the sake of tractability, we neglect these wider trade policy effects in this paper. We believe that the Vinerian approach remains a useful basis by which to organize initial empirical work on the issue.[2]

Clearly, the extent of trade diversion will be greater the higher the trade barriers maintained against non-participating countries are. Further, trade creation is likely to be more prevalent the greater the similarities in the production structures of the participating countries, yet the larger the differences in production costs. Similarly, the more the partner countries specialize in products which are imported from the rest of the world prior to the agreement, the more significant trade diversion may be. In other words, trade diversion in the EU market will only be important if Russia exports to the EU the same type of products as other countries export to the EU. Trade diversion in Russia will be more dominant if the EU exports to Russia products which correspond with those exported to Russia by other countries, such as the United States. In this paper, we examine the similarity, or degree of overlap, in the trade structures of different countries exporting to the EU and the Russian markets to provide an indication of the potential effects of free trade between the EU and Russia. We commence by looking at the EU market.

III. The Structure of Imports into the EU Market

The first column of Table A1 in the Appendix shows the value of EU (12) imports from major trading partners in 1994. The second column shows that Russia provided 2.9 per cent of EU imports, and as such Russia was the fourth most important supplier of EU imports behind the USA, Japan and China. The remaining CIS countries were not major suppliers to the EU market contributing about one half of one per cent of total EU imports in 1994. Of these CIS countries,

---

[2] We also abstract from a number of regularly cited but less quantifiable effects of regional integration, such as the impact on the attitudes and expectations of individuals and the implications for domestic and foreign investment.

Ukraine was the most important providing over 0.2 per cent of EU imports.

The third column of the table shows the coefficient of variation or the relative standard deviation (standard deviation/mean) for the product composition of EU imports from each country in 1994. This provides an indication of the extent to which imports are concentrated in a few product categories or are more widely spread. If imports were distributed equally between all the available product categories then the relative standard deviation would be one. Higher values of the relative standard deviation suggest increasing concentration. We compute this measure using data at the 4-digit level of the Harmonised System (HS), covering 1,241 different product categories. The data show that EU imports from Russia and the other CIS countries are much more concentrated than EU imports from other countries and the EU average. If these imports are concentrated upon similar products, then a free trade agreement with one country, such as Russia, could have severe implications for other CIS countries, depending on the level of the external tariff.

Before addressing this issue, we look at one further indicator of the nature of the trade structures of the various import suppliers to the EU market. In column four of Table A 1 is the proportion of the total number of product categories in which positive imports into the EU were recorded in 1994. Imports from Russia were recorded in 75 per cent of all the 1,241 4-digit categories. Thus, according to this measure the structure of EU imports from Russia is fairly diverse and covers a wider range of products than some Central and Eastern European countries and countries in Latin America and Asia. Other CIS countries, however, exhibit a very low degree of product coverage. Armenia, for example, records exports to the EU in only 3 per cent, or 34, of the 1,241 product categories. Belarus and, in particular, the Ukraine have the most diverse export structures within the CIS.

In this paper, we assess the degree of overlap between imports from different sources using the similarity index, first introduced by Finger and Kreinin (1979) to examine the potential of the Generalised System of Preferences (GSP) to divert trade; "if exports are dissimilar – i.e. subject to little or no "commodity overlap" – then there is little scope for trade diversion". The similarity index is used here to compare the structure of EU imports from Russia, r, with that of any other supplier of imports to the EU market, j,

$$S_{rj} = \sum_{l=1}^{n} \mathrm{Min}(w_{rl}, w_{jl}) \cdot 100, \tag{1}$$

where w_{rl} is the share of product l in total EU imports from Russia, and w_{jl} is the share of the same product in EU imports from country j. If the two countries have similar export structures, each product will tend to comprise a similar share of each country's total exports to the EU. In this case, the value of the index will be close to 100. If products which are important in one country's exports are of little significance in the other country's exports, then the value of the index will tend towards zero.[3]

The final column of Table A1 shows the value of the similarity index between EU imports from Russia and each country in Central and Eastern Europe, each country in the CIS and a number of other countries in Latin America, Asia, Africa and in the OECD. The trade data are again from 1994 and the index is computed at the 4-digit level of the HS.[4] The degree of similarity is highest for some of the former members of COMECON; the Baltic states, Poland, Belarus, Georgia, and Ukraine. There is also a high degree of overlap with other fuel-exporting countries, Mexico and Egypt. The degree of similarity between EU imports from Russia and countries in Asia is very low, for example: only 6 per cent of EU imports from China overlap with EU imports from Russia. Overall, this analysis suggests that, ceteris paribus, a free trade area between the EU and Russia, if it does influence EU trade with the rest of the world, will have the greatest impact upon EU imports from other CIS countries, rather than upon imports from other countries in the rest of the world, such as in Asia.

As we noted above, EU imports from Russia are highly concentrated. In fact, they are heavily concentrated upon fuels. In Table A2 in the Appendix, we report the results of applying this analysis to industrial products only. In terms of the Harmonised System, industrial products (Chapters 28–99) exclude from total trade agricultural products and fuels, but cover certain unprocessed commodities, such as metals and timber, as well as manufactured products. The first column of Table A2 shows the share of industrial products in EU imports from each of the countries. Industrial products comprise less than 50 per cent of EU imports from Russia and half of imports from Georgia. In Latin America and Egypt, fuels and/or agriculture comprise large proportions of exports to the EU. For the other countries,

---

[3] For another application of the similarity index see, for example, Greenaway and Milner (1993: chapter 11).

[4] The 4-digit level is used to provide some consistency with the analysis of the Russian import market where a further disaggregation of trade data is not available.

industrial products typically constitute over three quarters of exports to the EU.

Confining attention to industrial products shows much less concentration in EU imports from Russia, the relative standard deviation is of a similar order of magnitude to EU imports from countries in Asia and Latin America. The structure of EU imports from the other CIS countries is, however, much more concentrated than for other countries, the western republics of Belarus, Ukraine and Moldova being exceptions. The interpretation of the measure of industrial product coverage is as above; Russia exports to the EU in a wide range of product categories whilst most of the other CIS countries are dependent upon a very narrow range of products. As one would expect, the value of the similarity index declines for those countries where fuels are important, Georgia, Mexico and Egypt, and increases elsewhere. Again, the degree of overlap is highest when comparing EU imports from Russia with those from the CIS, the Baltics, and the Central and Eastern European countries. Relatively high values of the index are apparent for Brazil, South Africa and Canada. For other countries outside of Europe the degree of trade overlap is rather slight, typically around 10 per cent.

An additional way of trying to identify the potential for trade diversion is to highlight those products in which each country appears to be relatively efficient. It is assumed that competition between any two countries will be strongest for products in which they are both relatively efficient. The potential for trade diversion in an FTA will be greater the more important products are in which both the members and non-members appear to be relatively efficient.

A common approach is to assume that if a country is more efficient in producing one product relative to some other product this will be reflected in the structure of exports. We therefore use a measure of revealed comparative advantage in trade with the EU to identify those products which each country produces efficiently. A value of the index in excess of unity implies comparative advantage or relative efficiency. The index is defined as

$$\mathrm{RCA}_{il} = \frac{x_{il}}{\sum\limits_{l=1}^{n} x_{il}} \Bigg/ \frac{\sum\limits_{i=1}^{m} x_{il}}{\sum\limits_{l=1}^{n}\sum\limits_{i=1}^{m} x_{il}}, \qquad (2)$$

where x_{il} is the value of exports of product l from country i to the EU. There are n products and m exporting countries. The numerator shows the share of a particular product in the country's exports to the EU, whilst the denominator shows the share of this product in extra-EU imports. In other words, Russia, for example, would reveal a comparative advantage in trade with the EU in, say, footwear, if the share of footwear in total Russian exports to the EU exceeded the share of footwear in the exports of all countries to the EU. To examine the implications of a free trade agreement between the EU and Russia we calculate the share in EU imports from each trading partner of products in which both the country concerned *and* Russia reveal a comparative advantage in trade with the EU.[5]

An important issue is the level of disaggregation at which to apply the analysis. Should revealed comparative advantage be computed at the level of the industry, say HS chapters (2 digits), or at a much more detailed level, say HS 8 digits? The disadvantage of looking at the aggregate industry level is that strong advantages in specific products may be missed. For example, a country may reveal a strong comparative advantage in a particular type of machinery yet not appear to be relatively efficient in producing machinery as a whole. This phenomenon will be more important the greater the degree of product differentiation within an industry, and hence the larger the scope for countries to specialize in individual products.

The disadvantage of using the more detailed data is that at this level trade flows may be very sensitive to policy interventions. Restrictive trade policies in the importing country or industrial policies in the exporting country will distort trade and may lead to erroneous deductions concerning comparative advantage. At the aggregate level, the effect of these distortions is less apparent. We therefore compute the index of revealed comparative advantage at an intermediate level of disaggregation, the 4-digit level of the HS, sufficiently detailed to capture within industry specialization but not highly sensitive to product-specific policy distortions.

Table A3 in the Appendix shows the share of EU imports from each country of products in which that country and Russia reveal a comparative advantage in trade with the EU. This measure is computed separately for total trade, trade in industrial products, industrial products excluding base metals, and industrial products excluding base metals and iron and steel. The figures for Russia show the proportion of exports to the EU accounted for products in which

[5] Indicators of revealed comparative advantage (RCA) have been widely discussed. For a comprehensive treatment see Greenaway and Milner (1993: chapter 10).

Russia appears to be relatively efficient. The table shows that a very small proportion of EU imports from Asian countries is of products in which Russia and the relevant country both reveal a comparative advantage. The upshot of this is that, if a free trade agreement encourages Russia to further specialize in products in which a comparative advantage in trade with the EU is currently apparent, this will intensify competition for less than one tenth of exports from Asian countries to the EU.

In contrast, a very high proportion of EU imports from the CIS countries may face more intense competition following preferential access for Russia. All of EU imports from Tadjikistan, Turkmenistan and Uzbekistan are potentially vulnerable to more intense competition from imports from Russia. Over one-half of EU imports from the Baltic states are in products where the republics and Russia appear to be relatively efficient. Although, for these countries a free trade agreement with Russia would act to remove preferences currently granted to the Baltic countries under their Europe Agreements with the EU. The same issue relates to Central and Eastern European countries where approximately one-quarter of exports to the EU may be affected by the removal of tariffs and quantitative restrictions against imports from Russia.

The analysis above shows the share of EU imports from each country which may be subject to increased competition from Russia. The extent to which such competition will increase will depend upon the size of the current trade barriers for the products, the margin of preference that will be granted to Russian suppliers. If tariffs are close to zero, and there are no quantitative restrictions, then a free trade agreement will have little impact.

Table A4 in the Appendix shows that in general the key products exported by CIS countries to the EU face zero or very low import duties.[6] This is because the products concerned are mainly raw materials and fuels. Thus, although all of EU imports from Turkmenistan are products in which both this country and Russia reveal a comparative advantage, 90 per cent of this is cotton which enters the EU duty-free. A similar situation exists for Tadjikistan and Uzbekistan. Article XXIV of the GATT requires that "duties and other regulations of commerce" are not "higher or more restrictive" under an FTA.

[6] These duties are those applicable in 1994, the year corresponding to that of the trade data. The Uruguay Round agreement entails that many of these duties will fall further during the 1990s.

Thus, we can be certain that for products such as cotton where duties are already negligible, preferential trade agreements will have no effect.

Nevertheless, for certain products and certain countries, preferences for Russia could be important, for example, nitrogenic fertilizers from Belarus, ferro-alloys from Georgia and Kazakhstan, ammonia and certain iron and steel products from the Ukraine. If the EU is to proceed with negotiating free trade agreements with the western CIS countries then an important issue will be the relative timing of the implementation of trade barrier removal against imports from individual republics. Careful consideration would have to be given to extending the preferences granted to any one CIS country to all of the former republics. This suggests that an EU-CIS free trade area should be created rather than achieved in a piecemeal fashion that may generate economic difficulties for particular CIS countries.

IV. The Russian Market

The situation in the Russian market is different. Here, import barriers are much higher. Import policy in Russia is fairly transparent, the tariff is the principal policy and there do not appear to be any non-tariff barriers.[7] In 1994,[8] the unweighted average tariff was 12.3 per cent with a standard deviation of 17. The trade-weighted average tariff was around 10 per cent. Figure 1 shows the trade-weighted average tariffs for broad groups of products. Tariffs tend to be rather low for vegetable products, mineral products, chemicals and precision instruments. These products comprised over 30 per cent of Russian imports in 1994 but only 23 per cent of EU exports to Russia. The average tariff is highest for textiles where it exceeds 20 per cent. Textiles comprised about 3.5 per cent of Russian imports in 1994 and a similar proportion of imports from the EU. Imports from the EU are dominated by machinery and electrical appliances, which accounted for around one-third of the total in 1994. On average these products tend to face medium tariffs in the region of 10 per cent. Thus, an EU-Russia FTA is likely to have a more significant impact upon

---

[7] There is, however, mounting evidence that exporting to Russia faces significant administrative hurdles.

[8] A new tariff schedule was introduced on July 1, 1994. This forms the basis for the following calculations. There have been two subsequent changes to the tariff in July 1995 and July 1996 which have increased the average tariff to around 14.5 per cent.

Figure 1 – *Russian Average Import Tariffs by Product, 1994*

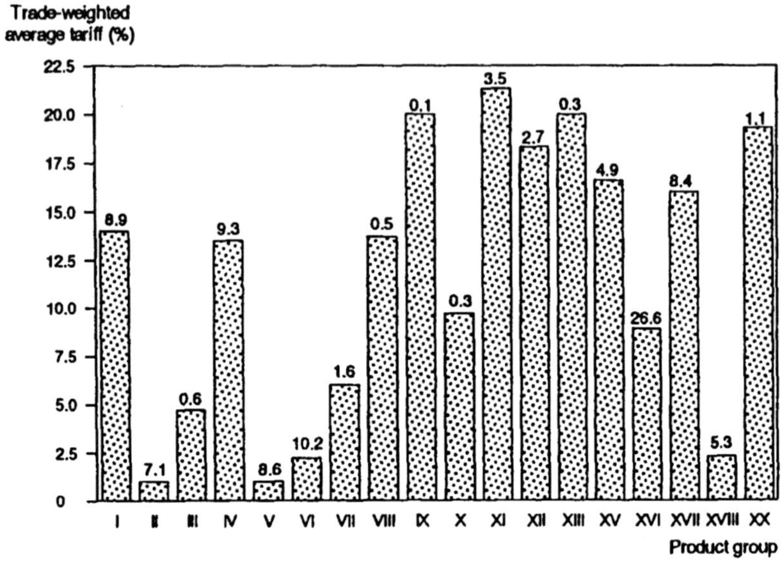

Note: The column numbers indicate the share of each product in total Russian imports.

I	Live animals, animal products	X	Pulp, paper and paperboard
II	Vegetable products	XI	Textiles
III	Animal or vegetable fats and oils	XII	Footwear
IV	Prepared foodstuffs, beverages, spirits, tobacco	XIII	Glass and glassware, articles of stone
V	Mineral products	XV	Base metals and articles thereof
VI	Chemicals	XVI	Machinery, electrical appliances
VII	Plastics and rubber	XVII	Vehicles and transport equipment
VIII	Hides and skins, leather	XVIII	Precision instruments
IX	Wood and wood manufactures	XIX	Miscellaneous manufactures

Precious stones (XIV) and arms and ammunition (XIX) which each comprise less than 1 per cent of imports are not included in the figure.

trade in the Russian market. Further, the revenue implications for Russia of an FTA will be much more important than for the EU.

Table A 5 in the Appendix presents the results of the analysis of the structure of the Russian import market. Again we concentrate upon the 4-digit level of the HS, but the Russian statistics only separately identify 543 codes. This reflects that Russian demand for imports has yet to achieve the diversity observed in EU imports.[9] The table shows that the EU is the principal supplier of imports to the Russian market,

[9] It may also be the result of initial difficulties in implementing the classification system, which was introduced in 1994.

accounting for 30 per cent in 1994. The CIS countries provided around one-quarter of Russian imports in 1994, with Ukraine alone responsible for 10 per cent of total Russian imports, and Belarus 5 per cent. Other major suppliers to the Russian market are the United States, Japan, Poland, China and Hungary. Since Russia has a free trade agreement with the CIS countries it is apparent that, in principle, the EU provides over 40 per cent of duty-generating imports.[10]

The third column shows the degree of product coverage of each of the suppliers to the Russian market. There is almost complete product coverage in imports from the EU and the United States. The Central and Eastern European countries also appear to export a wide range of products to Russia. In marked contrast to their exports to the EU, the CIS countries tend to have exports in the majority of product classifications. For example, EU imports from Kazakhstan are recorded in 182 of the 4-digit groups in the EU, but in the Russian market there are 513 products supplied from Kazakhstan. This may reflect either that the design and other supply characteristics of a wide range of products produced in the CIS are unsuitable for the EU market or that the reorientation of the trade of these countries towards the west has yet to take place.

This information on product coverage is reinforced by the data on the relative standard deviation for each supplier to the Russian market. Imports from the EU are the most widely dispersed across product categories. Imports from the Central and Eastern European countries, Belarus and the Ukraine, and the United States and Japan show relatively low levels of concentration upon a limited number of product categories. Thus, not surprisingly, those countries which export a wide range of products to Russia exhibit a diverse export structure, with relatively little concentration upon specific products.

The similarity index suggests a high degree of overlap, almost 50 per cent, between Russian imports from the EU and from the United States. There is a possibility that a free trade agreement between the EU and Russia could divert trade away from US suppliers. There is also a high degree of similarity between imports from the EU and from some of the Central and Eastern European countries, notably the Czech Republic and Poland. Negotiations for these countries

[10] In fact, the amount of tariff revenues derived from imports from the EU will be higher since the product structure of such imports is skewed towards products with higher tariffs. The weighted average tariff on Russian imports from the EU exceeds the weighted average duty on all Russian imports. The EU Commission argues that it is currently around 19 per cent.

to join the EU will commence at around the same time as free trade negotiations with Russia may occur. Thus, an important issue for these countries could be whether they accede before an agreement with Russia is reached, or how they are treated in an EU-Russia free trade agreement during a period of transition to accession.

A slightly different picture emerges from the information given by the analysis of revealed comparative advantage. Although there is a relatively high degree of similarity between Polish and EU exports to Russia, the analysis of comparative advantage suggests that an FTA would have less impact upon Poland. The proportion of Polish exports accounted for by products in which both Poland and the EU appear to be efficient is small, about 15 per cent. Thus, either Poland exports to Russia mainly products which cannot be produced relatively efficiently in the EU, and/or it exports products in which it has no apparent comparative advantage. In the first case, an FTA would have little impact upon Polish exports to Russia. If the second situation is the most relevant then Polish exports of such products to Russia would be expected to decline regardless of an FTA. Similar arguments can be applied to US exports to Russia.

In general, the data on revealed comparative advantage suggest that a wide range of countries in Central and Eastern Europe, the CIS and Asia, together with Japan and the United States, could be vulnerable to trade diversion effects in the Russian market if preferential treatment were granted to EU products. For many countries, over one-third of current exports to Russia are products which are produced relatively efficiently in that country as well as in the EU. The FTA will intensify competitive pressures in the market for these products.

V. Policy Implications

Tariffs in Russia are currently high and may be sufficient to generate significant trade diversion following a free trade agreement with the EU. The level of the tariff is therefore crucial in determining the magnitude of such trade diversion. The formation of the EEC is generally held to have led to very little trade diversion due to the lowering of the common external tariff as part of the global process of trade liberalization in the 1960s and pursued ever since. Similarly, the further liberalization of trade agreed in the Uruguay Round should help to ensure that the removal of remaining internal non-tariff trade barriers in the EU, to create the Single European Market, is not trade-diverting. For Russia, trade diversion arising from an FTA with the EU would be minimized if there was an accompanying reduction in import tariffs.

The situation is complicated somewhat by the desire of Russia to accede to the WTO. Accession negotiations typically involve the applicant offering product-by-product tariff bindings and may involve tariff concessions. Article XXIV of the GATT states that duties and other regulations affecting trade in the individual countries must not become more restrictive after the formation of a free trade area. Thus, if the FTA agreement with the EU were to precede WTO accession there would be little point in Russia binding tariffs at anything other than, or below, their level at the time of accession. However, it is likely that the US and other members of the WTO would strive for large reductions in the Russian tariff as the price for WTO membership, so as to reduce the preferential margin for the EU. Russia may also have less interest in maintaining high tariffs since they would essentially be preferential in favour of the EU. Thus, in practice if an FTA were to precede accession to the WTO then Russia would probably bind tariffs at levels lower than when the free trade agreement came into effect.

On the other hand, if GATT accession were to arrive before the FTA were to be implemented it is likely that all WTO members would seek commitments from Russia to bind tariffs at low levels, although the tenacity of the EU in seeking lower tariffs would be tempered by the imminence and probability of the conclusion of an FTA. One might conclude then that a firm rejection of the possibility of an FTA between the EU and Russia would facilitate the accession of Russia to the WTO. The United States and other WTO members would no longer be concerned about a preferential tariff in favour of the EU and the EU itself is unlikely to push Russia hard for substantially improved market access. The relative political priorities attached to accession to the GATT and an FTA with the EU in 1998 will be an important issue for both Russia and the EU.

The analysis above has been formulated in terms of the standard analysis of free trade areas. This can be extended to consider the implications for the terms of trade. If a free trade agreement generates a significant amount of trade diversion it will tend to improve the terms of trade of the parties to the agreement with an adverse impact upon the terms of trade of the rest of the world. Spilimbergo and Stein (1996) demonstrate how a free trade agreement between countries with greatly differing tariffs can reduce the terms of trade of the high-tariff country. For example, if Russia, with high tariffs, forms a free trade area with the EU and generates significant trade diversion in favour of EU producers, the terms of trade of both partners with respect to the rest of the world will improve. If the agreement leads to trade creation in Russia there will be a decline in sales by Russian firms in their domestic market. In the EU market, where tariffs are very low, trade diversion *and* trade creation are less likely to be significant. Thus, with no trade being created in the EU market the decline in domestic sales by Russian firms may not be offset by a rise in exports to the EU. Overall, the demand for goods produced in Russia may fall and its terms of trade could worsen. Note that in this case the EU benefits from an even larger improvement in its terms of trade.

These considerations suggest that prior to implementing a free trade agreement, Russia should be seeking to align its tariffs for industrial products more closely to those of the EU, which in turn would facilitate accession to the WTO. Further, Russia should seek to ensure that liberalization of any remaining non-tariff barriers to its exports to the EU is included in any agreement, so as to maximize the magnitude of trade creation in the EU market.

VI. Conclusion

The principal forces driving the EU and Russia towards a free trade agreement are political. However, the economic implications cannot be ignored and will in turn influence the political atmosphere in which any negotiations are conducted. In this paper, we have concentrated on the narrow issue of the potential for such an agreement to influence trade, and in particular, the degree to which trade may be diverted away from countries not party to the agreement. The basic conclusions from this analysis are, firstly, that the potential from trade diversion and trade creation in the EU market are slight because the common external tariff is already quite low. However, if there is any diversion it will most likely affect other CIS countries. Thus, an important issue will be the timing of separate agreements with the individual CIS countries and the position of CIS countries which currently have no commitment to discuss free trade arrangements with the EU.

Second, if the current relatively high tariffs are maintained in Russia, the implications of an FTA for trade and production are likely to be significant. A range of countries in Central and Eastern Europe, the CIS, and Asia, as well as Japan and the United States, may be affected by trade diversion towards EU suppliers. Such trade diversion may dominate the little trade created in the EU market for Russian producers. This negative effect for Russia may be compounded by adverse movements in the terms of trade. Difficulties may also arise from the loss of tariff revenue. Reductions in tariffs introduced as part of the process of accession to the WTO would have the additional effect of reducing possible economic losses from an FTA with the EU.

More generally, the paper tends to question the motivation for countries, such as Russia, in negotiating free trade agreements with the EU. It is difficult to identify economic benefits arising from the trade effects of such an agreement when EU tariffs are much lower than those in the prospective partner countries.

Appendix

Table A1 – *A Comparison between the Structure of EU Imports of All Products from Russia and Other Sources, 1994*

	Value (000 ECU)	Share of extra-EU imports	Relative std dev	Product coverage[a]	Similarity index
Russia	15,199,645	2.88	13.15	74.54	100.00
Baltic States					
Estonia	261,986	0.05	5.86	34.97	26.89
Latvia	703,281	0.13	15.14	34.25	30.25
Lithuania	726,266	0.14	12.32	42.95	28.33
Central and Eastern Europe					
Albania	125,707	0.02	10.77	25.54	11.51
Bulgaria	1,329,169	0.25	4.41	66.48	18.41
Czech Republic	6,210,292	1.18	2.72	88.40	15.88
Hungary	4,853,893	0.92	3.71	82.68	12.09
Poland	8,975,663	1.70	4.41	88.40	21.15
Romania	2,472,500	0.47	6.10	64.06	16.85
Slovenia	3,389,524	0.64	4.85	72.60	9.77
Slovakia	1,847,530	0.35	3.98	67.37	14.60
CIS					
Armenia	37,612	0.01	27.04	2.74	7.22
Azerbaijan	21,948	0.00	19.65	5.88	4.40
Belarus	419,700	0.08	6.96	34.57	24.46
Georgia	14,891	0.00	12.85	7.57	42.54
Kazakhstan	256,037	0.05	15.34	14.67	16.74
Kyrghistan	20,106	0.00	18.66	4.75	7.23
Moldova	49,783	0.01	8.89	11.68	8.65
Tadjikistan	87,902	0.02	31.56	3.06	8.38
Turkmenistan	190,871	0.04	31.78	4.83	6.54
Ukraine	1,235,600	0.23	6.79	50.36	33.86
Uzbekistan	517,353	0.10	24.62	6.61	4.39
Latin America					
Argentina	3,593,956	0.68	9.92	53.02	8.02
Brazil	10,532,483	1.99	7.82	77.20	15.23
Colombia	1,862,564	0.35	17.44	39.48	4.85
Mexico	2,522,934	0.48	11.26	62.13	35.12
Peru	1,276,896	0.24	11.24	30.78	9.77
Asia					
China	22,835,852	4.32	3.92	86.38	5.93
India	6,840,262	1.30	4.99	80.10	9.93
Indonesia	5,871,832	1.11	4.79	59.15	8.10
Malaysia	7,399,084	1.40	8.35	60.68	8.03
Philippines	2,011,199	0.38	6.30	49.07	4.44
Singapore	7,593,525	1.44	13.56	65.43	4.03
South Korea	8,425,345	1.60	6.21	70.35	5.14
Taiwan	10,184,500	1.93	8.22	75.34	3.50
Thailand	6,213,735	1.18	5.07	65.51	7.06
Vietnam	874,502	0.17	8.87	31.99	4.73
Other Developing					
Turkey	7,489,535	1.42	4.69	77.28	9.89
Morocco	3,690,286	0.70	6.14	55.60	8.29
Egypt	2,782,529	0.53	15.50	51.17	53.45
South Africa	6,458,497	1.22	11.77	76.55	16.66
Developed					
Canada	8,952,028	1.70	5.59	84.85	20.32
Japan	47,927,689	9.08	6.23	89.20	5.39
USA	87,032,863	16.48	4.65	99.03	14.35
Intra-EC	688,212,553		3.51	100.00	16.26
Extra-EC	528,068,114	100.00	3.70	100.00	30.94

[a] Number of product categories in which imports into the EU were recorded in per cent of total number of product categories (1,241).

Source: Comext Database.

Table A2 – *A Comparison between the Structure of EU Imports of Industrial Products from Russia and Other Sources, 1994*

	Share of ind prods	Value (000 ECU)	Share of extra-EU imports	Relative std dev	Product coverage[a]	Similarity index
Russia	45.36	6,894,437	1.70	6.42	80.37	100.00
Baltic States						
Estonia	76.76	201,102	0.05	5.67	38.03	31.89
Latvia	53.33	375,034	0.09	8.51	37.20	32.91
Lithuania	58.03	421,476	0.10	5.56	46.97	32.86
Central and Eastern Europe						
Albania	81.78	102,805	0.03	11.42	25.49	16.44
Bulgaria	81.08	1,077,755	0.27	4.45	70.50	25.96
Czech Republic	91.10	5,657,456	1.39	2.54	93.01	22.79
Hungary	82.21	3,990,252	0.98	3.64	86.64	17.58
Poland	79.62	7,146,486	1.76	4.27	92.09	27.82
Romania	91.39	2,259,685	0.56	5.82	69.78	20.32
Slovenia	97.71	3,311,894	0.82	4.37	78.52	14.81
Slovakia	93.54	1,728,150	0.43	3.63	72.46	23.26
CIS						
Armenia	99.97	37,600	0.01	23.95	3.19	14.85
Azerbaijan	95.33	20,923	0.01	18.19	6.68	7.47
Belarus	92.06	386,356	0.10	6.57	39.16	36.26
Georgia	50.00	7,446	0.00	10.90	8.22	22.09
Kazakhstan	95.31	244,032	0.06	14.23	15.93	24.76
Kyrghistan	98.28	19,760	0.00	16.80	5.45	11.66
Moldova	72.16	35,925	0.01	7.85	12.13	14.79
Tadjikistan	99.87	87,789	0.02	27.97	3.19	10.27
Turkmenistan	93.04	177,581	0.04	30.20	4.42	1.84
Ukraine	74.97	926,300	0.23	5.56	54.88	37.81
Uzbekistan	98.17	507,868	0.13	22.20	7.19	7.51
Latin America						
Argentina	20.29	729,157	0.18	8.87	53.55	13.46
Brazil	39.68	4,178,943	1.03	4.56	80.58	34.09
Colombia	10.76	200,379	0.05	8.00	40.90	13.08
Mexico	59.00	1,488,494	0.37	7.07	65.98	10.40
Peru	52.45	669,673	0.17	15.31	29.80	18.63
Asia						
China	92.76	21,182,383	5.22	3.70	90.44	8.39
India	83.43	5,706,701	1.41	5.08	84.89	16.10
Indonesia	71.89	4,221,044	1.04	4.80	61.87	8.71
Malaysia	90.31	6,682,430	1.65	8.09	65.26	13.53
Philippines	81.31	1,635,404	0.40	6.12	52.21	8.13
Singapore	98.21	7,457,229	1.84	12.22	70.91	5.06
South Korea	98.63	8,309,949	2.05	5.56	78.73	8.37
Taiwan	99.08	10,090,347	2.49	7.33	84.28	5.48
Thailand	76.77	4,770,244	1.18	4.49	68.86	10.06
Vietnam	78.52	686,667	0.17	8.90	30.94	5.01
Other Developing						
Turkey	75.33	5,642,056	1.39	4.73	80.16	11.50
Morocco	70.64	2,606,803	0.64	6.98	57.97	9.66
Egypt	38.93	1,083,224	0.27	8.60	52.72	20.06
South Africa	67.06	4,331,218	1.07	14.17	81.19	25.92
Developed						
Canada	74.88	6,703,190	1.65	6.05	88.08	30.76
Japan	99.54	47,707,767	11.76	5.53	95.07	8.62
USA	89.39	77,796,395	19.18	4.51	99.38	18.01
Intra-EC	81.47	560,696,302		3.70	100.00	20.10
Extra-EC	76.82	405,685,246	100.00	2.68	100.00	28.05

[a] Number of product categories in which imports into the EU were recorded in per cent of total number of product categories.

Source: Comext Database.

Table A3 – *Share of Exports to the EU in which the Country and Russia Reveal a Comparative Advantage in Trade with the EU*

	All goods	Industrial products	Industrial products less	
			metals group 1	metals group 2
Russia	92.04	88.24	86.21	88.34
Baltic States				
Estonia	57.56	63.54	58.36	60.83
Latvia	75.15	65.53	59.92	58.16
Lithuania	66.33	60.88	58.92	57.10
Central and Eastern Europe				
Albania	19.55	21.34	17.72	6.96
Bulgaria	29.00	35.91	30.86	24.68
Czech Republic	10.98	16.34	21.82	23.88
Hungary	9.88	13.51	14.25	14.91
Poland	16.30	19.98	24.01	30.36
Romania	18.08	18.04	18.83	22.63
Slovenia	3.94	8.12	18.60	22.60
Slovakia	17.77	20.23	27.72	29.11
CIS				
Armenia	85.98	93.82	11.12	11.69
Azerbaijan	59.63	74.91	74.12	74.32
Belarus	51.11	54.91	49.11	56.16
Georgia	73.76	85.44	83.93	55.14
Kazakhstan	62.23	67.82	88.00	84.44
Kyrghistan	42.98	93.45	76.97	73.06
Moldova	25.46	45.08	38.32	35.40
Tadjikistan	98.59	98.83	98.84	99.00
Turkmenistan	94.96	97.62	97.74	97.83
Ukraine	66.79	65.21	66.09	56.17
Uzbekistan	95.00	97.72	99.36	99.64
Latin America				
Argentina	15.61	52.04	51.26	51.39
Brazil	13.73	38.35	35.69	39.54
Colombia	2.78	33.65	33.73	25.82
Mexico	37.86	14.82	8.34	14.70
Peru	44.58	80.21	9.79	11.39
Asia				
China	2.27	3.23	4.09	4.14
India	12.10	15.10	7.38	7.87
Indonesia	7.63	10.27	14.01	16.30
Malaysia	7.42	7.70	7.65	7.66
Philippines	6.24	9.72	2.23	4.91
Singapore	0.60	0.33	0.54	0.54
South Korea	0.55	1.32	9.53	10.04
Taiwan	0.69	1.19	1.28	2.88
Thailand	5.46	5.13	2.96	4.14
Vietnam	1.54	0.20	11.20	11.96
Other Developing				
Turkey	5.10	6.34	7.68	8.80
Morocco	10.53	5.22	5.82	10.06
Egypt	63.96	28.70	19.18	35.24
South Africa	46.63	69.39	34.35	35.45
Developed				
Canada	28.20	36.85	36.48	37.05
Japan	0.93	0.94	15.27	15.83
USA	5.24	5.86	3.90	10.30

Note: Industrial Products cover HS 28 to 99 and exclude agricultural products and fuels. The third column (industrial products less metals group 1) further excludes base metals, pearls, copper, nickel, aluminium, lead, zinc, tin and other (HS 71, 74 to 81). The final column (industrial products less metals group 2) excludes in addition iron and steel (HS 72 and 73). The figures for Russia are the share of Russian exports to the EU accounted for by products in which Russia exhibits a RCA in trade with the EU.

Source: Comext Database.

Table A4 – *EU Import Duties (1994) for Key Products Imported from CIS Countries*

HS Code Description and country	Tariffs			
	% of imports	minimum	maximum	average
Armenia				
7102 Diamonds	76.2	0	1.9	0.6
7108 Gold	2.9	0	3.2	1.3
7110 Platinum	4.4	0	2.4	1.1
7404 Copper waste and scrap	1.9	0	0	0
Azerbaijan				
3104 Mineral or chemical fertilisers: potassic	1.8	0	0	0
5201 Cotton	52.7	0	0	0
7404 Copper waste and scrap	3.7	0	0	0
7901 Unwrought zinc	1	3	3	3
Belarus				
3102 Mineral or chemical fertilisers: nitrogenic	7.8	0	10.1	6.6
3104 Mineral or chemical fertilisers: potassic	2.5	0	0	0
4407 Wood ... of a thickness exceeding 6 mm	4.1	0	4.9	2.5
7102 Diamonds	4	0	1.9	0.6
7601 Unwrought aluminium	12.3	6	6	6
Georgia				
2709 Petroleum oils: crude	30	0	0	0
7118 Coin	3.9	0	0	0
7202 Ferro-alloys	10	0	7.6	4.6
7204 Ferrous waste and scrap	12.4	0	1.5	0.2
7502 Unwrought nickel	3.4	0	0	0
Kazakhstan				
2844 Radioactive chemical elements	2.4	0	6.7	1.4
5201 Cotton	3	0	0	0
7202 Ferro-alloys	7.9	0	7.6	4.6
7403 Unwrought copper	33.4	0	0	0
7901 Unwrought zinc	6.2	3	3	3
Kyrghistan				
2825 Hydrazine and hydroxylamine	3	0	9.9	5.6
2846 Compounds of rare earth metals	1.8	3.2	3.2	3.2
5201 Cotton	6.4	0	0	0
7207 Semi-finish. products of iron or non-alloy steel	4.4	2.4	4.8	3.2
7404 Copper waste and scrap	20.9	0	0	0
Moldova				
1206 Sunflower seeds	1.1	0	0	0
4101 Raw hides and skins	3.2	0	0	0
4104 Leather of bovine animals	3.3	0	6.8	2.4
7207 Semi-finish. products of iron or non-alloy steel	2.4	2.4	4.8	3.2
7404 Copper waste and scrap	10	0	0	0
Tadjikistan				
4104 Leather of bovine animals	1.9	0	6.8	2.4
5201 Cotton	89.5	0	0	0
7601 Unwrought aluminium	4.5	6	6	6
Turkmenistan				
2710 Petroleum oils: not crude	4.6	0	6	3.5
5201 Cotton	90.1	0	0	0
Ukraine				
1206 Sunflower seeds	6.9	0	0	0
2710 Petroleum oils: not crude	12	0	6	3.5
2814 Ammonia	5.6	9.9	9.9	9.9
7201 Pig iron	5.5	0	3.3	2.3
7207 Semi-finish. products of iron or non-alloy steel	5.1	2.4	4.8	3.2
Uzbekistan				
5201 Cotton	64.2	0	0	0
7108 Gold	27.4	0	3.2	1.3
Russia				
2709 Petroleum oils: crude	34.1	0	0	0
2710 Petroleum oils: not crude	10.2	0	6	3.5
2711 Petroleum gases	5.8	0	12.8	1.6
7403 Unwrought copper	5.6	0	0	0
7601 Unwrought aluminium	4.1	6	6	6

Source: Official Journal of the European Communities.

224 Weltwirtschaftliches Archiv 1997, Vol. 133 (2)

Table A 5 – *A Comparison between the Structure of Russian Imports of all Products from the EU and Other Sources, 1994*

	Value (000 $)	Share of Russian imports	Relative std dev	Product coverage[a]	Similarity index	RCA imports[b]
EU	11,652,553	30.15	2.08	96.69	100.00	
Baltic States						
Estonia	183,084	0.47	5.04	84.71	31.26	5.10
Latvia	177,982	0.46	3.84	87.29	38.02	34.37
Lithuania	249,069	0.64	4.85	88.95	38.70	30.78
Central and Eastern Europe						
Albania	253	0.00	16.89	10.31	4.86	26.52
Bulgaria	333,862	0.86	4.36	82.87	34.94	16.19
Czech Republic	374,961	0.97	2.97	82.50	47.23	15.62
Hungary	737,829	1.91	4.78	81.22	39.06	44.88
Poland	916,683	2.37	3.90	88.95	47.51	30.33
Romania	142,640	0.37	9.17	59.12	19.65	17.44
Slovenia	218,151	0.56	6.40	68.32	35.50	19.09
Slovakia	202,619	0.52	3.62	78.27	38.85	30.80
CIS						
Armenia	32,783	0.08	6.45	67.03	17.25	39.34
Azerbaijan	131,683	0.34	5.07	72.56	20.81	40.20
Belarus	1,951,743	5.05	4.04	95.76	32.13	10.96
Georgia	46,030	0.12	6.79	68.51	17.33	5.75
Kazakhstan	1,860,906	4.81	6.98	94.48	13.22	5.38
Kyrghistan	86,573	0.22	5.67	74.40	21.44	22.58
Moldova	463,422	1.20	6.02	82.69	23.91	70.84
Tadjikistan	81,873	0.21	5.36	65.01	12.67	46.45
Turkmenistan	51,672	0.13	7.93	61.14	6.63	53.20
Ukraine	3,947,904	10.21	2.80	98.71	38.68	9.44
Uzbekistan	781,676	2.02	9.47	87.66	15.08	11.56
Latin America						
Argentina	30,899	0.08	12.43	21.18	7.36	17.24
Brazil	192,168	0.50	12.97	16.94	9.05	8.89
Colombia	12,727	0.03	15.67	9.76	3.33	26.49
Mexico	6,035	0.02	13.22	11.05	6.04	23.33
Peru	13,516	0.03	19.41	12.71	5.17	4.34
Asia						
China	880,066	2.28	3.85	87.85	27.10	1.01
India	551,323	1.43	7.24	62.43	19.23	43.42
Indonesia	67,239	0.17	7.22	23.94	15.04	45.04
Malaysia	18,453	0.05	5.73	21.92	15.15	33.31
Philippines	5,458	0.01	10.07	12.52	8.48	18.90
Singapore	204,653	0.53	7.04	54.14	23.28	0.60
South Korea	410,670	1.06	4.46	78.27	35.59	43.37
Taiwan	130,686	0.34	11.17	41.62	19.68	19.20
Thailand	33,773	0.09	4.94	32.97	14.36	31.84
Vietnam	46,509	0.12	6.16	53.41	15.25	41.56
Other Developing						
Turkey	379,205	0.98	4.02	80.11	33.26	15.85
Morocco	15,551	0.04	22.03	6.08	2.32	95.50
Egypt	58,039	0.15	4.80	39.78	23.67	7.30
South Africa	23,670	0.06	14.99	19.34	7.67	30.91
Developed						
Canada	177,586	0.46	3.58	74.03	39.50	6.86
Japan	1,087,872	2.81	5.38	78.82	30.41	36.86
USA	2,006,397	5.19	4.40	93.00	48.45	21.74

[a] Number of product categories in which imports into Russia were recorded in per cent of total number of product categories (543). – [b] Share of imports in which country and EU have a revealed comparative advantage.

Source: Russian State Customs Committee.

References

Bagwell, K., and R. W. Staiger (1993). Multilateral Tariff Cooperation during the Formation of Customs Unions. Working Paper 4543. NBER, Cambridge, Mass.

Finger J. M., and M. E. Kreinin (1979). A Measure of "Export Similarity" and Its Possible Uses. *Economic Journal* 89 (December): 905–912.

Greenaway, D., and C. Milner (1993). *Trade and Industrial Policy in Developing Countries*. Basingstoke: Macmillan.

Gros, D., and A. Steinherr (1995). *Winds of Change: Economic Transition in Central and Eastern Europe*. London: Longman.

Kowalczyk, C. (1990). Welfare and Customs Unions. Working Paper 90-17. Dartmouth College.

Krugman, P. (1991). Is Bilateralism Bad? In E. Helpman and A. Razin (eds.), *International Trade and Trade Policy*. Cambridge, Mass.: MIT Press.

Perroni, C., and J. Whalley (1994). The New Regionalism: Trade Liberalization or Insurance? Working Paper 4626. NBER, Cambridge, Mass.

Spilimbergo, A., and E. Stein (1996). The Welfare Implications of Trading Blocs among Countries with Different Endowments. Working Paper 5472. NBER, Cambridge, Mass.

* * *

A b s t r a c t: The Potential Trade Effects of an FTA between the EU and Russia. – This paper analyzes some of the potential economic effects of free trade agreements between the EU and Russia and the other European CIS countries using standard indicators of trade patterns. It confirms that it would not be feasible for the EU to conclude such an agreement with Russia alone. It is also shown that, if the current high tariff levels are maintained in the CIS countries, they may not benefit from an agreement with the EU. More generally, the authors question the economic motivation for countries such as Russia in seeking free trade agreements with industrial countries which already have low levels of external protection. JEL no. F15, F14

*

Z u s a m m e n f a s s u n g: Die potentiellen Handelswirkungen einer Freihandelszone zwischen der EU und Rußland. – Die Verfasser untersuchen einige der potentiellen wirtschaftlichen Auswirkungen von Freihandelsabkommen zwischen der EU und Rußland und anderen europäischen Ländern der Gemeinschaft Unabhängiger Staaten (GUS), wobei sie Standardindikatoren für die Außenhandelsstruktur verwenden. Sie bestätigen, daß es für die EU nicht zweckmäßig wäre, solch ein Abkommen mit Rußland allein abzuschließen. Sie zeigen auch, daß die GUS-Länder, wenn sie die gegenwärtig hohen Zolltarife beibehalten, keinen Vorteil von einem Abkommen mit der EU hätten. Allgemein gesehen bezweifeln die Verfasser die ökonomische Begründung für Länder wie Rußland, Freihandelsabkommen mit Industrieländern anzustreben, die bereits einen niedrigen Außenschutz haben.

Journal of Common Market Studies
June 2001

Vol. 39, No. 2
pp. 265–84

Chapter 6

Technical Barriers to Trade in the European Union: Importance for Accession Countries*

PAUL BRENTON
Centre for European Policy Studies
JOHN SHEEHY
European Commission
MARC VANCAUTEREN
Centre for European Policy Studies

Abstract

With trade in industrial products between the EU and the countries of central and eastern Europe (CEECs) now essentially free of tariff and non-tariff restrictions, the principal impact of accession to the EU on trade flows will be through access to the single market of the EU. A key element of this will be the removal of technical barriers to trade. In this article we try to highlight the potential importance of technical barriers to trade between the EU and the various CEECs, distinguishing between sectors according to the different approaches to the removal of these barriers in the EU: mutual recognition, detailed harmonization (old approach) and minimum requirements (new approach). We use two sources of information on technical regulations: a sectoral classification from a previous study of the impact of the single market and our own detailed translation of EU product-related directives into the relevant tariff codes. The analysis suggests that the importance of technical barriers varies considerably across the CEECs. The adjustment implications of access to the single market are likely to be greatest for those most advanced in their accession negotiations.

* This research has been undertaken as part of the research project 'Accession, Differentiation and the Impact Upon Trade and Investment Flows in an Integrated Europe' financed by the European Commission under the ACE Research Programme 1997 (Project Number P97-8162R). We are grateful for the helpful comments of two anonymous referees.

Introduction

EU imports of industrial products from the central and eastern European countries (CEECs) are now free of tariffs and quantitative restrictions. This implies that the impact of the accession of these countries to the EU on trade will be determined by the removal of contingent protection measures, such as anti-dumping duties or undertakings,[1] but more importantly by their access to the single market of the EU. The full incorporation of the CEECs into the single market will provide for the complete freedom of movement of goods produced in the CEECs throughout all of the existing 15 EU member countries and the new Member States in central and eastern Europe. This will entail the removal of customs frontiers, and the associated costs of delays and documentation currently incurred when goods from the CEECs cross the EU border, equal access to government procurement contracts in EU countries, and the removal of barriers to trade imposed by differing technical regulations in the CEECs and in EU countries.

Previous analysis of the completion of the single market in the existing EU countries suggests that the removal of technical barriers to trade (TBTs) may be of great significance. The Commission (1998a) calculates that over 79 per cent of intra-EU trade may have been affected by technical regulations in 1996. In general, however, the issue of TBTs and their impact upon trade flows has received little attention in the literature on international trade despite the fact that it is recognized that these may constitute a substantial impediment to trade. This reflects in part problems relating to data. In many cases the impact of access to the single market has simply, and inadequately, been modelled as an ad hoc reduction in trade costs common to all suppliers.[2]

From a welfare point of view, the standard concepts of trade creation and trade diversion are relevant to the preferential removal of non-tariff barriers, as will occur with the accession of the CEECs to the EU. For a particular product in an EU or CEEC country, the reduction in the cost of imports from the EU or CEEC partner will entail imports displacing domestic production, or welfare-enhancing trade creation, if production in the partner is more efficient. The removal of technical barriers will also divert trade if suppliers in the rest of the world produce at lower cost than the partner and the costs related to technical barriers exceed their cost advantage. However, it is important to distinguish technical barriers to trade which simply raise costs from revenue-generating barriers such as tariffs. If the removal of revenue-generating

[1] For an analysis of the impact of the removal of EU anti-dumping measures against the CEECs, see Brenton (1999).

[2] For example, Gasiorek *et al.* (1991) and Brenton and Winters (1992) in different exercises assume that the completion of the single market implies a 2.5 per cent reduction in trade costs for all EU members. More recently, Francois (1998) takes accession to the EU for CEECs to entail an across the board reduction in trade costs of 10 per cent.

barriers causes trade diversion, then overall welfare could decline, since the country will lose real resources in the form of lost tariff revenue and this could outweigh the positive impact on welfare of trade creation. The removal of cost-increasing barriers will save real resources, and the country will simply forgo the possibility of further savings by maintaining barriers on third country suppliers (Pelkmans and Winters, 1988).[3] In this way the removal of technical barriers will be unambiguously welfare improving. However, as noted by Sapir (1990), if a tariff is levied on a product, then the preferential removal of cost- increasing technical barriers could reduce welfare since any trade diversion will lead to the loss of tariff revenue.

The framework outlined above provides the background to this article. However, to undertake a detailed and precise welfare analysis requires data on the *extent* to which technical regulations act as barriers to trade in terms of raising the costs of imports. Such information is generally not available as yet. In this article, we provide an initial look at the evidence concerning sectors and products where technical regulations are important, identify their prevalence in trade between the CEECs and the EU, and hence assess the potential impact of accession on trade between the two regions. Thus we assess the significance of sectors and products where technical barriers are likely to be present due to differences in national regulations and duplication of conformity assessment, but we are not able to calculate the magnitude of such barriers and their precise impact on trade.

We use two data sources. Firstly, we apply sectoral indicators of the presence of technical barriers and the particular approach to their removal adopted in the EU, as provided in the review of the impact of the single market in the EU (Commission, 1998a). We use these to identify the coverage of technical measures in the CEECs' exports to the EU and also to look at the pattern of comparative advantages in these sectors. Secondly, we use our own transcription of EU directives in terms of their coverage of detailed products (8-digit CN codes). This allows us to look at the similarity of each CEEC's exports to and imports from the EU of products subject to technical regulations in the EU. Our simple analysis confirms the importance of technical barriers to trade for the impact of the next enlargement and hence justifies additional, more sophisticated work to assess the potential impact on welfare. We start by briefly describing the approaches adopted in the EU to the removal of technical barriers to trade.

[3] Note, however, that external trade creation could arise if companies in the rest of the world are currently selling in both the EU and the CEECs, have to satisfy different technical regulations, and provide for conformity assessment, in each market. After the accession of the CEECs, the costs of the external suppliers will decline, since there will be a single set of technical regulations, or mutual recognition of differing partner regulations, and no need for duplication of conformity assessment.

II. The EU Approach to Technical Barriers to Trade

Sources of Technical Barriers to Trade

Technical barriers to trade can arise whenever an exporter has to alter his/her product in order to comply with differing partner country requirements, such as health, safety, environmental and consumer protection issues and/or when the product has to undergo multiple testing and certification procedures to be sold in both domestic and overseas markets. These requirements can be imposed by both governments (technical regulations) and non-governmental organizations (non-regulatory barriers, standards). The legal character of technical regulations distinguishes them from non-regulatory barriers or standards; namely, the latter are voluntary, not legally binding and arise from the self-interest of producers or consumers involved, for example, in improving the information in commercial transactions and ensuring compatibility between products. The former mainly relates to either technical specifications or testing and certification requirements such that the product actually complies with the specifications to which it is subjected (conformity assessment). Technical regulations are the focus of this article, although the boundary between mandatory and non-regulatory barriers is not always clear cut (Commission, 1998a).

Technical barriers strike at the heart of business operations affecting business pre-production, production, sales and marketing policies. The need for product design adaptation, reorganization of production systems and multiple testing and certification costs can entail a significant cost for suppliers of goods exported to a particular country, the magnitude of which differs across products. The removal of TBTs at the Community level is a central tenet of the single market since it is crucial for the provision of equal conditions of market access throughout the whole of the European Economic Area.

Instruments for Removing TBTs

The Community now has a widespread set of instruments to combat the market-segmenting effect of technical trade barriers. EU policy related to standards, testing and certification requirements is currently based on two approaches: enforcement of the Mutual Recognition Principle (MRP) and, if this fails, the harmonization of technical standards in each member country. Each approach will now be discussed in turn.

The Mutual Recognition Principle. The basic EU approach has been to promote the idea that products manufactured and tested in accordance with a partner country's regulations could offer equivalent levels of protection to those provided by corresponding domestic rules and procedures. However, this often requires accreditation of testing and certification bodies and a mutual recognition arrangement (MRA) between bodies because Member States often regulate for the same product risks in slightly different ways (or in the same way but requiring duplication of conformity assessment). 'Mutual Recognition' tends to apply where products are new and specialized and it seems to be relatively effective for equipment goods and consumer durables. It encounters difficulties, however, where the product risk is high and consumers or users are directly exposed.

The Harmonization Approach. Where 'equivalence' between levels of regulatory protection embodied in national regulations cannot be assumed, the only viable way to remove the TBT in question is for the Member States to reach agreement on a common set of legally binding requirements. Subsequently, no further legal impediments can prevent market access of complying products anywhere in the EU market. EU legislation harmonizing technical specifications has involved two distinct approaches, the 'old approach' and the 'new approach'. The old approach mainly applies to products (chemicals, motor vehicles, pharmaceuticals and foodstuffs) by which the nature of the risk requires extensive product-by-product or even component-by-component legislation and is carried out by means of detailed directives.

In the main, achieving this type of harmonization has been slow for two reasons. First of all, the process of harmonization became highly technical since it sought to meet the individual requirements of each product category (including components). This resulted in extensive and drawn-out consultations. Secondly, the adoption of old approach directives was based on unanimity in the Council. As a result the harmonization process proceeded extremely slowly. Indeed the approach was ineffective since new national regulations proliferated at a much faster rate than the production of EC-level directives on a limited set of products (Pelkmans, 1987).

It became increasingly recognized that there was a need to reduce the intervention of the public authorities prior to a product being placed on the market. Moreover, the decision-making procedure needed to be adapted in order to facilitate the adoption of technical harmonization directives by a qualified majority in the Council. This has been done by the adoption of the 'new approach' and applies to products, which have 'similar characteristics' and where there has been widespread divergence of technical regulations in EU countries. What makes this approach 'new' is that it indicates only 'essential requirements' and leaves greater freedom to manufacturers as to how to satisfy those requirements, dispensing with the 'old' type of exhaustively detailed directives.

The new approach directives provide for more flexibility than the detailed harmonization directives of the old approach, by using the support of the established standardization bodies (CEN, CENELEC) and the national standard bodies. The standardization work is achieved in a more efficient way, is easier to update and involves greater participation from industry. A further feature of the new approach is the use of market surveillance and the choice of attestation methods that are available: by self-certification against the essential requirements, by using generic standards or by using notified bodies for type approval and testing of conformity of type. We now proceed to assess the importance of technical regulations in the EU in terms of the amount of trade which is affected.

Technical Regulations, Conformity Assessment and Enlargement

The Europe Agreements between the EU and each of the candidate countries in central and eastern Europe provide for the widespread approximation of relevant laws in the CEECs with EU internal market legislation. These provisions have become of crucial importance given the subsequent drive towards membership and the inclusion in the criteria for membership[4] of 'the ability to take on the obligations of membership', that is, to adopt the legal and institutional framework of the EU, the *acquis*. Thus, the implementation of EU directives relating to technical regulations has become an essential element of the accession process. It is worth noting that there are more than 200 directives concerned with placing products on the market which will have to be adopted by the CEECs.

The effect of this is that individual CEECs may be granted sectoral access to the single market prior to accession following the necessary changes to domestic legislative systems. However, access will be dependent upon implementation as well as approximation of laws. A key element in this will be the institutional arrangements regarding testing and conformity assessment and market surveillance under the new approach. In other words, even when the relevant EU laws relating to technical regulations have been adopted in the CEECs, technical barriers will remain if duplication of conformity assessment procedures persists. The process of achieving access to the single market prior to accession is governed by mutual recognition agreements called the Protocols on European Conformity Assessment (PECAs). Individual CEECs can, following the satisfactory alignment of laws, negotiate sectoral access to the single market, subject to the technical competence of conformity assessment bodies being of a level equivalent to that in the EU and the acceptance by both parties of the results from notified conformity assessment bodies.

[4] As laid down by the Copenhagen European Council in December 1993. The White Paper of 1995 (*COM* (95) 163) provided precise detail on the directives concerned.

The European Commission has recently concluded agreements with Hungary and the Czech Republic[5] which are expected to enter into force early in 2001 following adoption by the Council. Both of these agreements cover machinery, electrical safety, electromagnetic compatibility, gas appliances, hot water boilers and good manufacturing practice for medicinal products. In addition, the Hungarian agreement covers good laboratory practice for medicinal products and medical devices whilst the agreement with the Czech Republic also includes personal protective equipment and equipment for use in potentially explosive atmospheres. Products from these sectors that satisfy conformity assessment by any notified body in the EU or the CEECs will have freedom of movement in the EU and the country concerned. The EU has also signed a framework agreement covering general principles with Latvia and is negotiating PECAs with Estonia, Lithuania, Slovenia and Slovakia.

The PECAs have primarily been concerned with those sectors where technical regulations have been harmonized in the EU. Little progress has been made on non-harmonized sectors where the principle of mutual recognition operates in the EU (Commission, 1998b). Hence, for certain products access to the single market will probably be delivered only with accession. The analysis below is based upon data from 1998 and earlier, and therefore captures the situation prior to the effective implementation of EU legislation in any of the CEECs. Thus, the analysis provides a first insight into the potential implications that the PECAs, and more complete access to the single market, will have for trade between the EU and the CEECs.

III. Technical Barriers and Trade between the EU and the CEECs

The Sectoral Incidence of Technical Barriers

Here we use information on the sectoral incidence of technical barriers and the particular approach adopted by the EU to their removal. The data come from the detailed study undertaken for the Commission's review of the impact of the single market in the EU (Commission, 1998a). This study provides information, at the 3-digit level of the NACE classification (about 120 manufacturing industries), of whether trade is affected by technical regulations and the dominant approach used by the Commission to remove such barriers in the EU.[6] For sectors where technical regulations affect trade, the study classifies them as those where the barriers are overcome using mutual recognition (MR),

[5] 'Commissioner Pascal Lamy initials agreements to facilitate trade in goods with candidate countries' «http://europe.eu.int/comm/trade/whats_new/facand.htm».

[6] Trade data according to the NACE classification were obtained from the COMEXT database. The NACE is the industrial classification used by the Statistical Office of the European Communities (Eurostat). A detailed definition of the classification is presented in Commission (1996).

and those sectors where mutual recognition is insufficient or unsuitable, so that either the old approach (OA) or the new approach (NA) to overcoming technical barriers is used. For these sectors it is assumed that all trade is affected by technical regulations and by the identified approach to the removal of the barriers. There are, however, a small number of sectors where a combination of approaches is identified. In the main, we ignore these in the analysis which follows.

The Trade Coverage of Sectors Subject to Technical Regulations. We start by showing the overall trade coverage of technical regulations in the EU and of the different approaches to their removal. In other words, we aggregate the value of imports of the EU-15 from different suppliers (each country's exports to the EU) across all the sectors which are not subject to technical barriers to trade. We then separately identify the proportion of total import value in sectors subject to old approach directives, new approach directives, mutual recognition, and finally a residual reflecting sectors where several approaches are relevant. We should stress here that these data allow us to identify the trade coverage of those sectors where technical barriers to trade are not important and then the coverage of sectors where technical regulations *may*, or are likely to, act as barriers to trade, in terms of requiring different product specifications for different markets and duplication of conformity assessment. We do not have information on the extent to which the presence of differing technical regulations actually restricts trade in these sectors.

In Table 1 we first show the breakdown of EU imports in 1998 from existing EU members and the accession countries in central and eastern Europe. The table demonstrates that a very large proportion of intra-EU trade is in sectors affected by technical regulations. On average less than one-quarter of intra-EU imports are in sectors where technical regulations are not important. The significance of these sectors ranges from around 41 per cent of EU imports from Greece to 20 per cent of EU imports from Germany and 15 per cent of EU imports from Ireland.

There is considerable variation across EU members in the share of trade affected by the different approaches to the removal of technical barriers. For example, sectors where mutual recognition is used comprise a relatively large share of EU imports from Ireland (32 per cent of total imports), Greece (30 per cent) and Portugal (29 per cent) but a small share of EU imports from Finland (5 per cent of the total), Sweden (10 per cent), Austria and Spain (both around 11 per cent). Sectors characterized by the new approach to the removal of technical barriers comprise a relatively large share of EU imports from Italy, Germany, Denmark Sweden and Austria, but are less important in EU imports from Greece, Ireland, the Netherlands, Portugal and Spain. Sectors where the

Table 1: The Importance of Different Approaches to Technical Barriers to Trade: Coverage of EU (15) Imports from Member States and Applicant Countries in 1998 (%)

	Old Approach	*New Approach*	*Mutual Recognition*	*No Technical Barriers*
EU Imports from Member States				
Austria	26.29	17.97	11.40	29.26
Bel-Lux	30.03	10.62	13.74	26.36
Denmark	24.98	17.39	16.54	27.14
Finland	38.89	12.20	5.04	21.53
France	30.74	11.12	17.32	26.68
Germany	31.12	17.53	14.70	20.18
Greece	17.28	5.60	29.65	40.75
Ireland	22.06	9.45	32.34	15.42
Italy	17.98	20.90	17.84	27.50
Netherlands	27.17	7.95	22.22	24.95
Portugal	25.32	8.92	28.78	26.93
Spain	39.73	8.86	11.31	28.84
Sweden	33.91	16.43	10.45	21.00
UK	21.29	14.08	24.61	23.31
Intra-EU	27.91	13.39	18.14	24.53
EU Imports from Accession Countries				
Bulgaria	5.73	9.61	29.72	37.51
Czech Republic	20.52	30.91	14.35	22.39
Estonia	34.40	13.06	14.06	34.68
Latvia	23.54	10.59	16.40	45.48
Lithuania	10.91	9.91	36.03	35.47
Poland	17.03	16.96	27.44	25.43
Hungary	30.45	13.45	24.98	14.95
Romania	2.38	9.13	49.44	28.74
Slovakia	37.87	13.43	19.82	17.35
Slovenia	26.46	23.18	16.90	19.82
Extra-EU	14.22	13.76	27.37	28.86

Note: the shares for each sector do not sum to 100 per cent since a small number of sectors where multiple approaches apply are excluded.

old approach applies comprise a relatively large share of EU imports from Spain, Sweden and Finland (over one-third of the total) and are also of particular importance for France, Germany, Belgium, Netherlands, Portugal and Austria (one quarter or more of the total). Thus, the principal conclusions to be drawn from Table 1 are of the overall importance of technical regulations to trade between EU countries and the variation across countries in the share of trade affected by the different approaches to the removal of the barriers caused by differing national regulations.

In the lower part of Table 1 we present a similar breakdown of EU imports from the applicant countries in central and eastern Europe, also in 1998. Here again there is considerable diversity across countries. Over one-third of EU imports from Bulgaria and Latvia in 1998 were in sectors where technical regulations pose no significant barriers to trade. Examples of such sectors include certain non-ferrous metals, footwear, and sawing and processing of wood. In contrast, less than one-fifth of EU imports from Hungary, Slovakia and Slovenia were in sectors free of trade restricting technical regulations in the EU. It is clear from the table that products subject to new approach directives in the EU form a much larger share of exports to the EU of the Czech Republic and of Slovenia than other CEECs. In this case the main sectors are those producing machinery. Old approach products are of greatest importance to Slovakia, Estonia and Hungary. For these countries the main sectors include motor vehicles and parts, prepared meats and petroleum products.

Table 1 also shows that on average the products of sectors subject to old approach directives comprise a relatively small share of EU imports from non-member countries relative to intra-EU trade. With regard to the CEECs, only in imports from Lithuania, Bulgaria and Romania does the share of old approach products fall below the average for extra-EU imports. In this sense the remaining CEECs are more similar to the existing EU countries than they are to non-member countries in terms of the importance of old approach products in their exports to the EU.

It is apparent from this table that the products of sectors subject to new approach directives form a larger share of EU imports from the Czech Republic, Slovenia, Poland, Hungary, and Slovakia than of average EU imports from existing Member States. For other CEECs such as Romania and Bulgaria, the share of new approach products does not differ substantially from that of EU Member States such as France and the Netherlands. Mutual recognition sectors, such as knitting and clothing industries, are particularly important in EU imports from the Balkan countries and Lithuania whilst they comprise a relatively small share of imports from the Czech Republic and Slovenia. Sectors where technical regulations are not important are a relatively high share of EU imports from the Balkan and Baltic States but are much less important for Hungary, Slovenia and Slovakia. Again, the figures reinforce the conclusion of considerable diversity amongst the CEECs of the importance of sectors subject to technical regulations, and of the share of sectors subject to the different approaches to the removal of technical barriers in the EU.

The Evolution of Trade Subject to Technical Regulations in EU Imports from and Exports to the CEECs. In Figure 1 we show the evolution of the shares of sectors subject to the various approaches to technical barriers in EU-12 imports from those countries where data permit a ten-year perspective. It is beyond the scope of this article to provide a full explanation of the changes that are observed.[7] Nevertheless, the trends that have emerged are interesting in showing the increasing importance of products subject to technical regulations in the EU for certain of the CEECs but not others. The graphs for Poland and Hungary clearly show the declining share of sectors where technical regulations are not significant. In 1988 around 50 per cent of EU-12 imports from Poland were of products where technical regulations are not a barrier to trade in the EU. By 1998 the share of such sectors had fallen to 25 per cent with the shares of new approach sectors and mutual recognition sectors rising. The share of old approach sectors remained fairly constant. For Hungary the share of sectors with no technical barriers fell from 34 per cent in 1998 to less than 15 per cent 10 years later. Here the share of new approach products increased from 10 to 14 per cent of the total and the share of mutual recognition products also increased, from 18 to 25 per cent. Again the importance of old approach sectors changed little.

For Bulgaria and Romania a very different picture emerges. For EU imports from Romania the share of sectors with no technical barriers to trade increased from 19 to 29 per cent. The share of these sectors in EU imports from Bulgaria remained fairly constant around 40 per cent. On the other hand, the share of old approach sectors collapsed, primarily during the period prior to 1992. Old approach sectors accounted for 24 per cent of EU imports from Bulgaria in 1988 but only 5 per cent in 1998. For Romania the share of these sectors fell from 35 per cent in 1988 to 3 per cent within the subsequent decade. In the case of Bulgaria this reflects a constant value of exports of old approach products amongst a growing value of total exports to the EU. For Romania, however, the value of exports of old approach products collapsed in the early 1990s, due primarily to a decline in exports of refined mineral oil products, motor vehicles and prepared meats. The share of new approach products in EU imports from

[7] For example, in 1988 EU imports from the CEECs in all sectors were subject to tariffs, which have subsequently been dismantled. The timetable for tariff removal under the Europe Agreements differed across products and agreements. Certain of the CEECs were implemented before agreements with others. Initial average tariffs are also likely to have differed across sectors subject to the different approaches to technical barriers.

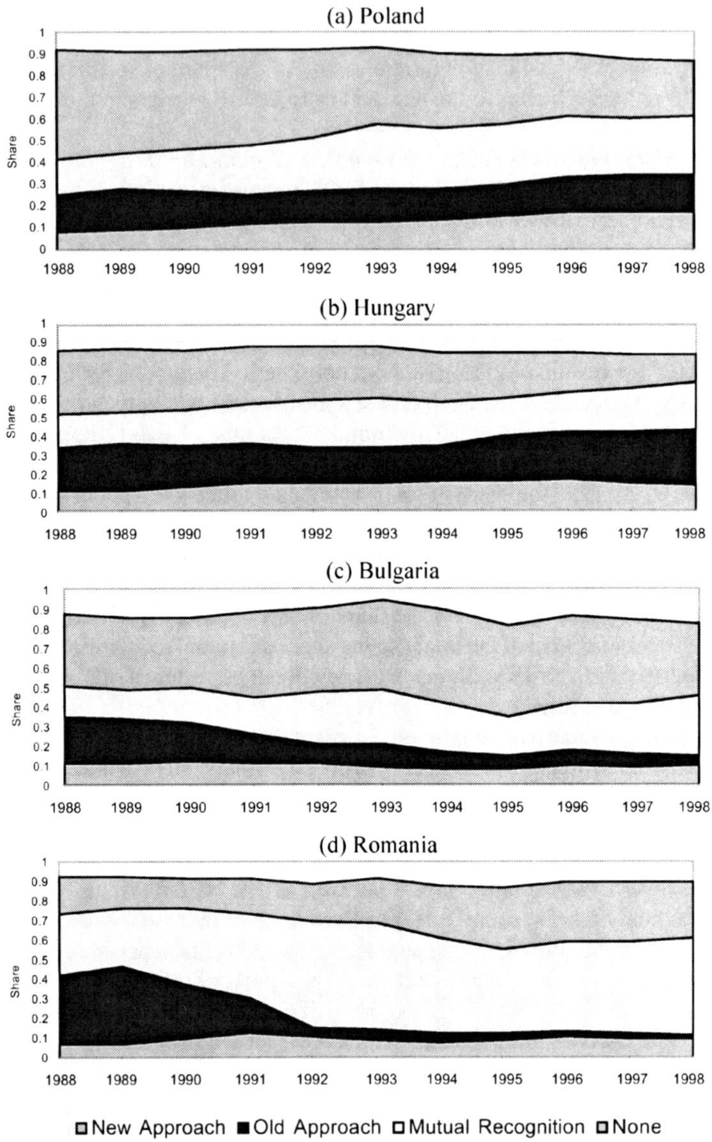

Figure 1: The Importance of Different EU Approaches to Technical Barriers to Trade: Coverage of EU (12) Imports, 1988–98

Note: the share of trade accounted for by these four categories does not sum to 1 due to the exclusion of some sectors where multiple approaches are applied. These sectors comprise the residual at the top of the graph.

these countries changed little over this period. The most notable change in share was that for mutual recognition products, which increased from 31 to over 45 per cent for Romania and from 16 to more than 25 per cent for Bulgaria.

Hence from the perspective of the importance of sectors subject to different approaches to technical regulations there have been major changes in the structure of EU imports from these CEECs since the onset of transition. The role that foreign direct investment (FDI) has played in the increasing importance of new approach sectors in EU imports from Poland and Hungary would be an interesting topic for further research. This would help to make an assessment of the extent to which countries such as Bulgaria and Romania will move into these sectors if they are able to attract significant amounts of FDI in sectors such as engineering. The constant or declining shares of old approach products in EU imports from the CEECs suggests that there are no strong comparative advantages in these sectors in central and eastern Europe, an issue to which we now turn.

Comparative Advantages and Technical Barriers. In Table 2 we show the results of an analysis of revealed comparative advantage for each of the CEECs in their trade with the EU, again classifying sectors according to the approach adopted to technical barriers in the EU. A graphical presentation for all ten CEECs is available in Brenton *et al.* (2000); here we summarize the main conclusions that arise for the CEECs as a group. Our index of revealed comparative advantage is defined as:

$$RCA_{il} = \frac{\dfrac{x_{il}}{\sum_{l=1}^{n} x_{il}}}{\dfrac{\sum_{i=1}^{m} x_{il}}{\sum_{l=1}^{n}\sum_{i=1}^{m} x_{il}}}$$

where x_{il} is the value of exports of sector l from country i to the EU. There are n products and m is the total number of countries exporting to the EU (including EU member countries). The numerator shows the share of a particular sector in the country's exports to the EU, whilst the denominator shows the share of this product in total EU imports. A value of the index in excess of one is taken to reveal a comparative advantage in the production and export of that sector.

For Table 2 we first identify sectors according to whether they are subject to old approach directives, new approach directives, mutual recognition or no significant barriers. Then we simply count the number of sectors in each category in which each of the CEECs reveals a comparative advantage in their trade with the EU.

Table 2: No. of Sectors in each Category where CEEC Country Reveals a Comparative Advantage in Trade with the EU in 1998

	Old Approach (22)[a]	*New Approach (19)*	*Mutual Recognition (22)*	*No Technical Barriers (51)*
Bulgaria	3	5	7	16
Czech Republic	3	17	11	23
Estonia	2	6	3	11
Hungary	4	5	7	12
Latvia	2	3	5	8
Lithuania	3	5	6	10
Poland	3	11	10	25
Romania	0	5	7	16
Slovakia	2	9	8	12
Slovenia	4	9	7	19

Note: [a] The numbers in brackets show the total number of sectors in each category.

In general the results suggest that for all of the CEECs there are relatively few old approach sectors where a comparative advantage in trade with the EU is revealed. None of the CEECs displays relative efficiency in more than four of the 22 old approach sectors. Bulgaria, Czech Republic and Poland each revealed a comparative advantage in three old approach sectors, whilst Romania revealed no comparative advantages for these sectors. This suggests that the accession of the CEECs and their access to the single market will have no great impact on EU imports of products from old approach sectors. In contrast, France reveals a comparative advantage (data not shown here) in 14 of the old approach sectors.

With regard to new approach sectors, the picture varies across the CEECs. Most of the CEECs reveal a comparative advantage in a limited number of new approach sectors, but usually to a greater extent than in old approach sectors. However, the Czech Republic reveals a comparative advantage in all but two of the 19 new approach sectors. Poland appears to be a relatively efficient producer of goods from 11 of the new approach sectors. Thus, this analysis suggests that if trade in new approach sectors between the EU and the CEECs is currently constrained by technical barriers to trade and the accession of the CEECs alleviates these barriers, then competition in the EU market for these products may intensify. We return to this issue below when we look in more detail at the similarity of products exported by the CEECs and the EU countries.

It may be, of course, that technical barriers to trade in the EU are distorting these measures of comparative advantage so that we may be underestimating the comparative advantages of the CEECs in old approach, new approach and mutual recognition sectors. However, the barriers in the EU faced by the different CEECs are likely to be similar so that our analysis here may give a reasonable picture of the relative comparative advantages of the CEECs across sectors. In addition, the decline in the share of old approach sectors in CEEC exports to the EU shown in Figure 1 occurred with unchanged policies for these sectors in the EU: harmonized standards were already in place. This suggests that the decline reflects domestic factors in the CEECs and the loss of comparative advantage.

Detailed Product Analysis of Old and New Approach Directives

The sectoral approach used above assumes that all products within a sector are covered by technical regulations. In this section we report the results from using alternative information on technical regulations in the EU. Here we have studied old approach and new approach directives, or used secondary information which has already undertaken such a task, to identify the precise product codes that are covered by the relevant technical regulations. The product classification that we use is the detailed trade classification of the EU, the Combined Nomenclature, which permits a direct link to the available trade data. We translate the old and new approach directives to the relevant 8-digit tariff line codes that are covered.[8]

These data allow for a much more detailed analysis of the nature of the exports of the CEECs to the EU of products subject to technical regulations in the EU and the extent to which they may be competing with products produced by EU member countries. The more similar is the product composition of CEEC and EU exports subject to technical barriers, the greater is the potential impact of the removal of those barriers with accession to the EU. Here we assess the degree of overlap between EU imports from different sources by using the similarity index. This was first introduced by Finger and Kreinin (1979) to examine the potential of the Generalized System of Preferences (GSP)[9] to divert trade: 'if exports are dissimilar – i.e. subject to little or no "commodity overlap" – then there is little scope for trade diversion'. The similarity index is used here to compare the structure of EU imports from any one supplier, r, with that of any other supplier of imports to the EU market, j:

$$S_{rj} = \sum_{l=1}^{n} \text{Min}\left(w_{rl}, w_{jl}\right) * 100$$

[8] There are over 10,000 codes in the EU classification. Details of the directives and other sources used to identify new and old approach products are presented in Brenton *et al.* (2000).

[9] The GSP is a scheme whereby the EU and other OECD countries offer non-reciprocal tariff preferences to developing countries.

where w_{rl} is the share of product l in total EU imports from country r, and w_{jl} is the share of the same product in EU imports from country j. The higher the value of the index the more similar are the two countries' export structures. On the other hand, if products which are important in one country's exports are of little significance in the other country's exports, then the value of the index will tend towards zero.

Here we apply this index to assess the degree of similarity between flows of new approach products and then separately between flows of old approach products. That is we take all those 8-digit codes which have been identified as new approach products and then assess the degree of overlap between intra-EU imports and EU imports from the CEECs and then between external EU imports and EU imports from the CEECs. We then repeat the exercise for old approach products. The results are summarized in Table 3.

EU imports from all of the CEECs exhibit a relatively low degree of similarity with both intra-EU imports and extra-EU imports. This conclusion applies to both new and old approach products. The Czech Republic shows the highest degree of similarity of trade structures with just over one-third of exports to the EU of new approach products matching EU imports from Member States with a slightly lower degree of overlap with EU imports from non-members. In contrast the degree of overlap between the structure of intra-EU imports of new approach products and extra-EU imports was 70 per cent in 1997. Hence these data suggest that the extent of trade diversion following the inclusion of the CEECs in the single market may be limited. In addition, if intra-EU trade flows are indicative of the structure of domestic production,

Table 3: Similarity of EU Imports of New and Old Approach Products in 1997

	New Approach Products		*Old Approach Products*	
	Similarity with Intra-EU Imports	*Similarity with Extra-EU Imports*	*Similarity with Intra-EU Imports*	*Similarity with Extra-EU Imports*
Intra-EU imports		70		56
Bulgaria	21	18	10	11
Czech Republic	37	32	48	36
Estonia	14	12	4	9
Hungary	36	31	29	28
Latvia	10	11	7	7
Lithuania	16	16	4	6
Poland	39	31	29	28
Romania	26	22	14	16
Slovakia	27	23	34	23
Slovenia	30	24	29	20

then there appears to be little potential for substantial trade creation. This suggests limited welfare gains to EU countries from the further liberalization of their imports from the CEECs, implied by the access of the latter countries to the single market.

Finally, in Table 4 we show the extent to which EU imports from the CEECs are similar to EU exports to the CEECs for both groups of products and compare this with Member States' intra-EU trade. It is clear that there is a low degree of similarity between EU imports from and EU exports to the CEECs of old approach and new approach products. Thus, for example, less than 10 per cent of Latvian exports of old approach and new approach products to the EU are matched by imports in similar product categories. For Bulgaria,

Table 4: Similarity of EU Imports and Exports in 1997

New Approach Products		*Old Approach Products*	
France	67.39	Germany	65.35
UK	65.65	France	62.28
Germany	65.31	UK	61.32
Netherlands	63.33	Bel-Lux	58.42
Extra-EU12	59.93	Spain	54.86
Bel-Lux	58.65	Netherlands	54.52
Spain	55.14	Extra-EU12	54.16
Italy	53.87	Italy	49.26
Austria	50.90	Czech Republic	46.40
Sweden	48.24	Sweden	45.45
Denmark	44.53	Austria	42.59
Czech Republic	42.82	Finland	38.75
Hungary	40.19	Portugal	34.79
Ireland	38.36	Ireland	28.41
Portugal	36.25	Denmark	26.68
Poland	33.97	Slovakia	24.46
Finland	31.57	Hungary	23.84
Greece	28.96	Poland	23.65
Slovakia	28.15	Romania	19.57
Romania	25.24	Greece	11.77
Bulgaria	20.61	Latvia	7.70
Lithuania	13.52	Bulgaria	6.00
Estonia	13.39	Estonia	4.39
Latvia	9.76	Lithuania	2.55

Romania and Slovakia there is a degree of overlap of between 20 and 30 per cent. Thus, to a large degree these countries are exporting different products, amongst the new approach and old approach products, to the EU than they are importing from the EU.

Amongst the CEECs the highest degree of similarity between exports to and imports from the EU is shown by Poland, Hungary and the Czech Republic where the degree of overlap lies between 30 and just over 40 per cent. This reflects in part country size. Small countries, such as Latvia, will tend to produce a narrower range of products than larger countries such as Poland. However, the values of the similarity index for the CEECs are much lower than the apparent degree of similarity for EU members of similar size. Compare the values for Poland and Spain, for example. This suggests that the adjustment implications of accession to the single market may not be as great as they would be if the CEECs were competing more directly with EU countries in the same product segments.

IV. Conclusions

One of, if not *the* most, important factor(s) affecting trade between existing EU members and new Member States in central and eastern Europe will be the removal of technical barriers to trade. To date there has been little attempt to assess the importance of such barriers to trade between the EU and the CEECs. In this article we have provided a very simple analysis, firstly using existing data sources of the sectoral incidence of technical regulations in the EU, and then using our own translation of the detailed product coverage of old and new approach directives. The general conclusions we reach are:

- that there is considerable diversity across the CEECs in the importance of sectors subject to technical regulations in the EU. Broadly, those countries currently most advanced in their accession negotiations are those where technical regulations are more important for their exports to the EU. This suggests that adjustment to the single market will be greater in these countries compared to, for example, the Balkan countries, where sectors for which technical barriers are not significant are much more important. Thus, for Romania and Bulgaria, a large share of their exports to the EU already faces market access conditions identical to those of existing EU members and where accession will have little direct impact. However, it is possible that the exports of these countries of products subject to technical regulations in the EU are being constrained by current access conditions and the lack of FDI into these countries.

- For all the CEECs there is little evidence from current trade flows of comparative advantage in sectors subject to old approach directives. For some of the CEECs, notably the Czech Republic and Poland, a comparative advantage is revealed in a wide range of sectors subject to the new approach in the EU.
- For new approach and old approach products the CEECs generally exhibit a low degree of similarity between their exports to the EU and their imports from the EU. This suggests different channels of specialization within the groups of new approach and old approach products. This will tend to mitigate the adjustment implications of accession in both the CEECs and the existing EU member countries. There is also a low degree of overlap between EU imports from the CEECs and EU imports from non-member countries. Thus, the magnitude of trade diversion when the CEECs have full access to the single market is likely to be limited.

This analysis has shown the importance of technical regulations to trade between the EU and the CEECs and some of the characteristics of such trade. It is apparent that the share of exports accounted for by products where there may be technical barriers to trade varies greatly across the CEECs. Thus, modelling the next enlargement as a common shock in all the CEECs does not appear to be appropriate. A key issue for additional research is to proceed to identify the extent to which the application of technical regulations in the EU actually constrains imports from the CEECs. Alternatively, to be able to assess the extent to which trade will expand on accession as technical barriers to trade are removed, we need to understand much better how the removal of these barriers in the EU with the creation of the single market affected intra-EU trade flows.

Correspondence:

Paul Brenton
Centre for European Policy Studies
Place du Congrès 1
Brussels 1000, Belgium
Tel: 00 322 229 3936 Fax:00 322 219 4151
email: paul.brenton@ceps.be

John Sheehy
European Commission
DG Internal Market
Rue de la Loi 200, Brussels
Tel: 00 322 299 3399
email: john.sheehy@cec.eu.int.

Marc Vancauteren
Centre for European Policy Studies
Place du Congrès 1
Brussels 1000, Belgium
Tel: 00 322 229 3936 Fax:00 322 219 4151
email: mvancauteren@ceps.be

References

Brenton, P.A. (1999) 'Anti-Dumping, Diversion and the Next Enlargement of the EU'. Working Document 129, CEPS, Brussels.

Brenton, P.A. and Winters, L.A. (1992) 'Estimating the International Trade Effects of "1992": West Germany'. *Journal of Common Market Studies*, Vol. 30, No. 2, pp. 143–56.

Brenton, P.A., Sheehy, J. and Vancauteren, M. (2000) 'Technical Barriers to Trade in the EU: Importance for Accession Countries'. Working Document 144, CEPS, Brussels.

Commission of the European Communities (1996) 'NACE Rev. 1, Statistical Classification of Economic Activities in the European Communities'. *Official Journal of the European Union*, L293.

Commission of the European Communities (1998a) 'Technical Barriers to Trade', Vol. 1, Subseries III Dismantling of Barriers, *The Single Market Review* (Luxembourg: OOPEC).

Commission of the European Communities (1998b) 'Central and Eastern European Countries: Report on Market Access'. MAAG-DOC.119 final, September, Brussels.

Finger, J.M. and Kreinin, M.E. (1979) 'A Measure of "Export Similarity" and its Possible Uses'. *Economic Journal*, No. 89, pp. 905–12.

Francois, J.F. (1998) 'Scale Economies, Imperfect Competition and the Eastern Expansion of the EU'. In Brockmeier, M., Francois, J., Hertel, T. and Schmitz, P. (eds) *Economic Transition and the Greening of Policies* (Kiel: Wissenschaftsverlag Vauk Kiel KG).

Gasiorek, M., Smith, A. and Venables, A. (1991) 'Completing the Internal Market in the EC: Factor Demands and Comparative Advantage'. In Winters, L.A. and Venables, A.J. (eds) *European Integration: Trade and Industry* (Cambridge: Cambridge University Press).

Pelkmans, J. (1987) 'The New Approach to Technical Harmonization and Standardization'. *Journal of Common Market Studies*, Vol. 25, No. 2, pp. 249–69.

Pelkmans, J. and Winters, L.A. (1988) 'Europe's Domestic Market'. Chatham House Papers No. 43 (London: Routledge/RIIA).

Sapir, A. (1990) 'Does 1992 Come Before or After 1990? On Regional Versus Multilateral Integration'. In Jones, R. and Krueger, A.O. (eds) *The Political Economy of International Trade – Essays in Honour of Robert Baldwin* (Oxford: Basil Blackwell).

Empirica **26:** 95–121, 1999.

Chapter 7

Economic Integration and FDI: An Empirical Analysis of Foreign Investment in the EU and in Central and Eastern Europe*

PAUL BRENTON and FRANCESCA DI MAURO
Centre for European Policy Studies, Brussels, Belgium
E-mail: paul.brenton@ceps.be; fdimauro@ceps.be

MATTHIAS LÜCKE
Kiel Institute of World Economics, Kiel, Germany
E-mail: mluecke@ifw.uni-kiel.de

Abstract. Recent evidence suggests that regional economic integration provides an important stimulus not only to trade, but also to FDI. In contrast, the available theory on FDI does not yet provide empirically testable propositions on the effects of concurrent trade and investment liberalisation. Moreover, given the limits of simulation models, which rely heavily upon parameter choice, in assessing the impact of such liberalisation, there is a need for empirical analysis to identify the principal features of FDI. This paper uses a 'gravity model' approach to assess the impact of the deepening integration between the EU and the CEECs on FDI flows in terms of three key issues. First, we provide systematic estimates of the expected long-term level of FDI in the CEECs. Second, we investigate whether FDI in the CEECs, on the one hand, and source country exports and imports, on the other hand, are complements or substitutes. Finally, we enquire whether an increase in the attractiveness of the CEECs to foreign investors has affected the magnitude of FDI going to other European countries.

Key words: Foreign direct investment, transition economies, gravity model

JEL codes: F15, F21, F23.

I. Introduction

Empirical evidence and initial modelling work suggest that regional economic integration can provide an important stimulus not only to trade, but also to foreign direct investment (FDI) within the region concerned. For example, Brenton (1996) found that the EU Single Market programme led to a significant increase in investment by EU firms in other EU countries in the late 1980s. However, the available theory on FDI has yet to provide clear and empirically testable propositions on the effects of both trade and investment liberalisation. Indeed, with different types of multinational firms, vertical and horizontal, the impact of preferential trade liberalisation and preferential investment liberalisation is difficult to deduce theoretically due to the high degree of dimensionality that is required. One approach to clarifying these effects is likely to rely upon the use of simulation models, but the results of which are dependent upon the choice of model specific parameters. Thus, there is a need, at present, for empirical analysis to identify the principal features of FDI and determine how these have evolved in an environment of increasing economic integration. Such work is important in informing the policy debate on FDI but may also be of use in highlighting the key issues and so helping to direct the development of theoretical work on FDI.

In this paper, we assess the impact of the deepening integration between the EU and the Central and Eastern European countries (CEECs) on FDI flows by addressing three major issues. First, we provide systematic estimates of the expected long-term level of FDI in the CEECs. The stock of FDI in Central and Eastern Europe (CEE) has grown rapidly since the beginning of systemic transformation in the early 1990s, particularly in the more advanced Central European transition economies. Nevertheless, Sinn and Weichenrieder (1997) assert in their influential article that the stock of FDI in the CEECs is still far lower than it should be, compared with countries having a similar level of income. Initial analysis of FDI flows (Brenton and Di Mauro, 1998) suggests that overseas investment in the more advanced CEECs, and particularly from Germany, is in fact high relative to other countries, after taking into account the main determinants of FDI flows. Here we assess whether similar conclusions can be derived when analysing the stock of FDI in central and eastern European countries. We employ a model of the determinants of bilateral FDI that is similar to the gravity model often used to explain bilateral trade flows.

The question of how much more FDI the CEECs can expect to receive as a result of their continuing transformation and future EU membership is important for both host and source countries.[1] From the host country perspective, the economic effects of FDI are usually regarded as unambiguously beneficial. FDI finances a substantial share of domestic investment in some CEECs and is probably less volatile than other international capital flows because of the essentially long-term orientation of investors. Furthermore, FDI represents an important source of managerial and technological knowledge which is particularly welcome in transition as in developing economies.[2]

By contrast, from the source country point of view, the immediate effect of growing FDI outflows is either to replace exports to the partner country by local production ('horizontal' FDI), or to enable firms in the source country to take advantage of lower labour costs abroad leading to the import of goods that were previously produced at home ('vertical' FDI). In either case, some structural change in the source country with the attending adjustment costs is likely to result. In contrast to this pessimistic scenario, however, nearly all empirical studies of the trade effects of FDI find that source country exports tend to increase along with FDI (see Graham, 1996 for a review of this literature). Our second objective in this paper, therefore, is to investigate whether FDI in the CEECs, on the one hand,

and source country exports and imports, on the other hand, are complements or substitutes.

Finally, we enquire whether an increase in the attractiveness of particular countries or regions to foreign investors, as a result of policy changes, such as the introduction of the Single Market in the EU and transition in Central and Eastern Europe and the integration agreements with EU countries, has affected the magnitude of FDI going to other European countries. Here we estimate our model of bilateral FDI on annual flow data and follow the evolution over time of the coefficients of dummy variables for countries such as the Scandinavian countries and Spain and Portugal.

The paper is organised as follows. Section II introduces the gravity-type model that forms the basis of the empirical analysis. Section III presents estimates of the long-term level of FDI in individual CEECs by major investing countries and compares these to current levels. Section IV analyses the relationship between FDI and trade. Section V investigates the possible impact of increasing economic integration between groups of countries upon FDI flows going to countries not directly included. Section VI concludes and provides some policy implications.

II. An Empirical Model of Bilateral FDI Flows

Until recently, the dominant paradigm for most empirical research on FDI has been the OLI framework. This identifies three broad conditions which are necessary before a firm will engage in direct investment abroad: advantages through ownership, location, and internalisation. An ownership advantage gives a multinational firm a cost advantage over local rivals in the foreign market, it can be in the form of a product or process, or intangibles such as a reputation for quality, a superior management and so on. There must also be a locational advantage which encourages the firm to produce the product, or provide the service, in the foreign country rather than producing it in domestic plants and exporting. Trade barriers, both natural (transport costs) and artificial (tariffs and quotas), cheap factors of production, and ease of access to consumers appear to be the principal locational advantages. The internalisation advantage leads the firm to set up a foreign subsidiary rather than exploit its ownership advantage in other ways such as licensing a foreign firm to produce the product or use the process.

Although this literature has provided a sound base for understanding why individual firms become multinationals and which factors at the level of the firm lead some industries being characterised by multinationals, the OLI framework has been sterile in explaining some of the key trends in FDI over the past three decades, such as the increasing volume of two-way investment between rich industrial countries, at a time of falling trade barriers. It has also been unable to generate empirical models conducive to a careful analysis of the effects of regional integration.

Recently, a small body of literature has emerged which has taken the key elements of ownership and locational advantages from the firm-based approach OLI (the issue of internalisation is largely ignored) and introduced them into general equilibrium trade models. In these models multinational firms arise endogenously and two-way FDI can occur between countries (see, for example, Brainard (1997) and Markusen and Venables (1995, 1996)). Here (horizontal) multinational activity is driven by the trade-off between the additional fixed costs of establishing an overseas plant against the costs of servicing this overseas market via exporting. As with the OLI approach trade and FDI are substitutes. Markusen et al. (1996) develop a model which allows for both vertical and horizontal multinational activity together with intra and inter industry trade. A feature of these theoretical models is that they demonstrate the role of country characteristics, such as, economic size, in explaining the pattern of FDI and trade flows.

This has stimulated some empirical studies of the bilateral distribution of FDI using the gravity model (Brainard, 1997; Eaton and Tamura, 1996; Brenton, 1996). The gravity model has proved to be popular and empirically successful in explaining bilateral trade flows. Since the evolution of FDI over the past three decades shares some common features with the evolution of trade, having become more intense between countries with similar relatively high income levels, and having grown faster than income, then the gravity model may also be useful in modelling the regional pattern of FDI.

Developed in the 1960s (Linnemann, 1966) the gravity model is typically applied to bilateral trade data for a single year (or average of years) pooled over origin countries. The model describes the flow from an origin i to a destination j in terms of supply factors in the origin (income and population), demand factors in the destination (again, income and population) and various stimulating or restraining factors relating to the specific flow, such as distance (as a proxy for trade costs) and trade preferences. Two recent contributions (Polak, 1996; Mátyás, 1997) have, however, suggested that the standard gravity model may be mis-specified. In both cases this mis-specification arises from pooling the data over source countries and/or over time and is not relevant when estimating the gravity model separately for each source country and for a single year. In this paper we apply the gravity model to data on the bilateral distribution of FDI, imports and exports for individual countries.

Our actual estimating equation takes the form:

$$\ln X_{ij} = \alpha + \beta_1 \ln Y_j + \beta_2 \ln \mathrm{POP}_j + \beta_3 \ln \mathrm{Dist}_{ij} + \sum \gamma_k D_{kij},$$

where X_{ij} is the value of any flow (FDI, imports or exports) or stock (FDI) from country i (source country) to country j (host country); Y_j is the income of country j; POP_j is the population of country j; DIST_{ij} is the distance between countries i and j; D_{kij} are dummy variables representing preferential preferential relationships between i and j which stimulate the flow/stock taken into account.

The volume of the relevant flow into a country is explained by the level of income of that country and its absolute size, as proxied by population. FDI and exports are expected to be positively related to the level of income, since they are both attracted by larger domestic markets, whilst negatively affected by country size. Large populous countries are expected to be more self-sufficient in terms of trade and investment. As for distance, theory suggests that firms will tend to prefer FDI to exports as trade costs, as proxied by distance, rise. More distant markets will tend to be served by overseas affiliates rather than by exporting. Nevertheless, this variable may also have a negative coefficient in the investment equations since the costs of operating overseas affiliates is likely to rise the further they are from the main headquarters (higher costs of placing personnel abroad, communication costs, language and cultural differences, informational costs on local tax laws and regulations, costs of being outside domestic networks, risks of exchange rate changes, etc.). Thus, distance will have a dampening effect on both trade and FDI, but the effect should be more pronounced for exports, a feature found in initial estimates of the gravity model applied to data for outflows from Japan and the US (Brainard, 1997; Eaton and Tamura, 1996) and from EU countries (Brenton, 1996).

For the three parts of our empirical analysis, we will use the gravity model in the following ways: first, in Section III we estimate a 'normal pattern' of bilateral FDI stocks of major European investing countries as well as the US, Japan and South Korea. This normal pattern may be thought of as reflecting FDI under conditions where stocks have been fully adjusted to any changes in the explanatory variables that have occurred in the past. The current, actual level of FDI from each of the source countries to the CEECs can then be compared to this 'normal pattern' through the use of dummy variables for the main groups of CEECs (first-round candidates for membership, and other CEEC candidate countries).

We then proceed to analyse the substitutability or complementarity between FDI and trade. We follow Graham (1996) and estimate gravity models for the exports and imports of each FDI source country in addition to the FDI stock. If trade and FDI are complementary, the residuals from the export or import regression should be positively correlated with the residuals from the corresponding FDI regression. If trade and FDI are substitutes, there should be a negative correlation.

Third, to assess the possible impact of investment and trade liberalisation between certain countries upon FDI going to excluded countries we estimate gravity equations using data on FDI flows over time (Section V) and investigate the time profile of dummy variables for particular host countries; for Portugal and Spain and for the three new Member-States (Austria, Finland and Sweden).

III. Actual vs. Expected FDI Stocks in Central and Eastern Europe

This section presents the results of a regression analysis of bilateral FDI *stocks* by major investing countries in the mid-1990s. The gravity model introduced in the preceding section is used to define a 'normal pattern' of bilateral FDI stocks. Dummy variables are included for two groups of Central and Eastern European economies (first- and second-round candidates for EU membership) to test for a possible divergence from this pattern. If the corresponding coefficients are significant and negative, the CEECs concerned can expect to benefit from further, large FDI inflows as foreign investors adjust their stocks to the new opportunities created by economic transformation. If the dummies are not significant, the future growth of the FDI stock can be expected to be in line with changes in the 'normal' determinants of FDI, especially GDP growth.

We also include in our regression equation an Economic Freedom Index, EFI (see Johnson et al., 1998). The index ranks annually more than 150 countries (with lower values standing for freer countries) and takes into account 10 factors of 'economic freedom': trade policy, taxation, government intervention in the economy, monetary policy, foreign investment, banking, wage and price controls, property rights, regulation and black market activity. It is therefore an indicator of the 'market-friendliness' of economic policies in the host country and from its definition we expect a negative sign for countries with a less favourable environment to foreign investors.

The regression results in Table I are arranged by investing country and show differences between three model specifications for each investing country. When only the three basic variables income, population, and distance are included (in addition to the CEEC dummies),[3] most coefficients have the expected signs: positive for income, negative for population and distance. When the Economic Freedom Index is added, its coefficient is nearly always significant and negative. At the same time, the sign of the population coefficient changes in many regressions because the index is highly negatively correlated with per capita income, which is implicit in the combination of the GNP and population explanatory variables. However, since the Economic Freedom Index adds considerably to the explanatory power of the model as measured by the adjusted R^2, we prefer this specification to the one including only the basic variables. This is justified in particular because we are interested in obtaining a normal pattern of bilateral FDI, rather than 'correct' estimates of the individual coefficients. The high explanatory power of the model with the Economic Freedom Index, with adjusted R^2 in the range from 0.52 to 0.79, leads us to conclude that these results represent fairly well the normal pattern of bilateral FDI stocks.

In order to explore the possible link between FDI and regional integration, a dummy for host country membership in the EU(15) is also included. The expected sign of the corresponding coefficient is not clear a priori. When the investing country is an EU member, both its trade and outward FDI may benefit from the reduced transaction costs and the liberalisation of financial flows. Therefore, if FDI and trade are substitutes, the impact of regional integration on FDI is not obvious. When the investing country is not an EU member, firms investing overseas might prefer an EU country over other potential host countries because it offers free access to the whole EU and EFTA markets. It is not clear, however, that this would raise FDI in all EU countries, which is what is tested by the dummy variable.

Table I. Regression results: Determinants of bilateral FDI, major OECD investing country (dependent variable: log of FDI)

Investing country	Log of GNP	Log of population	Log of distance	Economic freedom index	EU	CEE1st	CEE2nd	CIS	Wald test that CEE dummies are equal (F-stat.)	Adj. R^2	S.E.	Number of obs.
Austria	1.23***	−0.38	−0.81***			2.31**	0.46	−1.06	3.30**	0.53	1.57	43
	0.82**	0.09	−0.97***	−1.21*		2.05*	0.58	−0.50	1.79	0.55	1.54	43
	0.74*	0.15	−0.69*	−1.27*	1.07	2.96**	1.47	0.10	2.15	0.56	1.52	43
Finland	1.02***	−0.52	−1.25***			−2.15		−4.44**	1.18	0.49	1.74	35
	0.32	0.47	−1.68***	−2.35**		−2.45*		−4.12**	0.73	0.56	1.62	35
	0.36	0.43	−1.77***	−2.29**	−0.31	−2.71*		−4.39**	0.71	0.55	1.64	35
France	1.38***	−0.25	−0.59***			0.41	−0.61	−3.46***	4.49**	0.65	1.43	50
	0.91***	0.27	−0.71***	−1.36**		0.42	−0.40	−2.72**	3.02*	0.68	1.37	50
	0.88***	0.30	−0.63**	−1.37**	0.28	0.57	−0.28	−2.62**	3.03*	0.67	1.39	50
Germany	1.22***	−0.30*	−0.52***			0.15	−0.51	−1.74*	1.85	0.67	1.12	48
	0.87***	0.11	−0.63***	−1.03**		0.06	−0.25	−1.22	0.82	0.70	1.08	48
	0.81***	0.16	−0.41*	−1.08**	0.82	0.63	0.23	−0.83	1.10	0.70	1.06	48
Netherlands	0.94***	−0.19	−0.43***			−1.36**	−2.78**		1.48	0.69	1.06	42
	0.44**	0.37	−0.55**	−1.52***		−1.39**	−2.49**		1.17	0.77	0.91	42
	0.43*	0.37*	−0.52**	−1.53***	0.12	−1.32**	−2.41**		1.13	0.77	0.93	42
Norway	0.88**	−0.56	−0.96***			−1.33		−1.77	0.06	0.50	1.46	34
	0.33	0.16	−1.23***	−1.43*		−1.97	−1.63		0.04	0.53	1.41	34
	0.30	0.20	−1.09**	−1.50*	0.40	−1.64		−1.34	0.03	0.52	1.43	34
Switzerland	1.04***	−0.30**	−0.36***			−0.84		−5.22***	20.24***	0.79	0.81	40
	0.96***	−0.20	−0.39***	−0.25		−0.89		−5.13***	17.66***	0.79	0.82	40
	0.94***	−0.17	−0.31	−0.27	0.25	−0.69		−5.03***	17.15***	0.78	0.83	40

Table I. Continued

Investing country	Log of GNP	Log of population	Log of distance	Economic freedom index	EU	CEE1st	CEE2nd	CIS	Wald test that CEE dummies are equal (F-stat.)	Adj. R^2	S.E.	Number of obs.
UK	1.11***	−0.45**	−0.01			−2.55***	−3.47***	−2.37*	0.52	0.72	1.30	47
	0.53**	0.23	−0.21	−1.74***		−2.60***	−2.92***	−1.70	0.36	0.78	1.17	47
	0.49*	0.29	−0.02	−1.79***	0.72	−2.20***	−2.57***	−1.43	0.33	0.78	1.16	47
US	1.17***	−0.29**	−0.58			−0.59	−2.58**	−1.78	1.46	0.65	1.06	48
	0.71***	0.28	−1.02***	−1.55***		−0.69	−2.11**	−1.11	0.82	0.72	0.95	48
	0.78***	0.21	−1.04***	−1.49***	−0.27	−0.73	−2.12**	−1.18	0.72	0.72	0.95	48
Japan	0.95***	0.03	−0.99**			−2.95**	−4.12***	−2.23	0.45	0.59	1.68	40
	0.12	1.06**	0.05	−2.80***		−3.05***	−2.76**	−0.82	0.78	0.68	1.48	40
	0.52	0.64	0.08	−2.20**	−1.24**	−3.30***	−3.12**	−1.30	0.69	0.72	1.40	40
South Korea	0.51**	0.38	−1.26***			0.08	1.46	0.48	0.54	0.38	1.44	37
	−0.17	1.38***	−0.41	−2.45***		0.28	2.62**	1.69	1.89	0.52	1.28	37
	−0.30	1.53***	−0.40	−2.64***	0.44	0.37	2.74**	1.82	1.92	0.50	0.51	37

*** (**; *) Significant at the 1% (5%; 10%) level.

Notes: *Destination countries* include all OECD countries, plus Bulgaria, Romania, Russia, Slovenia, Slovakia, Ukraine, Argentina, Brazil, Chile, China, Hong Kong, India, Indonesia, Korea, Malaysia, Philippines, Singapore, Thailand. The country coverage is different for each source country, which explains differences in the sample size.

Dummy variables

- EU: all 15 EU Member States.
- CEE1st: Czech Rep., Hungary, Poland, Slovenia and 'Baltic Countries', since separate data for Estonia were not available.
- CEE2nd: Bulgaria, Romania and Slovakia.
- CIS: Russia and Ukraine.

As it turns out, the coefficient of the EU dummy is insignificant for all investing countries except Japan where it is negative. Thus these regression results convey the overall impression that host country membership in the EU does not significantly influence the stock of inward FDI. While this finding is not unexpected, a cautionary note is appropriate. The sample size for each source country is between 35 and 50 so that the roughly 15 EU countries can account for close to half of the sample. Since few other countries of similar per capita income are located in geographical proximity to the group, the EU dummy is likely to be correlated with the other explanatory variables. It is not entirely clear, therefore, whether the coefficient of the EU dummy provides an accurate measure of what FDI would be in the absence of European economic integration.[4]

With no other measure available, however, we now turn our attention to the coefficient estimates for the CEEC dummies. A distinction is made between first-round EU candidates (CEE1st – Poland, Hungary, Czech Republic), second-round candidates (CEE2nd - Slovakia, Bulgaria, Romania). For each investing country, the coefficients are not greatly affected by the specification of the underlying gravity model, i.e. the inclusion or not of the Economic Freedom Index and the EU dummy. Hence we limit ourselves to discussing the results for our preferred specification which includes only the Economic Freedom Index.

The coefficients of the CEEC dummies for the investing countries in Europe, except Norway and the UK, follow a pattern that differs notably from the remaining countries. Of the three coefficients, the one for the first-round EU candidates (CEE1st) always takes on the highest value, followed by CEE2nd and then by CIS. The Wald tests also reported in Table 1 reject the null hypothesis of equal coefficients for CEE1st, CEE2nd, and CIS only for France and Switzerland. Note that these tests are for individual countries and thus do not take into account that many of the European investing countries display the same basic pattern. Hence it seems safe to conclude that the CEE1st countries have been more successful than the rest of Central and Eastern Europe in terms of attracting FDI from Europe and Finland, even after controlling for differential progress in systemic transformation (through the Economic Freedom Index) and for geographical proximity (through the distance variable).

This finding is compatible with other evidence that the most advanced transition economies are increasingly hosting not only horizontal FDI aimed at their own domestic markets, but also vertical FDI that integrates local production into European production networks (Lankes and Venables, 1996; Szalavetz and Lücke, 1997). The ongoing accession to the EU of this group of countries may well have inspired international investors with sufficient confidence to rely on production in the CEE1st countries for their multinational sourcing. Furthermore, it is plausible that Central and East European transition economies are attractive locations for product sourcing mainly for European, rather than US or Japanese multinationals. For integration into production networks, geographical proximity to other production locations, ease of communication, and cultural affinity may well be of greater importance than for market-driven foreign investment. This could explain why the relatively favourable position of CEE1st countries is only found for investing countries in Europe.

We now turn to the question of whether FDI stocks in the three groups of CEECs are already close to their 'normal' levels, or whether significant further stock adjustment should be expected. The coefficient estimate for CEE1st is significant and negative for only four out of the total of eleven source countries for which data are available (Finland, Netherlands, UK, Japan). CEE2nd has significant and negative coefficient estimates for four out of eight source countries (Netherlands, UK, US, Japan); CIS for three out of ten countries (Finland, France, Switzerland). Hence, for most combinations of source and host countries, the stock of FDI in Central and Eastern Europe has largely adjusted to the level that would be expected among market economy host countries. These results complement the findings of Brenton and Di Mauro (1998) who found no evidence that FDI *flows* into the more advanced CEECs diverged significantly from the 'normal' level defined by the gravity model.

So the assertion by Sinn and Weichenrieder (1997) that FDI in Central and Eastern Europe is tiny, compared with developing countries, appears to be exaggerated when judged against this background. Any sustained, substantial growth of FDI in the CEECs will have to be stimulated to a large extent by growth of the host country and continuing economic reforms. As our regression results demonstrate, these two variables are closely linked and their relative importance is difficult to disentangle statistically.

IV. Trade and FDI: Complements or Substitutes?

We begin our analysis of the link between FDI and trade by estimating gravity equations for the exports and imports of the FDI source countries to and from the host countries in our FDI database. As in the previous section, various specifications with and without the Economic Freedom Index and the EU dummy have been tested. Dummy variables for the two groups of CEECs and the CIS are employed to test for any divergence of trade with the so-called countries from the 'normal pattern' established by the gravity model.

Selected regression results with and without the EU dummy are reported in Table II. The coefficient of the EU dummy variable is expected to be positive for EU reporting countries (i.e. the source countries of FDI) because regional integration is expected to reduce trade costs. Its expected sign is not clear for the remaining reporting countries. It turns out that, among European reporting countries, the coefficient estimates for the EU dummy variable are significant and positive only for German and Norwegian imports as well as for Dutch exports. Coefficient estimates are significant and negative for US and Japanese exports and imports.

These negative estimates are difficult to interpret with respect to the expected trade between the US and Japan on the one hand and future EU members among the CEECs on the other hand. Conceivably, the estimates might reflect a restrictive

Table II. Regression results for bilateral trade, major OECD countries

Reporting country	Dependent variable	Log of GNP	Log of population	Log of distance	Economic freedom index	EU	CEE1st	CEE2nd	CIS	Adj. R^2	S.E.	Number of obs.
Austria	Log of exports	0.80***	−0.02	−0.79***	−0.45*		0.64	0.34	−0.15	0.85	0.60	52
		0.81***	−0.03	−0.82***	−0.45	−0.13	0.54	0.26	−0.20	0.85	0.61	52
	Log of imports	0.50*	0.55*	−1.04***	−1.26**		−0.07	−0.04	0.21	0.64	1.21	52
		0.43	0.60**	−0.87***	−1.27**	0.68	0.46	0.44	0.53	0.64	1.21	52
Finland	Log of exports	0.51***	0.30**	−0.95***	−1.17***		0.23	−0.18	0.01	0.82	0.66	53
		0.48***	0.32**	−0.87***	−1.18***	0.26	0.39	−0.07	0.19	0.82	0.66	53
	Log of imports	0.57**	0.39	−0.96***	−1.39**		0.24	−0.15	0.22	0.58	1.30	53
		0.46	0.46	−0.67**	−1.44**	0.97	0.83	0.24	0.87	0.60	1.28	53
France	Log of exports	0.56***	0.13	−0.70	−0.41		−0.90***	−1.05**	−1.32***	0.82	0.57	53
		0.56***	0.12	−0.73***	−0.41	−0.09	−0.95***	−1.08**	−1.35***	0.85	0.57	53
	Log of imports	0.64***	0.17	−0.75***	−0.48		−0.75*	−0.59	−0.71	0.82	0.69	53
		0.63***	0.18	−0.72***	−0.48	0.12	−0.69	−0.55	−0.67	0.81	0.70	53
Germany	Log of exports	0.67***	0.09	−0.61***	−0.55***		0.24	0.14	−0.01	0.89	0.45	53
		0.65***	0.11	−0.53***	−0.56***	0.31	0.48	0.30	0.12	0.89	0.45	53
	Log of imports	0.57***	0.24*	−0.78***	−0.81***		0.19	0.20	−0.57	0.84	0.59	53
		0.53***	0.27**	−0.62***	−0.83***	0.61**	0.58	0.49	−0.31	0.85	0.57	53
Netherlands	Log of exports	0.62**	0.04	−0.73***	−0.59***		−0.32	−0.46	−0.40	0.89	0.51	53
		0.57***	0.08	−0.56***	−0.62***	0.67**	0.03	−0.19	−0.15	0.90	0.48	53
	Log of imports	0.63***	0.04	−0.52***	−0.53		−0.47	−0.62	−0.87	0.76	0.74	53
		0.63***	0.05	−0.52***	−0.53	0.02	−0.46	−0.61	−0.86	0.75	0.75	53

Table II. Continued

Reporting country	Dependent variable	Log of GNP	Log of population	Log of distance	Economic freedom index	EU	CEE1st	CEE2nd	CIS	Adj. R^2	S.E.	Number of obs.
Norway	Log of exports	0.85***	0.04	−1.15***	−0.81**		−0.78*	−1.10*	−0.90	0.85	0.79	53
		0.77***	0.09	−0.86***	−0.84**	0.84*	−0.23	−0.71	−0.41	0.86	0.77	53
	Log of imports	0.61**	0.47*	−1.13***	−1.33**		−0.30	−0.39	0.25	0.69	1.20	53
		0.48*	0.55**	−0.64**	−1.39***	1.39**	0.62	0.27	1.06	0.71	1.15	53
Switzerland	Log of exports	0.70***	0.02	−0.46***	−0.82**		−0.31	−0.07	−0.67	0.72	0.82	53
		0.70***	0.02	−0.45**	−0.81**	0.04	−0.28	−0.04	−0.66	0.72	0.83	53
	Log of imports	0.69***	0.22	−0.96***	−1.47***		−0.88	−0.33	−0.46	0.78	0.97	53
		0.64***	0.25	−0.75***	−1.42***	0.68	−0.42	0.02	−0.21	0.79	0.96	53
UK	Log of exports	0.61***	0.03	−0.46***	−0.91***		−0.92**	−0.82	−0.71	0.79	0.72	53
		0.57***	0.07	−0.32**	−0.93***	0.54	−0.65	−0.61	−0.53	0.80	0.71	53
	Log of imports	0.53***	0.21	−0.51***	−1.10***		−0.67*	−0.68	−1.32**	0.83	0.65	53
		0.49***	0.24*	−0.38***	−1.12***	0.50	−0.43	−0.49	−1.14**	0.83	0.64	53
US	Log of exports	0.31**	0.44***	−0.95***	−1.15***		−1.76***	−1.62***	−1.17*	0.80	0.74	53
		0.57***	0.23	−1.02***	−0.97***	−0.94***	−1.88***	−1.65***	−1.38**	0.84	0.65	53
	Log of imports	0.48***	0.34*	−0.87***	−0.89**		−1.46***	−1.13*	−0.91	0.71	0.90	53
		0.76***	0.12	−0.94***	−0.69*	−1.03***	−1.60***	−1.17**	−1.14*	0.76	0.81	53
Japan	Log of exports	0.43***	0.38**	−1.05***	−1.37***		−2.09***	−2.43***	−1.37**	0.88	0.72	53
		0.59***	0.25	−1.02***	−1.25***	−0.55**	−2.16***	−2.45***	−1.50**	0.89	0.69	53
	Log of imports	0.57**	0.23	−0.89**	−1.07**		−1.78***	−1.90**	−0.27	0.72	1.06	53
		0.87***	−0.02	−0.84**	−0.87*	−1.05***	−1.91***	−1.95***	−0.51	0.76	1.00	53
South Korea	Log of exports	0.06	0.73***	−0.68**	−1.67***		−0.43		−0.68	0.70	0.81	38
		0.21	0.61***	−0.67**	−1.53***	−0.49	−0.48		−0.79	0.70	0.80	38
	Log of imports	0.49**	0.19	−0.58	−0.90		−1.69**		0.18	0.58	0.98	38
		0.66**	0.06	−0.56	−0.73	−0.57	−1.76**		0.05	0.59	0.97	38

trade regime on the part of the EU leading to trade diversion to the disadvantage of the US and Japan. However, as we discussed above for FDI, the estimated negative coefficient might be the result of collinearity between the EU dummy and the other explanatory variables and might thus reflect low trade with Europe as a geographical region rather than the impact of institutional arrangements. In any event, the large absolute size of the negative coefficient estimates for the various CEEC dummies suggests that current US and Japanese trade with the CEECs is substantially lower than predicted and will probably increase just to attain the predicted (low) level of US and Japanese trade with EU members.

Given that few coefficient estimates for the EU dummy are statistically significant in the case of European reporting countries, plus the difficulty of interpreting the negative coefficient estimates for the US and Japan, the subsequent analysis will be based on the regressions without the EU dummy. Turning now to the level of trade between the European reporting countries and the CEECs, the coefficient estimates for the CEEC dummies are mostly insignificant, indicating that bilateral trade is close to the level expected among market economies. Important exceptions include French imports with large negative coefficients for all three groups of CEECs, UK exports to the first-round candidate countries (CEE1st), and UK imports from the second-round candidate countries (CEE2nd) as well as from Russia and Ukraine (CIS). Thus the trade of West European countries with the CEECs has largely adjusted to the regional pattern predicted on the basis of bilateral trade with market economies.[5]

In order to explore the possible impact of FDI on bilateral trade, we now include the residual from the FDI regressions in the gravity models for exports and imports. We follow the approach of Graham (1996) in assuming that if FDI substitutes for trade, then trade should be lower than 'normal' whenever FDI is higher than 'normal'. Hence, under the hypothesis of substitutability, the coefficient of the FDI residual in the gravity model for trade should be negative. For consistency, we use the same set of explanatory variables for calculating the FDI residual and in the gravity regression for trade. Also we allow the FDI residual to vary between the two groups of CEECs and the CIS and the remaining countries by adding the products of each CEEC dummy and the FDI residual as explanatory variables.

Table III reports the results for the extended gravity model for exports. The coefficient of the FDI residual is significant and positive for 7 out of 11 FDI source countries, and insignificant for the rest. Also, this coefficient differs only rarely between any of the three groups of CEECs on the one hand and the remaining countries on the other hand. A similar finding applies to imports (Table IV). The coefficient of the FDI residual is significant and positive for 5 out of the 11 FDI source countries and, again, differs little between the CEECs and CIS and the other countries. Hence we find no well-defined link between the stock of FDI and trade for France, Germany, the Netherlands, and Switzerland, nor between the stock of FDI on the one hand and Austrian and South Korean imports on the other. For the remaining countries, the stock of FDI and both exports and imports are found to be complementary. Complementarity is also found between FDI and Austrian and South Korean exports. Again, these results reinforce those of Brenton and Di Mauro (1998) who found, using a similar approach, complementarity between FDI *flows* and both import and exports.

In interpreting this finding, it is helpful to refer to the distinction between horizontal and vertical FDI. Most case studies of FDI find that the main motivation of foreign investors is to produce for the host country market or for export to other countries in the same region (horizontal FDI). While such investment may replace some final goods exports of the source country, it may also lead to exports of machinery and, subsequently, intermediate goods to the host country. This may explain the complementary relationship between FDI and exports for some source countries. Interestingly, however, calculations using the few available data on sectoral FDI for Germany, the US, and Japan suggest that even sectoral FDI and sectoral exports tend to be complementary.[6]

FDI may also be aimed at outsourcing production activities to the host country and exporting products (e.g. components) back to the source country. Such vertical FDI is perfectly compatible with the observed complementarity between FDI and imports. However, empirical studies, based mostly on enterprise surveys, find almost universally that vertical FDI plays only a small role as a proportion of total FDI, although its importance appears to have grown in Central European transition economies in recent years (Lankes and Venables, 1997).

One possible interpretation of the observed complementarity between FDI and both exports and imports is that FDI enhances the commercial presence of source country firms in the host country. The transfer of source country technology, the presence of source country nationals in the host country, the participation of host country nationals in training courses etc. in the source country, all serve to foster close commercial links that may affect trade in both directions.

If the main effect of FDI on trade is indeed through enhanced commercial presence, the fear found frequently in Western Europe of jobs being exported to Central and Eastern Europe through FDI is misplaced. It is by no means clear whether, in the absence of horizontal FDI from a particular source country, the host country would import the good in question from the source country. It may well import from another source, or the good might be produced by host country firms that might be domestically or foreign-owned.

V. Domino FDI?

Does economic integration between two countries or regions affect the amount of FDI being invested in third countries? The experiences of Spain and Portugal, upon joining the EU, and Mexico, following the decision to negotiate the NAFTA, suggest that joining a regional economic integration scheme can provide an impetus to inward FDI. This raises the question of whether these increases in incoming FDI affected the flows of direct investment going to other potential host countries

Table III. Regression results for exports with FDI residual, major OECD countries, mid-1990s

Investing country	Log of GNP	Log of population	Log of distance	Economic freedom index	FDI residual	FDI residual* CEE1st	FDI residual* CEE2nd	FDI residual* CIS	Adj. R^2	S.E.	Number of obs.
Austria	0.71***	0.00	−0.77***	−0.53**	0.11*	0.49**	0.01	0.30	0.86	0.54	42
Finland	0.38***	0.19	−0.85***	−1.14***	0.13**	−0.19		−0.52**	0.82	0.49	35
France	0.60***	0.13	−0.64***	−0.56**	0.11	−0.39	−0.03	0.36*	0.83	0.59	50
Germany	0.60***	0.11	−0.63***	−0.55***	0.09	0.10	−0.12	0.00	0.90	0.40	48
Netherlands	0.62***	0.01	−0.71***	−0.59***	0.12	0.12	0.44		0.90	0.47	42
Norway	0.87***	−0.10	−1.07***	−0.70*	0.35***	0.47		0.53	0.87	0.67	34
Switzerland	0.51**	0.25	−0.57***	−1.18**	−0.02	0.97		0.09	0.68	0.86	40
UK	0.64***	0.04	−0.41***	−0.93***	0.32***	0.05	0.21	−0.15	0.87	0.52	47
US	0.37**	0.44**	−0.98***	−1.33***	0.42***	0.42	0.00	−0.12	0.69	0.75	48
Japan	0.48***	0.46***	−1.08***	−1.82***	0.40***	0.06	0.88**	0.32	0.92	0.50	40
South Korea	0.24	0.44**	−0.91***	−0.98**	0.41***	−0.98*		−0.26	0.82	0.59	31

Table IV. Regression results for imports with FDI residual , major OECD countries, mid-1990s

Investing country	Log of GNP	Log of population	Log of distance	Economic freedom index	FDI residual	FDI residual* CEE1st	FDI residual* CEE2nd	FDI residual* CIS	Adj. R^2	S.E.	Number of obs.
Austria	0.72***	0.16	−0.85***	−0.86**	0.07	0.39	−0.01	−0.47	0.82	0.67	42
Finland	0.65***	0.00	−0.88***	−0.99***	0.15**	−0.10		−0.84***	0.84	0.57	35
France	0.72***	0.10	−0.68***	−0.45	0.04	−0.33	−0.14	0.34	0.80	0.70	50
Germany	0.58***	0.14	−0.74***	−0.77***	0.10	0.19	−0.09	0.46	0.87	0.50	48
Netherlands	0.66***	0.08	−0.44***	−0.78***	0.17	−0.25	0.13		0.81	0.61	42
Norway	0.87***	−0.14	−0.94***	−0.63*	0.19**	0.33		−1.51*	0.89	0.55	34
Switzerland	0.56**	0.41	−1.05***	−1.90***	−0.07	2.16		−0.11	0.80	0.94	40
UK	0.66***	0.14	−0.42***	−1.09***	0.27***	−0.21	0.01	−0.36	0.86	0.57	47
US	0.46**	0.46**	−0.96***	−1.28***	0.37**	0.49	0.33	−0.10	0.64	0.90	48
Japan	0.57**	0.38	−0.84*	−1.46**	0.43***	−0.01	0.26	−6.82	0.69	1.00	40
South Korea	0.54**	0.29	−0.49	−1.08	0.14	−1.43*		0.68	0.71	0.85	31

that did not offer the advantage of belonging to the regional integration scheme concerned. Baldwin et al. (1995) suggest that the creation of the Single Market in the EU 'probably led to investment diversion in the economies of the European Free Trade Association (EFTA) and investment creation in the EU economies', the latter being particularly prevalent in Spain and Portugal. This may, in turn, have encouraged these countries to seek access to the Single Market via the European Economic Area, and subsequently to request membership of the EU itself.

The question of whether discriminatory liberalisation between two countries affects investment in other countries suggests a possible parallel with the impact of regional integration on trade between partners and non-partners. Here, customs union theory has a long history and is relatively well developed. Free trade agreements are the archetypal example of the theory of second best, whereby the removal of one economic distortion (trade restrictions against future partners) in the presence of other distortions (trade restrictions against other countries) may actually reduce economic welfare. The standard Vinerian approach to such regional trade agreements identifies the welfare-enhancing increase in trade between the partners to the trade agreement (trade creation) against which must be considered trade diversion, the potential decline in trade with non-members (if they are more efficient producers), which is detrimental to welfare. More recently, this body of theory has been extended to allow for imperfect competition and the presence of scale economies. One key result is that regional integration can lead to agglomeration whereby economic activity becomes increasingly concentrated in countries or areas which contain, or are close to, the main pockets of demand.

The analysis of the effects of economic integration on FDI flows is much less developed. It is clear, however, that simple analogies with the literature on trade and, in particular, the terminology of creation and diversion, are not possible.[7] Most of the available reasoning concentrates upon the effects of trade liberalisation within regional agreements upon FDI flows. The crucial issue is whether trade and FDI are substitutes, as standard trade theory and much of the literature on FDI would suggest, or whether they are complements, which our analysis above would support. Under the former, the removal of trade barriers will entail that partners markets will be increasingly served by exports rather than by overseas production. Hence trade integration will dampen FDI flows. If trade and FDI are complementary then trade liberalisation will stimulate FDI flows.

However, the issue is further complicated if the regional integration involves investment liberalisation as well as trade liberalisation, as is clearly the case in the transition of the CEECs to market economies and their integration into the EU. Markusen (1997) has shown in a simple model with just two countries, that the two forms of liberalisation may have different effects on important variables, such as output and relative wages, and that both forms of liberalisation together may generate different impacts than when either is implemented alone.

The lack of clear theoretical prescriptions on the impact of economic integration on FDI flows requires that empirical analysis be used to identify the key mechanisms at work. Here we use the gravity model to look at the evolution over time of the bilateral distribution of the FDI flows of a particular investing country, rather than the stock of FDI as in the exercises above, and assess whether changes in FDI flows to regions which are economically integrating appear to be associated with changes in FDI flows to other regions. In particular, we look to see whether increasing EU integration in the late 1980s, adjustment to the Single Market and the accession of Portugal and Spain, had a negative impact upon FDI flows from EU countries going to the three European countries (EU3) which subsequently joined the EU in 1995, Austria, Finland and Sweden. We then try and assess whether the increased FDI flows from EU countries to the CEECs in the 1990s had any noticeable impact upon foreign investments by these countries in Portugal and Spain (EP).[8]

Our methodological approach is based upon that of Sapir (1997) who sought to identify whether a domino effect had characterised the impact of European integration upon bilateral trade flows. We use annual data on FDI outflows from France, Germany, Italy and the UK to a range of destination countries, both European and in the rest of the world. Initially, as in Sapir, we estimated a separate gravity equation for each investing country for each year and plotted the evolution of dummy variables for the EU3 and EP for 1982 to 1995 and for the CEECs from 1992 to 1995. However, many of the individual dummies were not well defined, reflecting in part the relatively small number of observations for each year and the variability in our FDI flow data. We then experimented by pooling the data over our sample period and including dummy variables for particular sub-periods: 1982 to 1986, 1987–1991, 1992–1995.

The model estimated is similar to that applied to the stock data except here we include a time trend (YEAR) to capture increases in FDI over time unrelated to income and population. The results, summarised in Table V, show that for all four source countries, GDP and distance are statistically significant, and, with the exception of the UK (a feature found before by Brenton (1996) and Brenton and Di Mauro (1998)), of the expected sign. Population has a negative impact upon the magnitude of FDI, but is only statistically significant for France and the UK. Adjacency also has a strong positive effect upon FDI flows. The fit of each of the equations is reasonably high, but in every case the standard error of the estimate is large. This suggests that some caution should be exercised with these results.

We now proceed to discuss the coefficients on the various dummy variables, the magnitude and significance of which are demonstrated in Figures 1 to 4. We include dummy variables for the EU10 (EU members prior to the Iberian enlargement), the EU3 (Austria, Finland and Sweden), EP (Spain and Portugal), the CEEC3 (the more advanced countries in central and eastern Europe – Czech Republic, Hungary and Poland), and the CEEC2 (those less advanced in the process of transition – Bulgaria and Romania), for each of three sub-periods, 1982 to 1986, 1987 to 1991 (the period after the announcement of the plan to create the Single Market and after the accession of Spain and Portugal), and 1992 to 1995 (the period covering the integration of the CEECs into the world market). The height of the bar in each

Table V. Gravity equation on FDI flows with country dummies

db 1982–1995	**France**		**Germany**		**Italy***		**UK**	
	Coefficient	*t Statistics*	*Coefficient*	*t Statistics*	*Coefficient*	*t Statistics*	*Coefficient*	*t Statistics*
R^2	0.6015		0.5457		0.4698		0.3316	
Standard error	1.4761		1.4757		1.7038		1.9982	
N. observations	403		514		304		454	
Intercept	−232.3743	*−4.6976*	−159.0660	*−3.9541*	14.9804	*0.2061*	−16.5497	*−0.2690*
LGDP	0.9708	*11.0749*	0.7253	*12.3489*	0.9183	*7.6823*	0.9803	*9.2344*
LPOP	−0.2969	*−3.7825*	−0.0873	*−1.4843*	−0.1697	*−1.3851*	−0.4014	*−4.0274*
LDIST	−0.4498	*−3.9484*	−0.4394	*−4.8660*	−0.7694	*−4.7514*	0.5542	*3.6793*
ADJ	0.5792	*2.1361*	0.5684	*2.4178*	0.2589	*0.6045*	2.1806	*3.5827*
YEAR	0.1151	*4.6112*	0.0795	*3.9291*	−0.0085	*−0.2345*	0.0027	*0.0871*
EU10P1	−0.4179	*−1.2245*	0.1432	*0.4417*	0.6110	*1.2722*	0.5044	*0.9752*
EU10P2	0.8761	*2.6220*	0.8665	*2.8175*	0.5437	*1.3282*	1.8143	*3.6419*
EU10P3	0.1834	*0.4850*	0.7164	*2.1115*	0.9677	*2.2340*	2.1613	*4.2146*
EU3P1	−2.2513	*−5.0885*	−0.8602	*−1.9275*			−1.1919	*−1.9183*
EU3P2	−1.3662	*−3.1576*	−0.0014	*−0.0032*	0.1032	*0.0925*	−1.2950	*−2.1322*
EU3P3	−1.0484	*−2.0097*	−0.0727	*−0.1548*	−1.7053	*−2.9115*	0.9777	*1.4465*
EPP1	0.4372	*0.9494*	0.8997	*1.7864*	0.1863	*0.2821*	1.8318	*2.5676*
EPP2	1.5823	*3.1138*	1.4767	*2.9969*	0.7871	*1.2995*	2.7054	*3.8829*
EPP3	−0.2068	*−0.3613*	1.2041	*2.1819*	2.1056	*3.2648*	0.6915	*0.9223*
CEEC3	0.8249	*1.5887*	3.0991	*5.6352*	1.2509	*2.1056*	1.1920	*1.7218*
CEEC2	−1.1429	*−1.8173*	0.1391	*0.2245*	−0.7091	*−1.0062*	0.2958	*0.3646*

* For Italy the EU3P2 dummy stands for 1990 only; no data were available prior to that year.

Notes

Destination countries include:

- All OECD countries – Bulgaria, Romania, Slovenia, Slovakia.
- Argentina, Brazil, Chile.
- China, Hong Kong, India, Indonesia, Korea, Malaysia, Philippines, Singapore, Thailand.

The country coverage is different for each source country, which explains differences in the sample size.
Dummy variables
Each dummy is followed by P1, P2 or P3, which stands for:

- period 1: from 1982 to 1986;
- period 2: from 1987 to 1991;
- period 3: from 1992 to 1995;
- EU10: Belgium–Luxembourg, Denmark, France, Germany, Greece, Ireland, Italy, Netherlands, UK;
- EP: Portugal and Spain;
- EU3: Austria, Finland and Sweden.
- CEEC3: Czech Rep., Hungary and Poland (only from 1992 to 1995);
- CEEC2: Bulgaria and Romania (only from 1992 to 1995).

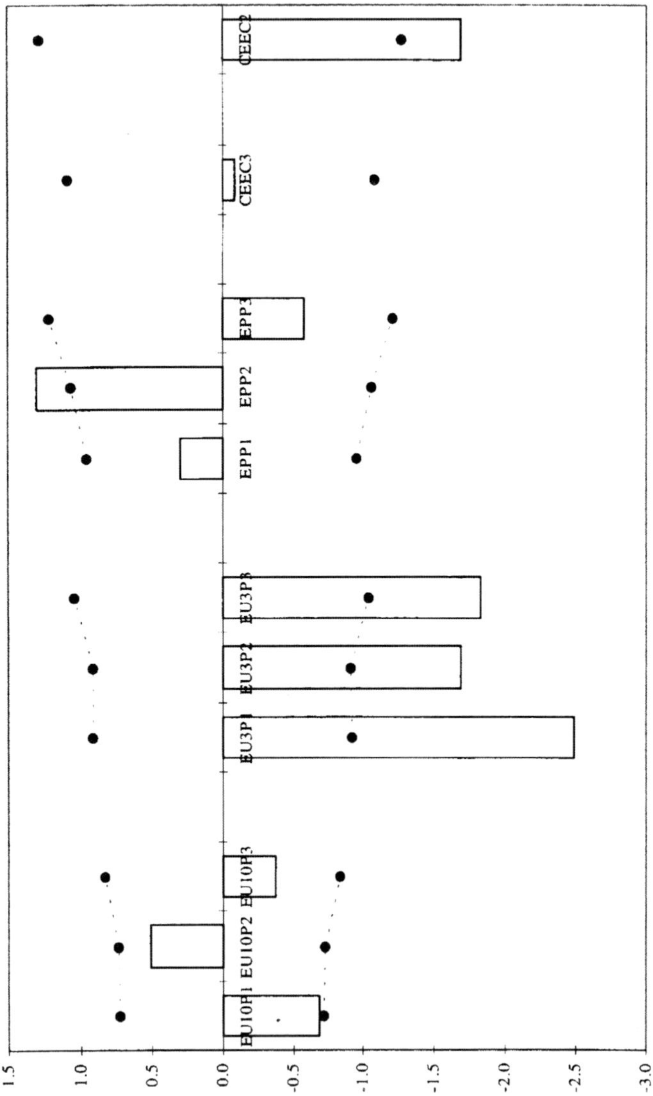

Figure 1. France – Evolution of the dummy variables in the 3 periods considered by group of partners.

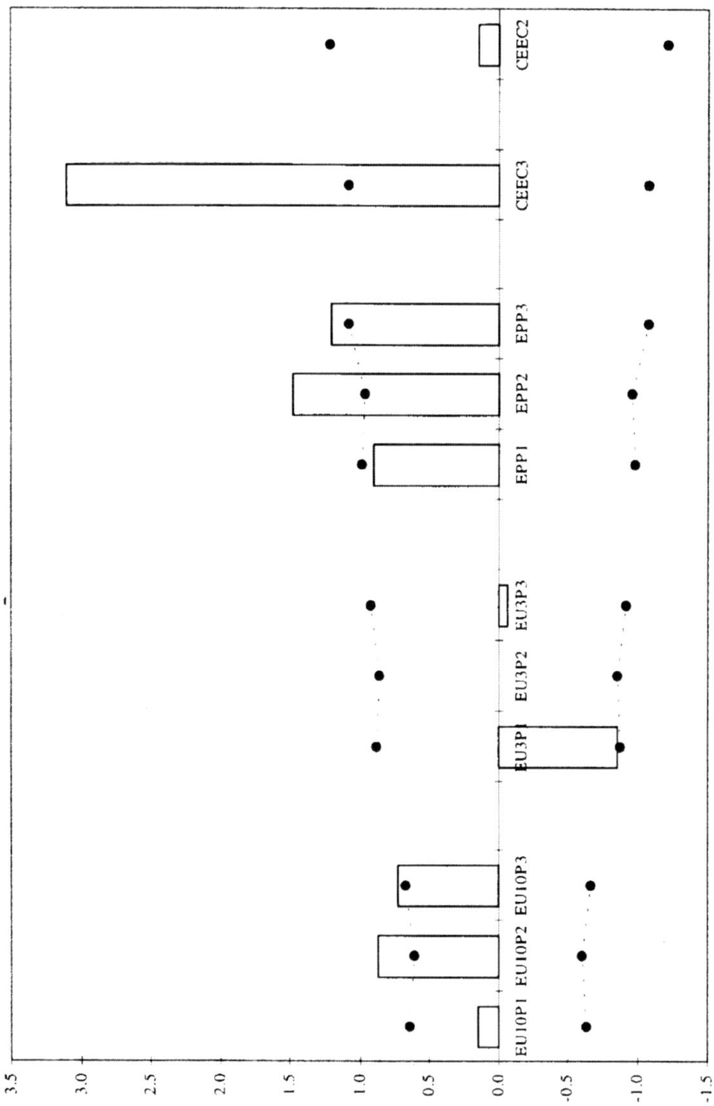

Figure 2. Germany – Evolution of the dummy variables in the 3 periods considered by group of partners.

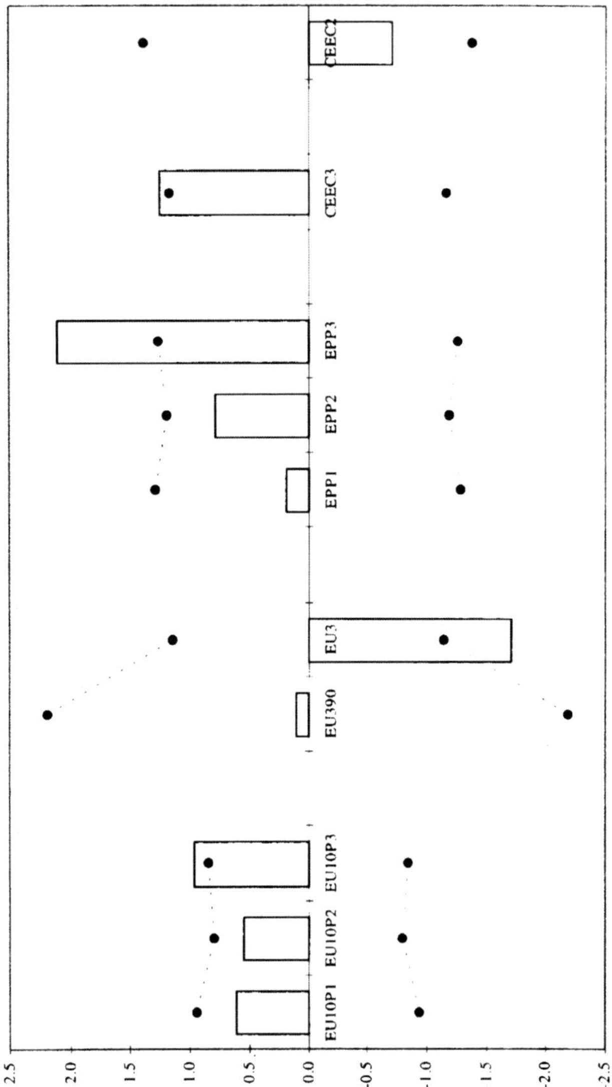

Figure 3. Italy – Evolution of the dummy variables in the 3 periods considered by group of partners.

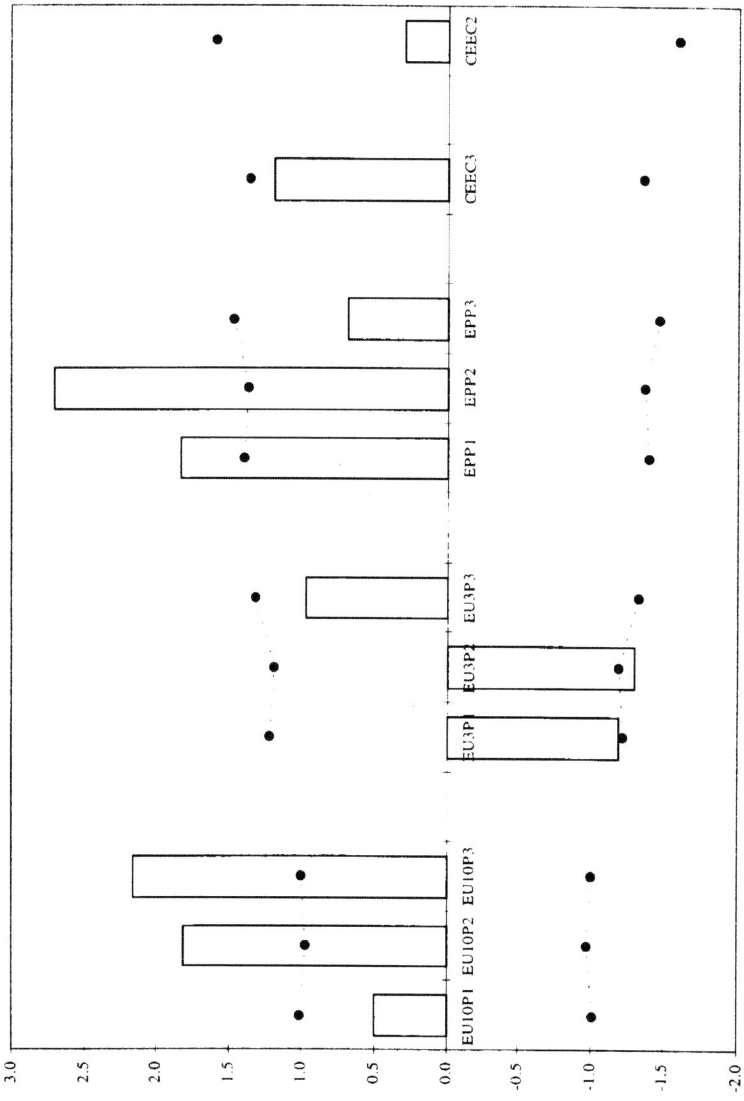

Figure 4. UK – Evolution of the dummy variables in the 3 periods considered by group of partners.

case shows the magnitude of the coefficient on the dummy whilst the small circles show the relevant (5 per cent) interval of significance. Thus, if the bar lies outside of the relevant circle then the estimated coefficient is statistically significant.

The results suggest that there has been an intensification of FDI in the EU10 countries since the introduction of the Single European Act. For France, Germany and the UK the EU10 dummy became significantly positive for the period 1987 to 1991, for the previous sub-period the intra-EU effect was small and statistically insignificant. In the subsequent period, 1992 to 1995, the strength of this effect has waned slightly in Germany, although it remains statistically significant, has become insignificant for France, but has intensified for the UK. In the case of Italy, the intra-EU effect became significant only for the last sub-period.

For Austria and the two Scandinavian countries we find no strong evidence that the two key developments in the latter half of the 1980s, the announcement of the Single Market and the Iberian enlargement, adversely affected the magnitude of inward FDI from EU countries. We do find that in the early 1980s these countries were receiving substantially less FDI than could be expected on the basis of their incomes and proximity to the EU. However, the magnitude of this 'under-potential' weakened in the late 1980s and in the first half of the 1990s. There is now no significant difference between the actual and potential flows of FDI into these countries from Germany and the UK. For France, the effect is still significantly negative but the magnitude is much smaller than in the early 1980s.

Next we look at the magnitude of FDI in Portugal and Spain, where the ratio of actual to potential FDI increased considerably in the period immediately after accession, whilst this effect has declined since 1991, with the exception of investment from Italy. We note that for Germany, where investment in the CEEC3 in the latest sub-period has been particularly strong, the strong positive and significant dummy for Portugal and Spain has remained. Similarly, for Italy, the presence of a positive and significant effect for investment in the CEEC3 is associated with an intensification of investment in Portugal and Spain. For the UK and France the CEEC3 dummy is not statistically significant, whilst for all four source countries actual investment in the CEEC2 does not differ significantly from its 'normal' level, in contrast to previous findings (Brenton and Di Mauro, 1998). Hence, our, albeit limited, analysis finds no evidence to suggest that the intensification of FDI in particular countries or regions, following integration with the EU, has had a discernible dampening effect on FDI flows going to other countries in Europe.

VI. Conclusions

In this paper we have utilised a very simple model of the bilateral distribution of a country's FDI to investigate issues regarding the economic integration of the CEECs with EU countries. We find that the stock of FDI in CEEC countries diverges little from the normal pattern we would expect after controlling for the main determinants of FDI stocks throughout the world. This, together with earlier research which suggested a similar conclusion for current flows of FDI to the CEECs, contradicts those who have argued that current FDI in the CEECs is very small compared to overseas investment in countries of similar income in different parts of the world. Thus, unlike these authors we do not expect a surge in FDI to the CEECs in future years. The key determinants of the growth of FDI to the region will be the pace of income growth and the success with which CEEC governments orient their policies to be conducive to business. We also find no empirical evidence to suggest that FDI has a direct impact upon the economy of the source country in terms of being a substitute for trade. This study reinforces previous empirical analysis which suggests a complementary relationship between FDI and trade. This is an issue which theoretical analysis of FDI can no longer ignore.

Finally, we investigated whether changes in FDI flows to particular countries or regions, in response to an increase in economic integration, had a noticeable impact upon the flows of FDI going to other, excluded, regions. Again, using the gravity model to explain the bilateral distribution of FDI flows over time, we found no evidence that increased investment in Spain and Portugal in the late 1980s significantly reduced investment flows to other European countries. Further, the flows of FDI going to the CEECs in the 1990s did not have a clear negative impact upon the amounts of overseas investment in Spain and Portugal. Additional integration between the EU and the CEECs, in the form of the accession of the latter, is therefore unlikely to substantially dampen the flows of overseas investment going to other European countries.

Notes

*. This research was undertaken with support from the European Union's Phare ACE Programme 1996, within a project on '*The Determinants of Financial Flows in the EU and the Associated States of Central and Eastern Europe and the Implications for Enlargement*'. Helpful comments by Daniel Piazolo and several participants at a workshop at CEPS in April 1998 are gratefully acknowledged. Data on distance between countries were kindly provided by Dieter Schumacher.

1. We do not consider here the potential flows of outward FDI from the transition countries. This is an interesting issue for the future and one which will become more relevant as incomes grow in the east.
2. Apart from FDI, there exist many other types of links between firms ('buyer-seller relationships') where such knowledge transfer takes place. FDI is prominent among these, first, because it is easier to measure. Second, to build up a close buyer-seller relationship requires substantial intangible investment from the partners. It is likely, therefore, that an environment conducive to FDI will also be conducive to other buyer-seller relationships, and that the evolution of FDI is a good indicator of knowledge transfer through inter-firm links more generally (Szalavetz and Lücke, 1996).
3. Where relevant we also found it necessary to include a dummy variable for the CIS countries – notably Russia and Ukraine.
4. As an alternative to the EU(15) dummy, separate dummies were also introduced for the 'core' EU of ten countries (EU10), the Iberian countries (Portugal and Spain; EU2), and the 'North European' recent entrants (Finland, Sweden, Austria; EU3). The point estimates for EU3 were

significant and negative for Korea and Japan. However, Wald tests did not reject the null hypothesis that the coefficients for the three separate EU dummies were equal.

5. This confirms the results of other studies, such as Brenton and Gros (1997). For a more detailed discussion see Piazolo (1997).
6. Space constraints prevent presentation of the results here, but they are available upon request.
7. Trade creation and trade diversion have a clear welfare interpretation. This is not the case if these terms are applied to FDI flows. Winters (1997) accordingly advises that the terms investment diversion and creation are dangerous and should be dropped from our vocabulary.
8. Greece is not separately identified since it has never been an important recipient of FDI from EU countries.

References

Baldwin, R.E., Forslid, R. and Haaland, J. (1995) 'Investment Creation and Investment Diversion: Simulation Analysis of the Single Market Programme', Discussion Paper 1308, CEPR, London.

Brainard, S.L. (1997) 'An Empirical Assessment of the Proximity-Concentration Trade-off Between Multinational Sales and Trade', *American Economic Review* **87**(4).

Brenton, P. and Di Mauro, F. (1998) 'The Potential Magnitude and Impact of FDI flows to CEECs', CEPS Working Document n. 116, February.

Brenton, P. and Gros, D. (1997) 'Trade Reorientation and Recovery in Transition Economies', *Oxford Review of Economic Policy* **13**(2), 65–76.

Brenton, P. (1996) 'The Impact of the Single Market on Foreign Direct Investment in the EU', Report for DGII, European Commission.

Eaton, J. and Tamura, A. (1996) 'Japanese and US Exports and Investment as Conduits of Growth', NBER Working Paper 5457.

Graham, E.M. (1996) 'On the Relationship Among Foreign Direct Investment and International Trade in the Manufacturing Sector: Empirical results for the United States and Japan', WTO Staff Working Paper RD-96-008.

Johnson, B.T., Holmes, K.R. and Kirkpatrick, M. (1998) '1998 Index of Economic Freedom', The Heritage Foundation, The Wall Street Journal.

Linnemann, H. (1966) 'An Econometric Study of International Trade Flows', Amsterdam: North-Holland.

Lankes, H.-P. and Venables, A.J. (1996) 'Foreign Direct Investment in Economic Transition: The Changing Pattern of Investments', *Economics of Transition*, **4**(2), 331–347.

Markusen, J.R. (1997) 'Trade Versus Investment Liberalisation', *Nota di Lavoro* 75.97, FEEM, September.

Markusen, J.R. and Venables, A.J. (1996) 'The Theory of Endowment, Intra-Industry and Multinational Trade', CEPR Discussion Paper N. 1341, February.

Markusen, J.R. and Venables, A.J. (1995) 'Multinational Firms and the New Trade Theory', NBER Working Paper 5036.

Markusen, J.R., Venables, A.J., Konan, D.E. and Zhang, K.H. (1996) 'A Unified Treatment of Horizontal Direct Investment, Vertical Direct Investment, and the Pattern of Trade in Goods and Services', NBER Working Paper 5696, Cambridge MA, August.

Mátyás L. (1997) 'Proper Econometric Specification of the Gravity Model', *The World Economy*, **20**, 363–368.

Polak, J.J. (1996) 'Is APEC a Natural Regional Trading Bloc? A Critique of the 'Gravity Model of International Trade'', *The World Economy* **19**(5), 533–43.

Piazolo, D. (1997) 'Trade Integration between Eastern and Western Europe: Policies Follow the Market', *Journal of Economic Integration* **12**(3), September, 259–297.

Sapir, A. (1997) 'Domino Effects in Western European Trade, 1960–92', CEPR Discussion Papers N. 1576, February.

Sinn, H.W. and Weichenrieder, A.J. (1997) 'Foreign Direct Investment, Political Resentment and the Privatization Process in Eastern Europe', *Economic Policy* **24**, 179–210.

Szalavetz, A. and Lücke, M. (1997) 'Export Reorientation and Transfer of Know-how and Technology – The case of Hungarian Manufactured Exports', Kiel Working Papers, No. 801, Kiel Institute of World Economics, March. Forthcoming in Conference Volume.

Winters, L.A. (1997) 'Assessing Regional Integration Arrangements', *mimeo*, World Bank, Washington D.C.

World Trade Review (2011), 10: 2, 249–276
 doi:10.1017/S1474745610000509

Chapter 8

Assessing the adjustment implications of trade policy changes using the Tariff Reform Impact Simulation Tool (TRIST)

PAUL BRENTON*
Lead Economist, World Bank
CHRISTIAN SABOROWSKI
Consultant, World Bank
CORNELIA STARITZ
Junior Professional Officer, World Bank
ERIK VON UEXKULL
Economic Officer, International Labour Organization

Abstract: TRIST is a simple, easy to use, country focused tool to assess the short-term adjustment implications of trade reform. It has been developed to improve the information available to policy makers in developing countries. It has the following key features: projections are based on revenues actually collected at the tariff line level rather than simply applying statutory rates, as in currently available tools; it is transparent, runs in Excel, with formulas and calculation steps visible to the user, and is open-source with users free to change, extend, or improve according to their needs; it has high policy relevance because it projects the impact of tariff reform on total fiscal revenue from imports (including VAT and excise taxes) and results are available at the product level so that sensitive products or sectors can be identified; the tool is flexible and can incorporate tariff liberalization scenarios involving any group of trading partners and any schedule of products. This paper describes the TRIST tool and provides a range of examples that demonstrate the insights that the tool can provide to policy makers on the short-term adjustment impacts of reducing tariffs.

1. Introduction

Careful analysis of the adjustment impacts of trade reform is essential to policy makers in developing countries as they seek to improve the structure of incentives

* Correspondence to Paul Brenton, email: pbrenton@worldbank.org
We would like to thank Ian Gillson, Anneke Hamilton, Bernard Hoekman, Jamus Jerome Lim, Themba Munalula, Juan Sebastian Saez, Philip Schuler, David Tarr and Peter Walkenhorst for valuable comments. Financial support for TRIST has been provided by the governments of Finland, Norway, Sweden and the United Kingdom through the Multi-donor Trust Fund for Trade and Development. The views expressed here are those of the authors and should not be attributed to the World Bank.

within an outward looking trade and competitiveness strategy. An immediate concern, especially in low-income countries, is the impact of tariff liberalization on tax revenues. Tariffs are typically an important source of tax revenues in low-income countries, often reflecting the weakness of the domestic tax base and of other tax instruments. In addition, changes in output in different sectors and associated impacts on employment are likely to be an important aspect of the political economy driving support and opposition to trade reform. Further, trade reform entails changes in prices and an important consideration is how these will affect households, especially the poorest. A good understanding of the potential adjustment implications of trade reform can contribute to the design of better trade reform strategies and to the discussion and implementation of policies that can reduce the impact of adjustment, especially when the costs are concentrated upon particular groups in society. The latter is of particular importance in countries that lack social safety nets with broad coverage.

In response, the World Bank has developed a simple spreadsheet tool called TRIST (Tariff Reform Impact Simulation Tool) that can be used in client countries to analyze the short-term adjustment implications of tariff reform.[1] The tool was developed to provide better estimates to policy makers and trade negotiators in developing countries of the impact of changes in tariffs on government revenues, imports, protection, and prices in the short run, taking advantage of the more detailed information on imports that is increasingly available at the country level from computerized customs systems. TRIST does not require any proprietary software, programming skills or internet access. It is free and easy to use, transparent, with a simple underlying trade model, and flexible in that it can quickly address different trade policy scenarios. It uses detailed data on actual revenues collected on imports, whereas other tools use hypothetical revenues from applying duty rates on paper. It can take into account all official taxes levied on imports at the border, not just tariffs, and show the change in trade tax revenues, which is more relevant than the change in tariff revenues alone. When suitable data are available, it can provide information on the short-term relative vulnerability of different sectors in the domestic economy in terms of output and employment. It can also be linked to household budget data to trace the influence of changes in prices following trade reform to household expenditures and the costs of attaining a given consumption bundle.

TRIST is a partial equilibrium model and there are naturally issues that the model is not well suited to answer. It cannot be used to project the aggregate impact of tariff reform. Thus, it cannot provide an assessment of whether a particular policy change is beneficial or not. This would require a more sophisticated economy-wide model.

This paper provides a description of the TRIST tool and gives examples of its use. Section 2 discusses the objective behind the development of TRIST and

1 Brenton *et al.* (2007) describes the initial motivation, development, and application of the model.

outlines crucial advantages compared to existing tools. Section 3 presents the trade model underlying the tool and discusses the intuition behind the calculation steps. In Section 4, some examples of the analysis of short-term adjustment costs using TRIST are presented. Section 5 concludes.

2. The purpose of TRIST

The TRIST software is open-source and free of charge. The tool is Excel based and does not require any additional proprietary software, hardware (other than minimal disk space), or programming expertise. The origin of TRIST lies in the limitations of existing tools in providing support to policy makers in developing countries in assessing the implications of tariff reforms and the opportunities created by the increasing use of computerized customs systems to deliver data that are more relevant for detailed analysis of revenue impacts. There are three main features of TRIST:

1. Most tools for trade policy analysis use statutory tariff rates (those on paper) and recorded trade flows. This can lead to a lack of precision in predicted impacts since a common feature of import regimes of developing countries is the widespread use of tariff exemptions. For example, a range of institutions including the government, international agencies, embassies, and NGOs (non-governmental organizations) usually do not pay duties on products imported for official purposes. It is important that these imports are excluded since they do not generate revenue for the government, do not enter the domestic market in free circulation, and cannot be used for commercial purposes. Exemptions are also granted on imported intermediate products and capital goods to provide incentives for exports and for domestic and foreign investment. Hence, it is important to take these exemptions into account and assess their importance.[2] TRIST is designed to use both statutory and applied tariff data and is able to assess the impact of tariff exemptions. In this regard, for the low-income countries for which TRISTs have been developed, we find that exemptions can amount to 40–50 % of total revenue collected. These numbers illustrate that a better understanding of the magnitude and structure of tariff exemptions is crucial in determining the adjustment implications of tariff reform on fiscal revenues.

Using statutory rather than actually applied duties to investigate the impact of tariff liberalization scenarios will typically lead to a substantial overestimation of the impact of tariff liberalization on trade flows and revenues. Table 1 shows how

2 The use of collected rather than statutory revenue also identifies when imports that are eligible for duty-free (or reduced duty) access are actually subject to full duties. This will probably occur when there is lack of awareness of the duty-free scheme and preferences are not requested, or due to rules of origin. Different scenarios regarding these revenues can be explored in TRIST. The scenarios presented in this paper typically adopt the assumption that the proportion of imports of a particular product from a country eligible for preferential access that actually pay duties is maintained.

Table 1. Highlighting the features of TRIST[1]

A: Change in tariff revenue for an EPA (elimination of all tariffs on imports from the EU)[2]

	Based on applied tariffs		Based on statutory tariffs		Based on applied tariffs and removal of all exemptions	
	Local currency mln.	%	Local currency mln.	%	Local currency mln.	%
Ethiopia	−461	−17.2	−873	−32.6	−123	−4.6
Madagascar	−21	−28.5	−31	−41.8	−9	−11.5
Malawi	−560	−6.5	−732	−8.5	2,255	26.2
Zambia	−99,135	−17.7	−129,940	−23.2	137,781	24.6

B: Change in total trade tax revenue for an EPA (elimination of all tariffs on imports from the EU)[2]

	Based on applied tariffs		Based on statutory tariffs		Based on applied tariffs and removal of all exemptions	
	Local currency mln.	%	Local currency mln.	%	Local currency mln.	%
Ethiopia	−506	−3.4	−953	−6.4	−119	−0.8
Madagascar	−23	−3.9	−32	−5.3	−10	−1.6
Malawi	−613	−0.8	−842	−1.1	2,527	3.3
Zambia	−107,589	−1.7	−145,562	−2.3	145,573	2.3

Notes: 1 The demand elasticity is set to 0.5, the exporter substitution elasticity is set to 1.5.
2 EPA scenario: zero tariffs with EU. For all other trading partners, tariffs are unchanged.

tariff and total trade tax revenue in selected Common Market for Eastern and Southern Africa (COMESA) countries would be affected by the removal of tariffs on imports from the EU under an economic partnership agreement (EPA). We assume here that the EPA entails reducing all tariffs on products imported from the EU to zero. In practice, there are likely to be a range of products that are excluded that will reduce the revenue effect, so that the estimates here will provide an upper bound on actual impacts.[3] Column one in part A of the table shows that the predicted changes in tariff revenues when using applied tariff rates amount to around 17%–18% for Ethiopia and Zambia, 30% for Madagascar, and 6% for Malawi. The next column in part A presents the tariff revenue loss predicted when statutory tariff rates are used as in previous studies. It is clear that the predicted losses are now substantially higher. The final column in part A of Table 1 examines

3 Because of data limitations for the countries under review, we assume the absence of a domestic substitution effect between imports and domestic production (see below for a detailed discussion).

a scenario in which the respective countries attempt to recover the revenue loss they incur due to the EPA by abolishing all tariff exemptions on products that enter the domestic market. The numbers show that the resulting tariff revenue loss is much lower and there is even a gain in revenues in Zambia and Malawi.

2. A second major challenge in investigating the impact of trade policy reform is to account not only for statutory and applied tariff rates, but also for the interplay between tariffs and other forms of taxes levied on imports. Whilst customs duties are a key source of revenue in developing countries, they represent just one of potentially many taxes and charges levied on imports. Most countries also apply excise taxes as well as a VAT or sales tax.[4] Often these will generate significantly more revenue than customs duties. In fact, our estimates show that in most countries tariff revenue constitutes substantially less than 50 % of overall revenue collected at the border, for example Bolivia (20 %), Kenya (25 %), Mozambique (32 %), and Burundi (39 %). In practice, the domestic tax base – for VAT in particular – tends to be very small in developing countries. Thus, it is very important to take into account changes in VAT and excise receipts that follow the reform of customs duties, since it is total revenues from trade that are of interest to policy makers.

Part B of Table 1 presents the impact of the EPA policy scenario on overall import tax revenues. The predicted percentage change in overall tax revenues at the border is substantially less than the percentage change in tariff revenues that is typically presented in studies of the revenue impact of trade reform. The total revenue losses increase slightly in the case of all four countries considered in Table 1. However, it is not clear *ex-ante* whether the effect of trade liberalization on VAT and excise revenue will be positive, due to increased imports, or negative, due to a reduction of the tax base, since VAT is usually levied on the tariff inclusive value of imports. Changes can also result from trade diversion if the collection rate for these taxes varies significantly between imports from different trading partners. Either way, studies that focus solely on changes in customs duties will provide only a partial and potentially misleading picture.

3. A third major motivation for the development of TRIST is the limitations that arise from using aggregated and unwieldy models in a dynamic policy environment. New options and proposals for trade policy emerge frequently and require adjustments to the scenarios used for projections. Further, trade policy discussions typically concern detailed products, such as identifying lists of sensitive products that are excluded from liberalization scenarios. Thus, disaggregated results that break down the revenue impact by detailed product and trading partner are a crucial input to trade policy formulation. An important aim of TRIST is to provide a simple and flexible tool that can be easily and quickly used and adapted to reflect

4 TRIST can also accommodate import surcharges and other taxes on imports as well. For example, a number of countries in the Caribbean impose environmental taxes on imported goods.

specific country circumstances as well as to allow the user to define relevant reform scenarios, exclusion lists, etc. Of course, such a tool has its limitations. Using a simple partial equilibrium model like TRIST involves trade-offs compared to using more aggregated less flexible economy-wide general equilibrium (GE) models. TRIST addresses questions related to detailed trade policy changes, but it does not capture inter-sectoral effects or long-term aggregate impacts.

One example of the need for such flexibility is the definition of sensitive product lists for EPAs. The EC Commission interpreted the GATT requirement that preferential trade agreements, such as EPAs, lead to the gradual removal of tariffs and non-tariff barriers on 'substantially all trade' as allowing ACP countries (African, Caribbean and Pacific Group of States) to exempt up to 20 % of their imports from tariff reductions.[5] The detailed tariff line level data available in TRIST allow policy makers to thoroughly analyze the implications of choosing different lists of exempted products. In particular, countries may want to exclude products from liberalization for which the policy reform will generate the largest reduction in revenue or protection. To give a few examples, the projected tariff revenue loss from an EPA with the EU falls from 14.4 % to 2.1 % in Tanzania, from 19.4 % to 5.1 % in Kenya, and from 17.1 % to 5.4 % in Ethiopia when the sensitive product list is chosen according to the revenue sensitivity of the products imported from the EU (see Table 3 below, accompanied by a fuller discussion). At the other extreme, it is interesting to analyze the revenue impact of the reduction of very high tariffs only, since reducing such tariff peaks will remove an important distortion in the importing regime of the economy. As an example, capping all tariffs at a maximum rate of 25 % is projected to result in moderate tariff (overall import tax) revenue losses of 0.5 % (0.1 %), 3.8 % (1.1 %), and 10.1 % (4.6 %), in Zambia, Tanzania, and Ethiopia respectively.[6]

TRIST is developed on a country-by-country basis using detailed data typically obtained in a collaborative approach with officials from the statistical departments of national Customs authorities and Ministries of Trade.[7] Most other available tools are cross-country models that access data from large international databases, such as TRAINS (Trade Analysis and Information System) (as is the case for the SMART model[8]), or global models that focus on particular sectors and cannot assess the whole of the tariff schedule (such as GSIM (Global Simulation Model)).

5 The EC Commission interprets substantially all trade as covering 90 % of mutual trade. Since the EU countries will liberalize 100 % of their imports from ACP countries under an EPA, the EC Commission has deemed that the ACP countries must liberalize at least 80 % of their imports from the EU.

6 For the simulations underlying the results presented in this paragraph, a demand elasticity of 0.5 and an exporter substitution elasticity of 1.5 were used.

7 TRIST is being used by the COMESA secretariat to estimate revenue losses emanating from trade reforms for which countries can subsequently be compensated. In Nigeria, an analysis of the revenue implications of an EPA with the EU (Andriamananjara *et al.*, 2009) has influenced the decision of whether to engage in negotiations on such an agreement. TRIST has also been used to provide similar information on tariff policy options in Côte d'Ivoire (Hoppe, 2010).

8 For a description of the SMART model, see Jammes and Ollareaga (2005).

TRIST is not designed for broad cross-country or global analysis. Updating TRAINS or developing global sectoral datasets to include applied duties and other tax levies on imports would be a major undertaking that has not yet commenced.[9]

3. The methodology used in TRIST

TRIST consists of two Excel files: the first is the *Data Aggregation Tool* which organizes and appropriately formats the data to be imported into the second, the *Simulation Tool*. The *Data Aggregation Tool* allows the user to create country and product groups that are relevant to the formulation of trade policy scenarios in the country-specific context. For example, the analysis of the revenue implications of joining a free trade agreement (FTA) requires defining the members of the FTA as a separate trading partner group. In the *Simulation Tool*, the user defines the tariff reform scenarios, can choose the parameters of the trade model underlying the calculations, and reviews the simulation results both at the aggregate, the sectoral, and at the tariff line levels.

In order to implement a TRIST for a given country, detailed and complete data on import transactions for the most recent year are required (data averaged across a number of years can also be used). For each import transaction, the data must identify the type of product (tariff line level, typically HS 8 digit), the country of origin of the trade flow, the customs procedure code (CPC) defining the customs regime under which the good enters the country,[10] the import value of the transaction, the statutory tariff, the tariff actually applied (to calculate tariff exemptions) as well as the value of VAT, excise, and other import taxes. These data are typically readily available from the customs authorities in countries that have implemented computerized customs systems, such as Asycuda and TradeNet. The cleaned and reorganized data can directly be imported into the *Data Aggregation Tool* via a drop-down menu that requires only a few mouse clicks from the user.

Figure 1 gives an overview of the structure of TRIST and how it works. First, the data from customs are organized within the *Data Aggregation Tool* and then uploaded into the *Simulation Tool*, within which the user defines the relevant tariff reform scenarios for each trading partner and parameterizes the elasticities of the trade model underlying TRIST, which we discuss below. A separate worksheet within the *Simulation Tool* presents the results of the chosen reform scenario. It illustrates the impact on tariff, excise, and VAT revenues as well as on prices at the sector level. When available, production data can be read directly into the

9 TRIST also has the advantage that it can be applied in countries that do not currently submit trade data to the UN statistical system, such as the DR Congo.

10 The CPC code allows government, transit, and temporary imports to be identified and excluded. These types of import transactions should be excluded from the analysis as they do not enter the domestic market and/or are not subject to import duties and other taxes applied at the border. Studies that simply use total imports inclusive of these official and temporary imports will underestimate the degree of protection in the economy and overstate the importance of exemptions.

Figure 1. How TRIST works

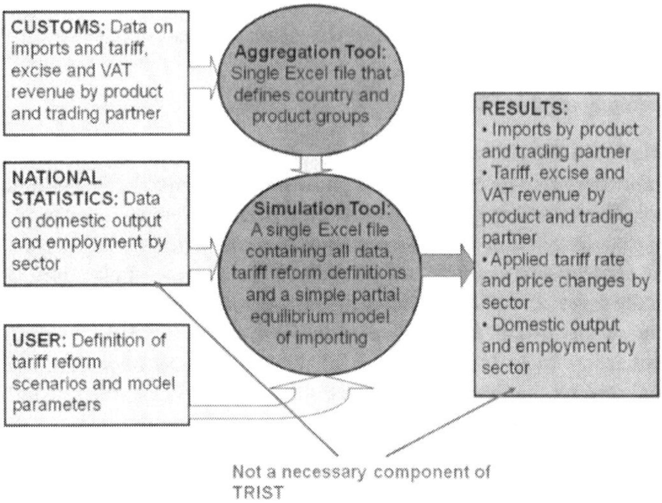

Simulation Tool. This additional information is however not required for TRIST to function.

An integral part of TRIST is the trade model that underlies the quantification of the effects of trade reform scenarios on imports, revenues, and production. The trade model in TRIST is based on four core assumptions: First, the model is derived from standard consumer demand theory and utilizes elasticities to determine the magnitude of the demand response to the price changes that result from a tariff reform.[11] Second, the calculations are based on the standard Armington (1969) assumption of imperfect substitution between imports from different trading partners since consumers distinguish products by the place of production. This intuitive assumption is standard in empirical international trade work and implies that a fall in the price of imports from country A relative to country B will only lead to a partial and not complete substitution of imports from country B with imports from country A.

Third, the model does not allow for direct substitution between different products. In other words, each product is modeled as a separate market and in isolation from other markets. This is perhaps the strongest assumption used in the model. However, a relaxation would not only complicate computations but would

11 Given that the elasticities determine percentage changes in imports, this implies that zero trade flows remain zero before and after any given reform and there is no market entry of new trading partners.

also generate a need for a range of additional ad-hoc assumptions regarding the precise design of the additional substitution effect and its parameterization. In the light of our goal to keep the model simple and transparent and to facilitate country ownership of the tool, we regard this simplifying assumption a sacrifice worth making.

Fourth, it is assumed that all changes in tariffs are fully passed on and that the world price for each product remains unchanged. That is to say that we assume an infinite supply elasticity of imports so that changes in demand in the importing country have no effect on the world price of the product; a realistic assumption for small low-income economies.

Let us now have a closer look at the three calculation steps (see Figure 2) determining the import response in our trade model.[12] In the first stage we model the allocation of given expenditure on imports of a product across different country suppliers and how this allocation changes when tariffs and duties are amended. The *exporter substitution effect* defines how imports from exporter A are substituted for imports from exporter B when the price of imports from exporter A relative to B declines, for example following a preferential trade reform that includes exporter A but not exporter B. The extent to which a given change in relative prices translates into a change in relative imports depends on a user-defined exporter substitution elasticity. In order to isolate the exporter substitution effect, total imports are held constant in this step.

In the second calculation step, total expenditure on a given product is allocated between domestic sources and imports. The *domestic substitution effect* allows for a demand shift between domestic production and imports when the relative price of imports changes.[13] The extent to which the share of imports in domestic consumption changes depends on a user-defined domestic substitution elasticity. The change in imports is then distributed across all importers according to their share of the import market. This calculation step can only be modeled if data on domestic production are available. If this is not the case, domestic substitution is not modeled and the domestic substitution elasticity becomes irrelevant.

The third and final calculation step allows for an overall *demand effect* in response to the change in the average price of domestic consumption of the good. The average price change is computed as an average of the price change in imports and the price change in domestic production, weighted by their relative shares in domestic consumption. A decrease/increase in the average price of the product leads to a percentage increase/decrease in overall consumption of the product, proportionately distributed between imports and domestic production. The extent

12 For detailed formal calculation steps, consult the Appendix.

13 When calculating the impact on employment it is also necessary to make an additional assumption that there are no second round effects, i.e. that the domestic output–employment ratio does not change in response to the trade policy change. In practice, over the medium to longer term, tariff reform leads changes in efficiency that will further influence the impact of employment.

Figure 2. The trade model in TRIST

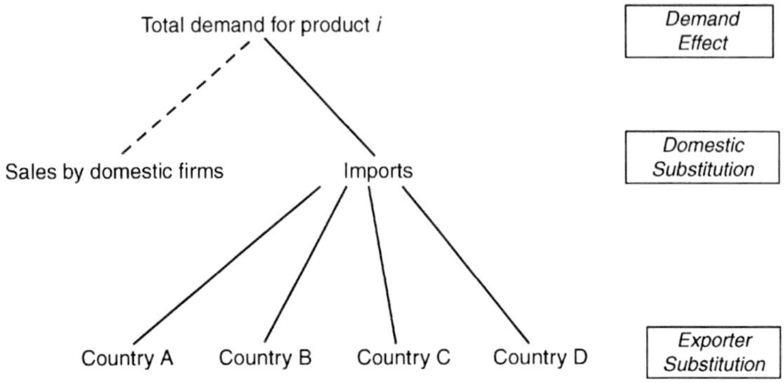

to which imports change for a given change in the overall price depends on a user-defined import demand elasticity.

This description of the three calculation steps has outlined the crucial role played by elasticities as the parameters of the model. Elasticities are notoriously difficult to estimate, and so detailed and robust estimates of the three elasticities (exporter substitution, domestic substitution, demand) are not readily available in the literature. TRIST includes default values for each of these three parameters that are common across products and import suppliers. The sensitivity of the results can be easily assessed by changing the values of the elasticities with the option to vary them both across products and suppliers.

When detailed local knowledge on these elasticities is available, TRIST allows users to define trading partner and product-specific elasticities. Furthermore, there is an option to include the most well-known estimates of elasticities in the literature. First, the user can choose to incorporate the import demand elasticities estimated in Kee *et al.* (2004). However, these elasticities are not available for all product groups (HS 6 digit). Second, the user can choose to use the product-specific import demand elasticities used in SMART.[14] For exporter substitution elasticities or domestic substitution elasticities, there are no estimates available at the level of product detail that TRIST uses.

14 It is good practice to experiment with different sets of elasticities as robustness checks. The default elasticities used in this paper are 1.5 (exporter substitution), 1 (domestic substitution), and 0.5 (demand). To illustrate how the projections change when Kee *et al.* (2004) or SMART elasticities are used, we consider the revenue impact of an EPA between Nigeria and the EU. A once and for all reduction in Nigerian tariffs on EU imports is projected to lead to a 16.8% reduction in overall Nigerian trade tax revenues according to our default elasticities, a 14.6% reduction when using the Kee *et al.* (2004) estimated demand elasticities, and a 14.3% reduction when using the SMART elasticities.

4. Examples of policy issues that can be addressed in TRIST

In this section, we will give some examples of how TRIST can be used to determine the magnitude of short-term adjustment costs to tariff reform. We begin by focusing on the revenue implications and then move on to show how TRIST can be used to provide insights into the potential short-term impact of tariff reforms on domestic production and employment. In the following, we go through some examples of unilateral, bilateral, and regional trade reforms[15] that have been analyzed using TRIST.

Example 1: The COMESA customs union[16]

A pressing trade policy issue currently facing COMESA members is the impact of joining the customs union (CU). We choose three countries to analyze the revenue impact of such a scenario, Malawi, Kenya, and Zambia. The trade policy scenario is defined as follows: all the remaining non-zero intra-COMESA tariffs are set to zero. This implies assuming that a complete COMESA Free Trade Agreement (FTA) is put in place before the implementation of the customs union. Preferential tariffs with SADC members remain the same. The COMESA common external tariff (CET)[17] is applied to all remaining trading partners. However, in order to account for tariff exemptions, statutory tariffs in the CET schedule are multiplied by the current ratio of collection efficiency, i.e. the tariff revenue that has been collected divided by the revenue that should have been collected according to the current statutory rates.

Table 2 presents results of revenue losses from the above-defined COMESA CET scenario. We choose two sets of elasticity values: the default values and higher values to assess sensitivity. In Malawi, the implementation of the CET is projected to lead to a moderate reduction in protection as the import weighted average tariff rate falls from 5.4 to 5.1 %. Tariff revenues are projected to fall by US$3.6 million with the default elasticities and by US$6.6 million with the higher elasticity values corresponding to losses of between 4.8 % and 8.7 % of tariff revenue. Total trade revenue losses from tariffs, excises, and VAT are projected to be between US$5.2 and US$6.6 million, a fall of about 2–2.5 % in overall trade tax revenues.[18] Zambia and Kenya would lose proportionately more revenue as a result of the implementation of the CET. The tariff revenue loss is predicted to be between 17 % and 20 % in Zambia and between 24 % and 27 % in Kenya. The total trade revenue loss is projected as being between 4.6 % and 5 % in Zambia and between 6.3 % and 6.8 % in Kenya.

15 TRIST only analyzes imports. It does not include trade policy changes related to subsidies or changes to export taxes which also impact on government revenues.

16 The following results are taken from Brenton *et al.* (2007).

17 We use the COMESA CET schedule as of 24.10.2008 as provided by the COMESA secretariat.

18 A higher demand elasticity will accentuate the impact of tariff reductions on the level of overall imports and therefore the positive impact on VAT and excise revenues.

Table 2. Predicted revenue implications of a COMESA common external tariff[1] (millions of US$)

Country	Malawi		Zambia		Kenya	
Elasticities[2]	default	high	default	high	default	high
Initial imports	1416.0	1416.0	3930.9	3930.9	10057.5	10057.5
New Import	1416.6	1419.0	3949.5	3972.5	10097.7	10117.8
Change	0.6	2.9	18.6	41.7	40.2	60.3
% change	0.0%	0.2%	0.5%	1.1%	0.4%	0.6%
Initial tariff revenue	75.9	75.9	245.8	245.8	443.0	443.0
New tariff revenue	72.2	69.3	203.0	196.0	335.4	323.8
Change	−3.6	−6.6	−42.8	−49.8	−107.6	−119.2
% change	−4.8%	−8.7%	−17.4%	−20.3%	−24.3%	−26.9%
Initial excise revenue	78.8	78.8	98.5	98.5	525.3	525.3
New excise revenue	78.4	79.0	98.0	98.5	525.3	525.3
Change	−0.4	0.1	−0.5	−0.1	0.0	0.0
% change	−0.6%	0.2%	−0.5%	−0.1%	0.0%	0.0%
Initial VAT revenue	117.0	117.0	684.7	684.7	810.3	810.3
New VAT revenue	115.9	116.9	680.1	683.5	806.2	807.9
Change	−1.2	−0.1	−4.5	−1.1	−4.1	−2.4
% change	−1.0%	−0.1%	−0.7%	−0.2%	−0.5%	−0.3%
Initial total revenue	271.8	271.8	1029.0	1029.0	1778.6	1778.6
New total revenue	266.5	265.2	981.2	977.9	1666.5	1657.7
Change	−5.2	−6.6	−47.8	−51.0	−112.1	−120.9
% change	−1.9%	−2.4%	−4.6%	−5.0%	−6.3%	−6.8%
Initial collected tariff rate	5.4%	5.4%	6.3%	6.3%	4.4%	4.4%
New collected tariff rate	5.1%	4.9%	5.1%	4.9%	3.3%	3.2%

Notes: 1 The COMESA CET scenario assumes zero tariffs among COMESA partners, unchanged tariffs for SADC partners. For all other trading partners, the new CET rate is applied but deflated by the current ratio of collection efficiency (collected tariff rate / statutory tariff rate) to account for tariff exemptions. In the few cases of tariff lines for which no final agreement has been reached yet the lowest tariff rate under consideration is used.
2 The default scenario assumes 0.5 for import demand elasticity, 1.5 for exporter substitution elasticity. High scenario assumes 1 for import demand elasiticity, 5 for exporter subsitution elasticity.

Example 2: An economic partnership agreement (EPA) with the EU[19]

An important challenge for many low-income countries is the negotiation and implementation of EPAs with the EU. In contrast to the previous Cotonou and Lome Agreements, these new agreements call for the reciprocal elimination of tariffs on imports from the EU. In many African, Caribbean, and Pacific countries, lack of information about the potential magnitude of the adjustment costs that will

19 The following results are taken from a TRIST-based World Bank report for the secretariat of COMESA (Brenton *et al.*, 2007).

Table 3. Predicted revenue implications of an economic partnership agreement (EPA) with the European Union (millions of US$)

	Tanzania			Kenya			Ethiopia		
Country	EPA	Sensitive list	exemptions cut	EPA	Sensitive list	exemptions cut	EPA	Sensitive list	exemptions cut
Initial imports	5802.8	5802.8	5802.8	10057.5	10057.5	10057.5	3589.7	3589.7	3589.7
New Import	5819.4	5805.5	5770.2	10093.3	10057.7	9984.0	3610.9	3589.8	3576.5
Change	16.6	2.7	−32.7	35.8	0.2	−73.5	21.2	0.2	−13.2
% change	0.3%	0.0%	−0.6%	0.4%	0.1%	−0.7%	0.6%	0.0%	−0.4%
Initial tariff revenue	270.3	270.3	270.3	443.0	443.0	443.0	291.7	291.7	291.7
New tariff revenue	231.4	264.7	318.6	357.2	420.3	537.8	241.8	275.6	305.6
Change	−38.9	−5.7	48.2	−85.7	−22.6	94.8	−49.9	−16.0	13.9
% change	−14.4%	−2.2%	17.8%	−19.4%	−5.7%	21.4%	−17.1%	−5.5%	4.8%
Initial excise revenue	294.4	294.4	294.4	525.3	525.3	525.3	68.9	68.9	68.9
New excise revenue	294.0	294.4	294.3	524.2	525.3	525.2	70.1	68.9	70.0
Change	−0.4	0.0	−0.1	−1.1	−0.1	−0.1	1.2	0.0	1.1
% change	−0.1%	0.0%	0.0%	−0.2%	−0.0%	−0.0%	−1.7%	−0.0%	−1.6%
Initial VAT revenue	528.5	528.5	528.5	810.3	810.3	810.3	297.1	297.1	297.1
New VAT revenue	525.3	528.3	528.6	803.7	809.1	803.4	293.8	296.3	295.5
Change	−3.2	−0.1	0.1	−6.6	−1.2	−6.9	−3.2	−0.8	−1.5
% change	−0.6%	0.0%	0.0%	−0.8%	−0.2%	−0.9%	−1.1%	−0.3%	−0.5%
Initial total revenue	1093.2	1093.2	1093.2	1778.6	1778.6	1778.6	657.7	657.7	657.7
New total revenue	1050.8	1087.4	1141.4	1685.1	1754.7	1866.4	605.7	640.8	671.1
Change	−42.4	−5.8	48.2	−93.5	−23.9	87.8	−52.0	−16.8	13.4
% change	−3.9%	−0.5%	4.4%	−5.3%	−1.5%	4.9%	−7.9%	−2.6%	2.0%
Initial collected tariff rate	4.7%	4.7%	4.7%	4.4%	4.4%	4.4%	8.1%	8.1%	8.1%
New collected tariff rate	4.0%	4.6%	5.5%	3.5%	4.2%	5.4%	6.7%	7.8%	8.5%

arise from removing tariffs against imports from the EU has led to considerable uncertainty and apprehension concerning these agreements.[20]

Table 3 contains simulation results for trade reform scenarios related to the implementation of the EPAs. We consider three countries for which EPAs are currently high on the policy agenda: Tanzania, Kenya, and Ethiopia. For each of the three countries, the first column of the table considers an EPA scenario in which all tariffs on products from the EU are set to zero. As discussed earlier, countries are being allowed to exclude around 20% of their imports from the EU from liberalization. The revenue losses predicted in this first exercise should thus be seen as an upper bound on the likely impact of the agreement.

20 There are many studies in the literature that have attempted to estimate the revenue implications of EPA agreements between the European Union and various African countries. These include Brenton *et al.* (2007), Busse and Grossmann (2004), Karingi *et al.* (2005), Khandelwal (2004), and Milner *et al.* (2005) to name a few. Brenton *et al.* (2007) discuss the relative merits of the methodologies used.

Table 4. Sources of tariff revenue in Ethiopia (2005)

	COMESA (FTA)	COMESA (non-FTA)	EU27	Other	Total
Share of imports	1.2 %	3.2 %	23.2 %	72.3 %	100.0 %
Share of total tariff revenue	0.0 %	4.3 %	16.2 %	79.5 %	100.0 %
Share of tariff revenue/ total tax revenue*	0.0 %	0.8 %	3.1 %	15.3 %	19.2 %
Share of total trade tax revenue*	1.8 %	4.7 %	17.6 %	75.9 %	100.0 %
Share of trade tax revenue / total tax revenue*	0.8 %	2.1 %	7.6 %	32.9 %	43.3 %
Trade weighted average applied tariff	0.0 %	10.8 %	5.7 %	8.9 %	8.1 %
Trade weighted average statutory tariff	0.9 %	16.0 %	10.7 %	11.5 %	11.4 %
Trade weighted average tariff exemptions	0.8 %	5.2 %	5.1 %	2.6 %	3.2 %
Tariff collection rate	5.1 %	67.6 %	52.8 %	77.4 %	71.5 %

Note: *Based on IMF data on total tax revenue.

As a result of removing tariffs on imports from the EU, the average level of protection falls in all countries, with average import weighted collected tariff rates falling from 4.7 % to 4.0 % in Tanzania, from 4.4 % to 3.5 % in Kenya, and from 8.1 % to 6.7 % in Ethiopia. All three countries loose more than 10 % of tariff revenue due to the EPA and there are overall trade tax revenue losses of 3.9 % in Tanzania, 5.3 % in Kenya, and 7.9 % in Ethiopia.[21]

In the following, we chose Ethiopia as an example to consider the results of the simulation exercise in somewhat more detail. Table 4 presents some of the basic summary statistics for Ethiopian imports that TRIST automatically produces. The first row shows the share of each of the four main groups of import suppliers in Ethiopian imports. The EU accounts for just under a quarter of Ethiopian imports. COMESA countries, on the other hand, are relatively small suppliers of the Ethiopian market, with other countries contributing the vast majority of imports. The second row shows that the share of the EU in tariff revenue was 16.2 %, and thus less than its share in imports, with the opposite being the case for imports from other countries. Tariffs on total imports account for 19 % of Ethiopia's total tax revenue, with tariffs on imports from the EU contributing 3.1 % of tax revenues.[22] When VAT and excise taxes levied on imports are taken into account, imports from the EU contribute 7.6 % of tax revenues, while total imports provide 43.3 % of revenues. Trade is clearly a key source of tax revenues in Ethiopia.

The trade weighted average applied tariff is 5.7 % for the EU, below the overall average of 8.1 %. Conversely, the tariff actually levied on imports from other COMESA countries and the rest of the world is above the overall applied average,

21 Karingi *et al.* (2005) using older data predict a loss of revenue for Ethiopia from an EPA that would be equivalent to 6.7 % of total tax revenues.

22 The data for total tax revenue were taken from IMF Article IV reports. The remaining entries in Table 4 are TRIST output.

while applied tariffs to member countries of the COMESA FTA are close to zero even though Ethiopia is not yet a member of the FTA. It should be noted that these are trade weighted tariff averages, so a higher number reflects the fact that imports are concentrated on products with a high level of protection. The tariff collection rate (the ratio of actual tariff revenue to hypothetical tariff revenue had the statutory tariff rate been applied) is 52.8 % for imports from the EU, which is below the average for all imports (71.5 %), and highlights the importance of taking into account exemptions when analyzing trade policy changes towards the EU.

Finally, we provide more detail on the commodity and sector concentration of the estimated impacts of an EPA. Table 5 identifies the ten top tariff lines that account for the largest revenue losses following the removal of tariffs on imports from the EU (change in revenue on a given product category divided by total change in revenue). Typically, these products are characterized by a combination of relatively high imports from the EU coming in under high applied tariffs, resulting in a relatively high amount of tariff revenue collected.[23]

Table 5 shows that the products with the highest revenue losses typically have a medium share of imports from the EU. There is a conceptual reason for this in the trade model underlying TRIST: if imports from the EU are 0 % for a product, liberalization with the EU will not lead to revenue losses. However, if the import share from the EU is 100 %, all tariff revenue on these imports will be lost, but there will not be any substitution away from other exporters. Thus, in relative terms, the revenue losses per unit of EU imports are the highest if only around half of the imports of a product come from the EU. Note that these results are based on the same demand and substitution elasticities across products, thus the differences between products are not driven by the value of elasticities.

Table 6 aggregates the estimated changes in prices at the ISIC (International Standard Industrial Classification) Rev. 3 industry level to obtain industry level changes in overall import prices. These figures give an indication of the sectors that are likely to face the stiffest increase in competition as tariffs on the EU are removed. For Ethiopia, import prices for tobacco products and forestry products fall by around 15 %. For all other sectors, the competition effect is likely to be milder with price changes of imports of less than 5 %.

As mentioned previously, countries often negotiate to exclude particular products from tariff removal commitments. In TRIST, any user-defined list of products can be selected to be excluded from the EPA or any other trade agreement since the model is based on data at the tariff line level. As an example, we look at the case in which countries choose the exclusion list to minimize the adverse revenue impact on the agreement. In TRIST, we can simply run the EPA scenario

23 Note that a large proportion of the tariff lines that generate the largest losses in revenues are vehicles and cigarettes. These are products for which there is a straightforward policy response to declining revenues from tariff removal: an increase in non-discriminatory excise taxes. This tax mechanism is already available and thus would be easy to administer.

Table 5. Top ten products in terms of revenue loss from free trade with the EU

Description	hscode	Share in total revenue loss	Share in total imports from EU	Collected tariff rate on EU imports	Share in total tariff revenue from EU	Share of imports of product coming from the EU
Iron/steel bars & rods,hotrolled ...	72142000	4.4%	1.4%	19.5%	2.5%	22.7%
Vehicles with spark-ignition engine of cyl.capC 1000<C_C<1300CC	87032210	3.9%	0.6%	34.2%	2.0%	47.4%
Parts and accessories, nes, for vehicles...	87089900	2.8%	1.1%	15.2%	2.0%	37.9%
Cigarettes containing tobacco	24022000	2.3%	0.4%	34.7%	1.3%	85.9%
Pub. transport type vehicle(diesle/semi-d) seat capacity <15 pass.	87021010	1.9%	0.2%	33.3%	0.8%	21.4%
Vehicles with diesel/semi-d engine cylinder capacity>2500CC	87033390	1.9%	0.5%	19.8%	1.7%	29.3%
Goods vehicle with dis/semi-dengines, GVW <=5 TONNE	87042190	1.5%	1.1%	8.5%	1.0%	39.8%
Medicaments of other hormones, for retail sale, nes	30043900	1.4%	3.3%	2.6%	1.5%	47.4%
Other food preparations of flour etc...	19019090	1.4%	0.2%	30.0%	0.7%	16.5%
Vehicles with spark ignition engine of cylinder capacity >1800CC ...	87032390	1.3%	0.3%	24.7%	1.0%	21.6%

Table 6. Ethiopian import price changes by sector under EPA scenario

ISIC Rev. 3 industry	Import weighted average price change	Share in total imports
16 – Manufacture of tobacco products	−15.9 %	0.1 %
02 – Forestry, logging and related service activities	−14.9 %	0.1 %
13 – Mining of metal ores	−4.4 %	0.0 %
26 – Manufacture of other non-metallic mineral products	−3.3 %	1.0 %
34 – Manufacture of motor vehicles, trailers and semi trailers	−2.8 %	6.8 %
...		
18 – Manufacture of wearing apparel; dressing and dying of fur	0.0 %	1.9 %
01 – Agriculture, hunting and related service activities	0.0 %	7.8 %
11 – Extraction of crude petroleum and natural gas ...	−0.1 %	0.4 %
23 – Manufacture of coke, refined petroleum products and nuclear fuel	0.0 %	16.2 %
40 – Electricity, gas, steam and hot water supply	0.0 %	0.0 %

without an exclusion list and then rank products by the ratio of overall trade tax revenue loss to import value from the EU. We then select the sensitive products beginning with those that have the highest ratio until we reach a cumulative share of 20 % of imports from the EU.

The results from this scenario are presented in the second column of Table 3 and show that the fall in tariff revenues compared to the initial EPA scenario without the exclusion list is considerably reduced by between 12 and 14 percentage points for the three countries. The overall trade tax losses under this scenario amount to 0.5 % (Tanzania), 1.5 % (Kenya), and 2.6 % (Ethiopia). For some countries, official exclusion lists for a potential EPA have already been determined. Among these are the EAC (East African Community) member states Tanzania and Kenya. Table 7 contrasts the impact of an EPA under the revenue loss minimizing scenario outlined in column two of Table 3 with a scenario in which the official EAC exclusion list is used. In the case of Tanzania, the projected 1.5 % loss in trade tax revenue is only slightly higher than the losses projected for the revenue loss minimization case, whereas revenue losses for Kenya are closer to the projected impact for an EPA without an exclusion list. This indicates that the EAC exclusion list may have been determined to respond more closely to Tanzanian rather than Kenyan revenue concerns.

Another policy response to declining tariff revenues due to trade liberalization is the removal of tariff exemptions. In Table 3, the third column presents the impact of a scenario in which all tariffs with the EU are set to zero, with no exclusion list, and tariff exemptions are cut to zero. All three countries gain substantial amounts of tariff and overall trade tax revenue by cutting exemptions despite the fact that all tariffs with the EU are set to zero. Similarly, in all three countries the reform

Table 7. Tanzanian and Kenyan EPA with official EAC exclusion list

Tanzania

	EPA with 80% sensitive list	EPA with official EAC exclusion list
Total number of tariff lines	4,393	4,393
Number of excluded product lines	1,581	1,078
% change in imports	0.0%	0.1%
% change in tariff revenue	−2.2%	−6.4%
% change in total revenue	−0.5%	−1.7%
Old collected tariff rate	4.7%	4.7%
New collected tariff rate	4.6%	4.4%

Kenya

	EPA with 80% Sensitive List	EPA with official EAC exclusion list
Total number of tariff lines	4,363	4,363
Number of excluded product lines	1,597	1,075
% change in imports	0.1%	0.3%
% change in tariff revenue	−5.7%	−17.8%
% change in total revenue	−1.5%	−4.8%
Old collected tariff rate	4.4%	4.4%
New collected tariff rate	4.2%	3.6%

actually leads to an increase (of between 2% and 4%) rather than a decrease in import weighted average collected tariffs. However, the removal of tariff exemptions could exacerbate the negative, trade diverting, impact of the preferential trade agreement. It is important that a country also seeks to reduce its MFN (most favoured nation) tariffs to reduce the possible distortions that arise from removing tariffs against particular suppliers and not others. Hence a commitment to reduce tariffs against the EU should be coordinated with the removal of tariff exemptions. For example, removing all tariff exemptions would allow Tanzania to cut its MFN tariffs by more than 30% at the same time as implementing the EPA agreement without any adverse revenue impact. Similarly, Ethiopia could cut its MFN tariffs by more than 20% and Kenya by more than 40%.

Example 3: 'Trade diversion' and 'trade correction'[24]

A preferential tariff liberalization will reduce prices of imports from the beneficiary country. This creates a potential for trade diversion if the good is produced less efficiently in the preferred source than in countries subject to the full tariff. The

24 These calculations were carried out by the authors using a TRIST for Nigeria as well as a prototype of the supplementary tool for the calculation of trade diversion vs. trade correction.

Table 8. Trade diversion vs. trade correction for a Nigerian FTA with China

	in billions of Nigerian Nairs								
	Trade diversion			Trade correction			Total trade re-sourced		
	win	lose	net	win	lose	net	win	lose	net
ECOWAS	0.0	−11.2	−11.2	0.0	−2.8	−2.8	0.0	−14.0	−14.0
AFRICA	0.0	−0.1	−0.1	0.0	−0.1	−0.1	0.0	−0.1	−0.1
EU	0.0	0.0	0.0	0.0	−8.4	−8.4	0.0	−8.4	−8.4
USA	0.0	−1.5	−1.5	0.0	−0.3	−0.3	0.0	−1.8	−1.8
CHINA	12.8	0.0	12.8	11.6	0.0	11.6	24.4	0.0	24.4
TOTAL	12.8	−12.8	0.0	11.6	−11.6	0.0	24.4	−24.4	0.0

topic of trade creation vs. trade diversion, and the resulting welfare implications, is well-known, and can be addressed in TRIST in a standard way similar to existing tools like SMART with the help of an easy to install add-on tool.

However, TRIST adds an additional dimension to this type of analysis by also looking at what can be referred to as trade correction: the reversal of previous trade diversion. Consider the following example: after the EU is granted tariff free market access, it takes over some of the market share that was previously held by other trading partners who already enjoyed tariff free market access prior to the EU being granted the tariff reduction. This would not be trade diversion as it would actually imply a move of consumption towards a more efficient producer that was previously disadvantaged in terms of market access.

As a practical example, we consider a sequential scenario: we assume that Nigeria has liberalized all tariffs on imports from the EU to zero as part of an EPA. The resulting import allocations and tariff rates are taken as the 'base scenario' for the following policy experiment, namely an FTA between Nigeria and China. Table 8 shows how different trading partners would be affected in terms of their exports to Nigeria if Nigerian tariffs on all Chinese imports were preferentially driven to zero as part of the FTA. The table distinguishes two categories of re-sourced trade as outlined above: diverted trade that is welfare reducing (trade diversion) and changes in response to a decrease in preferences previously granted which is not welfare reducing (trade correction).

Table 8 shows that Nigeria now imports an additional 24.4 billion Naira worth of goods from China. Imports from all other trading partners decline, with trade diverted away from the EU being entirely due to trade correction. The reason is that imports from China increase at the expense of EU goods in product categories in which Chinese exports were initially disadvantaged by preferences given to EU exports under the EPA. For all other partners some of the decline in exports to Nigeria is classified as trade diversion and some is classified as trade correction. This is because some, but not all Chinese products had initially been subject to significant discrimination from preferences given to other trading partners.

Example 4: The impact of specific and complex duties[25]

TRIST can also deal effectively with specific and complex tariffs. Specific tariffs are those in which the duty is related to the volume or other physical characteristics of the product rather than its value, while complex tariffs combine different types of duties such as ad valorem and specific tariffs. A key feature of specific and complex tariffs is that the level of protection given by the statutory rate is not transparent and in practice will vary across different transactions of the same product. These tariffs tend to be regressive since higher proportional rates of protection are applied to the lower value transactions that are consumed by poor households. Footwear is a good example of a product that is often subject to specific duties – often a fixed amount per pair. In Mauritius, for example, in 2007 there was a specific duty of 125 rupees per pair on certain types of footwear with uppers of leather and outer soles of rubber, plastics, leather, or composition leather. The ad valorem impact of such a fixed tax will be much greater on relatively cheap shoes from India than on a pair of Jimmy Choo's! Indeed, the data in TRIST show that in 2007, the ad valorem equivalent tariff on imports of such footwear from India (39.8 %) was more than double that on imports from the EU (19.2 %), while the ad valorem equivalent tariff on the small quantity of imports from Italy was 9.4 %.

The data in TRIST are based on actual revenues collected and so TRIST automatically computes ad-valorem equivalents of specific and complex tariffs for each product by country import flow. Hence, TRIST can show the revenue and other adjustment implications of removing specific and complex tariffs or of strategies to convert them into ad valorem rates. Other tools that are based on statutory rates rather than collected revenues use formulas to calculate approximate ad valorem equivalents. For example, in WITS (World Integrated Trade Solution), for simple specific tariffs, the ad valorem equivalent is calculated by dividing the specific duty by the unit value (value divided by quantity). The unit value is based either on the importing countries total imports of the product from the world or the global imports of OECD countries (Stawowy, 2001). The use of these more aggregated unit values reflects concerns with the quality of the information on the quantity of individual import flows. However, there remain many gaps in the WITS database regarding ad valorem equivalents of specific duties. For example, in WITS, the duties levied by Mauritius on leather footwear are reported as zero whichever method of calculation is used.

Table 9 shows statutory complex tariffs in the Tanzanian tariff schedule and Figure 3 illustrates the revenue implications of converting them to ad-valorem equivalents and subsequently reducing these. Again, there is an important difference

25 The results in examples 4 and 5 are from unpublished World Bank presentations, P. Brenton, J. Kweka, and E. von Uexkull, 'Tanzania: Trade and Competitiveness Policies to Propel Growth' (May 2007) and P. Brenton and E. von Uexkull, 'Mauritius: Adjusting to Trade Reform' (February 2008).

Table 9. Specific tariffs in Tanzania[26]

Product	Tariff	Collected tariff from 2008 TRIST data
Rice in the husk (paddy or rough)	75 % or USD 200/MT whichever is higher	76.5 %
Husked (brown) rice	75 % or USD 200/MT whichever is higher	60.8 %
Semimilled or wholly milled rice ...	75 % or USD 200/MT whichever is higher	71.5 %
Broken rice	75 % or USD 200/MT whichever is higher	9.5 %
Cane sugar	100 % or USD 200/MT whichever is higher	100.1 %
Worn clothing and other worn articles	45 % or USD 0.30/kg whichever is higher	54.3 %

Figure 3. Revenue implications of replacing specific with ad-valorem tariffs in Tanzania

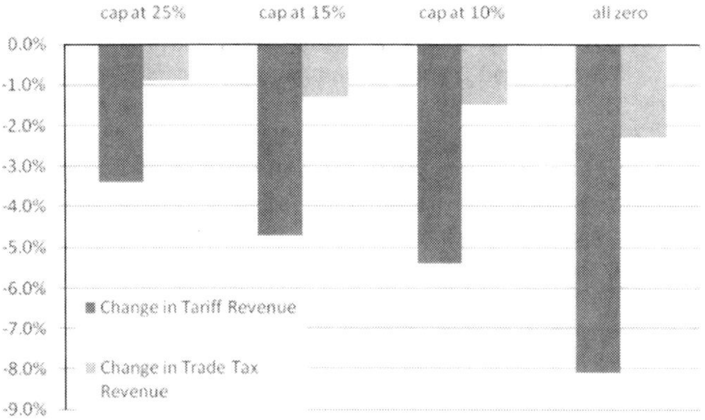

in the projected changes in tariff revenues and changes in total import tax revenues, with the percentage change in the former being around four times greater than that of the latter. The contribution of such taxes to trade revenues is relatively small, such that conversion to an ad valorem rate of 25 % (the maximum rate in the common external tariff of the East African Community) would lead to import tax revenue losses of less than 1 %. Complete abolition of these duties would result in trade revenue losses in the order of 2 %. These losses would need to be judged relative to the distortion of trade created by these duties, their regressive impact on poor households, and the additional administrative costs for customs in applying them relative to ad valorem duties.[27]

26 Specific tariffs may be subject to exemptions. This is why the average collected tariff is lower than the minimum in rows 2, 3, and 4.

27 Specific duties will typically require a higher prevalence of physical inspections than ad valorem duties. On the other hand, specific duties may be useful where lack of capacity in Customs prevents

Example 5: The impact of trade reforms on output and employment

Up to this point, this paper has focused on the analysis of revenue changes in response to trade policy reforms. Yet, revenue effects are not the only adjustment cost policy makers may need to address. The following analysis shows how TRIST can be extended to provide input to an analysis of the short-term impact of trade reforms on domestic production and employment.

However, again, it is important to note that TRIST uses a partial equilibrium model and thus does not take into account inter- and intra-sectoral linkages and the economy-wide impacts of tariff changes. The results presented below are based on tariff line level partial equilibrium simulations which do not take into account the various economy-wide resource constraints and reallocations, or any inter- and intra-sectoral economic linkages that may be important for the medium- to long-term impacts of the respective reforms. One of the core benefits of trade liberalization is that it removes the anti export bias in economies with high levels of protection which will depreciate the real exchange rate and allow export sectors to compete more effectively for domestic factors of production. This not only implies that export intensive sectors might benefit disproportionately from trade liberalization and are likely to expand in the medium to long term, but also that an assessment of the short-term aggregate impact of a liberalization scenario on domestic production may be subject to a systematic upward bias.[28]

These concerns are less of an issue with respect to relative sectoral impacts of tariff reform. Given its nature as a partial equilibrium model, the purpose of TRIST in contributing to the analysis of trade reform adjustment costs in terms of output and employment is thus to identify sectors that are likely to be hardest hit as part of the direct short-term adjustment to increased competition in import markets, to assess the magnitude of these differences, and to contribute to the design of policy interventions that seek to cushion these direct adjustment costs.[29]

The impact of trade reforms on domestic production, and in particular on employment, has been one of the most politically sensitive issues in the discussion on adjustment costs. In the long run, trade liberalization leads to the reallocation of

application of standard valuation techniques. We also stress again that TRIST cannot provide an estimate of the economy-wide welfare effects of removing such duties.

28 The export response is unlikely to occur in the short run and to be slower than the response of imports to a tariff reduction. On the other hand, the real exchange rate impact of a given reform may occur quickly in countries that face serious foreign exchange constraints, thus limiting the negative impact on import competing sectors in the absence of (foreign exchange depletion –) offsetting export expansion.

29 Another reason why TRIST cannot be used to assess the aggregate impact of trade reform on output and employment is that the data are typically available for industry only and exclude output and employment in agriculture and services – by far the biggest sources of employment in most developing countries. There are several partial equilibrium models that assess the impact of changes in agricultural trade policy, such as ATPSM (Agricultural Trade Policy Simulation Model). Also, the latest version of the GTAP (Global Trade Analysis Project) database contains data on output and employment for agricultural and service sectors in 113 countries. However, the data are only available at an aggregated level. The lack of consistent output and employment data at a detailed sector level in many low-income countries remains an important constraint on policy relevant trade analysis in these countries.

production factors (labor and capital) to more productive uses, and thus changes in the pattern of production and employment among and within firms, industries, and regions. In the short run, production in import competing sectors will tend to decline, which may have social and political costs. A better understanding of these effects is central to effective sector- and region-specific trade policy making that mitigates these adjustment costs.

A first indication of those sectors that are likely to be most affected by short-term adjustment costs to tariff reform can be gained by looking at changes in prices for each sector. These will be larger for sectors where average tariffs fall the furthest. However, this analysis can be considerably enhanced and deepened if there are detailed data at the sector level on domestic sales (production minus exports) and employment. These can be uploaded into the *Simulation Tool* and TRIST will automatically amend the model to include the domestic substitution effect as well as present sectoral changes in domestic production and employment that result from the tariff reform scenario of interest. The short-term impact of a tariff reform on output and employment will be determined by the size of the change in the tariff at the sector level, the short-run elasticity of supply, and the initial size of the sector. The exercise will show that large sectors facing significant tariff reductions are likely to face the greatest adjustment in the short term.[30]

A country for which a TRIST has been developed and for which the necessary data on sectoral domestic production (at the 4-digit level) are available is Mauritius. Table 10 presents selected results illustrating the impact of a duty-free island trade policy scenario on output and employment. The move towards a tariff free island reduces the share of output directed towards the domestic market because of higher competition from imports. Employment results are based on the assumption that the number of full-time equivalent jobs in companies declines proportionately with output. We do, however, control for the fact that in some sectors – especially textiles and wearing apparel – production for the domestic market is more labor intensive than export oriented production.[31] The table presents changes in domestic production and employment in the ten sectors that are projected to be most severely affected (in terms of output losses) by the reform scenario. These are the manufacture of furniture, wearing apparel, soap and detergents, bakery products, preserving of fruits and vegetables, and wine.

The results suggest that short-run employment adjustments are likely to be concentrated on two sectors, with more than three-quarters of the projected loss of

30 Production data are generally not available at the same level of disaggregation as tariff data which reduces the accuracy of TRIST when extending it to production and employment data. Hence, there is a trade-off between including production and working at a less disaggregated level, or excluding production and being able to capture disaggregated impacts on trade and trade-related taxes. While the level of disaggregation of the output and employment data impacts on the calculations of the domestic substitution effect, the remainder of the calculations continues to be conducted at the tariff line level.

31 The differences in labor productivity between exporting and non-exporting firms in each sector were calculated using data from the World Bank's Enterprise Survey.

Table 10. Duty-free island in Mauritius: 15 most affected sectors[32]

	Output (Mln. Rupees)		Employment (full-ime equivalents)	
Sectors sorted by predicted output loss	Change	% change	Change	% change
1552 – Manufacture of wines	−30	−6.2%	−19	−6.0%
2424 – Manufacture of soap and detergents, etc.	−59	−5.6%	−55	−5.6%
3610 – Manufacture of furniture	−114	−3.8%	−415	−3.8%
1513 – Processing and preserving of fruit and vegetables	−32	−3.2%	−19	−3.2%
1541 – Manufacture of bakery products	−53	−3.1%	−88	−3.1%
2710 – Manufacture of basic iron and steel	−26	−1.4%	−7	−1.4%
1554 – Manufacture of soft drinks; production of mineral waters	−23	−1.0%	−25	−1.0%
1810 – Manufacture of wearing apparel, except fur apparel	−109	−0.6%	−397	−1.0%
1511 – Production, processing and preserving of meat and meat products	−21	−0.5%	−7	−0.5%
01 to 09 – Agriculture, forestry and fishing, excl. sugar cane	−23	−0.3%	−88	−0.3%

employment occurring in furniture and apparel. This analysis supported the government in introducing a program to assist adjustment of the furniture sector.

5. Conclusions

TRIST is a simple, easy to use country focused model that brings substantial advantages in simulating the impact of trade reforms and thus in evaluating different trade policy options. It contributes to a better understanding of trade-related adjustment implications which is crucial to design a reform agenda that maximizes benefits from greater openness while minimizing and adequately cushioning adjustment costs. While TRIST has been developed to simulate the short-term implications of trade reform on fiscal revenue, TRIST can be extended to estimate the differences between trade creation, diversion, and correction with the resulting welfare implications as well as the initial impact of trade reform on domestic production and employment in import competing sectors.

The key features of TRIST compared to previous studies and models are that it uses collected tariff rates at the tariff line level, which leads to greater accuracy than using statutory rates; it takes into account all taxes collected levied on trade, not only tariff revenue, but also revenue from VAT and excise taxes; it works at a highly disaggregated and policy relevant level, breaking down results for detailed products and trading partners; it is transparent, open, and flexible and does not require sophisticated software or specific programming skills. The overarching

32 The percentage changes in the table refer to the change in output (employment) in a sector relative to total output (employment) in that sector.

goal of TRIST is to provide a tool to government agencies and other stakeholders that can use it to support an informed discussion of the possible short-term consequences of tariff reforms.

It is hoped that free access to the spreadsheet tool will allow researchers and government officials to fine tune TRIST to reflect country circumstances, and will enable them to analyze the impact of proposals for trade policy reform as they arise. An aim of this paper and tool is also to encourage the collection of more accurate and detailed data on production, employment, and consumption. This is important to allow for more systematic analysis of the impact of trade (and other) policy changes on output, employment, consumption, and poverty so as to help motivate positive interventions that limit the adjustment costs, and so maximize the overall positive economic benefits, of trade reform.

TRIST templates as well as a TRIST manual, additional information, and links to publications using TRIST are available at http://go.worldbank.org/2P8FPC0760.

References

Andriamananjara, S., P. Brenton, E. von Uexkull, and P. Walkenhorst (2009) 'Assessing the Economic Impacts of an Economic Partnership Agreement on Nigeria', World Bank Policy Research Working Paper 4920.

Armington, P. (1969), 'A Theory of Demand for Products Distinguished by Place of Production', *IMF Staff Papers*, 16, pp. 159–178.

Brenton, P., M. Hoppe, E. v. Uexkull (2007), 'Evaluating the Revenue Effects of Trade Policy Options for COMESA Countries: the Impacts of a Customs Union and an EPA with the European Union', mimeo, World Bank, http://siteresources.worldbank.org/INTRANETTRADE/Resources/239054-1196261607599/4442906-1253912908321/COMESA.pdf

Busse, M. and H. Grossmann (2004), 'Assessing the Impact of ACP/EU Economic Partnership Agreement on West African Countries', HWWA Discussion Paper 294, Hamburg Institute of International Economics.

Hoppe, M. (2010) 'Estimating the Fiscal Impact of the Côte d'Ivoire-EU Economic Partnership Agreement', Africa Trade Policy Notes 4, World Bank, http://siteresources.worldbank.org/INTAFRREGTOPTRADE/Resources/4_CI_TRIST_Policy_Note_FINAL.pdf

Jammes, O. and M. Ollareaga (2005), 'Explaining SMART and GSIM', mimeo, World Bank, http://wits-old.worldbank.org/witsweb/download/docs/Explaining_SMART_and_GSIM.pdf

Karingi, S., R. Lang, N. Oulmane, R. Perez, M. Sadni Jallab, and H. Ben Hammouda (2005), 'Economic and Welfare Impacts of the EU–Africa Economic Partnership Agreements', African Trade Policy Centre work in progress, 10.

Kee, H., A. Nicita, and M. Olarreaga (2004), 'Import Demand Elasticities and Trade Distortions', CEPR Discussion Papers 4669.

Khandelwal, P. (2004), 'COMESA and SADC: Prospects and Challenges for Regional Trade Integration', IMF Working Paper 04/227.

Milner, C., O. Morrissey, and A. McKay (2005), 'Some Simple Analytics of the Trade and Welfare Effects of Economic Partnership Agreement', *Journal of African Economies*, 14(3): 327–358.

Stawowy, W. (2001), 'Calculation of Ad Valorem Equivalents of Non-Advalorem Tariffs – Methodology Notes', mimeo UNCTAD, http://wits.worldbank.org/witsweb/Doc/default.aspx

Appendix: Detailing the calculation steps in the trade model

The trade response to a change in tariffs for a given product from a given exporter is calculated based on the resulting percentage change in the duty inclusive price. It is assumed that all changes in tariffs are fully passed on and that the world price remains unchanged (infinite supply elasticity). For a change in the tariff (with VAT and excise rates unchanged), the percentage change in the price of good i from exporter j is calculated as follows (subscript i is omitted for all arguments in the formula)

$$\frac{\Delta p_j}{p_j^{old}} = \frac{(1+t_j^{new})(1+ext_j)(1+vat_j)-(1+t_j^{old})(1+ext_j)(1+vat_j)}{(1+t_j^{old})(1+ext_j)(1+vat_j)} = \frac{t_j^{new}-t_j^{old}}{(1+t_j^{old})}$$

where

Δp_j is the change in price of imports from country j,
p_j^{old} is the price of imports from j before tariff reform,
p_j^{new} is the price of imports from j after tariff reform,
p_{wld} is the world market price,
t_j^{old} is the tariff rate applied to imports from country j before reform,
t_j^{new} is the tariff rate applied to imports from country j after reform,
ext_j is the excise tax rate applied to imports from j, and
vat_j is the VAT rate applied to imports from j.

The trade response for a particular product is modeled in three consecutive steps. In the first stage, we model the allocation of given expenditure on imports of a product across different country suppliers and how this allocation changes when tariffs and duties are amended. To isolate this substitution effect, total imports are held constant (product subscript i is omitted for all arguments in the formula)

$$q_j^{ES} = \left[\frac{\Delta p_j}{p_j^{old}} * \gamma_j^{ES} + 1\right] q_j^{old} * \frac{\sum_{j=1,\dots,n}\left(q_j^{old}\right)}{\sum_{j=1,\dots,n}\left(\left[\frac{\Delta p_j}{p_j^{old}} * \gamma_j^{ES} + 1\right] q_j^{old}\right)}$$

Where q_j^{ES} is the imported quantity from j after exporter substitution step,
q_j^{old} is the imported quantity from j before reform, and
γ_j^{ES} is the exporter substitution elasticity for imports from country j.

In the second step, total expenditure on the product is allocated between domestic sources and imports. The change in imports resulting from this step is then distributed across all importers according to their share of the import market. By definition total domestic consumption remains constant in this stage

$$\frac{\Delta \overline{P}}{\overline{P}^{old}} = \sum_{j=1,\ldots,n} \left[\frac{q_j^{old}}{\sum_{j=1,\ldots,n} \left(q_j^{old}\right)} * \frac{\Delta P_j}{P_j^{old}} \right]$$

$$q_j^{DS} = q_j^{ES} + \left[Q_{imp}^{DS} - Q_{imp}^{old}\right] * \left[\frac{q_j^{old}}{\sum_{j=1,\ldots,n} \left(q_j^{old}\right)} \right]$$

$$Q_{imp}^{DS} = \left[\frac{\Delta \overline{P}_{imp}}{\overline{P}_{imp}^{old}} * \lambda^{DS} + 1 \right] Q_{imp}^{old}$$

where

Q_{imp}^{old} is the initial total imported quantity,
Q_{imp}^{DS} is the total imported quantity after substitution with domestic output,
q_j^{DS} is the quantity imported from supplier *j* after substitution between imports and domestic output,
λ^{DS} is the domestic substitution elasticity for imports from exporter *j*, and

$\frac{\Delta \overline{P}}{\overline{P}^{old}} = \sum_{j=1,\ldots,n} \left[\frac{q_j^{old}}{\sum_{j=1,\ldots,n} \left(q_j^{old}\right)} * \frac{\Delta P_j}{P_j^{old}} \right]$ is the change in price of total imports.

In the third and final step, the demand effect, the change in the price of imports leads to an overall change in the price of the product (given by the change in the aggregate price of imports weighted by the share of imports in domestic consumption), which in turn results in a change in domestic consumption of a good. The additional consumption resulting from this effect is distributed across both imports and domestic production according to initial shares of total consumption of the product.

$$Q_{TD}^{new} = \left[\frac{\Delta \widetilde{P}}{\widetilde{P}\ old} * \mu^{D} + 1 \right] Q_{TD}^{old}$$

$$Q_{imp}^{new} = Q_{imp}^{DS} + \left[Q_{TD}^{new} - Q_{TD}^{old}\right] * \left[\frac{Q_{imp}^{old}}{Q_{imp}^{old} + Q_{dom}^{old}} \right]$$

$$q_j^{new} = q_j^{DS} + \left[Q_{imp}^{new} - Q_{imp}^{DS}\right] * \left[\frac{q_j^{old}}{\sum_{j=1,\ldots,n}\left(q_j^{old}\right)}\right]$$

where Q_{TD}^{old} is the initial total demand for product *I*,
Q_{TD}^{new} is the total demand after the change in the overall price of product *I*,
Q_{dom}^{old} is the initial quantity of demand for domestic output,
Q_{dom}^{new} is the final demand for domestic output
Q_{imp}^{new} is the final demand for imports of product *I*,
q_j^{new} is the quantity imported from supplier *j* after all three effects from changes in import prices (the substitution between different sources of imports, between imports and domestic output, and the demand effect for the product as a whole),
μ^D is the demand elasticity for product *I*, and

$$\frac{\Delta\tilde{P}}{\tilde{P}^{old}} = \left[\frac{Q_{imp}^{old}}{Q_{imp}^{old} + Q_{dom}^{old}} * \frac{\Delta\overline{P}}{\overline{P}^{old}}\right]$$

is the change in the price of total domestic consumption.

Section 2:
Trade, Wages and Adjustment

Bulletin of Economic Research 51:4, 1999, 0307-3378

Chapter 9

OUTSOURCING AND LOW-SKILLED WORKERS IN THE UK*

Bob Anderton and Paul Brenton

ABSTRACT

Outsourcing is proxied by constructing import penetration terms for groups of countries (distinguishing between imports from industrialized countries and imports from low-wage countries) for each four-digit industry within the broader categories of textiles and non-electrical machinery. The results show that imports from low-wage countries have made a significant contribution to the decline in the wage-bill share and relative employment of the less-skilled in the UK. The degree of outsourcing may differ between industries, and large currency appreciations may have a disproportionately large impact on the economic fortunes of the less-skilled.

I. INTRODUCTION

The declining relative economic fortunes of unskilled workers in the USA over the past two decades has been extensively documented and analysed.[1] Studies based on traditional neoclassical trade theory have tended to conclude that the increase in imports from low-wage countries has played, at most, a minor role in this. However, more recent econometric research based on the notion of *outsourcing*, where firms

* We are extremely grateful to Mary O'Mahony for supplying us with *Census of Production* and capital stock data. We are in debt to two anonymous referees and one Managing Editor of the *Bulletin of Economic Research* whose comments and efforts substantially improved the paper, but any errors remain the responsibility of the authors. This research forms part of the Globalisation and Social Exclusion project funded by the European Community under the Targeted Socio-Economic Research (TSER) Programme.

[1] See, for example, the summer 1995 and spring 1997 issues of the *Journal of Economic Perspectives*.

reduce costs by moving low-skill-intensive production activities to low-wage countries, does find a significant impact of trade on the relative employment and wages of unskilled workers in the USA (Feenstra and Hanson, 1995, 1996). Casual but direct evidence also suggests that outsourcing plays a significant role in modern production. For example, Nike employs just 2500 persons in the USA for marketing and other headquarters services, whereas about 75 000 persons are employed in Asia producing shoes that are sold to Nike; and General Electric currently *imports* all of the microwaves marketed under its brandname from Samsung in Korea (Magaziner and Patinkin, 1989). Outsourcing is also claimed to be an important activity in industries such as footwear (Yoffie and Gomes-Casseres, 1994, case 7), textiles[2] (Waldinger, 1986; Gereffi, 1993), and electronics (Alic and Harris, 1991). Many of the above examples – such as the General Electric case – also illustrate that outsourcing applies to *finished* goods as well as *intermediate* inputs.[3]

In the UK the relative wages and employment of the low-skilled also fell dramatically during the 1980s. During that decade the real earnings of the top tenth of male earners in the UK rose at a rate five times faster than that of the earnings of the bottom tenth of male earners.[4] The unemployment rate of less-skilled males in the UK rose from 6.4 per cent in the mid-1970s to 18.2 per cent by the mid-1980s, whereas over the same period the unemployment rate of skilled males rose only from 2.0 per cent to 4.7 per cent (Nickell, 1996). Although the rise in UK wage inequality occurred in a number of directions, the most significant widening of relative wages has been between skilled and unskilled workers.

Research into the causes of this deterioration in the economic fortunes of the less-skilled in the UK typically finds that increased trade with the low-wage countries has had very little impact on either the employment or relative wages of low-skilled workers (e.g. Machin *et al.*, 1996; and Haskel, 1996a,b).[5] However, in this paper we follow a different approach to previous UK studies and examine the impact of outsourcing on the relative wages and employment of the less-skilled in the UK. In contrast to previous studies of the USA, which use total imports to proxy outsourcing, we separately identify imports from industrial countries, and those from low-wage countries (as outsourcing to industrial

[2] *Textile World* (1994) provides an idea of the relative level of wages in various low-wage countries in the textiles sector in 1993. For example, medium-income countries such as South Korea and Mexico have hourly compensation levels of around one-quarter to one-third of those in the USA, whereas low-income countries such as India, China and Bangladesh have average textile wage rates under 5 per cent of US levels.

[3] Slaughter (1995) finds that multinational outsourcing contributed very little to the increase in wage inequality in the USA. Differences in the definition of outsourcing partly explain why the results of Feenstra and Hanson differ from those of Slaughter.

[4] Source: *OECD Employment Outlook*, July 1993, pp. 157–84, Table 5.3.

[5] The work of Wood (1994) is one obvious major exception.

countries is unlikely directly to adversely effect the relative fortunes of unskilled workers). In Anderton and Brenton (1998a) we showed that during the 1980s and early 1990s the low-wage countries increased their shares of UK imports across a whole range of sectors, including those typically treated as skilled intensive, such as machinery, but that this growth was uneven across industries. Hence we also investigate whether the impact of outsourcing has been the same across both skilled and unskilled-intensive sectors.

II. THEORETICAL FRAMEWORK AND METHOD

II.1. Theoretical framework

Two main explanations are frequently offered for the apparent shift in demand away from low-skilled workers in industrial countries, which, it is commonly perceived, has contributed to an increase in wage inequality in countries with relatively flexible labour markets (the USA and the UK) and a rise in unemployment for such workers in countries with more rigid labour markets (continental Europe). Firstly, it is suggested that skill-biased labour-saving technical progress has reduced the relative demand for unskilled workers; and second, that increased international trade with nations with an abundant supply of low-skill and low-wage labour has decreased the demand for low-skilled workers in the advanced industrialized countries. Standard trade theory suggests that both of these factors could be responsible for the decline in the fortunes of low-skilled workers in industrial countries and that empirical analysis is required to identify the relative importance of each.[6]

Traditional trade theories primarily explain movements in relative wages *across* industries, whereas what also needs to be explained is the dramatic fall in the relative wages and employment of unskilled workers *within* sectors. Indeed, the observed shift away from the use of unskilled labour within industries is in contradiction with trade being the cause of rising inequality in the traditional model. If trade with low-wage countries has reduced the relative wage of unskilled labour, then firms within all sectors have an incentive to use relatively more of this now cheaper factor. This has led a number of authors to conclude by deduction that biased technological change must be the principal cause of the shift away from the use of unskilled labour. However, the impact of globalization appears to be more complicated than is allowed for within the confines of standard factor proportions trade theory. We need to look more carefully at how firms within sectors respond to the more

[6] For a review of the standard Hecksher–Ohlin and Stolper–Samuelson issues concerning the links between trade and relative wages, see Brenton (1998).

intense competition provided by increased imports from low-wage countries.

One explanation of how trade with low-wage countries may push down the relative wages and employment of unskilled workers *within* industries is provided by the notion of 'outsourcing'. Outsourcing occurs where firms take advantage of both the low-wage costs of relatively labour-abundant countries and modern production techniques whereby the process of manufacturing a product can be broken down into a number of discrete activities – by moving the low-skill-intensive parts of production abroad, but continue to carry out the high-skill-intensive activities themselves.[7] Once the low-skill activities have been performed the goods are then imported back from the low-wage countries and either used as intermediate inputs or sold as finished goods. Hence, trade with the low-wage countries via this route will shift employment away from less-skilled towards skilled workers in countries such as the UK, and put downward pressure on the relative wages and employment of low-skilled workers *within* industries.

Feenstra and Hanson (1995) used industry import shares – imports as a share of consumption in each industry – as a proxy for outsourcing in the USA, and the share of non-production workers in the total wage bill to proxy the relative demand for skilled workers in each industry. Using these variables, Feenstra and Hanson estimate that the growth of imports over the period 1979–87 explains 15–50 per cent of the increase in the share of non-production labour in the USA. In this paper, we seek to assess empirically whether outsourcing has been an important phenomenon in the UK. We concentrate on the relative pay and employment of UK non-manual and manual workers in two broad sectors, textiles and non-electrical machinery. In common with most studies on this issue we define non-manual workers as skilled and manual workers as less-skilled. Textiles are typically seen as requiring the intensive use of unskilled labour, whilst the production of non-electrical machinery is usually treated as using relatively large inputs of skilled labour. Figures 1 and 2 below show the proportions of the total wage bill and total employment accounted for by non-manual workers in our two sectors for the sample period 1970–86. The charts clearly show that in both sectors non-manual workers increased their share of the wage bill and employment during the sample period.

Our approach is to estimate econometrically the impact of outsourcing using a proxy variable similar to Feenstra and Hanson's (1996). However, they proxy outsourcing by the share of imports in total

[7] 'Moving the low-skill-intensive parts of production abroad' does not necessarily mean that the firm is involved in outward foreign direct investment; it can also mean that the low-skill parts of production are closed down and replaced by imports, of intermediate or finished goods, from low-wage countries.

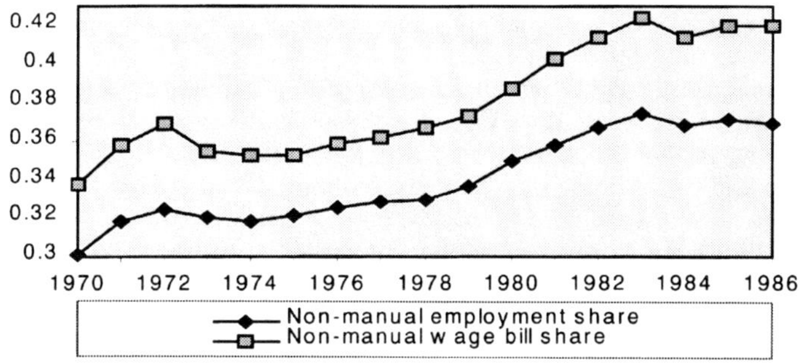

Fig. 1. Non-electrical machinery production

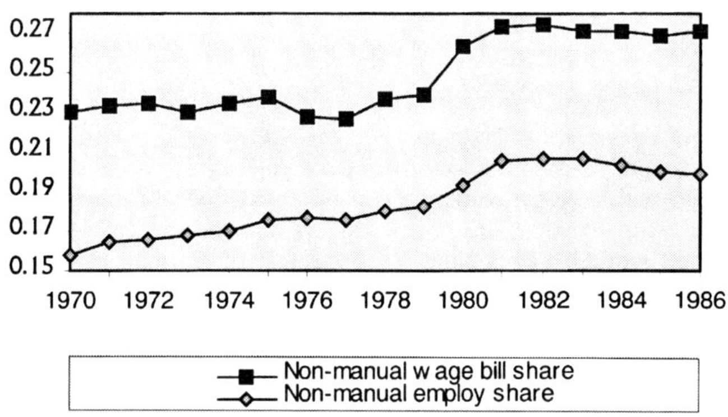

Fig. 2. Textiles production

USA consumption from *all* countries, which implicitly captures the outsourcing of USA production to advanced industrialized countries as well as to the low-wage countries. On the other hand, there is no obvious reason why firms would outsource *low-skill-intensive* activities, which is a key mechanism by which outsourcing may affect the demand for the less-skilled, to advanced industrialized countries which are relatively abundant in skilled labour. Consequently, in this paper we examine whether the source of imports matters. We therefore disaggregate UK imports according to individual supplier countries and construct an import share term for different groups of countries – i.e. industrialized and low-wage countries – for each four-digit industry within the broader categories of textiles and non-electrical machinery. Thus, we explicitly identify imports *solely from low-wage countries* and use this as a variable for explaining changes in the relative wages and employment of the low-skilled in the UK, and thereby more accurately proxy outsourcing to low-wage countries.

We also investigate two other closely related hypotheses. First, given that one might expect low-skill-intensive industries (such as textiles) to be more prone to outsourcing than high skill-intensive sectors, we investigate whether the degree of outsourcing differs across industries. Second, we also consider whether the large appreciation of sterling in the early 1980s had a disproportionate impact on outsourcing owing to factors such as switching costs (i.e. if there are costs involved in moving from domestic sources of supply to a foreign source then a large appreciation of the currency of the importing country may result in a price differential *vis-à-vis* low-wage country suppliers which is large enough to compensate for the switching costs), and whether this mechanism has any impact on the economic fortunes of the less-skilled by increasing the 'threat' of outsourcing.

II.2. Econometric analysis

Following Feenstra and Hanson (1995, 1996), we seek to assess whether industry import shares have contributed significantly to the determination of the within-sector relative wages of low-skilled workers in the UK. We also estimate equations which explain the relative employment of low-skilled workers. Following the approach of Berman *et al.* (1993, 1994), and assuming capital to be a fixed factor of production, we start from a variable cost function in translog form:

$$\begin{aligned}\ln C_i = {} & \alpha_0 + \alpha_Y \ln Y_i + \tfrac{1}{2}\alpha_{YY} \ln(Y_i)^2 + \beta_K \ln K_i + \tfrac{1}{2}\beta_{KK} \ln(K_i)^2 \\ & + \sum_j \gamma_j \ln W_{ij} + \frac{1}{2}\sum_j \sum_k \gamma_{jk} \ln W_{ij} \ln W_{ik} + \sum_j \delta_{YJ} \ln Y_i \ln W_{ij} \\ & + \sum_j \delta_{KJ} \ln K_i \ln W_{ij} + \rho \ln Y_i \ln K_i + \lambda_T T_i \\ & + \frac{1}{2}\lambda_{TT} T_i^2 + \lambda_{YT} T_i \ln Y_i + \lambda_{KT} T_i \ln K_i + \sum_j \phi_{iwj} T_i \ln W_{ij} \qquad (1)\end{aligned}$$

where C_i is variable costs in industry i, Y_i is output in industry i, K_i is the capital stock in industry i, W_{ij} is the price of variable factor j, and T represents technology in industry i.

Cost minimization generates the following linear equations for the factor shares (S):

$$S_{ij} = \alpha_j + \delta_{Yj} \ln Y_i + \delta_{Kj} \ln K_i + \sum_K \gamma_{jk} \ln W_{ik} + \phi_{iwj} T_i. \qquad (2)$$

Finally, differencing (denoted by d) generates

$$dS_{ij} = \phi_{iwj} dT_i + \delta_{Yj} d \ln Y_i + \delta_{Kj} d \ln K_i + \sum_k \gamma_{jk} d \ln W_{ik}. \qquad (3)$$

Assuming homogeneity of degree one in prices imposes

$$\sum_K \gamma_{iK} = \sum_j \gamma_{iK} = \sum_j \delta_{iK} = \sum_j \delta_{Yj} = 0 \qquad (4)$$

which generates, with two variable factors j and k:

$$dS_{ij} = \phi_{ij} dT_i + \delta_{Kj} d \ln K_i + \delta_{Yj} d \ln Y_i + \gamma d \ln(W_j / W_k). \qquad (5)$$

In our empirical application of the above model we have two variable factors of production, low-skilled (manual) workers and higher-skilled (non-manual) workers, and adopt a similar approach to Machin *et al.* (1996) by estimating the following wage-bill share equation using disaggregated industry data pooled over both time and 11 four-digit industries:

$$dSW_{it} = \alpha d \ln K_{it} + \beta d \ln Y_{it} + \rho (R\&D/Y)_{it-1} + \lambda d \ln MS_{it} + \gamma D_{it} + U_{it} \qquad (6)$$

where WB_{it}^{hs} is the wage bill of the higher skilled, WB_{it}^{ls} is the wage bill of the lower skilled, and SW_{it} is the share of the wage bill of the higher skilled (i.e. $WB_{it}^{hs}/(WB_{it}^{hs} + WB_{it}^{ls})$). $R\&D_{it-1}$ is research and development expenditure which is included as a proxy for technological change, MS_{it} is the share of the value of domestic demand for the output of industry i accounted for by imports, D_{it} is a set of time dummies included to capture any company preferences for non-manual or manual workers common across industries for a given year, and U is an error term.

The MS term is included to capture the impact of outsourcing at the industry level. Following the discussion above, in addition to including the share of *total* imports we also disaggregate imports by their source and experiment with two other versions of MS:

- MSI = imports from industrialized countries;
- MSV = imports from the NICs and very-low wage countries, that is, Singapore, S. Korea, Taiwan, Hong Kong plus the former Comecon countries, China and other Asian developing countries, Latin America and African countries.

Feenstra and Hanson justify the inclusion of the MS term in the wage-bill share equation by arguing that merely including the factors derived from a traditional translog cost function will not capture other factors, such as outsourcing, which may influence a firm's demand for skilled labour. Given that outsourcing to low-wage countries is claimed to push the range of activities performed by domestic industry away from low-skill towards high-skill tasks, the MS term can be interpreted as representing a reduced-form relationship between outsourcing and a firm's unit input requirement for skilled labour.[8]

Note that our wage-bill share equation does not include the relative wage rates for the two types of labour, mainly because relative wages are unlikely to be exogenous and there is also the problem of the definitional relationship between the dependent variable (the share of the wage bill) and the relative wage term. In addition to the wage share equations we also estimate the following employment share equation:

$$dSE_{it} = \alpha d\ln K_{it} + \beta d\ln Y_{it} + \rho(R\&D/Y)_{it-1} + \lambda d\ln MS_{it} + \omega d\ln RW_{it} + \gamma D_{it} + U_{it} \quad (7)$$

where SE_{it} is the share of high-skilled workers in total employment in sector *i*, and RW_{it} is the wage of the high-skilled workers relative to the low-skilled. Although the derivation of this equation is less satisfactory from a theoretical point of view, it should provide interesting empirical insights in addition to the wage bill equations and allows us to compare our results with those of previous studies, such as Machin *et al.* (1996), who also estimate employment share equations.

II.3. Data

We use disaggregated wage and employment data, taken from the UK *Census of Production* and converted to the International Standard Industrial Classification (ISIC), for the two broad UK sectors, textiles and non-electrical machinery. Changes in technology are proxied by expenditures on R&D as a proportion of GDP (source: OECD ANBERD database). The capital stock data are from O'Mahoney *et al.* (1994), whilst imports and domestic production are taken from the bilateral trade dataset derived by Brenton and Winters (1992). The period of analysis is 1970 to 1986. The trade, production, employment and wage data are all obtained at the four-digit level of the ISIC and the period of analysis is 1970 to 1986. In order to provide sufficient observations for estimation, we pool the data across 11 ISIC sectors (six in the textiles industry and five in the non-electrical machinery production industry) and apply panel estimation techniques. Given that we lose one observation because we estimate a first-difference model, our estimation period 1971–86 therefore provides us with 176 observations. Estimates including the R&D term are based on 143 observations over the sample period 1974–86 (as the R&D data only begin in 1973).[9]

[8] However, a more rigorous derivation of equation (6) could begin by including either labour in low-wage countries as another factor of production, or outsourced intermediate goods (represented in either price or quantity terms) in the cost function. Such an approach is beyond the scope of this paper, but we hope to carry out a more complete derivation in future work.

[9] A more comprehensive description of the data are available in Anderton and Brenton (1998b), and the Appendix provides details of the 11 four-digit sectors.

III. EMPIRICAL RESULTS

We begin by examining the importance of our different measures of import penetration in explaining changes in the share of the wages and employment of the higher-skilled in the UK textiles and non-electrical machinery sectors. We first estimate our basic equations (6) and (7) using *total* import penetration, but we exclude the R&D term from our specifications (owing to apparent multicollinearity with the capital stock term – this is discussed in more detail below). The results, shown in columns 1a in Tables 1 and 2 for the wage-bill and employment share specifications respectively, suggest that total import penetration has not significantly affected changes in the relative wages and employment of the low-skilled in our limited sample of UK sectors. We then investigate the role of imports from specific groups of countries by experimenting with our import penetration measures for industrial and low wage countries. We consistently find that only the import penetration term for the low-wage countries is positively signed and statistically significant (a positive sign means that an increase in import penetration from low-wage countries pushes down the relative wage bill and employment shares of the less-skilled).[10] For example, the results in columns 1c of Tables 1 and 2 show that imports from the low-wage countries (*MSV*) have a statistically significant influence on the share of the wage income and employment of the less-skilled, whereas the results in columns 1b show that imports from the industrialized countries (*MSI*) have no effect on the relative economic fortunes of the less-skilled. Both sets of results are therefore consistent with our *a priori* expectations regarding the impact of outsourcing.

Our results therefore differ from those of Feenstra and Hanson (1995, 1996) – who find a significant role for *total* imports in explaining wage inequality in the US – as we demonstrate that for the UK it is important to disaggregate UK imports according to the country of origin. However, the difference between these two sets of results may be explained by differences in the structure of trade for the two countries. For example, almost one-half of total US imports currently come from non-industrial countries, whilst only 24 per cent of UK imports came from these countries. So, even though low-wage countries typically comprise a relatively small share of UK imports, increased trade with these countries appears to have had a significant impact on the relative wage and employment opportunities of the less-skilled.

The wage-bill share equations (Table 1) show that a change in output is negatively signed and a change in the capital stock is positively signed, but

[10] This was true for all of the specifications shown in Tables 1 to 4.

TABLE 1

Wage-bill share equations (dSW_{it})

Equation	*(1a)*	*(1b)*	*(1c)*	*(2)*
C	0.32×10^{-2}	0.31×10^{-2}	0.32×10^{-2}	0.12×10^{-3}
	(0.75)	(0.72)	(0.75)	(0.03)
$d \ln Y_{it}$	-0.34×10^{-2}	-0.59×10^{-2}	-0.63×10^{-2}	-0.81×10^{-2}
	(0.42)	(0.73)	(1.03)	(1.28)
$d \ln K_{it}$	0.097	0.093	0.089	—
	(1.09)	(1.03)	(1.04)	
$(R\&D/Y)_{it-1}$	—	—	—	0.143
				(1.06)
$d \ln MS_{it}$	0.013	—	—	
	(1.21)			
$d \ln MSI_{it}$	—	0.75×10^{-2}	—	—
		(0.71)		
$d \ln MSV_{it}$	—	—	0.014	0.015
			(3.23)	(3.25)
N	176	176	176	143
R^2	0.2999	0.2957	0.3374	0.3309
SEE	0.01332	0.01336	0.01296	0.01325

Notes: (i) OLS estimation (full set of time dummies included); (ii) t-statistics are in parentheses; (iii) C=intercept; SW_{it}= non-manual wage bill in sector i; Y_{it} = real output in sector i; K_{it}=capital stock for sector i; $(R\&D/Y)_{it-1}$ = R&D expenditure divided by nominal GDP for sector i; MS_{it}=value of total UK imports divided by UK domestic sales plus total imports for sector i; MSI_{it}=as for MS but only imports from advanced industrialised countries; MSV_{it}=as for MS but only for imports from the NICs and the very low-wage countries; SE_{it}=employment of non-manual relative to manual workers in sector i; RW_{it}=wage rate of non-manual workers relative to manual workers in sector i.

both variables are not statistically significant.[11] The signs for these two variables conform with our priors as we expect complementarities between capital and skill and a short-run decline in output tends to hurt the wages and employment of the less-skilled relative to the skilled.[12] Furthermore, the employment share equation (Table 2) shows that an increase in the

[11] F-tests on our basic specifications show that we can jointly restrict both the intercept and slope parameters to be equal across all of the sectors at the 5 per cent level of significance, hence panel estimation by pooling the data across all 11 sectors is acceptable. For example, the F-tests for equation (1) are [$F(40,132)=1.2857$] and [$F(50,121)=1.1093$)] for the wage-bill and employment share equations, respectively (these are the F-tests for the unrestricted versus the pooled specifications as we test whether $A, B = A_i, B_i$, where A represents the intercept and B the slope parameter).

[12] Kraft (1994) argues that the ratio of skilled to unskilled workers will vary counter-cyclically because skilled workers will be retained by a firm during a recession because they are costly to train. Hence, primarily unskilled workers will be laid-off during a recession.

TABLE 2
Employment share equations (dSE_{it})

Equation	*(1a)*	*(1b)*	*(1c)*	*(2)*
C	0.41×10^{-2}	0.39×10^{-2}	0.41×10^{-2}	0.14×10^{-3}
	(1.28)	(1.23)	(1.36)	(0.41)
$d \ln Y_{it}$	0.12×10^{-2}	-0.17×10^{-2}	0.28×10^{-3}	-0.11×10^{-2}
	(0.21)	(0.29)	(0.06)	(0.22)
$d \ln K_{it}$	0.071	0.064	0.067	—
	(1.07)	(0.95)	(1.07)	
$d \ln RW_{it}$	−0.041	−0.041	−0.037	−0.049
	(2.25)	(2.22)	(2.13)	(2.38)
$(R\&D/Y)_{it-1}$		—	—	0.119
				(1.19)
$d \ln MS_{it}$	0.88×10^{-2}	—	—	
	(1.11)			
$d \ln MSI_{it}$	—	-0.27×10^{-2}	—	—
		(0.34)		
$d \ln MSV_{it}$	—	—	0.013	0.013
			(4.06)	(3.83)
N	176	176	176	143
R^2	0.2592	0.2539	0.3247	0.3099
SEE	0.00987	0.00993	0.00942	0.00991

See the notes under Table 1.

relative wages of skilled workers does indeed decrease the relative demand for skilled workers. In general, the equations perform fairly well with an R^2 usually exceeding those reported in Machin *et al.* (1996).[13]

Columns 2 in Tables 1 and 2 shows the results when we include the R&D technology proxy along with the *MSV* term, but we exclude the capital stock term as the inclusion of both terms tends to decrease the *t*-statistic of both variables (possibly owing to multicollinearity).[14] It can

[13] In general, we experiment with various versions of key variables (i.e. lagging variables or using log versions, etc.) and the results reported in the tables are for the best performing versions. For example, we experimented with equations (6) and (7) by using a non-logged version of the import penetration term. The non-logged *MSV* import penetration terms remained strongly significant with parameters (*t*-statistics) of 0.4368 (2.28) and 0.4446 (3.18) for the wage-bill and employment shares, respectively, and the parameters and *t*-statistics of the other variables in the equation remained virtually unchanged (however, in subsequent equations we prefer to use the logged version of the *MSV* term as this delivers a higher R^2).

[14] Consequently our procedure throughout this paper is to show the results including the capital stock and R&D terms separately, not together. This procedure has the added advantage that whenever we exclude the R&D terms we also benefit from a longer sample period.

be seen that the R&D term has a positive sign in both specifications which is consistent with the idea that skill-biased labour-saving technological progress has damaged the relative economic fortunes of the less-skilled – but it is not statistically significant (although the t-statistic is usually above 1). Again, the low-wage country import penetration term is strongly significant and positively signed regardless of whether or not the R&D term is included.

Our earlier tests showed that it is acceptable to impose a common slope parameter across all of the different sectors, but this is a joint test of *all* of the slope parameters and it may be the case that some of the parameters differ between the textiles and non-electrical machinery production industries. Therefore, in contrast with previous empirical studies in this area, which usually assume that trade with low-wage countries affects all industries equally, we examine whether there are differences across sectors. In particular, we investigate whether non-electrical machinery production is less prone to outsourcing relative to the textile industry (which is possible given that textiles is usually viewed as low-skill-intensive and machinery as high-skill-intensive).

The first two columns in Tables 3 and 4 show estimates of equations (6) and (7) (the first including the capital stock, the second with the R&D term) but with a dummy variable for import penetration from low-wage countries in non-electrical machinery production (that is, $d \ln MSV_{nem,t} = d \ln MSV_{it}$ multiplied by a dummy variable with a value of 1 for non-electrical machinery production sectors and 0 otherwise). Both the wage bill and employment share equations show a negative parameter for $d \ln MSV_{nem,t}$ suggesting that non-electrical machinery production may be less prone to outsourcing relative to textiles. The parameter on $d \ln MSV_{nem,t}$ is roughly half the magnitude of that on the aggregate $d \ln MSV_{it}$ term (however, it should be noted that $d \ln MSV_{nem,t}$ is only sometimes statistically significant at the 10 per cent level).[15]

We also investigated the impact of import *prices* by replacing the import penetration variable (MSV) with disaggregated *relative price* (RP) terms; i.e. the price of UK imports relative to the UK domestic price for the same product broken down into the same three categories as the import penetration terms (total imports, imports from industrial countries and imports from low-wage countries).[16] None of the relative price terms was statistically significant. Thus, whilst we find that the

[15] If we replace the non-electrical machinery dummy with a textiles dummy we obtain the expected *positive* sign.

[16] The relative price term can be interpreted as representing price incentives to outsource. We expect such a term to have a negative sign as a decline in the price of imports from low-wage countries relative to UK domestic prices may encourage outsourcing to low-wage countries, thereby decreasing the demand for less-skilled relative to high-skilled workers. The price of imports is, as usual, proxied by the unit value (value per tonne), whilst domestic prices are derived from producer price information.

TABLE 3
Wage-bill share equations (dSW_{it})

Equation	(1)	(2)	(3)	(4)
C	0.34×10^{-3}	-0.81×10^{-4}	0.38×10^{-2}	-0.13×10^{-2}
	(0.81)	(0.18)	(0.94)	(0.29)
$d \ln Y_{it}$	-0.66×10^{-2}	-0.86×10^{-2}	-0.61×10^{-2}	-0.82×10^{-2}
	(1.09)	(1.38)	(1.01)	(1.33)
$d \ln K_{it}$	0.106	—	0.138	—
	(1.22)		(1.60)	
$(R\&D/Y)_{it-1}$	—	0.191	—	0.219
		(1.38)		(1.62)
$d \ln MSV_{it}$	0.018	0.020	0.016	0.019
	(3.23)	(3.48)	(3.11)	(3.34)
$d \ln RPV80_{tx,t}$	—	—	−0.065	−0.061
			(2.71)	(2.55)
$d \ln MSV_{nem,t}$	-0.91×10^{-2}	−0.013	-0.79×10^{-2}	−0.012
	(1.15)	(1.45)	(1.03)	(1.33)
N	176	143	176	143
R^2	0.3429	0.3419	0.3728	0.3744
SEE	0.01295	0.01319	0.01269	0.01291

Notes: $d \ln MSV_{nem,t} = d \ln MSV_{it}$ multiplied by a dummy variable with a value of 1 for non-electrical machinery sectors and 0 otherwise; $d \ln RPV80_{tx,t} = d \ln RPV_{i,t}$ multiplied by a dummy variable with a value of 1 for textile sectors in 1980 and 0 otherwise.

quantity of imports from low-wage countries affects relative wages and employment for the low-skilled in the UK, import prices do not seem to matter.[17]

However, given that Figures 1 and 2 show a distinctly large increase in inequality in the early 1980s, we also investigated whether there was a disproportionate response to the decline in relative import prices resulting from the large appreciation of sterling at this time.[18] If there

[17] This may be due to changes in product *quality* factors. For example, in the earlier stages of product development, 'learning by doing' may enable low-wage countries to increase the quality of their products without changing product prices and thereby encourage an increase in UK imports of their manufactures. Hence, the correlation between changes in import prices and changes in imports of low-wage country products might be weak (whereas the import penetration term provides a more accurate measure of how successfully low-wage country products are competing with UK products).

[18] Between the first quarter of 1979 and the first quarter of 1981, the sterling effective exchange rate rose by around 30 per cent, but, by the end of 1983, virtually all of the appreciation had been reversed (i.e. the annual value of the effective exchange rate was almost exactly the same in both 1979 and 1983). Anderton and Brenton (1998c) show that the rise in inequality in the USA in the early 1980s was associated with the dramatic rise in the dollar.

TABLE 4

Employment share equations (dSE_{it})

Equation	*(1)*	*(2)*	*(3)*	*(4)*
C	-0.44×10^{-2}	-0.81×10^{-3}	0.49×10^{-2}	0.48×10^{-2}
	(1.46)	(0.08)	(1.65)	(0.15)
$d \ln Y_{it}$	-0.32×10^{-4}	-0.16×10^{-2}	0.56×10^{-4}	-0.99×10^{-3}
	(0.01)	(0.33)	(0.001)	(0.22)
$d \ln K_{it}$	0.084	—	0.111	—
	(1.33)		(1.79)	
$d \ln RW_{it}$	−0.035	−0.048	−0.031	−0.043
	(2.01)	(2.37)	(1.87)	(2.19)
$(R\&D/Y)_{it-1}$	—	0.159	—	0.183
		(1.54)		(1.82)
$d \ln MSV_{it}$	0.017	0.018	0.016	0.017
	(4.24)	(4.04)	(4.16)	(3.93)
$d \ln RPV80_{tx,t}$	—	—	−0.051	−0.052
			(3.21)	(2.92)
$d \ln MSV_{nem,t}$	-0.97×10^{-2}	−0.011	-0.89×10^{-2}	-0.97×10^{-2}
	(1.70)	(1.61)	(1.59)	(1.49)
N	176	143	176	143
R^2	0.3370	0.3241	0.3787	0.3676
SEE	0.00936	0.00985	0.00909	0.00957

See the notes under Table 3.

are *switching costs* involved in moving from a domestic source of supply to a foreign source (note that the 'domestic supply' includes components and semi-finished products made in-house), then a large appreciation may result in a substantial price differential between these competing sources sufficient to cover these costs and encourage a disproportionate rise in outsourcing (alternatively, the increased price differential may be sufficient to compensate for product quality differences between low-wage countries and the UK).[19] We therefore replaced the import penetration variables in our basic wage-share and employment equations with terms comprising the relative price multiplied by annual dummies from 1978 onwards. Again the relative price effects did not have a statistically significant impact upon wage-bill or employment shares. However, a particularly large negative effect, sometimes statistically significant at the 10 per cent level, was found for the year 1980 which

[19] For example, producers will incur costs if they have to change or modify their machinery or production techniques when switching from domestically supplied goods to foreign goods. Furthermore, such a change will be difficult to reverse even if the large appreciation is fully reversed as UK producers are now familiar with the quality of goods not previously imported.

represents the peak of the sterling appreciation (again, this was only for the term capturing the relative price of imports from *low-wage* countries).

Given that the UK textile industry was particularly badly hit by the appreciation of sterling in the early 1980s,[20] we tested for differences in relative price elasticities across sectors by re-estimating our equations and incorporating a single 1980 relative price dummy for the textiles industry alone (i.e. $d \ln RPV80_{tx,t} = d \ln RPV$, the relative price of imports from low-wage countries, multiplied by a dummy variable with a value of 1 for the textile sectors in 1980 and 0 otherwise). The $d \ln RPV80_{tx,t}$ term was statistically significant and indicates that the textile industry may have been disproportionately affected by outsourcing owing to the large deterioration in UK relative price competitiveness against low-wage countries in the early 1980s.[21] Of course, this effect should be picked up (at least partly) by an increase in the import penetration term, so we then added the $d \ln RPV80_{tx,t}$ term to equations 1 and 2 of Tables 3 and 4 to see whether the relative price term was still significant even when the import penetration term is included, and the results are shown in columns 3 and 4.[22] The $d \ln RPV80_{tx,t}$, and $d \ln MSV$ terms are both statistically significant, suggesting that the relative price term captures other effects in addition to the increase in import penetration. It may be the case that the relative price term in columns 3 and 4 captures the 'threat' of increased competition from low-wage countries (and the associated 'threat' of increased opportunities for reducing labour costs via outsourcing) arising from the large appreciation of sterling. Therefore, as an alternative to reducing labour costs by outsourcing, this increased 'threat' may have encouraged other firms to implement measures which restrain the wages – and perhaps terminate the employment – of less-skilled workers in order to remain competitive against low-wage countries. At the same time, the 'threat' of outsourcing may have made it considerably easier for firms to obtain the agreement of their workforce for the implementation of such measures.

IV. COMPARISONS WITH PREVIOUS WORK

Feenstra and Hanson (1995, 1996) conclude that outsourcing may explain 15–50 per cent of the increase in the wage bill share of skilled

[20] Anderton (1997) shows that approximately one quarter of a million jobs were lost between 1979 and 1984 in the UK textiles sector.

[21] A similar term for the non-electrical machinery sectors was not statistically significant.

[22] It is worth noting that the capital stock and R&D terms both become statistically significant at the 10 per cent level in the employment share equation when these sector-specific dummies are included. Thus, equation (4) in Table 4 suggests that investment in R&D, which proxies technological change, may also explain some of the decline in the relative employment opportunities of low-skilled workers in these sectors.

workers in the USA. For, the period 1970 83 (Figures 1 and 2 show that most of the change in the relative wages and employment of the less-skilled in the UK occurred between these dates), we estimate that outsourcing may account for around 40 per cent of the rise in the wage-bill share of skilled workers and approximately one-third of the increase in their employment share in the UK textiles sector.[23]

In contrast to our results, neither Haskel (1996a,b) nor Machin *et al.* (1996) find a significant impact of trade on the wage-bill share and relative employment of the less-skilled in the UK. However, neither study uses trade data which separately identifies imports from low-wage countries, nor do they test for differences across sectors.[24] Haskel (1996a,b) and Machin *et al.* (1996) conclude that technology and changes in labour market institutions explain the bulk of the declines in the economic fortunes of the less-skilled in the UK (both studies find that declines in union density are associated with a decline in the relative employment and wage-bill share of less-skilled workers). However, one might argue that the bulk of the decline in the relative employment of the less-skilled occurred too early in the 1980s to be caused by a decline in union power proxied by the fall in union density. Indeed it seems more plausible that the decline in trade union density was the *outcome* of the relative employment decline of production workers, which begs the question as to what caused the job losses of the less-skilled in the UK in the early 1980s. This paper suggests that 'outsourcing' to low-wage countries provides a significant part of the answer.

In this paper we have demonstrated that imports from low-wage countries are associated with a decline in the relative demand, and a fall in the wage-bill share, for less-skilled labour within UK manufacturing sectors. But it is beyond the scope of this paper to identify to what extent this, and other sources of changes in demand for the less-skilled, have influenced the wage premium of the skilled. The latter is a *general equilibrium* consequence that depends on, for example, the specialization of the economy or the sector where technological change occurs (see Haskel and Slaughter, 1998). Further work is therefore required to integrate concepts such as outsourcing into a general equilibrium analysis of the rise in wage inequality in the UK.

[23] For simplicity these calculations are based upon the change in the non-logged *MSV* term between 1970 and 1983, and then multiplying this value by the appropriate parameter (i.e. 0.4368 and 0.4446 for the wage-bill and employment shares, respectively) and expressing this as a proportion of the change in the wage bill and employment shares of non-production workers in the Textiles sector during the same period.

[24] However, it should be noted that the Haskel and Machin *et al.* studies may give different results for other reasons (i.e. both studies use different sample periods; Haskel uses the New Earnings Survey Panel Dataset and Machin *et al.* use United Nations data to construct relative employment and earnings series).

V. SUMMARY

Although it should be noted that this study looks only at a small part of UK manufacturing, we do find some evidence that outsourcing may have damaged the economic fortunes of the less-skilled in the UK. We have shown that when assessing the impact of outsourcing the source of imports matters. For the UK, it seems that using aggregate imports to capture outsourcing may be misleading and that disaggregation of imports in order to identify low-wage country sources of supply is necessary. In addition, we find some evidence that low-skill sectors such as textiles are more likely to be influenced by outsourcing than higher-skill sectors and that large currency appreciations may have a disproportionate impact on the economic fortunes of the less-skilled, partly by creating an increased 'threat' of outsourcing.

National Institute of Economic and Social Research, London, UK

Centre for European Policy Studies, Brussels, Belgium

Received October 1997
Final version accepted 1 October 1998

REFERENCES

Alic, J. A. and Harris, M. C. (1991). 'Appendix: The NBER immigration, trade and labor markets data files', in: Borjas, G. and Freeman, R. (eds), *Immigration, Trade and the Labour Market*. University of Chicago Press and NBER, Chicago, pp. 407 20.

Anderton, R. (1997). 'UK trade performance and the role of product quality, innovation and hysteresis: some preliminary results', National Institute discussion paper 102.

Anderton, R. and Brenton, P. (1998a). 'Trade with the NICs and wage inequality: evidence from the UK and Germany', in: Brenton, P. and Pelkmans, J. (eds), *Global Trade and European Workers*, Macmillan, London.

Anderton, R. and Brenton, P. (1998b). 'Did outsourcing to low-wage countries hurt less-skilled workers in the UK?', in: Brenton, P. and Pelkmans, J. (eds), *Global Trade and European Workers*, Macmillan, London.

Anderton, R. and Brenton, P. (1998c). 'The dollar, trade, technology and inequality in the USA', *National Institute Economic Review*, no. 166, October.

Berman, E., Bound, J. and Griliches, Z. (1993). 'Changes in the demand for skilled labor within US manufacturing industries: evidence from the Annual Survey of Manufactures', National Bureau of Economic Research working paper 4255.

Berman, E., Bound, J. and Griliches, Z. (1994). 'Changes in the demand for skilled labor within US manufacturing: evidence from the Annual Survey of Manufactures', *Quarterly Journal of Economics*, vol. CIX, no. 2, May.

Brenton, P. (1998). 'Rising trade and falling wages: a review of the theory and the empirics', in: Brenton, P. and Pelkmans, J. (eds), *Global Trade and European Workers*, Macmillan, London.

Brenton, P. and Winters, L. A. (1992). 'Estimates of bilateral trade elasticities and their implications for the modelling of 1992', Centre for Economic Policy Research discussion paper 717.

Feenstra, R. C. and Hanson, G. H. (1995). 'Foreign investment, outsourcing and relative wages', National Bureau of Economic Research working paper 5121.

Feenstra, R. C. and Hanson, G. H. (1996). 'Globalization, outsourcing and wage inequality', *American Economic Review*, vol. 86, no. 2, pp. 240–45.

Gereffi, G. (1993). 'The role of big buyers in global commodity chains: how US retail networks affect overseas production patterns', in: Gereffi, G. and Korzeniewicz, M. (eds), *Commodity Chains and Global Capitalism*, Praeger, Westport, CT, pp. 95–122.

Haskel, J. (1996a). 'The decline in unskilled employment in UK manufacturing', Centre for Economic Policy Research discussion paper 1356.

Haskel, J. (1996b). 'Small firms, contracting-out, computers and wage inequality: evidence from UK manufacturing', Centre for Economic Policy Research discussion paper 1490.

Haskel, J. and Slaughter, M. (1998). 'Does the sector bias of skill-biased technological change explain changing wage inequality?', unpublished paper, Queen Mary and Westfield College, University of London, and Dartmouth College.

Kraft, K. (1994). 'Wage differentials between skilled and unskilled workers', *Weltwirtscaftliches Archiv*, Vol. 130(2), pp. 329–49.

Machin, S., Ryan, A. and van Reenen, J. (1996). 'Technology and changes in skill structure: evidence from a panel of international industries', Centre for Economic Policy Research discussion paper 1434.

Magaziner, K. and Patinkin, M. (1989). 'Fast heat: how Korea won the microwave war', *Harvard Business Review*, Jan/Feb, pp. 83–92.

Nickell, S. (1996). 'Unemployment and wages in Europe and North America', *The Labour Market Consequences of Technical and Structural Change* discussion paper series 6 (sponsored by the Leverhulme Trust).

O'Mahony, M., Wagner, K. and Paulsen, M. (1994). 'Changing fortunes: an industry study of British and German productivity growth over three decades', National Institute Report Series 7.

Slaughter, M. (1995). 'Multinational corporations, outsourcing, and American wage divergence', National Bureau of Economic Research working paper 5253.

Waldinger, R. D. (1986). *Through the Eye of the Needle*, New York University Press, New York.

Wood, A. (1994). *North–South Trade, Employment and Inequality: Changing Fortunes in a Skill-Driven World*. Oxford University Press, Oxford.

Yoffie, D. B. and Gomes-Casseres, B. (1994). *International Trade and Competition*, McGraw-Hill, New York.

DATA APPENDIX: FOUR-DIGIT SECTORS

We pool the data across 11 ISIC sectors (six in the textiles industry and five in the non-electrical machinery production industry) over an annual sample period from 1970 to 1986. Given that we lose one observation because we estimate a first-difference model, our estimation period 1971–86 therefore provides us with 176 observations (i.e. 16×11). Estimates including the R&D term are based on 143 observations over the sample period 1974–86 (as the R&D data begin only in 1973). The four-digit ISIC sectors used in the estimation are as follows:

ISIC3211	Spinning, weaving and finishing textiles
ISIC3212	Manufacture of made-up textile goods, except wearing apparel
ISIC3213	Knitting mills
ISIC3214	Manufacture of carpets and rugs
ISIC3215	Cordage, rope and twine industries
ISIC3219	Manufacture of textiles not elsewhere classified
ISIC3821	Manufacture of engines and turbines
ISIC3822	Manufacture of agricultural machinery and equipment
ISIC3823	Manufacture of metal and woodworking machinery
ISIC3824	Manufacture of special industrial machinery and equipment except metal and woodworking machinery
ISIC3829	Machinery and equipment except electrical not elsewhere classified.

UK data from the *Census of Production* are first classified to a common UK SIC as the data are defined in terms of the 1968 UK SIC (i.e. Minimum List Headings: MLH) for the first part of the sample period but defined in terms of the 1980 UK SIC (Activity Headings: AH) in the latter part of the sample period. Therefore, the first task is to compile consistent industry series for the whole sample period by linking the MLH and AH series. This was achieved by following the CSO's *Standard Industrial Classification Revised 1980: Reconciliation with Standard Industrial Classification 1968* (CSO, 1980) which gives the correspondence between the AH and MLH series. In cases where only a proportion of the MLH should be allocated to the appropriate AH, we calculate the relevant proportion by using the 1979 *Census of Production* data which were published on the basis of both SIC 1968 and SIC 1980 (hence we have an overlapping observation for the SIC 1968 and 1980 classifications). The second step was to 'map' the consistent UK SIC series to the above ISIC classifications (using a similar methodology to that in Anderton (1997).

Chapter 10
What's Trade Got to Do with It? Relative Demand for Skills within Swedish Manufacturing

By

Robert Anderton, Paul Brenton, and **Eva Oscarsson**

Contents:

I. Introduction

The issue of skill upgrading within the manufacturing sectors of various countries has been given much attention during the 1990's. One possible reason for the deteriorating position of unskilled workers is a shift in demand towards skilled workers. The two major competing explanations for this shift are technological change that is biased against unskilled workers and increasing international trade with low-wage countries that are abundant in unskilled workers. The relative impact of these two forces pushing industrial countries towards greater inequality is an empirical issue, which has been primarily addressed with regard to the experience of the United States, while similar work on European countries is evident only recently (Brenton and Pelkmans 1998; Greenaway and Nelson 2001). In general, there is no conclusive evidence of significant changes in the relative price of unskilled compared to skilled-intensive products in industrialized countries, as required under the standard Heckscher–Ohlin–Samuelson (HOS) model for trade with low-wage countries to affect labour-market outcomes. Similarly, factor content studies, which translate changes in the quantity

---

Remark: This research has been performed as part of the TSER project on "Globalisation and Social Exclusion". Financial support from the European Commission is gratefully acknowledged. Oscarsson has also been supported by the Swedish Foundation for International Cooperation in Research in Higher Education. We are grateful for the comments and suggestions of Par Hansson and participants at the conference on "Globalisation and Social Exclusion in the EU" at CEPS in December 2000. All views expressed in this paper are the authors' and do not necessarily reflect those held by the European Central Bank, the Centre for Economic Policy Studies or the Dept. of Economics, Stockholm University.

of trade into changes in demand for the different types of labour, generally conclude that the impact of trade, whilst not insignificant, is small relative to that of technology. Borjas et al. (1992), for example, suggest that trade accounted for only 15 per cent of the increase in inequality in the United States in the 1980s.

However, empirical studies that adopt a non-standard framework for analysis tend to apportion a bigger role to the impact of inequality. Wood (1994) argues that many of the products imported from low-wage countries have no close domestically produced substitute in the industrial countries, so that the typical approach of applying the same factor input coefficients for both imports and exports is incorrect. Accordingly, when factor input coefficients for production in the low-wage countries are used, the computed quantity of labour displaced by imports from low-wage countries in the industrial countries is of a magnitude 10 times greater than previous studies.

Meanwhile, the standard HOS approach cannot explain why much of the observed increase in the ratio of skilled to unskilled workers has occurred *within* industries.[1] One explanation for this is that technological progress has led to a splitting up of the production chain into various stages within industries and that the unskilled-intensive activities have been *'outsourced'* to low-wage countries. Feenstra and Hanson (1996) suggest that outsourcing may account for up to 50 per cent of the increase in the demand for skilled relative to unskilled workers that occurred in United States manufacturing industry in the 1980s. Anderton and Brenton (1999) conclude that outsourcing to low-wage countries may have contributed to 40 per cent of the rise in the share of wages paid to skilled workers in the UK textiles sector during the 1980s and 1990s. This latter study also showed the importance of distinguishing between imports from low-wage countries and imports from other OECD countries in empirical analysis.

This suggests that to accurately identify the impact of globalization we need to look deeply *within* broad industrial sectors. In this paper, we examine the effect of technological change and international trade on skill upgrading within the Swedish manufacturing sector. We adopt an approach that allows us to identify the impact of outsourcing. A key feature of the work is the level of industry detail in the data used for testing for the impact of trade and technology. Compared to other studies

[1] Berman et al. (1998) suggest that between 70 and 80 per cent of the increase in the wage-bill share of skilled workers in OECD countries occurred within, rather than between, industries.

which use more aggregate data, our highly detailed data may more accurately capture the within-sector adjustments in skilled and unskilled labour inputs that have occurred.

Sweden is an interesting case, since it is much smaller and more open than the United States and the United Kingdom and has implemented fundamentally different labour market policies than the latter two countries, which are typically held up as paragons of flexible labour markets. Nevertheless, all three countries have all experienced a shift away from unskilled towards skilled workers within the manufacturing sector. The paper is organized as follows. In Section II, we describe changes in the wage and employment shares of skilled and unskilled workers in Swedish manufacturing since the 1970s and the available explanations for these trends. Sections III and IV present our empirical model and the estimation results, respectively. Section V provides some concluding remarks.

II. Skill Upgrading in Swedish Manufacturing

Figure 1 shows the evolution of the share of the total wage bill for non-production workers – which in common with other studies we treat as being analogous to skilled workers – and the non-production worker share of total employment.[2] The non-production worker share of employment increased from 27 to 35 percent between 1970 and 1993, with a sharp increase from around 1990 onwards (when Sweden experienced a deep recession). The share of the total manufacturing wage bill for non-production workers increased from 36 to 43 percent during the same period.

The large proportionate change in the employment share compared to the wage-bill share of skilled workers suggests that the increase in inequality between skilled and unskilled workers in Sweden has arisen primarily in terms of employment opportunities rather than in the form of greater disparities in wages. This is confirmed by data which show that, in contrast to the United States and the United Kingdom, the relative wage of non-production to production workers in Sweden remained constant (with a premium of about 50 per cent) throughout the 1970s and 1980s and actually *fell* during the recession of the early 1990s.

[2] See Sachs and Shatz (1994) for a discussion about alternative definitions of skill levels. They argue that the use of non-production and production workers serves well as proxies for skilled and unskilled workers.

Figure 1: *Wage and Employment Shares for Non-Production Workers within Swedish Manufacturing, 1970–1993*

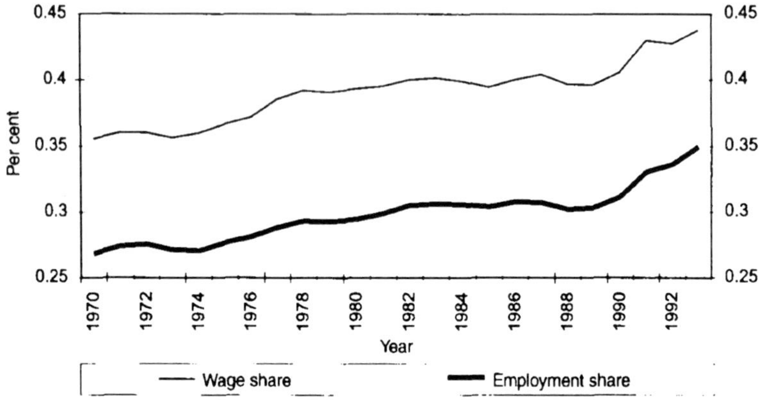

Source: Manufacturing, various issues, Statistics Sweden.

On the other hand, the ratio of non-production to production workers employed increased steadily from around 38 per cent in the mid-1970s to 45 per cent at the end of the 1980s with a big increase to 55 per cent in the early 1990s recession (Table 1).

Structural labour market rigidities may explain why most of the adjustment took place on the employment side, while relative wages remained stable. For example, the Swedish labour market is characterized by 'strong' trade unions (around 80 per cent of employees were union members in 1991; see Edin and Holmlund 1995). As is well known, wage bargaining in Sweden was highly centralized during a considerable part of our sample period. The trade unions pursued a solidarity wage policy, until the breakdown of centralized wage bargaining in 1983, with the guiding principle of equal pay for equal work irrespective of the ability to pay among firms or industries. Such an institutional framework tends to compress wage differentials between skill groups, with the result that a decrease in the relative demand for the less skilled will be reflected in a fall in relative employment rather than relative wages – which is consistent with labour market outcomes in Sweden. Accordingly, the Swedish experience appears to match the description of mainland Europe as being characterized by rigid labour markets, while the United States and United Kingdom represent flexible labour markets: declining demand for the less skilled will encourage a fall in relative wages in the United States and United Kingdom,

Table 1: *Employment Structure of the Swedish Manufacturing Sector, 1975 and 1993*

ISIC	Description	Total empl 1975	%	Rel empl NP/P	Total empl 1993	%	Rel empl NP/P
31	Food beverages and tobacco	72,076	7.8	0.33	59,583	10.9	0.38
32	Textile, wearing app and leather	57,066	6.2	0.23	12,332	2.3	0.35
33	Wood and wood products	76,758	8.3	0.20	38,427	7.1	0.25
34	Paper, paper prod, print and publishing	104,145	11.3	0.41	72,449	13.3	0.64
35	Chemicals, plastic prod and petroleum	68,372	7.4	0.53	49,376	9.1	0.74
36	Non-metallic mineral products	33,127	3.6	0.33	14,823	2.7	0.42
37	Basic metal industries	70,702	7.6	0.34	31,505	5.8	0.33
381	Fabricated metal prod except mach and equip	87,175	9.4	0.29	47,988	8.8	0.35
382	Machinery and equipment	133,164	14.4	0.48	74,534	13.7	0.70
383	El machinery, apparatus appliances and supplies	81,134	8.8	0.56	42,895	7.9	0.85
384	Transport equipment	124,963	13.5	0.41	81,840	15.0	0.51
385	Instruments and photo equipment	10,151	1.1	0.57	16,897	3.1	1.57
38	Fabricated metal prod	436,587	47.2	0.43	263,613	48.4	0.61
39	Other manufacturing	6,466	0.7	0.32	2,424	0.4	0.67
3	Manufacturing	925,299	100	0.38	544,532	100	0.54

Source: Manufacturing 1975 and 1993, Statistics Sweden.

but cause rising unemployment for the less skilled in continental Europe.[3]

Table 1 gives a more detailed sectoral overview of the Swedish manufacturing sector and shows changes in both total employment and the ratio of skilled to unskilled workers. In 1975 the Swedish manufacturing sector employed nearly one million workers, around 23 per cent of total employment. The largest 2-digit sector, measured by employment, is manufacturing of fabricated metal products followed by paper, paper products, printing and publishing.

Between 1975 and 1993, total employment in the manufacturing sector fell by 41 per cent and its share of total employment decreased to around 14 per cent. The reduction in employment was especially pro-

[3] Indeed, Hansson (2000) finds that the difference between the unemployment rates of unskilled and skilled labour (those with more than 12 years of education) had an upward sloping trend during 1970–1998.

nounced in Ship and Boat Building and Repair (ISIC 3841), where the employment of production and non-production workers decreased by 90 and 80 per cent, respectively. Another industry well known to face strong international competition is Textile, Wearing Apparel and Leather Industries (ISIC 32), where production worker employment decreased by 80 per cent and non-production worker employment by 70 per cent between 1975 and 1993. Expanding industries in terms of employment are hard to find, but examples are the low-skill-intensive industries Alcoholic Beverages (ISIC 3131), Other Paper and Board Products (ISIC 3419) and the higher-skill-intensive industries of Drugs and Medicines (ISIC 3522) and Instruments and Photo Equipment (ISIC 3851 and 3852).

Table 1 also shows that employment reductions were generally more extensive for production workers than for non-production workers. Skill upgrading was particularly evident in the high-skill sectors such as Machinery and Equipment (ISIC 382), Electrical Machinery, Apparatus Appliances and Supplies (ISIC 383) and Instruments and Photo Equipment (ISIC 385) as well as in the lower-skill sector of Textile, Wearing Apparel and Leather (ISIC 32). The pronounced skill upgrading in high-skill sectors is illustrated in Figure 2, which shows that the wage and employment share for skilled workers (i.e. non-production) increased to a greater extent within high-skill industry groups when compared to low-skill industry groups, particularly at the end of the period (1990–1993). This important feature of the Swedish experience is captured in the empirical analysis reported below.

The increase in skill intensity in Swedish manufacturing can be decomposed into a 'between industry' component and a 'within industry' component. The 'between industry' effects are caused by shifts in the relative size of skilled-intensive and unskilled-intensive sectors over time, while the 'within industry' effects are caused by skill upgrading within each industry. Previous work on the Swedish manufacturing sector has shown that the vast majority of the increased skill intensity has been generated by skill upgrading within industry and even within plants (Hansson 1997, 2000; Machin and Van Reenen 1998).[4]

International trade can cause both of these effects. The traditional explanation is that trade with low-wage countries shifts production from

---

[4] Hansson (1997) shows that the changes in employment composition within manufacturing between 1986–1993 were totally dominated by the within-plant component. An analysis of firm entry and exit shows that in Sweden in the early 1990s the share of skilled workers was higher in entering plants, while the skill share in exiting plants was about the same as in surviving plants.

Figure 2: *Wage and Employment Shares for Non-Production Workers within Swedish Manufacturing 1970–1993: High-Skill Sectors (HS) and Low-Skill Sectors (LS)*

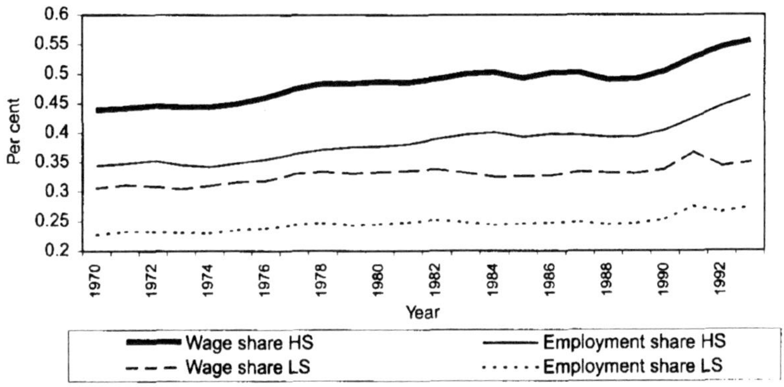

Note: High-skill industries are ISIC 342, 35, 382, 383 and 385.

Source: Manufacturing, various issues, Statistics Sweden.

unskilled-intensive sectors to sectors intensive in skilled workers via 'Stolper–Samuelson' effects (see Anderton and Brenton 1998a; Sachs and Shatz 1996). But international trade may also stimulate specialization within industries, either with respect to activities or goods through outsourcing (see Anderton and Brenton 1998b, 1999; Feenstra and Hanson 1996). An industry is composed of a whole range of production activities that vary in skill intensity and an industry can also produce a range of goods from high-skill- to low-skill-intensive goods. Outsourcing is one way for the firm to take advantage of low foreign wage costs by moving the low-skill-intensive parts of production to low-wage countries, then importing the goods back and using them either as intermediate inputs or to sell them as final goods.

In their case study analysis, Anderton and Schultz (1999) find that outsourcing of production to low-wage countries is quite common in the medical equipment industry in both Germany and the United Kingdom and that the emergence of the new democracies of eastern Europe has created further outsourcing opportunities for Germany because of the geographical proximity of these low-wage countries. With regard to more sophisticated medical equipment – such as diagnostic, monitoring and therapy equipment – it seems that the basic parts of production (such as metal casings) are sometimes outsourced to low-wage countries, while the more complex parts of the production process are performed domestically. By contrast, the domestic production by some firms of lower-tech medical equipment, such as simple surgical instruments, was frequently supplemented by importing similar finished products from low-wage countries and reselling them on the domestic market after carrying out simple tasks such as quality control procedures and packaging. Some of the price differentials in this sector are extremely large; for example, simple scalpels sold by one UK firm for 25 pounds can be purchased from Pakistani companies for 1 pound! Hence the price incentives to outsource can be quite significant.

Previous studies have found only small effects of trade on wages and employment in Sweden. Machin et al. (1996) study the period 1973–1989 and find evidence of capital-skill complementarity, meaning that increases in the wage bill and employment shares of skilled workers are positively correlated with investments in physical capital. There is also evidence of new technology and skills complementarity, where new technology is measured as the ratio of R&D expenditures to value added. In that study, over 80 per cent of the increase in the wage bill share of skilled workers is attributed to the R&D effect in Sweden. The study also finds weak evidence that import-intensive industries had a faster increase in the wage bill share of skilled workers.[5]

Hansson (2000) concludes that the decline in relative wages for skilled labour during 1970–1985 was caused by growth in the relative supply of skilled labour outstripping the relative demand.[6] Whereas during 1986–1993 both relative wages and the rate of skill upgrading increased, which suggest an increase in the relative demand for skilled labour within Swedish manufacturing. Hansson claims that this coincides with a stronger complementarity between knowledge (R&D) capital and skills, and large investments in R&D during the same period. This study also finds that the impact of intensified competition from the South (non-OECD countries) on the relative demand for skilled labour was small and the effect was limited to the textile industry.

In this paper we use an approach first introduced by Berman et al. (1994), where a reduced-form labour demand equation at the industry level is estimated. This approach was later elaborated upon by Feenstra and Hanson (1995, 1996), and has been widely used by, among others,

---

[5] In the later study by Machin and Van Reenen (1998) that result is however not statistically significant.

[6] Hansson refers to standardized relative wages for skilled and unskilled workers based on educational levels.

Machin et al. (1996), Machin and Van Reenen (1998), Anderton and Brenton (1998b, 1999) and Hansson (1997, 2000). This paper advances on existing work in this area by using highly disaggregated industry, trade, wage and employment data. The data are for individual industries at the 4 digit ISIC-level, covering 41 manufacturing industries, which allows for a far more accurate distinction between high-skill and low-skill-intensive industries in comparison to previous analyses, which focus on *broad* industrial sectors. Our trade data are also disaggregated by import supplier which, in contrast to most other studies in this area, allows us to separately identify imports from low-wage countries. In addition, we also investigate the definition and specification of the import penetration term typically used to proxy the impact of international outsourcing. Previous studies have all specified this term in *values*. By contrast, this study suggests that it is more appropriate to measure import penetration in *volume* terms. We also experiment with relative import price terms. Another innovative aspect of this study is that we use patenting activity, as well as R&D expenditure, as our proxy for new technology and innovation.

III. The Empirical Model

In this section, we outline the theoretical model underlying our empirical specifications and then econometrically estimate the impact of trade with low-wage countries and changes in technology on the Swedish wage-bill and employment shares for non-production workers. We use highly disaggregated wage, employment and production data and define non-production workers as skilled and production workers as less skilled. We experiment with two alternative proxy variables for technological change: first, patenting activity; second, R&D expenditure as a proportion of sales. The capital stock data are from Statistics Sweden. The bilateral Swedish imports data were obtained from the OECD on an SITC basis and converted to the ISIC REV2 classification. Trade, production, wage and employment data are all disaggregated to the 4-digit ISIC level (hence all variables are on an ISIC basis and further details of the 4-digit sectors used in the analysis are given in the data appendix). In order to provide enough observations for 'panel estimation', we pool the data across 4-digit ISIC sectors using annual data for the sample period 1975–1993 (imposing, in effect, the same parameters across the different 4-digit sectors).[7]

[7] More details concerning the data are given in the Appendix.

Following Feenstra and Hanson (1995, 1996), we seek to assess whether increased competition from low-wage countries has contributed significantly to the determination of the within-sector wage bill and employment shares of low-skilled workers in Sweden. We start from a variable cost function in translog form and assume capital to be a fixed factor of production (see Berman et al. 1994):

$$\begin{aligned}\ln C_i = {} & \alpha_0 + \alpha_y \ln Y_i + \frac{1}{2}\alpha_{YY} \ln (Y_i)^2 + \beta_K \ln K_i \\ & + \frac{1}{2}\beta_{KK} \ln (K_i)^2 + \sum_j \gamma_j \ln W_{ij} \\ & + \frac{1}{2}\sum_j \sum_k \gamma_{jk} \ln W_{ij} \ln W_{ik} + \sum_j \delta_{Yj} \ln Y_i \ln W_{ij} \\ & + \sum_j \delta_{Kj} \ln K_i \ln W_{ij} + \rho \ln Y_i \ln K_i + \lambda_T T_i \\ & + \frac{1}{2}\lambda_{TT}(T_i)^2 + \lambda_{YT} T_i \ln Y_i + \lambda_{KT} T_i \ln K_i \\ & + \sum_j \varnothing_{Tw_j} T_i \ln W_{ij} \end{aligned} \tag{1}$$

where C_i is variable costs in industry i,
Y_i is output in industry i,
K_i is the capital stock in industry i,
W_{ij} is the price of variable factor j and
T_i represents technology in industry i.

Cost minimization followed by differencing, and the imposition of homogeneity of degree one in prices generates the following equations for factor shares (S) in the case of two variable factors, j and k:

$$\begin{aligned} dS_{ij} = {} & \varnothing_{Tw_j} dT_i + \delta_{Kj} d \ln K_i + \delta_{Yj} d \ln Y_i \\ & + \gamma d \ln \left(\frac{W_j}{W_k} \right). \end{aligned} \tag{2}$$

In our empirical application of the above model we have two variable factors of production, low-skilled (production) workers and higher-skilled (non-production) workers, and adopt a similar approach to Machin et al. (1996) and Anderton and Brenton (1998b, 1999) and estimate the following Swedish wage bill and employment share equations:

$$dSW_{it} = \alpha d \ln K_{it} + \beta d \ln Y_{it} + \rho TECH_{it} + \lambda d \ln MS_{it} + \gamma D_t + U_{it} \quad (3)$$

$$dSE_{it} = \alpha d \ln K_{it} + \beta d \ln Y_{it} + \rho TECH_{it} + \lambda d \ln MS_{it} + \ell d \ln(W^{hs}/W^{ls})_{it} + \gamma D_t + U_{it} \quad (4)$$

where SW_{it} is the share of the wage bill of the high skilled $WB^{hs}_{it}/(WB^{hs}_{it} + WB^{ls}_{it})$,

SE_{it} is the employment share of the high skilled (similarly derived as SW_{it}),

WB^{hs}_{it} is the wage bill of the higher skilled (i.e. non-production workers),

WB^{ls}_{it} is the wage bill of the lower skilled (i.e. production workers),

W^{hs}/W^{ls} = relative wage rates of high and low-skilled workers,

K_{it} is the capital stock,

Y_{it} is real output,

$TECH_{it}$ is the proxy variable for technological change,

MS_{it} is the share of the value of domestic demand for the output of industry i accounted for by imports from low-wage countries,

D_t is a set of time dummies included to capture changes in demand for non-manual relative to manual workers common across industries for a given year,

U_{it} is an error term.

Subscript represents industry i.

Note that in the wage share equation the relative wage term is dropped due to potential endogeneity and the problem of the definitional relationship between the dependent variable (the share of the wage bill) and relative wage rates. In this paper we also experiment with patenting activity as a proxy for technological change, while previous work tends to use R&D expenditure. One advantage of using patents is that they are an *output* of the innovation process, whereas R&D expenditure is simply an expenditure *input*, which may never come to fruition in terms of practical application.

The *MS* term represents Swedish import penetration from low-wage countries and can be interpreted as a proxy for outsourcing.[8] In this paper, we follow the approach of Feenstra and Hanson (1995, 1996)

[8] Low-wage countries are defined as non-OECD countries, with the OECD taken as those members prior to 1994 (i.e. excluding recent members such as the Czech Republic, Hungary, Poland, South Korea and Mexico).

and justify the inclusion of the *MS* term in the wage bill share equation by arguing that merely including the factors derived from a traditional translog production function will not capture other factors – such as outsourcing – which may influence a firm's demand for skilled labour. Given that outsourcing to low-wage countries is claimed to push the range of activities performed by domestic industry away from low-skill towards high-skill tasks, the *MS* term can be interpreted as representing a reduced-form relationship between outsourcing and a firm's unit input requirement for skilled labour.

In this study we use data on sectoral imports from low-wage countries to capture the outsourcing of the low-skill elements of the production process. An alternative proxy is to use information on intermediate inputs from input-output tables and then multiply this by the ratio of imports to total consumption. We prefer using the direct import measure, since this also captures the outsourcing of what are measured as final products in the customs statistics. For example, footwear and clothing products are sold under brand names in Europe but produced in low-wage countries.[9] Further, in practice the variables generated by these two alternative approaches are likely to be very similar since input-output tables are compiled infrequently, typically every five years, so that all of the variation in the imported intermediate term will be due to changes in import penetration.

Most studies that use this approach specify the import penetration variable as the *value* of imports divided by the value of domestic sales plus imports and an increase in this import penetration term is then deemed to reflect greater competitive pressure from external suppliers. However, if import prices fall, the change in this import penetration value term will depend upon the magnitude of the import demand elasticities (i.e., a small elasticity will result in a *fall* in import penetration expressed in value terms). In addition, if domestic producers respond to greater import competition by increasing the quality of their products, it is feasible that greater import competition could be accompanied by a fall in import penetration in value terms.[10] By contrast, import penetration measured in volume terms does not suffer from these problems: a fall in import prices will always lead to an increase in import penetration in

[9] It might also be argued that in addition to measuring the actual amount of intermediate inputs that are imported the import penetration term captures the incentive to firms to outsource, in terms of pressure of competition in the market for the final product.

[10] That is, if the value of the denominator of the import penetration term increases due to an increase in the quality of domestic production, then an import penetration term defined in values may decline despite a rise in imports.

volume terms. Accordingly, in this study we include an index of import penetration in volume terms in our estimating equations as an alternative to the value term.

Diehl (1999) has argued that in a proper application of the cost function framework it should be the relative price of internationally outsourced products that enter the estimating equation rather than the import penetration ratio. However, in an application to German manufacturing industries Diehl concludes that the import penetration ratio (in value terms) is a better indicator of competitive pressures than relative import prices, although in his application the relative price of imported intermediate imports from all sources is used, while the import penetration variable measures only the share of low-wage countries. In an application to data for UK textiles and engineering sectors, Anderton and Brenton (1999) also find that import penetration terms provide a statistically significant contribution to rising wage inequality whilst relative import prices are insignificant. Here again we experiment with an import price term defined as the price of imports from low-wage countries relative to Swedish producer prices (PM/PD) for each ISIC sector.[11] Thus, in this paper we assess three proxies for the impact of globalization: relative import prices, import values and import quantities.

IV. Econometric Results

During our econometric analysis, we consistently found that import penetration by low-wage countries measured in value terms was not statistically significant in any of our regressions. This is consistent with previous studies of the impact of globalization in Sweden. By contrast, import penetration measured as an index of relative volumes as well as the relative price of imports from low-wage countries tend to be statistically significant throughout our analysis. By contrast, the relative price of imports from high-wage OECD countries was not statistically significant when separately included whilst, interestingly, import penetration in both value and volume terms by OECD countries was estimated to have a negative effect on the share of skilled workers in employment and total remuneration.[12] Hence, it would appear that skilled workers in

[11] Actual measures of import prices by country and sector are not available and hence, in common with most studies which use measures of trade prices, we utilize unit values (value per unit of volume) to approximate import prices. These are calculated using data (in tonnes) initially collected at the 5-digit level of the SITC.

[12] Including OECD relative prices or import penetration in volume or value terms did not qualitatively change the estimated coefficients on other explanatory variables.

Sweden are in direct competition with other skilled workers in OECD countries, whilst what matters for unskilled workers are imports from developing countries. We now present the results in detail.

Columns (A), (B) and (C) in Table 2 show our results for the initial specifications of equation (3), for the wage-bill share, whilst the first three columns of Table 3 present the analogous results for equation (4),

Table 2: *Results from the Swedish Wage-Bill Equations*

Equation	(A)	(B)	(C)	(D)	(E)	(F)	(G)
C	0.005 (2.52)	0.008 (3.81)	0.008 (4.28)	0.001 (0.33)	0.004 (1.68)	0.002 (0.85)	0.004 (1.77)
$D \ln Y_{it}$	−0.016 (2.17)	−0.023 (2.98)	−0.013 (1.75)	−0.025 (3.29)	−0.023 (2.89)	−0.022 (2.94)	−0.020 (2.55)
$D \ln K_{it}$	0.062 (3.21)	0.067 (3.42)	0.064 (3.34)	0.054 (2.84)	0.056 (2.94)	0.054 (2.87)	0.057 (2.97)
PAT/Y	0.483 (3.59)	0.447 (3.17)	0.341 (2.50)	0.455 (3.43)	0.310 (2.31)	0.402 (3.07)	0.247 (1.81)
$R\&D \times D90–93$	–	–	–	0.065 (4.31)	0.071 (4.62)	0.067 (4.44)	0.072 (4.74)
$d \ln(VM/VD)_{it}$	–	0.001 (0.25)	–	–	–	–	–
$d \ln(QM/QD)_{it}$	–	–	0.009 (4.46)	–	0.009 (4.68)	–	0.008 (3.58)
$d \ln(PM/PD)_{it}$	−0.018 (5.51)	–	–	−0.018 (5.43)	–	−0.012 (3.59)	–
$DUM_{HS} \times d \ln(QM/QD)_{it}$	–	–	–	–	–	–	0.013 (2.59)
$DUM_{HS} \times d \ln(PM/PD)_{it}$	–	–	–	–	–	−0.038 (4.81)	–
N	721	721	721	721	721	721	721
R^2	0.3320	0.305	0.3224	0.3492	0.3424	0.3702	0.3487
SEE	0.0212	0.0216	0.0213	0.02091	0.0210	0.0206	0.0209

Note: The dependent variable is dWS, the change in wage-bill share of non-production workers; (i) OLS estimation for annual data sample period of 1976–1993 (full set of time dummies included); (ii) t-statistics are in parentheses; (iii) VM/VD is import penetration in value terms while QM/QD is an index of the volume of non-OECD imports relative to the volume of domestic output, the former is measured in tonnes, the latter is derived as the value of domestic output divided by the producer price index for each sector; (iv) PM/PD = import price of goods from non-OECD countries relative to Swedish producer prices. DUM_{HS} = dummy variable with value of 1 when sector is high-skill-intensive and 0 otherwise. All regressions use the Least Squares Dummy Variables technique (LSDV) weighted by annual employment shares in manufacturing for each industry to minimize the impact of small industries. Time dummies are included but their parameter estimates are not presented here. The number of observations reflects that data for certain sectors were not available for some observations at the start of the sample period. Precise details are available from the authors upon request.

the employment share equation. We show, separately, the results with the inclusion of the relative import price and import penetration in value and volume terms. All variables except import penetration in value terms are correctly signed and significant in the wage-bill share specification. The change in output is negatively signed which is in line with our expectation that a short-run decline in output tends to reduce the demand for the less skilled relative to the skilled. The capital stock term is positively signed and confirms our prior that complementarities exist between capital and skill. Similarly, the technology term is also positively signed and statistically significant, implying that an increase

Table 3: *Results for Swedish Employment Share Equations*

Equation	(A)	(B)	(C)	(D)	(E)	(F)	(G)
C	0.007 (4.39)	0.009 (5.64)	0.009 (5.85)	0.004 (2.13)	0.006 (3.24)	0.004 (2.39)	0.006 (3.35)
$d\ln Y_{it}$	−0.002 (0.28)	−0.007 (1.12)	−0.002 (0.28)	−0.009 (1.39)	−0.009 (1.36)	−0.008 (1.22)	−0.006 (0.98)
$d\ln K_{it}$	0.042 (2.64)	0.046 (2.81)	0.045 (2.76)	0.036 (2.32)	0.039 (2.42)	0.037 (2.35)	0.039 (2.45)
$d\ln RW_{it}$	−0.071 (7.22)	−0.068 (6.75)	−0.072 (7.11)	−0.075 (7.62)	−0.076 (7.56)	−0.080 (8.10)	−0.075 (7.57)
PAT/Y	0.567 (5.10)	0.558 (4.81)	0.485 (4.28)	0.544 (4.94)	0.458 (4.08)	0.511 (4.66)	0.40 (3.50)
$R\&D \times D90\text{–}93$	–	–	–	0.049 (3.94)	0.053 (4.17)	0.051 (4.07)	0.055 (4.32)
$d\ln(VM/VD)_{it}$	–	−0.001 (0.38)	–	–	–	–	–
$d\ln(QM/QD)_{it}$	–	–	0.005 (2.73)	–	0.005 (2.96)	–	0.003 (1.81)
$d\ln(PM/PD)_{it}$	−0.013 (4.64)	–	–	−0.012 (4.58)	–	−0.009 (3.35)	–
$DUM_{HS} \times d\ln(QM/QD)_{it}$	–	–	–	–	–	–	0.013 (3.05)
$DUM_{HS} \times d\ln(PM/PD)_{it}$	–	–	–	–	–	−0.021 (3.11)	–
N	721	721	721	721	721	721	721
R^2	0.3964	0.3791	0.3844	0.4097	0.3994	0.4178	0.4073
SEE	0.0175	0.0178	0.0177	0.0173	0.0175	0.0172	0.0174

Note: The dependent variable is dES, the change in employment share of non-production workers. See also notes to Table 2.

in technology will lead to a rise in the ratio of skilled workers in the production process.

The relative price of imports from low-wage countries is also statistically significant and negatively signed, implying that a decline in the price of imports from low-wage countries relative to the price of Swedish products, results in a decline in the wage-bill and employment share of the less skilled. The import volume penetration term also has a sign consistent with our a priori expectations and is statistically significant. An increase in the quantity of imports from low-wage countries relative to the quantity of sales produced domestically raises the share of total remuneration going to skilled workers. The import value penetration term is not statistically significant.

Similar results hold for the employment share specification (columns (A)–(C) of Table 3), that is, the technology, import volume penetration and relative import price terms are statistically significant and correctly signed – with the exception that the change in output is not statistically significant. As expected, the relative wage term in the employment share equation is negatively signed and statistically significant.

Given that Sweden showed a sharp rise in both inequality and R&D expenditure during 1990–1993, we experimented by dummying the technology terms over these last few years of the sample period in order to evaluate whether or not there was an additional technology effect over these years. Although we could not find any additional effect from patenting activity, the dummied R&D term was statistically significant in both the wage-bill and employment share equations (see equations (D) and (E) in Tables 2 and 3).[13] This suggests a much stronger impact of technology on inequality during the recession years of 1990–1993. Given that this period was extremely unusual – that is, following a long period of stable unemployment the number of people without jobs increased dramatically – it seems likely that this was an opportunity for a substantial restructuring of production, probably associated with an increase in the intensity of competition between firms as they attempted to sustain demand for their products in a shrinking domestic market.

Consequently, one explanation for the greater impact of technology on inequality over this period might be that firms had to become more high-tech which necessitated increased R&D expenditure along with complementary, and rapid, skill upgrading. An alternative interpretation

[13] In fact, using R&D intensity alone as a proxy for technological change (without interacting with the dummy for 1990–1993) the technology effect was insignificant.

might be that this was simply a compositional effect within sectors whereby the severe recession and increased competition resulted in the survival of the 'better' firms, which in this case are high-tech/high R&D/high-skill-intensive firms, while the low-tech/low R&D/low-skill-intensive firms simply went out of business. Under such a scenario, the rise in R&D expenditure during 1990–1993 would also be associated with an increase in the wage-bill and employment shares of the higher skilled.

Finally, recalling our earlier charts which showed that the largest rises in inequality actually occurred in the high-skill sectors, we decided to test whether the above estimated parameters differ across sectors. Accordingly, we created a dummy variable (DUM_{HS}) which has a value of 1 for the high-skill sectors and 0 otherwise. We then re-estimated equations (3) and (4) and added extra terms by multiplying each variable by DUM_{HS}. The only statistically significant dummy variables were those on the import penetration variables ($DUM_{HS} \times d\ln(PM/PD)_{it}$ and $DUM_{HS} \times d\ln(QM/QD)_{it}$). These results suggest that the impact of trade with low-wage countries on Swedish inequality is *larger* for high-skill sectors compared to low-skill sectors (see columns (F) and (G) of Tables 2 and 3).

Ostensibly, this seems a somewhat surprising result as one might expect low-skill sectors to be more affected than high-skill sectors by relatively lower-priced goods from low-wage countries. This expectation seems reasonable if firms can substitute low-skilled workers with outsourcing by importing the necessary intermediate or finished products from low-wage countries. Firms can easily do this regardless of whether they are low-skill/low-profit or high-skill/high-profit. By contrast, if outsourcing requires foreign direct investment in low-wage countries – involving the manufacture of specific components/products possibly requiring supervision and technical expertise from the investing company – then this may only be possible for high-skill/high-profit firms. In other words, under these circumstances, high-skill/high-profit firms would have a greater ability to outsource – which is consistent with the larger parameter for relative import prices for the high-skill sectors.

In addition, the scope for outsourcing depends upon the degree to which production of the final product can be fragmented into discrete stages with substantially different factor intensity ratios. This will be determined by technological conditions in the industry. Thus, although the incentive to outsource will be greater in low-skill-intensive sectors where low-skilled workers comprise a substantial portion of total production costs, the capacity and ability to outsource may be greater in high-technology, skill-intensive sectors.

V. Conclusions and Policy Implications

Many studies suggest that there has been a decline in the demand for less-skilled labour across OECD countries. In the case of Sweden, there is evidence to support this view as both the wage-bill and employment shares of high-skilled labour rose from the mid-1970's to early 1990s. However, this rise in Swedish inequality is primarily due to a sharp increase in the relative employment of the higher skilled as, in contrast to other countries such as the United States and United Kingdom, relative wages between non-production and production workers remained fairly stable. Labour market rigidities, associated with high trade union density and centralized wage bargaining, may explain why most of the adjustment took place on the employment side.

This paper has sought to statistically assess the factors responsible for this increase in inequality, and particularly to what extent it represents a decline in demand for the less skilled due to trade and technology effects. In contrast to the majority of other studies on Sweden, our econometric results show that trade with low-wage countries has significantly contributed to the rise in inequality in Swedish manufacturing. We believe that there are two main features of our approach that may explain this difference.

First, we apply a now fairly standard model of outsourcing but at a much more disaggregated level than in previous studies. Thus, our data allow for a more accurate identification of the determinants of the within-sector shifts in relative demands for skilled and unskilled workers in OECD countries which appear to characterize the recent period of globalization. Second, our proxy for outsourcing is specified in terms of relative prices or the level of import penetration in volume terms. Previous studies have used import penetration in value terms. The latter may not be a good proxy for increased incentives to outsource if short-run demand elasticities are such that a fall in import prices is accompanied by a decline in the value of import penetration and if domestic firms respond by raising the quality of their products, such that the value of domestic sales rises faster than the value of imports even though the relative quantity of imports has increased. In the data used in this exercise there is a very low correlation (−0.09) between the proportionate change in relative import prices for low-wage countries and the proportionate change in import penetration measured in value terms. On the other hand, the correlation between changes in relative import prices and changes in import penetration measured in volume terms is much higher (−0.54). This supports our argument that import penetration in volume terms is the more appropriate measure of outsourcing.

We also find evidence to suggest that imports from low-wage countries have a larger impact on inequality in the higher-skill industries when compared with the low-skill industries. We suggest some reasons why this may be the case, for example: the financial resources of high-skill sectors are such that they are better able to incur the fixed costs that may arise with a switch to outsourcing overseas, but this is an issue which requires some further research.

Finally, whilst we do find that trade with low-wage countries has been an important determinant of rising inequality in Swedish manufacturing sectors, our results also demonstrate that technological change, as proxied by patenting activity and expenditures on R&D in the 1990s, also played a major role. Our results roughly suggest that outsourcing to low-wage countries accounted for around 25 per cent of the average sectoral increase in the wage share of skilled workers in Sweden over our sample period and for around 15 per cent of the increase in the employment share.[14] Technological change on the other hand was the dominant factor accounting for well over half of the average increase in wage and employment inequality in Sweden.

From a policy perspective, our analysis reveals that, in a world of fragmented production, international trade in the form of outsourcing can act to increase inequality between skilled and unskilled workers even within *advanced* industries in which a country may appear to have a strong comparative advantage. However, economists believe strongly that trade restrictions are not an appropriate policy response and that superior measures to combat inequality and social exclusion are available to governments in advanced industrialized countries. However, these instruments should not be targeted only at those unskilled workers who have lost their jobs or suffered substantial declines in relative wages in traditional unskilled intensive industries, unskilled workers in skilled-intensive industries may also require assistance.

---

[14] This crude calculation was made by multiplying the regression coefficient for the change in import penetration variable by the mean value of this variable and then dividing by the mean of the dependent variable, the change in the employment share of the skilled workers.

Data Appendix

Employment and wages
To categorise labour into different skill groups is problematic. Skills are difficult to measure and there is an ongoing discussion about the problems related to the use of various variables. In this study manufacturing data are used where the workers are categorised as non-production and production workers, respectively.[15]

The manufacturing data come from an annual survey where the information is collected from all establishments with 10 or more employees.[16] The following variables are used:

- number of production workers
- number of non-production workers
- wage sum for production workers excluding payroll taxes
- wage sum for non-production workers excluding payroll taxes.

From these data annual wages are calculated for production workers and non-production workers, respectively. In the analysis annual data is used covering the period 1975–1993 for industries at the 4-digit ISIC code level.

Import prices
The Centre for Economic Policy Studies (CEPS) has recently produced unit values using the OECD trade database.[17] The trade data is converted from product categories in the trade classification (SITC) to industrial sectors (4-digit ISIC code level).

Producer prices
Producer price index from Statistics Sweden at the 4-digit ISIC code level.

Sales
Sales values from Statistics Sweden at the 4-digit ISIC code level. Sales values are defined as total operating income from industrial production.

Capital stocks
Stocks of fixed assets at replacement costs from Statistics Sweden. They include buildings and machinery. The level of aggregation varies between 2- and 4-digit ISIC codes.

Patent data
The original patent data were supplied by the US Dept. of Commerce, Patent and Trademark Office. They were converted from the US patent classification

---

[15] Wage earners and salaried employees, respectively.

[16] Manufacturing, various issues, Statistics Sweden. Starting in 1992, the first 14 days of an employee's illness are covered by "sick-wages" from the employer and not by the social insurance system. These "sick-wages" are included in the wage sums for 1992–1993, which disturbs comparison of wages per employee over time somewhat. However, leave-of-absence due to illness decreased a lot at the same time, which diminishes the problem to some extent.

[17] Globalisation and Social Exclusion project, funded by the EC under the TSER programme.

system to the ISIC system. The converted data provide information on twenty ISIC categories. The level of aggregation varies between 2- and 4-digit ISIC codes. Where 4-digit data is unavailable we apply the patent intensity from the 2-digit level across the 4-digit sub-groups. Five-year averages are used. The patent data are "whole counts" by "date of patent grant". The variable used is patents divided by sales times 1000.

R&D investments
Expenditure on research and development by sector from the OECD ANBERD database. It covers around 35 industries. The level of aggregation varies between 2- and 4-digit ISIC codes. Where 4-digit data is unavailable we apply the R&D intensity from the 2-digit level across the 4-digit sub-groups. The variable used is R&D expenditure divided by sales.

Import penetration
Import penetration in value terms is measured as imported value from non-OECD countries in relation to domestic demand (sales plus imports minus exports) per industry (4-digit ISIC code level). Imported and exported value is from the CEPS trade data set and the sales value from Statistics Sweden.

Import penetration in volume terms is derived as an index of imported volume, initially measured in tonnes and taken from the CEPS trade data set based on OECD data, divided by an index of the volume of domestic sales, taken as the value of domestic sales divided by the producer price index for each sector.

Industries included in the regression analysis

High-skill sectors (HS):
3522 Manufacture of drugs and medicines
3825 Manufacture of office, computing and accounting machinery
3831 Manufacture of electrical industrial machinery and apparatus
3832 Manufacture of radio, television and communication equipment and apparatus
3833 Manufacture of electrical appliances and housewares
3839 Manufacture of electrical apparatus and supplies not elsewhere specified

Low-skill sectors (LS):
3111 Slaughtering, preparing and preserving of meat
3112 Manufacture of dairy products
3113 Canning and preserving of fruit and vegetables
3114 Canning, preserving and processing of fish, crustacea and similar foods
3115 Manufacture of vegetable oils and fats
3116 Grain mill products
3117 Manufacture of bakery products
3118 Sugar
3119 Manufacture of cocoa, chocolate and sugar confectionary
3121 Manufacture of food products not elsewhere specified
3122 Manufacture of prepared animal feeds
3133 Malt liquors and malt
3134 Carbonated water industries and soft drinks

3140 Tobacco manufactures
3211 Spinning, weaving and finishing of textiles
3212 Manufacture of made-up textile goods other than clothing
3213 Knitted goods
3214 Manufacture of carpets and rugs
3215 Cordage, rope and twine industries
3219 Manufacture of textiles not elsewhere specified
3220 Manufacture of wearing apparel except footwear
3233 Manufacture of leather products except footwear and apparel
3240 Manufacture of footwear except rubber or plastic footwear
3610 Manufacture of pottery, china and earthware
3620 Manufacture of glass and glass products
3691 Manufacture of structural clay products
3692 Manufacture of cement, lime and plaster
3699 Manufacture of non-metallic mineral products, not elsewhere specified
3710 Iron and steel basic industries
3720 Non-ferrous metal basic industries
3811 Manufacture of cutlery, hand-tools and general hardware
3812 Manufacture of furniture and fixtures primarily of metal
3813 Manufacture of structural metal products
3819 Manufacture of fabricated metal products except machinery and equipment, not elsewhere classified
3843 Manufacture of motor vehicles and parts

References

Anderton, R., and P. Brenton (1998a). Trade with the NICs and Wage Inequality: Evidence from the United Kingdom and Germany. In P. Brenton and J. Pelkmans (eds.), *Global Trade and European Workers*. Basingstoke: Macmillan.

Anderton, R., and P. Brenton (1998b). The Dollar, Trade, Technology and Inequality in the USA. *National Institute Economic Review* 166: 78–86.

Anderton, R., and P. Brenton (1999). Outsourcing and Low-Skilled Workers in the UK. *Bulletin of Economic Research* 51: 267–286.

Anderton, R., and S. Schultz (1999). Explaining Export Success in the UK and Germany: A Case Study of the Medical Equipment Industry. Anglo-German Foundation Report. London.

Berman, E., J. Bound, and Z. Grilliches (1994). Changes in the Demand for Skilled Labor within U.S. Manufacturing: Evidence from the Annual Survey of Manufactures. *Quarterly Journal of Economics* 109: 367–398.

Berman, E., J. Bound, and S. Machin (1998). Implications of Skilled Biased Technological Change: International Evidence. *Quarterly Journal of Economics* 113: 1245–1280.

Borjas, G., R. Freeman, and L. Katz (1992). On the Labour Market Effects of Immigration and Trade. In G. Borjas and R. Freeman (eds.), *Immigration and the Work Force: Economic Consequences for the United States and Source Areas*. Chicago: University of Chicago Press.

Brenton, P., and J. Pelkmans (eds.) (1998). *Global Trade and European Workers*. Basingstoke: Macmillan.

Diehl, M. (1999). The Impact of International Outsourcing on the Skill Structure of Employment: Empirical Evidence from German Manufacturing Industries. Kiel Working Paper 946. Kiel Institute for World Economics, Kiel.

Edin, P., and B. Holmlund (1995). The Swedish Wage Structure: The Rise and Fall of Solidarity Wage Policy? In R. Freeman and L. Katz (eds.), *Differences and Changes in Wage Structures*. Chicago: University of Chicago Press.

Feenstra, R., and G. Hanson (1995). Foreign Investment, Outsourcing and Relative Wages. Working Paper 5121. NBER, Cambridge, Mass.

Feenstra, R., and G. Hanson (1996). Globalization, Outsourcing and Wage Inequality. *American Economic Review, Papers and Proceedings* 86 (2): 240–245.

Greenaway, D., and D. Nelson (2001). Globalisation and Labour Market Adjustment. Special issue of *Oxford Review of Economic Policy* 16.

Hansson, P. (1997). Trade, Technology and Changes in Employment of Skilled Labour in Swedish Manufacturing. In J. Fagerberg, P. Hansson, L. Lundberg, and A. Melchior (eds.), *Technology and Trade*. Cheltenham: Edward Elgar.

Hansson, P. (2000). Relative Demand for Skills in Swedish Manufacturing: Technology or Trade? *Review of International Economics* 8: 533–555.

Machin, S., and J. Van Reenen (1998). Technology and Changes in Skill Structure: Evidence from Seven OECD Countries. *Quarterly Journal of Economics* 111: 195–226.

Machin, S., A. Ryan, and J. Van Reenen (1996). Changes in Skill Structure: Evidence from an International Panel of Industries. Discussion Paper 1434. CEPR, London.

Sachs, J., and H. Shatz (1994). Trade and Jobs in U.S. Manufacturing. *Brookings Papers on Economic Activity* (1): 1–69.

Sachs, J., and H. Shatz (1996). US Trade with Developing Countries and Wage Inequality. *American Economic Review, Papers and Proceedings* 86: 234–239.

Wood, A. (1994). *North-south Trade, Employment and Inequality*. Oxford: Clarendon Press.

***

Abstract: What's Trade Got to Do with It? Relative Demand for Skills within Swedish Manufacturing. – This paper seeks to identify the contribution of trade and technological change to the increase in inequality between skilled and unskilled workers in Sweden since the 1970s. An empirical approach is adopted which allows for the outsourcing of the low-skill parts of the production chain to low-wage locations and is applied to detailed industry and bilateral trade data, the latter distinguishing between low-wage sources of imports and OECD countries. The paper finds that, in contrast to previous studies, trade with low-wage countries may have contributed to the rise in inequality in Swedish manufacturing. The empirical results also suggest that the increased use of technology also played a role in creating greater inequality between skilled and unskilled workers in Sweden, with the magnitude of this impact increasing in the 1990s. JEL no. F160, J31, O33

Scottish Journal of Political Economy, Vol. 49, No. 1, February 2002

Chapter 11

TRENDS IN DISAGGREGATED IMPORT AND EXPORT PRICES IN EUROPE: IMPLICATIONS FOR THE TRADE AND WAGES DEBATE

*Paul Brenton and Anna Maria Pinna**

ABSTRACT

We consider carefully the evidence from traded prices (as proxied by unit values) concerning the transmission of the effects of globalisation to domestic labour markets. Using standard index number techniques we decompose changes in sectoral import and export unit values into movements due to changes in pure prices of the initial bundle of goods imported or exported and changes due to upgrading of that bundle. Looking at the imports of selected European countries of textiles, clothing and footwear relative to engineering products we find evidence of strongly falling pure prices of the unskilled intensive products relative to the skilled products in the 1980s. This reinforces the view that import prices can capture the impact of globalisation in terms of falling relative prices for products produced with the intensive use of unskilled labour. However, the trends are not common across all the unskilled sectors; footwear is clearly an exception. In the absence of detailed domestic data, we look for reactions by domestic firms to increased import competition in movements in the price and composition of exports. We find evidence of stiff price competition from imports being associated with similar movements in export prices and no support for the view that import competition from low-wage countries has led to upgrading of the quality of exports.

I INTRODUCTION AND BACKGROUND

To what extent has trade with labour abundant low wage economies affected western labour markets? During the 1980s and 1990s there has been a well-documented increase in wage inequality between skilled and unskilled workers in the US and to some extent in the UK. In continental Europe the gap between skilled and unskilled wages has not widened appreciably. However, there has been a substantial increase in unemployment propensities for unskilled workers in these countries. The principal causes of these labour market developments have been subject to considerable debate and research but as yet no clear-cut conclusions have been reached.

*Centre for European Policy Studies, Brussels

Standard economic trade theory demonstrates that more open international trade can cause the sort of changes in labour markets in OECD markets that have been observed in the last two decades. It is changes in the price of low-skilled labour intensive goods relative to the price of skilled-labour intensive products that lie at the heart of the traditional (Stolper-Samuelson) economic explanation of the impact of globalisation on domestic labour markets. However, trade is not the only identifiable culprit for the increasing wage inequality or falling employment opportunities to have bedevilled unskilled workers in the OECD countries. Much of the debate on the impact of globalisation has revolved around empirical analysis of the relative importance of trade with low-wage countries and the impact of changes in technology. In this paper we concentrate upon the trade explanation.

The main conclusion from existing empirical studies of movements in relative prices is that although inequality across skills started to increase during the early 1980s, the domestic prices of unskilled-labour intensive products have shown no clear decline relative to those of skilled intensive products (Slaughter, 1998). Movements in producer prices in the US, on the contrary, highlight the 1970s as the Stolper-Samuelson decade (Leamer, 1996). The evidence for European countries (Lawrence, 1996; Lucke, 1997; Anderton and Brenton, 1998) suggests that producer prices of unskilled-labour-intensive goods did not decline by more than those of skilled-labour-intensive products in neither the 1970s nor the 1980s.

One possible explanation for these results is that sectoral producer prices are unable to capture the relevant trade shock faced by the industrialised economies because they are too aggregated. Wood (1997, 1998), for example, argues that heterogeneity of goods in standard statistical definitions of sectors and changes in quality over time (which maybe correlated with the skill intensity of production) could engender substantial errors into available producer price series. If sub-sectors within industries are different, in terms of requiring different amounts of skilled and unskilled labour, then more open trade may reduce the prices of some goods but raise the prices of others, leaving the industry aggregate price unchanged. Ideally, one would use highly disaggregated series on producer prices to address this issue, but unfortunately they are not available.

In addition, countries such as the NICs and other Asian economies, which initially emerged into the international context by penetrating unskilled-labour-intensive sectors, have recently diversified their production into unskilled-labour-intensive activities across a range of unskilled *and* skilled intensive industries. Some countries (primarily the NICs) have also been able to shift into skilled-intensive activities. The use of producer price measures at the industry level will not enable such within industry adjustments to be discerned.

Wood points instead to changes in the prices of imports and exports, which do suggest a rising relative price of skilled-intensive products in the 1980s (but not in the 1970s). However, issues of measurement pertain to import and export prices, just as to producer prices. In particular, the problems of aggregating over sub-categories and of quality upgrading remain. For example, the rising relative trade price of skilled-intensive goods could reflect quality upgrading within this group of products relative to unskilled-labour intensive goods. Here, however, further analysis is possible since highly detailed trade data are readily available.

The aim of this paper is to evaluate more carefully the information contained in trade prices and to assess what this contributes to our understanding of the impact of globalisation. Trade prices are the conduit by which globalisation affects domestic labour markets. We look at movements in import and export unit values (which as usual are used to proxy import and export prices) within two skilled-intensive sectors (electrical and non-electrical machinery) and three key unskilled intensive sectors (textiles, clothing and footwear). Machinery is typically taken as a skilled intensive sector in which OECD countries possess a comparative advantage. Textiles, clothing and footwear are more traditional manufacturing sectors where the intensity of unskilled labour in production is higher and it is generally accepted that comparative advantage has shifted to the labour-abundant developing countries. Textiles, clothing and footwear are generally those sectors expected to be most affected by increased competition from low-wage countries.

We utilise data, covering the period 1976–1994, at the most detailed (tariff-line) level of disaggregation for five European countries (UK, France, Germany, Belgium-Luxembourg and Italy). For each of these importing countries we consider trade with five regions: OECD, Central and Eastern European Countries, the NICs, other Asian countries and the rest of the world. If globalisation has had a significant impact upon labour markets in industrial countries this should be apparent in movements in prices for finely defined categories of traded products.

A key feature of our work is that we allow for quality upgrading within sectors by using fairly standard index number techniques to decompose movements in unit values into two components: pure changes in prices and variations across time in the bundle of goods. The paper has two key objectives. Firstly, we assess the extent to which the pure prices of unskilled-labour intensive products have changed relative to the pure prices of skilled intensive products. In other words we take the bundle of goods in each sector imported at the start of the period as fixed and investigate the extent to which the price of this bundle has changed relative to the price of the fixed bundle for the other sectors.

As mentioned above, the issue of the impact of globalisation would ideally be analysed using detailed data on domestic output prices. The second objective of this paper is, in the absence of such disaggregated information on domestic prices, to look to see whether we can identify responses to globalisation by domestic firms from changes in the price and composition of the bundle of goods exported. It is here that detailed product specific data are available. In particular, we look to see if increasing import competition is associated with a response by domestic firms to raise the quality of the output they produce. The concept of defensive innovation, discussed by Wood (1994, 1998), explains the intra-industry skill upgrading of employment as a defensive strategy against increased competition in international markets. In this situation we should observe quality upgrading of domestic production and exports precisely in those sectors characterised by greater competition in international markets. We check for this by seeing whether there has been a tendency for import prices to be correlated with upgrading of the bundle of goods exported.

The paper commences by briefly reviewing the evidence regarding movements in relative producer prices and import prices over the past 30 years. We then proceed to analyse the detailed tariff line trade data and discuss the implications of the information contained in these data for the debate over the role of trade in increasing inequality between skilled and unskilled workers in Europe and North America. The final section presents some conclusions.

II The Price Puzzle: Trends in Sectoral Producer and Import Prices

Figure 1 shows indices of the domestic prices (price of value-added) of the two high skilled intensive sectors, non-electrical machinery and electrical machinery, relative to the price of textiles, clothing and footwear, unskilled intensive activities, for seven European countries and the US. There is some evidence of a slight upward trend in the ratio of the price of electrical machinery relative to textiles, clothing and footwear for certain countries. However, the picture from the non-electrical sector is even more clouded and no overall pattern across these countries can be deduced. In some countries the price ratio has fallen over a large part of the sample period!

Figure 2 shows relative import prices (unit values) for these European countries. The figures show the ratio of the import price of engineering products as a whole relative to the aggregate import price of textiles, clothing and footwear. We show separately the ratio of the import price of engineering products from OECD countries relative to the import price of textiles, clothing and footwear from non-industrial countries as well as the price ratio of total engineering imports relative to total textiles, clothing and footwear imports. Interestingly, there do not appear to be significant differences between the two series suggesting that for these countries the import price of low skilled products is determined by trade with the South and that the import price of engineering products is determined by trade with the North.

With the exception of France, these figures suggest more strongly an upward trend in the relative price of engineering products, at least since the early 1980s. Hence, as in previous studies the information from the import prices is more indicative of a fall in the relative price of unskilled intensive products. We now proceed to investigate more carefully the extent to which changes in these aggregate unit values capture the true competitive effect from imports, and hence the potential impact of trade upon the domestic labour market. We do this by investigating the extent to which movements in import prices might be clouded by changes in the product composition of the sectoral indices.

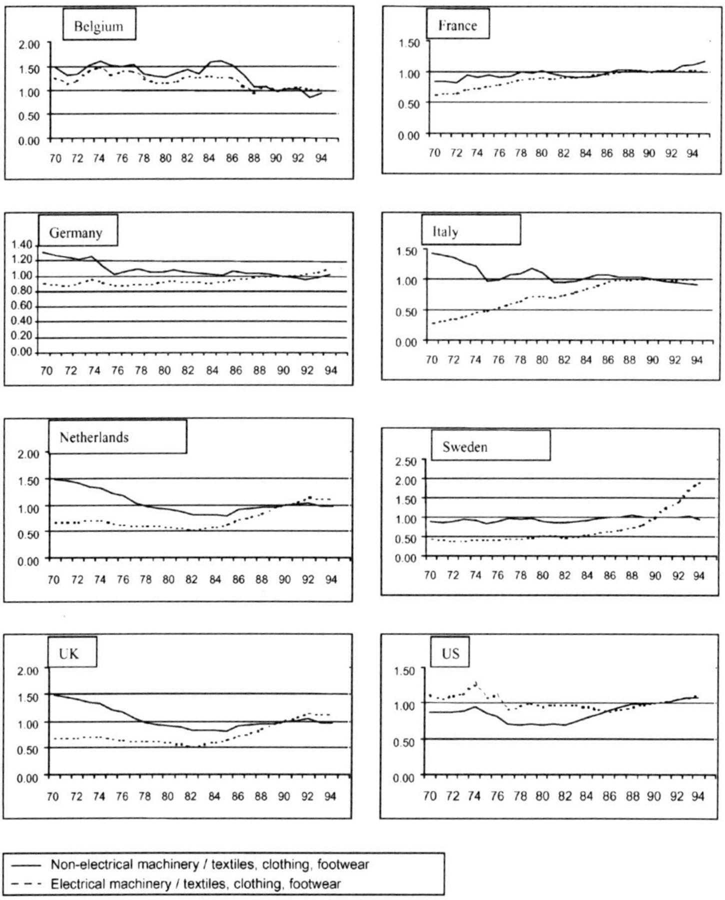

Figure 1. Relative domestic prices: price of value-added of machinery relative to textiles, clothing and footwear in selected European countries and the US (1990 = 1)
Source: OECD STAN Database.

III Price Movements and Quality Upgrading

Adjustments for quality are crucial when computing price movements for skilled intensive sectors, particularly if sector-biased technological change is prevalent, as previous studies would suggest. As we shall see quality upgrading may also be an important feature of sectors typically thought of as unskilled intensive. We start from the observation that the price (proxied throughout by unit

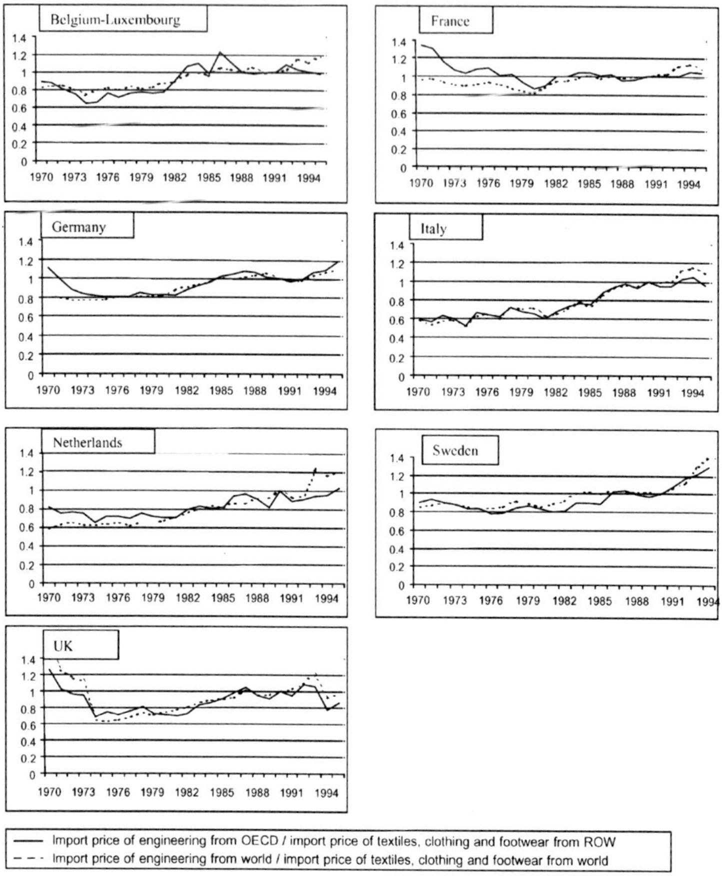

Figure 2. Relative import prices: unit value of engineering products relative to textiles, clothing and footwear (1990 = 1).

Source: Derived from OECD trade data.

value—value per unit of volume)[1] of an imported or exported commodity often varies across different countries (or regions). Such price differences are a first indication that, even for fairly standardised products, product differentiation and differences in quality are important. This implies that care must be taken in interpreting changes in the price of traded products across countries. Anderton and Brenton (1998), for example, show that for both the UK and Germany

[1] Import and export prices are not available for most European countries at a detailed product level.

movements in import prices for many sectors over the 1980s would have been different from that observed if the share of the different country suppliers of imports had remained constant.

When considering total imports of a particular product it is not possible to distinguish whether an increase in the price mirrors a pure price increase or the switch to a more expensive supplier, which is able to provide a higher quality variant of the product. In the following analysis we crudely control for this country composition effect by considering several different regions as sources of imports or as export destinations, but take each region to be relatively homogeneous in it's country composition. That is we assume that products from the different countries within the same region are very similar in terms of quality. Shifts in the country composition of imports from a particular region, *ceteris paribus*, are not expected to have a substantial impact upon the unit value for that region.

Changes in sectorally aggregated unit values for each region also need careful interpretation. Changes in the indices can be caused by pure price movements at the disaggregate commodity level but also by quality upgrading in terms of changes in the commodity composition of the bundle imported from the region, that is, by a move towards commodities characterised by higher prices. The unit value index of imports from, or exports to, a particular country for a sector g at time t is:

$$P_g(t) = \frac{\sum_{i=1}^{n} V_i(t)}{\sum_{i=1}^{n} Q_i(t)} = \frac{\sum_{i=1}^{n} P_i(t) \cdot Q_i(t)}{\sum_{i=1}^{n} Q_i(t)}, \tag{1}$$

where V_i and Q_i are respectively the value and quantity traded of each commodity i in the sector, and there are n commodities in the sector. The change in the aggregate unit value index is measured by:

$$\Delta P_g(t) = \ln P_g(t) - \ln P_g(t-1). \tag{2}$$

Let's consider the case where the total quantity traded in the sector is constant in time. A price change from t to $t+1$ for the aggregate can therefore be caused either by a change in any of the P_i or by a change in any of the Q_i. The latter being a change in the composition of sectoral imports or exports. So a shift in demand towards more expensive commodities in the sector will lead to an increase in the aggregate import or export price even if none of the individual prices (P_i) change. In this paper we attempt to identify from changes in sectoral import or export prices movements due to adjustments in the composition of the bundle of commodities and changes due to movements in actual prices. That is, we seek to derive a measure of pure price changes within the sector analysed together with a quantification of quality upgrading in the sector.

To achieve this we have applied the Divisia index number methodology introduced by Chinloy (1980) and applied by Aw and Roberts (1986) to calculate the impact of quantitative restrictions in promoting substitution within the imported bundle towards higher-priced products and sources. The Tornqvist price index for a group of products is defined as the value-share weighted sum of the growth of the individual import product prices:

$$\Delta P_g{}^*(t) \equiv \sum_i^n S_i(t)\Delta P_i(t), \tag{3}$$

where:

$$S_i(t) \equiv \frac{1}{2}\left[\frac{V_i(t)}{\sum_i^n V_i(t)} + \frac{V_i(t+1)}{\sum_i^n V_i(t+1)}\right],$$

and:

$$\Delta P_i(t) \equiv \ln\left(\frac{V_i(t+1)}{Q_i(t+1)}\right) - \ln\left(\frac{V_i(t)}{Q_i(t)}\right).$$

As shown by Aw and Roberts (1986) the difference between the aggregate unit value index, (2), and the Tornqvist index, (3), will measure the growth in import and export prices due to the recomposition of the bundle among the different products. When there is a shift towards relatively more expensive goods in the bundle index (2) will be higher than index (3). In other words the distance between the two indices provides a measure of the bias created from the fact that the unit-value index is a quantity-weighted average where greater weight is given to the prices of those goods whose change in quantity between t and $t+1$ has been highest.

IV The Data

We consider for each of five EU countries (Belgium-Luxembourg, France, German, Italy, UK) trade with five regions: OECD, CEEE (Central and Eastern European Economics), NICs (4 tigers), RoA (Rest of Asian Countries) and RoW (Rest of the World). The last four groups are chosen to capture the competitive pressure from low-wage economies amongst heterogeneous regions. For each region we have computed the standard import and export unit values (as in (2)) and then corrected these for changes in the commodity composition of the bundle of traded goods belonging to each sector (as in (3)). Within each region the difference between (2) and (3) will be interpreted as a measure of within industry quality upgrading since it reveals changes in the composition of the bundle of goods traded towards more expensive varieties of the goods.

Data have been collected at the highest level of disaggregation (6-digit-Nimexe for the 1976–87 period and 8-digit-CN for the 1988–94 period) for the imports and exports of the two skilled and three unskilled labour intensive sectors. More precisely 853, 560 and 67 activities belonging respectively to the textiles, clothing and footwear sectors enter our calculations whilst 1698 and 847 activities define the non-electrical and electrical machinery sectors in the period 1976–87. Following the revision of the trade classification used by the EU, 815, 451, 95, 1041, 749 activities enter our calculations for the period 1988–94 for the textiles, clothing, footwear, non-electrical and electrical machinery respectively.[2]

We implicitly assume that products are homogeneous at the tariff line level and that quality upgrading is reflected by shifts between products at the tariff line level. If the quality of the individual tariff line products were to change this would be captured as a movement in price. It should be remembered, that here we are using the most detailed data that is available, further disaggregation is not possible.

V The Results

We have considered movements in relative import prices between the sub-periods 1976–81, 1981–87 and 1988–94. Such temporal decomposition is aimed to capture better the differences between the 1970s and the 1980s suggested by the changes in aggregate import and export prices, but also reflects the change of trade classification in the EU in 1988. Our aim here is to disentangle pure price and quality upgrading effects due to increased international competition within aggregate import and export price movements.

Corrected relative unit values—movements in pure prices

In Figure 3 we compare changes in the (quality corrected) unit values of imports of the skilled intensive sectors from the OECD countries with those of imports of unskilled intensive products from the four low-wage regions (comparison sets will be defined as OECD-NICs, OECD-RoA, OECD-RoW and OECD-CEEE).[3] In each part of the figure we show separately the changes in the pure price of non-electrical machinery, electrical machinery, textiles, clothing and then footwear. The first objective is to assess whether these changes in 'pure prices' have been larger for the skilled intensive sectors than for the unskilled intensive sectors. Price changes for imports from OECD of both skilled and unskilled intensive sectors (Figure 3E) are also presented to allow movements in the prices of unskilled intensive products imported from the South to be compared to movements in the prices of the same products imported from the North.

[2] The difference between the number of products belonging to the same sector is due to a change in the international trade classification adopted by Eurostat. In 1988 the Combined Nomenclature was introduced, replacing the previous Nimexe classification. The CN is an extension of the Harmonised System, whereby additional codes with 2 digits added, are used. Therefore each commodity in the CN is characterised by an 8-digit code.

[3] Calculations have also been performed using unit values of exports of skilled products to OECD countries. The use of either export or import unit values to compute movements in prices in the skilled intensive sectors leads to the same broad conclusions.

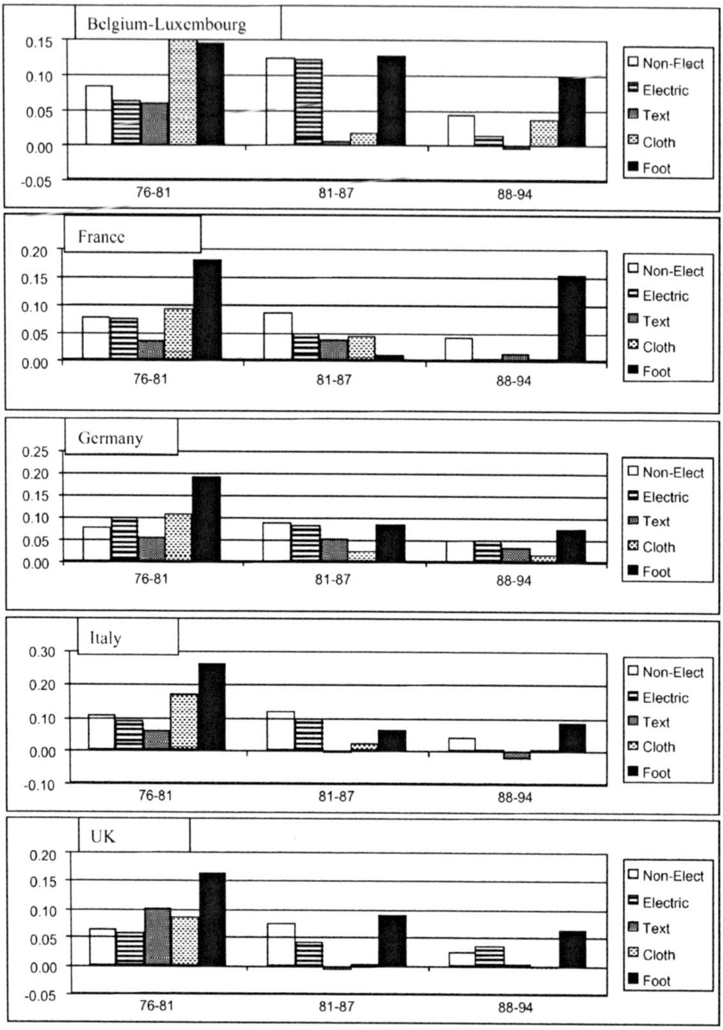

Figure 3. Changes in the pure price of imports (unit values corrected for quality change). A: Comparison between imports of engineering products from OECD countries and textiles, clothing and footwear from the NICs.

Source: Own calculations based upon data from Comext database.

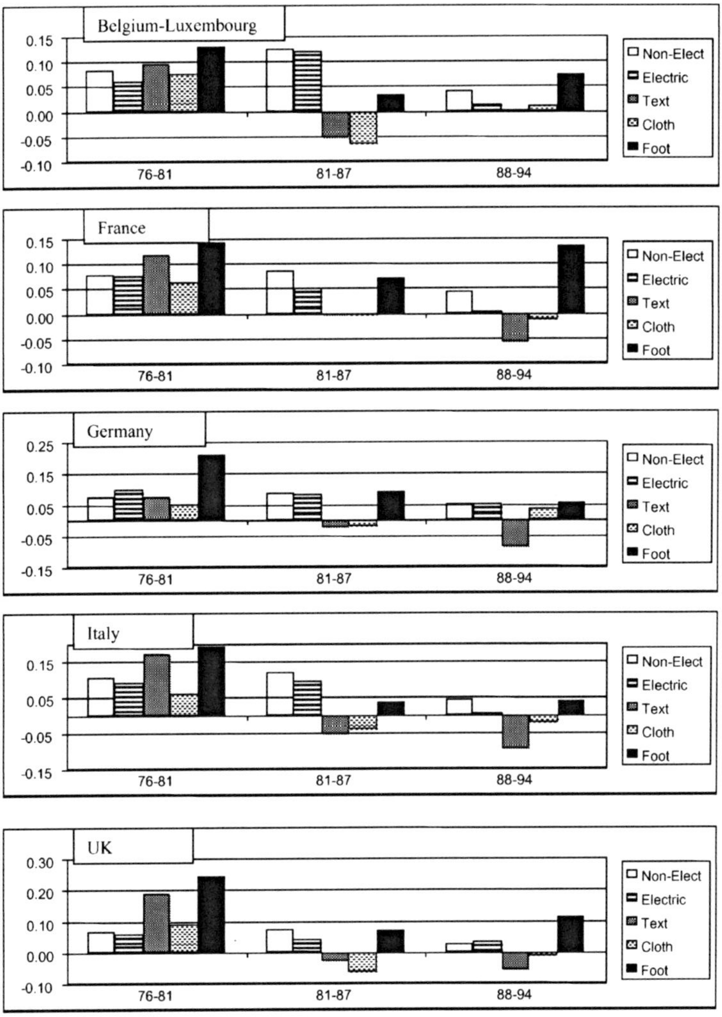

Figure 3. Changes in the pure price of imports (unit values corrected for quality change).
B: Comparison between imports of engineering products from OECD countries and textiles, clothing and footwear from the rest of Asia.

Source: Own calculations based upon data from Comext database.

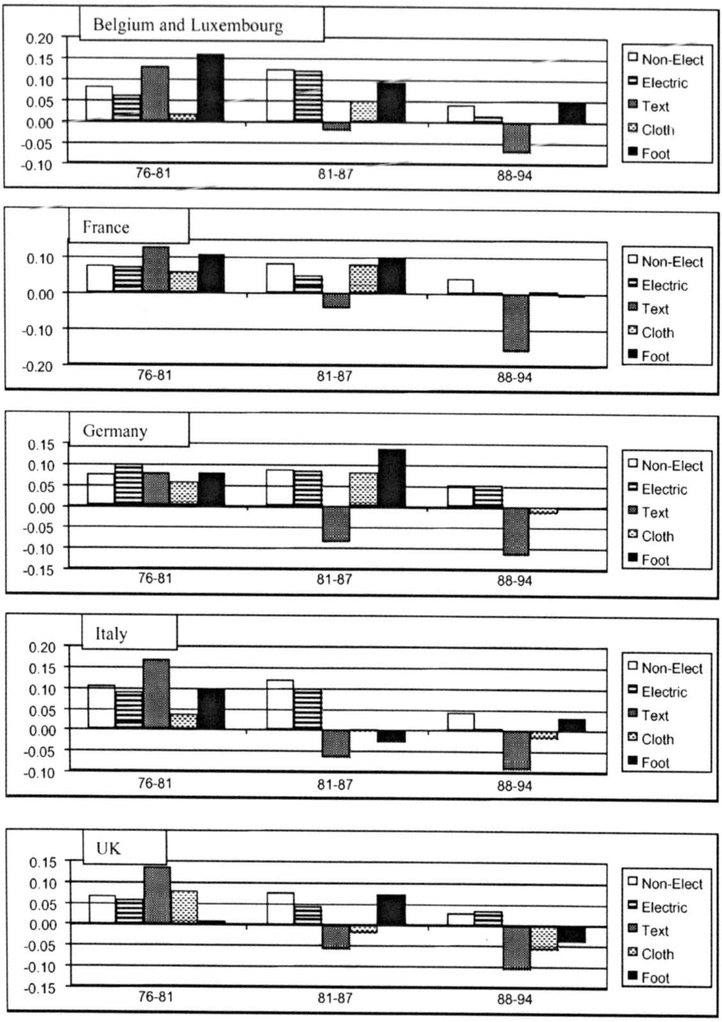

Figure 3. Changes in the pure price of imports (unit values corrected for quality change). C: Comparison between imports of engineering products from OECD countries and textiles, clothing and footwear from the rest of world.

Source: Own calculations based upon data from Comext database.

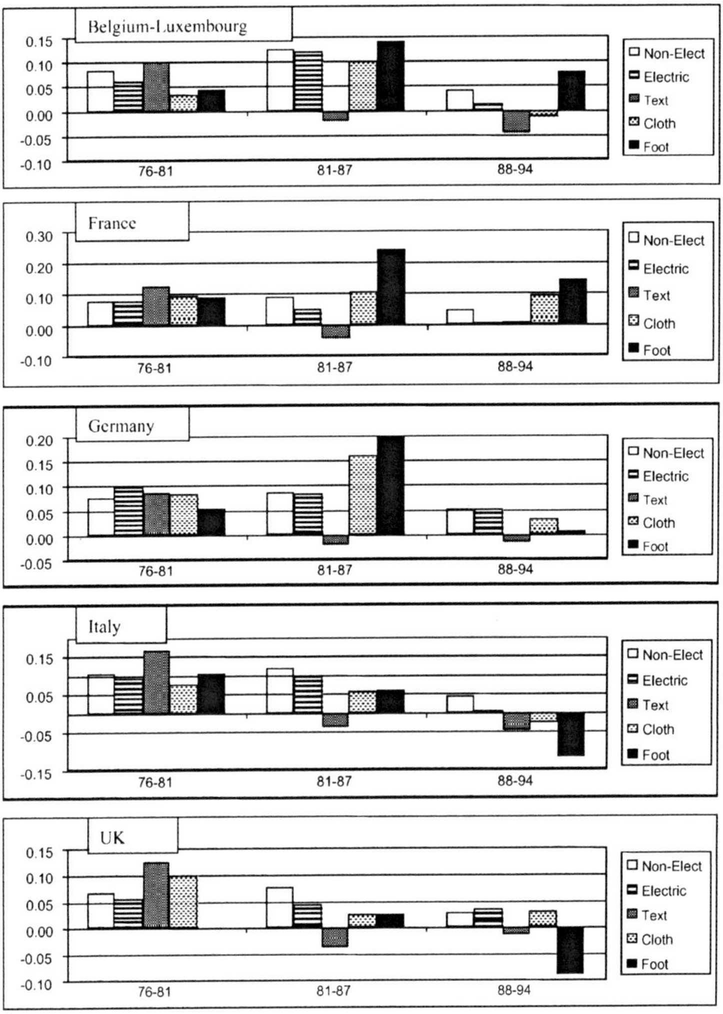

Figure 3. Changes in the pure price of imports (unit values corrected for quality change). D: Comparison between imports of engineering products from OECD countries and textiles, clothing and footwear from CEEE.

Source: Own calculations based upon data from Comext database.

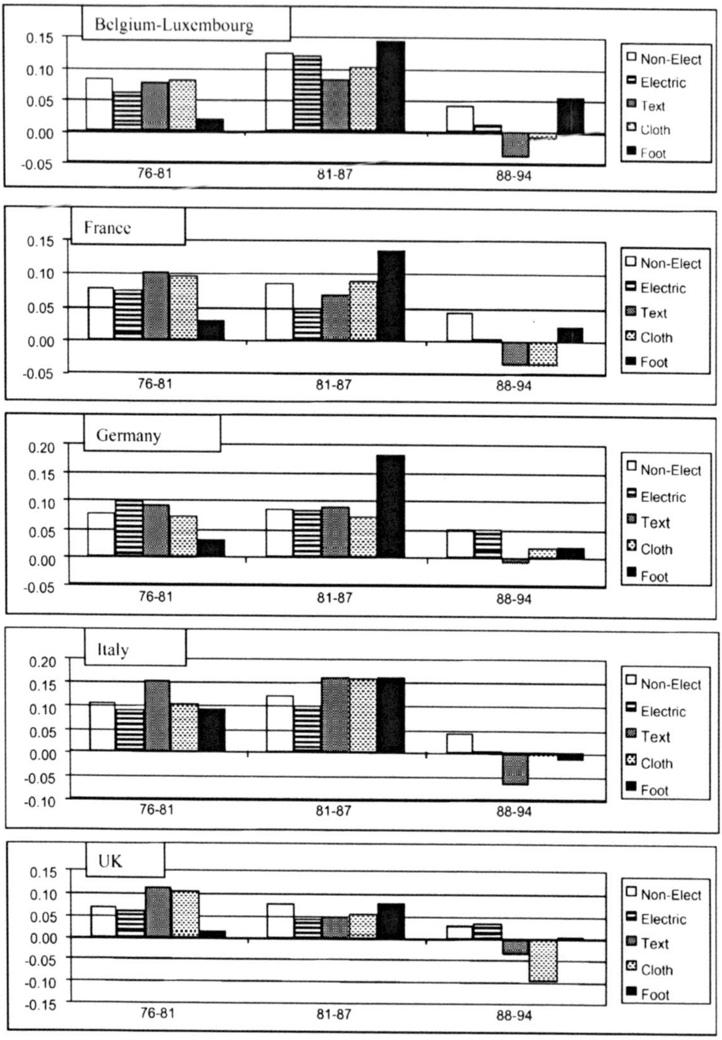

Figure 3. Changes in the pure price of imports (unit values corrected for quality change). E: Comparison between imports of engineering products from OECD countries and textiles, clothing and footwear from OECD countries.

Source: Own calculations based upon data from Comext database.

In the first period (1976–81) the picture revealed is one of increases in corrected unit values for the unskilled intensive commodities being typically higher than the corresponding changes for the skilled intensive sectors. However, somewhat different patterns for the unskilled products are apparent across the sources of imports. Figure 3A shows large increases between 1976 and 1981 in pure prices of clothing and footwear imports from the NICs, relative to imports of engineering products from the OECD countries. On the other hand, the pure price of textile imports from these countries to fell relative to the price of engineering imports from the OECD countries. Figure 3B shows relative increases in the pure price of textile and footwear imports from the Rest of Asia, but often a fall in the price of clothing from this region relative to imports of engineering products from OECD countries. A similar picture emerges for imports from the Rest of the World, shown in Figure 3C. For the CEEE region (Figure 3D) the picture is a little more mixed, but there is no indication of an overall fall in the relative price of the unskilled intensive products.

Thus, these results suggest that the relative price of skilled intensive products decreased rather than increased in the second part of the 1970s in all the importing countries and trading regions considered here. However, the figures do reveal a varied picture for the different unskilled intensive activities. The increase in the pure price component of footwear import unit values was generally the highest, whilst a comparison between textiles and clothing suggests that competitive pressure from the NICs was mostly apparent in the textile sector with competition from RoA, RoW and CEEE being particularly important in clothing products. The aggregate import prices discussed in Section II do not reveal these trends. They suggest, in general, a slow upward trend in the ratio of skilled to unskilled import prices, reflecting, in part at least, the contrasting movements in pure price changes between different unskilled intensive activities from low-wage economies.

The analysis of the data for the later periods clearly suggests an opposite trend in movements in pure prices within the aggregate import unit values for each region. Pure import prices of textiles and clothing from the low-wage regions generally rose by much less than the equivalent prices of imports of engineering products from the OECD countries. In some cases the price of the bundle of unskilled intensive goods imported at the start of the period actually fell in absolute terms. It is interesting that the conclusion that the relative pure price of unskilled activities declined in the 1980s and 1990s is evident in the comparison between electrical machinery and the unskilled intensive activities. This machinery sector includes products of the computer industry, the prices of which are generally deemed to have fallen strongly during these periods.[4] Our simple data analysis would therefore suggest that, in contrast to Leamer (1996), the 1980s, and

[4] Computers and computer components are included in sector 85 (electrical machinery). The literature has extensively discussed whether computers should be included in the price analysis, since computer prices appear more sensitive than other sectors' prices to the influence of quality upgrading. For example, Sachs and Shatz (1994) introduce a dummy for the computer industry in their regression analysis whilst Feenstra and Hanson (1997) omit the computer industry from their sample.

not the 1970s, are the Stolper-Samuelson decade in terms of movements in the price of skilled intensive products relative to unskilled intensive products.

It is also apparent from Figure 3 that for the 1980s and 1990s there are considerable differences between changes in the pure price of imports of footwear and changes in the pure price of imports of the other unskilled activities. Increases in import prices are typically higher for footwear than for textiles and clothing and in many cases changes in footwear prices have been of a similar magnitude to the changes in prices for the skilled intensive commodities. Thus, for footwear there has been no change or even an increase in pure import prices relative to the pure price of imports of skilled intensive products from the OECD countries. Initially, we speculate here that this may have something to do with the structure of the footwear industry and the increasing importance of sports footwear and the role of companies such as Nike and Adidas. But this is an issue that requires more serious attention.

Another interesting feature that is evident from Figure 3 is the difference between regions in movements in prices of the different categories of unskilled intensive products. In the textiles and clothing sectors relatively stronger import competition, in terms of falling relative pure prices, came first from the RoA region and then subsequently from the RoW region (particularly in the textiles sector where large declines in prices are recorded in the 1980s and 1990s). Not surprisingly more intense competition from the CEEE region is most apparent in the 1988–94 period.

The principal conclusion which emerges from looking at developments for the OECD region alone (Figure 3E) is that pure prices of imports of textiles and clothing from the OECD increased by a similar order of magnitude to the changes in the prices of the skilled intensive products in the first two sub-periods. However, in the period since 1987 imports of textiles and clothing from the OECD in all the European countries have been characterised by both relative and absolute declines in pure prices.

So competitive pressure from RoA and RoW countries in the early 1980s, as reflected by large negative pure price changes in textile and clothing imports, may have led to declining relative prices of unskilled intensive products in industrial countries. This may then have contributed to the decline in the relative wage, or the fall in relative employment opportunities, of unskilled labour in those countries. The decline in the price of textiles and clothing imports from the OECD in the most recent period may also reflect the increasing role of outsourcing in industrial countries. OECD countries have responded to more intense competition by moving the unskilled activities of the production process in textiles, clothing or footwear to low-wage economies. This has led to prices falling for those products, given that the weight of unskilled activities is particularly high in these sectors.

Responses to international competition—quality upgrading

In this part of the analysis we briefly look at the evolution over time of changes in the sectoral unit value index due to shifts in the composition of the bundle imported, which we refer to as quality upgrading. We expect that the nature of foreign competition, whether exercised in terms of downward pressure on prices for the unskilled intensive products or in terms of quality upgrading, will have different implications for domestic labour markets. In a perfect competition framework, wages are clearly anchored to product prices. However, with product differentiation it is more complex to predict the effects of import competition, either in the form of lower prices or quality upgrading, on domestic wages. Relative product prices still matter, but the extent to which domestic relative prices are influenced by developments abroad (for example via an increase in the availability of cheap labour) depends upon the degree to which imports compete with the domestic varieties of the product. If, in the face of the increased competition from low-wage economies, domestic production moves towards unskilled intensive commodities of a higher quality then the relevant product price for unskilled wages at home is that of the domestic variety.[5] Given this, we also present data on quality upgrading of exports (the move to more expensive varieties in the bundle) to proxy changes in the domestic production structure.

We proceed firstly by looking at the strength of any associations between changes in the pure prices of the bundle of goods imported and the composition of that imported bundle in terms of quality upgrading. We then try and identify if there are any significant links between price and quality movements of imports and changes in the price and composition of the bundle exported. This is an indirect approach, given the lack of suitable domestic data, to assessing how domestic production might have reacted to changes in the nature of import competition.[6]

For this part of the analysis we use data aggregated across all the trading regions since a change in competitive conditions due to movements in the price and quality of imports from one particular source may not necessarily be reflected in changes in exports to that specific destination. Therefore we now calculate pure movements in price as changes in unit values after netting out quality upgrading due to changes in both the country and product composition of imports. Thus, our index (3) is calculated as:

$$\Delta P_g{}^*(t) \equiv \sum_{c}^{5} \sum_{i}^{n} S_{ci}(t)\Delta P_{ci}(t), \qquad (3')$$

where, c refers to each of the five regions considered. The difference between (3′) and index (2) calculated for total imports or exports of each sector trade gives the change in the unit value due to quality movements resulting from a change in supplier or a change in the product composition of the bundle.

[5] As pointed out by Slaughter (1998) the Stolper Samuelson theorem also applies under the assumption of imperfect competition as long as price-cost markups are constant. In our scenario there can still be a negative effect on wages for the unskilled if the move to higher quality and higher priced varieties is also associated with higher price-cost margins.

[6] Brenton and Pinna (2000) provide a more detailed graphical analysis of quality upgrading by sector and by importing region.

Table 1 shows, for the unskilled intensive sectors, simple correlation coefficients between changes in the pure price of imports and exports (Pimp, Pexp), between changes in the quality of imports and exports (Qimp, Qexp) and between changes in the price of imports and changes in the quality of imports, and likewise for exports. The coefficients in the upper left-hand matrix in the table are based on data for all five importing countries, all three sectors and all three periods (1976–81, 1981–87 and 1988–94). The correlation coefficients here have therefore been calculated with 45 observations. The coefficients are not high but those which are significant indicate that movements in pure prices of imports are positively correlated with changes in pure price of exports (a coefficient of 0·58) and that improvements in the quality of exports are correlated with quality upgrading of imports (a coefficient of 0·43). There is no

TABLE 1
Correlations between pure price movements and quality upgrading for both imports and exports

	Total Trade				Trade without imports from OECD			
All sectors								
	Pimp	Qimp	Pexp	Qexp	Pimp	Qimp	Pexp	Qexp
Pimp	1·00				1·00			
Qimp	0.36*	1·00			0.30*	1·00		
Pexp	0.58*	0·14	1·00		0.38*	0·07	1·00	
Qexp	0.34*	0.43*	0·19	1·00	0·21	0·28	0·19	1·00
Textiles								
	Pimp	Qimp	Pexp	Qexp	Pimp	Qimp	Pexp	Qexp
Pimp	1·00				1·00			
Qimp	0·76*	1·00			0·76*	1·00		
Pexp	0·60*	0·81*	1·00		0·63*	0·71*	1·00	
Qexp	0·31	0·11	−0·20	1·00	0·19	−0·21	−0·20	1·00
Clothing								
	Pimp	Qimp	Pexp	Qexp	Pimp	Qimp	Pexp	Qexp
Pimp	1·00				1·00			
Qimp	0·69*	1·00			0·26	1·00		
Pexp	0·64*	0·47	1·00		0·53*	0·35	1·00	
Qexp	0·65*	0·77*	0·53*	1·00	0·42	0·52*	0·53*	1·00
Footwear								
	Pimp	Qimp	Pexp	Qexp	Pimp	Qimp	Pexp	Qexp
Pimp	1·00				1·00			
Qimp	−0·07	1·00			0·18	1·00		
Pexp	0·68*	−0·10	1·00		0·28	−0·15	1·00	
Qexp	0·25	0·20	0·19	1·00	0·30	0·18	0·19	1·00

Notes:
Pimp = change in pure price of imports, Pexp = change in pure price of exports, Qimp = quality upgrading of imports, Qexp = quality upgrading of exports.
*Coefficient significant at 5%

evidence here that increasing import price competition is associated with significant upgrading of the quality of exports. Pure price movements are positively and significantly correlated with quality upgrading of exports.

Thus, we find that where import competition has been strongest in terms of relatively small increase or declines in pure prices there have generally been small pure price increases of exports, and a limited degree of quality upgrading of both imports and exports. Moreover, when imports have been characterised by strong quality upgrading there has been also upgrading of exports. We also present separate correlations for each of the three unskilled intensive sectors, but here are limited to 15 observations only. All the sectors are characterised by the positive and significant association between movements in pure import prices and changes in the pure price of exports. But only in clothing is there a significant correlation between changes in the price of imports and changes in the quality of exports, but again the association is positive. No correlation between quality upgrading of imports and exports is revealed in the footwear sector.

We have made some limited attempts to check the robustness of these associations. What we find is that the key price-price and quality-quality correlations remain, firstly, when imports from the OECD are excluded so that we calculate movements in the prices of imports from only low wage regions (right hand column of Table 1), and secondly, when bilateral associations are investigated (results are not reported here but are available). The latter case provides for an increase in the number of observations in each period and in each sector.[7]

This correlation analysis is rather weak and further work is required to extend the data to provide for the more formal testing of hypotheses regarding the impact of globalisation. However, we interpret these results as indicating possible important linkages between developments in the international and national markets. In general import price competition seems to have been positively associated with movements in the price of exports, whilst quality upgrading of imports seems to be linked to movements in the quality of exports.[8] We do not find any convincing evidence from the changing structure of exports of defensive innovation leading to a higher quality bundle of exports in response to stiff price competition from imports.

VI Conclusions

In this paper we have sought to delve into sectoral import and export prices to separate out changes due to pure price movements for a given bundle of goods and changes due to adjustments to the bundle of goods imported or exported.

[7] Germany was the only country where none of the correlations in any sector were significant.

[8] We very simply considered the issue of causality by assessing the links between movements in import prices in one period and movements in export prices in the following periods. Both at the aggregate and the sectoral level the correlations were higher when the import data were associated with the export data of the following period.

We feel this is useful in attempting to identify more clearly whether the prices of unskilled intensive activities have fallen relative to that of skilled intensive activities. It has also allowed us to consider the nature of the response to more intense international competition, as reflected in falling relative pure prices and upgrading of the quality of imports, in terms of changes to the price and composition of the bundle of goods exported.

Specifically we report three key conclusions:

1. With respect to the issue of relative prices our analysis reveals important differences between the 1970s and the 1980s in the impact of trade with low-wage countries on European economies. Our analysis of changes in pure import prices suggests that the 1980s are the Stolper-Samuelson decade, when the price of unskilled intensive products fell relative to that of skilled intensive goods. Relative prices of unskilled compared to skilled intensive goods changed little in the 1976 81 period. However, in the period 1981 94 we observe a drastic fall in the pure price of imports of textiles and clothing from low-wage regions relative to the pure price of imports of engineering products from the OECD countries.
2. Pure price movements in the imported bundles have generally been accompanied by price movements in the same direction in the exported bundle of the same sector. A positive association is also apparent between upgrading of the quality of imports and improvements in the quality of exports. In other words, import price competition seems to be associated more with movements in the price rather than the quality of exports. Along the same lines, when imports have been characterised by quality upgrading there has also tended to be upgrading of the quality of exports.
3. Considerable heterogeneity among unskilled intensive sectors is revealed. The impact of trade with low-wage countries on relative import prices is not common across all unskilled intensive sectors. We find behaviour in the footwear sector to be quite different to that in the textiles and clothing sectors.

In general, our results support the view that using relative import prices identifies more clearly an impact of globalisation in Europe. An issue for further reflection is why these changes in import prices do not show up in changes in relative domestic output prices; is it simply a matter of data or does it reflect the nature of production and distribution in European countries?

In this work we have not been able to link the changes in relative import prices to developments in domestic factor markets in Europe. However, our analysis would suggest caution in rejecting globalisation as a significant factor in explaining the outcomes for unskilled workers in European countries over the past 20 years. Substantial movements in relative prices revealed by the import data are consistent with trade having played a significant role in affecting the fortunes of unskilled workers in Europe. From a policy perspective we subscribe to the view that even though trade may have played an important role in affecting these workers in Europe the most suitable response is in terms of facilitating adjustment of these workers to alternative areas of activity.

Appropriate intervention would appear to be in the form of retraining, enhancing labour market flexibility and promoting the mobility of labour via, for example, measures affecting the housing market.

ACKNOWLEDGEMENTS

This paper has been prepared under the research project 'Globalisation and Social Exclusion' financed by the European Commission under the Targeted Socio-Economic Research (TSER) Programme. The paper has benefited from the comments of other team members. The authors are also grateful for the comments of Kimberly Clausing. An earlier version of this work was presented at the Conference of the European Trade Study Group in Rotterdam, 24–26 September 1999. The authors thank the participants for some useful comments. The usual disclaimer applies.

REFERENCES

ANDERTON, R. and BRENTON P. (1998). Trade with the NICs and wage inequality: evidence from the UK and Germany. In P. Brenton and J. Pelkmans (eds), *Global Trade and European Workers*. London, Macmillan, pp. 39–68.

AW, B. Y. and ROBERTS, M. J. (1986). Measuring quality change in quota-constrained import markets. The case of US Footwear. *Journal of International Economics*, 21, pp. 45–60.

BRENTON, P. and PINNA, A-M. (2000). 'Trends in Disaggregated Import and Export Prices in Europe: Implications for the Trade and Wages Debate'. Working Document 141. Brussels, Centre for European Policy Studies.

CHINLOY, P. (1980). 'Sources of quality change in labour input', *American Economic Review*, 70, 108–119.

LAWRENCE, R. (1996). *Single World, Divided Nations?* Paris, OECD Development Centre.

LEAMER, E. (1996). In search of Stolper-Samuelson effects on US wages. Working Paper 5427. Cambridge MA, National Bureau of Economic Research.

LUCKE, M. (1998). European trade with lower-income countries and the relative wages of the unskilled: an explanatory analysis for West Germany and the UK. In P. Brenton and J. Pelkmans (eds) *Global Trade and European Workers*. London, Macmillan, pp. 69–95.

SLAUGHTER, M. (1998). International trade and labour market outcomes: results, questions, and policy options. *Economic Journal*, 108, pp. 1452–62.

WOOD, A. (1994). *North-South Trade, Employment and Inequality: Changing Fortunes in a Skill-Driven World*. Oxford, Clarendon Press.

WOOD, A. (1997). Openness and wage inequality in developing countries: the Latin American challenge to East Asian conventional wisdom. *World Bank Economic Review*, 11, pp. 33–57.

WOOD, A. (1998). Globalisation and the rise in labour market inequalities. *Economic Journal*, 108, pp. 1463–82.

Date of receipt of final manuscript: 12 March 2001.

Chapter 12

Adjustment to globalisation

A study of the footwear industry in Europe

Paul Brenton, Anna Maria Pinna and Marc Vancauteren

Introduction

Most of the economic literature on globalisation has concentrated upon the impact of trade upon relative wages and relative employment opportunities for unskilled relative to skilled workers in OECD countries.[1] This has been based upon the observed worsening of the fortunes of less-skilled workers in many industrial countries and the textbook Hechscher-Ohlin-Samuelson (HOS) model of international trade. This theory, including the Stolper-Samuelson link between changing product prices and changing relative wage rates, has been widely adopted despite rather shaky empirical support. In this framework globalisation leads to a reallocation of resources in OECD countries from import competing, low-skill-intensive industries to the high-skill-intensive sectors in which these countries have a comparative advantage. Most economists conclude that the role of policy in this context is to assist this reallocation by providing training and increasing the quantity of skilled labour.

However, a number of observed features suggest that this paradigm is inappropriate for a complete appraisal of the impact of globalisation in OECD countries. First, for many of the unskilled intensive sectors, as the import penetration ratio has increased so has the ratio of exports to output. In the standard HOS model countries either import or export products, not both. Hence, even in low-skill-intensive sectors product differentiation exists. This then provides another means of adjustment to globalisation not possible within the standard model, the within sector adjustment to produce different and higher quality products. Second, there appears to be a range of experience across countries in the evolution of low-skill-intensive sectors. In some OECD countries certain sectors have maintained employment and output whilst in other countries production has declined dramatically. If the trade shock from globalisation is common across countries then this suggests that a variety of responses to globalisation are available to firms in OECD countries.

Industrial adjustment to globalisation is the focus of this chapter. Here we concentrate upon one particular sector, footwear, which bears the characteristics of a typical low-skill intensive manufacturing sector where comparative advantage has decisively shifted to low-wage labour abundant countries. We do not provide a comprehensive overview of developments in the footwear sector but highlight a number of key issues which are apparent from an analysis of footwear but which do not often figure in general discussions of globalisation. We concentrate upon how adjustment to globalisation has taken place in those European countries which were major footwear producers at the start of the 1970s and discuss the diversity of experiences across Europe. We start with the standard trade model and analyse the changes in trade flows which have affected the footwear industry in Europe. We then proceed to discuss the main changes in the industry which are apparent over the last 20 years. We first look at developments in employment, distinguishing between skilled and unskilled workers, before looking at changes in wages and some data concerning the nature of unemployment of footwear workers in one EU country; Belgium. Finally, we look for evidence of strategies used by firms to successfully adjust to the increased international competition from low-wage countries, including discussion of productivity growth, technological adaptation, upgrading of product quality and finally the development of industrial districts and flexible organisation.

Globalisation and EU trade in footwear products

Traditional trade theory, in the form of the Stolper-Samuelson theorem, suggests that changes in the relative price of unskilled labour intensive products, such as footwear, lie at the heart of traditional explanations of the link between trade, changes in relative wages and structural adjustment. Much of the empirical literature on this issue has failed to find convincing evidence that the price of products, such as footwear, has fallen relative to the price of products skilled-intensive products, such as machinery (Lawrence, 1996; Lucke, 1997; Slaughter, 1998; Anderton and Brenton, 1999a).

One possible explanation for these results is the sectoral producer prices which as typically analysed are unable to capture the relevant trade shock faced by the industrialised economies because they are too aggregated. Wood (1997, 1998), for example, argues that heterogeneity of goods in standard statistical definitions of sectors and changes in quality over time (which maybe correlated with the skill intensity of production) could engender substantial errors into available producer price series. If sub-sectors within industries are different, in terms of requiring different amounts of skilled and unskilled labour, then more open trade may reduce the prices of some goods but raise the prices of others, leaving the industry aggregate price unchanged. This is likely to be the case for footwear when thinking of standardised mass-produced varieties and fashion sensitive high quality shoes, for example. Ideally, one would use highly disaggregated series on producer prices to address this issue, but unfortunately they are not available. Wood points instead to changes in the prices of imports and exports, which do suggest a rising relative price of skilled-intensive products in the 1980s (but not in the 1970s).

However, Brenton and Pinna (2000), who use highly disaggregated import data to separate out changes in quality (defined as movements to higher value products) from pure price movements within the bundle of imported footwear products, suggest there was no change or even a decrease in the import prices of the skilled intensive machinery industries relative to footwear. Thus, the traditional trade theory link from falling relative prices to falling relative wages is difficult to support in the case of footwear, but these authors do find support for falling relative import prices for textiles and for clothing.

Imports used in the earlier exercise were measured at the border and hence the calculated prices did not capture tariffs and the impact of non-tariff barriers. Thus, even if border prices did not change, producer and consumer prices may have fallen if trade barriers have been reduced. However, in the EU there has been little change in the degree of tariff protection of footwear producers over the past thirty years. Footwear remains a relatively highly protected industry. The average tariff on EU imports of industrial products is now around 3 per cent whilst for leather footwear the tariff is 8 per cent and for footwear with non-leather uppers the tariff is currently equal to 17 per cent. In 1976 the tariff on finished leather footwear was 8 per cent whilst that on non-leather footwear was 20 per cent, the latter has only declined since 1994.

In addition to customs duties, imports of footwear into EU countries have often been subjected to non-tariffs measures including quantitative restrictions and voluntary export restraints and anti-dumping measures. Prior to the creation of the Single Market in the EU there were a number of bilateral trade restrictions on imports of footwear. For example, the French and Italian footwear industries pleaded successfully with the Commission to be allowed to impose VERs in the mid-1980s on imports of non-leather footwear from Asian countries, specifically Taiwan and Korea. The Commission justified this action on the basis that different types of footwear are substitutable in demand and that the sharp rise in imports of synthetic and textile footwear contributed directly to the fall of more than 70 million pairs in Community production of leather footwear.[2] The removal of border and customs formalities that was necessitated by the Single Market implied that bilateral restrictions could no longer be maintained. Thus, the bilateral restrictions on imports into Italy and France were reformed into an EC-wide quota system, though this has subsequently been removed.

Evidence for the UK suggests that non-tariff trade barriers have not been successful in preserving total employment in the footwear sector and have been an extremely expensive means of protection. Brenton and Winters (1993) and Winters and Takacs (1991) model the effects of a number of quantitative restrictions imposed by the UK in the late 1970s and early 1980s on imports of non-leather footwear from the Far East and imports of leather footwear from Central and Eastern European countries. Their findings suggest that in 1979 (when all of these restrictions were in place) the total cost of a job saved in the UK footwear sector was nearly 12 times annual wages every year for each year that the protection was in place.

This all suggests that trade liberalisation in the form of reductions in tariffs or removal of NTBs cannot be at the heart of explanations of the decline in footwear employment in Europe. In addition the view that high tariffs and non-tariff barriers are a useful tool to protect domestic industries from low-cost foreign competition or to allow time for adjustment to the new competition receives little support from the experience of footwear. We now proceed to look in more detail at changes in the quantity of footwear imported into the EU market.

Import penetration and export intensity in the EU footwear sector

According to Wood (1995), developed countries have shifted from 'manufacturing autarky', in which they produced all the manufactures demanded domestically (skilled-labour-intensive and unskilled-labour-intensive products) to specialisation in the production of the skilled-intensive activities within all sectors and reliance upon imports from developing countries to supply their needs of labour intensive commodities. Thus, not all types of footwear that are imported compete with domestically produced shoes. In this framework, a fall in the world price of the imported unskilled intensive products would no longer affect skilled and unskilled workers as factors of production in industrial countries. Relative wages are not tied to relative world prices and instead both benefit from a lower price of goods they consume. Relative wages are only determined by domestic factor demand and supply conditions. Hence, trade volumes and not relative product prices matter. The trade effect on wages and employment in the industrial countries has to be measured by calculating the quantities of skilled and unskilled labour embodied in imports and export flows. According to this view, wages in the footwear sector have been driven down because footwear activities (not only finished pairs of shoes, but especially components) formerly undertaken by unskilled workers in industrial countries are increasingly being purchased from low-wage developing countries.

Figure 6.1 shows the trend in the quantity (metric tons) of footwear traded within the EU12 market (intra-EU) and imported by the EU12 from the extra-EU region. It is clear that the trend rate of growth of imports from both external and EU countries increased after the mid-1980s but that the rate of growth of extra-EU imports was greater than that of internal EU trade.[3] Hence import penetration of the EU footwear market from external sources increased considerably after the mid-1980s.

In the 1990s, for the first time, the volume of footwear imported from outside of the EU has exceeded internal trade in footwear. Imports from non-EU countries increased by 41 per cent between 1976 and 1981. Between 1986 and 1994 extra-EU imports rose by 168 per cent whilst the volume of EU production increased by 25 per cent and domestic consumption was 43 per cent higher.

Figure 6.2 illustrates import penetration as well as the export intensity ratio for each of the main EU producing countries, Italy, Germany, France and the UK, along with Spain and Portugal, whose shares of European production have increased since the 1980s. The Italian, UK, German and French markets have been increasingly penetrated by imports since the mid-1970s whilst in Spain and Portugal import penetration increased considerably only after 1986.

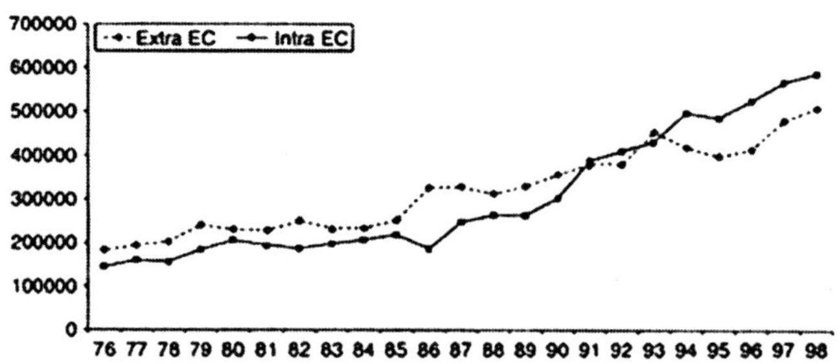

Figure 6.1 EU12 intra-EC and extra-EC and imports of footwear by volume, 1976–1998.

Source: Comext Database.

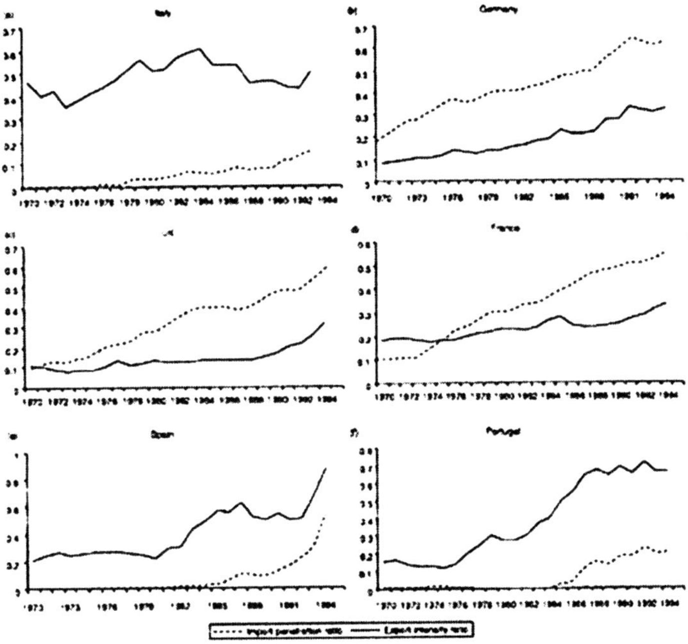

Figure 6.2 Import penetration and export intensity in the European footwear industry: (a) Italy; (b) Germany; (c) UK; (d) France; (e) Spain; (f) Portugal.

Source: OECD STAN Database.

In all of these European countries the share of production devoted to exports has risen, with this increase being particularly strong for Spain and Portugal. In 1994, Spain exported more than 80 per cent of total production, whilst at the beginning of the 1980s only 20 per cent of production was exported. Italy has seen some variability in the amount of production exported but was already a major exporter of footwear in the early 1970s. Nevertheless, a substantial proportion of Italian footwear output continues to be exported. Moving to the remaining countries, the common picture is one of a concurrent increase in import penetration and export intensity. For the UK, France and Germany a substantially higher proportion of output is now exported relative to the 1970s.

Clearly, this rise in the export propensity reflects in part the decline in the amount of production of footwear in Europe. However, it is clear that EU producers are now exporting more footwear than 20 years ago: the volume of footwear exported has increased. This is difficult to reconcile with standard trade theory. Loss of comparative advantage should affect sales in all countries not just those in the domestic market. The trade data also show that the volume of footwear exported outside of the EU has grown faster than exports to other EU countries. Hence the explanation for rising exports cannot be increased trade between members behind a protective external wall.

This growth in the amount of EU footwear that is exported entails that EU producers are selling shoes that are differentiated from those of the low wage producers who have increasingly penetrated the EU domestic market and/or that the amount of outsourcing of footwear has increased. Some information on this issue can be gleaned from comparing the volume of exports of footwear measured in tonnes and the volume of exports measured in pairs. In the EU trade statistics finished shoes are recorded in both pairs and tonnes, whilst parts of footwear tend to be measured only by weight. Over the past 20 years exports of footwear measured in tonnes and measured in pairs have both increased but the amount of tonnes of exports has grown at a much faster rate than exports of footwear measured in pairs. Thus, unless there has been a substantial increase in the weight per pair of shoes exported (unlikely unless exports have been concentrated upon boots with an ever increasing size of steel toe cap), then not only has there been an increase in exports of finished differentiated footwear from Europe but there has been a more significant increase in outsourcing, where parts are exported from the EU for further processing abroad. We return to the issue of outsourcing later.

To consider more carefully how the increase in import penetration may have affected the nature of production of EU footwear we proceed to consider the geographical composition of EU imports, and in particular, how the share of low-wage countries has changed. Figure 6.3 illustrates the trend in the share of EU12 imports of total footwear from the NICs (4 Asian tigers), RoA (rest of Asian countries), CEEE (Central Eastern European Economies) and RoW (rest of the World trade). The data show a clear increase in the penetration of imports from less-developed, low-wage regions in the period after the mid-1980s, which coincides with the rapid increase in the volume of EU imports of footwear identified

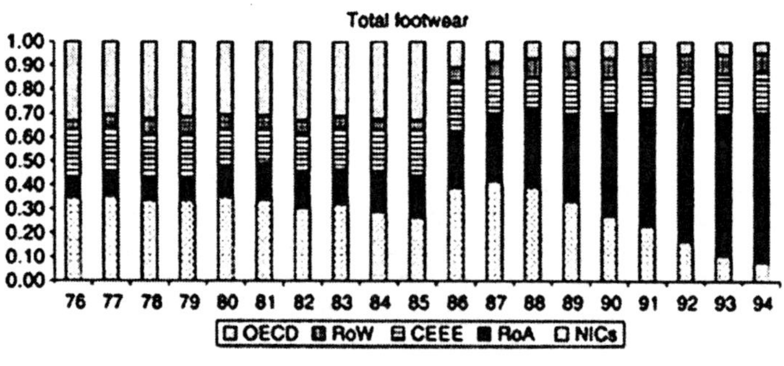

Figure 6.3 Shares of extra-EC 12 imports by region of origin.

in Figures 6.1 and 6.2. This occurred first, at the expense of the OECD countries and has subsequently been associated with a decline in the share of the NICs themselves. This reflects in part the relocation of activity in Asia away from the NICs towards countries such as the Philippines and Thailand but, in particular, China.

Until 1985, trade with OECD countries accounted for around 30–35 per cent of total extra-EU12 imports. This share has subsequently been reduced considerably to less than 10 per cent. Such changes in the composition of imports may reflect, at least partially, another aspect of the globalisation process whereby firms in OECD countries have relocated their production to low-wage regions. Sales by OECD firms of finished products in the EU market which are produced in low-wage locations overseas will be recorded as imports from the developing country where production took place.

Thus the past 15 years have seen important changes in the magnitude of import penetration on the EU footwear market and that of each member country. This has been accompanied by substantial adjustments in the source of extra-EU imports. At the more detailed product level the data confirm a substantial increase in the penetration of imports of final footwear products by low-wage countries and the re-sourcing of parts and components away from OECD countries to the Central and Eastern European countries and to countries in Asia (excluding the NICs).

We now address how exports of the different categories of footwear have developed, and in particular, finished products relative to parts and components. Much of the discussion on how globalisation has affected labour market outcomes in OECD countries has concentrated upon the impact of the increased availability of cheaper products imported from low-wage economies. However, a world of more integrated economies implies not only the possibility to export the national variety of a product but also the option to partially or completely relocate domestic production to low-wage locations. The two developments are linked if relocation occurs as a defensive strategy to the availability of cheaper imports.

Finished footwear products exported from the EU are mainly sold in other OECD countries, although the importance of the OECD has been declining and the Central and Eastern European countries have risen in prominence as a market for finished EU footwear. Changes in the geographical composition of exports of parts and component segments follow the same pattern but their magnitude has been much greater. For example, uppers of leather and other parts made of leather were mainly exported to OECD countries during the 1970s and the first part of the 1980s, but by 1994 less than 20 per cent of EU12 exports were directed to the OECD region. In 1994 the majority, over 70 per cent, of such parts and components were exported to Central and Eastern European countries. These changes in the geographical structure of exports of parts and components may be linked to the relocation of production out of the EU12 in response to increasing import competition from low-wage regions, which brings us to the issue of outsourcing.

Outsourcing occurs when firms take advantage of low-wage costs in labour abundant countries by moving the low-skill-intensive parts of the production process abroad, but continue to carry out the high-skill activities themselves in the domestic economy. Trade with low-wage countries via this route shifts employment away from less-skilled workers in industrial countries and puts downward pressure on the relative wages and employment of less-skilled workers within industries. The phenomenon has been investigated by Feenstra and Hanson (1996a, b) using data on imports of intermediate inputs by domestic firms. The underlying intuition is that intermediate inputs are associated with unskilled labour activities which domestic firms choose to move abroad to cheap labour locations as a response to more intense import competition from low-wage countries.

One feature that is apparent for the EU is that the value per unit of imports of parts and components is greater than the unit value of exports of parts and components, both in total and for various sub-categories. Such a difference, moreover, has increased over time. This is consistent with the view that an important feature of manufacturing trade over the last two decades has been the increasing division of the value chain (Krugman, 1995b) and the relocation of certain activities (the most unskilled-intensive) to low-wage economies. Here the evidence suggests that the value-added embodied in European exports of parts and components of footwear is less than that embodied in European imports of footwear parts and components, suggesting that additional value to parts and components is added outside of Europe. We now proceed to look at how the domestic nature of the footwear industry in Europe has changed over the past 30 years in the light of these developments in trade.

Changes in employment and wages in the footwear sector

Employment in footwear

Table 6.1 shows the tremendous changes in the use of labour in the footwear sector that have occurred since 1970. However, it is clear that the pattern of

Table 6.1 Change in total labour input in footwear in selected countries: 1970=100

1997	*US*	*Italy*	*Spain*	*Portugal*	*UK*	*Germany*
1970	100	100	100	100	100	100
1980	78.92	97.52	121.36	108.21	91.49	62.54
1985	51.96	96.18	104.40	124.02	68.81	54.07
1990	37.74	91.53	61.92	n.a.	52.27	36.50
1995	29.65	101.14	53.15	n.a.	42.32	20.8
1997	31.85	101.78	57.16	n.a.	42.98	19.56

Source: ISIS.

changes in labour input varies substantially across countries. In the UK, the US and Germany the amount of persons employed in footwear has been declining continuously since 1970. For these countries between one-tenth and one-third of the jobs in footwear in 1970 had been lost by 1980. Employment loss continued throughout the 1980s and by 1997 the number of footwear jobs in the US was only 32 per cent of the level in 1970. In Germany in the same year employment in footwear was less than one-fifth of the level of 1970, whilst in the UK only 43 per cent of the number of jobs at the start of the period remained.[4]

For Italy, employment in footwear remained roughly constant throughout the 1970s and early 1980s. Between 1985 and 1992 there was a 10 per cent reduction in the level of employment in the Italian footwear sector. However, there has subsequently been an increase in employment with a return to the numbers employed in the early 1970s. For Spain the level of employment in the footwear sector increased during the 1970s and then declined from 1980 to 1988 with some subsequent stabilisation. Between 1985 and 1988 one-third of footwear jobs in Spain was lost. The period of employment loss in Spain coincides with accession to the EU and there is some evidence of a period of relocation by Spanish footwear manufactures to Portugal during this period. Footwear employment in Portugal itself has increased continuously since 1970. In 1989 the number of footwear jobs in Portugal was double the number which existed in 1970.[5]

In addition to looking at changes in total employment it is also important, as trade theory suggests, to consider changes in the relative employment of skilled and unskilled workers in the footwear sector. Unfortunately, the available data do not clearly define skilled and unskilled workers and so, in common with other studies of globalisation, we have to use definitions based upon manual and non-manual workers (Table 6.2).

In all countries except Portugal and Italy, there has been a substantial loss of manual employment in the footwear industry. This loss of manual employment has occurred consistently since the 1970s although it has generally been more pronounced in the period since 1985, when import penetration has increased most strongly. The final rows of Table 6.2 show a substantial decline in the ratio of unskilled to skilled footwear workers in all countries, including Italy where the fall in the employment of unskilled workers has been less significant, even though there was a much higher ratio of unskilled to skilled workers in Italy at the start

Table 6.2 The composition of employment in footwear: manual and non-manual workers (number)

	Germany		*Spain*		*Portugal*		*Italy*		*UK*		*France*	
	Manual	*Non-man*	*Manual*	*Non-man*	*Manual*	*Non-man*	*Manual*	*Non-man*	*Manual*	*Non-man*	*Manual*	*Non-man*
1970	78,450	11,250	45,510	7,125	14,050	2,120	88,531	7,300	76,000	12,900	65,210	8,972
1975	61,025	9,425	55,320	8,560	15,242	2,255	79,251	7,200	70,727	11,150	58,464	8,845
1980	47,850	8,250	48,700	6,250	17,604	2,450	79,250	7,100	70,285	11,050	50,337	7,412
1985	41,250	7,250	36,250	4,985	25,045	2,564	78,250	6,920	54,287	6,885	40,524	6,432
1990	26,147	6,596	26,786	4,659			68,412	8,812	40,343	6,125	33,414	7,994
1995	14,152	4,521	24,202	5,802			77,121	15,213	31,250	6,372	25,847	5,451
1997	13,252	4,293	23,654	5,594			72,221	11,421	30,145	8,064	24,510	4,854
Percentage changes												
1970–1985	−47,42	−35,56	−20,35	−30,04	78,26	20,09	−11,61	−5,21	−28,57	−46,63	−37.86	−28.31
1985–1997	−67,87	−40,79	−34,75	12,22			−7,70	65,04	−44,47	17,12	−39.52	−24.53
Ratio of manual to non-manual												
1970	6.97		6.39		6.63		12.13		5.89		7.27	
1997	3.08		4.23				6.32		3.74		5.05	

Sources: Eurostat, ILO, ISTS.

of the period relative to other countries. In Spain, Italy and the UK there has been an absolute increase in the employment of non-manual workers since 1985, whilst manual employment has continued to plummet. This is difficult to reconcile with standard trade theory, where given the fall in the price of unskilled labour, the unskilled/skilled labour ratio is expected to increase. It may reflect a somewhat different response to international competition since the mid-1980s. The observed increase in the relative use of skilled labour could reflect an attempt by European footwear producers to upgrade their production and to concentrate upon the production of high quality footwear and/or upon design-intensive activities. We return to this issue later, when we discuss evidence of upgrading from data on exports by EU footwear producers. It may also reflect the impact of outsourcing, which we suggest above has been an important feature of the adjustment to globalisation, as low-skill-intensive activities are moved overseas whilst the skill-intensive parts of the production process are retained in Europe.

Developments in wages

Globalisation may lead to social exclusion even for workers who remain employed if there is a significant deterioration in their relative and more importantly their real wage. Here, in Table 6.3 we present the available data on percentage changes in wages for the unskilled and changes in salaries for the skilled workers employed in the footwear sector in various countries during the 1980s and early 1990s. In most cases the average wage of the unskilled footwear worker has increased proportionately less than the average salary of skilled workers. This is as one would expect. Intense competition from low-wage sources of supply would be expected to put downward pressure on the relative wage of the unskilled footwear workers in Europe. However, in Germany the returns to skilled and unskilled workers have risen at similar rates whilst in Portugal the unskilled footwear worker has fared much better than the average skilled footwear worker.

It is also important to compare the wage performance of footwear workers relative to that of other workers employed in manufacturing. Table 6.3 also shows changes in wages and salaries in manufacturing as a whole. These data demonstrate that in Germany, the UK, Italy and Spain unskilled footwear workers have done less well in terms of wage increases than other workers in manufacturing. In Portugal, France and the US unskilled footwear workers have received larger increases in wages than unskilled workers in general. Similarly, in all countries for which data are available, with the exception of France and the US, skilled workers in footwear have obtained lower increases in salaries than skilled workers on average in manufacturing.

The final rows of Table 6.3 also show that, with the exception of Spain over the short 5-year period for which data is available, wages of unskilled workers employed in the footwear industry in Europe have increased at a faster rate than the general price index since 1980. In this sense we find no evidence from these data that unskilled footwear workers in Europe or the US have suffered from the compression of real wages experienced by unskilled workers in general in the US.

Table 6.3 Changes in wages and salaries in footwear and in manufacturing, 1980–1994

United States		*Germany*		*Portugal*		*UK*		*Spain*		*Italy*		*France*	
Unskill	*Skill*	*Unskill*	*Skill*	*Unskill*	*Skill*	*Unskill*	*Skill*	*Unskill*	*Skill*	*Unskill*	*Skill*	*Unskill*	*Skill*
Percentage change in wages and salaries in footwear 1980–1994													
100.4[a]	110.3[a]	64.13	64.66	659.18	542.6	146.51	165.53	24.69[b]	39.06[b]	101.02[c]	122.84[c]	132.27	146.7
Percentage change in wages and salaries in manufacturing: 1980–1994													
73.6[c]	93.2[c]	76.96	75.48	512.5	796.09	168.33	195.30	92.59[b]	91.59[b]	127.1[c]	141.1[c]	120.80	121.0
Percentage change in consumer price index: 1980–1994													
75.27[c]		51.28		560.19		115.66		31.16[b]		93.62[c]		94.31	

Sources: EUROSTAT, US Bureau of Labour Statistics and IMF *International Financial Statistics*.

Notes

a 1980–1993 All footwear, leather-related products except rubber footwear,

b 1989–1994.

c 1980–1993.

a 1983–1994.

More surprisingly the data do suggest a decline in the real wage of skilled footwear workers in Portugal. So, although unskilled footwear workers in Europe have not suffered a real wage reduction, in general, their wage relative to that of other unskilled workers in Europe has fallen.

For footwear it is clear that the group of production or unskilled workers is far from homogeneous, as is often assumed in discussions of the impact of globalisation. The process of making footwear can be broken down into distinct stages of production. Accordingly, this division of production stages has brought about a division of labour, which requires a variety of skills from within the unskilled labour force. For example, the cutting of the leather, in which the varying texture of the material must be taken into consideration, is the most highly skilled and best paid job within the group of production workers in the factory. This is further illustrated by Table 6.4, which shows the range of wage costs for manual workers according to skill types in both Belgium and Italy.

It would appear that wage levels reflect the skill intensity of manual workers in the leather footwear industry. Cutters, vampers, Goodyear stitchers, and so on, are of the highest order of skill and receive the highest hourly wages. This reflects not only that the nature of the job is quite complex, but also that it takes years of experience to work up to full efficiency (Blim, 1983). In Italy those at the highest levels within the group of production workers receive almost 60 per cent more in hourly wages than those at the bottom of the skill spectrum. In Belgium the ratio is smaller at around 16 per cent. Table 6.5 looks at the picture over time and presents the ratio of the wages of the most skilled manual workers (level 1) to those classified as less skilled. The lack of significant change in these ratios over time reflects the institutional structure of wage setting in both of these countries.

Table 6.4 Hourly wages for Italian and Belgian labourers according to level of skills in the leather footwear industry in 1999 (in EURO)

Level	*Classifications*	*Italy*	*Belgium*
1	Cutting parts of the upper and the sole, stitching of the inside sole, Goodyear stitchers	8,55	8,78
2	Stretching the completed upper over a wooden form (the last)	7,97	8,56
3	Attaching the sole to the upper, tying up out-soles	7,21	8,56
4	Includes all tasks of level 1, 2, 3 at the experience level between 3 and 6 months	6,89	8,26
5	Includes all tasks of level 1, 2, 3 at the experience level of 0–2 months	6,6	8,06
6	Completely perforating, stitching of front-feet, inspecting the shoe, tempering heel stock, pulling out tacks	6,33	7,99
7	Not-completely perforating and stitching, polishing and packing	6,05	7,89
8	Includes all tasks of level 6, 7 at the experience level of 0–2 months	5,43	7,59

Sources: Committee of Social Affairs (Belgium 1997), FILTA (1999).

Table 6.5 Ratio of hourly wages for Italian and Belgian labourers according to level of skills in the leather footwear industry, 1981–1999 (skill level 1=1)

	Skill level							
	1	*2*	*3*	*4*	*5*	*6*	*7*	*8*
Italy								
1999	1	0.93	0.84	0.81	0.77	0.74	0.71	0.64
1995	1 1	0.94	0.85	0.83	0.80	0.77	0.74	0.69
1989	1	0.98	0.90	0.85	0.82	0.80	0.76	n.a.
1985	1	0.92	0.86	0.84	0.81	0.78	n.a.	n.a.
1981	1	0.90	0.83	0.81	0.78	0.76	n.a.	n.a.
Belgium								
1999	1	0.97	0.97	0.94	0.92	0.91	0.90	0.86
1995	1	0.97	0.96	0.94	0.92	0.91	0.90	0.88
1989	1	0.97	0.96	0.94	0.92	0.91	0.89	0.88
1985	1	0.97	0.96	0.94	0.91	0.90	0.89	0.87
1981	1	0.97	0.95	0.93	0.91	0.90	0.88	0.86

Sources: Committee of Social Affairs (Belgium 1997), FILTA (1999).

If there has been a change in the relative demand for these different types of manual workers it is likely to have been reflected in changes in employment since wage adjustment appears constrained. In addition, if outsourcing reduces the employment of the least skilled within the group of production workers at a greater rate than employment of the more skilled cutters then the average recorded wage for production workers could rise.

It is also apparent that footwear produced within the key categories of leather, plastic, rubber and textile shoes is far from homogeneous. Thus, the extent to which production workers employed in the footwear industry in Europe compete with unskilled labour elsewhere in the world depends on the quality of the shoes produced. Higher quality shoes and more elaborate footwear styles require better workmanship and so the need for firms to retain those with the highest degree of skills among the production workers. In general, most EU countries producing leather footwear have oriented their production towards skilled labour, while EU firms producing synthetic shoes have sought to exploit the large endowment of low skilled, low wage labour in developing countries such as China, South Korea (CEC, 1997). In other words, where the quality of the footwear is important and it reflects the quality of the labour input then the forces pushing towards localisation of production can outweigh those of globalisation. At the same time these considerations also suggest that where quality is important the scope for mechanisation of the tasks of the production workers is likely to be limited.

Unemployment of footwear workers

The 'trade and labour' debate, both in the US and Europe, has firmly focused on the issue of how much inequality, either in terms of wages or unemployment, can

Table 6.6 Duration of unemployment in footwear and total manufacturinga in Belgium

	Less than 1 month	*1–3 months*	*3–6 months*	*6–12 months*	***STU/TOTU*** [b]	***LTU/TU*** [c]
1. Cutting, stitching and pinning-footwear						
1988	0.02	0.04	0.03	0.17	0.25	0.75
1998	0.04	0.03	0.04	0.05	0.16	0.84
2. Not completely perforating and stitching and polishing-footwear						
1988	0.07	0.06	0.14	0.12	0.40	0.60
1998	0.03	0.04	0.08	0.14	0.28	0.72
3. Spinning, weaving and knitting-textiles						
1988	0.03	0.04	0.05	0.10	0.22	0.78
1998	0.02	0.05	0.06	0.09	0.22	0.78
4. Manuals-total industry						
1988	0.04	0.06	0.07	0.13	0.30	0.70
1998	0.04	0.06	0.07	0.14	0.31	0.69
5. Non-manuals-total industry						
1988	0.05	0.07	0.09	0.22	0.43	0.57
1998	0.06	0.07	0.08	0.18	0.39	0.61

Source: Belgian Federal Ministry of Labour.

Notes

a based on number of job searchers registered,

b ratio short term unemployed/total unemployed,

c ratio of long term unemployed/total unemployed.

be attributed to increased competition from low-wage countries. None of the other dynamics of labour markets linked to social exclusion, such as the length of unemployment for those who are made redundant, or the mobility of different types of workers between wage classes, has been directly considered in relation to the emergence of less-developed countries in international markets.

An important element in the extent to which the decline in employment opportunities for manual workers in the footwear sector translates into social exclusion is the adjustment costs that such workers face in obtaining employment elsewhere in the economy. If workers released by the footwear sector are quickly re-employed in other sectors then the decline in employment in the footwear sector is unlikely to be a significant factor creating social exclusion.[6] On the other hand if footwear workers spend long periods without work, due perhaps to the sector specificity of the skills that they possess or locational factors, then the social costs of the decline in the footwear industry will rise.

Table 6.6 illustrates the duration of unemployment of two groups of manual footwear workers in Belgium and compares these with a group of manual workers in the textiles industry and then with all manual and all non-manual workers in Belgium. As shown in the table above differing wage levels reflect the skill intensity of manual workers in the footwear industry which suggests a degree of heterogeneity within the manual labour force employed within the footwear sector. We have selected the two groups of manual workers with the highest and lowest levels of skill according to the wage rate; respectively, those involved with (1) cutting, stitching and pinning and (2) those manuals who are partially involved in the stitching, and undertake perforating and polishing.

Table 6.6 shows the proportion of total unemployment in each category of worker by duration. We distinguish primarily between short-term unemployment, defined as those unemployed for twelve months or less, and the long-term unemployed, those without a job for more than one year. Thus, for footwear workers previously employed in cutting, weaving and pinning 75 per cent of the total number of unemployed had been without a job for more than one year in 1988. The principal conclusions which emerge from these data for Belgium are that

- Since 1988 the proportion of unemployed manual footwear workers who have been unemployed for more than one year has increased whereas the proportion of total unemployed manual workers in Belgium who are long-term unemployed has remained constant.
- A higher proportion of the more skilled manual footwear workers becomes long-term unemployed than do the least skilled manual workers. Those footwear workers who have the lowest level of skill find alternative employment more quickly than those manual workers with higher skills and higher wages. What is not apparent is whether this reflects skill specificity or wage inflexibility of this group of manual workers.
- The duration of unemployment of the least skilled footwear workers is, on average, less than that of the group of manual textile workers.
- The duration of unemployment of non-manual workers in Belgium is considerably less than that of manual workers.

It is also interesting to note that there may be considerable differences in the unemployment propensities of different skill categories of manual workers. For example, in Belgium in 1991 for every cutter and pinner, the most skilled manual worker, employed in the footwear sector there were more than two unemployed persons who previously worked as cutters and pinners in footwear. On the other hand, for every 8 finishers, the least skilled of the manual workers, employed in the footwear sector there was 1 unemployed former footwear finisher. Further, the ratio of employed to unemployed increased between 1981 and 1991 for finishers but declined for cutters and pinners. A similar feature is apparent for the textiles industry in Belgium: the ratio of employed to unemployed is higher for the least skilled manual workers and the propensity for the more skilled production workers to be unemployed has increased during the 1990s whilst that of the least skilled production workers has declined.[7]

So, for the footwear sector we find a degree of heterogeneity within the group of workers classified as manual both in terms of wage rates and unemployment duration. In Belgium, those manual footwear workers who receive the highest wage rates are also likely to experience longer terms of unemployment. This finding, which needs to be supported by data for other countries and other industries, is suggestive that training programmes which seek to upgrade the skills of manual workers to aid their re-entry into employment, could be more efficient if targeted at particular groups of manual workers, those which have a higher degree of skill which may be highly sector specific.

Responses to increased international competition

We now proceed to look at certain key factors which have affected the performance of the footwear industry in Europe in the light of globalisation and how European footwear producers have reacted to increasing foreign competition. We concentrate upon technological change, the upgrading of product quality and reorganisation of the industry to adopt flexible production methods and the development of industrial districts. In the earlier section, we showed that, in general, adjustment of the labour input in Europe has taken the form of reductions in the quantity employed and that large changes to the relative price of labour employed in footwear are not apparent.

We start by looking at technological change. In much of the debate over the causes of increasing inequality between skilled and unskilled workers the focus is upon identifying the relative impact of trade relative to technological change. However, improvements in technology may be both a cause of increased trade flows, by allowing the outsourcing of low-skill activities, for example, as well as a defensive response by producers in industrial countries to increasing competition from low-wage countries. Here we simply seek to identify the extent of technological change in the footwear sector.

Technological change

Measuring technological change is obviously very difficult. One simple approach is to look at the share of equipment in total investment and to check, as one might suspect, that the share of equipment increases substantially during periods in which technological change transforms the production process. Table 6.7 shows that, in general, the share of investment devoted to machinery has not changed substantially when the 1990s are compared with the early 1970s, although the data for certain countries show quite high volatility from year to year.

Table 6.7 Index of the share of investment in machinery in total investment in footwear (1970=100)

	Germany	*Portugal*	*Spain*	*UK*	*Italy*
1970	100,00	100,00	n.d.	100,00	100,00
1975	127,12	109,04	n.d	104,17	104,40
1980	112,10	88,27	n.d	104,17	109,24
1985	126,38	100,00	n.d.	100,96	84,36
1990	91,47	98,83	95,81	142,66	98,28
1994	112,99	28,68	96,93	90,00	118.20

Source: ISIS.

Table 6.8 The use and impact of computer-aided technologies in the footwear industry (percentage of respondents)

	France		*Germany*		*Italy*		*UK*		*Portugal*	
	CAD[a]	*CAS*[b]	*CAD*	*CAS*	*CAD*	*CAS*	*CAD*	*CAS*	*CAD*	*CAS*
In use	67	73	85	46	23	10	41	64	9	4
Negative impact on employment	20	33	38	38	12	20	9	55	9	13
Requires new abilities	67	40	85	31	40	30	59	45	48	43
Positive impact on quality	60	80	85	69	29	28	50	77	43	43

Source: DG V-EU data 'Social Study on the European Footwear Industry' (questionnaire).

Notes

a Computer-aided design.

b Computer-aided stitching.

Further indicators of technological development are provided in Table 6.8 which shows the responses of 250 firms to a survey carried out in 1999 concerning the application of two new technologies, computer-aided design (CAD) and computer-aided stitching (CAS). The responses suggest that the use of CAD, which is related to the design of the product, is far more widespread than the more production related technology, CAS. The data also suggest important differences across countries in the application of these technologies.

In general, CAD and CAS are applied more widely in France, Germany and the UK than in Italy and Portugal. In Germany, 85 per cent of respondents report that they are applying CAD techniques whilst 46 per cent of respondents are using computer-aided stitching. In the UK, nearly two-thirds of respondents confirm that they are using CAS. In Italy and Portugal these technologies appear to be much less widely applied, perhaps reflecting the nature of the sector in these locations; a large number of small firms and the preponderance of fashion-oriented leather-uppered footwear. Only 10 per cent of respondents in Italy and 4 per cent of respondents in Portugal report that they are using CAS techniques.

The questionnaire also asked respondents if the application of these technologies had had a negative impact upon employment. About 40 per cent of German firms, just over half of UK firms and one-third of French firms responded that the use of CAS had reduced employment. Responses in France and the UK suggest that the use of CAS has a more significant negative impact upon employment than application of CAD; only 9 per cent of UK respondents reported that CAD reduced employment levels. For Germany the same proportion of firms report a negative impact of CAD on employment as reported a negative employment impact of applying CAS.

Thus, we observe that loss of employment in footwear has not been evenly distributed amongst European countries. On the basis of the available data we find that those countries which had the lowest levels of labour productivity in footwear at the start of the period in 1970 experienced the sharpest falls in employment in footwear. In addition, there is some indication that these countries have more widely adopted the most recent technological advances that are relevant to the sector. We can, however, say nothing about the direction of causality concerning these developments or the extent to which the application of these technologies represents a response to more intense international competition.

Quality upgrading

We noted earlier that at the same time as import penetration ratios have increased so have export to output ratios. This is not possible to reconcile with traditional trade theory where products are assumed to be homogeneous wherever they are produced. Clearly, with the magnitude of the wage differentials between the EU countries and the developing countries, it is unlikely that EU producers could compete in the same market segments. Thus, one response from EU producers to intense international competition from low-wage countries would be to differentiate their product in terms of higher quality and in terms of design and fashion. It is interesting to note that the success of this response is likely to depend in part upon access conditions in other industrial countries. The principal markets for high quality footwear will be the OECD countries. Thus, in principle constraints upon exports of footwear to other OECD countries may constrain adjustment to more intense competition from low-wage countries. Here the role of regional integration may be important in the face of high barriers in other rich country markets.

A recent survey of global buyers of footwear products (Schmitz and Knorringa, 1999) highlights the importance of innovative design in the ability of Italy to compete with other countries who exhibit superiority in terms of price, such as China, India and Brazil. This study also shows the importance of flexibility in meeting orders in influencing buyers decisions. Italy's leading position in the industry is maintained by 'first, its innovative design capability, and second, its strong component industry' (Schmitz and Knorringa, 1999, p. 13), this is enhanced by fast response and high quality in supplying relatively small orders. China on the other hand is considered as a place of cheap shoes of reliable quality. China is also seen to be strong in responding to massive standardised orders.

Assessing the extent of quality upgrading is difficult. Data on production is collected at too aggregate a level to be useful. Given this, Brenton and Pinna (2000) look at upgrading of the exports of European countries as reflecting possible strategies by domestic footwear producers to increase the quality of their output. Using detailed (8-

digit) trade data these authors take quality upgrading to be a shift within the bundle of commodities exported towards higher value products. This analysis provides little evidence of a marked upgrading of the bundle of footwear products exported by EU countries in the 1980s and 1990s when import competition has become more intense. In fact exports of most of the EU countries, including Italy, to other OECD markets were downgraded after 1988.

Brenton and Pinna (2000) find no evidence of more intense import competition from low-wage countries in the footwear sector being statistically associated with export upgrading. The only significant correlation that they find suggests a positive relation between movements in the pure price of imports (after correcting for quality upgrading) and changes in pure price of exports. Thus, where import competition has been strongest in terms of pure prices there appear to have been smaller pure price increases of exports.

Thus, to date, despite much survey and anecdotal support, there is no comprehensive evidence from industry or trade data of quality upgrading being used as a response to globalisation in the footwear sector in Europe. However, the approach above will not pick up increases in quality which occur for all of the most detailed product categories. Hence, the Italian advantage in innovation in design could result in a higher quality of all the footwear produced in Italy. This will not appear as quality upgrading in the export bundle unless there is a shift to products which have a higher value at the start of the period under investigation.

Industrial districts and flexible organisation

Clearly the response to globalisation, and to greater competition generally in the footwear sector, has not been uniform across EU countries. In some countries, such as Germany, investment abroad has played a very important role and domestic employment has declined sharply. Elsewhere, in Italy, for example, domestic output and employment have been maintained. An important aspect of the apparent success of the footwear industry in Italy is the way that the industry has become organised, and in particular the adoption of flexible production methods and the emergence of locational concentration of firms in industrial districts. It is to this issue that we finally turn.

Storper and Scott (1990) define flexible production as the *'variety of ways in which producers shift promptly from one process and/or product to another, or adjust their output upward and downward in the short run without strongly deleterious effects on productivity'*. This flexibility can be achieved within the firm and between firms. The former can be derived from the use of general-purpose equipment and machinery and through the more effective adjustment of labour inputs. Flexibility between firms is achieved from the fragmentation of the production process into many units in different firms. This provides for rapid change in the combinations of vertical and horizontal linkages between the various units and allows for quick adjustment of output levels and of product specifications. It is clear that the footwear industry in Italy has benefited from a high degree of specialisation based upon the division of the production cycle, with several firms specialised in different phases of production (Rabellotti, 1995). Crucial in this structure is a well-developed network of backward-linked firms producing components and raw material. This organisation of the sector has led to a high degree of flexibility and ability to adjust to changing market conditions.

Flexibility in production is often closely linked with labour flexibility. Storper and Scott (1990) identify three main areas where employers seek flexibility from the labour input: (i) to make wage rates adjustable downwards and to determine wages on a worker-by-worker basis rather than with occupational groups (ii) redeployment of the workforce (internal flexibility) across the shop-floor and (iii) develop strategies that allow for rapid adjustments in the quantity of labour input (external flexibility). The latter can typically be achieved through labour turnover, including temporary lay-off and recall, through the use of more temporary workers, more part-time workers and via subcontracting. Internal flexibility of labour can be associated with a higher level of job security if firms seek to retain the high level of firm specific human capital that is involved. External flexibility will in general have an adverse effect upon employment security, although again cases can be found where, for example, high levels of subcontracting stabilise the level of production.

In such an industry, skilled workers will typically be required to move frequently from task to task and from job to job. However, this is not usually associated with long periods of unemployment. Unskilled labour, on the other hand, whose wages are generally low, often face considerable employment instability. Thus, although flexible production methods have been an important response to changing international conditions, and seem to have played a crucial role in the success of the footwear industry in Italy, there are significant implications for labour, primarily unskilled labour, in terms of employment security.

Flexibility in production often results in rapid increases or decreases in labour input and has led firms to increase the number of workers, temporary or part-time, who enjoy lower levels of employment security. This results in income variation for workers over time due to their changing access to employment. Finally, workers with lower levels of employment security are likely to have less bargaining power than more secure workers. Thus, production and labour flexibility may have played an important role in widening wage differentials between skilled and unskilled workers.

Flexible production methods result from the fragmentation of the production process into many specialised units linked together in a network of supplier-buyer and subcontracting relationships. The close inter-relations between suppliers entails that many firms tend to be located in close proximity which has led to the development of industrial districts. Rabellotti (1995) provides evidence of the nature of footwear districts from two Italian regions; Brenta and Marche. Of fundamental importance to these districts is the presence of strong backward-linkages. That is, the existence of a well-developed system of suppliers and subcontractors which can provide a wide variety of products with short delivery times. This has a number of advantages including, smaller stocks of inputs for producing final shoes, the progressive reduction of the time between order and delivery, and an increase in the capacity of final shoe producers to diversify their products. Collaboration between the suppliers of inputs and the producers of shoes is an important aspect of the way that footwear industrial districts are organised since it allows fashion decisions to be taken together.

The Italian footwear districts are characterised by a high level of subcontracting with a wide network of enterprises specialised in particular aspects of the production process. According to Varaldo (1988), more than 80 per cent of Italian footwear firms subcontract the production of soles, insoles and heels, around 70 per cent subcontract the production phases of edging and sewing of uppers and about half of the firms subcontract the cutting phase. This splitting up of the production process allows the use of specialised machines and specific labour skills for particular tasks and provides for larger scale economies than are possible in shoe production itself. In the survey of Rabellotti (1995) the key reason for subcontracting is to reduce costs. Nearly three quarters of the surveyed firms report this as the catalyst for their decision. In addition, for 50 per cent of the firms subcontracting is seen as an important means of increasing flexibility. As subcontractors are more specialised, and are more able to reap the available economies of scale, they are seen as providing better products at lower cost and with shorter delays.

Most of the shoe producers surveyed in Italy chose subcontractors within the same area. The key issue in terms of our discussion of globalisation, is why it is in Italy that subcontracting has mainly been allocated to other firms in the region and not overseas to even lower cost suppliers. A key feature of industrial districts is the maintenance of stable and continuous linkages between shoe producers and subcontractors. Despite having been given prominence in a number of previous studies of industrial districts, local government was of little importance in the footwear districts of Italy.

Several authors observe a link between the characteristics of the local labor market and industrial clusters. The learning process which usually takes place inside the firm, becomes a collective process in the industrial district, based on common knowledge which accumulates in people rather than in firms. Knowledge, which is transmitted from one generation to the next, enhances local innovation through labour mobility, which circulates the know-how of one firm to the other.

Interestingly, the Italian model of the industrial district in the footwear sector is not replicated elsewhere. In the case of Mexico, Rabellotti (1995) observed a substantial difference in the linkages between firms. The relationship between suppliers and manufacturers are mainly 'market linkages', simply based on a factor of price and not through cooperation, as in Italy. Hing (1998) explores regional clustering in Taiwan and focuses on the existing key role of trading companies, which did not play an important role in Italy. The connection of these companies with international markets helped to keep Taiwan's small and medium sized shoe manufacturers up to date with rapidly changing fashion trends and technologies. Trading companies serve as a hub of information regarding managerial, technical and financial conditions in shoe factories.

In conclusion, a key feature of the footwear industry in Italy has been the increasing flexibility of production and the strong links between producers of components and the producers of final shoes within industrial districts. This has enabled Italian producers to maintain market share and output in the high quality, design intensive, and fashion sensitive part of the footwear market. The flexibility of production and labour input have enabled footwear firms to respond quickly to changing demands and to efficiently and effectively meet small scale orders for quality footwear. Clearly, such a response to increased competition would not be appropriate in the case of the mass production of standardised shoes. Nevertheless, the use of subcontracting to local firms and the flexibility of small firms have been a crucial aspect of the success of the Italian footwear industry. The response elsewhere in Europe, for example in the UK, of increasing firm size has not provided a basis for effective competition in the global market.

Nevertheless, the precise role that flexibility and industrial districts play in relation to social exclusion is not yet entirely clear. Flexibility in the use of labour often means the increasing use of temporary, part-time and cottage workers. The lack of employment stability for these workers can be reflected in rising wage differentials compared to skilled workers with higher job stability. In addition, these are workers who can miss the social safety net which is in place for permanent, full-time workers.

Conclusions

Footwear is often perceived as a standard labour-intensive manufactured product in which comparative advantage has decisively shifted from OECD countries to low-wage developing countries. In Europe as a whole there has been a substantial contraction of the sector over the past thirty years with a considerable loss of jobs. However, this decline is not uniform across EU countries. Italy, for example, has been able to maintain employment in footwear roughly at 1970 levels throughout the subsequent period.

What is apparent is that developments in the footwear sector have varied across EU countries. It would seem that Germany, for example, has been characterised by a substantial shift to production in overseas locations and the outsourcing of parts of the production process. Countries such as Italy, for example, have not shifted production overseas in this manner and have instead maintained domestic output and employment levels. An important feature of this has been the shift to ever-higher export intensities at the same time as import penetration has increased. Thus, one might conclude that globalisation, as well as creating additional competitive pressures in the domestic market, provides increased opportunities for sales overseas. An important part of the response to low-wage competition in countries which have maintained domestic output and employment would appear to be success in reorienting sales towards foreign markets. A key element in the relative success of the industry in countries such as Italy has been the move towards more flexible modes of production and the development of industrial districts. The role that policy can make in facilitating this adjustment is something which requires further attention.

Finally, this study highlights that even within a fairly standard sector such as footwear, unskilled or manual labour appears to be far from homogeneous. Within this group of workers there are significant differences in wages paid to certain types of workers. One interesting finding, which needs to be further substantiated, is that those manual workers with the highest level of skills and the highest wages tend to experience longer periods of unemployment than the least skilled footwear workers. This would suggest some attention be given to the need to target retraining schemes amongst unemployed manual workers and that within the group of unskilled workers there may be particular market imperfections which reduce the flexibility of certain types of manual workers and so raise the costs of adjustment for these workers to new economic conditions.

Acknowledgement

This work has been prepared under the research project 'Globalisation and Social Exclusion' financed by the European Commission under the Targeted SocioEconomic Research (TSER) Programme.

Notes

1 See Wood (1998) and Slaughter (1998) for an overview.

2 Commission of the European Communities, Official Journal no. 161/16, 27.

3 The dip in intra-EU trade after 1993 may reflect the change in the measurement of trade after the creation of the Single Market.

4 The data for Germany incorporate the eastern part of the country after 1990, hence there was an even greater decline in employment in the western part of the country in the 1990s than is shown in these data.

5 Due to an apparent change in the recording of footwear employment in Portugal after 1989 we cannot continue the employment series into the 1990s. Recorded employment in 1990 was double that recorded in 1989 yet output remained at roughly the same level.

6 Unless the quality of these new jobs, in terms of wages and other conditions, is considerably inferior to those in the footwear sector and this contributes to the problem of social exclusion.

7 These data come from: NIS, Belgium: 'Volkstelling' (Census), 1981–1991 (ten-yearly survey, data available for 1961–1971–1981–1991) and Ministry of Labour.

Section 3:
Trade and Development

Journal of World Trade 37(3): 623–646, 2003.

Chapter 13

Integrating the Least Developed Countries into the World Trading System: The Current Impact of European Union Preferences Under "Everything But Arms"

Paul BRENTON*

Trade preferences are a key element in industrial countries' efforts to assist the integration of the least developed countries (LDCs) into the world economy. This article provides an initial evaluation of the impact of the European Union's recently introduced "Everything But Arms" (EBA) initiative on the products currently exported by the LDCs. It shows that the changes introduced by the EBA in 2001 are relatively minor for the currently exported products, primarily because over 99 percent of EU imports from the LDCs are in products which the European Union had already liberalized and the complete removal of barriers to the key remaining products, rice, sugar, and bananas has been delayed. The paper proceeds to look at the role EU preferences to LDCs in general have been playing and could play in assisting the integration of the LDCs. It shows that there is considerable variation across countries in the potential impact that EU preferences can have given current export structures. There is a group of the LDCs for whom EU trade preferences on existing exports are not significant since these exports are mainly of products where the most-favoured-nation (MFN) duty is zero. Export diversification is the key issue for these countries. For other LDCs, EU preferences have the potential to provide a more substantial impact on trade. However, the paper shows that only 50 percent of EU imports from non-ACP LDCs which are eligible actually request preferential access to the European Union. The prime suspect for this low level of utilization are the rules of origin, both the restrictiveness of the requirements on sufficient processing and the costs and difficulties of providing the necessary documentation. More simple rules of origin are likely to enhance the impact of EU trade preferences both in terms of improving market access and in stimulating diversification towards a broader range of exports.

I. INTRODUCTION

Trade preferences are seen by many as an essential element in integrating the developing countries, and particularly the least developed countries, into the world

* Paul Brenton, International Trade Department, The World Bank, Washington DC; e-mail: <pbrenton@worldbank.org>. The views expressed are those of the author and should not be attributed to the World Bank. The author is very grateful for the comments of Andrea Rossi, Claire Thirriot, Robert Kirk, Larry Hinkle, and participants of a trade seminar at the World Bank.

trading system. Trade preferences in Organization for Economic Co-operation and Development (OECD) countries are expected to encourage the importation of products from developing countries, raising the export earnings of these countries, stimulating investment and growth. Initial preference schemes were introduced in the 1970s under the Generalized System of Tariff Preferences (GSP). Over the past three decades the exports of some of the developing countries, particularly those in east Asia, have grown strongly. However, export success has not been uniform and some developing countries, those at the lowest levels of income, have been left behind. In response there have been a number of recent initiatives in OECD countries to further discriminate in favour of the least developed countries (LDCs). Most notable among these are the European Union's Everything But Arms (EBA) initiative and the African Growth and Opportunity Act (AGOA) of the United States.

This article takes a look at the initial impact of the EBA, which came into effect in March 2001, although as we shall show the vast majority of imports from the LDCs were already entering the European Union duty and quota free. The impact of the changes introduced in 2001 on the products currently exported were therefore relatively minor and as such they should be seen as the final, but small, step in a longer term process that the European Union has implemented to provide complete duty and quota free access to the LDCs. The article goes on to look more broadly at the impact of EU preferences and seeks to assess the scope, actual and potential, that the EBA, broadly defined as covering all products with duty-free access to the European Union, can play in integrating the least developed countries into the world economy.

The focus of the article is on those products currently exported by the LDCs. For a group of the poorest countries it is clear that under current trade structures preferences are of no real value since almost all exports are concentrated in products for which the EU external tariff is zero. For these countries the key issue is to what extent the EU scheme of preferences can assist in stimulating diversification into a broader range of exports. For other countries the value of EU preferences under the current structure of exports is more significant due to a higher export share of dutiable products and the larger magnitude of available preferences. However, it appears that improvements in market access are often constrained by the nature of the rules which govern the granting of preferences. The adoption of more simple rules of origin would be of particular benefit to many of these LDCs.

II. The Everything But Arms Initiative

Figure 1 shows the evolution of the exports of the LDCs to the European Union since 1988. The period from 1989 to 1993 was one of absolute decline in the value of exports to the European Union. Subsequently there has been moderate but sustained growth in the value of exports, with a very substantial increase of over 35 percent in 2000. Nevertheless, the figure shows that the relative decline of LDC exports to the European Union continued throughout the 1990s with a slight recovery in 2000 and

FIGURE 1: LDC EXPORTS TO THE EU, 1968–2001

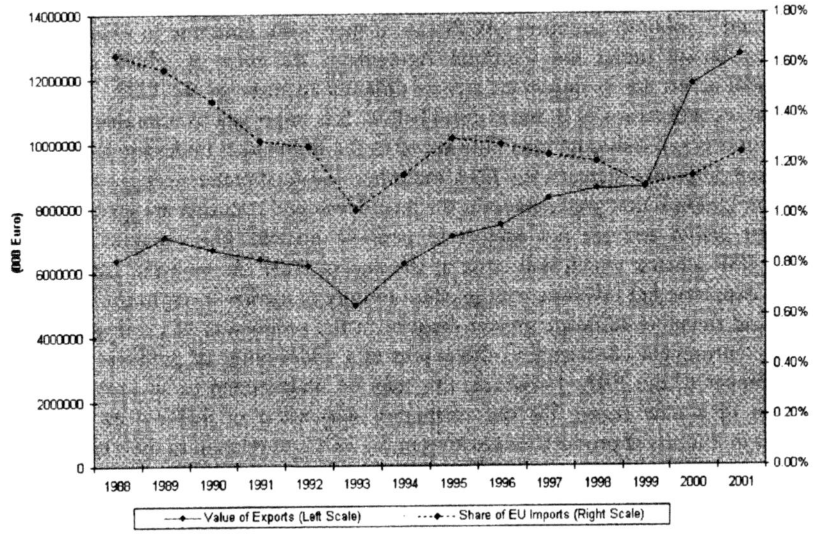

2001. In 2001 the LDC share of the EU import market was about 25 percent lower than in 1988. It is against this background that we now consider the possible impact of the changes introduced in 2001 by the EBA initiative and then consider more broadly the importance of EU preferences to the LDCs.

The EBA regulation grants duty-free access to imports of all products from the least developed countries, with the exception of arms and munitions, and without any quantitative restrictions. The European Union has argued that "this *significantly* enhances export opportunities and hence potential income and growth for these countries" (CEC (2002) emphasis added). Liberalization was immediate except for three products: fresh bananas, rice, and sugar where tariffs will be gradually reduced to zero (in 2006 for bananas and 2009 for rice and sugar). There are duty-free tariff quotas for rice and sugar which will be increased annually. It is important to note that the majority of products from these countries already received duty-free treatment under the GSP or Cotonou Agreement. The EBA proposal extended tariff and quota-free access to the EU market to the remaining 919 (of these 44 tariff lines were products with full liberalization delayed) of the 10,200 tariff lines.[1] The vast majority of these 919 products are agricultural products, including certain meat products, vegetables, fruits, wines, and prepared foodstuffs, such as biscuits and jams.

[1] For some product categories liberalization had already been implemented for the ACP countries while for other categories zero-duty access was already available for the non-ACP LDCs.

An important feature of the EBA is that it is embedded in the EU's GSP scheme and access to the EU market is governed by the rules of that scheme. At present the African and Caribbean countries (ACP) can, if they wish, continue to export to the European Union under the Cotonou Agreement, the rules of which governing preferential access are in important aspects different to those of the GSP. This is an issue that we will return to in more detail below. It is important to note that the non-ACP countries can only gain zero duty access to the EU market under the EBA.

A key difference between the EBA and other unilateral preferences granted by the European Union is that preferences for the least developed countries are granted for an unlimited period and are not subject to periodic review. This contrasts with the current GSP scheme which will cease at the end of 2004. As such the EBA should provide exporters and investors with greater certainty of market access to the European Union and therefore stimulate greater capacity in the production of existing products and an environment conducive to the export of a wider range of products. This is a crucial aspect of the EBA. However, this may be undermined to an extent by the inclusion of a new reason for the temporary suspension of preferences: "massive increases in imports of products originating in the LDCs in relation to their usual levels of production and export capacity." This could act as a constraint upon large-scale investment that transforms production capacities in a particular country and may limit diversification into new products.[2]

Of the 919 product lines liberalized under the EBA, imports from the LDCs[3] were recorded in just 80 of the tariff lines in 2000, with 13 of these lines being bananas, sugar and rice where full liberalization is delayed. Imports of these 80 product lines amounted to 73.6 million euros in 2000, equivalent to around 0.5 percent of total LDC exports to the European Union, but 63 million euros of these imports were in products with delayed liberalization (Table 1).[4] In 2001 the LDCs exported to the European Union again in 80 of the categories liberalized by the EBA, with 11 of these being products with delayed liberalization. Exports to the European Union of products liberalized in 2001 amounted to 3.7 million euro, a substantial decline from the exports of 10.7 million euros of such products in 2000. However, driving these figures was a decline from 7.2 million euros in 2000 to 0.8 million euros in 2001 of imports of grain sorghum from Sudan. Excluding this exceptional item trade in products liberalized under the EBA in 2001 fell from 3.5 million euros to 2.9 million euros. The value of exports of products with delayed liberalization fell slightly from 62.9 million euros to 60.7 million euros. Table 1 also shows that the vast majority of exports of products liberalized under the EBA emanate from the ACP countries. Very small flows of these products currently come from the non-ACP countries.[5]

---

[2] This clause was initially discussed in the context of combating fraud; however, this is not made clear in the legislation and it would appear that it could be invoked in more general circumstances.

[3] Myanmar is currently excluded from preferences for political reasons. Senegal also became eligible for EBA preferences from the start of 2002 but is not included here.

[4] The key product here is sugar, exports of which to the EU amounted to 47.9 million euros in 2000.

[5] However, UNCTAD (2001) suggests some export potential in these products for countries such as Bangladesh.

TABLE 1: OVERALL IMPACT OF THE EBA IN 2001

	Exports of products liberalized under the EBA in 2001	Exports of products under the EBA with delayed liberalization (bananas, rice, sugar)	Exports of all products covered by the EBA	Total exports of all products
Exports to the EU of all LDCs (000 euro)				
2000	10,657	62,963	73,620	11,733,712
2001	3,658	60,670	64,328	12,858,993
Exports to the EU of ACP countries (000 euro)				
2000	10,505	62,904	73,409	7,764,664
2001	3,344	60,596	63,940	8,634,365
Exports to the EU of non-ACP countries (000 euro)				
2000	152	59	214	3,969,048
2001	313	74	387	4,225,518

Total exports to the European Union of the LDCs, on the other hand, increased by 9.6 percent in 2001. Thus, it is difficult to postulate that liberalization under the EBA has stimulated this increase in total trade. Indeed within this overall total there is wide variation in the growth of exports to the European Union among the LDC countries. For 12 of the LDCs, exports to the European Union fell by more than 30 percent between 2000 and 2001. For another 16 countries exports fell but by less than 30 percent. Exports to the European Union increased for 19 LDCs, with nine of these experiencing growth of more than 30 percent. Thus, for the majority of the LDCs exports to the European Union declined in 2001. This demonstrates that market access is just one of a range of factors, which include price volatility for primary products and domestic supply constraints, that are influencing the value of LDC exports to the European Union.

The direct impact of the liberalization provided by the EBA in 2001 is shown in more detail in Table 2, which shows for each of the LDCs the value of exports to the European Union in products for which there was liberalization of EU trade barriers in 2001. In general the amount of trade in products liberalized in 2001 is very small reaching almost 1 percent of total exports to the European Union for Haiti and amounting to three one-hundredths of 1 percent of total LDC exports to the European Union in 2001. The table also shows the amount of exports to the European Union which were eligible for these improved preferences and which requested preferential access to the European Union under the EBA initiative. None of the eligible imports from the ACP countries actually requested and therefore were not granted preferential access under the EBA. It would appear that the EBA has had no immediate impact on EU imports from the ACP countries. This is in contrast to the non-ACP countries where three-quarters of the exports of products for which tariffs were removed in 2001 were actually granted duty-free access under the EBA. We assume that for various reasons to be discussed in more detail below imports from the ACP countries are still entering the European Union under the Cotonou Agreement rather than under the EBA.

TABLE 2: THE IMPORTANCE OF PRODUCTS LIBERALIZED IN 2001 UNDER THE EBA (000 EURO)

	Total exports to EU	Eligible exports of products liberalized in 2001	Exports of products liberalized in 2001 requesting access under EBA	Exports of rice, sugar, bananas	Share of exports liberalized in 2001 in total exports to EU (%)	Export share of items with delayed liberalization (%)
ACP						
Angola	1,944,630	91 (91)*	0	0	0.00	0.00
Congo	941,784	7 (7)	0	50	0.00	0.01
Equatorial Guinea	754,865	0	0	0	0.00	0.00
Liberia	736,973	10 (10)	0	0	0.00	0.00
Madagascar	600,912	72 (42)	0	8,500	0.01	1.41
Guinea	579,518	41 (28)	0	0	0.01	0.00
Mozambique	530,174	248.5 (2)	0	991	0.05	0.19
Tanzania	395,283	35 (35)	0	6,648	0.01	1.68
Sudan	303,550	778 (778)	0	13,982	0.26	4.61
Mauritania	258,568	6	0	6	0.00	0.00
Uganda	242,524	116.3 (49)	0	55	0.05	0.02
Malawi	194,903	0	0	22,617	0.00	11.60
Ethiopia	159,389	12(11)	0	968	0.01	0.61
Zambia	158,375	1,359 (1,359)	0	6,675	0.86	4.21
Central African Republic	152,804	0	0	0	0.00	0.00
Niger	119,613	6	0	0	0.00	0.00
Benin	63,698	69 (69)	0	0	0.11	0.00
Burkina Faso	63,052	52 (44)	0	0	0.08	0.00
Djibouti	61,494	38 (22)	0	0	0.06	0.00
Togo	58,591	26 (26)	0	26	0.04	0.02
Chad	57,638	1 (1)	0	0	0.00	0.00
Mali	45,726	67 (60)	0	0	0.13	0.00
Sierra Leone	38,420	72 (2)	0	0	0.19	0.00
Rwanda	21,782	5.5 (4)	0	78	0.03	0.36
Comoros	20,770	3	0	0	0.00	0.00
Gambia	20,679	41 (41)	0	0	0.00	0.00
Burundi	19,474	19 (19)	0	0	0.10	0.00

TABLE 2: CONTINUED

	Total exports to EU	Eligible exports of products liberalized in 2001	Exports of products liberalized in 2001 requesting access under EBA	Exports of rice, sugar, bananas	Share of exports liberalized in 2001 in total exports to EU (%)	Export share of items with delayed liberalization (%)
Lesotho	12,797	0	0	0	0.00	0.00
Haiti	16,356	158 (158)	0	0	0.97	0.00
Vanuatu	13,653	0	0	0	0.00	0.00
Cape Verde	11,803	10 (10)	0	0	0.11	0.00
Sao Tome	8,009	0	0	0	0.00	0.00
Eritrea	6,737	1 (1)	0	0	0.01	0.00
Solomon Islands	4,975	0	0	0	0.00	0.00
Guinea Bissau	4,542	0	0	0	0.00	0.00
Somalia	3,047	0	0	0	0.00	0.00
Samoa	2,206	0	0	0	0.00	0.00
Kiribati	728	0	0	0	0.00	0.00
Tuvalu	390	0	0	0	0.00	0.00
Non-ACP						
Bangladesh	3,318,865	69	68	5	0.00	0.00
Cambodia	482,480	0	0	0	0.00	0.00
Laos	143,716	74	74	42	0.05	0.03
Nepal	135,119	0	0	0	0.00	0.00
Yemen	83,596	169	91	0	0.20	0.00
Maldives	37,377	1 (1)	0	0	0.00	0.00
Afghanistan	23,813	0	0	0	0.00	0.00
Bhutan	552	0	0	27	0.00	4.89
Total	12,859,883	3,658 (2,870)	234	60,670	0.03	0.47
Total ACP	8,634,365	3,344 (2,869)	0	60,596	0.04	0.70
Total non-ACP	4,225,518	313 (1)	234	74	0.01	0.00

Note: *The number in brackets is the value of exports in products liberalized under the EBA but which were not recorded as being eligible for EBA preferences in EU customs statistics. One possibility is that imports entered the EU in the first two months of the year prior to the implementation of the EBA. However, cursory investigation for some of these products suggests that imports occurred throughout the year. Mis-recording of the data is also possible but maybe worth investigating whether imports of these products were denied preferences to which they were eligible.

The table also shows the value of exports to the European Union in 2001 of bananas, rice and sugar, products which will be fully liberalized under the EBA but with some delay. Here the potential impact of the EBA is more significant for particular countries. For example, due to the importance of sugar, almost 12 percent of the value of Malawi's exports to the European Union in 2001 was from products which will be subject to future liberalization. Significant shares of the exports of Bhutan, Sudan, and Zambia are also in products where market access *may* improve in the future. Overall, bananas, rice and sugar comprised almost 0.5 percent of total LDC exports to the European Union in 2001. These products are much more important in the exports of the ACP countries than in the exports of the non-ACP countries. Thus, of the products which had not been fully liberalized under the GSP or the Cotonou Agreement it is precisely those products which are of more importance to the LDCs where full liberalization has been delayed. However, it is worth noting that on the basis of current exports to the European Union most of the LDC will be unaffected by future liberalization under the EBA. Thirty-two of the LDCs did not export any bananas, rice or sugar to the European Union in 2001.

Thus we conclude from an analysis of the exports of LDCs of products liberalized in 2001 that the direct impact of the EBA has not so far been significant: very small amounts of exports are concerned and for all the ACP countries exports of products which have been liberalized have not entered the EU market under the EBA. It may be that adjustment to the new regime will take some time as different documentation is required than under the Cotonou Agreement. It could also be that substantial investment is required for these new preferences to be exploited, for example, if the products concerned are subject to demanding technical regulations or private standards. Thus, the reduction of barriers and the greater certainty of the EBA could stimulate new trade from the LDCs in the future. However, even a substantial increase in the volume of exports of products liberalized in 2002 will have little impact on overall exports. The impact of the future liberalization of bananas, rice, and sugar could have a more profound impact on particular countries, but not the ACPs in general, since the majority do not export these products. This impact will be determined by the extent to which current tariff quotas are binding on trade.

The small impact of the EBA in 2001 reflects that the vast majority of EU imports from the LDCs (99.5 percent in 2001) were already eligible for tariff and quota free access. Hence, we now proceed to look at trade in all products covered by EU preferences, including those previously liberalized under the GSP and the Cotonou Agreement to try and assess what role EU trade preferences in general have been playing and could play in assisting the integration of the LDCs into international markets. We start by looking at two broad measures of the potential impact of the EBA, now defined more broadly as EU trade preferences in general, on the exports of the least developing countries: first, the coverage of the EBA for each country, that is, the importance of exports that are subject to preferences in relation to total exports to the European Union and second, the extent to which the available preferences are actually utilized. On the first point, if a country mainly exports to the EU products that are already subject to zero or low MFN tariffs then the preference scheme will have little direct short-term impact on exports. The key contribution that may arise is if the scheme encourages a degree of export diversification into products where preferential margins remain. As noted above, the EBA is potentially an important step forward in this respect due to its unlimited duration. On the second point, preferences are only valuable from an economic point of view to the extent that they are actually granted. A scheme which offers preferential access but which contains rules that constrain or prevent delivery of improved access will be of little importance.

III. The Potential Impact of EU Trade Preferences with Current Trade Structures

Table 3 classifies each of the LDCs along these two dimensions on the basis of data on exports to the European Union in 2001. We look first at the importance of products for which preferences, whatever their magnitude, are available and allocate countries according to whether such products comprise less than 5 percent of total exports, for which we deem the initiative to be having no direct impact given the current structure of exports, when such products comprise between 5 and 30 percent of total exports to the European Union we take the initiative to be of low relevance, and when products subject to preferences amount to more than 30 percent of exports we take the initiative to be of high relevance given current exports. These dimensions are shown in the rows of Table 3. For seven countries, Angola, Central African Republic, Chad, Congo, Liberia, Niger, and Vanuatu, products eligible for preferential access to the European Union under the EBA comprised less than 5 percent of total exports to the European Union in 2001. It is worth noting that none of these countries currently export bananas, rice or sugar and so further liberalization under the EBA is likely to have no immediate impact. For these countries exports are dominated by products where the MFN duty is already zero. Specifically, for each country in 2001 the key products were: Angola (oil/diamonds), Central African Republic (diamonds/wood), Chad (cotton), Congo (diamonds), Liberia (sea-going vessels/wood), Niger (uranium), and Vanuatu (sea-going vessels).

For these countries the key issue is export diversification. The extent to which preference schemes such as the EBA assist in the process of export diversification is worthy of further study. For this particular group of countries, for whom extensive trade preferences have been available under the Cotonou Agreement, there has been little apparent export diversification, although diversification may have been stymied by the weak contractual nature of the preferences. Preferences under the EBA provide for greater certainty. This is a crucial issue and one where it would be useful if there were to be monitoring of the impact of the EBA on export diversification and careful analysis of constraints upon the export of a broader range of products. Such constraints

TABLE 3: THE RELEVANCE OF EBA AND THE DELIVERY OF PREFERENTIAL ACCESS TO THE EU MARKET IN 2001

	Extent of Preferential Access		
	No take-up of preferences	Low take-up of preferences	High take-up of preferences
No relevance of EBA	Angola, Central African Republic, Chad, Democratic Republic of Congo, Liberia, Niger, Vanuatu		
Low relevance of EBA	*Bhutan*, Burundi, Djibouti, Equatorial Guinea, Guinea, Kiribati, Mali, Rwanda, Solomon Islands, Sudan	*Afghanistan*, Sierra Leone	Haiti, Samoa, Lesotho
High relevance of EBA	Benin, Burkina Faso, Cape Verde, Comoros, Eritrea, Gambia, Guinea Bissau, Madagascar, Malawi, Mauritania, Mozambique, Sao Tome, Somalia, Tanzania, Togo, Tuvalu, Uganda, Zambia	Ethiopia, *Maldives*	*Bangladesh*, *Cambodia*, *Laos*, *Nepal*, *Yemen*

Notes: No Relevance of EBA – Exports eligible for preferences <5% of total exports to the EU
Low Relevance of EBA – 5%< Exports eligible for preferences <30% of total exports to the EU
High Relevance of EBA – Exports eligible for preferences >30% of total exports to the EU
No take-up of preferences – exports requesting preferences <5% of exports eligible for preferences
Low take-up of preferences – 5%< exports requesting preferences <30% of export eligible for preferences
High take-up of preferences – exports requesting preferences >30% of exports eligible for preferences
The non-ACP LDCs are in italic.

are likely to include technical regulations and standards in overseas markets and the costs of transport and other trade-related infrastructure.

A further 15 countries are classified as those where EU trade preferences are of low relevance given current exports since the share of exports of products where preferences are available comprises a significant but not substantial share of total exports to the European Union, that is, between 5 and 30 percent. With the exceptions of Afghanistan and Bhutan, all of these countries are from the ACP region. Finally, the majority of LDCs, 25 countries, comprise the group for which products subject to preferences account for more than 30 percent of current exports. The remaining non-ACP countries all fall into this category.

Hence this classification gives a crude first indication of the potential importance of trade preferences for the various ACP countries with current export structures. However, it is important to go further and look at the magnitude of the preferences that are being granted. This is provided in Figures 2 to 4, which show the average margin of preference in the EU market if all available preferences were fully utilized (as will be discussed later, this cannot be stressed enough). This was computed as the implicit transfer (the sum across all products of the MFN tariff[6] multiplied by the value of exports) divided by the value of total exports to the European Union in 2001.[7] This is equivalent to the trade weighted average tariff that would arise if MFN duties were applied. The three figures group countries according to a perceived insignificant current value of preferences, a potential transfer of less than 1 percent of the value of exports to the European Union, countries for whom the potential value of preferences is currently low, of the order of between 1 and 5 percent of exports, and countries for whom the current value EU preferences is potentially substantial, that is, equivalent to more than 5 percent of the value of current exports to the European Union.

Figure 2 shows the countries where EU preferences are currently insignificant and comprises all seven countries identified above as having a share of preferential exports in total exports of less than 5 percent. These countries are joined in this figure by six other ACP countries and Bhutan. While these countries' exports are characterized by a higher proportion of products which are subject to preferences, the MFN tariffs on these preferences are low. For example, the majority of preferential exports by Mali are hides and skins where the average EU tariff is only 2 percent. In general, EU preferences for this group of countries are unlikely to have any substantial impact on exports under current trade structures.

[6] Throughout we use the post-Uruguay Round *ad valorem* tariffs and the *ad valorem* equivalents of specific duties. For some products, such as confectionery, the duty is complex being based upon an *ad valorem* tariff and specific rates according to sugar and milk contents. For these products, without further information, the *ad valorem* equivalents of the specific duties for average sugar and milk contents were applied.

[7] This does not include the value preferences for the delayed liberalization products of bananas, rice and sugar. For these products the value of preferences depends upon the extent to which exports exceed the tariff-free quota. Thus, for those countries which are significant exporters of these products, Malawi, Sudan, Madagascar, Zambia, and Tanzania, the potential transfer could be higher than shown here. Nevertheless, since three of these five countries are classified as having a high potential transfer under the EBA the omission of sugar, rice and bananas will not distort the overall picture given by Figures 2 to 4.

FIGURE 2: COUNTRIES FOR WHOM THE POTENTIAL VALUE OF EU PREFERENCES IS INSIGNIFICANT

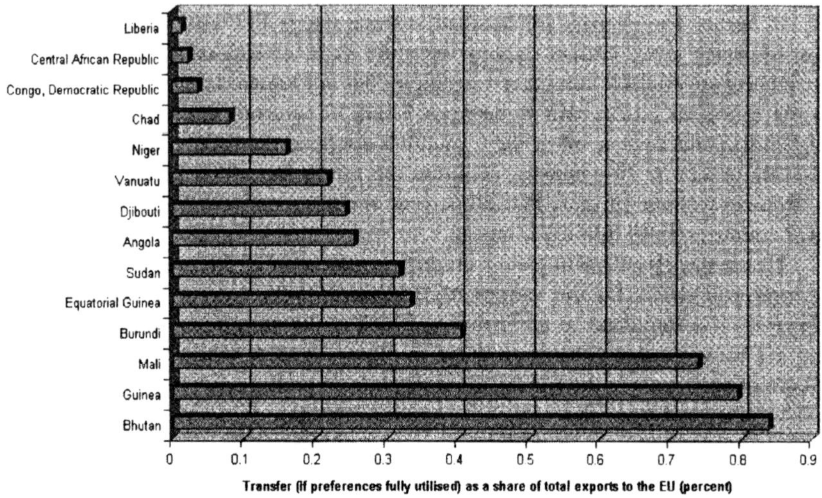

FIGURE 3: COUNTRIES FOR WHOM THE POTENTIAL VALUE OF EU PREFERENCES IS LOW

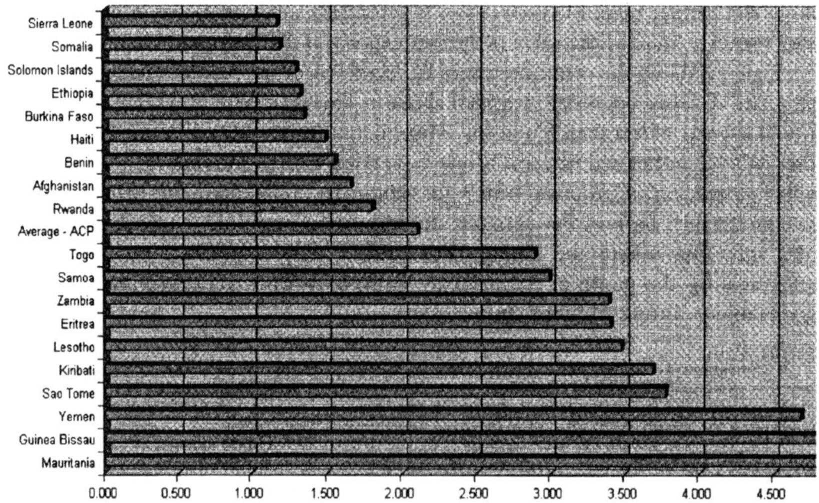

FIGURE 4: COUNTRIES FOR WHOM THE POTENTIAL VALUE OF EU PREFERENCES IS HIGH

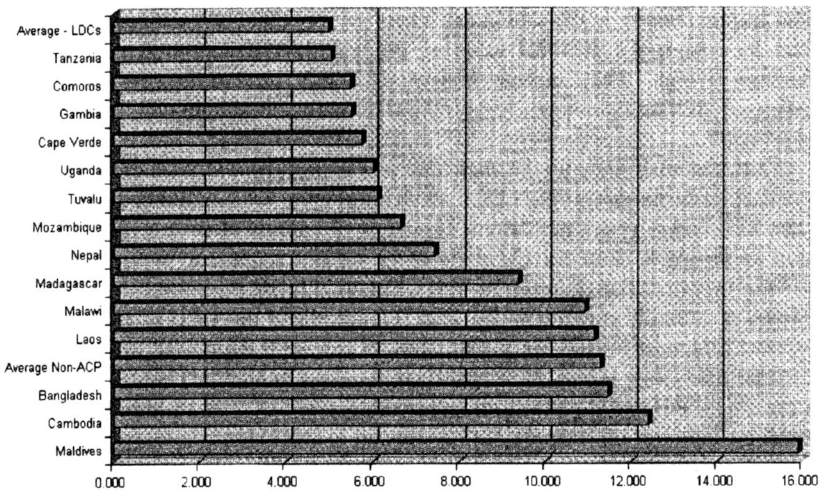

Figure 3 shows the group of countries for whom the potential value of EU preferences with the current structure of exports lies between 1 and 5 percent of the value of exports in 2001. The figure also shows that the average for the ACP countries lies at just over two percent. If fully exploited EU preferences to ACP countries amounted to a transfer equivalent to approximately 1.92 billion euros in 2001. To reiterate, the actual transfer would have been less than this due to the fact that only a proportion of exports from the ACP countries to the European Union would have been granted preferential access to the European Union. Some exports would have paid the MFN tariff.

Figure 4 shows the group of countries for whom EU trade preferences are of greater significance under current trade structures, which in our very crude breakdown is defined as when the value of the potential transfer exceeds 5 percent of the value of exports in 2001. Figure 4 highlights the substantial impact that EU trade preferences could be having on the non-ACP LDCs. For these countries, the current potential transfer on average is equivalent to 11.26 percent of the value of exports in 2001. In general, this reflects the high share of clothing products in the exports of these countries to the European Union, for which the EU tariff is typically 12 percent. The very high value of the potential transfer for the Maldives reflects the importance of clothing exports but also exports of prepared tuna, for which the EU tariff is 24 percent. The Maldives also highlight the importance of taking account of the amount of exports which are actually granted preferences, since for this country, the value of the actual transfer in 2001 was no more that 5.5 percent of the value of exports in 2001. For Nepal, Laos, Cambodia, and Bangladesh, the potential transfer under EU preferences is also substantial. There are a number of ACP countries in the group for whom the potential value of EU trade preferences with current trade structures is high. They include Malawi, primarily due to exports of tobacco, Madagascar (fish and clothing), Mozambique (unwrought aluminium), Uganda (fish and tobacco).

Thus, this analysis shows the vastly different impact that EU trade preferences can potentially make for the various LDCs which are eligible for duty and quota free access to the EU market under the current structures of exports of these countries. For a group of the ACP countries EU preferences are not significant with the products currently exported. For countries such as Chad and Liberia the potential value of EU preferences currently amounts to less than 0.1 percent of the value of exports to the European Union, reflecting that the structure of exports is dominated by products for which the MFN duty is zero. However, there are also a number of countries for whom the potential value of EU preferences is currently substantial. The analysis shows a clear distinction between the non-ACP countries on average, for whom preferences are potentially of high significance and the average for the ACP countries, where EU trade preferences are typically much less important under current trade structures. This analysis has been based on the importance of EU preferences if all exports from the LDCs were granted preferential access to the EU market. We now proceed to look at the available information on the actual take-up of preferences under the EBA.

IV. The Utilization of Preferences

The take-up of preferences is the other key factor which defines the impact of trade schemes such as the EBA. The columns of Table 3 show the allocation of the LDCs according to the share of exports which requested[8] preferential access to the EU market under the EBA in the value of exports which were eligible for preferential access, the later being the value of exports for which the MFN duty is non-zero (with the exception of bananas, rice, and sugar). Again we present a crude breakdown according to whether there is no take-up of preferences (exports requesting preferences were less than 5 percent of the value of exports eligible for preferences), low take-up of preferences (the ratio of requesting zero duty access over eligible between 5 and 30 percent), and high utilization of preferences (more than 30 percent of exports eligible for preferences requested to enter the EU market duty free).

[8] Thus, the amount actually granted preferential access could be less than this figure. We suspect that the main reason why traders forego the financial incentives that are available and do not request preferences is that the costs of attaining them exceed their value. The key factors raising the costs of obtaining preferences are the rules of origin and the administrative costs of proving conformity with those rules. There is some suspicion regarding the data provided by the Netherlands which may understate (to an unknown extent) requests for preferences. This will not distort the key findings that are presented.

It is striking from Table 3 that for almost all of the ACP countries there is no take-up of preferences under the EBA. Lesotho, is a notable exception. In contrast, for the majority of the non-ACP countries there is a high take-up of preferences. We suspect that the very low utilization of preferences under the EBA by the ACP countries reflects that most of the exports from these countries entered the European Union under the Cotonou Agreement rather than under the EBA in 2001. This begs the question of why these countries are still using the Cotonou Agreement rather than the EBA to access the EU market. On the one hand this may just reflect the delay in adjusting to the new scheme and also, as discussed above, the majority of exports from ACP countries were already entering the European Union duty free under Cotonou and at present there is no incentive to change to EBA, particularly given that different documentation is required to use the EBA (Form A) and the Cotonou (EUR1). Although, as noted above (see Table 2), that even for products where the EBA offers better access than Cotonou there has been no take-up of preferences under EBA.

- On the other hand, the lack of use of EBA may reflect some important differences between the two schemes. Most notable among these are differences in the rules of origin. Although the required degree of processing tends to be the same for each product category, a number of the general rules vary substantially:

  Cumulation: Cumulation allows inputs from specified countries to be treated as originating materials. The EBA is contained within the EU's GSP scheme and therefore is governed by the rules of origin specified in the GSP. Under the GSP diagonal cumulation can take place within four regional groupings: ASEAN, CACM, the Andean Community, and SAARC. Diagonal cumulation allows originating materials (those which satisfy the EU rules of origin for that product) from regional partners to be further processed in another country in the group and treated as if the materials were originating in the country where the processing is undertaken. However, this flexibility in sourcing is constrained by the requirement that the value-added in the final stage of production exceeds the highest customs value of any of the inputs used from countries in the regional grouping.

  Cumulation under the EBA is not available to the ACP countries. Such cumulation is a possibility for Cambodia and Laos within ASEAN and for Bangladesh, Bhutan, Maldives, and Nepal within SAARC. Thus, for example, the standard rule of origin states that clothing products must be made from yarn. In other words, the fabric from which the clothes are cut and made-up must be woven in the beneficiary country or the European Union. With diagonal cumulation clothing producers in Cambodia can use fabrics from Indonesia (provided they are originating, that is produced from the stage of fibres) and still receive duty-free access to the European Union. Similarly, producers in Nepal can import originating fabric from India. This provides for slightly more freedom in sourcing decisions than is available under the basic rule of origin.[9]

However, UNCTAD (2001) shows how the value-added requirement can render regional cumulation of little value. For example, value-added in the making up of clothing in Bangladesh ranges from between 25 and 35 percent of the value of exports. However, value-added in the production of fabrics in India is around 65 to 75 percent. Regional cumulation allows clothing produced in Bangladesh from Indian fabrics preferential access to the European Union but not at the zero rate (for which Bangladesh is eligible) but at the rate for which India is eligible, which is only a 20 percent reduction from the MFN rate, that is a tariff of 9.6 percent.

Under the Cotonou Agreement full cumulation[10] (Inama (2002)) can occur with any of the ACP countries and there is no requirement concerning value-added in the final stage relative to the customs value of inputs used. There is also the possibility for cumulation with South Africa, provided that the value-added exceeds the value of materials from South Africa, and with neighbouring non-ACP developing countries, although highly constrained for textile and clothing products. Hence it is possible that ACP countries using materials from other ACP countries qualify for duty-free access to the EU market under the Cotonou Agreement but not under the EBA.

- *Tolerance Rule/Minimum Processing*: Under the EBA non-originating materials which according to the specific rules of origin cannot be used in the manufacture of a product may nevertheless be used provided that their value does not exceed 10 percent of the ex-works price of the product. Under Cotonou non-originating materials up to a total value of 15 percent of the ex-works prices can be used.[11]
- *Fish*: For a number of the ACP countries (Angola, Benin, Eritrea, Gambia, Guinea, Guinea Bissau, Madagascar, Mauritania, Mozambique, Sao Tome, Togo, Tanzania, Uganda) fish are a major export. Although the basic processing rule is the same under the EBA and Cotonou, all products used must be wholly obtained, the conditions pertaining to the vessels which catch the fish are more liberal under Cotonou (see Annex 1).

[9] For certain textile and clothing products, but subject to quantitative limits, Cambodia, Laos, and Nepal have requested and been granted a derogation from the rules for certain textiles and clothing products such that originating inputs from any countries belonging to the SAARC, ASEAN, or the ACP can count as originating materials.

[10] The most advanced form of cumulation, full cumulation, allows for any working or processing (even if it does not confer origin) undertaken in one country to be carried forward to another country and counted as if it were undertaken in the country of final processing. For example, a clothing product made in one country from fabric produced in a regional partner which in turn was made from non-originating yarn would be eligible for duty-free access to the EU under full cumulation but not under diagonal cumulation since the fabric would not be deemed to be originating (the rule of origin for the fabric requires manufacture from fibres).

[11] In both cases this is predicated on specific rules on maximum values of non-originating materials not being violated. For example, the rule of origin for preparations of vegetables, fruits, etc., preserved by sugar (HS 2006) requires that materials of Chapter 17 (sugar) do not exceed 30 percent of the ex-works price.

Hence, there are several reasons why the ACP countries may not be utilizing the duty-free preferences under the EBA and are still using the Cotonou Agreement to access the EU market.

For the non-ACP LDCs we can analyse the issue of the take-up of preferences in more detail since exports from these countries can only achieve duty-free access to the EU market under the EBA. Given our data on the amount of exports eligible for preferences which actually requested duty-free access we can derive (the lower bound on) the amount of exports which actually pays the MFN duty rate.

Table 4 shows that on average 50 percent of exports from the non-ACP countries requested duty-free access to the EU market in 2001. This implies that at least half of exports from these countries to the European Union did not receive preferential access and paid the MFN tariff rate. The take-up of preferences varies from less than 10 percent for Afghanistan and Bhutan to 36 percent for Cambodia, 50 percent for Bangladesh and over 70 percent for Nepal and Yemen. The next column of the table shows the value of the implied transfer for the exports that may have entered duty free, that is, the value of exports which requested duty-free access multiplied by the MFN tariff. On the basis of exports in 2001 this amounted to a transfer of 232 million euros.[12] The table shows that, given the size of overall exports, most of this transfer went to Bangladesh, which received 187 million euros.

The next column of the table shows the value of the transfer that was foregone, that is, the additional transfer that would have arisen if all exports from these countries had entered the EU market with zero duties. Thus, if the EBA had delivered duty-free access to all of the exports recorded as having come from Bangladesh then there would have been an additional transfer of 193 million euros. The table then shows the delivery ratio, the value of preferences that requested duty-free access compared to the total available transfer if all preferences were utilized. This will be lower than the ratio of exports requesting access to exports eligible for preferences if the take-up of preferences tends to be lower for higher tariff products. With the exception of Afghanistan and Bangladesh this is not the case, although the weight of Bangladesh entails that the delivery ratio for the group as a whole is lower.

The penultimate column of the table shows the value of the total potential transfer (the actual transfer plus the transfer foregone) as a proportion of exports to the European Union in 2001. These are the data that were presented in Figures 3 and 4. Thus, on average the EBA could deliver a transfer equivalent to 11 percent of the exports of the non-ACP LDCs in 2001. The final column shows the transfer foregone as a proportion of exports to the European Union, which is equivalent to the trade weighted average tariff that the exports of these countries actually faced. The difference between the two columns shows that value of the transfer actually made as a proportion of exports to the European Union. For Bangladesh, the EBA led to a

[12] This is assuming that all of the transfer goes to the exporter. Olarreaga and Ozden (2003) suggest that a substantial part of this transfer could be going to the importers.

TABLE 4: EXPORTS TO THE EC UNDER THE EBA FROM NON-ACP COUNTRIES

	Total exports to EU (000 euro)	Exports to EU eligible under EBA (000 euro)	Exports to EU requesting duty-free access (000 euro)	Exports requesting duty-free access as a proportion of total eligible exports (%)	Maximum value of preferences granted (000 euro)	Transfer foregone (000 euro)	Delivery ratio	Total potential transfer as a proportion of exports to the EU	Transfer foregone as a proportion of exports to the EU
Afghanistan	23,813	5,705	307	5.38	15.76	378.38	4.00	1.66	1.59
Bangladesh	3,318,865	3,265,831	1,637,514	50.14	187,426.55	192,610.83	49.32	11.45	5.80
Bhutan	552	109	2	1.65	0.12	4.51	2.51	0.84	0.82
Cambodia	482,480	477,700	171,865	35.98	228,30.63	36,980.56	38.17	12.40	7.66
Laos	143,716	133,872	78,878	58.92	9,536.50	6,491.26	59.50	11.15	4.52
Maldives	37,377	37,152	9,732	26.20	2,064.14	3,876.08	34.75	15.89	10.37
Nepal	135,119	123,406	88,130	71.42	7,237.67	2,807.27	72.05	7.43	2.08
Yemen	83,596	38,262	29,213	76.35	3,280.23	635.11	83.78	4.68	0.76
Total non-ACP LDCs	42,25,518	4,082,037	2,015,641	49.38	232,391.59	243,784.01	48.80	11.27	5.77

transfer (or a margin of preference) equivalent to 5.65 percent. However, the lack of full utilization of the available preferences entails that Bangladesh faced a trade-weighted average tariff of 5.8 percent, which is far in excess of the trade-weighted average tariffs paid by many non-preferential exporters to the European Union! Cambodia, Laos and the Maldives all faced relatively high average tariffs when exporting to the European Union after taking into account that only a proportion of exports could have entered the European Union duty free.

If we assume that the same factors which constrain the take-up of preferences by non-ACP countries also afflict the ACP countries and that the utilization of preferences by the ACP countries was on average similar to that of the non-ACP countries then the value of EU preferences under current export structures becomes even less for these countries with an implicit transfer of around 1 percent of the value of exports to the European Union in 2001.

V. Reasons for the Under-Utilization of Preferences

Brenton and Manchin (2003) argue that the prime suspects for the lack of utilization of EU trade preferences are the rules of origin, both in terms of the nature of the rules defining specific processing requirements, with the constraints that this entails for international sourcing from the lowest cost locations, and the costs of providing the necessary documentation to prove conformity with the rules. The costs of documentation related to the rules of origin are compounded by the requirement that goods for which preferences are requested are shipped directly to the European Union and that if they are in transit through another country, which will be the case for most of the LDCs, then documentary evidence must be provided to show that the goods remained under the supervision of the customs authorities of the country of transit, did not enter the domestic market there and did not undergo operations other than unloading and reloading. In practice it may be very difficult to obtain the necessary documentation.

Rules of origin are required to prevent trade deflection, whereby products from non-beneficiary countries are re-directed through LDCs to exploit the preferences that are available. This is indeed necessary but the rules of origin should be no stricter than is required to fulfil this function. Rules of origin which are more strict than is necessary will act to protect producers in the preference granting country and undermine the value of the preference scheme for the LDCs. Unfortunately there appears to be no analytical work that assesses the optimal rule of origin from a practical point of view that would prevent trade deflection. One suspects that in most cases a simple change of tariff heading would suffice, compared to the complex rules in most preferential trade schemes.

The fact that only a proportion of exports which are eligible for preferences are requesting preferences suggests that much more than trade deflection is at hand. Deflected trade would request preferences. This in turn suggests that on average 50 percent of recorded exports from the non-ACP LDCs which are eligible for zero-duty access to the EU market and which are not deflected trade from non-eligible countries are not getting that preferential access. If the reason for this lack of take-up of preferences is inability to satisfy the rules of origin or the high costs of proving origin, which are the prime suspects, then clearly the rules are restrictive relative to the objective of preventing trade deflection.

A reason which has been used to justify strict rules of origin is that they encourage the development of integrated production structures within developing countries to maximize the impact on employment and to ensure that it is not just low value-added activities which are undertaken in the LDCs. This is not a reasonable justification for the strict rules of origin that are applied by the European Union and the other OECD countries. First, such rules discriminate against small countries where the possibilities for local sourcing are limited or non-existent (Hewitt *et al.* (1995)). Since most LDCs are small countries they are particularly disadvantaged by restrictive rules of origin relative to larger developing countries. Regional cumulation provisions have been introduced to reduce the constraining effect of the current rules of origin. Nevertheless, they still hamper the choice of sourcing, the ACP countries can source materials from each other but not from low-cost locations in Asia, for example, and as noted earlier there are further restrictions, in terms of value-added requirements on the extent to which cumulation can be used.

Second, there is no evidence that strict rules of origin over the past 20 years have done anything to stimulate the development of integrated production structures in developing countries. Third, this argument would be much more convincing if the rules of origin were defined by a process of discussion with the developing countries to identify what would be appropriate. They are not. They are defined and imposed by the European Union, the United States and so on. It seems very difficult to argue that the double or triple processing requirements (yarn or fibre forward rules) that dominate both EU and US preference schemes were introduced for the benefit of textile producers in developing countries as opposed to the benefit of textile producers in the European Union and the United States. Finally, globalization and the splitting up of the production chain does not allow the luxury of being able to establish integrated production structures within countries. Strict rules of origin act to constrain the ability of firms in LDCs to integrate into these global production networks and in effect act to dampen the location of any value-added activities in these countries.

VI. Conclusions

The EBA initiative is an important step forward in the treatment of products from LDCs in the EU market. It sends a clear signal that all products from LDCs will be eligible for duty and quota free access to the EU market and that such access will be maintained indefinitely.[13] This is where the main impact of the changes introduced by the EBA will

[13] There are, however, the concerns over the provisions for the suspension of preferences in the agreement and the uncertainty that these may introduce.

be felt in the future, that is, in the extent to which they provide for the diversification of the exports of LDCs, which has been so lacking in the past. Such a policy should be more broadly adopted by all OECD countries, preferably bound under the auspices of the WTO and with a common and more liberal approach to rules of origin.

The direct impact of the EBA in 2001 was negligible since a very small proportion of exports from the LDCs was involved and for the least developed ACP countries even those products which were eligible for improved access did not enter the EU market under the EBA. The principal impact of the changes introduced by the European Union in 2001 on products currently exported will arise for products for which full liberalization was delayed: bananas, sugar, and rice. However, these products are important only for a minority of the LDCs and accounted for just a half of 1 percent of the exports to the European Union of the LDCs as a group in 2001.

For several of the least developed ACP countries, under current export structures, EU tariff preferences in general can play nothing more than a minor role in integrating these countries into the world economy. The average tariff that these countries would pay if preferences were removed, the average margin of preference, is less than 1 percent. Thus, for these countries the paramount trade policy issue is that of trade diversification rather than that of market access for the bundle of products currently exported. For trade preferences in the European Union to be of real value they must facilitate the export of a broader range of goods.

The lack of trade diversification of many LDCs despite duty-free access to the European Union for more than a decade for the vast majority of tariff lines under the Lome Convention and the GSP is not encouraging in this respect. However, the EBA is different since the preferences are not time limited, providing greater certainty for investors and traders. It is important that the impact of the EBA on diversification be monitored and constraints on the export of a broader range of products identified and alleviated. In many cases supply constraints are drastic and it is these which should be the focus of trade-related technical assistance.

Nevertheless, with the preference scheme attention needs to focus on the rules of origin and the extent to which these limit the possibilities for export diversification. The rules of origin are particularly restrictive for simple manufactured products, such as clothing, and for processed food products, precisely those manufactured products where export diversification may be feasible for these LDCs. This group of countries stands out as a case for the current complex rules of origin to be replaced with a more simple requirement to confer origin for all products, such as change of tariff heading. For other LDCs, EU preferences are of more significance under current export structures by providing a more substantial margin of preference. However, the available evidence from the non-ACP countries suggests that there are constraints upon the ability of these LDCs to fully exploit the available preferences in the EU market.

So, although EU trade preferences do entail a significant margin of preferences for many of the LDCs the full potential of the scheme is not being realized. The under-utilization of preferences, which is probably linked to difficulties in satisfying the rules of origin, entails that a substantial proportion of exports of LDCs to the European Union pay the full MFN tariff. Since the products exported by many of the LDCs are subject to relatively high MFN tariffs, such as those applied to clothing, exports from the LDCs can still face substantial tariff barriers to access the EU market. This has a number of implications for the modelling of the impact of trade liberalization. Models which assume the full take-up of preferences under trade schemes such as the EBA will overstate the economic benefits of such schemes to the LDCs due to the under-utilization of preferences in practice. It then follows that estimates of the impact of preference erosion following multilateral liberalization in a successful WTO round will overstate the negative impact on LDCs. Modelling exercises which show the impact of more liberal rules of origin would be particularly useful.

The ACP countries are now in the process of negotiating changes to their trade relationships with the European Union. Under current EU proposals the least developed ACP countries must contemplate the end of the Cotonou Agreement and either establish economic partnership agreements with the European Union and regional partners or revert to the preferences that are available under the EBA. The analysis presented here shows that for a number of the least developed ACP countries EU preferences are currently of little value given the existing structure of trade since the majority of their exports are concentrated in products with a zero MFN duty. Hence for these countries the end of the Cotonou Agreement will only be of relevance to their access to the EU market to the extent that the more favourable rules of origin under Cotonou compared to the EBA provides a stimulus to future trade diversification. The possibilities for cumulation between ACP countries under Cotonou but not under the EBA may be of particular importance in this context.

For other ACP LDCs the information on the utilization of the EBA in 2001 suggests that for the vast majority of trade the Cotonou Agreement was the preferred vehicle for accessing the EU market. This may reflect some inertia and lack of knowledge of the new scheme. However, it may also reflect the more liberal rules of origin under the Cotonou Agreement. Further studies on this issue would be very useful, for if the rules of origin are encouraging the use of Cotonou rather than EBA then there may be significant costs in shifting to the EBA. At this point, it would appear that the EBA is not a substitute for the Cotonou Agreement. This also highlights that rules of origin should be a key issue for countries which decide to enter into negotiations to establish economic partnership agreements with the European Union.

Finally, the European Union has provided an important lead to other developed countries in opening up its market to all the products exported by the LDCs. The United States has recently implemented the Africa Growth and Opportunity Act which offers improved access to certain African, but not Asian, LDCs. However, the US scheme is less than fully comprehensive, is time limited and its impact is also constrained by restrictive rules of origin.[14] Canada has recently proposed its own

[14] See Mattoo *et al.* (2002).

scheme of duty-free access for LDCs, but again certain agricultural products are excluded. The proposed Canadian scheme does appear to have more flexible rules of origin. For example, for textiles and clothing the scheme allows cumulation among all developing countries (including China and India) with a 25 percent value-added requirement. What would be of immense value would be for the developed countries to come together at the WTO and co-ordinate their positions on market access for developing countries and in particular to address the issue of the under-utilization of trade preferences. The prime suspects for this are the rules of origin; at the very least it is time they were brought in for questioning!

References

Brenton, P. and M. Manchin (2003), *Making EU Trade Agreements Work: The Role of Rules of Origin*, World Economy, forthcoming

CEC (undated), "EU Trade Concession To Least Developed Countries, Everything But Arms Proposal: Possible Impacts On The Agricultural Sector", mimeo, at <europa.eu.int/comm/trade/pdf/eba_ias.pdf>.

CEC (2000), "Products to be Liberalized for LDC Countries", mimeo, at <europa.eu.int/comm/trade/pdf/ebaprodlist.pdf>.

Hewitt, A., A. Koning and M. Davenport (1995), "The Impact of the Uruguay Round Agreements on Manufactured Products of the African, Caribbean and Pacific Group", (UNIDO).

Inama, S. (2002), *Market Access Issues for LDCs: Issues to be Addressed*, 36 Journal of World Trade 1 (February), 85–116.

Mattoo, A., D. Roy and A. Subramanian (2002), "The Africa Growth and Opportunity Act and its Rules of Origin: Generosity Undermined?", World Bank Policy Research Working Paper 2908.

Olarreaga, M. and C. Ozden (2003), "AGOA and Apparel: Who Captures the Rents in the Presence of Preferential Market Access?", mimeo, World Bank

UNCTAD, Commonwealth Secretariat (2001), *Duty and Quota Free Market Access for LDC's: An Analysis of Quad Initiatives*, at <www.unctad.org/en/docs/poditctabm7.en.pdf>.

ANNEX 1: SIMPLE COMPARISON OF THE RULES OF ORIGIN REGARDING VESSELS UNDER THE EBA AND COTONOU AGREEMENT

- Under the EBA the vessel must be registered in the beneficiary country or the European Union. Under Cotonou the vessel must be registered in the European Union or any ACP state.
- Under the EBA the vessel must sail under the flag of the beneficiary country or the European Union. Under Cotonou the vessel must sail under the flag of any ACP country or the European Union.
- Under the EBA the vessels must be at least 50 percent owned by nationals of the beneficiary country or the European Union or by companies with a head office in either the beneficiary or an EU state of which the chairman and the majority of the board members are nationals of those countries. Under

Cotonou these provisions are extended to cover all ACP states. Under certain conditions the European Union will accept vessels chartered or leased by the ACP state under the Cotonou Agreement.

- Under the EBA the master and officers must be nationals of the beneficiary country or an EU Member and at least 75 percent of the crew must be nationals of the beneficiary country or the European Union. Under Cotonou 50 percent of the crew, and the master and officers must be nationals of any ACP state or the European Union.

Chapter 14

Making EU Trade Agreements Work: The Role of Rules of Origin

Paul Brenton and Miriam Manchin

1. INTRODUCTION

FREE trade and preferential trade agreements are a major element in EU foreign policy and are at the forefront of EU policy towards developing countries and neighbouring countries in Europe, including the countries of South-east Europe. As Pelkmans and Brenton (1999), amongst others, note, economic factors are often only one of many which propel the EU towards such agreements. This reflects that free trade partners are often economically very small relative to the EU. For free trade partners, on the other hand, improved access and security of access are key elements in the desire for an agreement with the EU. For the EU, free trade agreements are a means of increasing economic integration through improved access to the EU market, which is seen as important in achieving other political, foreign policy and security objectives. This entails that a key element of the EU's free trade and preferential trade agreements is the extent to which they *deliver* improved market access.

This paper argues that the degree of improved market access, in terms of the amount of a country's exports to the EU which are actually granted favourable treatment, delivered by current EU trade agreements is much less in practice than on paper. This is not a new finding, but very little or nothing has been done to try and change this situation. So, for example, it is clear that the much vaunted 'Everything but Arms' agreement with the 48 least developed countries will not deliver duty free access for all exports from these countries to the EU. Similarly, trade preferences and free trade agreements with the Balkan countries, as a means to promote stability and integration, will not provide for all exports from these countries to enter the EU market free of duties. In fact it is quite possible that a free trade agreement will have very little impact on access to the EU

PAUL BRENTON is from the International Trade Department of the World Bank, Washington DC. MIRIAM MANCHIN is from the Centre for European Policy Studies, Brussels. The views expressed in this paper are those of the authors and should not be attributed to either the World Bank or the Centre for European Policy Studies. The authors are grateful to Daniel Gros, Jacques Pelkmans and an anonymous referee for helpful comments.

market for the majority of a partner country's exports to the EU. It is agreements with these two groups of countries that are the focus of this paper, due to their current importance in EU foreign policy. The arguments are, however, equally pertinent to the recent agreements with South Africa and the revised Meds agreements and prospective agreements with Ukraine, Russia and Moldova on the soon to be enlarged EU's Northern borders.

We argue that the EU should adopt a more rigorous approach to monitoring whether its objectives with regard to free trade agreements are actually being met, and, in particular, whether the agreements are actually fostering economic integration and increasing access to the EU market. We show that the precise impact of a free trade or preferential trade agreement, especially for small countries that have a narrow industrial base, depends very much upon the detailed rules that the EU imposes to govern eligibility for preferential treatment. These rules are very strict in key sectors for the developing countries and countries in the Balkans, such as textiles and clothing and footwear, and severely limit the amount of exports from these countries that receive improved access to the EU market. It is clear that what matters is not just the level of border barriers but the rules that govern the way they are administered. Unfortunately, there is little transparency or discussion of the latter, discussion is too often avoided on the grounds that these are technical matters, whereas in practice such rules can be just as restrictive as tariff barriers.

2. MAKING FREE TRADE AGREEMENTS WORK: ATTENTION AT THE BORDER

a. The Effectiveness of the GSP

How will stabilisation or free trade agreements promote market access and economic integration between the Balkans and the EU? If they do little to improve access to the EU market then they will contribute little to the EU's foreign policy objectives for the region. How will the 'Everything but Arms' agreement improve the treatment of exports from Least Developed Countries to the EU? To address this issue we look at previous EU preferential trade policies towards developing countries and some of the countries in the Balkans region. The EU has had a scheme of preferences for developing countries since 1971 known as the Generalised System of Preferences (GSP). Prior to the signing of stabilisation agreements with the EU, some countries in the Balkans had preferential access to the EU under the GSP. Albania had full access to GSP preferences whilst the former republics of Yugoslavia have had preferential access only for certain agricultural products since 1996 but also had special treatment for textiles and clothing products under different arrangements.

The GSP is a scheme that allows for duty reductions on certain products from particular countries subject to the products meeting the requirements stipulated by the EU, which we will discuss in more detail below. A new GSP scheme has recently been agreed for the period starting in 2002. Here we look at information regarding the previous scheme. The key issue is that the rules governing eligibility for preferences under both the old and the new scheme are very similar. Products under the old GSP were classified according to four headings according to the extent of duty reductions: very sensitive, where the duty applicable was 85 per cent of the MFN rate; sensitive – 70 per cent of the MFN rate; semi-sensitive – 35 per cent of the MFN rate; and non-sensitive, where products entered duty free.

For the GSP scheme in aggregate in the year 1999 only one third of EU imports from developing countries which were eligible for preferences actually entered the EU market with reduced duties. This primarily reflects the treatment of textiles and clothing products, which accounted for over 70 per cent of EU imports from countries covered by the GSP but where the utilisation rate (the ratio of imports receiving preferences to eligible imports) was only 31 per cent. It is worth noting here that the coverage rate of the EU scheme is very comprehensive: over 99 per cent of imports from developing countries of products that are subject to duties in the EU are eligible for preferences. The striking feature of the EU scheme is the low utilisation of these preferences. The US scheme in contrast has a much higher utilisation rate (over 76 per cent in 1998) but is much less comprehensive in terms of coverage (only 53 per cent of dutiable imports from developing countries are eligible for preferences). This is because textiles and clothing products are essentially excluded from the US scheme. They are included in the EU scheme but only a small proportion of imports covered actually receives any preferences.

The overall impact of the two schemes appears similar. In the EU scheme around 33 per cent of dutiable imports from developing countries receive preferential treatment, whilst 41 per cent of US dutiable imports from developing countries are actually granted preferences, although if mineral products (mainly fuel oils) are excluded from the US scheme (fuel oils face a zero duty in the EU) then only 4 per cent of dutiable imports from developing countries receive preferential treatment in the US. Hence, in practice the EU and the US GSP schemes have only been delivering improved market access to a minority of imports from developing countries. The US scheme has provided virtually no preferential access for manufactured products made in developing countries.

For developing countries in general the textiles, clothing and footwear sectors are key sectors which provide the base for industrialisation and participation in the global economy. This is because production in these sectors is based upon the intensive use of labour, which is relatively cheap in developing compared to developed countries. Clothing and footwear appear to be of particular importance in the globalising economy of the 21st century. The establishment of a clothing sector does not require massive capital investment by firms or particularly large

TABLE 1
The Extent of Preferential Treatment (GSP) of EU Imports from Albania[1]

Period	*EU Imports (in 1000 Euro)*	*Per Cent of Total Imports from Albania*	*Eligible*	*Granted*	*Per Cent Granted*
Clothing (CN 61–63)					
1998	74596.0	34.5	74841.3	1980.1	2.6
1997	57719.0	30.2	57176.2	7465.2	13.1
1996	56443.0	28.6	56315.7	964.9	1.7
1995	43568.0	28.8	43592.2	2840.9	6.5
1994	25508.0	20.8	25588.2	1388.0	5.4
Footwear (CN 64)					
1998	63981.0	29.6	63928.50	960.70	1.5
1997	51047.0	26.7	51055.29	1479.75	2.9
1996	60637.0	30.7	60502.98	1030.73	1.7
1995	34187.0	22.6	34067.30	764.90	2.2
1994	35078.0	28.6	34818.20	973.30	2.8

Note:
[1] The coverage of the GSP for Albania was limited to agricultural products from July 1999, and it was replaced by exceptional trade measures for countries and territories participating or linked to the EU's Stabilisation and Association process (Council Regulation No. 2007/2000) from September 2000.

Source: *Eurostat*.

investments in infrastructure by governments, relative to other sectors such as machinery or chemicals. Further, the fragmentation of production of these sectors in OECD countries and the outsourcing of low-skilled labour activities, such as the making-up of articles of clothing, to low wage locations offers the opportunity for developing countries to effectively participate in trade. Clothing was classed as a very sensitive product in the earlier GSP scheme and thus a reduction of only 15 per cent of the applied tariff was applicable. Nevertheless, given that the average EU tariff on clothing is around 12 per cent the GSP scheme potentially offered a significant transfer, and important source of hard currency, to the exporting country.

For all the Balkan countries clothing products are a major export category, accounting for over one third of total exports to the EU of Macedonia, Bosnia-Herzegovina and Albania and one quarter of Croatian exports to the EU in 1998. Table 1 shows for Albania the extent to which exports of clothing and footwear, which comprise over two thirds of exports to the EU were eligible for GSP preferences between 1994 and 1998 and the extent to which those products actually benefited from lower duties in the EU market. It is striking that the GSP has had almost no effect in delivering improved market access to the EU for Albania for these products. Because of the importance of these products to Albania this entails that the GSP had very little impact on Albania's exports to the EU in total. In 1998, almost 84 per cent of total Albanian exports to the EU were eligible for preferential treatment under the GSP and only 2 per cent of these exports were actually granted preferential access, hence only a very small share of the total amount of exports eligible for GSP preferences actually entered the EU market at a preferential rate.

It is interesting to note that similar conclusions emerge from analysis of the utilisation of GSP preferences for textiles and clothing products by Central and Eastern European countries in the early 1990s. For all countries, with the exception of Bulgaria, only about 10 per cent of products eligible for duty reductions actually entered the EU market at a preferential rate. For Bulgaria around one fifth to one quarter of eligible products received preferential treatment. Thus, even for countries such as Hungary, at much higher levels of income and development, the utilisation of available preferences in 1992 was very low.

Western Balkan countries (Albania, Bosnia and Herzegovina, Croatia, Kosovo and Macedonia) have, since 2000, been offered improved autonomous trade preferences by the EU including exports of textiles and clothing products. Limited and specific trade preferences were also made available in 2000 for particular industrial products originating in the Federal Republic of Yugoslavia. Certain textiles and clothing products can be exported to the EU free of duty up to specified quantitative limits. Although we do not have data about the extent to which imports from these countries have directly benefited from these preferences, it appears that the majority of trade has taken place under another scheme, outward processing, which we discuss in more detail below. Normal imports were considerably below their ceilings. At the same time imports under the outward processing scheme were significantly higher than imports under the preferential scheme for almost all product categories. This suggests that many companies chose the OPT scheme instead of benefiting from preferences using normal imports.[1]

Understanding the reasons for this failure to benefit from GSP and duty reductions on textiles and clothing products is important in assessing the extent to which the free trade provisions of the 'Everything but Arms' agreement and the stabilisation agreements with the Balkan countries will actually deliver improved access to the EU market. If factors which prevented the utilisation of GSP benefits and other preferences remain under these agreements then the direct effect upon exports from the 49 least developed countries and the Balkans region is likely to be very muted.

b. The Role of Rules of Origin

So why have producers in developing countries, Balkans producers or EU importers not been exploiting the incentives of the GSP or the preferential access

[1] More details of the utilisation of GSP preferences by Central and Eastern European countries in the early 1990s and the magnitude of imports of textiles and clothing products from Balkan countries in 2000 are presented in Brenton and Manchin (2002).

for textiles and clothing products for the Balkan countries? We believe that if these preferences were costlessly available then they would be fully exploited. Economic operators are notoriously good at exploiting available incentives. Thus, there must be cost-raising factors or structural impediments which are constraining the uptake of such benefits.

One of the key factors underlying the difficulties in obtaining preferential access to the EU is likely to be the specific rules, and particularly the rules of origin, which the EU attaches to all of its trade agreements. Rules of origin define the conditions that a product must satisfy to be deemed as originating in the country from which preferential access to the EU is being sought. The main justification for rules of origin is to prevent trade deflection, whereby products from non-participating countries destined for the EU market are redirected through free trade partners of the EU to avoid the payment of EU customs duties. Similar reasoning applies to the need for rules of origin in the EU's free trade partner. When products are produced in a single stage then the origin of the products should be relatively easy to establish. Proof that the product was produced in the free trade partner should be sufficient. For all other cases the rules of origin define the methods by which it can be ascertained that the product has undergone sufficient working or processing in the free trade partner to qualify for preferential access. The specification of rules of origin has become particularly important in recent years as technological progress and globalisation have led to the increasing fragmentation of the production process into different stages or tasks which are undertaken in different locations. In practice the higher the level of working that is required by the rules of origin the more difficult it is to satisfy those rules.

A number of general approaches to determining origin are available. In the EU's bilateral trade agreements the basic rule that it adopts is that of the change in tariff heading at the 4-digit level of the Harmonised System (HS) of tariff classification. However, in a very large number of cases this basic rule is supplanted by often restrictive specific requirements. These other requirements can be a minimum percentage of local value added in the originating country, or a technical requirement which requires that the product undergoes specific manufacturing operations in the country.

For example, with the basic rule of change in tariff heading, a country which imports woven cotton fabric (HS 5208) to produce cotton shirts (6105) would satisfy the rule of origin and qualify for preferential reduction of the tariff on cotton shirts. However, in this specific case in EU free trade agreements the change of tariff classification is replaced with a requirement that the product has been manufactured from yarn. In effect this imposes the requirement that two stages of production must be undertaken in the partner or qualifying area to confer origin – not only the sewing together of the fabric but also the production of the fabric itself! Clothing products made in free trade partners of the EU but which are made-up of fabrics imported from third countries, such as China, will not satisfy the EU origin rules and will not qualify for tariff reduction.

The rules of origin defined by the GSP, the Europe Agreements, the Stabilisation and Association Agreements and by the regulations on autonomous trade preferences to Western Balkan countries are almost identical. The agreements state a general change of tariff heading rule, however, annexes specify, for listed products, requirements other than change in tariff classification. The value-added criterion is very rarely applied, the specific requirements listed in the annex mainly define technical requirements. These annexes typically stretch to over 80 pages, although the scope of technical requirements is even greater than this suggests since in certain cases (for example, Chapter 60 – knitted or crocheted fabrics) a specific technical requirement is set for the whole chapter.

The technical requirements defined in the annexes are more specific and more restrictive than the change in tariff heading rule. In the case of textile, clothing and footwear, the annex never specifies value-added requirements, it only lays down technical requirements. In the case of textiles, only 14 per cent of the product headings require a change in heading to satisfy origin, while the remaining 86 per cent must meet specific technical requirements to qualify for preferential access. In the case of clothing, for 95 per cent of the products the rules do not permit change of heading but require specific working and processing. Similarly for footwear, most of the products have to fulfil technical requirements. Hoekman (1993) notes that as these rules become technical they offer scope for the participation of industries in setting restrictive rules of origin.

The rules of origin in the GSP relating to textiles and clothing are very similar to those in the EU's free trade agreements including those with the Central and Eastern European Countries – for example, to qualify for duty reductions, clothing products must be made from yarn. An example of the restrictiveness of these rules has been the request, and the granting (up to a quantitative limit), of a derogation from the rules of origin by Lao PDR, Nepal and Cambodia. In 1997 only 6 per cent of Lao textile and clothing exports to the EU benefited from GSP duty exemption (Lao PDR is classified as a least developed country and is eligible for duty free access to the EU market for many industrial products). The Commission accepted that the Lao textile and clothing industry was unable to satisfy the EU rules of origin. Thus, the 'Everything but Arms' agreement with the same rules of origin as the GSP is unlikely to deliver any substantial improvement in access to the EU market for clothing products from countries such as Laos.

It is rules of origin, such as those discussed above, which underlie the analyses of Krueger (1995) and Krishna and Krueger (1995) who demonstrate how rules of origin can act as 'hidden protectionism' and induce a switch in demand in free trade partners from low-cost external inputs to higher-cost partner inputs to ensure that final products actually receive duty free access. With the apparent aim of preventing trade deflection, rules of origin can be used to protect a domestic industry from unwanted competition based in the partner, even in conditions where trade deflection is unlikely (Falvey and Reed, 1998). Note that in this situation the EU is unlikely to exert pressure on the trade partner for the general liberalisation of tariffs against other trading partners. James (1997) argues that as the degree of protection offered by the common external tariff in the EC has diminished increasingly restrictive rules of origin have become commonplace.

Thus, for example, in small developing countries where there is no domestic textile industry but a competitive clothing industry, clothing producers will be faced with the choice of importing fabrics from the EU and therefore satisfying the EU origin rules and receiving preferential access to the EU market or importing fabrics from a non-qualifying source and having to pay the full duty. This choice will be influenced by the tariff in the EU on the final product and the country's tariff on imported fabrics. If clothing producers in the country are induced to shift from a third country source to an EU source of fabrics there will be trade diversion (fabrics will be imported from a less efficient source and there will be a loss of tariff revenue) which will offset any gains from improved access to the EU market for the final clothing product. Given the importance of the textiles and clothing sectors and that the rules of origin in EU trade agreements may stimulate such trade diversion, it is possible that such agreements will actually reduce economic welfare in developing-country partners and partner countries in the Balkans!

It is sometimes suggested that the restrictive nature of rules of origin can be reduced if the agreement allows diagonal cumulation across other free trade or preferential trade partners. In the GSP there is limited regional cumulation. For the stabilisation agreements in the Balkans there is no regional cumulation, only bilateral cumulation with the EU is allowed. However, cumulation will only be important if a lower cost (than the EU) provider of the intermediate input is included in the area of cumulation. For example, in the case of clothing, cumulation will be meaningless if none of the countries included have an efficient textile industry. So long as the rules of origin prevent domestic producers in the partner country from sourcing inputs from the most efficient global suppliers the value of any preferential access to the EU market will be reduced or eliminated.

The restrictiveness of satisfying rules of origin may also be compounded by the costs of actually proving origin. In a widely quoted study Herin (1986) found that the costs for EFTA producers of proving origin led to one quarter of EFTA exports to the EU paying the applied most favoured nation (MFN) duties. The costs of proving origin involve satisfying a number of administrative procedures so as to provide the documentation that is required and the costs of maintaining systems that accurately account for imported inputs from different sources to prove consistency with the technical rules. The ability to prove origin may well require the use of, what are for small companies in developing and transition economies, but not for companies in the EU, sophisticated and expensive accounting procedures. Without such procedures it is difficult for companies to show precisely the geographical breakdown of the inputs that they have used.

The costs of proving origin may be even higher, and possibly prohibitive, in countries where customs mechanisms are poorly developed. Thus, even if producers can satisfy the EU's rules of origin, in terms of meeting the technical requirements, they may not receive preferential access to the EU because the customs authorities do not accept their proof of origin or the costs of proving origin are high relative to the duty reduction that is available. The latter suggests that the economic impact of preferential tariff reduction may be discontinuous. Initial reductions in tariffs will have little impact since they will be less than the costs of proving origin. It is only once the gap between the preferential tariff and the MFN rate exceeds the costs of proving origin that there will be a stimulus to trade. However, as we will discuss below even with free trade agreements the difficulties and costs of proving origin may preclude duty free access to the EU.

The World Bank and the European Bank for Reconstruction and Development jointly developed a Business Environment and Enterprise Performance Survey (BEEPS). The survey is based on face-to-face interviews with firm managers and owners. The questionnaire included the following question: 'how problematic are customs/foreign trade regulations for the operation and growth of your business?'. The answers suggest that these regulations still constitute important obstacles, especially for small companies, where the number of employees was between 1 and 49. For example, in Croatia only 39 per cent of firms said that these regulations generated no obstacles, in Albania only 15 per cent, in Bosnia and Herzegovina the same figure was 31 per cent while in Macedonia it was 23 per cent.

3. RULES OF ORIGIN AND OUTWARD PROCESSING ACTIVITIES

Further evidence that rules of origin and the costs of origin are important comes from the importance of outward processing traffic (OPT) and interestingly the fact that for Europe Agreement countries OPT activities have continued even after the complete removal of tariffs. OPT has been an important feature of the development of trade between the EU and the countries of Central and Eastern Europe and is equally, if not more, important for countries in the Balkans. OPT in textiles and clothing may have been initially stimulated in the early 1990s by the presence of quotas imposed under the Multi-Fibre Agreement or bilaterally imposed by the EU. However, few of those quotas appear to have been binding.

Under normal or fiscal OPT procedures, EU trade policy encourages processing overseas by EU firms by providing relief from import duties on the compensating value of imports after processing abroad. The amount of duty payable is calculated from the value of the product imported multiplied by the appropriate tariff for that product minus the hypothetical duty that would have been paid on the intermediate products exported under the processing scheme, that is the value of the exports for processing abroad multiplied by the appropriate EU tariff for that product. Thus, an EU firm which exports textiles under an OPT scheme and re-imports clothing products would have to pay the duty on the clothing product but would be refunded the duty that would be applicable to the value of the textile products exported.[2]

Within outward processing in textiles and clothing the EU has provided for a specific scheme known as 'economic outward processing' where, often up to specific limits and/or subject to surveillance, imports after processing enter the EU duty free. Economic outward processing was introduced to 'enable the textile and clothing industry to adapt to the conditions of international competition'. Under this regime, goods temporarily exported from the EU for processing must be in free circulation within the Community and must have EU origin. Although, if products of Community origin are insufficient, derogation can be granted from these rules, but for no more than 14 per cent of the total value of the goods for which prior authorisation is requested. There are further requirements in the regulation to protect the industry in the Community, such as, commitments to maintain production and employment in the Community and maximum processing rules. The latter are the converse of the rules of origin in free trade and preferential trade agreements, which stipulate minimum processing requirements.

Furthermore, the economic outward processing procedure should only be applied if there are quantitative limits or surveillance with regard to imports of textile and clothing products from the country where the processing would take place. However, for the Czech Republic, the Slovak Republic, Hungary, Poland, Romania and Bulgaria the procedure was applicable for products even when there were no import limitations or specific measures. Imports after economic outward processing for these countries could enter the EU with zero duties.

Table 2 shows the importance of products that have been processed abroad in EU imports of clothing from the Balkan and Central and Eastern European countries in 1998 and 2000. For Albania and Serbia the vast majority of clothing exports to the EU, 92 per cent and 85 per cent respectively, had involved the processing of EU inputs under an outward processing scheme. For Bosnia, Croatia and Macedonia around one half or more of clothing exports to the EU had been part of an OPT operation for an EU company. Overall between 10 and 20 per cent of EU imports from Macedonia, Bosnia and Croatia have involved the processing of temporarily exported EU inputs, whilst nearly two thirds of EU imports from Albania were after outward processing. Hence, outward processing,

[2] The EU has recently revised the scheme so that now tariffs are paid on the value-added overseas.

TABLE 2
Importance of Economic OPT and Fiscal OPT in EU Exports of Textiles and Imports of Clothing

	Share of EU Imports of Clothing after Processing Abroad					
	2000			*1998*		
	Total	*Economic*	*Fiscal*	*Total OPT*	*Economic*	*Fiscal*
Turkey	0.5	0.1	0.4	1.5	1.0	0.5
Romania	33.6	7.1	26.5	51.8	13.7	38.1
Bulgaria	46.2	6.6	39.6	51.4	9.9	41.5
Albania	92.1	23.1	69.0	94.3	19.6	74.7
Croatia	54.4	23.9	30.5	60.6	21.6	39.0
Bosnia-Herzegovina	49.4	13.5	35.9	66.8	22.6	44.2
Serbia-Montenegro	85.0	25.3	59.7	83.9	20.9	63.0
FROM	58.8	13.9	44.9	61.1	17.3	43.8
Poland	35.5	6.9	28.6	57.0	9.4	47.6
Slovakia	18.2	6.3	11.9	49.4	11.0	38.4
Hungary	40.7	21.0	19.7	47.6	11.3	46.3
Slovenia	28.8	5.0	23.8	57.8	14.4	43.4
Czech Rep.	25.8	7.4	18.4	39.7	9.0	30.7

Source: *Eurostat*.

particularly of clothing and footwear products, is an important feature of EU trade relations with the Balkan countries.

It is also informative to look at the evolution of OPT for those countries which now have duty and quota free access to the EU market through the Europe Agreements. In 2000 imports after outward processing accounted for over 35 per cent of EU imports of clothing from Poland, over 40 per cent of EU imports from Hungary, 34 per cent from Romania and more than 45 per cent from Bulgaria. EU tariffs on imports of clothing from Poland, Hungary, Bulgaria and Romania were removed in 1997. So why should EU companies incur all the administrative costs associated with registering for outward processing in products where they should be able to import the final product free of duties?

We postulate here that the cost of paying the full duty on the imported clothing products minus the duty that is calculated on the exported inputs is less than the costs of proving origin (including the risk that even valid documents are rejected at the customs point) or that origin cannot be proved due to the strict nature of the rules of origin. If this is the case then OPT amongst preferential trade partners is a mechanism for reducing duty payable without having to incur the costs of proving origin or is a mechanism for avoiding having to prove origin. This argument is supported by the data for Turkey, which shares many of the features of the countries in this region, in terms of relative labour costs and comparative advantage in the production of clothing products. A notable difference, however, is that Turkey has signed a customs union agreement with the EU, under which, due to the common external tariff, there is no need to prove origin. Outward processing between the EU and Turkey is negligible.

Hence, EU bilateral trade policies, particularly with regard to the textiles and clothing sectors, act as a mechanism to lock partners into the processing of EU inputs and where this is not feasible preferential access is prevented. Restrictive technical rules of origin ensure that clothing products produced in partners from third country fabrics do not qualify for preferential treatment. For neighbouring countries the restrictiveness of the rules of origin and the costs of proving conformity with those rules can be overcome by participation in the outward processing schemes established by the EU. For developing countries that are further away even this does not seem to be a practical option. Nevertheless, whilst it may be in the interest of the industry in the EU to participate in these processing operations it is not clear whether it is in the best interests of the partner. Thus, an important issue for consideration in the EU should be whether these outward processing schemes are helping the EU to achieve its foreign policy objectives with regard to neighbouring countries and whether alternative policies would be more effective in stimulating trade and economic integration.

Given the apparent importance of rules of origin in influencing the economic impact of free trade areas it is of interest to look at the process of negotiation that leads to their inclusion. In fact, however, it appears that there is no process of negotiation. The EU presents its specification of rules of origin, which potential free trade partners either accept or accept! But how does the EU arrive at its specification of rules of origin? Given that economic integration is an element in achieving foreign policy objectives are these rules designed in a way to minimise any hindrance to the exports of the free trade partner? Our initial analysis suggests not: rules of origin are a significant factor in constraining exports from free trade partners of the EU. Conversely, are the rules primarily reflecting the interests of EU producers? It would be easier to assess this proposition if the process by which the EU defines rules of origin were transparent. But it is not. The information we have been able to obtain suggests that the current set of rules of origin, which are very similar across different free trade partners, are applied simply because they have been applied in the past. The exact origins of the specification of the rules of origin and their rationale are not clear but one cannot rule out that they primarily reflect the interests of particular groups of EU producers, who are quite happy to see such rules remain. There does not appear to have been any attempt to assess whether rules of origin specified a decade or more ago are relevant to the current economic climate.

Thus, what we can conclude is that the EU imposes an existing set of rules of origin with little regard to their potential economic impact on free trade partners. UNCTAD (2001) points out that arguments concerning the restrictiveness of rules of origin have been regularly made since the inception of the GSP scheme almost 30 years ago but the rules have changed little and the problems in fulfilling the origin requirements persist. Preferential rules of origin have passed through a number of rounds of global trade talks under the GATT and then the WTO untouched and subject to no effective discipline.

4. CONCLUSIONS

Developing countries and the countries of the Balkans are specialised in the production of labour intensive products. The ability to increase export revenues in the short-run and to increase the degree of economic integration with the EU will be determined by export capacity and market access for products such as clothing and footwear. This is the background to the 'Everything but Arms' and the Stabilisation Agreements that the EU is signing in the Balkans region. In this paper we suggest that economic integration, which is stated by the EU as an important element of its foreign policy initiatives towards these countries, will be hampered by the nature of the administrative rules that the EU applies to implement free trade agreements. At the forefront of these are rules of origin, which govern access to preferential treatment. Preferences under the GSP have not been exploited in the past because of the difficulties of satisfying the restrictive technical rules that the EU applies to define origin and because of the actual costs of proving origin and difficulties in passing through customs.[3]

Thus whilst the EU likes to portray its agreements with the Central and Eastern European and now the Balkan countries as asymmetric, with trade liberalisation being undertaken at a faster rate in the EU, in practice this may not be the case. At best the nature of the rules of origin that the EU imposes upon free trade partners ensures that producers in these countries are locked in to using high cost inputs from the EU if they wish to benefit from reduced tariff barriers on their exports to the EU. This clearly reduces the value of the tariff concessions. However, there is evidence to suggest that the restrictiveness of the rules of origin make it very difficult for companies in these preferential partners to actually obtain duty reductions and improved market access. In effect, to obtain improved market access requires a degree of sophistication in terms of being able to satisfy origin rules and to prove conformity with those rules. This makes asymmetric liberalisation by the EU with relatively poorer countries difficult to achieve through preferential or free trade agreements. One way of avoiding these problems and of guaranteeing improved access to the EU market would be to sign customs unions rather than free trade agreements where rules of origin are not

[3] Of course, if the real objective of the EU has been to protect EU industry and shift sourcing patterns in developing countries towards EU suppliers whilst offering improved market access then it could be argued that the agreements have been quite successful.

necessary due to a common external tariff, provided that a suitable means of allocating tariff revenues is implemented.

What could be done to reduce the restrictiveness of rules of origin in EU preferential trade agreements? Currently, the EU approach assumes that all trade partners are equally susceptible to trade deflection and so are treated in the same restrictive manner. This is clearly far too draconian. If the EU were to relax its rules of origin by, for example, requiring a single production step in the production of clothing, it is obvious that we would not see a flood of imports from third countries being re-directed through each and every one of the EU's free trade and preferential partners. There may be some propensity for trade deflection, although this is declining due to tariff reductions and the removal of quotas, but this is most likely to be concentrated on specific locations. Thus, a more targeted policy such as a carefully designed flexible safeguards policy is likely to be more effective in preventing trade deflection without constraining imports from a wide range of preferential suppliers.

In this light we make the following recommendations:

- There is a need for monitoring by the EU of the extent to which its trade agreements actually deliver improved market access to partner countries. This would not be difficult to achieve. Thus, under the stabilisation agreements the EU should collect statistics on the amount of imports from Balkan countries that actually receive duty free treatment. Similar provision should be made for the 'Everything but Arms' agreement. The EU has established a strong capacity for monitoring overseas market access for EU companies. It would be useful if a similar capacity were established to monitor to what extent EU offers to third countries of improved market access actually materialise, and if not, why not. This is crucial if economic integration is to play the role envisaged for it in the EU's foreign policy towards developing countries and regions such as the Balkans.
- The EU should make available information on the amount of tariff revenue collected on imports from preferential and free trade partners. Such funds should be added to the technical assistance budget for each country. The revenue that the EU collects on imports from duty free or preferential trade partners should not enter the general EU budget.
- There should be a complete reconsideration of the explicit rules of origin in EU trade agreements. For products of particular importance to the developing and the Balkan countries, where products are clearly not receiving preferential access there could be derogation from the current rules of origin. More generally, the EU should consider at least implementation of a one-step rule for clothing products together with a sensible safeguards policy. Ideally, the simple change of tariff heading rule should be applied to all products.

- Attention should be given to the administrative costs for companies of proving origin. A simpler and less demanding system would make it easier for small companies in developing and transition countries to actually gain preferential access to the EU market.
- The Balkan countries and developing countries should bear in mind the potential restrictive nature of rules of origin when devising their own free trade agreements.[4] In Europe a quick move towards less restrictive pan-European rules of origin should be implemented. In the Balkans, careful consideration should be given to the benefits of establishing a customs union with the EU, which will avoid the problems addressed in this paper.

REFERENCES

Brenton, P. and M. Manchin (2002), 'Making EU Trade Agreements Work: The Role of Rules of Origin', Working Document 183 (CEPS, Brussels).

Falvey, R. and G. Reed (1998), 'Economic Effects of Rules of Origin' *Weltwirtschaftliches Archiv*, **134**, 209–29.

Flatters, F. (2002), 'SADC Rules of Origin: Undermining Regional Free Trade', Paper presented at the TIPS Forum, Johannesburg, September 2002 (http://qed.econ.queensu.ca/faculty/flatters/writings/ff_sadc_roo_tips_forum.pdf).

Herin, J. (1986), 'Rules of Origin and Differences Between Tariff Levels in EFTA and in the EC', Occasional Paper 13, Economic Affairs Department (EFTA, Geneva).

Hoekman, B. (1993), 'Rules of Origin for Goods and Services, Conceptual Issues and Economic Considerations', *Journal of World Trade*, **27**, 4, 81–99.

James, W. E. (1997), 'APEC and Preferential Rules of Origin: Stumbling Blocks for Liberalization of Trade?', *Journal of World Trade*, **31**, 3, 113–34.

Krishna, K. and A. Krueger (1995), 'Implementing Free Trade Areas: Rules of Origin and Hidden Protection', Working Paper 4983 (National Bureau for Economic Research).

Krueger, A. (1995), 'Free Trade Agreements Versus Customs Unions', Working Paper 5087 (National Bureau for Economic Research).

Pelkmans, J. and P. Brenton (1999), 'Free-Trade with the EU: Driving Forces and the Effects', in O. Memedovic, A. Kuyvenhoven and W. Molle (eds.), *Multilateralism and Regionalism in the Post-Uruguay Round Era: What Role for the EU?* (Kluwer: Boston).

UNCTAD (2001), 'Improving Market Access for Least Developed Countries', UNCTAD/DITC/TNCD/4 (Geneva).

[4] See Flatters (2002) for a discussion of the potential impact of restrictive rules of origin in the Southern African Development Community.

Chapter 15

WATCHING MORE THAN THE DISCOVERY CHANNEL TO DIVERSIFY EXPORTS

Paul Brenton and Richard Newfarmer

In seeking to accelerate export diversification, much of the focus in the past has been on increasing the number of products that are exported. Hausmann and Rodrik (2003) continue in this vein and focus on the "discovery process" of exporting, contending that firms in developing economies tend to underinvest in discovery because would-be first movers into export markets fear their initially high returns would be eroded by subsequent new entry, and they thus underinvest in searching for new export activities. A policy corollary is that governments can usefully deploy industrial policies to stimulate discovery and hence diversification.

Klinger and Lederman (2004) create a model to test the hypothesis that the threat of imitation inhibits the rate of "discovery." They proxy barriers to entry by using the average time it takes to register a formal firm (from the World Bank's *Doing Business* surveys), and find that indeed barriers to entry are associated with increased discovery and diversification. From this they deduce that some type of subsidy to the discovery process is warranted.

While discovery of new export products may be important to the process of export growth, one must look at the whole export product cycle. For example, what are the obstacles to sustaining new product exports? Brenton, Pierola and von Uexküll (2009, chapter 7 in this volume) show that lower-income developing countries do fairly well in generating new product exports ("births"), but that a high proportion do not survive to maturity ("deaths"). This finding suggests that activity during the acceleration phase of the export product might be as important as the discovery phase.

Policy that is focused solely on the discovery phase may miss other important opportunities for driving export growth. Hence, it is necessary to understand the contribution of various sources of export growth in developing countries before drawing strong policy conclusions regarding one particular element of the growth process. To this end, this chapter asks the question, Are countries with rapidly growing exports performing well because they are intensifying existing exports to existing markets or because they are bringing new products to market or because they are extending the reach of existing products to markets in third countries? After reviewing the export performance of a wide group of developing countries during the period 1995–2004, the chapter explores the importance of, and the potential for, the growth of existing exports to new markets.

OLD-GROWTH EXPORTS VERSUS NEW-GROWTH EXPORTS

Over time, the growth of exports can be divided into the expansion of existing products to old markets (the intensive margin) and the expansion of existing and new products to new geographic markets, as well as the expansion of new products to old markets (the extensive margin). This study builds upon previous analyses of the role of the intensive and extensive margins in export growth (such as those by Evenett and Venables 2002, Besedes and Prusa 2007, and Zahler 2007) by using data for a broader set of developing-country exports to a wider group of importers and for a more detailed commodity breakdown.

Our examination of the growth of exports from 99 developing countries to 102 developed- and developing-country markets over 1995–2004, accounting for 87 percent of imports from the developing-country exporters, shows the preponderance of growth at the intensive margin.[1] For a list of the countries in the study, see annex 6A. For the 99 exporters as a whole, the intensive margin accounted for 80 percent of the contribution to total export growth, while the extensive margin contributed only 20 percent (figure 6.1).

Within the intensive margin, existing export flows that experienced an increase (equivalent to 105 percent of total export growth) were slightly offset by those export flows that fell (20 percent of total export growth) or disappeared (4 percent of total export growth). Within the

Figure 6.1 Decomposition of Export Growth for 99 Developing Countries, 1995–2004

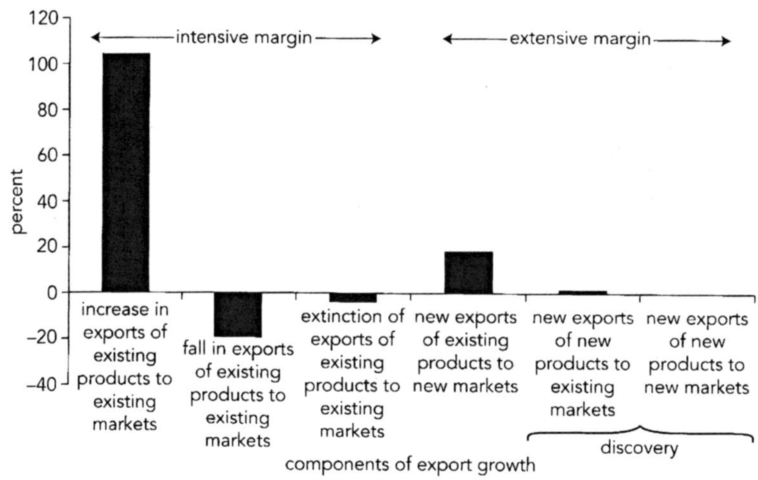

Source: Authors' calculations based on U.N. Comtrade (Commodity Trade Statistics Database).
Note: Each bar equals the change in exports for the category divided by the change in total exports.

extensive margin, the export of existing products to new markets accounted for about 18 percent of total export growth, while the export of new products accounted for only 1 percent of growth.

These conclusions largely hold for each of the geographic regions. In all geographic regions, the intensification of existing export flows makes the largest contribution to export growth, in most regions offset only slightly by the decline or extinction of existing flows (table 6.1). The decline and extinction of existing export products are somewhat more important in sub-Saharan Africa, which is also the only region where the extensive margin made a larger contribution to export growth than the intensive margin. In none of the regions was the export of new products a significant source of export growth between 1995 and 2004. These results are also consistent across income groups, where export growth is dominated by the intensive margin. (We also repeated the exercise for an earlier period to determine if the results were consistent, and they were; see annex 6B.)

Table 6.1 Contribution of the Intensive and Extensive Margins to Export Growth, by Region (percent)

	Intensive margin			Extensive margin			Total = 100%	
Region	Increase in exports of existing products to existing markets	Fall in exports of existing products to existing markets	Extinction of exports of existing products to existing markets	New exports of existing products to new markets	New exports of new products to existing markets	New exports of new products to new markets	Intensive	Extensive
Africa	106.9	–37.7	–25.9	46.1	10.2	0.4	43.3	56.7
Middle East and North Africa	92.1	–16.9	–7.6	30.1	2.4	0.0	67.6	32.4
Europe and Central Asia	89.8	–14.7	–7.3	29.8	2.4	0.0	67.8	32.2
Latin America and the Caribbean	105.7	–21.9	–8.6	23.1	1.6	0.0	75.3	24.7
South Asia	104.3	–21.6	–5.0	20.8	1.5	0.0	77.7	22.3
East Asia and Pacific	106.7	–19.3	–1.7	13.8	0.5	0.0	85.7	14.3

Source: Authors' calculations based on U.N. Comrade.

EXPLOITING THE EXTENSIVE MARGIN

Countries that are already producing in many markets and have highly diversified export portfolios obviously have less potential to increase exports at the extensive margin and therefore a broader base for the intensive margin to propel growth. However, countries with a less-developed productive base have, as Besedes and Prusa (2007) suggest, enormous opportunities to further exploit the extensive margin for growth.

One way to measure that geographic potential for a specific country is to look at the products it exports, compare that to the number of countries importing those products around the world, and then measure the share of geographic markets the country actually reaches. This we call the *index of export market penetration.*[2] For the given range of products that a country exports, the index will be higher for countries that service a large proportion of the number of national markets around the world that import that product. Countries that export only to a small number of the overseas markets that import the products that the country exports will have a low value on the index.

Indeed, by this measure, countries with higher per capita incomes tend to have more success in exploiting the available markets for the goods that they export. This is illustrated in figure 6.2, which shows a positive correlation between the log of the index of export market penetration and the log of GDP (gross domestic product) per capita (table 6.2). Further, the positive

Figure 6.2 Export Market Penetration and per Capita Income

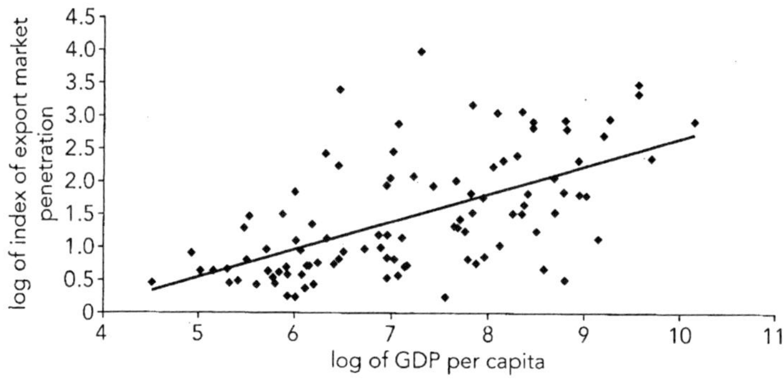

Source: Authors' calculations.

and significant relationship between export market penetration and GDP per capita remains after controlling for economic size (log of GDP).[3]

Example: Albania Reaches Fewer Markets than Does the Czech Republic

A specific example helps in understanding the large differences in export market penetration between countries of different income levels. Albania, with a per capita income of $2,400 in 2004, exported 955 products, about one-third of the number exported by the Czech Republic, with a per capita income of $10,500 (column 2 of table 6.3). These 955 products generated 2,050 bilateral export flows for Albania. In contrast, the Czech Republic's 2,863 exported products generated over 50,000 bilateral flows. Thus, the number of bilateral export flows for Albania was only 4 percent of that for the Czech Republic (column 3 of table 6.3), even though the number of potential flows for Albania is around 35 percent of that of the Czech Republic (column 4). Thus, Albania is

Table 6.2 Regression Results for Dependent Variable Log of Index of Export Market Penetration

Log of GDP per capita	0.42	0.09
	(0.06)	(0.04)
Log of GDP		0.38
		(0.03)
Adjusted R^2	0.35	0.77

Source: Authors' calculations.

Note: Standard errors are in parentheses.

Table 6.3 Export Market Penetration for Albania and the Czech Republic, 2004

Country	Number of products exported	Actual number of export relationships	Potential number of export relationships	Export market penetration
Albania	955	2,050	90,350	2.27
Czech Republic	2,863	50,187	258,904	19.38
Ratio	0.35	0.04	0.35	

Source: Authors' calculations based on U.N. Comtrade.

currently exploiting just 2 percent of the potential bilateral flows for the products that it exports, while the Czech Republic is exploiting almost 20 percent of its available export opportunities (column 5).[4]

What could explain why countries such as Albania exhibit a much lower number of bilateral trade flows for their export products than countries with higher levels of income per capita? Here the recently developed model of trade with heterogeneous firms (Melitz 2003) is useful in highlighting critical parameters that can limit the number of trade flows. In the Melitz model, there is a distribution of firms within a country with differing productivities and hence differing marginal costs. Exporters must incur the fixed costs of entering markets (both the domestic and overseas markets) and variable trade costs (such as transportation and tariffs).

For every market in the world, including the domestic market, local firms face a cutoff condition that is defined as the highest marginal cost at which firms can enter the market. Because sales to the domestic market do not incur trade costs, the domestic cutoff marginal cost, conditioned by domestic demand, will determine the number of firms that enter the local market. Exporters need not necessarily serve the local market since local demand may not exist or be sufficient. However, in activities with scale economies, producing for the domestic market may enable firms to expand output to an extent that reduces marginal costs below the threshold to export to overseas markets. Hence, policies that raise the fixed costs of entry into the local market and the marginal costs of selling domestically can affect the number of firms and the potential number of exporters. This points to the importance of the overall incentive regime governing investment, the business climate, labor regulations, and the costs of key inputs. The latter will be determined by the trade regime and the efficiency of ports and customs for firms dependent on imported inputs, as well as by the provision of backbone services such as telecommunications, energy, water, and finance.

Bilateral exports will be stimulated by a fall in the fixed costs of entering overseas markets and by a decline in trade costs. Fixed costs are likely to emanate from the costs of obtaining market information, marketing in overseas markets, and producing to the standards of that market. Trade costs will arise from the costs of clearing customs and ports in the exporting and importing countries, transport costs, tariffs and other restrictions on market access, and the costs of conformity assessment for the overseas market.

In a world in which firms differ in their productivities, trade costs allow low-productivity firms that sell only to the domestic market to survive. Thus, a fall in trade costs induces a reallocation of resources within sectors away from low-productivity firms that exit the industry toward the most productive nonexporting firms that are now able to expand through exporting and to existing high-productivity exporters that can increase overseas sales further. As a result, industry productivity expands and incomes rise (Bernard and others 2003).

Possible Market Interventions to Boost the Rapid-Growth Phase

In this context, are there market imperfections that might justify government intervention in the rapid-growth phase, much as Hausmann and Rodrik posit exist in the discovery phase? Indeed it is possible to hypothesize several.

- Factor market imperfections: Costs of capital may prevent sufficient expansion of supply from reaching new export markets, and labor market regulations may prevent flexible deployment of labor.
- Informational asymmetries: Costs of gathering information about opportunities in new export markets may be high because few firms in a developing country export to that new market relative to competing suppliers from other countries.
- Imperfection in domestic services markets: Costs of key input services—telecommunications, transportation, and finance—are often high, in many instances because of policy barriers to entry (state monopolies prevent entry, for example).
- Transportation imperfections: Costs of transport to third markets may be high because the low quantity of total exports from a given developing country deprives exporters of scale economies in transport. Similarly, cartel arrangements in shipping drive up prices—and more so to developing countries (World Bank 2002).

Other imperfections could undoubtedly be identified. The point is that given the importance of the intensive margin, any strategy for using exports to grow would be remiss if it focused only on the discovery channel.

CONCLUSIONS: POLICIES AND OPEN QUESTIONS

Because of the importance of existing exports in the overall growth performance of a country's exports, policies that focus excessively on the discovery phase—to the exclusion of attention to existing products—are bound to miss opportunities to propel growth. Moreover, in the search for new markets, exploring the obstacles to penetrating new geographic markets is arguably as worthy of a priori policy attention as is exploring obstacles to discovery of new product exports.

How can policies remedy the types of market failures that may impede expansion into third markets? In many cases, these constraints to competitiveness require specific interventions and institutions. Supply-side constraints may impede firms from satisfying demands in existing markets—and typically infrastructure reliability and cost are crucial among these. Moreover, weak performance in the index of export market penetration, as shown in this study, underscores the importance of export promotion agencies—and even the need for economic officers in foreign embassies—in overcoming informational asymmetries that impede the search for third markets. Investment promotion regimes, standards bodies, and customs agencies are likely to be important to support innovation and clustering. Finally, diagnosis of underperformance in all these areas should result in policy initiatives to overcome obstacles. To be effective, experience suggests that these initiatives should be brought together within a strategy for competitiveness rather than as a series of ad hoc interventions.

This chapter opens up other interesting questions of research on diversification. At the intensive margin, have successful countries performed well because, during the mature stage of a product, they have invested in raising quality and introducing differentiation that allows them to exploit the intensive margin? At what stage in the export cycle did firms choose to seek new geographic markets—at a point when growth in existing markets began to slow, or in an earlier acceleration phase? Also, the findings on product deaths merit closer scrutiny and might be amenable to policy remedies. Why do low-income countries with apparent success in the discovery phase of the export cycle experience a greater rate of premature product demise? A recent article (Besedes and Prusa 2006) argues that sustaining growth in the first two to four years is crucial to moving into the acceleration phase. All of this suggests that watching more than the discovery channel might lead to a more comprehensive policy vision.

ANNEX 6A: COUNTRY COVERAGE

Table 6A.1 Developing-Country Exporters, by Income Level

Low income	Lower middle income	Upper middle income	High income
Bangladesh	Albania	Argentina	Korea, Rep. of
Benin	Algeria	Chile	Singapore
Burkina Faso	Angola	Costa Rica	Slovenia
Burundi	Armenia	Croatia	Taiwan, China
Cambodia	Azerbaijan	Czech Republic	
Central African Republic	Bolivia	Equatorial Guinea	
Chad	Brazil	Estonia	
Ethiopia	Bulgaria	Gabon	
Gambia, The	Cameroon	Hungary	
Ghana	Cape Verde	Latvia	
Guinea	China	Lithuania	
Guinea Bissau	Colombia	Malaysia	
India	Dominican Republic	Mauritius	
Kenya	Ecuador	Mexico	
Kyrgyz Republic	Egypt, Arab Rep. of	Panama	
Lao PDR	El Salvador	Poland	
Madagascar	Georgia	Romania	
Malawi	Guatemala	Slovak Republic	
Mali	Guyana	South Africa	
Mauritania	Honduras	Trinidad	
Mongolia	Indonesia	Turkey	
Mozambique	Jamaica	Uruguay	
Nepal	Jordan	Venezuela, R. B. de	
Niger	Kazakhstan		
Nigeria	Morocco		
Pakistan	Nicaragua		
Rwanda	Paraguay		
São Tomé and Principe	Peru		
Senegal	Philippines		
Sierra Leone	Sri Lanka		
Sudan	Thailand		
Tajikistan	Tunisia		
Tanzania	Turkmenistan		
Togo	Ukraine		
Uganda			
Uzbekistan			
Vietnam			
Zambia			

Source: World Bank data.

Table 6A.2 Importing Countries and Economies

Algeria
Argentina
Australia
Austria

Bahrain
Bangladesh
Barbados
Belgium
Bolivia
Brazil
Burkina Faso
Burundi

Cameroon
Canada
Chile
China
Colombia
Costa Rica
Croatia
Cyprus
Czech Republic

Denmark
Dominica

Ecuador
Egypt, Arab Rep. of
El Salvador
Estonia

Finland
France

Gambia, The
Germany
Greece
Guatemala

Honduras
Hong Kong, China
Hungary

Iceland
India
Indonesia
Ireland
Israel
Italy

Japan
Jordan

Kazakhstan
Kenya
Korea, Rep. of
Kyrgyz Republic

Latvia
Lithuania
Luxembourg

Macao, China
Macedonia
Madagascar
Malawi
Malaysia
Maldives
Malta
Mauritius
Mexico
Moldova
Morocco

Netherlands
New Zealand
Nicaragua
Norway

Oman

Pakistan
Paraguay
Peru
Philippines
Poland
Portugal

Qatar

Romania

Saudi Arabia
Seychelles
Singapore
Slovak Republic
Slovenia
South Africa
Spain
St. Kitts and Nevis
St. Lucia
St. Vincent and the Grenadines
Sudan
Sweden
Switzerland

Taiwan, China
Tanzania
Thailand
Togo
Trinidad and Tobago
Tunisia
Turkey

Uganda
United Kingdom
United States
Uruguay

Venezuela, R. B. de

Zambia
Zimbabwe

Source: World Bank data.

ANNEX 6B: DECOMPOSITION OF EXPORT GROWTH OVER A DIFFERENT TIME PERIOD

To help assess the robustness of the results discussed above, we applied the decomposition of exports to a different period. We want to maintain the same developing-country exporters, but moving to an earlier growth period reduces the number of import-reporting countries. To maintain a large sample, we chose the period 1993–2002, for which there are 78 reporting importers.

Figure 6B.1 shows that the broad conclusions from the main analysis are replicated in this different growth period. The main driver of export growth for the developing countries in the sample was the increase in exports of existing products to existing markets. Growth at the intensive margin again dominates growth at the extensive margin. Within the latter, it is exports of existing products to new markets that is most important. Products that were not exported in 1993 but that were exported in 2002 did not contribute significantly to export growth.

Figure 6B.1 Decomposition of Export Growth of 99 Developing Countries: 1993–2002

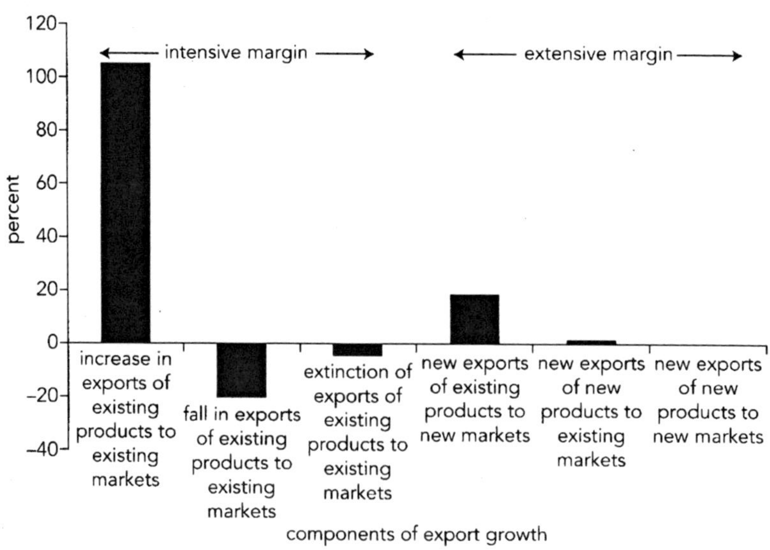

Source: Authors' calculations based on U.N. Comtrade.

NOTES

1. Small island economies, Middle East oil exporters, and a number of other countries, typically African countries in conflict, were excluded. There are 3,078 products, after removing gas, crude petroleum, and 34 specific steel products for which there is clearly a problem of data consistency over time. The data are import data reported for the Standard International Trade Classification (SITC) from partner countries in U.N. Comtrade (Commodity Trade Statistics Database). Data reported for the SITC are used rather than data reported for the Harmonized System, because the former has more countries for the 10-year period analyzed (102 versus 95) and because the latter has been subject to two revisions that may have introduced inconsistencies, despite efforts to establish a consistent time series. The numbers discussed here are essentially trade-weighted averages of the various components of export growth. The conclusions are not sensitive to the inclusion or exclusion of China (the country with the greatest weight in the sample).
2. This index is defined as the ratio of the actual number of bilateral trade flows to potential bilateral trade flows. Formally, for exporter j, for whom I_{ij} is the set of products (i) in which positive exports are observed, we define $Y_{ijk} = 1$ for $X_{ijk} > 0$, else $Y_{ijk} = 0$; and $Z_{ik} = 1$ for $M_{ik} > 0$, else $Z_{ik} = 0$, where X_{ijk} is the value of exports of product i from exporter j to importer k, and M_{ik} is the value of imports of product i by importer k. Then our index of export market penetration is given by $IEMP_j = \sum_{i \in I_{ij}} \sum_k Y_{ijk} \Big/ \sum_{i \in I_{ij}} \sum_k Z_{ik}$.
3. Note that the relationship between export market penetration and relative income is robust to different thresholds of exports (we also run these regressions for an index of export market penetration for exports that exceed \$10,000 and also for exports in excess of \$1 million).
4. Again, conclusions remain with the different thresholds for exports, as discussed in the previous footnote.

REFERENCES

Bernard, A., J. Eaton, B. Jensen, and S. Kortum. 2003. "Plants and Productivity in International Trade." *American Economic Review* 93: 1268–90.

Besedes, Tibor, and Thomas Prusa. 2006. "Ins, Outs, and the Duration of Trade." *Canadian Journal of Economics* 39 (1): 266–95.

———. 2007. "The Role of Extensive and Intensive Margins and Export Growth." Working Paper 13628, National Bureau of Economic Research, Cambridge, MA.

Brenton, Paul, Martha Denisse Pierola, and Erik von Uexküll. 2009. "The Life and Death of Trade Flows: Understanding the Survival Rates of Developing-Country Exporters." In *Breaking Into New Markets: Emerging Lessons for Export Diversification*, ed. Richard Newfarmer, William Shaw, and Peter Walkenhorst, 127–44. Washington, DC: World Bank.

Evenett, Simon, and Anthony Venables. 2002. "Export Growth in Developing Countries: Market Entry and Bilateral Trade Flows." Working paper, University of St. Gallen, Berne.

Hausmann, Ricardo, and Dani Rodrik. 2003. "Economic Development as Self-Discovery." *Journal of Development Economics* 72: 603–33.

Klinger, Bailey, and Daniel Lederman. 2004. "Discovery and Development: An Empirical Exploration of 'New' Products." Policy Research Working Paper 3450, World Bank, Washington, DC.

Melitz, Marc. 2003. "The Impact of Trade on Intra-Industry Reallocations and Aggregate Industry Productivity." *Econometrica* 71: 1695–725.

World Bank. 2002. *Global Economic Prospects*. Washington, DC: World Bank.

Zahler, A. 2007. "Decomposing World Export Growth and the Relevance of New Destinations." Working paper, Center for International Development, Harvard University, Cambridge, MA.

Chapter 16

THE LIFE AND DEATH OF TRADE FLOWS: UNDERSTANDING THE SURVIVAL RATES OF DEVELOPING-COUNTRY EXPORTERS

Paul Brenton, Martha Denisse Pierola, and Erik von Uexküll

One of the distinguishing patterns in export diversification concerns the life and death of trade flows.[1] Countries with rapidly diversifying export portfolios seem to outperform countries that are diversifying more slowly—not in the number of new export flows that emerge, but rather in the survival rates of these new flows once they are introduced. Can low-income countries adopt policies that improve the chances of survival of new export flows and thereby boost exports?

To answer this question, this chapter first provides data on the frequency with which trade in specific partner country and product categories fails to occur (represented by zeroes in bilateral trade matrices). We then look to past writings for insights explaining the survival or death of new export flows. This work suggests that initially small flows tend to have a lower chance of survival than flows that are larger initially. To dig deeper, we build on an initial analysis of the duration of U.S. import flows by Besedes and Prusa (2006) and investigate the survival rates of detailed product flows from a broader sample of 44 exporting countries over the period 1985 to 2006. This is complemented with a small case study for Ecuador that utilizes firm-level data and investigates firm entry into exporting and subsequent survival. This review allows us to hone in on key factors that explain variations in the probability of survival of export flows and, in a final section, draw some policy implications.

THE FREQUENCY OF ZEROES IN BILATERAL TRADE MATRICES

Recent studies have noted the preponderance of zeros in bilateral trade flow statistics. For example, Baldwin and Harrigan (2007) find that of the potential export flows of the United States (defined by the matrix of the 8,880 goods with positive exports at the 10-digit level of the U.S. trade classification and the 100 largest import markets), 70 percent of the entries are zero. In other words, relatively few countries are importing the goods that the United States exports. The incidence of these zeros is found to be positively correlated with distance and negatively related to the size of the import market. Brenton and Newfarmer (2007) construct an index of export market penetration that captures the extent to which a country is selling its exports to the countries that import these products. The index takes a value of 100 if a country serves all of the markets that consume products of the type the country is exporting, and is lower to the extent that these consuming countries do not buy the exporting country's products. The 2004 median value of this index for 99 developing-country exporters is 3.6 percent (so 96.4 percent of potential bilateral export flows are zero). They also find that values of the index are positively correlated with GDP per capita: higher-income countries tend to exploit a larger number of the available trade flow opportunities.

The preponderance of bilateral trade zeroes in part reflects the frequency of exit. Besedes and Prusa (2006) find that a large proportion of U.S. bilateral import flows at a detailed product level are short-lived, with a median duration of between two and four years. Alvarez (2002) finds that of the more than 1,900 firms reporting export activity in a survey of Chilean manufacturing firms over 1990–96, only 20 percent reported exporting in every year of the sample.

TRADE THEORY, ZEROES IN BILATERAL TRADE MATRICES, AND ENTRY AND EXIT IN TRADE MARKETS

The large number of bilateral trade flows that are equal to zero focuses attention on the conditions that encourage the initiation of trade flows (entry into the market) and the disappearance of flows (exit). Recent trade theory has devoted considerable analysis to the determinants of entry, but less has been written on exit. One important insight: it is difficult to reconcile the frequency of zeroes in bilateral trade matrices with traditional explanations of international trade.[2] Models of international trade that incorporate the costs involved in entering and sustaining exporting, including those related to obtaining information, have had more success in elaborating the conditions that govern the sustainability of export flows.

Exporting Firms' Lack of Information on Costs

Uncertainty about the fixed costs of exporting may result in firms with relatively low productivity entering a market, only later to discover that they are unable to survive. Indeed, firms may deliberately enter export markets to discover the exact nature of these costs and withdraw if they are unexpectedly high. In this case initial entry is likely to take place on a small scale and exit is likely to be prevalent. Short-term entry may reflect the search processes that are necessary to match suppliers and buyers in the overseas market. "Sometimes their product isn't right for the market, or the country they chose was not a good fit, or their approach or agents are not right," one export consultant said (Rauch 1996). By contrast, when information on the costs of exporting is available or can be obtained at little cost, then entry is likely to be on a larger scale, and exit after a short period should be less prevalent. Such information is likely to be easier to obtain the greater the presence of exporters of other products to the particular overseas market and the greater the overall experience in exporting the specific product.

Buyers Lack of Information on Exporters

Rauch and Watson (2003) emphasize that buyers in developed-country markets incur search costs in finding developing-country suppliers and may be uncertain about the supplier's ability to deliver large orders to the buyer's specifications. The buyer may obtain information about the capacity of the supplier by starting with small orders that generate no profits but that reveal whether the establishment of a longer-term relationship, which may require costly investments in training the supplier, is likely to succeed. The model suggests that the higher the search cost and the lower the probability that the supplier will be able to meet the buyer's requirements, the more likely buyers in importing countries are to start a relationship with an exporter with small orders. The model also predicts that export flows that begin with large orders will tend to have longer duration. That is because buyers tend to initiate large orders with suppliers that have lower production costs and are less likely to look for an alternative supplier.

The Implications of Contract Enforcement

Araujo and Ornelas (2007) focus on the importance of credibility in an environment of weak contract enforcement. Potential exporters look for partnerships with distributors in overseas markets, but where the institutional environment is weak, some distributors with little concern for the future will behave opportunistically and default. Distributors can improve their access to exporters by establishing a reputation for reliability, and export flows will increase over time (and exporters' costs decline) as exporters become better aware of the trustworthiness of the distributor. The probability of exit from exporting declines the longer the partnership with a distributor continues. Improvement in the institutions for contract enforcement has a direct and positive effect on exports by reducing uncertainty and improving the expected return of the exporter.

Search Costs and Policy Consistency

Edwards (2007) shows that search costs tend to bias exporters to continue existing relationships. In addition, firms with established relationships are likely to be less sensitive to changes in the relative prices of different suppliers than are firms and distributors that are still looking for a satisfactory partner. This finding suggests that inappropriate trade policies, even if reversed, can have long-run adverse impacts. For example, preferential import liberalization may lock in trade diversion (resulting from information costs) even after a subsequent multilateral reduction of tariffs has removed tariff preferences.

Product Quality

Imperfect information and contract enforcement are likely to be of greater significance for buyers searching among suppliers providing products of different quality.[3] In other words, the matching of exporters and buyers tends to be easier for standard and homogeneous products. Much of the discussion concerning export diversification in developing countries centers on how to increase exports of differentiated products, especially manufactures, and reduce the importance of homogeneous products, particularly commodities. Rauch (1999) presents tentative evidence that search costs are higher; matching is more difficult; and proximity, common language, and colonial links are more important for differentiated products than for homogeneous products that are traded on organized international exchanges. Quality considerations underline the importance of institutions governing metrology, testing, and conformity assessment, where weak facilities in developing countries increase uncertainty and may entail additional costs in sending products to more-developed countries for assessments of quality and conformity with private or public standards.

EMPIRICAL SUPPORT FOR THEORIES EXPLAINING THE PREVALENCE OF ZEROES IN BILATERAL TRADE MATRICES

To investigate conditions governing the sustainability of trade flows, we adopt a simple model that builds on the theoretical insights discussed above. This model assumes that firms differ in productivity; that entry costs to exporting are fixed and are related to the costs of obtaining information; and that differences in quality among similar export products mean that only firms that can produce goods of sufficiently high quality are able to export to distant markets. This model has two important implications. First, bilateral trade zeroes will be more frequent the larger the distance between markets; because trade costs rise with distance, firms with lower productivity will not find it profitable to serve more distance markets. Second, bilateral trade zeroes will be less frequent the larger the importing country: as the size of the foreign market increases, the ability of lower-productivity firms to incur the fixed costs of exporting will improve. To investigate whether export survival is more difficult for exporters from developing countries than for those from high-income countries, we test these hypotheses using cross-country bilateral trade data at a detailed product level. We complement this with an analysis of entry and exit into exporting at the firm level using a survey of Ecuadoran manufacturers.

Data Sets Employed

We track the sustainability of export flows by observing the evolution of bilateral trade flows at a detailed product level over time: a positive trade flow followed by a zero entry indicates exit from exporting. Two data sets are used. The first involves reports by importing countries (import data are generally viewed as more reliable than export data, particularly when measuring developing countries' exports) at a detailed commodity classification that is consistent over time, so that changes in trade flows cannot be attributed to changes in classification. Taking into consideration the maximum number of importers available, at the most detailed commodity level, with consistent data for a 21-year period, our data set involves 44 exporters to 56 importers for 1,271 product categories at the Standard International Trade Classification 5-digit level.[4] We exclude very small values and treat an export occurrence in excess of $1,000 as a flow, but we do test the sensitivity of our conclusions to flow size.[5] The analysis is expressed in terms of the *hazard rate*, or the probability that a positive export flow in one period is followed by zero exports in the next (the hazard rate is defined in annex 7C).

We also investigate an alternative source of information at the firm level. The data set used for this analysis is from the continuous manufacturers survey carried out by the National Institute of Statistics of Ecuador. The survey covers 2,771 firms from 1993 to 2003, of whom 805 were exporters at some point. The sectors included in the sample accurately represent the main manufacturing sectors in the Ecuadoran economy, including food and beverages, textiles, apparel, wood, rubber and plastic, paper, and automobiles.

Description of Survival Rates

Both data sets reveal that the probability that an export flow will disappear declines the longer the duration of the export flow. Figure 7.1 shows the estimated survival rates of export flows at 1, 5, 10, and 20 years for each exporting country, ordered by per capita income. For low-income countries, hazard rates are particularly high in the first years of the duration of a trade flow. For Malawi, just 35 percent of flows survive beyond a year. For Taiwan, China, and the Republic of Korea, around 60 percent of trade flows survive for more than a year. The survival rate at 10 years is around 30 percent for Taiwan, China, and Korea and around 15 percent for the low-income countries in Africa. Figure 7.2 confirms a positive correlation between export survival and per capita income in the exporting country. Export flows from low-income countries have a lower probability

Figure 7.1 Survival Rates of Export Flows, Selected Countries, 1985–2005

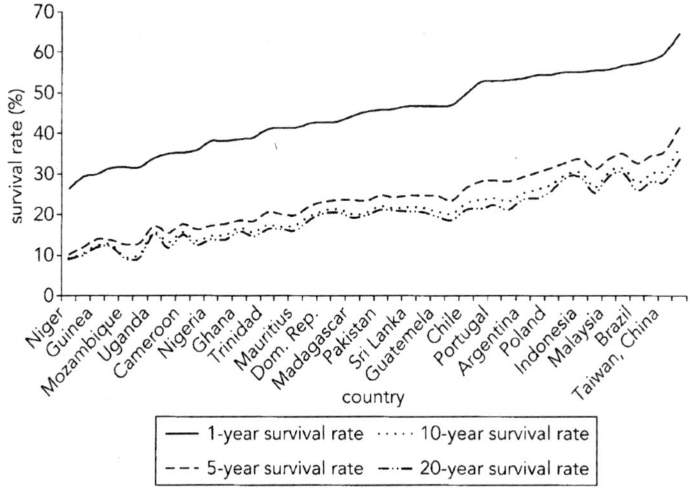

Source: Authors' calculations.

Figure 7.2 Ten-Year Survival Rates of Export Flows, 2004

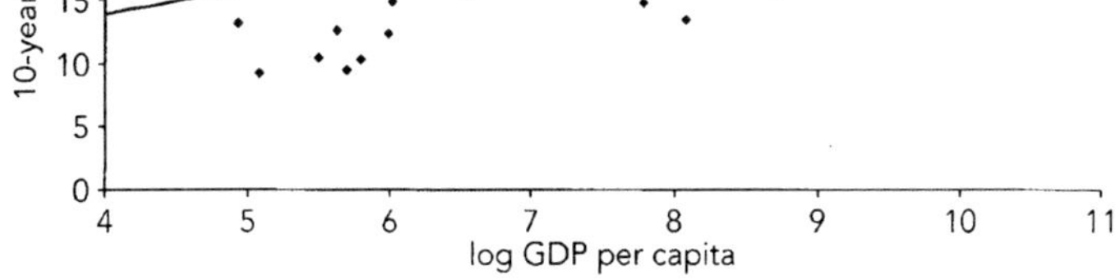

Source: Authors' calculations, based on World Development Indicators database.

of survival than flows from higher-income countries. Limiting the sample to trade flows above $50,000 (to reduce the likelihood of misclassification and to exclude observations attributable solely to the reexport of imported goods[6]) tells the same story: hazard rates are lower the longer the duration of the export flow, and survival rates and country income are positively correlated.

The data from Ecuador's manufacturing survey confirm the prevalence of export spells of short duration (figure 7.3). Of the 1,014 episodes of exporting during the sample period, 27 percent survived for just one year. Less than half of the episodes of exporting lasted more than four years. Firms that export for longer periods have a much lower hazard rate than firms with less export experience.

Investigation of Factors Affecting Export Survival

We now proceed to investigate factors that may explain differences in hazard rates. In particular, we explore why export flows in low-income countries have substantially higher hazard rates than those for higher-income countries.

Figure 7.3 Survival Rates for Ecuadoran Exporters

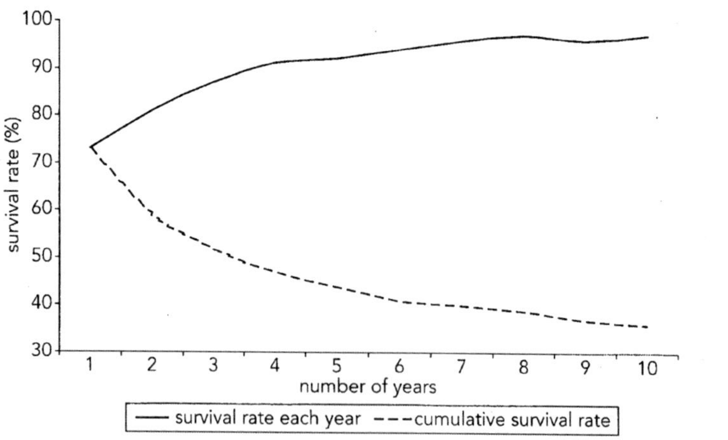

Source: Authors' calculations.

The independent variables that influence hazard ratios are

- the initial value of exports;
- distance as an indicator of trade costs;
- country variables that influence the cost of searching (proximity, common language, colonial ties);
- the total value of exports of the product, to capture experience with exporting a product;
- the size of the overall bilateral export flow, to capture knowledge of the particular import market; and
- the size of total imports of a product (there are likely to be a larger number of buyers in bigger markets, increasing the chance of the exporter supplier finding a suitable match).

We also include a number of policy variables, such as

- a measure of the variability of the bilateral exchange rate around the time that the flow is initiated;
- a measure of the deviation of the bilateral exchange rate in the year of entry from the period average, as a crude proxy for exchange rate misalignment; and
- measures of tariffs and trade preferences (the average tariff at the five-digit level over the available observations, a measure of the change in tariffs before and after 2000, and the presence of a preferential agreement between the two countries).[7]

Finally, we experiment with dummy variables for trade between poor countries and other countries in the sample to assess whether, after controlling for the variables above, exporters from low-income countries still face higher hazard rates.

The results reported in annex 6B show the impact of a one-unit change in an independent variable on the ratio of the estimated hazard function to base hazard function. The key issue is whether the value of the coefficient is significantly greater than 1 (meaning the variable increases the hazard) or less than 1 (meaning the variable reduces the hazard). For example, a coefficient of 1.1 would mean that a one-unit increase in the independent variable increases the hazard by 10 percent in any period t.[8] Care has to be taken when comparing the relative magnitudes of estimated coefficients because interpretation depends upon the definition of the variable.

The analysis of cross-country bilateral trade flows strongly supports the prediction that the larger the initial export flow the lower the hazard rate. The results also show that the hazard rate increases with distance. Similarly, the data from the Ecuadoran survey show a very strong positive impact of the size of the initial export on the firm's export survival rate. We also found a strong correlation between the size of the firm (in total sales) and the size of exports upon entry into exporting. This last finding suggests that relatively large firms are more likely to succeed in exporting than smaller firms.

Variables included to proxy information, search costs, and ease of matching all influence the hazard ratio significantly. Trading with a neighbor, common language, and colonial ties all reduce the hazard rate significantly. It is interesting that the size of overall exports of a product reduces the hazard, as does the size of the overall bilateral trade flow. Hence, increases in exports of existing products can help to reduce the hazard rate of exporters entering new markets. The size of the import market for a particular product is also a significant determinant of the hazard rate, but the size of the impact appears to be less important than the size of exports of the product and the magnitude of bilateral trade.

Without controlling for the other variables, the parameters on the dummy variables for rich to poor, poor to poor, and poor to rich country trade relationships are all significantly greater than one, suggesting that exports from poor countries and exports to poor countries face a higher hazard rate than exports between rich countries. However, once we control for initial size of exports, distance, and the proxies for information and search costs, the size of the parameters on these dummies declines substantially, indicating that most of the difference in hazard ratios between rich and poor countries can be explained by variables in the model.

The exchange rate terms, especially the term designed to capture variability, substantially increase the hazard rate. The tariff variables, although statistically significant, are very close to unity, while the preferential trade variable suggests that preferential access to an overseas market reduces the hazard faced by exporters.

These results appear to be robust to the, albeit crude, treatment of left censoring and when the sample is restricted to larger trade flows.[9] In this exercise, we include multiple episodes of exporting for the same product exporter-importer flow. To check the robustness of our results to the presence of these multiple spells, we also estimate the model including just one randomly selected episode of exporting for each product exporter-importer combination. This does not change the results in any substantive way.[10]

Treating these multiple spells more effectively is a challenge for our future work. Currently we treat all export episodes in the same way.

However, subsequent entries into exporting may not be independent of previous failed attempts. If information spills over, then firms may learn from the failures of others. We also need to allow for the possibility of cross-product and cross-market spillovers. An exporter of a particular product may learn from the export success or failure of other similar products. An exporter to a particular market may learn from experience in another similar or neighboring market.

CONCLUSIONS AND POLICY IMPLICATIONS

Successful export growth and diversification require not only entry into exporting but survival and subsequent growth. Our analysis confirms the conclusions of Besedes and Prusa (2006) that introducing new export flows appears to be less of a problem for developing countries than sustaining them over time. Survival rates are considerably lower for export flows of short duration, especially in the first five years of the life of a flow for developing countries. Our analysis suggests that the size of the initial export flow and measures relating to information and search costs, together with exchange rate volatility, are important factors explaining differences in hazard rates of export flows.

The importance of the initial size of exports is consistent with work by Brenton and von Uexküll (2007), who find that technical assistance targeted at specific export products tends to be more effective, in terms of the subsequent growth of exports, for larger export flows. The high hazard rate for initially small flows suggests caution in public policy interventions that are aimed specifically at exporters that start small. Reasoning along similar lines to Rauch (2007), we find that broad institutional changes favoring small firms relative to large firms in an economy are likely to have a relatively small impact on trade relative to reforms that favor entry of large firms.

The high hazard rate for initially small export flows also indicates that governments, through their export promotion agencies and trade consulates around the world, should pay particular attention to supporting new exports from their countries in new markets. Active engagement with exporters may well identify policy obstacles that, if removed, would increase the survival rate of exports.

Our analysis also suggests that the size of total exports of a product and the overall level of trade between two countries are important to the survival of new entrants in a market. Hence, the expansion of exports of existing products is important in allowing for future export growth and diversification.

Finally, policy measures that create a bias for or against exports of existing key products may affect the fate of prospective exports. On the negative side, for example, an export tax on a raw material or intermediate export, designed to support exports of the finished product, may actually act to constrain export diversification by limiting the flow of information from overseas markets and the experience of exporting. Similarly, taxing existing exports to fund an export promotion agency may not be appropriate.

On the positive side, experiences in several successful countries underscore the importance of maintaining a competitive real exchange rate, especially for several initial years after an export push has begun. Beginning with a depreciated exchange rate and holding the real value of the currency in check for several years has been a hallmark for nearly all countries that have managed to increase their export growth rate significantly over a sustained period. This approach allows time for products to penetrate several geographic markets, for exporters to develop transportation and other economies of scale, and for entrepreneurs to learn about new markets.

ANNEX 7A: EXPORTER AND IMPORTER COVERAGE

Table 7A.1 Importers Covered

Argentina	Greece	Oman
Australia	Guatemala	Panama
Austria	Honduras	Paraguay
Barbados	Hong Kong, China	Peru
Belgium and Luxembourg	Iceland	Philippines
Belize	India	Portugal
Bolivia	Indonesia	Singapore
Brazil	Ireland	Spain
Canada	Israel	St. Lucia
Chile	Italy	Sweden
Colombia	Jamaica	Thailand
Costa Rica	Japan	Trinidad and Tobago
Cyprus	Jordan	Tunisia
Denmark	Korea, Rep. of	Turkey
Ecuador	Malaysia	United Kingdom
Egypt, Arab Rep. of	Mexico	United States
Finland	Morocco	Uruguay
France	Netherlands	Venezuela, R. B. de
Germany	New Zealand	

Table 7A.2 Exporters Covered

Argentina	Indonesia	Pakistan
Bangladesh	Ireland	Poland
Brazil	Jamaica	Portugal
Burkina Faso	Kenya	Singapore
Cameroon	Korea, Rep. of	Sri Lanka
Chile	Madagascar	Taiwan, China
Dominican Republic	Malawi	Tanzania
Ecuador	Malaysia	Thailand
Egypt, Arab Rep. of	Mali	Trinidad and Tobago
France	Mauritius	Tunisia
Ghana	Mexico	Turkey
Guatemala	Morocco	Uganda
Guinea	Mozambique	Uruguay
Honduras	Niger	Zambia
Hungary	Nigeria	

ANNEX 7B: TECHNICAL ANNEX

Dealing with Censored Data in Econometric Estimates

As is common in studies of survival, the available data are censored. First, we observe flows in the first year of our sample but do not know for how long they have been in existence. Second, we observe flows in the final year of our sample but do not know how long they will continue to exist. The problem of right-censoring is easily resolved by the Kaplan-Meier and Cox estimation procedures applied in this chapter that extract the valuable information contained in these observations while avoiding bias. For example, a right-censored observation that is three years old at the cutoff year of the sample still gives valuable information about survival in its first two years of existence but should not be counted as a failure event in year three. Left-censoring presents a more serious problem. The literature provides some suggestions for procedures to deal with left-censoring,[11] but most of them rely on either quite extensive assumption or supplementary data that are not available in our case. Thus, for this preliminary work, our approach is simply to examine two sets of results, one where we simply ignore left-censoring and one where we drop all left-censored observations as a robustness test. A second issue is that duration or time-to-event data are typically skewed and making assumptions about underlying distributions is difficult. Hence, applying standard parametric statistical methods is unlikely to be appropriate.

Defining Indicators of Export Survival

Based on Keifer (1988), the probability distribution of duration can be defined as $F(t) - \Pr(T < t)$.

This specifies the probability that a random variable T is less than a value t. The corresponding density function is $f(t) = dF(t)/dt$.

The survivor function is most commonly used in analyzing duration data: $S(t) = 1 - F(t)$.

This gives the probability that T will equal or exceed some value t. Another useful function is the hazard function, $\lambda(t) = f(t)/S(t)$, which shows the rate at which spells will be completed at time t, conditioned on their lasting until t.

Define h_j as the number of export flows that are observed to have completed spells of duration t_j, for $j = 1$, and K as the number of years in our sample, 21. Define n_j as the number of flows that are at risk at time t_j. The Kaplan-Meier estimator is the nonparametric maximum likelihood estimate of $S(t)$ and takes the form $\hat{S}(t_j) = \prod_{i=1}^{j} (n_i - h_i)/n_i$, which is essentially obtained by equating the estimated conditional probability of completing a spell at t_j with the observed relative frequency of completion at t_j. The corresponding estimator for the hazard function is $\hat{\lambda}(t) = h_j/n_j$.

Dependent Variable Used in Investigating the Determinants of Export Survival

Following many studies of duration data and the Besedes and Prusa (2006) study of U.S. imports, we implement a semiparametric approach to the hazard function in order to analyze the determinants of the longevity of trade relationships. We estimate a Cox proportional hazard model, which assumes that variables influencing longevity have a proportionate impact on the base hazard function, that is, a change in variable z would increase or reduce the hazard function by the same factor in any period. The mathematical form of the hazard function in the Cox (1972) model is $\lambda(t, z) = \lambda_0(t)e^{\beta z}$, where $\lambda(t, z)$ is the hazard function, $\lambda_0(t)$ is the base hazard function, $\mathbf{z}$ is a vector of variables that have a proportional impact on the hazard function, and β is a vector of coefficients to be estimated that characterizes how $\mathbf{z}$ impacts the hazard function.

ANNEX 7C: RESULTS OF HAZARD RATE ESTIMATIONS

Table 7C.1 Semiparametric Results for Full Sample

	Hazard ratio					
Variable	**1**	**2**	**3**	**4**	**5**	**6**
VAL	0.828	0.860		0.860	0.859	0.867
	(0)*	(0)*		(0)*	(0)*	(0)*
DIST	1.088	1.107		1.108	1.101	1.115
	(0)*	(0)*		(0)*	(0)*	(0)*
BORDER	0.826	0.806		0.801	0.786	0.824
	(0)*	(0)*		(0)*	(0)*	(0)*
COMLANG	1.079	0.939		0.936	0.939	0.938
	(0)*	(0)*		(0)*	(0)*	(0)*
COLONY	0.895	0.948		0.953	0.951	0.843
	(0)*	(0)*		(0)*	(0)*	(0)*
EXP_PRODUCT		0.924		0.923	0.923	0.924
		(0)*		(0)*	(0)*	(0)*
IMP_PRODUCT		0.987		0.991	0.993	0.991
		(0)*		(0)*	(0)*	(0)*
TOTALTRADE		0.936		0.936	0.936	0.932
		(0)*		(0)*	(0)*	(0)*
PP			1.265	1.048	1.042	0.999
			(0)*	(0)*	(0)*	(0.779)
PR			1.226	0.971	0.969	0.947
			(0)*	(0)*	(0)*	(0)*
RP			1.111	1.048	1.046	1.034
			(0)*	(0)*	(0)*	(0)*
DE3					1.501	1.272
					(0)*	(0)*
REL_E					0.977	0.969
					(0)*	(0)*
PTA						0.925
						(0)*
AVTARIFF						1.001
						(0)*
DAVTARIFF						1.001
						(0)*
Number of observations	1,218,063	1,218,063	1,218,063	1,218,063	1,212,504	740,756

Source: Authors' calculations.

Note: VAL = initial export value; *DIST* = distance; *EXP_PRODUCT* = the value of all exports of the product by the exporter; *IMP_PRODUCT* = the value of all imports of the product by the importer; *TOTALTRADE* = the value of all exports between the export and the importer; *PP, PR,* and *RP* = dummy variables for exports from poor to poor countries, poor to rich, and rich to poor, respectively; *DE3* = a measure of the variability of the exchange rate; *REL_E* = a measure of deviation of exchange rate; *PTA* = membership in a free trade agreement; AVTARIFF and DAVTARIFF = measures of the average and the dispersion of tariffs. All specifications are stratified by product, left-censored observations included. Numbers in parentheses indicate the p-values; zero indicates a p-value of 0.0004 or less.

* Significant at the 1 percent level.

NOTES

1. A trade flow is the movement of a particular product to a specific market. The birth of a trade flow, one that was previously zero, entails a firm or firms entering that market for the product concerned. The death of a trade flow signifies that a firm or firms have exited from that market for the particular product. This chapter has benefited from discussions with Peter Walkenhorst.
2. Baldwin and Harrigan (2007) conclude that models of trade-based monopolistic competition are inconsistent with the presence of zeros and that those based on comparative advantage are not consistent with the observed tendency of zeros to decrease with the size of the import market. Models with heterogeneous firms (meaning that productivity differs among firms) and fixed entry costs to exporting (Melitz 2003) can be consistent with zero bilateral trade entries that decline with distance and size of the market. However, such models need to be amended to take into account product quality to explain another important observation—export prices increase with distance.
3. The importance of quality in influencing the pattern of bilateral trade flows has also been stressed by Schott (2004) and Hallak (2006).
4. The exporters and importers are listed in annex 7A. The need for consistent import data over 21 years means that most African countries and transition economies are absent from the importer group.
5. The econometric tests are complicated because we do not know how long flows in the first year of our sample have been in existence, nor for how long flows in the last year are sustained. These issues are briefly discussed in annex 7B.
6. For example, Brenton and Hoppe (2005) find that mirror statistics suggest the apparent export of a number of manufactured products from Sierra Leone, including electrical machinery, vehicles, and clothing. The export of passenger vehicles to Greece, to take one example, is simply not credible. Conversations with government officials, private organizations, and individual business persons confirmed that there was currently no significant manufacturing export capacity in the country. Thus, these apparent exports are either misclassified by product or origin (they could have been incorrectly allocated to the Sierra Leone country code in the process of compiling the relevant statistics) or they could be reexports of formerly imported products (including materials brought in by the peacekeeping forces of the United Nations or the Economic Community of West African States).
7. Caution is required with the tariff variables. We lose a large number of observations (almost 40 percent) from lack of data.
8. In some specifications, we stratify the sample, allowing for hazard functions to differ between the strata.
9. See annex 7B for further discussion.
10. These results are presented in detail in Brenton, Pierola, and von Uexküll (2007).
11. See, for example, D'Addio and Rosholm (2002).

REFERENCES

Alvarez, Roberto. 2002. "Determinants of Firm Export Performance in a Less Developed Country." Anderson Graduate School of Management, University of California, Los Angeles.

Araujo, Luis, and Emmanuel Ornelas. 2007. "Trust-Based Trade." CEP Discussion Paper 820, Centre for Economic Performance, London School of Economics, London.

Baldwin, Richard, and James Harrigan. 2007. "Zeros, Quality, and Space: Trade Theory and Trade Evidence." Working Paper 13214, National Bureau of Economic Research, Cambridge, MA.

Besedes, T., and T. Prusa. 2006. "Ins, Outs, and the Duration of Trade." *Canadian Journal of Economics* 104: 635–54.

Brenton, Paul, and Mombert Hoppe. 2005. "Trade Policy in Sierra Leone: Capacity, Strategy and Market Access." Paper prepared for the Sierra Leone Diagnostic Trade Integration Study, World Bank, Washington, DC.

Brenton, Paul, and Richard Newfarmer. 2007. "Watching More than the Discovery Channel: Export Cycles and Diversification in Development." Policy Research Working Paper 4302, World Bank, Washington, DC.

Brenton, Paul, Martha Denisse Pierola, and Erik von Uexküll. 2007. "The Life and Death of Trade Flows: Understanding the Survival Rates of Developing Country Exporters." World Bank Development Economics Group, Washington, DC.

Brenton, Paul, and Erik von Uexküll. 2007. "Product Specific Technical Assistance for Exports: Has It Been Effective?" World Bank, Washington, DC.

Cox, D. 1972. "Regression Models and Life-Tables." *Journal of the Royal Statistical Society* 34, no. 2: 187–220.

D'Addio, Anna Christina, and Michael Rosholm. 2002. "Left-Censoring in Duration Data: Theory and Application." Working Paper 2002-5, University of Arhus, Denmark.

Edwards, Huw. 2007. "Trade Search and Its Implications." Photocopy. Centre for the Study of Globalisation and Regionalisation, University of Warwick, Country, UK.

Hallak, Juan. 2006. "Product Quality and the Direction of Trade." *Journal of International Economics* 68: 238–65.

Keifer, Nicholas M. 1988. "Economic Duration Data and Hazard Functions." *Journal of Economic Literature* 26: 646–79.

Melitz, Marc. 2003. "The Impact of Trade on Intra-Industry Reallocations and Aggregate Industry Productivity." *Econometrica* 71: 1695–725.

Rauch, James. 1996. "Trade and Search: Social Capital, Sogo Shosha, and Spillovers." Working Paper 5618, National Bureau of Economic Research, Cambridge, MA.

———. 1999. "Networks versus Markets in International Trade." *Journal of International Economics* 48: 7–35.

———. 2007. "Development through Synergistic Reform." Working Paper 13170, National Bureau of Economic Research, Cambridge, MA.

Rauch, James E., and Joel Watson. 2003. "Starting Small in an Unfamiliar Environment." *International Journal of Industrial Organization* 21: 1021–42.

Schott, Peter. 2004. "Across-Product versus Within-Product Specialization in International Trade." *Quarterly Journal of Economics* 119: 647–78.

Chapter 17

What Explains the Low Survival Rate of Developing Country Export Flows?

Paul Brenton, Christian Saborowski, and Erik von Uexkull

Successful export growth and diversification require not only entry into new export products and markets but also the survival and growth of export flows. For a cross-country dataset of product-level bilateral export flows, exporting is found to be a perilous activity, especially in low-income countries. Unobserved individual heterogeneity in product-level export flow data prevails even when a wide range of observed country and product characteristics are controlled for. This questions previous studies that used the Cox proportional hazards model to analyze export survival. Following Meyer (1990), a Prentice-Gloeckler (1978) model is estimated, amended with a gamma mixture distribution summarizing unobserved individual heterogeneity. The empirical results confirm the significance of a range of product- as well as country-specific factors in determining the survival of new export flows. Important for policy-making is the finding of the value of learning-by-doing for export survival: experience with exporting the same product to other markets or different products to the same market is found to strongly increase the chance of export survival. A better understanding of such learning effects could substantially improve the effectiveness of export promotion strategies. Export survival, Cox proportional hazard, low-income countries. JEL codes: F10, F14, C41

In a seminal study, Besedes and Prusa (2006b) conclude that for developing countries the key element in achieving faster aggregate export growth is higher survival rates for existing trade flows. Brenton, Pierola, and von Uexkull (2009) show that poorly performing developing countries are not inferior to stronger performing countries in introducing new trade flows but that these countries

Paul Brenton (corresponding author, pbrenton@worldbank.org) is a lead economist at the World Bank. Christian Saborowski (csaborowski@worldbank.org) is a consultant at the World Bank. Erik von Uexkull (vonuexkull@ilo.org) was a junior professional associate at the World Bank when this article was written and is now an economic officer at the International Labour Organization. The authors would like to thank Joel Horowitz for useful comments and advice on different versions of this article. They are also grateful to Claudio Montenegro for excellent technical support and to Maria Lucia Guerra Bradford, Jan Loeprick, Richard Newfarmer, Denisse Pierola, Peter Walkenhorst, and seminar participants at the World Bank for improving the quality of this work. All remaining errors are solely the responsibility of the authors. The views expressed are those of the authors and should not be attributed to the organisations with which they are affiliated.

THE WORLD BANK ECONOMIC REVIEW, VOL. 24, NO. 3, pp. 474–499 doi:10.1093/wber/lhq015
Advance Access Publication December 14, 2010

experience much lower rates of survival. It is these low survival rates that undermine the expansion of export flows.

From a practical policy perspective, it is important to understand not only the factors driving entry into exporting but also the processes that sustain new exports and expand export volume. Are there factors that are amenable to public policy interventions that affect the survival of a particular exporter or export flow? Do these factors impinge particularly on firms in low-income countries?

This article extends the empirical analysis of export survival to provide a basis for answering these questions, building on Besedes and Prusa's (2006b) initial study of the determinants of export flow duration.[1] First, it investigates a novel, more detailed dataset of product-level trade flows comprising a large number of both developing and developed country imports and exports that includes low-income as well as middle- and high-income exporters. Second, it pursues a more rigorous empirical approach that examines the reliability of the continuous time proportional hazards model that has been used unquestioningly to assess the determinants of the survival rates of new export flows (Besedes and Prusa 2006b; Blyde 2008). This model is misspecified in the presence of unobserved heterogeneity, a strong possibility with export data—for example, from the unobserved quality of the management of the underlying exporting firms.

The findings of the empirical analysis provide strong evidence against the validity of the proportional hazards assumption in the Cox model. A possible explanation is the presence of unobserved individual heterogeneity that is not accounted for in the estimation. Given the nature of the trade flow data, which group survival rates into annual observations and have many tied failure rates, a Prentice-Gloeckler (1978) model is used to provide a discrete time equivalent of the Cox proportional hazards model. The model is augmented with a gamma mixture distribution to address unobserved individual heterogeneity (Meyer 1990). The analysis reveals that these methodological improvements are indeed important. The coefficients change strongly in switching from the Cox to the Prentice-Gloeckner model, and the estimated impact on the hazard rate of most variables rises. Augmenting the Prentice-Gloeckner model with a gamma mixture distribution further increases the impact of all variables. For most of the variables of interest, this change is economically significant.

In general, failure to account for unobserved heterogeneity, if it is indeed important, will overestimate the degree of negative duration dependence in the (true) baseline hazard and underestimate the degree of positive duration dependence. Moreover, the proportionate effect of a given regressor on the hazard rate is no longer constant and independent of survival time, and the proportionate response of the hazard to variation in each regressor at any survival time is attenuated. All of this is precisely what is observed in the data.

1. Blyde (2008) provides another application of the basic approach used by Besedes and Prusa (2006b).

The empirical results confirm that cultural and geographic ties between trading partners as well as market size and exporting experience are important to the survival of new export flows. Moreover, the results suggest that exporting experience is product and region specific, particularly for developing country exporters. In line with standard findings in the literature, variables designed to capture search costs as well as cultural and geographic ties between trading partners matter more for differentiated than for homogeneous products, based on the classification proposed in Rauch (1999). A range of alternative models and specifications test the robustness of all these results. Finally, the significance of unobserved heterogeneity in product-level export flows points to the importance of using firm- as well as product-level data to understand export survival.

The article is organized as follows. Section I presents the dataset and provides descriptive statistics on the global pattern of duration dependence in the data as well as differences in the determinants across product groups. Section II briefly reviews the theoretical and the empirical literature on export market entry and exit. Section III discusses the econometric specification of a hazard model that incorporates country- and product-specific factors that influence export survival, and presents the empirical results, including a battery of robustness checks. Section IV outlines the need for additional research.

I. Data and Patterns of Export Survival

The empirical results of this article are based on a novel dataset that is more comprehensive in a number of important dimensions than those used in previous studies of trade flow survival. It includes data on export flows at the five-digit level of the Standard International Trade Classification (SITC) from 82 exporting countries to 53 importers. This amounts to a total of 2,861,394 export lifetime spells.[2]

The level of product detail in this dataset is finer than that of previous studies. It considers 1,271 products (petroleum products are excluded), whereas Blyde's (2008) dataset had 625 products and Besedes and Prusa's (2007) had 380.[3] While it is interesting to see whether the conclusions of these previous studies hold for more detailed products, the more detailed product data are likely to better capture the dynamics of export entry and exit.

Coverage of exporters is also broader in this dataset than in previous studies, with the explicit intention of including countries with a wider range of income levels—in particular, including more Sub-Saharan African countries. Blyde (2008) has 47 high- and middle-income exporters and no low-income exporters, whereas Besedes and Prusa (2006b) investigate export survival

2. This study considers an export occurrence to be a flow greater than $1,000, but it also tests the sensitivity of the conclusions to flow size.

3. Besedes and Prusa (2006b) and Nitsch (2007) use very detailed data at or close to the tariff-line level but analyze only the duration of exports to a single market, the United States and Germany, respectively.

patterns in 46 countries, only 1 of them (Madagascar) is low income. The dataset compiled for this study covers 82 exporters including 22 low-income countries and 22 Sub-Saharan African countries.

It is widely accepted that import data are more reliable than export data, especially for developing countries. Therefore, the dataset is based on mirror statistics from importing countries. It spans the 20 years from 1985 to 2005, sufficient to undertake meaningful survival analysis. From the United Nations Commodity Trade Statistics Database (Comtrade), all importers were included that reliably report annual data at the desired level of disaggregation over the entire sample period. This means that the number of importers in this dataset set is lower than in previous studies.[4] This condition seeks to avoid the erroneous attribution of export entries and exits to a country that result from failing to report in a particular year.

Inevitably, some of the data are left or right censored. This is the case for about a quarter of the flows in the sample. Left censoring means that a flow is observed in the first year of the sample period but with no indication of when it came into existence. Right censoring implies that a flow is observed in the final year of the sample but with no indication of how long it will continue to exist. Right censoring is less of a problem since the duration estimation techniques use the information on the time of survival up to the censoring point but do not make any inference about what will happen to the export spell subsequently. Left censoring is a more serious problem because econometric techniques that deal efficiently with left-censored spells typically rely on strong additional assumptions or supplementary data, which are not available in this case.[5] While left-censored observations are included in the descriptive statistics so as to present a complete picture of export survival rates, they are excluded from the sample for the econometric analysis. Strictly speaking, therefore, the

4. The need for consistent import data over 21 years means that most African countries and transition economies are absent from the importer group. The UN Comtrade database reveals that the largest sample of importers could be obtained for data reported according to the Standard International Trade Classification (SITC) as opposed to the Harmonised System, which was introduced more recently. Working with the SITC allows for the longest possible time dimension. As the SITC has been twice revised during the sample period, the data were combined using backwards concordance to Revision 1. In general, backwards concordance leads to more consistent product-level data over time but at the price of less detail. There is an issue regarding a small number of product categories that are joined together in subsequent revisions. There are around 100 categories where backwards concordance appears to be problematic, as shown by the appearance of zeros in the aggregate of imports from all countries in the sample. Including these product categories may therefore introduce some bias into the analysis of survival. On the other hand, the fact that these product categories are aggregated over time suggests that they have become less important and indeed may not contain important information. An extreme example is the product code for steam engines.

5. See, for example, D'Addio and Rosholm (2002).

conclusions about the determinants of export survival refer only to new exports rather than to all export flows in the sample.[6] This strategy has been followed in much of the literature, although the distinction has not always been made clear.

Another analytical challenge concerns how to deal with one-year interruptions of export flows. Some researchers (Blyde 2008; Besedes and Prusa 2006b) have chosen to ignore interruptions of one year, since they may reflect simply reporting errors. This arbitrary strategy may create more problems than it solves. For the benefit of transparency, such gaps in the data are not ignored in analysis here, although the robustness of the results to their exclusion is examined.

Plotting the average death rate of export flows over the sampling period for each country against per capita GDP (natural log) shows clearly that death rates are high across the sample (figure 1). The death rate is defined as the number of trade flows that cease to exist in a given year divided by the total number of trade flows and thus reflects the unconditional probability that an export flow disappears in that year. On average, about 15 percent of all export relationships in a given year disappear before the beginning of the next year. There is a strong negative correlation between death rates and per capita GDP. Death rates are below 10 percent in developed countries but as high as 50 percent and more in developing countries (in Mozambique and Zimbabwe, for example).

To gain a better understanding of the pattern of duration dependence in the data, a nonparametric estimate of the survivor function is investigated. The data on the duration of export flows are expressed in annual observations, indicating only that an export flow was recorded during the year. For flows that cease in a particular year, all that is known is their duration expressed in annual increments. For flows that survive, the available information is that their duration exceeded the lower limit of the last observed duration. In effect, the data can be interpreted as grouped survival time data, and so the life table method is appropriate to estimate the survival function nonparametrically. This method is based on the same idea as the Kaplan-Meier (1958) product-limit estimator for continuous time data but adjusts the estimate of the survivor function for the possibility that export flows could have ended at any point during the time interval. This boils down to using an average estimate centered on the midpoint of the interval.

The survivor function $S(t)$ is defined as the cumulative probability of surviving up to some point in time t, and T denotes the time to a failure event for a particular trade flow. Defining d_j as the number of failures observed in interval i_j, N_j as the number of spells at risk of failure at the start of the interval and n_j

6. In this study, the sample period of 20 years entails that some proportion of these "new exports" have existed for many years. Indeed, even datasets with longer sample periods will still be concerned only with "new exports."

Figure 1. Relationship of Death Rate of Exports and per Capita GDP, 1985–2005

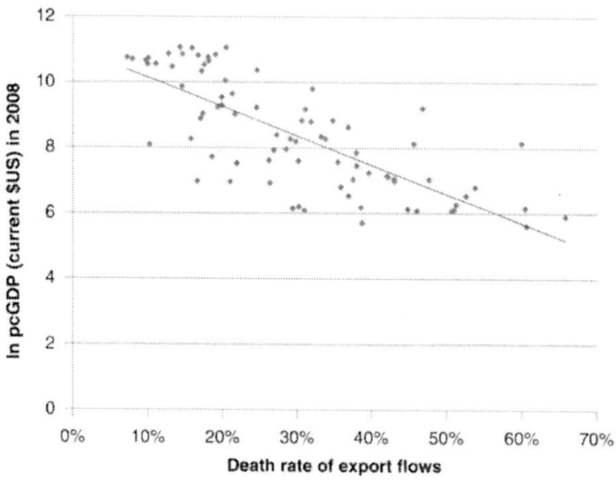

Source: World Bank various years and regression results based on data from UN Comtrade.

as the adjusted number of spells at risk of failure at the midpoint of the interval, one can write n_j as $n_j = N_j - \frac{d_j}{2}$ and the life table estimator of the survivor function as

$$\hat{S}(t_j) = \prod_{i=1}^{j}(1 - \frac{d_i}{n_i}) \tag{1}$$

A plot of the life table survival function for the entire sample shows clear evidence of negative duration dependence throughout the lifetime of the trade flows (figure 2). In other words, the probability that an export flow will disappear falls the longer the duration of the flow. During the first five years of the emergence of a given trade flow, hazard rates are particularly high. Only about a third of all export spells survive this initial period; a fifth survive the first 20 years. This finding is in line with previous results in Besedes and Prusa (2006a) and Blyde (2008), among others.

Examination of the estimated rates of survival across income groups immediately reveals the presence of negative duration dependence (table 1). The estimates suggest that export flows are more likely to survive longer in richer countries. This finding holds for the entire sample and for each one-digit SITC sector.[7] For high-income countries, 59 percent of trade flows

7. Similar patterns of survival rates within each sector suggest that the finding of lower survival rates for developing countries is not due simply to the types of products these countries tend to export.

FIGURE 2. Survival Rates of Export Flows, 1985–2005

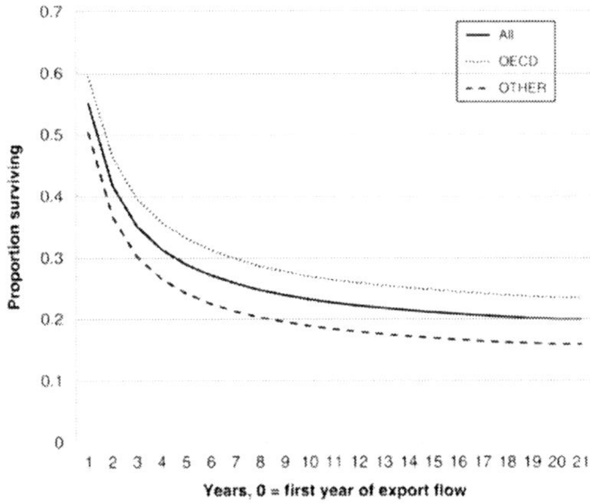

Source: Regression results based on data from UN Comtrade.

survive longer than one year. For low-income countries, only 39 percent do. After 20 years, 23 percent of export flows survive for high income countries, but only 8 percent do for low-income countries. Survival rates for middle income countries fall in between, but closer to the upper end of the interval between high- and low-income countries. This could suggest that the problem of export survival is more relevant for countries moving from low- to middle-income status than for those moving from middle- to high-income status. A similar finding is that the survivor function for Organisation for Economic Co-operation and Development (OECD) countries lies consistently above the survivor function for the remaining countries (see figure 2).

Results are similar for individual countries, with 70 percent of export flow spells surviving for more than one year for the United States but less than 30 percent for Burkina Faso. Within 10 years of initiation, some 41 percent of export flows survive for the United States, but only 17 percent for Argentina, 12 percent for Egypt, and 4 percent for Burkina Faso.

The evidence in this section is suggestive. Section III investigates more deeply the factors that might shorten or lengthen the life of an export flow and explain differences in survival rates. The focus is on why export flows in low-income countries have substantially lower survival rates than those for middle- and high-income countries. But before this econometric analysis of the trade flow data, a review of the literature on the determinants of the duration of export flows sets the context.

TABLE 1. Export Survival Rates by One-Digit Standard International Trade Classification and Country Income Group, 1985–2005 (percent)

	All goods			SITC 1			SITC 2			SITC 3			SITC 4		
Years	Low income	Middle income	High income	Low income	Middle income	High income	Low income	Middle income	High income	Low income	Middle income	High income	Low income	Middle income	High income
1	39	51	59	39	51	57	43	49	52	49	52	55	43	52	56
5	15	25	32	15	24	31	15	21	24	23	24	27	18	24	29
10	11	19	26	11	18	24	9	15	17	18	18	19	12	18	22
15	9	18	24	8	16	21	7	13	14	16	16	16	11	15	19
20	8	17	23	7	14	19	6	12	13	15	15	15	9	15	18
21	8	17	23	7	14	19	6	12	13	15	15	15	9	15	18
	SITC 5			SITC 6			SITC 7			SITC 8			SITC 9		
Years	Low income	Middle income	High income	Low income	Middle income	High income	Low income	Middle income	High income	Low income	Middle income	High income	Low income	Middle income	High income
1	36	52	59	39	51	58	34	50	62	40	52	60	46	52	58
5	13	26	33	16	25	31	10	24	38	17	27	35	20	26	32
10	9	20	26	12	19	25	7	20	33	13	22	29	14	21	25
15	7	18	24	10	17	22	6	18	31	12	20	27	11	18	23
20	6	17	23	9	16	21	5	18	30	11	19	26	10	17	22
21	6	17	23	9	16	21	5	18	30	11	19	26	10	17	22

Source: Authors' calculation based on data from UN Comtrade.

II. THE LITERATURE ON THE DETERMINANTS OF EXPORT SURVIVAL

International trade theory says little about the duration of trade flows. Recent developments in trade theory have focused on heterogeneous firms and entry into exporting and on how reductions in trade costs shift resources from lower productivity firms to higher productivity exporters. There has been little attention to why some firms cease exporting within a short time of starting to export. Similarly, the literature on export behavior, based extensively on firm surveys, has concentrated on differences between exporters and nonexporters and on whether the observed higher productivity of exporters is a cause or result of entry into foreign markets. Much less information is available on the evolution of exporters after they enter into trade activities, reflecting in part the lack of continuous surveys.

Besedes and Prusa (2006b) were the first to investigate the duration of U.S. import trade, showing that short survival times are consistent with a search model of international trade. In particular, the high number of short trade relationships appears to reflect uncertainty in the formation of trade relationships. Both higher reliability and lower search costs lead to larger initial purchases and longer relationships. This finding is confirmed in follow-up studies such as Blyde (2008) and is investigated in detail by Besedes (2008).

Market knowledge and other information needed for successful entry into exporting are likely to be important in explaining exit. With less than perfect information about the fixed costs of exporting a particular product to a particular market or some uncertainty about the value of these costs, lower productivity firms that are marginal entrants into exporting may not survive. Indeed, firms lacking full market information may use entry into export markets as cost-discovery mechanism for exporting to a particular market and withdraw if they find that incurring the fixed costs of exporting to that market is unprofitable. Initial entry is likely to be small scale and exit prevalent. Short-term entry may also reflect the search processes that are necessary to match suppliers and buyers in overseas markets.

When information on the costs of exporting is readily available or obtainable at little cost, larger scale entry is more likely and rapid exit should be less frequent. The greater the export activity in a particular overseas market—the more exporters of other products to that market and the greater the overall experience with exporting a particular product—the easier it should be to obtain such information. Several recent studies have sought to formalize the influence of imperfect information on the dynamics of export entry and exit.

Rauch and Watson (2003) look at the initiation of export flows from the perspective of developed country buyers that are uncertain about the long-term prospects of a potential partnership with developing country suppliers. The buyer is unsure whether the supplier will be able to deliver large orders to the buyer's specifications even if the buyer invests in training the supplier. The buyer may glean information about the capacity of the supplier before making such an investment by starting with small orders that generate no profits but that reveal whether the training is likely to be successful. In other words, the buyer has the choice of starting big or small. Finally, the buyer has the option of continuing a supplier relationship or abandoning it and searching for a new supplier. Once a successful relationship is in place, the buyer can access a network of other suppliers and can obtain information on new firms without incurring search costs.

The model suggests that buyers in importing countries are more likely to start a relationship with an exporter with small orders the higher the search cost and the lower the probability that the supplier will be able to meet the buyer's requirements. But the model also predicts that export flows that commence with large orders will last longer— because buyers tend to initiate large orders with suppliers with lower production costs and will be less likely to look for an alternative supplier.

Araujo and Ornelas (2007) characterize information costs relating to exporting in terms of weak contract enforcement. Potential exporters look for partnerships with buyers in overseas markets, but the weak institutional environment allows some buyers with little concern for the future to behave opportunistically and to default. In such a climate, forward-looking buyers seek to differentiate themselves from myopic buyers by building a reputation over time. Hence, information costs decline as exporting experience accumulates. Initially small export flows increase over time as the exporter learns more about the buyer's trustworthiness and probability of defaulting on the contract. Thus, the longer the partnership with the buyer continues, the lower the probability of exiting from exporting.

Improving the institutions for contract enforcement has a direct, positive effect on exports by reducing uncertainty and raising the expected return of the exporter. However, there is also an indirect negative impact on the size of exports since stronger contract enforcement reduces the value of future reputation compared with the situation under weaker enforcement. In other words, it becomes more difficult for a buyer that has built a reputation to differentiate itself from other buyers that are now less likely to default because of the threat of a more effective legal challenge. The latter effect will tend to be stronger in cases of initially weak enforcement. Stricter enforcement of contracts also increases the level of initial exports in a new partnership and supports relationships of longer duration.

In a recent study, Albornoz, Pardo, and Corcos (2010) suggest that firms discover their profitability as exporters only after engaging in exporting. Firms adjust quantities and decide whether to exit or to serve new destinations based on what they learn about themselves through exporting experience. Edwards (2007) discusses the impacts of trade liberalization in a situation of search costs and matching of producers and buyers in overseas markets. Once a search process has been under way for a long time, a proportion of firms and buyers will be matched and so will be less sensitive to new potential trade partners. This would explain the negative duration dependence found by Besedes and Prusa (2006b); once a flow has been established for a while, the probability of failure drops. Firms in established relationships are likely to be less sensitive to changes in the relative prices of different suppliers than are firms and distributors that are still looking for a satisfactory partner. This suggests time dependency and that inappropriate sequencing of trade policy reforms can have adverse long-run impacts. For example, preferential import liberalization may lock in trade diversion (due to information costs) even after subsequent multilateral tariff reductions have removed tariff preferences.

Information asymmetries and formal institutions for contract enforcement tend to be more important for buyers searching among suppliers providing products of different quality. Put differently, matching suppliers and buyers will tend to be easier for standard and homogeneous products. Much of the discussion on export diversification in developing countries centers on increasing exports of differentiated products, especially manufactures, and reducing the importance of homogeneous products, particularly commodities. Rauch (1999) presents evidence, albeit tentative, that search costs are higher and matching is more difficult for differentiated products and that proximity, common language, and colonial links are more important for differentiated products than for homogeneous products that are traded on organized international exchanges.

Quality introduces another set of institutions that might influence bilateral trade. Poor quality metrology, testing, and conformity assessment facilities in developing countries mean that exporters will incur additional costs for assessing quality and conformity with private or public standards when exporting products to more developed countries or that some uncertainty will surround issues of quality and standards. The buyer may have additional uncertainty about the ability of the exporter to consistently deliver the specified product quality. These concerns about information and quality are likely to be most important for trade between countries with different quality preferences and different stages of development of the institutions responsible for contact enforcement and quality.

The discussion above and the studies by Besedes and Prusa (2006b), Blyde (2008), and Brenton, Pierola, and von Uexkull (2009) suggest that the following variables likely influence the hazard rate of export flows:[8]

- The initial value of the trade relationship is a crude proxy for the level of confidence the trading partners originally had in the profitability of the trade relationship.
- The distance between the exporter and the importer captures two types of costs that a firm might encounter in a trade relationship: trade costs and

8. Precise definitions of these variables are provided in appendix 1. The reference year for all variables is the year in which the trade relationship starts or, in the case of left-censored observations, 1985, the beginning of the sampling period.

the initial cost of searching for an appropriate trading partner. These costs are likely to be lower for neighboring countries that share a common language or common border and countries with past colonial ties.

- For both trading partners, larger economic size and greater wealth should facilitate the survival of trade flows. Bigger markets are likely to have a larger number of buyers, thus increasing the likelihood that the exporter will find a suitable match. This effect is captured by the inclusion in the model of the trading partners' GDP (this effect is analyzed more closely through robustness tests).
- Exporting experience in general and at the product and industry level in particular is captured by the amount of total exports to the market and total exports of the product (to all markets). Other important determinants are the size of the import market and the exporter's knowledge of the market. To account for these factors, the total value of trade between the trading partners and the global value of the importer's imports of the product concerned are included. The larger these flows are, the greater the potential spillovers of information to new entrants.
- If market experience with a product is specific to the importing region, existing export relationships with countries that border the import market should facilitate survival in a new market. A test is conducted for whether exporting experience follows a geographic pattern. A dummy variable indicates whether the exporter is already exporting the product concerned to a neighboring country of the importing country.
- Trial and error patterns of learning to export to a market are captured by a dummy variable indicating whether there have been previous exporting spells of the product to the importer.
- Several policy variables are included: a measure of the variability of the bilateral exchange rate when the flow is initiated; a measure of the deviation of the bilateral exchange rate from the period average in the year of entry into the exporting relationship, as a crude proxy for exchange rate misalignment; and a dummy variable for the presence of a preferential trade agreement between the trading partners, as an indicator of trade policy restrictiveness. While it would be preferable to include the actual tariff rate in the import market for each product, this information is available only for a subset of countries and years. Including this information would come at the expense of a greatly reduced sample size.

III. Econometric Specification and Empirical Results

Previous studies of export survival, including those by Besedes and Prusa (2006a, b) and Blyde (2008), have used the continuous time proportional hazards model proposed by Cox (1972), which is widely used in survival analysis. This model is based on the assumption that variables influencing survival have a proportionate impact on the base hazard function; that is, a change in variable z would raise or lower the hazard function by the same factor in any period. The mathematical form of the hazard function for export flow i in the Cox model is

$$\lambda_i(t) = \lambda_0(t)\exp(Z_i(t)'\beta) \quad (2)$$

where $\lambda_0(t)$ is the baseline hazard at time t, $z_i(t)$ is the vector of covariates for flow i that have a proportional impact on the hazard function, and β is a vector of coefficients to be estimated that characterizes how z affects the hazard function.

The Cox model is widely used because it enables estimating the relationship between the hazard rate and a set of explanatory variables using a partial likelihood approach without having to assume anything about the shape of the baseline hazard function. This is why the model is often referred to as a semi-parametric model. However, this convenience relies heavily on the assumption that the baseline hazard function summarizing the pattern of duration dependence can be separated from the individual specific non-negative function of covariates. Hence, the function of covariates scales the baseline survivor function with a constant factor independent of survival time. If the data are not consistent with this assumption, the model is misspecified. Possible reasons for the failure of this assumption could be the omission of relevant time-dependent variables or the presence of unobserved individual heterogeneity. Previous studies of export flow survival at the product level have not tested the proportional hazards assumption and have not investigated unobserved individual heterogeneity.

The first step is to estimate a simple Cox model. The sample is stratified by the 1,271 product categories. Hence, the estimation does not insist that the baseline hazard be proportional across products but allows a separate baseline hazard function for each product group. The number of observations in the dataset makes it possible to use such fine stratification without incurring a problematic drop in degrees of freedom.

The Cox estimation results are presented in the first set of columns in table 2 for the preferred specification. The coefficient estimates are not discussed at this point as the purpose of this estimation is to test for the validity of the model specification—the validity of the proportional hazards assumption. A comprehensive discussion of applicable testing procedures for the Cox model can be found in Horowitz and Neumann (1992). An interesting first descriptive check is a plot of the log of nonparametric estimates of the hazard function against time for different subgroups of trade flows in the sample. If the proportional hazards assumption is appropriate, the plots should move in parallel. Although not reported here, different subgroups of the sample were analyzed, and the evidence from these plots does not support the proportional hazards assumption.

TABLE 2. Estimation Results, 1985–2005

Variable	1. Cox (1972) proportional hazards model			2. Prentice-Gloeckner model without unobserved heterogeneity[a]			3. Prentice–Gloeckner model with unobserved heterogeneity, gamma distribution[a]			4. Prentice-Gloeckner model with unobserved heterogeneity, gamma distribution[a]			5. Multiple spells excluded			6. Small trade flows excluded (< $55,000)		
	Exp(b)	*p*-value	25th-> 75th percentile[b] (%)	Exp(b)	*p*-value	25th-> 75th percentile[b] (%)	Exp(b)	*p*-value	25th-> 75th percentile[b] (%)	Exp(b)	*p*-value	25th-> 75th percentile[b] (%)	Exp(b)	*p*-value	25th-> 75th percentile[b] (%)	Exp(b)	*p*-value	25th-> 75th percentile[b] (%)
Initial value	0.908	0.000	-22.5	0.966	0.000	-8.3	0.968	0.000	-7.7	0.967	0.000	-8.0	0.987	0.000	-3.1	1.155	0.000	37.9
Distance	1.074	0.000	10.2	1.191	0.000	26.3	1.254	0.000	35.0	1.224	0.000	30.8	1.310	0.000	42.7	1.280	0.000	38.5
Border	0.831	0.000	-16.9	0.670	0.000	-33.0	0.595	0.000	-40.5	0.627	0.000	-37.3	0.544	0.000	-45.6	0.556	0.000	-44.4
Common language	0.895	0.000	-10.5	0.739	0.000	-26.1	0.672	0.000	-32.8	0.701	0.000	-29.9	0.637	0.000	-36.3	0.679	0.000	-32.1
Colony	0.988	0.001	-1.2	0.976	0.000	-2.4	0.976	0.000	-2.4	0.977	0.000	-2.3	0.975	0.040	-2.5	1.073	0.000	7.3
GDP product	0.979	0.000	-5.6	0.946	0.000	-14.3	0.928	0.000	-19.1	0.936	0.000	-16.9	0.909	0.000	-24.2	0.929	0.000	-18.7
Total exports	0.989	0.000	0.0	0.974	0.000	0.0	0.968	0.000	0.0	0.971	0.000	-14.7	0.964	0.000	-17.8	0.965	0.000	-17.4
Industry exports	0.997	0.000	-1.4	0.981	0.000	-7.4	0.965	0.000	-14.0	0.972	0.000	-11.3	0.956	0.000	-17.8	0.952	0.000	-19.4
Product exports	0.942	0.000	-22.8	0.863	0.000	-54.3	0.835	0.000	-65.3	0.848	0.000	-60.1	0.816	0.000	-72.9	0.811	0.000	-75.0
Product imports	0.984	0.000	-5.7	0.929	0.000	-26.0	0.905	0.000	-34.9	0.915	0.000	-31.1	0.886	0.000	-41.6	0.907	0.000	-34.0
Bilateral trade	0.965	0.000	-10.6	0.958	0.000	-12.7	0.946	0.000	-16.4	0.951	0.000	-14.7	0.947	0.000	-16.2	0.936	0.000	-19.3
Neighbor	0.881	0.000	-11.9	0.729	0.000	-27.1	0.682	0.000	-31.8	0.703	0.000	-29.7	0.600	0.000	-40.0	0.628	0.000	-37.2
Previous spell	0.842	0.000	-15.8	0.351	0.000	-64.9	0.274	0.000	-72.6	0.305	0.000	-69.5				0.315	0.000	-68.5
FX volatility	1.007	0.000	0.5	0.992	0.000	-0.6	0.990	0.000	-0.8	0.990	0.000	-0.8	0.997	0.169	-0.3	0.991	0.006	-0.7
FX misalignment	1.000	0.160	0.0	0.996	0.000	-0.4	0.997	0.000	-0.3	0.997	0.000	-0.3	0.998	0.003	-0.2	0.992	0.000	-0.8
PTA	0.999	0.599	-0.1	0.961	0.000	-3.9	0.955	0.000	-4.5	0.957	0.000	-4.3	0.912	0.000	-8.8	0.959	0.000	-4.1
logtime				0.893	0.000		1.186	0.000										
No. of observations	2,861,394			2,861,394[c]			2,861,394[c]			2,861,394[c]		2,702,156			1,762,595			
LogL				-2,133,032			-2,121,082			-2,123,406		-968,098			-400,017			
gamma variance																		
Exp(b)							0.471			0.291		1.364			0.795			
p-value (Exp (b))							0.000			0.000		0.000			0.000			
LR test																		
chi^2							23899			25197		116,813			11,205			
p-value (chi^2)							0.000			0.000		0.000			0.000			

Note: See appendix 1 for variable sources and definitions.

a. The Prentice-Gloeckner regressions include a set of biannual calendar time dummy variables (not reported).

b. Percentage change in the hazard ratio if the value of the exogenous variables increases from the 25th percentile to the 75th percentile of all observations in the dataset. In the case of dummy variables, the impact of a change from 0 to 1 is reported.

c. For the Prentice-Gloeckner estimation, the dataset is modified from one observation per export spell to one observation per year with export spell, which increases the number of observations to 7,234,950.

Source: Regression results based on data from UN Comtrade.

Kay (1977) suggests another testing procedure. He derives residuals for the Cox model and tests the proportional hazards assumption by plotting these so-called Cox-Snell (1968) residuals against the Nelson-Aalen cumulative hazard function (Nelson 1972; Aalen 1978). For the proportional hazards assumption to be valid, the plot should deviate little from the 45 degree line. This condition is clearly violated in the data (figure 3). This result holds independently of whether the sample is stratified. Different combinations of covariates, including interaction terms and time-dependent variables, were used to capture as much information as possible, and all led to the same conclusion.

A formal statistical testing procedure of the proportional hazards assumption in the Cox model is based on residuals derived by Schoenfeld (1982) that do not vary over time if the model specification is correct. Table 3 presents the results of testing for a zero slope of the plot of the Schoenfeld residuals against survival time both globally and for each covariate. The test statistics and the associated *p*-values reveal that the null hypothesis of a constant slope is rejected with confidence for the model as a whole and for all but two covariates individually.

These results constitute strong evidence for the failure of the proportional hazards assumption in the data. In the above testing procedures, both time-dependent covariates and interaction terms appeared to be neither the reason for this problem nor its solution. Another possible cause of the failure of the proportional hazards assumption is the presence of unobserved individual heterogeneity—which could arise, for example, from omitted firm-specific variables, such as managerial capacity—that captures the risk of failure in addition to that captured by the observed covariates.

In general, failure to account for unobserved heterogeneity will, if it is indeed important, lead to overestimating the degree of negative duration

FIGURE 3. Kay (1977) Test of Proportional Hazards Assumption, 1985–2005

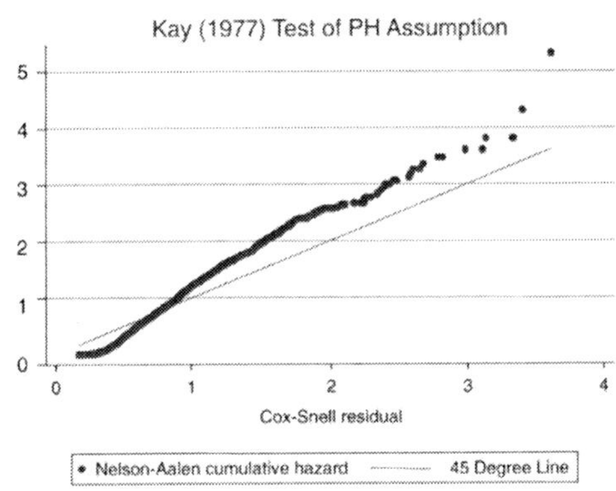

Source: Regression results based on data from UN Comtrade.

TABLE 3. Schoenfeld (1982) Test of Proportional Hazard Assumption, 1985–2005

Variable	Chi^2	*p*-value
Initial value	513.75	0.000
Distance	691.09	0.000
Border	248.71	0.000
Common language	149.33	0.000
Colony	1.41	0.200
GDP product	4,451.92	0.000
Total exports	4,634.23	0.000
Industry exports	167.37	0.000
Product exports	628.62	0.000
Product imports	240.02	0.000
Bilateral trade	266.56	0.000
Neighbor	124.87	0.000
Previous spell	436.64	0.000
FX volatility	0.000	0.900
FX misalignment	865.75	0.000
PTA	11.54	0.000
Global	14,551.38	0.000

Source: Regression results based on data from UN Comtrade.

dependence in the (true) baseline hazard and underestimating the degree of positive duration dependence. In other words, the coefficient on the functional representation of analytical time will be biased downward for export flow data that are subject to negative duration dependence in the hazard. Moreover, in the presence of unobserved and unaccounted for individual heterogeneity, the proportionate effect of a given regressor on the hazard rate is no longer constant and independent of survival time, and the proportionate response of the hazard to variation in each regressor at any survival time is attenuated.

The next step is to estimate a model that addresses unobserved heterogeneity. A discrete time model is more appropriate for trade flow data than the continuous time model applied by Besedes and Prusa (2006b) and followed by others such as Blyde (2008). As discussed above, the data are organized in annual observations. There are also many tied failure times. Such data are properly accommodated in the framework of discrete duration models (see Lancaster 1990). For this reason, an appropriate starting point for the estimations is the Prentice-Gloeckler (1978) model,[9] which is a discrete time equivalent of the continuous time proportional hazards model. If unobserved heterogeneity is assumed to take a multiplicative form, the hazard function can

9. The Prentice-Gloeckler model is an interesting complement to the Cox model, as both estimators make no assumption about the shape of the baseline hazard. For suitably re-organized data in export flow–period format, the Prentice-Gloeckler log-likelihood function is the same as the log-likelihood function for a generalized linear model of the binomial family with a complementary log-log link (Jenkins 1995).

be expressed as

$$\lambda_i(t) = \theta_i \lambda_0(t) \exp(Z_i(t)'\beta) \tag{3}$$

where θ_i is an unobserved random variable that is assumed to be independent of $z_i(t)$, the vector of covariates for flow i. Maximum likelihood estimates of the parameter vector and baseline hazard can be obtained by conditioning the likelihood function on θ_i and then integrating over the distribution of θ. This approach requires specifying a distribution function for θ. Following Meyer (1990), a common approach is to use the gamma distribution with mean 1 and variance σ^2, which gives a closed form expression for the likelihood function.

Table 2 also presents the results from estimating the preferred specification using both the Prentice-Gloeckler model and the Prentice-Gloeckler model incorporating a gamma mixture distribution summarizing individual heterogeneity.[10] The log of time was introduced as an additional variable into one specification to directly capture the pattern of duration dependence (second and third set of columns in table 2), although the benchmark specification (discussed below) does not contain this variable. As can be observed, the results are not very sensitive to the exclusion or inclusion of this additional variable. Finally, biannual calendar time dummy variables are also included in all regressions with the Prentice-Gloeckner model to account for the possibility that the survival of export flows is sensitive not only to analytical time but also, for instance, to cyclical downturns in global demand.

A first glance at the results reveals two key findings. First, the p-values for all variables are virtually zero and the likelihood ratio test strongly rejects the null hypothesis of the absence of unobserved individual heterogeneity in the data. This result is confirmed when a normal distribution is used instead of the gamma mixture distribution to summarize unobserved heterogeneity (not reported). Second, the proportional response of the hazard to changes in almost all of the regressors is underestimated in the basic Prentice-Gloeckler model. Furthermore, the degree of negative duration dependence in the hazard is overestimated when unobserved individual heterogeneity is not taken into account. In fact, the models indicate that the strongly negative duration dependence found in the survivor functions in the previous section is well explained by the regressors once unobserved heterogeneity is taken into account. The coefficient on the log of time suggests a slightly upward sloping baseline hazard.

The heterogeneity terms are significant when examining different product or income groups and when excluding very small trade flows or trade flows with previous spells in the sample (last two sets of columns in table 2). Learning more about the source of the heterogeneity is thus an important avenue for future research. It is likely that it can be found in the failure to account for

10. Throughout this article, the estimated coefficients are presented in exponential form.

firm-specific characteristics in product-level data. It is interesting that recent application of a discrete time proportional hazards model to firm-level export data for Spain (Esteve-Perez, Pallardo, and Requena 2008) indeed found no evidence of unobserved heterogeneity.

The remainder of this section discusses the results of the preferred specification, the Prentice-Gloeckler model using a gamma mixture distribution to summarize unobserved individual heterogeneity (fourth set of columns in table 2). To help interpret the economic significance of the results, the predicted percentage change in the hazard ratio resulting from a move from the 25th percentile to the 75th percentile of the distribution of a given control variable (or from 0 to 1 in the case of dummy variables) is shown in table 2. It shows, for example, that the hazard rate is 31 percent higher for a trade relationship with a country in the 75th percentile of the distance variable than with a country in the 25th percentile.

Figure 4 links changes in the hazard rate to the share of export flows that survive for 20 years or more assuming a hazard rate identical to the one for the sample as a whole. It shows that the number of export relationships surviving after 20 years falls from about 20 percent to around 12 percent with a 31 percent increase in the overall hazard rate for the dataset. The impact of a

FIGURE 4. Impact of a Change in the Hazard Rate on Survival Time of Trade Flows

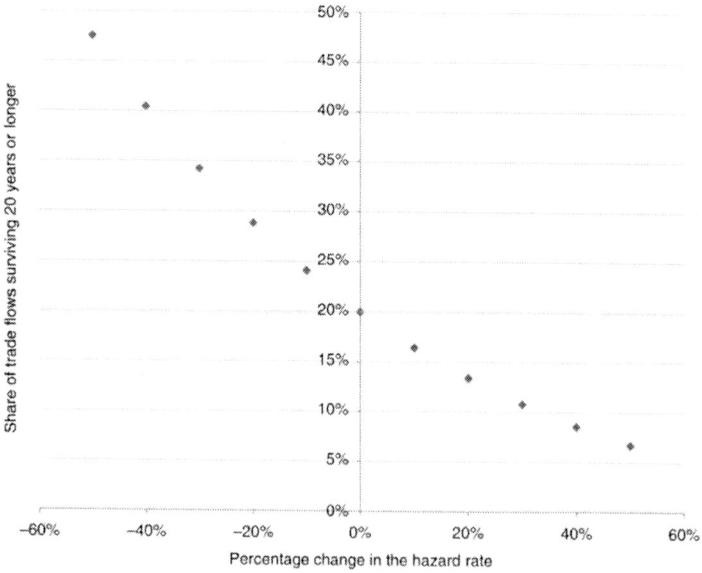

Source: Authors' calculation.

given percentage change in the hazard rate on a country's overall export performance will of course depend on several additional factors, such as the country's individual hazard rate, the number of existing and new trade relationships in each year, and the assumed growth rate of export flows that survive.

The results support the prediction that hazard rates are lower for export flows with larger initial values. Moving from the 25th to the 75th percentile for initial export values reduces the hazard rate by 8 percent. However, this effect is much weaker than the one predicted by the Cox model (−23 percent).[11] The hazard rate is higher for initially small flows, and this result holds until all trade flows with initial values smaller than $55,000 are excluded from the sample (sixth set of columns in table 2). The hazard rate also increases strongly with distance. Intuitively, trade costs would be expected to be the main driver of this effect. A common language (−30 percent) and a common border (−37 percent) significantly reduce the hazard rate, whereas colonial ties have only a small impact (−2 percent). Qualitatively, all these results are consistent with those found by Besedes and Prusa (2006a) and Blyde (2008). However, the coefficient estimates differ markedly in some cases.

The results also support the hypothesis that previous export experience is important in maintaining a trade relationship. Having previous export spells in the same product category decreases the hazard rate by 70 percent. Moreover, the results suggest that exporting experience is product rather than market specific. A move from the 25th to the 75th percentile for a country's total exports of goods within the same five-digit product category translates into a 60 percent reduction in the hazard rate. The impact of industry-specific and global export experience is weaker but not negligible. The size of the importer's market for a given product also appears to matter. Finally, these results also support the assumption that the economic size of both trading partners contributes to trade flow facilitation and to trade flow survival (see Blyde 2008 and Baldwin and Harrigan 2007, for example). A likely reason is that the number of possible matches between firms increases with the size of the two economies.

The analysis also finds that the hazard rate is reduced (by 30 percent) if the exporter already sells the product to other countries in the same region as the importer. This suggests that the regional nature of exporting experience should not be neglected. There appear to be learning effects specific to the product and the importing regions that help exporters sustain their trade relationships. This complements the finding of Roberts and Tybout (1995), who show that experience matters for initiating trade flows as well.

The results also provide evidence that both an initial overvaluation of the exporter's exchange rate and higher exchange rate volatility during initiation of

11. The importance of the initial size of exports is consistent with work by Brenton and von Uexkull (2009), who find that technical assistance targeted to specific export products tends to be more effective for the subsequent growth of exports for larger export flows.

export flows decrease hazard rates, but these effects do not seem to be economically significant. Finally, the coefficient on the preferential trade agreement dummy variable (*PTA*) indicates that a preferential trade agreement between the exporter and the importer reduces hazard rates by about 4 percent. This effect seems weaker than one would expect ex ante. In fact, the true effect may be attenuated by the definition of the variable, which gives the reference year for the *PTA* dummy variable as the starting year of the trade relationship. This implies that trade flows that become subject to a trade agreement after they are initiated are recorded as not being subject to the agreement.[12]

Two robustness checks were performed for the preferred specification (last two sets of columns in table 2). The first test excludes multiple spells from the analysis; doing so does not have a strong effect on the results. The second test excludes initially small trade flows (less than $55,000), which reverses the results for the impact of the initial value. This suggests that the positive impact of the initial export value is driven by a large number of observations with very small initial values and short duration but that once the initial size exceeds a certain threshold, the impact is reversed. A large share of these very small trade flows may be trial and error attempts at exporting, with firms exporting small amounts (or buyers ordering small amounts) initially to test whether a trade relationship is viable. This effect is no longer relevant in the data once these very small transactions are excluded. To the contrary, some trade flows with the largest initial values in the sample also have very short duration, which explains why the coefficient on the initial value is reversed once small initial value trade flows are dropped.

Previous research has argued convincingly that factors such as common language, common border, proximity, and other indicators of search barriers to trade may play a greater role for differentiated goods than for homogeneous goods (see Besedes and Prusa 2006a). This notion is investigated formally by dividing the sample into three sub-samples, each corresponding to one of the product categories classified in Rauch (1999).[13] The differences across product categories are small but generally confirm that factors such as distance, common border, common language, and colonial ties that influence trade costs play a more decisive role in the survival pattern of differentiated products than of homogeneous products (table 4). Intuitively, differentiated products are not traded on organized exchanges, so the exporter has to gather information and engage in an extensive search process, both in initiating trade flows and in sustaining them. Factors facilitating this search then contribute to a higher probability of trade flow survival.

12. This is particularly problematic for trade relationships that last for the entire sampling period. Many have a 0 for the PTA dummy because the number of preferential trade agreements in 1985 was much lower than it is today. As an illustration, only about 16 percent of trade relationships in 1985 were under a preferential trade agreement, whereas 40 percent were in 2005.

13. Experiments with both of Rauch's classification schemes shows that the results are not sensitive to the classification scheme chosen. Results are reported for the conservative classification.

TABLE 4. Results by Product Category at Preferred Specification (Prentice-Gloeckner model with unobserved heterogeneity, gamma distribution), 1985–2005

	Rauch: diversified					Rauch: reference priced					Rauch: homogeneous				
Variable	Exp(b)	95% confidence interval		*p*-value	25th–> 75th percentile[a] (%)	Exp(b)	95% confidence interval		*p*-value	25th–> 75th percentile[a] (%)	Exp(b)	95% confidence interval		*p*-value	25th–> 75th percentile[a] (%)
Initial value	0.943	0.941	0.945	0.000	−13.9	0.934	0.931	0.937	0.000	−16.0	0.969	0.963	0.975	0.000	−8
Distance	1.241	1.235	1.248	0.000	33.2	1.244	1.233	1.254	0.000	33.6	1.219	1.197	1.241	0.000	30
Border	0.621	0.609	0.633	0.000	−37.9	0.632	0.615	0.650	0.000	−36.8	0.635	0.601	0.671	0.000	−36
Common language	0.698	0.691	0.705	0.000	−30.2	0.700	0.689	0.711	0.000	−30.0	0.749	0.724	0.775	0.000	−25
Colony	0.950	0.934	0.965	0.000	−5.0	1.029	1.004	1.054	0.023	2.9	1.029	0.978	1.083	0.271	3
GDP Imp x Exp	0.921	0.918	0.923	0.000	−21.0	0.945	0.941	0.950	0.000	−14.4	0.954	0.944	0.964	0.000	−12
Total exports	0.969	0.968	0.969	0.000	−15.5	0.977	0.976	0.978	0.000	−11.4	0.987	0.985	0.989	0.000	−6
Industry exports	0.989	0.988	0.990	0.000	−4.4	0.966	0.964	0.968	0.000	−13.6	0.989	0.984	0.994	0.000	−4
Product exports	0.828	0.827	0.829	0.000	−68.2	0.866	0.864	0.868	0.000	−53.3	0.883	0.878	0.887	0.000	−46
Product imports	0.916	0.915	0.918	0.000	−30.6	0.936	0.934	0.938	0.000	−23.5	0.960	0.955	0.964	0.000	−15
Bilateral trade	0.940	0.938	0.942	0.000	−18.1	0.945	0.942	0.949	0.000	−16.5	0.936	0.927	0.944	0.000	−19
Neighbor	0.730	0.725	0.736	0.000	−27.0	0.711	0.703	0.720	0.000	−28.9	0.706	0.687	0.725	0.000	−29
Previous spell	0.315	0.312	0.317	0.000	−68.5	0.315	0.312	0.319	0.000	−68.5	0.291	0.284	0.298	0.000	−71
FX volatility	0.990	0.987	0.993	0.000	−0.8	0.994	0.989	0.998	0.008	−0.5	1.013	1.003	1.023	0.010	1
FX misalignment	0.995	0.994	0.996	0.000	−0.5	0.998	0.996	0.999	0.002	−0.2	0.990	0.987	0.993	0.000	−1
PTA	0.968	0.960	0.976	0.000	−3.2	0.957	0.945	0.970	0.000	−4.3	0.996	0.967	1.025	0.763	0
No. of observations	4,745,333					1,707,599					347,020				
LogL	−1,302,371					−543,221					−121,643				
Exp(b)	0.230					0.320					0.450				
p-value (Exp(b))	0.000					0.000					0.000				
chi^2	1,001					8,734					3,928				
p-value (chi^2)	0.000					0.000					0.000				

Note: All regressions include a set of biannual calendar time dummy variables (not reported).

a. Percentage change in the hazard ratio if the value of the exogenous variables increases from the 25th percentile to the 75th percentile of all observations in the dataset. In the case of dummy variables, the impact of a change from 0 to 1 is reported.

Source: Regression results based on data from UN Comtrade.

It also appears that the importance of the initial trade value to the length of survival is lower for homogeneous products, which may be due to less need for a trial and error search process for a commodity traded on an organized international exchange. Similar arguments can be made for the variables characterizing the exporting experience at the product level, economic size of both trading partners, and the size of the import market for the given product. The negative effect of the *PTA* dummy variable on the hazard rate also becomes markedly weaker for homogeneous goods, perhaps because a preferential trade agreement might be less important in facilitating trade for homogeneous goods typically traded on organized exchanges.

Finally, the analysis considers exporters from different income groups (table 5). The goal here is to understand whether the factors affecting export survival influence exports from developing countries more strongly than exports from richer countries. The results suggest that both regional exporting experience and previous trade relationships between two trading partners are more important for low-income exporters. The differences in point estimates are substantial, as evidenced by the absence of any overlap of confidence intervals between the estimates for high- and low-income exporters. Similarly, it is perhaps not surprising to find that past colonial ties help high- and middle-income exporters much less than low-income exporters in sustaining their export flows; again, the confidence intervals do not overlap. A common border between trading partners has a significantly smaller positive impact on the probability that a trade flow will survive when the exporter is a developing country. This suggests that low-income countries still have a long way to go to fully exploit the advantages of lower trade costs when trading with neighboring countries.

Although perhaps not economically significant, the size of the initial trade flow has a positive effect on the hazard rate for low-income exporters. In nonreported regressions, this issue was further investigated by interacting the initial export value with the product category according to Rauch (1999). As it turns out, the slightly positive effect is driven only by homogeneous products that are traded on organized exchanges and that constitute a high share of developing country exports. One explanation could be that the recorded sources and destinations of these exports change frequently as buyers regularly switch purchases between different source countries.

Furthermore, the relationship between the *PTA* dummy variable and the hazard rate changes sign when the sample is restricted to low-income exporters. This finding is somewhat surprising. Although not reported here, this was analyzed further by interacting the *PTA* dummy variable with characteristics of the importing country. It appears that the effect of a preferential trade agreement on the hazard function is only positive for preferential trade agreements between low-income exporters and low-income importers. It could be that a preferential trade agreement between low-income countries encourages exports to more hazardous partner markets.

TABLE 5. Results by Exporter Country Category at Preferred Specification (Prentice-Gloeckner with unobserved heterogeneity, gamma distribution), 1985–2005

	High-income exporters					Middle-income exporters					Low-income exporters				
Variable	Exp(b)	95% confidence interval		*p*-value	25th–> 75th[a] (%)	Exp(b)	95% confidence interval		*p*-value	25th–> 75th[a] (%)	Exp(b)	95% confidence interval		*p*-value	25th–> 75th[a] (%)
Initial value	0.961	0.958	0.962	0.000	−9.6	0.974	0.971	0.977	0.000	−6.3	1.021	1.014	1.028	0.000	5
Distance	1.141	1.134	1.147	0.000	19.4	1.331	1.321	1.340	0.000	45.6	1.264	1.238	1.291	0.000	36
Border	0.663	0.645	0.682	0.000	−33.7	0.715	0.701	0.729	0.000	−28.5	0.766	0.703	0.834	0.000	−23
Common language	0.730	0.721	0.739	0.000	−27.0	0.761	0.751	0.771	0.000	−23.9	0.859	0.835	0.884	0.000	−14
Colony	0.938	0.922	0.954	0.000	−6.2	0.996	0.973	1.020	0.758	−0.4	0.777	0.746	0.809	0.000	−22
GDP product	0.959	0.956	0.962	0.000	−10.8	0.941	0.937	0.944	0.000	−15.6	0.915	0.908	0.923	0.000	−22
Total exports	0.976	0.974	0.977	0.000	−12.2	0.974	0.973	0.975	0.000	−12.9	0.980	0.979	0.981	0.000	−10
Industry exports	0.972	0.971	0.974	0.000	−11.1	0.958	0.956	0.960	0.000	−16.8	0.962	0.959	0.966	0.000	−15
Product exports	0.845	0.843	0.846	0.000	−61.6	0.840	0.838	0.842	0.000	−63.5	0.839	0.834	0.843	0.000	−64
Product imports	0.920	0.919	0.922	0.000	−29.2	0.919	0.917	0.921	0.000	−29.8	0.935	0.931	0.939	0.000	−24
Bilateral trade	0.914	0.911	0.917	0.000	−25.9	0.938	0.935	0.941	0.000	−18.7	0.978	0.973	0.984	0.000	−7
Neighbor	0.752	0.746	0.757	0.000	−24.8	0.658	0.651	0.664	0.000	−34.2	0.629	0.611	0.648	0.000	−37
Previous spell	0.321	0.319	0.323	0.000	−67.9	0.297	0.295	0.300	0.000	−70.3	0.270	0.264	0.276	0.000	−73
FX volatility	0.975	0.972	0.979	0.000	−1.9	1.039	1.034	1.043	0.000	3.0	1.008	1.002	1.014	0.014	1
FX misalignment	1.003	1.002	1.004	0.000	0.3	0.990	0.989	0.992	0.000	−0.9	0.977	0.973	0.982	0.000	−2
PTA	0.893	0.885	0.902	0.000	−10.7	0.976	0.966	0.986	0.000	−2.4	1.155	1.126	1.184	0.000	15
No. of observations	4,094,474					2,596,781					317,203				
LogL	−1,162,169					−764,662					−130,293				
Exp(b)	0.156					0.400					0.410				
p-value	0.000					0.000					0.000				
chi2	3,895					1,578					5,840				
p-value	0.000					0.000					0.000				

Note: All regressions include a set of biannual calendar time dummy variables (not reported).

a. Percentage change in the hazard ratio if the value of the exogenous variables increases from the 25th percentile to the 75th percentile of all observations in the dataset. In the case of dummy variables, the impact of a change from 0 to 1 is reported.

Source: Regression results based on data from UN Comtrade.

However, the small number of low-income country importers in the sample requires caution in interpreting this result.

IV. Discussion and Conclusions

Exporting is a perilous activity, particularly in low-income countries. Understanding the determinants of export survival rates is therefore an important challenge for empirical analysis. A policy focus only on entry into exporting will miss a fundamental aspect of the dynamics of exporting. A strategy for increasing and sustaining export growth rates should address factors that contribute to the low export survival rates.

This article extends the path-breaking studies of export survival by Besedes and Prusa (2006a, b) by applying statistical survival techniques to a broad dataset of bilateral export flows with a high level of product and export-country detail. It formally tests, and rejects, the assumption of proportional hazards that underlies the standard Cox (1972) model typically used in the literature. The finding of the importance of accounting for unobserved heterogeneity points to the need for survival analysis with firm-level data to complement studies using product-level flow data in modeling export survival. The study also finds that both regional- and product-specific experience matter most for low-income economies and that these countries appear to insufficiently exploit the advantages of trading with neighboring economies.

The aim of this article was to extend the empirical analysis of export survival. There is still a way to go before clear policy recommendations can be derived, however. That will require more detailed country- and firm-specific analysis of the factors influencing export survival. The high prevalence of export failures suggests some caution regarding policy messages about constraints to exporting drawn from surveys of existing exporters. It is also important to derive information from exporting firms that have failed.

References

Aalen, Odd. 1978. "Non Parametric Inference for a Family of Counting Processes." *Annals of Statistics* 6: 701–26.

Albornoz, Facundo, Hector Calvo Pardo, and Gregory Corcos. 2010. "Sequential Exporting." *University of Birmingham Discussion Paper 10-08*. Birmingham, UK.

Araujo, Luis, and Emanuel Ornelas. 2007. "Trust Based Trade." *CEP Discussion Papers 0820*. Centre for Economic Performance, London.

Baldwin, Richard, and James Harrigan. 2007. Zeros, Quality, and Space: Trade Theory and Trade Evidence. *NBER Working Paper Series 13214*. Cambridge, MA: National Bureau of Economic Research.

Besedes, Tibor. 2008. "A Search Cost Perspective on Formation and Duration of Trade." *Review of International Economics* 16 (5): 835–49.

Besedes, Tibor, and Thomas Prusa. 2006a. "Product Differentiation and Duration of U.S. Import Trade." *Journal of International Economics* 70 (2): 339–58.

———. 2006b. "Ins, Outs, and the Duration of Trade." *Canadian Journal of Economics* 104 (1): 635–54.

Blyde, Juan. 2008. "What Drives Export Survival? An Analysis of Export Duration in Latin America." *Inter-American Development Bank*, Washington, DC.

Brenton, Paul, Martha Pierola, and Erik von Uexkull. 2009. "The Life and Death of Trade Flows: Understanding the Survival Rates of Developing-Country Exporters." In *Breaking into New Markets: Emerging Lessons for Export Diversification*, eds. Newfarmer Richard, Shaw William, and Walkenhorst Peter. Washington, DC: World Bank.

Brenton, Paul, and Erik von Uexkull. 2009. "Product Specific Technical Assistance for Exports—Has It Been Effective?" *Journal of International Trade and Economic Development* 18 (2): 235–54.

CEPII (Centre d'etudes prospectives et d'informations internationales). Various years. BACI International Trade Database at the Product Level. www.cepii.fr/anglaisgraph/bdd/baci.htm

Cox, David. 1972. "Regression Models and Life Tables." *Journal of the Royal Statistical Society Series B* 34 (2): 187–220.

Cox, David, and E. Joyce Snell. 1968. "A General Definition of Residuals." *Journal of the Royal Statistical Society* B 30: 248–75.

D'Addio, Anna, and Michael Rosholm. 2002. "Left-Censoring in Duration Data: Theory and Application." Economic Working Papers 2002-5. School of Economics and Management, Aarhus University, Aarhus, Denmark.

Edwards, Huw. 2007. "Trade Search and Its Implications." *Centre for the Study of Globalisation and Regionalisation*, Warwick, UK.

Esteve-Perez, Silviano, Vicente Pallardo, and Francisco Requena. 2008. "The Duration of Trade: Spanish Firms and Export Partners." Paper presented at European Trade Study Group Conference, September 11–13, Warsaw.

Horowitz, Joel, and George Neumann. 1992. "A Generalized Methods of Moments Specification Test of the Proportional Hazards Model." *Journal of the American Statistical Association* 87 (417): 234–40.

IMF (International Monetary Fund). Various years. World Economic Outlook Database. Washington, DC: International Monetary Fund.

Jenkins, Stephen. 1995. "Easy Estimation Methods for Discrete-Time Duration Models." *Bulletin of Economics and Statistics* 57 (1): 129–38.

Kaplan, Edward, and Paul Meier. 1958. "Nonparametric Estimation from Incomplete Observations." *Journal of the American Statistical Association* 53: 457–81.

Kay, Richard. 1977. "Proportional Hazard Regression Models and the Analysis of Censored Survival Data." *Applied Statistician* 26 (3): 227–37.

Lancaster, Tony. 1990. The Econometric Analysis of Transition Data. Cambridge, UK.: Cambridge University Press.

Meyer, Bruce. 1990. "Unemployment Insurance and Unemployment Spells." *Econometrica* 58 (4): 757–82.

Nelson, Wayne. 1972. "Theory and Applications of Hazard Plotting for Censored Failure Data. *Technometrics* 14: 945–66.

Nitsch, Volker. 2007. "Die Another Day: Duration in German Import Trade." *CESifo Working Paper 2085*. CESinfo, Munich.

Prentice, Ross, and Lynn Gloeckler. 1978. "Regression Analysis of Grouped Survival Data with Application to Breast Cancer Data." *Biometrics* 34 (1): 57–67.

Rauch, James. 1999. "Networks versus Markets in International Trade." *Journal of International Economics* 48 (1): 7–35.

Rauch, James, and Joel Watson. 2003. "Starting Small in an Unfamiliar Environment." *International Journal of Industrial Organization* 21 (7): 1021–42.

Roberts, Mark, and James Tybout. 1995. "An Empirical Model of Sunk Costs and the Decision to Export." *Policy Research Working Paper 1436*. World Bank, Washington, DC.

Schoenfeld, David. 1982. "Partial Residuals for the Proportional Hazards Regression Model." *Biometrika* 69 (1): 239–41.

United Nations, Statistics Division. Various years. United Nations Commodity Trade Statistics Database (Comtrade). http://comtrade.un.org/

World Bank. Various years. World Development Indicators. Washington, DC.

Appendix. Sources and Definitions of Variables

Appendix 1. Variable sources and definitions

Variable	Definition	Source
Initial value	Log of the trade value in first year of spell	UN Comtrade
Distance	Log of the distance in kilometers between most populous cities in exporting and importing countries	CEPII
Border	Dummy variable, 1 if shared border	CEPII
Common language	Dummy variable, 1 if common language	CEPII
Colony	Dummy variable, 1 if exporter is a former colony of importer	CEPII
GDP Imp x Exp	Product of GDP of importer and exporter in purchasing power parity terms	IMF
Total exports	Log of total exports of the exporter	UN Comtrade
Industry exports	Log of exporter's total exports in industry	UN Comtrade
Product exports	Log of exports of the product to all countries by the exporter in first year of trade relationship	UN Comtrade
Product imports	Log of imports of the product from all countries by the importer in the first year of trade relationship	UN Comtrade
Neighbor	Dummy variable, 1 if exporter exports the same product to a neighboring country	UN Comtrade
Bilateral trade	Log of exports of all products from exporter to importer in the first year of trade relationship	UN Comtrade
Previous spell	Dummy variable, 1 if previous spells within sample period	UN Comtrade
FX volatility	Average absolute value of the monthly percentage change in the exchange rate between exporter and importer in years t = -1, 0 and 1 around the beginning of the trade relationship	IMF
FX Misalignment	Exchange rate between exporter and importer in the year the trade relationship starts relative to the period average.	IMF
PTA	Dummy variable, 1 if exporter and importer are in a preferential trade agreement when trade flow commences	World Bank

The Journal of International Trade & Economic Development
Vol. 18, No. 2, June 2009, 235–254

Routledge
Taylor & Francis Group

Chapter 18

Product specific technical assistance for exports – has it been effective?

Paul Brenton* and Erik von Uexkull

International Trade Department, The World Bank, MSN MC2-201, 1818 H Street St. NW, Washington, DC 20433, USA

(*Received July 2007; final version received February 2008*)

The international community is placing increasing emphasis on aid for trade to assist low income countries to integrate into the global economy and to address their domestic constraints to export driven growth. There is, however, scant information on the effectiveness of previous support for export development to inform the design of new initiatives. In this paper, we exploit information on product specific technical assistance for trade and estimate a simple partial equilibrium model to assess the impact on the key measurable outcome – exports of the product subject to assistance. We apply a difference in differences approach to isolate the impact of the policy interventions and draw four main conclusions: on average, export development (ED) programs have coincided with or predated stronger export performance; such programs appear to be more effective where there is already significant export activity; there is some concern about the additionality of the programs and that support may be being channeled to sectors that would have prospered anyway; ultimately, conclusions strongly depend on what one postulates would have happened in the absence of the policy intervention, so the definition of a credible counterfactual is of utmost importance for the evaluation of technical assistance for exports.

Keywords: aid for trade; export development; difference in differences; developing countries

Introduction

The Doha Declaration (2001) states that 'well targeted, sustainably financed technical assistance' has an important role to play for developing countries to enable them to 'share in the growth of world trade commensurate with the needs of their economic development'. While progress has generally been slow in the Doha Round, this particular call has not remained unanswered: donors have increased their trade-related aid commitments by about 50%

*Corresponding author. Email: pbrenton@worldbank.org

ISSN 0963-8199 print/ISSN 1469-9559 online

DOI: 10.1080/09638190902916444
http://www.informaworld.com

between 2001 and 2004, when they reached a total of roughly US$3 billion (OECD 2006). Almost US$1 billion of this has been estimated to go into projects that directly support the supply capacity of private enterprises for exports (Cali 2007).

A number of studies on policy variables and trade have demonstrated the opportunities for well designed technical assistance to support export growth and diversification in developing countries. Just to mention a few, Wilson et al. (2003) use a gravity model to analyze trade facilitation in terms of port efficiency, customs environment, regulatory environment and electronic business-usage and find improvements in these fields significantly increase trade. Francois and Manchin (2006) emphasize the importance of institutional quality and infrastructure and show that they significantly impact exports. Using microlevel data from the World Bank's Investment Climate Assessment, Yoshino (2006) finds an important role for trade credit, internet access and other factors that facilitate linkages with international markets. This suggests that policy measures and public sector investment can have a strong impact on export performance and underline the case for technical assistance in countries that have weak capacity and limited financial resources to address the relevant constraints.

Recent evaluations state that many aid-for-trade programs have been successful in raising awareness and knowledge of trade policy issues or facilitating integration into the multilateral trading system (OECD 2006). However, with respect to export development, results are much less clear. Some programs are found to have improved the environment for trade or encouraged exports in non-traditional sectors, but generally evaluators found it difficult to measure impact, especially in the long run (OECD 2006). In an evaluation of European Commission sponsored technical assistance projects, ADE s.a. (2004) finds that the quantitative impact of projects on exports was small in the countries' export portfolios, but may have had a significant quality effect. Te Velde et al. (2006) echo this, concluding that 'the impact of EC's TRA in terms of expansion and diversification of external trade and FDI has been disappointing in all case studies except Vietnam, although the analysis of macroeconomic variables is too complex to allow for a clear-cut causal relation on this.'

The Policy and Operations Evaluation Department of the Dutch Ministry of Foreign Affairs, in its 2005 review of technical assistance delivered by international organizations, criticizes a general lack of measurable outcome indicators in such programs.

Nevertheless, the impact of technical assistance on exports and export diversification should be the key measurable outcome of the projects financed by these activities. This paper seeks to enhance our understanding of the effectiveness of aid for trade by taking an initial look at the impact of product specific export development (ED) programs. This has one big advantage compared with previous evaluations: by focusing on programs that are targeted to a specific product, we have a measurable outcome variable: exports of that product.

The difficulty, as in all empirical studies of the impact of a specific policy change, is in defining the counterfactual to which actual performance can be compared. Simply comparing before and after performance is not sufficient since it is necessary to identify what would have happened to the exports of those receiving treatment in the absence of this technical assistance. In this paper, we use a very simple partial equilibrium model of the evolution of exports and apply a difference in differences approach,[1] comparing countries that receive technical assistance with control groups of other counties. We start by discussing our data and then look at some specific examples of technical assistance for exports that are characteristic of the observations in our data set. We then present and discuss our empirical results before drawing general conclusions in the final section.

Data on technical assistance for export development

We use data on ED programs from two different sources. First, the Doha Development Agenda Trade Capacity Building Database (TCBDB) provided by the OECD and WTO. This database contains comprehensive information on trade-related technical assistance by all important donors. Unfortunately, data are only available back to 2001. Second, we use data we received from GTZ[2] on technical assistance projects that have been delivered between 1975 and 2000. Unfortunately, we were not able to get comparable data from other donors involved in technical assistance, so the only pre-2000 ED programs in our dataset are those reported by GTZ.

From these two sources, we select product-specific ED programs through a keyword search on typical export products for developing countries. We then select all programs for which the description of content indicates that they specifically target exports of a particular commodity. This leaves us with a list of 88 ED programs in 48 different countries.[3] Most programs are for textiles (15), followed by coffee (12) and wood articles (10).[4]

Table 1 provides summary statistics on the size and nature of the technical assistance projects in our sample. The mean project value is $2.3 million for a mean duration of 2.7 years. However, the data are widely dispersed and skewed to the right since the median project value is just over a third of a million dollars. Hence, our data reflect a large number of relatively small technical assistance projects with a few projects that have substantial funding. The table also shows the average funding according to whether initial exports are above or below average prior to the technical assistance project. The biggest projects in terms of funding are focused on larger initial exports. Again, there is substantial dispersion. The mean project value for initially large exports is almost US$4 million, whilst the median value is around half a million dollars. The average size of a technical

Table 1. Summary statistics for project values.

	Project value (1000 US$)		Project duration (years)	
	Mean	Median	Mean	Median
Full sample	2,264	343	2.7	1
Above median initial exports	3,782	517	3.2	1
Below median initial exports	594	254	2.1	1
Projects in low income countries	1,252	371	3.0	1
Projects in medium income countries	3,229	300	2.3	1

Note: Three country-product pairs excluded due to outlier value data.

assistance project for smaller initial exports is substantially less and with lower dispersion.

The last two rows of Table 1 present a breakdown of project values by the income level of the host country. We find projects in middle income countries tend to have a higher value (around US$3.2 million) than projects in low income countries (US$1.3 million).

The next step is to merge the information on ED programs with export data from the United Nations COMTRADE database. We use mirror export data for the years 1975 to 2005. We assume that there were no ED programs other than those reported by GTZ in place for the products and countries we select before 2001 (where we do not have information from TCBDB). Thus, our counterfactual to technical assistance is defined by data for a large number of country-product pairs with no technical assistance and a small number (possibly zero) of country-product pairs with technical assistance that we have not identified. This could lead to a small downward bias in our results.

There is considerable variation in the initial volume of exports of industries that receive technical assistance. ED programs have been implemented in export industries of below $10,000 (honey from Uganda, fruit from Senegal), but also for multi hundred million dollar export industries, such as, textiles from Turkey and Egypt and coffee from Colombia.

Some examples of technical assistance for exports

Vietnam, a low income country, already exported textiles of around US$300 million per year when the ED program started in 2001. After implementation, export growth in textiles was much stronger than before. However, Vietnam also experienced high growth in other relevant export industries during these years and thus there is no noticeable positive effect of the ED program on the export share of textiles (Figure 1).

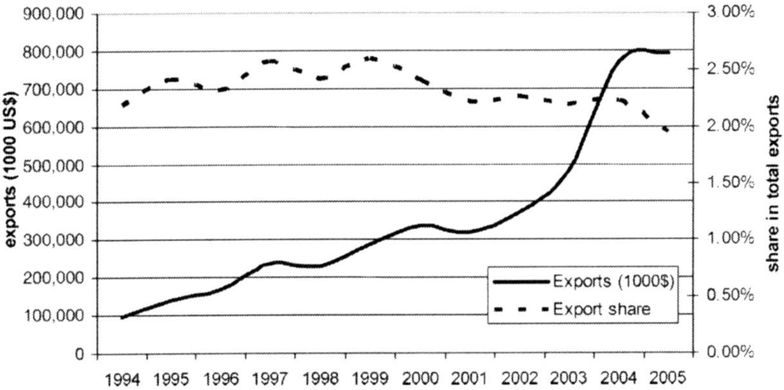

Figure 1. Textile exports from Vietnam.

The PDR of Lao, a low income country, hardly exported any corn before 2003 when the ED program started. In 2003, and the following two years, corn exports grew tremendously, also increasing their share in the country's overall export portfolio from almost zero to 0.45%. It seems unlikely that this effect was triggered entirely by the relatively small amount of the ED program so this could be an example for an ED program being delivered in an industry that is already set to take off (Figure 2).

Cameroon, a lower middle income country, had previously exported onions in low and unstable quantities when the ED program started in 2003. In this year, there was a spike in onion exports, but in the following year, they went back to close to zero. This is an example for a highly unsustainable program. We do not know if the program had a positive impact on the domestic market, but in terms of export development, it appears to have failed (Figure 3).

Cut flowers had been a growing export industry in Uganda (a low income country) for a decade when the ED program started in 2003. After the ED program, exports made a jump to a new level, almost tripling their export value within one year. Although other Ugandan exports also rose strongly at this time, cut flowers significantly increased their export share (Figure 4).

Mongolia, a low income country, had traditionally been an exporter of wool products. However, exports declined and lost share in the export portfolio in the late 1990s and early 2000s. After the ED program in 2003, exports of wool products entered a steady growth path, outperforming overall export growth in 2005 (Figure 5).

Methodology

Our analysis is based on a simple partial equilibrium adjustment model of exports. Given the initial nature of our inquiry and the limitations of the

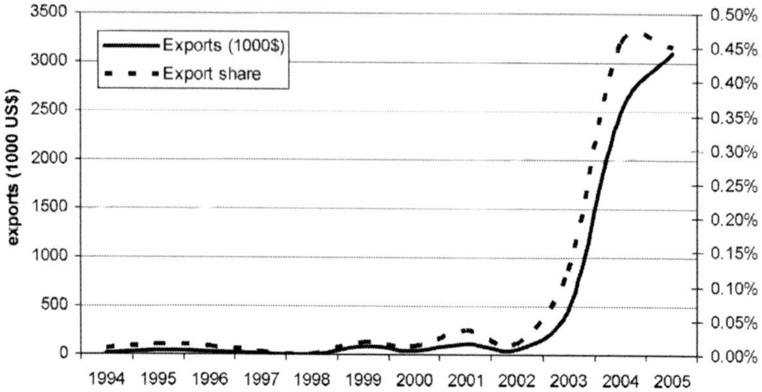

Figure 2. Corn exports from Lao PDR.

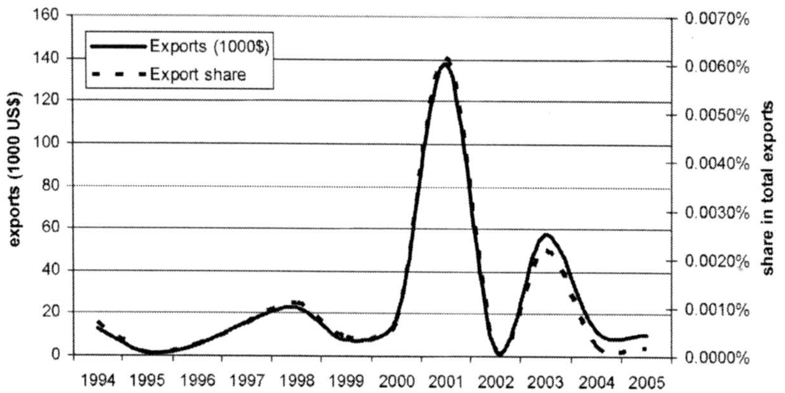

Figure 3. Onion exports from Cameroon.

available data, a simple model of exports is most appropriate. Our approach is similar to that adopted to investigate the impact of anti-dumping actions (see e.g. Prusa 1997, and Brenton 2001). The basic model that we estimate is

$$\ln(X_{ijt}) = \beta_0 + \beta_1 \ln(X_{ijt-1}) + \sum_{s=0}^{4} \delta_s ED_{ijt-s} + C_j + Y_t * P_i + \varepsilon_{ijt}$$

Exports X of product i by country j in period t are a function of exports of the same product by the same country in the previous period. We then add a vector of dummy variables ED which take the value of 1 if an ED program is started in period $t = 0,1,2,3,4$. ε is an error term and β_0 is a constant.

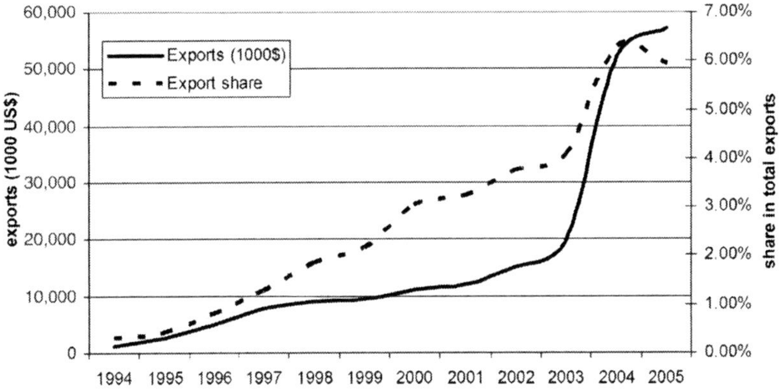

Figure 4. Cut flowers exports from Uganda.

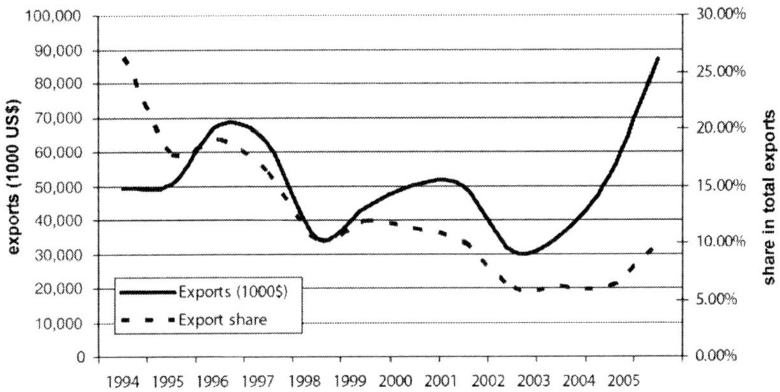

Figure 5. Wool products exports from Mongolia.

We include country fixed effects C and an interaction term for year and product fixed effects ($Y*P$). The country fixed effects control for fixed country specific factors such as size, climate, and population. The year-product fixed effects control for any changes that are specific to a product in any given year. Here, we mainly think of supply or demand shocks that have a strong influence on the world market price and quantities exported. Ultimately, the choice of fixed-effects is a question of which counterfactual scenario one wants to use as a benchmark for effectiveness and other choices could certainly also be justified.

We also estimate a model specification in which we replace logged exports by the logged share of good i in total exports of country c on both sides of the equation so as to control for general trends in a country's export performance. As with the fixed effects, the preference between the two models depends on the question of what one would consider a more adequate benchmark of comparison to evaluate the effectiveness of technical assistance. The interpretation of the δ coefficients is straightforward: a significantly positive δ_s indicates that an ED program has led to additional export growth in the years after its implementation.

To identify properly the impact of a particular policy intervention or 'treatment' we need to be able to identify the potential outcome for those receiving assistance if they had not been treated. A common response is to adopt a difference in differences approach whereby we assume that in the absence of a policy intervention, exports of a country would grow in line with the average of a group of comparator countries. The main problem we face in analyzing the effect that 'treatment' with an ED program has on a country is thus the selection of an adequate 'without treatment' control group. We use two approaches. First, we compare the country with the ED program to all other developing countries in the world that export the product for which ED was given. This is fairly straightforward and not very demanding of the data. However, this could bias our results because the decision to implement an ED program is not exogenous to other factors that determine export performance. For example, technical assistance to export a particular commodity will only be implemented in countries that have the necessary prerequisites to produce this commodity (for example, the climate conditions to grow a certain crop). On the other hand, technical assistance will typically target countries that face constraints in their export performance or have a particularly strong need to diversify.

In order to mitigate these problems, our second approach is to select the control group by pairing our 'treatment' observations with other countries that exhibit similar observable characteristics. We select the pairing countries using the following procedure, which is similar to that used by Girma et al. (2004) for matching firms. First, we estimate the probability of a country to export the good in question based on a number of general determinants of a country's export portfolio such as its level of development, its factor endowments and its climate conditions.[5] Then, we pair each country that has an ED program for product i with the country that is closest to it in terms of the predicted likelihood to export product i. This is clearly more demanding of the data. Our pairing gives us a panel of 167 country–product pairs.[6] One further issue of concern in working with panel data is the potential presence of unit roots. We test for unit roots in both the full and the paired dataset using the Fisher test suggested by Maddala and Wu (1999). In both cases, the presence of a unit root is clearly rejected.

Results

We now present the results of estimating the above log-linear equation for each of our different approaches to selecting the control group. With this dataset an important issue is how to deal with the zero values that are present. Simply deleting these observations would lose important information and unbalance the panel. Completely excluding cases where exports are zero would lead to selection bias, and so, within the confines of the estimating equation, we simply add a small constant to the export variables to enable them to be subject to logarithmic transformation. Later we apply a different functional form and estimator to check the robustness of the results obtained from least squares estimation of the log-linear model. In non-reported regressions, we also experimented with a purely linear specification to avoid the problem of the zeros. Results are roughly consistent with the reported results for the log-linear specification. However, given the strong differences in initial size of exports discussed in the data section, we consider the linear model to be less appropriate as it puts excessive weight on the naturally larger absolute changes in exports from countries that are already large exporters. In

Table 2. (a) OLS estimation for full sample with all exporters as control group.

	All observations	Dropping outliers	All observations	Dropping outliers
	$\ln(X_{i,c} + 0.01)$, (1000\$)		$\ln(X_{i,c}/X_{tot,c} + 0.000001)$	
Dependent variable in t-1	0.731 (0.000)***	0.867 (0.000)***	0.794 (0.000)***	0.916 (0.000)***
ED program in t	0.870 (0.000)***	0.398 (0.001)***	0.556 (0.000)***	0.236 (0.002)***
ED program in $t+1$	0.778 (0.000)***	0.248 (0.069)*	0.522 (0.000)***	0.239 (0.002)***
ED program in $t+2$	0.833 (0.000)***	0.289 (0.005)***	0.534 (0.000)***	0.179 (0.018)**
ED program in $t+3$	1.052 (0.000)***	0.479 (0.000)***	0.592 (0.000)***	0.174 (0.010)**
ED program in $t+4$	1.000 (0.000)***	0.454 (0.000)***	0.645 (0.000)***	0.277 (0.000)***
Fixed Effects	country, year*product	country, year* product	country, year* product	country, year* product
Constant	2.875 (0.000)***	1.226 (0.000)***	−1.292 (0.000)***	−1.027 (0.000)***
Observations	100.142	91,575	100,142	93,648
R-squared	0.792	0.926	0.793	0.931

P values based on heteroskedasticity-consistent standard errors in parentheses.
*Significant at 10%; **significant at 5%; ***significant at 1%.

all specifications of the model the coefficient for lagged exports (or export share) are positive and highly significant. In what follows, we concentrate on discussing the coefficients on the dummies entered to capture the impact of the product-specific technical assistance for exports.

Control group = all exporters

In the specification with all exporters as control group (Table 2(a)), we find a very strong and highly significant impact of ED programs in the years $t = 0,1,2,3,4$ after their implementation. The effect is slightly lower, but still significant if we use the export share as our dependent variable. These results would suggest extreme increases of around 90% in exports and 60% in export shares in each of these years, which seems hardly believable. We then apply a simple procedure to detect and delete potential outliers that might drive these results. After running the initial regression, we drop all observations for which the studentized residual is more than two standard

Table 2. (b) OLS estimation for treatment countries with above median initial exports and all exporters as control group.

	All observations	Dropping outliers	All observations	Dropping outliers
	$\ln(X_{i,c} + 0.01)$, (1000\$)		$\ln(X_{i,c}/X_{tot,c} + 0.000001)$	
Dependent variable in t-1	0.737 (0.000)***	0.878 (0.000)***	0.790 (0.000)***	0.914 (0.000)***
ED program in t	1.031 (0.000)***	0.343 (0.000)***	0.688 (0.000)***	0.227 (0.000)***
ED program in $t+1$	1.103 (0.000)***	0.431 (0.000)***	0.690 (0.000)***	0.261 (0.000)***
ED program in $t+2$	1.165 (0.000)***	0.459 (0.000)***	0.772 (0.000)***	0.346 (0.000)***
ED program in $t+3$	1.293 (0.000)***	0.549 (0.000)***	0.762 (0.000)***	0.227 (0.002)***
ED program in $t+4$	1.225 (0.000)***	0.484 (0.000)***	0.736 (0.000)***	0.200 (0.002)***
Fixed Effects	country, year*product	country, year*product	country, year*product	country, year*product
Constant	3.517 (0.000)***	1.260 (0.000)***	−0.806 (0.000)***	−0.595 (0.000)***
Observations	56,816	51,910	56,816	53,071
R-squared	0.792	0.932	0.784	0.927

P values based on heteroskedasticity-consistent standard errors in parentheses.
*Significant at 10%; **significant at 5%; ***significant at 1%.
Note: The treatment group comprises all country-product pairs who had an ED program with initial exports above the median. The control group comprises country-product pairs of all those developing countries that export the products that are contained in the treatment group.

deviations away from the mean. We then re-run the regression with only the remaining observations. After doing this, the magnitude of the estimated coefficients on the technical assistance dummies fall considerably but remain significant (at a 10% or higher level) for all years. The annual increase in exports due to technical assistance is now estimated at around 40% and for export shares around 20%, which still seems very high. In this particular application, there are some concerns in applying this procedure regarding outliers since a successful technical assistance project that increases exports from close to zero to a substantial amount in a short period of time might appear statistically as an extreme value.

As shown in Table 1, in our sample, the size of technical assistance projects tends to be bigger the larger are existing export flows. In addition, technical assistance delivered to an already large and existing export industry might face very different problems and opportunities than technical assistance delivered to export industries in their infancy. To further explore these differences, we split the treatment group into countries with above and

Table 2. (c) OLS estimation for treatment countries with below median initial exports and all exporters as control group.

	All observations	Dropping outliers	All observations	Dropping outliers
	$\ln(X_{i,c} + 0.01)$, (1000$)		$\ln(X_{i,c}/X_{tot,c} + 0.000001)$	
Dependent variable in t-1	0.725 (0.000)***	0.860 (0.000)***	0.788 (0.000)***	0.910 (0.000)***
ED program in t	0.749 (0.035)**	0.429 (0.049)**	0.450 (0.055)*	0.250 (0.071)*
ED program in $t+1$	0.502 (0.055)*	0.071 (0.776)	0.357 (0.051)*	0.225 (0.112)
ED program in $t+2$	0.566 (0.012)**	0.127 (0.448)	0.307 (0.054)*	0.025 (0.835)
ED program in $t+3$	0.929 (0.000)***	0.446 (0.011)**	0.461 (0.002)***	0.104 (0.344)
ED program in $t+4$	0.855 (0.000)***	0.470 (0.003)***	0.607 (0.000)***	0.376 (0.004)***
Fixed Effects	country, year*product	country, year*product	country, year*product	country, year*product
Constant	2.923 (0.000)***	1.319 (0.000)***	−1.328 (0.000)***	−0.696 (0.000)***
Observations	94,716	86,532	94,716	88,557
R-squared	0.793	0.925	0.792	0.929

P values based on heteroskedasticity-consistent standard errors in parentheses.
*Significant at 10%; **significant at 5%; ***significant at 1%.
Note: The treatment group comprises all country-product pairs who had an ED program with initial exports below the median. The control group comprises country-product pairs of all those developing countries that export the products that are contained in the treatment group.

below median initial export levels in the sample. Table 2(b) reports the results for the above median group. These suggest even higher impacts on both export levels and export shares than in the full sample. Here, too, coefficients are considerably lower when outliers are dropped. The results for the below median export group are shown in Table 2(c). Here, we find lower and less significant coefficients than for the full sample. Before dropping outliers, coefficients are still significant at a 10% level for all years $t = 0,1,2,3,4$ but after dropping outliers, they are only significant in the years $t = 0,3,4$ for exports and $t = 0,4$ for export shares.

These results suggest that ED programs in countries with high initial export levels tend to have a higher impact on the growth of exports and export shares. We also split the sample into low income and middle income countries. The results, which are not reported here, show for the low-income country sub-sample a positive and significant impact of ED programs for all years with point estimates and significance levels similar to the full sample estimations. For the middle income countries, coefficient estimates are lower and after dropping outliers they become insignificant for some years.

Table 3. (a) OLS estimation for full sample with matched exporters as control group.

	All observations	Dropping outliers	All observations	Dropping outliers
	$\ln(X_{i,c} + 0.01)$, (1000\$)		$\ln(X_{i,c}/X_{tot,c} + 0.000001)$	
Dependent variable in t-1	0.766 (0.000)***	0.908 (0.000)***	0.834 (0.000)***	0.929 (0.000)***
ED program in t	0.319 (0.060)*	0.024 (0.772)	0.152 (0.143)	0.027 (0.700)
ED program in $t+1$	0.160 (0.290)	−0.005 (0.962)	0.110 (0.289)	0.060 (0.402)
ED program in $t+2$	0.255 (0.112)	0.033 (0.741)	0.193 (0.065)*	0.041 (0.576)
ED program in $t+3$	0.468 (0.002)***	0.210 (0.026)**	0.202 (0.037)**	0.075 (0.287)
ED program in $t+4$	0.463 (0.005)***	0.207 (0.067)*	0.231 (0.072)*	0.138 (0.167)
Fixed Effects	country, year*product	country, year*product	country, year*product	country, year*product
Constant	1.811 (0.486)	−1.530 (0.271)	−0.886 (0.080)*	−1.594 (0.012)**
Observations	4,778	4,481	4,778	4,540
R-squared	0.911	0.977	0.921	0.976

P values based on heteroskedasticity-consistent standard errors in parentheses.
*Significant at 10%; **significant at 5%; ***significant at 1%.

Control group = matched exporters

We now move to the results obtained when the countries receiving technical assistance are more closely pair-wise matched with other countries that have similar characteristics in terms of the likelihood to export this product. Table 3(a) presents the results for the full sample. The results still provide support for a significant impact of technical assistance on exports in the years $t = 3$ and 4 after implementation at about 45% per year (around 20% per year when dropping outliers). With respect to the export share, the estimations show positive and significant coefficients suggesting an effect of ED programs of around 20% in the years $t = 2,3,4$ but all coefficients become insignificant once outliers are dropped. One conclusion from the strong difference between these and the previous results is that the implementation of ED programs is in fact endogenous to other factors that influence a country's export performance and much of the export growth we observe after implementation of these programs might have happened anyway.

Tables 3(b) and (c) report results for the above median and below median initial exports groups, respectively. Here, we see a significantly

Table 3. (b) OLS estimation for treatment countries with above median initial exports and matched exporters as control group.

	All observations	Dropping outliers	All observations	Dropping outliers
	$\ln(X_{i,c} + 0.01)$, (1000\$)		$\ln(X_{i,c}/X_{tot,c} + 0.000001)$	
Dependent variable in t-1	0.821 (0.000)***	0.941 (0.000)***	0.863 (0.000)***	0.949 (0.000)***
ED program in t	0.140 (0.200)	−0.004 (0.949)	0.100 (0.269)	0.025 (0.655)
ED program in $t + 1$	0.325 (0.036)**	0.170 (0.015)**	0.085 (0.422)	0.117 (0.044)**
ED program in $t + 2$	0.099 (0.499)	0.096 (0.331)	0.113 (0.203)	0.019 (0.805)
ED program in $t + 3$	0.482 (0.000)***	0.228 (0.014)**	0.221 (0.062)*	0.139 (0.097)*
ED program in $t + 4$	0.182 (0.321)	−0.174 (0.094)*	−0.132 (0.328)	−0.180 (0.053)*
Fixed Effects	country, year*product	country, year*product	country, year*product	country, year*product
Constant	2.120 (0.000)***	0.815 (0.000)***	−0.264 (0.039)**	0.052 (0.586)
Observations	2,489	2,379	2,489	2,397
R-squared	0.918	0.980	0.939	0.984

P values based on heteroskedasticity-consistent standard errors in parentheses.
*Significant at 10%; **significant at 5%; ***significant at 1%.

positive impact in the years $t = 1,3$ for both export levels and shares that is robust to dropping outliers for the above median exporters. However, we also see significantly (at a 10%, but not at a 5% level) negative coefficients in year $t = 4$ for both export levels and shares after dropping outliers. For the below median initial exporters, we find a strong and significant impact in the years $t = 3,4$ for export levels and $t = 4$ for export shares. Two findings strike us as interesting here. First, for the matched specification, effects of ED programs are weaker and usually only occur after a time lag of two to three years. Second, unlike in the full sample specification, we do not find the impact of technical assistance to be stronger for countries with higher initial export levels (if anything, the opposite holds true for this specification). We will discuss some potential explanations for these findings in the conclusions section.

Another issue with our estimations is that we are trying to draw general conclusions on the impact of ED programs that vary significantly in terms of size, duration, methodology etc. While it is not possible to take into account all these differences, we did run a specification of our model that takes into account the monetary value of an ED program. To do this, in addition to our

Table 3. (c) OLS estimation for treatment countries with below median initial exports and matched exporters as control group.

	All observations	Dropping outliers	All observations	Dropping outliers
	$\ln(X_{i,c} + 0.01)$, (1000$)		$\ln(X_{i,c}/X_{tot,c} + 0.000001)$	
Dependent variable in t-1	0.554 (0.000)***	0.685 (0.000)***	0.634 (0.000)***	0.767 (0.000)***
ED program in t	0.479 (0.183)	0.247 (0.248)	0.240 (0.276)	0.158 (0.313)
ED program in $t + 1$	0.144 (0.588)	0.006 (0.977)	0.235 (0.168)	0.093 (0.571)
ED program in $t + 2$	0.390 (0.220)	0.124 (0.585)	0.261 (0.209)	0.024 (0.876)
ED program in $t + 3$	0.652 (0.035)**	0.364 (0.097)*	0.339 (0.118)	0.173 (0.306)
ED program in $t + 4$	0.549 (0.043)**	0.473 (0.044)**	0.415 (0.044)**	0.428 (0.023)**
Fixed Effects	country, year*product	country, year*product	country, year*product	country, year*product
Constant	2.511 (0.303)	0.815 (0.393)	−2.609 (0.000)***	−1.507 (0.005)***
Observations	2,321	2,178	2,321	2,195
R-squared	0.905	0.962	0.908	0.965

P values based on heteroskedasticity-consistent standard errors in parentheses.
*Significant at 10%; **significant at 5%; ***significant at 1%.

ED dummy, we include an interaction term between the ED dummy and the log of the value of a program, and scale this by the recipient country's per capita GDP to allow for meaningful cross-country comparisons. In this specification, there is no clear interpretation for the coefficients of the ED dummy. However, the coefficients of the interaction terms can be interpreted as the percentage increase in exports due to a 1% increase in the relative endowment of an ED program, conditional on an ED program being in place. Our estimates, not reported here, show some positive and significant coefficients for the relative program value, but in no case is the significance of this coefficient robust to dropping outliers. Thus, we do not find clear evidence that the relative size of an ED program has a significant impact on its effectiveness.

Fixed-effects Poisson estimator

Finally, we address our concerns about the log-linear model and the way this compels us to treat the zeros in the data set by specifying the relationship in multiplicative form and using a fixed-effects Poisson estimator with the variables in their initial state.[7] This allows us to keep the zeros in the data set without transformation. In this specification (Table 4), we find a strong and

Table 4. Fixed-effects Poisson estimation for all treatment countries, all exporters and matched exporters as control group.

	All exporters	Matched exporters	All exporters	Matched exporters
	$X_{i,c}$, (1000$)		$X_{i,c}/X_{tot,c}$	
Dependent variable in t-1	0.000	0.000	3.366	3.464
	(0.000)***	(0.000)***	(0.000)***	(0.000)***
ED program in t	−0.048	0.248	0.029	0.037
	(0.808)	(0.009)***	(0.772)	(0.708)
ED program in $t+1$	0.282	0.400	−0.013	−0.007
	(0.254)	(0.000)***	(0.846)	(0.914)
ED program in $t+2$	0.663	−0.018	0.090	0.098
	(0.002)***	(0.958)	(0.461)	(0.426)
ED program in $t+3$	0.706	0.359	0.097	0.129
	(0.079)*	(0.004)***	(0.259)	(0.130)
ED program in $t+4$	0.335	0.172	0.196	0.221
	(0.340)	(0.455)	(0.158)	(0.108)
Fixed Effects	country, product	country, product	country, product	country, product
Constant				
Observations	99,688	4,712	99,688	4,712
R-squared				

P values based on heteroskedasticity-consistent standard errors, based on Wooldridge (1999) in parentheses.
*Significant at 10%; **significant at 5%; ***significant at 1%.

significant impact of ED programs on exports in years $t = 2{,}3$ at around 70% when running the regression on the full sample. For the matched sample, we find a strong and significant impact in the years $t = 0{,}1{,}3$. For export shares, we do not find a significant impact for any of the years.

Conclusions

Our model, simple as it is, has delivered some interesting but at this stage initial insights. First, exports have on many occasions increased significantly under ED (export development) programs. While questions remain on the issue of causality and the adequate benchmark scenario to judge an ED program's effectiveness, there can be little doubt that, on average, ED programs have coincided with or predated stronger export performance in the targeted commodities. Second, the initial size of an export sector may matter for the effectiveness of technical assistance. When splitting the full sample into above and below median initial export levels, we find a much stronger performance of programs delivered to industries with initially high export levels. It may be that the constraints facing the growth of existing exports are easier to identify and alleviate in technical assistance projects than are the constraints to new exports. In addition, it may be more appropriate for technical assistance to assist exporters that have previously shown a capacity to penetrate overseas markets but are currently facing particular constraints in terms of management, marketing, product design, market information and so on. However, the difference between the results for high and low initial exports sub-samples disappears in the specification with matched exporters that we use to control for endogeneity of the selection of countries and industries for an ED program. This suggests that the better performance of ED programs in high initial export industries is mainly because technical assistance is directed towards industries that are already set to take off.

Third, the strong difference in the size and significance of coefficients between our full and matched sample suggests that the export growth observed after the implementation of an ED program often might not be a direct result of the program, but rather reflect the fact that ED programs target sectors with promising prospects for the future. While this can be justified in some cases, it raises the concern that technical assistance might allocate funds to already successful export sectors that could be better used to address constraints in sectors that lag behind.

Finally, this paper demonstrates that the key issue in identifying the impact of technical assistance is to define carefully the counterfactual situation of what would have happened without it. We adopted a difference in differences approach using a set of observed outcomes from a population that has not been subject to the policy under scrutiny and assume that the average outcome for this group would have pertained to the treated group if they had not received the treatment. However, the outcome of any assessment of effectiveness ultimately depends on what one considers as an adequate benchmark scenario.

This initial exercise has been limited by the confines of the data set and especially our limited information on product specific technical assistance for exporters prior to 2001. We hope to be able to obtain addition information from donors that will enable us to extend and expand the data set. As the information set increases it should be possible to look more closely at the characteristics of ED programs and at the recipients of such assistance that are related to the success of technical assistance in delivering sustained increases in exports. There is also scope for further work to be done in refining the process of selecting the control group and in the matching of countries. In addition, it would be useful to complement this work by ex post case study analysis of the impact of specific technical assistance projects and the reasons for their success and failure. The analysis of the impact of technical assistance for exports would be facilitated by more comprehensive and rigorous project completion and assessment reports that identify the expected and actual impact of the project on exports.

Acknowledgements

The authors are very grateful for the helpful comments of Richard Newfarmer, Ben Shepherd, Milan Nedeljkovic and an anonymous referee and to Jana Hoeffken who compiled the data on technical assistance delivered by GTZ for us.

Notes

1. See Meyer (1995) for a review of the difference in differences approach.
2. Gesellschaft für Technische Zusammenrbeit.
3. Table A1 in the Appendix shows the distribution of the ED programs among countries.
4. Table A2 provides a breakdown of ED programs by products.
5. The variables used are distance from the equator, per capita GDP, telephone mainlines per 1000 inhabitants, literacy ratio, life expectancy at birth, percentage of land that is arable, labor force/arable land.
6. This is slightly lower than twice the number of ED programs identified for two reasons: first, we have to drop three country-product pairs because we do not have all the data necessary for the matching process. Second, in three cases, the same country-product pair is selected to the control group for two different treatment countries.
7. Wooldridge (1999) shows that the fixed effects Poisson estimator is fully robust, requiring only a simple structural conditional mean assumption. We use the methodology suggested by Wooldridge to compute the robust standard errors reported in Table 4.

References

ADE s.a. 2004. *Evaluation of trade-related assistance by the European Commission in third countries*. Final report, Brussels.

Brenton, P. 2001. Anti-dumping policies in the EU and trade diversion. *European Journal of Political Economy* 17: 593–607.

Cali, M. 2007. Scale and types of funds for aid for trade. ILEAP Negotiation Advisory Brief No. 12.

Francois, J., and M. Manchin. 2006. Institutional quality, infrastructure, and the propensity to export. http://www.uni-kiel.de/ifw/konfer/staffsem/manchin.pdf (accessed 12 March 2007).

Girma, S., D. Greenway, and R. Kneller. 2004. Does exporting increase productivity? A microeconometric analysis of matched firms. *Review of International Economics* 12: 855–66.

Maddala, G., and S. Wu. 1999. A comparative study of unit root tests with panel data and a new simple test. *Oxford Bulletin of Economics and Statistics* 61: 631–52.

Meyer, B. 1995. Natural and quasi-experiments in economics. *Journal of Business and Economic Statistics* 13: 151–61.

OECD. 2006. Trade-related assistance: What do recent evaluations tell us? Paris: DCD-DEV Secretariat Study.

Policy and Operations Evaluation Department (IOB) of The Netherlands Ministry of Foreign Affairs. 2005. Aid for trade? An evaluation of trade-related technical assistance. Amsterdam: IOB Evaluation.

Prusa, T. 1997. The trade effects of US anti-dumping actions. In *The effects of US trade protection and trade promotion policies*, ed. R. Feenstra, 191–213. Chicago: University of Chicago Press.

Te Velde, D.W., M. Cali, A. Hewitt, and S. Page. 2006. A critical assessment of the EU's trade related assistance to third countries – lessons from the past, policy options for the future. Study for the International Trade Committee of the European Parliament. http://www.odi.org.uk/iedg/Projects/TRA_Final_Draft_ODI.pdf (accessed 9 May 2007).

Wilson, J., C. Mann, and T. Otsuki. 2003. Trade facilitation and economic development. World Bank Policy Research Working Paper 2988.

Wooldridge, J. 1999. Distribution-free estimation of some nonlinear panel data models. *Journal of Econometrics* 90: 77–97.

Yoshino, Y. 2006. Trade facilitation, domestic constraints and export performance in regional and global markets: Firm-level evidence in African manufacturing sector. *World Bank Regional Program of Enterprise Development*.

Appendix

Table A1. Host countries of ED programs in sample.

Country	Income level	No. of programs
Bangladesh	Low income	1
Bolivia	Lower middle income	2
Bosnia and Herzegovina	Lower middle income	1
Brazil	Lower middle income	1
Cambodia	Low income	2
Cameroon	Lower middle income	2
Cape Verde	Lower middle income	1
China	Lower middle income	2
Colombia	Lower middle income	1
Congo, Rep.	Lower middle income	1
Cuba	Lower middle income	1
Ecuador	Lower middle income	4
Egypt, Arab Rep.	Lower middle income	2
El Salvador	Lower middle income	1
Eritrea	Low income	1
Ethiopia	Low income	5
Ghana	Low income	1
Guatemala	Lower middle income	1
Guinea	Low income	1
Honduras	Lower middle income	1
India	Low income	2
Jamaica	Lower middle income	1
Kenya	Low income	3
Lao PDR	Low income	4
Lesotho	Lower middle income	1
Mali	Low income	1
Mexico	Upper middle income	2
Mongolia	Low income	2
Morocco	Lower middle income	2
Mozambique	Low income	1
Namibia	Lower middle income	1
Nicaragua	Lower middle income	2
Pakistan	Low income	2
Peru	Lower middle income	5
Poland	Upper middle income	1
Rwanda	Low income	1
Senegal	Low income	2
Seychelles	Upper middle income	1
Sri Lanka	Lower middle income	2
Tanzania	Low income	3
Thailand	Lower middle income	2
Timor-Leste	Low income	2
Trinidad and Tobago	Upper middle income	1
Uganda	Low income	3

(*continued*)

Table A1. (*Continued*).

Country	Income level	No. of programs
Uruguay	Upper middle income	1
Uzbekistan	Low income	1
Vietnam	Low income	3
Zambia	Low income	4
Total		88

Table A2. ED programs in the sample by product.

Coding system	No. ED programs	Product code	Product name
HS 92	1	41	Raw hides and skins (other than fur)
HS 92	10	44	Wood and articles of wood
HS 92	4	51	Wool, fine/coarse animal hair
HS 92	2	409	Natural honey
HS 92	2	603	Cut flowers and flower buds
HS 92	1	702	Tomatoes, fresh or chilled.
HS 92	2	703	Onions, shallots, garlic, leeks
HS 92	1	801	Coconuts, brazil nuts and cashew nuts
HS 92	3	803	Bananas, including plantains, fresh
HS 92	1	807	Melons (including watermelons)
HS 92	4	808	Apples, pears and quinces, fresh
HS 92	2	809	Apricots, cherries, peaches
HS 92	12	901	Coffee, whether or not roasted
HS 92	3	902	Tea, whether or not flavored
HS 92	1	905	Vanilla
HS 92	1	1701	Cane or beet sugar
HS 92	5	1801	Cocoa beans, whole or broken, raw or roasted
HS 92	1	2204	Wine of fresh grapes
HS 92	1	2401	Unmanufactured tobacco
ISIC Rev. 2	15	321	Manufacture of textiles
ISIC Rev. 2	8	322	Manufacture of wearing apparel, excl. footwear
ISIC Rev. 2	5	323	Manufacture of leather and products of leather
ISIC Rev. 2	3	324	Manufacturing of footwear

Development Policy Review, 2009, 27 (3): 243-267

Chapter 19

Carbon Labelling and Low-income Country Exports: A Review of the Development Issues

Paul Brenton, Gareth Edwards-Jones
and Michael Friis Jensen*

This article discusses the carbon accounting and carbon-labelling schemes being developed to address growing concerns over climate change. Its particular concern is their impact on small stakeholders, especially low-income countries. The popular belief that trade is by definition problematic is not true; carbon efficiencies elsewhere in the supply chain may more than offset emissions from transportation. Indeed, low-income countries may offer important opportunities for carbon emission reductions because of their favourable climatic conditions and use of low energy-intensive production techniques. However, their effective inclusion in labelling schemes will require innovative solutions to provide low-cost data collection and certification.

Key words: Carbon footprint, carbon labelling, low-income countries, exports, standards, certification

1 Introduction

In response to growing anxiety about climate change, policy-makers, firms and consumers are considering ways in which to reduce greenhouse gas emissions. A possible mitigation mechanism undergoing rapid development is carbon[1] labelling. This involves measuring greenhouse gas emissions from the production of products or services and conveying that information to consumers and those making sourcing decisions within companies. Well-designed schemes will create incentives for production of different parts of the supply chain to move to lower emission locations. Thus, carbon labelling enables consumers to join the battle against climate change by using their shopping trolley.

Firms are eager to cater to consumers' demands and to reduce their own carbon footprints. Global retail giants are developing carbon measurement and labelling

* Paul Brenton and Michael Friis Jensen are in the International Trade Department, World Bank, 1818 H Street NW, Washington, DC 20433 (pbrenton@worldbank.org), and Gareth Edwards-Jones is in the School of Environment and Natural Resources, Bangor University, Wales. The authors are grateful for the comments of Tom Brewer, Mona Haddad, Paul Hodson, Andreas Kopp, Brian Levy, Muthukumara Mani and Philip Schuler. This work is funded in part by the Multi-Donor Trust Fund for Trade and Development supported by the UK, Swedish and Norwegian governments. The views expressed reflect solely those of the authors and not necessarily the views of the funders, the World Bank Group or its Executive Directors.

1. We follow common usage here and use carbon to refer to all greenhouse gases. Appendix 1 provides a brief overview of the relevant terminology.

Published by Blackwell Publishing, Oxford OX4 2DQ, UK and 350 Main Street, Malden, MA 02148, USA.

schemes and major manufacturers are following suit. However, the strong desire to act on carbon labelling has been running ahead of the challenges of measurement and the problems of effective communication through labelling that must be addressed for schemes to be successful. As a result, a growing number of standards are being developed with little effort to co-ordinate and generally little or no voice given to small players, such as low-income countries (LICs).

This article aims to draw attention to the potential impact of carbon measurement, footprinting and labelling schemes on the exports of LICs in a context in which such schemes are actually being developed and applied. To date, the major practical initiatives in this area have been led by retailers, and as a result are product-focused. There are at least three potential ways in which a product-focused approach can be operationalised. First, through a consumer-facing carbon label. Second, through the provision of product information via other means, for example, on a website. Thirdly, producers could offer to reduce their greenhouse gas (GHG) emissions related to their products through some form of social contract. Such commitments by producers are part of the methodologies of both the Carbon Trust in the UK and of carboNZero in New Zealand. Because such organisations are already implementing schemes, a discussion of the likely impacts of these approaches is pertinent. However, we do not seek to provide here a discussion of carbon labelling in the context of identifying optimal policies to mitigate climate change. In the future there will probably be a mix of policy responses using a range of complementary instruments, which may include market-based mechanisms such as carbon taxes, but these instruments are not yet operational, whereas carbon footprinting and labelling are.

Fears have been raised that low-income countries will face greater difficulties in exporting in a climate-constrained world where carbon emissions need to be measured and certification obtained to enable participation in carbon labelled trade. This discussion centres on *transportation* and the common presumption that products produced locally will have an advantage in terms of carbon emissions, and on the effects of *size*. Exports from LICs typically depend on long-distance transportation and are produced by relatively small firms and tiny farms which will find it difficult to participate in complex carbon-labelling schemes. However, the scientific evidence shows that carbon efficiencies elsewhere in the supply chain of a product may more than offset the emissions associated with transportation, while the disadvantages of small size can be accommodated by innovative solutions to low-cost data collection and certification.

Carbon labelling needs to be based on a sound, well-developed and independent scientific base. At present the available scientific evidence is small, but growing. It is too early to make specific predictions of how the exports of LICs will be affected, but it is timely to identify the major issues. This article starts by providing a brief overview of the intersection between carbon labelling and international trade. It then proceeds with two empirical sections. Section 3 presents the main conclusions and key issues raised by studies that have sought to measure carbon emissions or energy used along international supply chains, while Section 4 gives an overview of the emerging carbon-labelling initiatives. Both sections identify the key characteristics from a low-income country perspective. Section 5 is more analytical and discusses how LICs' export interests interact with the ongoing process of designing carbon-labelling schemes and how the schemes that emerge create challenges and opportunities for future trade. Conclusions are offered in Section 6.

2 Carbon labelling and trade

The role of carbon labelling is to provide information to consumers and purchasers who are concerned about the impact of their choices on global warming. It is one instrument available to mitigate climate change that includes other trade measures, such as carbon taxes and countervailing duties, and specific regulatory requirements. The purpose here is not to compare and judge carbon labelling relative to other instruments but rather to investigate the key implications of emerging labelling schemes for a particular constituency: low-income countries.

An important aspect of carbon accounting and labelling is that schemes are actually being developed *and* implemented. As will be discussed in more detail in Section 4, there is a strong momentum within the corporate sector towards labelling initiatives. At present it is unclear if and when carbon taxes will be applied. While a tax on fossil fuels, in proportion to the carbon emitted in their use, would be relatively straightforward to apply, it would not address a number of important issues related to global warming. First, such a tax would only target emissions of CO_2 and not other greenhouse gases such as nitrous oxide and methane. Second, and related, a carbon tax would not deal with emissions due to changes in land use, such as deforestation. These two points are particularly important when considering agriculture, as typically the greatest impact on climate change from this sector arises from nitrous oxide from soils and methane from ruminants (Edwards-Jones et al., 2008). Finally, without global agreement on a carbon tax it appears that countries applying such a tax would seek to impose import taxes on products from countries that do not participate. Given the nature of globalisation and cross-border production networks in which a finished product typically contains components from an array of countries, there would need to be some form of carbon accounting to implement such an approach. Labelling schemes can therefore complement the more traditional approaches of taxation and regulation. For example, carbon labelling is an integral part of the proposed EU regulation on biofuels, discussed in more detail below.

The development of carbon labelling was predated by discussions of 'food miles'. While food miles have been discredited as an accurate measure of the impact of food products on climate change,[2] discussions of how carbon labelling can attain the necessary precision to be effective are still ongoing. That is the scientific side of the discussion. The economics is complex and involves: consideration of how labels may bring down transaction costs in a supply chain by increasing transparency with regard to relevant product attributes (in this case emission efficiency); the costs of providing and verifying the necessary information; and how labelling will change consumer and producer behaviour.

2. Food miles, a metaphor for the evolution of the global food industry, are difficult to apply. Calculations show that transporting apples by sea, for example, causes less than 1% of the carbon dioxide emissions if they are flown; but the food miles concept tells us nothing about how the apples are transported.

The way in which information on carbon emissions is presented is a key issue on which consensus is far from achieved. Exploratory schemes giving detailed numerical information similar to nutritional information, have not proved successful. Simple labels can be misleading and inconsistent with the policy objective of reducing emissions. Alternatives being investigated include labels signifying that some minimum achievement has been attained (or a commitment to do so), or labels that certify observance of an appropriately defined 'good environmental practice'. At the same time, companies are exploring ways of distributing information internally so as to achieve objectives regarding their carbon footprint.

Measurement costs are a critical issue for small stakeholders. Low-income countries have predominantly small firms and tiny farms, hence any size bias in the carbon-labelling schemes, in terms of the costs of measuring emissions and of verifying those measurements, will translate into a heavy burden on the competitiveness of such small players. A feature of the last two decades of development in agro-food industries has been the implementation of strict trade standards, like the imposition of the GlobalGAP standard by a group of primarily UK and Dutch retailers. The cost of this standard is generally thought to be a major reason behind the marginalisation of small farmers from horticultural export markets (Dolan and Humphrey, 2000; Gibbon, 2003; Graffham et al., 2006; Graffham and MacGregor, 2006).

The provision of credible information is essential if a carbon-labelling scheme is to serve as a guideline for buyers and consumers when choosing emission-efficient products. Certification is one way to target this problem. Given that costs must be incurred by firms in certifying their emissions, the success of carbon labelling requires that consumers are willing to pay a premium to protect the global environment. Further, by allowing consumers and company purchasers to demonstrate their willingness to pay to reduce their carbon footprints, labelling may initiate a process by which firms in the production chain innovate so to acquire or maintain an existing advantage in terms of carbon emissions.

In principle, such labelling schemes could play an important role in achieving emission reductions and be a useful complement to other environmental policies. However, as with other eco-labels, there is concern that such schemes may, in practice, unfairly restrict trade, especially with LICs. This may arise if the labelling criteria reflect local technologies and tend to exclude 'acceptable products' produced with different processes in overseas locations, as might occur if the process of developing the labelling scheme is liable to capture by domestic interests.[3] Similarly, there may be discrimination against imported products if the carbon emissions of particular products are indirectly derived using parameters based on data in the importing country and which may overestimate the emissions in the producing country (Deere, 1999). Both these concerns are likely to impact most heavily on LICs, where production processes tend to differ from those in rich countries and for which parameters derived in rich countries will be most inappropriate. In addition, as noted above, the costs of

3. Here we can make an analogy to the rules of origin that industrial countries have applied to determine eligibility for trade preferences. In the past, the specification of these rules has been far from transparent, has excluded key stakeholders and been strongly influenced by domestic industry, resulting in excessively restrictive rules limiting the value of preferences and constraining the degree of new competition faced by domestic producers.

certification are likely to impinge especially heavily on producers in LICs and if these costs lead to the exclusion of low emission producers from developed-country markets, then the whole labelling scheme would be undermined.

3 Carbon emissions throughout an international supply chain

Concern about climate change has stimulated interest in estimating the total amount of carbon emitted during the production, processing and distribution of a product. The final outcome of this exercise is called the product's 'carbon footprint' and the exercise itself is known as 'carbon accounting'.[4] A product's carbon footprint is different from a company's as the former includes the carbon emitted by consumption (and disposal) of the product itself as well as of all inputs necessary to produce it. It is therefore called an embedded (or embodied) footprint.

Methods are already established for measuring, reporting and verifying carbon emitted during production.[5] One scientific method typically applied is Life Cycle Analysis (LCA).[6] In principle, this should imply adding up all carbon emissions throughout a product's life from the production of inputs to final consumption and disposal of waste. The methodological difficulties of putting this intuitively appealing idea into practice are, however, immense and the lack of standardised methods heavily influences the usefulness and comparability of existing studies.

Nevertheless, a small but rapidly growing literature analyses product-level carbon footprints. Needless to say, carbon accounting is becoming increasingly difficult in today's globalised world where supply chains grow longer and ever more complex.

There is little doubt that this complexity accounts for the dominance of agricultural supply chains in the scientific literature since many foods are subject to little processing and pass through relatively simple supply chains. Other products that have been subject to carbon measurement studies include transport fuels and forestry products, where again the supply chains are relatively straightforward. Nevertheless, carbon accounting may also be implemented for more complex products such as industrial products, although studies are still rare.

---

4. Carbon footprints are expressed in units of CO_2 equivalents (CO_2e). This is because different GHGs have different impacts on the atmosphere – so-called radiative forcing. The most important GHGs in agriculture are carbon dioxide (CO_2), nitrous oxide (N_2O) and methane (CH_4). Currently it is estimated that 1kg of CH_4 is equivalent to 25kg of CO_2, and 1kg of N_2O equivalent to 298kg CO_2 over a 100-year time horizon (IPCC, 2007). However, as scientific knowledge on global warming has progressed so these conversion factors have been amended over time. Previously the Intergovernmental Panel on Climate Change (IPCC) had suggested that 1kg of CH_4 was equivalent to 23kg of CO_2, and 1kg of N_2O was equivalent to 296kg CO_2 (IPCC 2001), while before that IPCC (1995) had suggested GWP conversion factors of 21 for CH_4 and 310kg for N_2O. This is not a problem from a scientific point of view; however, some legislation and treaties may have adopted earlier IPCC conversion factors, and care should be taken to ensure equivalence in any calculations. The degree of radiative forcing of a GHG depends on several factors including how long they survive in the atmosphere, their current concentration in the atmosphere and their ability to capture infrared radiation.
5. Defined in the World Business Council for Sustainable Development/World Resource Institute GHG Protocol and ISO 14064 on GHG quantification and reporting.
6. LCA is defined in ISO 14040-44 standards and associated guidelines. Its methodology should not be used for regulatory purposes.

Table 1: Lifecycle analyses relevant to low-income country exports

Study	Case	Outcome	Comments
Williams (2007)	Kenyan and Dutch roses consumed in UK	Air freight-related emissions counteracted by higher energy use by Dutch greenhouses	Comparison of one Dutch with one Kenyan farm. Comparison may not be typical. Data not verified independently
Jones (2006)	Kenyan and UK beans consumed in UK	Kenyan and European on-farm energy consumption similar. Kenyan 12 times higher than UK due to air freight	No UK primary data, so basis for comparison is questionable.
Sim et al. (2007)	Kenyan, Guatemalan and UK runner beans consumed in UK	Kenyan and Guatemalan global warming potential 20-26 times higher than UK due to airfreight	As no UK primary data were collected it is hard to compare overall emissions
Fogelberg & Carlsson-Kanyama (2006)	Frozen South and Central America broccoli compared with fresh Swedish broccoli consumed in Sweden	Transportation-related emissions counteracted by lower use of fossil fuels in South and Central America production systems. In terms of carbon emissions, no substantive differences between the two origins	Only aggregated data presented in graphs, so hard to understand data collection and manipulation methods. Attempts made to normalise results to account for nutritional differences – a non-standard approach.
Fogelberg & Carlsson-Kanyama (2006)	Brazilian and Swedish chicken consumed in Sweden	Analyses trade-off between shipping feed from Brazil to produce chicken in Sweden and producing both in Brazil and shipping chicken to Sweden. Differences in emissions small	Only aggregated data presented in graphs, so hard to understand data collection and manipulation methods
Blanke & Burdick (2005)	German and Southern hemisphere apples consumed in Germany	Energy needed to store Northern apples almost as great as that needed to transport from overseas	Relies on modelling supply chains rather than primary data collection. Studies one month only, and only energy use (correlated with but not identical to carbon emissions)

Mila i Canals et al. (2007a)	EU and Southern hemisphere apples consumed in EU	Southern hemisphere apples as energy efficient as EU apples during EU Spring and Summer due to energy needed for storage counteracting that needed for transportation by ship	Considers whole calendar year. Only studies energy use (correlated with but not identical to carbon emissions). Incorporates variation in energy use in supply chains to present a more realistic range of energy use than normal LCA approach of one figure per supply chain
Mila i Canals et al. (2007b)	UK and Spanish lettuce consumed in UK	Spanish Winter production plus refrigerated road transport more 'carbon efficient' than UK Winter greenhouse production. Fertilisers important source of emissions in all systems	Primary data collected through field surveys on farms. However, sample size still too small to claim that results are statistically representative. Highlights variation between farms in emissions/kg lettuce produced
Schlich & Fleissner (2005)	German, Brazilian and New Zealand fruit juices and lamb consumed in Germany	Large global companies better able to exploit opportunities for reducing energy inputs from greater scale. Outweighs transportation-related emissions	
Saunders et al. (2006)	New Zealand and UK lamb consumed in UK	New Zealand's more extensive farming systems outweigh transportation-related emissions	Methodologically flawed in many ways: analysed 7 NZ farms as compared with standard data for one UK farm-type: did not consider all GHGs. NZ source found to be 4 times more 'carbon efficient' than UK production
Barrett et al. (2002)	Food consumed in York (UK)	Meat and dairy products have highest carbon emissions, horticultural products 3 to 5 times lower (per kg basis)	Ecological Footprinting used as methodological basis; specifically used Energy Analysis Program (EAP) to model carbon emissions
Wallén et al. (2004)	Food consumed in Sweden	Cheese, coffee, frozen fish and meat have highest carbon emissions, horticultural products 3 to 12 times lower (per kg basis)	Data taken from secondary sources, including suppliers. In absence of some data a series of assumptions made
Kramer et al. (1999)	Food consumed in the Netherlands	Meat and dairy products account for 50% of food-related carbon emissions, fruit and vegetables account for 15% of emissions	

Relatively few complete LCAs or carbon footprints for entire supply chains are published in the peer reviewed literature, with even fewer covering activities in a developing country. Similarly, studies that consider alternative supply chains for the same good, namely, a good supplied to the same market place via different supply chains, are very scarce. A larger grey literature is often produced by parties with commercial interests. To make things even more difficult, studies differ in their methodologies, making comparison difficult. Table 1 presents an overview of the main studies. With these caveats in mind, the rest of this section will present the available evidence and distil the lessons for LIC export opportunities.

3.1 Carbon emission patterns are highly complex

The literature illustrates a number of ways in which different carbon-emitting activities interact to provide an overall carbon footprint. An important implication of this is that geographical location alone is a poor proxy for overall emissions; favourable production conditions may more than offset a disadvantage in transport.

Williams (2007) estimated the carbon footprint of cut roses supplied to the UK market from companies in Kenya and the Netherlands and found that, even after taking into account the emissions from air transport, the Kenyan roses produced considerably lower emissions than Dutch glasshouse production, owing to the electricity and heat used in Kenyan greenhouses being derived from geothermal energy rather than fossil fuels. Fogelberg and Carlsson-Kanyama (2006) point out the trade-off between the high use of diesel in Swedish broccoli production and carbon emissions from long-distance transportation of broccoli from South and Central America where, on the other hand, the agricultural technologies used are less mechanised and primary fossil fuel consumption is much lower. Schlich and Fleissner (2005) explore the trade-off between close-to-market but small-scale fruit juice production and far away carbon efficient large-scale production, and find that better use of scale economies outweighs transportation-related emissions.

The exact structure of emissions is likely to be highly specific to the given supply chain under scrutiny, and the limited body of existing evidence offers few rules of thumb. Mila i Canals et al. (2007a) find that the balance between emissions from refrigeration of local apples and from transporting apples from the other side of the globe shifts throughout the year. In the European Spring and Summer, long-distance trade is most efficient, but when European apples are in season the balance tips and local apples are most efficient. Emissions from the use of imported inputs that have been transported long distances are important in comparing the carbon footprints of products from different locations. Fogelberg and Carlsson-Kanyama (2006) compare chicken consumed in Sweden from two sources: Sweden and Brazil. Two key differences are highlighted. First, energy consumed in Brazilian production is lower than that in Sweden due to the more clement climate. Second, the feed used in Sweden is produced partly from imported soy meal (which may come from Brazil). In Brazil, all ingredients in the feed are obtained domestically.

Thus, the complexity of carbon emissions discredits simplistic but intuitively appealing concepts such as food miles and buy-local campaigns. Such concepts may be more relevant when particular food qualities such as freshness and authenticity are sought by the consumer. But the available evidence lends little support to the notion that they have much to offer in terms of climate-change mitigation.

3.2 Transportation is one source of carbon emissions among many

The popular belief is that trade, by definition, is problematic from an environmental perspective since it necessitates transportation. But this is generally not true; transportation is one source among many. Carbon emissions per tonne-km vary with the different types of transport and generally fall in the order of air freight, road, ships. However, while aviation emissions are widely known to be high, some discussion remains as to what they actually are. Energy use differs between short and long-haul flights (23.7MJ/tonne-km and 8.5MJ/tonne-km, DEFRA, 2005) and also between freight carried in the belly of a passenger plane and in a dedicated freight plane. As a result, there are a variety of emission factors available for air transport.

Emissions from ocean-going ships are considerably lower. Indeed, Jones (2006) estimates that if beans were transported from Kenya to the UK by ship (Mombasa to Southampton), the energy use would be 1.7MJ/kg, 56MJ/kg less than the air freight from Nairobi to London. However, given that the journey by sea would take 11-12 days it would be necessary to chill, or otherwise treat, the beans in order to render them saleable on arrival. In a similar set of calculations, Wangler (2006) estimates that the emissions from transporting 1kg of produce from Cape Town to London by air would be 14.9 kg CO_2e, and by ship from Cape Town to Southampton between 0.1 and 0.12kg CO_2e.

Thus, air transport is a carbon hotspot and the airfreight of fresh fruit and vegetables is clearly responsible for a substantial, if not the major, proportion of carbon emissions in the supply chains to wholesalers (Edwards-Jones et al., 2009; Sim et al., 2007). However, the transport emissions are perhaps more evident in these supply chains than in other food items. Supply chains of fresh produce are relatively simple, since they contain few other intermediate inputs. Other foodstuffs, such as processed dairy products like yoghurts and meat items like sausages, tend to require more sophisticated processing, have longer production chains and use multiple inputs. All of these entail greenhouse gas emissions. As a result, the overall carbon footprint of fresh produce tends to be amongst the lowest for any food category (Barrett et al., 2002; Wallen et al., 2004), and transport tends to be a proportionally higher contributor to it than in other foodstuffs.

Nevertheless, the vast majority of low-income country exports, and of international trade in general, is transported by ships for longer distances and roads for shorter distances. Notably, sea transport has become highly energy efficient (measured on a tonne-km basis) and for most products it is unlikely that transportation will be a disproportionate source of carbon emissions. This is particularly relevant for processed food and industrial products, for which energy-consuming processing weighs more heavily than for the relatively simple products analysed in LCAs so far.

3.3 LICs' carbon competitiveness needs to be explored

The potential of LICs to participate in global trade in a climate-constrained world in which carbon emissions carry a larger cost than today has not been investigated in any detail. The few existing studies suggest that LICs may remain competitive in sectors where they have traditionally done well (see Edwards-Jones et al., 2009), as is the case for Kenyan roses and presumably for many traditional bulk commodities transported by sea.

Some studies have shown that one particular agricultural process is extremely energy-intensive: protected production. Examples include production under glass or in polytunnels in the case of horticulture. This arises because of the use of energy for heat and light, whereas it is inputs of natural light and heat that are used in non-protected agriculture. In addition, substantial emissions in the cultivation of protected agriculture arise from the production of the materials used to build the glass houses and polytunnels; steel, glass, plastics.[7] Hence, LICs are likely to have an advantage in competing with protected production in richer Northern countries. The source of energy is also important. This was highlighted in the case of roses produced using thermal energy in Kenya but energy generated from fossil fuels in the Netherlands.[8]

3.4 Carbon accounting is complex and costly

The data requirements for detailed carbon accounting can be daunting. In the extreme, it would be necessary to measure the carbon emissions at every point along every production chain. Clearly this is impossible, and schemes have to deal with the issue of how practically to collect relevant information.

However, over-simplification and generalisation also carry problems, and schemes must be comprehensive enough to represent real supply chains and also enable identification opportunities for emission savings along a supply chain, including those involving LICs. This issue is further complicated, as low-cost approaches to obtaining data and certification are needed to ensure that small players can afford to participate. So far a mere handful of products have been labelled, and it is in the step towards general application that this issue will have to be addressed. It is worthwhile noting that the process of carbon accounting is common to all climate-change instruments that work around products. So, regardless of the nature of any final set of instruments, labels, taxes or standards, the issues associated with collecting accurate data at the right scale and at an affordable cost will be common.

4 Emerging carbon-labelling initiatives

This section takes a closer look at existing schemes of carbon labelling, discusses attempts to standardise and simplify measurement methodologies and highlights some

7. See the studies of protected lettuce and strawberries presented in Lillywhite et al. (2007).
8. Whilst such energy does not lead to global warming potential, it is likely that a label signifying that a product had been produced with energy from nuclear sources would influence the purchasing decisions of some consumers (cf. the example of Eurostar which is driven in England largely by nuclear energy).

emerging innovative solutions to data collection and certification. There is clearly a need for additional scientific studies to shed light on the nature of emissions along typical production chains and discuss representative values for particular regions and types of producer. 2007 became a boom year for discussions of carbon labelling, with a number of new initiatives emerging, often backed by large commercial players, and, in the case of the UK and France, by the government. Most approaches have been based on the development of voluntary standards. The following identifies their key characteristics.

4.1 Carbon labelling has great momentum

The combination of a strong private-sector push and public support has propelled carbon-labelling initiatives forward in the UK. For example, the supermarket Tesco announced plans in January 2007 to carbon-label all products (estimated at 70,000 items).[9] A trial of about 20 products has been available in Tesco stores since April 2008. The stated objective is to allow consumers to integrate carbon emissions into their purchasing decisions by providing information in the same easily accessible way as for nutritional value or price. So far no more than a handful of products have been carbon-labelled, although an interim system puts a small airplane symbol on air-freighted products, under the assumption that airfreight is a major source of the carbon emissions in a product's lifecycle. The airplane symbols have also been used by Marks and Spencer and the Swiss supermarket Coop.

The French supermarket Casino has developed its own labelling scheme addressing issues of climate change and waste management; the former is mainly an application of the food miles concept rather than proper carbon accounting. Casino's own-brand food products will be marked with both a traffic-light system indicating environmental friendliness as well as a specific number giving the amount of carbon dioxide emitted during the transport stage of the product's life cycle. The French government is reported to have asked all French retailers to look into a system similar to Casino's (Casino et al., 2007; Ministère de l'Ecologie, du Développement et de l'Aménagement durables and FCD, 2008; Market New Zealand, 2008).

The Carbon Trust, a private company in statute set up by the UK government in response to the climate-change threat, has developed a pilot methodology to measure the carbon footprint of products as well as a label to display the information on individual products (Carbon Trust, 2007). Walker's cheese and onion crisps was the first product to be carbon-labelled in July 2007. The Trust is now working with the British Standards Institution and DEFRA to produce a standardised methodology to measure embodied carbon footprints using as a base the Trust's own pilot methodology.

9. The definition of what would actually be an 'item' is unclear. It is likely that 70,000 is an underestimate. Fresh produce like lettuce or apples, for instance, varies significantly in carbon footprint according to season, as do many other products, including manufactures. Electricity may be provided by hydropower in the rainy season in tropical countries, for instance, while relying on fossil fuels in the dry season. Two manufactured products may therefore have different footprints depending on the timing of production, despite being undistinguishable in appearance. This raises the issue of the time period over which emissions should be measured and whether emission information should be consignment-specific or averaged over a number of batches.

The initiative runs under the name of PAS 2050 (BSI, 2008). A PAS, or Publicly Available Specification, is a type of fast-track standard that should not be mistaken for a true British Standard, though it may serve as the basis for a future, more authoritative, British Standard. The methodology is currently being tested on approximately 75 product ranges from 20 different companies.[10]

The Soil Association, the major organic standard-setter in the UK, suggested excluding air-freighted products from organic certification on the assumption that air-freighted goods are major emitters of carbon relative to goods transported by other means. This led to a strong reaction from development agencies and from the Kenyan horticultural industry, a major source of off-season fresh vegetables and cut flowers.[11] The Soil Association subsequently decided to 'ensure that organic food is only air freighted to the UK if it delivers genuine benefits for farmers in developing countries' (Press release, 27 October 2007). From January 2009 air-freighted organic food will have to meet the Soil Association's own Ethical Trade standards or the Fairtrade Foundation's standards, and licensees will be required to develop plans for reducing any remaining dependence on air freight (Soil Association, 2008).

The UK debate has to a large extent focused on food, probably due to the fact that the idea of 'Food Miles' was born in the UK, and presumably because the low degree of processing of many foods makes calculating embodied carbon emissions relatively tractable. The development of carbon labelling is, however, far from restricted to the UK. A number of major US retailers and brand-name manufacturers are also in the process of developing their own schemes (for more details of the range of initiatives see Appendix 2).

Most often activities to analyse and label the carbon emissions of products take place within the larger context of a declared company goal to reduce carbon footprint and are often coupled with carbon offsetting schemes that companies are using to proclaim an ultimate goal of carbon neutrality. The methodologies used for measurement as well as the degree to which third-party verification is applied are often unclear. Some initiatives have also been taken in continental Europe. The Swedish organic standard-setter, KRAV, is in the process of developing a carbon-labelling scheme for food (organic as well as conventionally produced). Similar initiatives are being developed by Swiss standard-setters specifically for organic food (Gibbon and Bolwig, 2007).

Many of the recent initiatives emphasise the public relations element and downplay the practical problems of implementing these schemes. The motivation is to give a company a green profile and to target environmentally sensitive market segments. Broader issues of methodological rigour and how to develop cost-effective solutions on a scale greater than the individual company are naturally not addressed by those who are concentrating on the interests of their own shareholders. As such, the

10. The Carbon Trust recently announced its plan to open an office in Beijing to assist the Chinese business sector in reducing its carbon footprint.

11. An International Trade Centre-commissioned study found that 50-60 producer-exporters worldwide would be affected by a ban and that at least 21,500 livelihoods in developing countries would be compromised. Furthermore, the environmental impacts themselves may be ambiguous as organic growers would be tempted to convert to conventional products in order to keep growing for export markets (Gibbon and Bolvig, 2007).

approaches have been developed with little co-ordination and a lack of transparency. The attempts to define common standards in PAS 2050 and by KRAV indicate a concern amongst stakeholders that too many standards may provide few benefits as they will confuse users such as consumers with conflicting messages. There is a real danger of fragmentation. Governments may start to take more interest as the use of carbon labelling expands and the scope for abuse of labels becomes greater.[12]

Measurement and display standards are likely to become more established as business and standard-setters respond. However, as soon as a standard is established it becomes much more difficult to influence its design; hence the immediate need to ensure that the process of developing these standards is open and transparent and reflects the interests of all stakeholders large and small. We discuss the issue of the participation of low-income countries in carbon-labelling schemes in the next section, which concentrates not only on the challenges of developing effective and comprehensive carbon-labelling schemes but also on cost-effective methods of collecting and certifying the necessary information.

5 Development issues in carbon labelling

The state of the art of carbon labelling is that a number of schemes are emerging in an unco-ordinated fashion. These schemes are based partly on political and commercial desires to act on climate change and partly on scientific knowledge about emission patterns. It is fair to say that they are still far from being broadly applicable. Currently, they will be costly to implement and science has not yet produced the data upon which widely applicable schemes can be built. However, the situation is likely to change rapidly over the next few years.

We do not have sufficient knowledge to make strong predictions on how exactly low-income countries will be affected by carbon labelling. In standard-setting, the devil is typically found in the detail. But it is possible to identify key issues and to suggest appropriate responses that will push carbon labelling in a development-friendly direction. Naturally, carbon labelling is by design an environmental instrument. The development angle to this is to ensure that carbon-labelling schemes include the capacities of LICs in mitigating climate change as well as the reality regarding the ability of firms and farms in poor countries to measure and certify their carbon emissions.

5.1 Measurement methodology

There are four key elements of the approach to determining the carbon footprint of a product or service, and all can have a critical impact in determining the quality and

12. The European Parliament, for example, passed a resolution in 2007 calling for 'the introduction of WTO compatible common standards and labelling schemes regarding the GHG implications of different products, including at the production and transport stages'; 'a procedure to assess and label these ecological footprints and to develop software in order to enable businesses to calculate the quantity of GHG emitted from every production process'; and 'the development of a scheme based on sound life-cycle data which includes finished goods, such as cars and electronic equipment' (European Parliament, non-legislative resolution T6-0576/2007).

reliability of the study: the use of primary versus secondary data, the use of emission factors, the treatment of land-use change and setting the system boundary.

In general, it is preferable to use *primary data* (process-specific data collected from part or all of the supply chain) rather than *secondary data* (data obtained from sources other than direct measurement of the supply chain being investigated). The Carbon Trust pilot methodology and the draft PAS 2050 both recommend the use of primary data to the extent possible.[13] However, the collection of primary data can be expensive and time-consuming, particularly for supply chains that cross international boundaries. Very few studies have collected primary data from low-income countries. For this reason, many companies prefer a more standardised approach in which secondary data from well recognised sources are used in conjunction with standard databases of emission factors to estimate the carbon footprints of particular supply chains. Such an approach will be relatively resource-efficient and easy to implement, and will tend to encourage the use of similar methodologies across different supply chains.

However, the available studies question the reliability of using secondary data and the representativeness of data obtained from specific or a limited number of suppliers. For example, using secondary data from producers in rich countries to estimate the carbon emissions of producers in LICs will not capture the fact that the technologies being applied in rich countries are unavailable or unsuitable. Even within countries, information from one farm or production unit may not reflect practices from others. Any method which assumes standard emissions will fail to capture this variation. While this may not be important to firms such as retailers, it is important to both individual producers, such as farmers, and consumers.

Rewarding the carbon-efficient producer serves simultaneously to encourage innovation and to bring about reduced atmospheric pollution. The development of a carbon label is potentially an excellent way of communicating the relative efficiencies of different supply chains and production units to the consumer. However, to achieve this would require calculating the carbon footprint of each individual producer. Further, consumers could only really respond to carbon labels in this way for relatively unprocessed goods such as fruit, vegetables, primary cuts of meat and some dairy produce (such as liquid milk). Here the carbon label would be able to reflect the management practices on individual farms or plants. However, for goods which utilise produce from more than one farm or production unit this becomes much more difficult to present.

Another critical issue concerns the choice of baseline year(s) for data collection; this will tend to have an impact on the outcome, particularly if the year was not typical of long-term conditions. Consider, for example, the variation in both inputs to crops between years (more fungicides on wheat in wet years) and also crop yields due to annual variation in weather.

13. The Carbon Trust methodology 'allows for use of secondary data (i.e. from secondary sources) where collection of primary data (i.e. actual data collected from supply chain) is not feasible' (Carbon Trust, 2007: 7) The draft PAS 2050 states that '[p]rimary data sources are preferable to secondary data sources as the data will reflect the specific nature/efficiency of the process, and the GHG emissions associated with the process' (BSI, 2008: 4).

The amounts of carbon emitted during particular parts of the manufacture and/or use of products are termed *emission factors*. These are usually expressed in terms of kg of CO_2-equivalents. If the emission factors for the manufacture, transport and use of a certain amount of product are known, and the amount of that product in a given process is also known, then the total carbon emission arising from the use of that product in that process can be estimated, by the simple multiplication of the amount of product used by the relevant emission factors. If this process is repeated for all products relevant to that process, then the total carbon emissions for the entire process can be calculated. However, some emission factors are location-specific. For example, a country generating a large proportion of its electricity from renewable sources should have a significantly smaller emission factor for electricity than one dependent on power-generation technologies which emit large amounts of GHGs, such as coal-powered generation. These differences can then have knock-on effects on the carbon footprint of products. So nitrogen fertiliser generated in an economy largely dependent on renewable energy should have a lower emission factor than the same fertiliser produced in a more coal-dependent country. This level of detail currently remains relatively underdeveloped in carbon footprinting methodology.

Further complications arise from a consideration of soils. All growing plants sequester atmospheric CO_2 in photosynthesis and when they die the carbon within them enters the soil as soil organic carbon. As a result of this ongoing process soils have come to represent a major stock of carbon. This store is not necessarily permanent, and through bacterial and chemical activity soils can also be emitters of GHGs (typically nitrous oxide and carbon dioxide, but also methane in some locations, such as paddy rice). Given the difficulties in measuring these fluxes accurately in the field, the IPCC undertook a meta-analysis[14] of all the available experimental data to produce standard emission factors from soils (Bouwman and Taylor, 1996). This emission-factor approach is based on a limited number of data points and is applied worldwide for agricultural soils, regardless of variations in soil characteristics, land management or climate (Roelandt et al., 2005). This is obviously a crude approach that can have little relevance to local conditions (Smith et al., 2002).

The difficulties associated with emissions from soil are evident when considering issues of *land-use change*. For example, changing from forest to grassland or grassland to crop land can result in the release of large amounts of GHGs from the soil. Here the issue is not only how to measure the emissions; a decision also has to be made on how many years this 'one-off' increase in emissions should be spread over.

Currently gaseous emissions from soil are difficult to incorporate in LCAs, and the absence of up-to-date and locally specific emission factors introduces a degree of uncertainty into the magnitude of the estimated carbon emissions for a product or process. Hence, when standardised emission factors are used it would be appropriate to present the variation in published emission factors to derive upper and lower bounds for any carbon footprint. But this further complicates the task of presenting information to consumers in a clear and simple way.

14. Meta-analysis provides a means of assessing and combining empirical results from different studies. The approach takes as individual observations the point estimates of relevant parameters from different studies, which are then used to derive an overall estimate of the relevant variable.

The *system boundary* defines the extent of processes that are included in the assessment of GHG emissions, and estimates of the carbon footprint of a system will depend on where the system boundary is drawn. In the absence of an agreed framework for calculating a carbon footprint, there is the potential to draw the boundary in different ways.[15] For example, when considering agricultural activities the system boundary should include emissions arising from the manufacture and distribution of farm inputs, and the transport of these inputs to the farm, as well as any impacts related to their direct use on-farm (such as emissions related to the use of fertiliser). However, the boundary could be extended to include emissions from soils related to fertiliser use and manure management and further to consider the flow of GHGs into and out of soils and plants in the productive and non-productive areas of the farm, such as woodlands.

Decisions have to be made on whether to include, *inter alia*, manufacture of capital goods, such as tractors, buildings, and transport equipment, routine maintenance of machinery, transport of employees, transport of consumers to retail stores and transport of the produce to consumers' homes. Such decisions will have important implications for the outcomes of carbon footprinting. For example, the methodology proposed by the Carbon Trust excludes emissions from the production of capital equipment; this will tend to favour capital-intensive techniques over labour-intensive processes and hence will be to the disadvantage of LICs. The same methodology also excludes emissions from worker transportation. LIC workers generally walk or take public transport to work, while richer countries' workers commute in cars.

5.2 LICs' carbon efficiencies

The choice of data sources, emission factors and system boundaries will influence LIC trade, but at the current state of knowledge it is not possible to foresee the direction of this influence. We simply do not know enough about the carbon efficiency of LIC production systems. We have much better knowledge about the transportation segment and, although air freight will often be a critical element, transportation in general does not look like a big problem.

The issue of the location of processing activities and how this affects the overall carbon footprint of a product may arise. In the case of the consumption of chicken in Sweden reviewed in Section 3 above, it may be more efficient from a carbon perspective to process the chicken close to the origin of the feed and then ship to the final consumer rather than ship the feed and process the chicken closer to the consumer. Traditionally, the location of the point of processing in agro-food supply chains has been based on a range of criteria, one of which being energy costs. With climate-change considerations on the rise, energy use will become more costly and the location of processing might change to low-income countries in some instances. Local processing will save on transport-related emissions, as the final product will contain much less

15. One has to be aware that the discussion of system boundaries is only relevant for process-based lifecycle and hybrid analyses. Input-output-based lifecycle analysis avoids this problem as it relies on a complete description of the whole economic system (Minx et al., 2007; Hendrickson et al., 1998; Leontief and Ford, 1970).

waste. For example, in the case of meats, only a fraction of the feed is converted into meat.

Relocation of processing to LICs is more likely when fewer carbon-emitting sources of energy are utilised to process the product. The evidence of Fogelberg and Carlsson-Kanyama (2006) further calls into question the 'buy local' campaign's claims that local sourcing is carbon-efficient. In today's globalised world, so-called local products rely on transported intermediary inputs, for instance, oil. There is no reason to expect, *a priori*, that the carbon emissions of local production plus transport of inputs are lower than foreign production plus transport of the end product. The final outcome of carbon accounting for processed products including agri-foods is likely to be supply-chain-specific.

The information we currently have on the domestic segment of the supply chain is piecemeal. However, it may be useful to speculate on its potential implications. The agricultural capacities and technologies of LICs are likely to give rise to new opportunities for exports to rich countries if carbon emission considerations and effective labelling schemes render the use of carbon-intensive inputs such as agro-chemicals and fertiliser by producers in rich countries a constraint upon competitiveness, compounded by dependence on fossil fuels.

Fertilisers tend to be used much less intensively in countries with lower incomes. Similarly, production is less mechanised, with much smaller use of tractors and other equipment using fossil fuels. In low-wage countries production is typically labour-intensive, and energy-using capital equipment, which also embodies energy expended in its production, is used much less intensively than in higher-wage countries. Livestock rather than machines are often used for a number of agricultural tasks.

5.3 LIC representation

The strong desire to act on carbon labelling has been running ahead of consideration of the methodological difficulties of measurement and the problems of effective communication through labelling. A growing number of standards are being developed with little effort to co-ordinate and generally little or no voice given to small stakeholders and to LIC concerns, with large players dominating discussions. The technical capacity and the resources needed to participate in standard development are considerable and may be the main cause of the lack of involvement so far.[16]

The development of appropriate standards for environmental and social purposes is difficult, due to the many opposing interests involved. The Code of Good Practice developed by the ISEAL Alliance has become the 'gold standard' for how such

16. The Kenyan fresh produce and flower industry has participated in the discussion in the UK on carbon and organic labelling. The National Taskforce on Horticulture of Kenya made a formal submission to the Soil Association pointing to the industry's renewable energy use and the importance of export horticulture for the country. The industry also commissioned the lifecycle analysis of Kenyan and Dutch flowers discussed earlier. It has also created its own campaign entitled 'Grown under the sun' that seeks to inform the consumer about the Kenyan industry and the role it plays in climate change and in poverty eradication efforts in the country. However, the Kenyan example is the exception, and most carbon-labelling initiatives are currently being developed with little input from LICs.

standards should be set.[17] To develop an effective standard, in terms of meeting the objective set and of achieving the acceptance of the companies and consumers supposed to use the standard, requires a healthy mix of stakeholder consultation and use of good science. Most carbon-labelling standards are currently being developed in a way far from ISEAL-type requirements. Some are being developed in an open structured manner, notably the publicly or semi-publicly developed standards such as the Carbon Trust pilot methodology, BSI's PAS 2050, the standards of the Soil Association and KRAV. On the other hand, many emerging standards are private requirements where most of the details about their development are unavailable.

5.4 Impact assessment and emerging solutions

Another issue of concern is the lack of impact assessment of the evolving standards. The costs of compliance remain unknown and therefore there are no efforts to identify ways in which these may be lowered by adopting appropriate strategies of compliance or by modifying the standards themselves. The debate surrounding the potential exclusion of air-freighted products from the organic certification of the Soil Association is the only example of an attempt to consider the consequences of implementing carbon-labelling standards. The debate remains locked at a technical level centred on setting the standards that on paper would yield an impact of carbon emissions, but it fails to consider how they would function in the real world of implementation and compliance costs. It is important to emphasise that cost-effective standards are not just a purely economic consideration but will in the end determine their environmental effectiveness in mitigating climate change, since cost considerations will be a key driver behind their adoption by market players.

So, it is clear that carbon labelling involves complex technical issues and faces a number of challenges if it is to be a useful tool for reducing carbon emissions in a way that does not exclude small players. There is a need to support an emerging body of independent scientific evidence to ensure that standards are soundly based, whilst allowing for all stakeholders to participate effectively in the standard-setting process. A number of recent initiatives dealing with environmental and sustainability issues have addressed some of the critical issues that face carbon labelling, in terms of design and process. These can provide important insights for the development and practical implementation of carbon-labelling schemes.

17. The ISEAL Alliance is an open membership association for international social and environmental standard-setting and conformity-assessment organisations that seek to meet objective criteria for credible operating practices. Its Code of Good Practice stipulates, among other things, that standards be developed according to documented procedures including published work programmes, with enquiry points to which comments may be submitted, and with well published periods for commenting and a procedure for taking account of comments submitted. Furthermore, the standard-setting process must strive for consensus among a balance of interested parties, and standards must be published and subject to periodical review. The aim of following such codes of good practice is to ensure that a final standard meets the intended objective and will be acceptable to its targeted end users among companies and consumers rather than ending up as a tailor-made instrument for the use of vested interests. The Carbon Trust has begun a collaboration with the ISEAL Alliance.

While most activity on carbon labelling has been undertaken in the context of voluntary standards, the EC Commission has recently proposed a new regulation that includes mandatory requirements for measuring the carbon footprints of biofuels (Commission of the European Communities, 2008). Biofuels have been subject to controversy as claims have been made that biofuels grown under certain conditions may actually lead to more carbon emissions than they save.

The EC Commission has designed a scheme to ensure that the use of biofuels does have climate-change benefits. By 2020, it proposes that 20% of overall energy consumption should come from renewable energy, while 10% of fuels used for transport should come from biofuels. Biofuels used for compliance with the regulatory requirements (and that are entitled to benefit from national support systems) will be required to fulfil criteria for environmental sustainability, namely: (i) they must lead to at least 35% carbon savings; (ii) they must not be produced on land with high carbon stock; and (iii) they must not be produced on land with high biodiversity value. The last two requirements have been introduced to address concerns about emissions from changed land-use patterns and fears that relying on biofuels may harm other social objectives, notably biodiversity.

The EU scheme bears many resemblances to carbon-labelling schemes, although its nature is quite different since compliance is mandatory. It has already defined a methodology to measure the carbon footprint of biofuels as well as a way to use the measurements, including attempts to keep down the administrative costs. The proposed legal text allows for the use of default values laid down for common biofuel production pathways on the basis of typical values derived from independent scientific analysis.[18] These default values vary by region. Producers of biofuels are entitled to claim the level of carbon savings established by these default values. However, if a producer feels that they are more efficient than implied by the relevant default value, they may use actual values if they use the LCA method defined in the regulation.

A number of other approaches to environmental issues provide examples of how developing countries can be effectively included. For example, the Roundtable of Sustainable Palm Oil, which has sought to deal with the issue of land-use changes although carbon emissions are not covered, has considerable developing-country participation and is addressing the concerns of small developing-country producers, for example, through the establishment of a smallholder task force.

6 Conclusions

There is clearly a momentum behind the idea of carbon labelling from consumers, producers and increasingly policy-makers. What is uncertain is precisely where it will lead. What is apparent is that simple, cost-effective methodologies for measuring carbon emissions will be required for carbon labelling to be broadly applied. But carbon-

18. The proposed directive does incorporate results for pathways of relevance to developing countries: sugar cane and palm oil. With regard to the potential carbon efficiencies of developing countries, it is interesting to note that sugar cane ethanol is identified as the best-performing technology in terms of carbon reductions. This supports the notion that a comprehensive approach to LCA in carbon labelling schemes is likely to identify developing countries as a low emissions source of agricultural products.

labelling schemes must also be designed so as to capture the complexity of carbon emissions and the many opportunities for reducing emissions that exist along international supply chains. Emissions from transport can be more than offset by efficiencies in other stages of production and distribution. Hence, intuitively appealing concepts such as food miles and buy-local campaigns cannot address the complexity of carbon emissions, will distort trade and may even increase emissions. Geographical location alone is a poor proxy for overall emissions; favourable production conditions may more than offset a disadvantage in transport. Hence, these concepts have nothing to offer in terms of climate-change mitigation.

Given their favourable climate and the use of technologies that are typically less carbon-intensive than elsewhere, the interests of low-income countries must be properly reflected in the design and implementation of carbon-labelling schemes. However, the potential for LICs to exploit the relative emission efficiencies that they possess depends on their ability to measure and verify emissions in a cost-effective way.

The development community can play a positive role on three fronts. First, with regard to knowledge, through support for the expansion of the scientific base and dialogue upon which the standards are being built. Second, on the advocacy front, it needs to ensure that the interests of LICs are properly represented in the debate and design of carbon-labelling standards. Finally, on the operational front, it should assess the capacity of LICs to participate in carbon-labelled trade and help ensure that new opportunities for exports are exploited. Effective participation in carbon-labelled trade will require the infrastructure and institutions that provide the necessary measurement and certification mechanisms that are often lacking in low-income countries.

first submitted August 2008
final revision accepted January 2009

References

Barrett, J.; Vallack, H.; Jones, A. and Haq, G. (2002) *A Material Flow Analysis and Ecological Footprint of York - Technical Report*. York: Stockholm Environment Institute.

Blanke, M. M. and Burdick, B. (2005) 'Food (Miles) for Thought: Energy Balance for Locally-grown Versus Imported Apples Fruit', *Environmental Science and Pollution Research* 12: 125-7.

Bouwman, A. F. and Taylor, J. A. (1996) 'Testing High-resolution Nitrous Oxide Emission Estimates Against Observation Using an Atmospheric Transport Model', *Global Biogeochemical Cycles* 10: 307-18.

BSI (2008) 'PAS 2050 – Specification for the Measurement of the Embodied Greenhouse Gas Emissions in Products and Services'. Working Draft. London: British Standards Institute.

Carbon Trust (2007) 'Carbon Footprint Measurement Methodology'. Version 1.3, 15 March 2007. Carbon Trust.

Casino, Bio IS and ADEME (2007) 'Un nouvel étiquetage des produits de grande consommation'. Paris: Casino, Bio Intelligence Service and Agence de l'Environnement et de la Maîtrise de l'Energie.

Commission of the European Communities (2008) 'Proposal for a Directive of the European Parliament and of the Council on the Promotion of the Use of Energy from Renewable Sources'. COM(2008) 19 FINAL, 2008/0016(COD). Brussels.

Deere, C. (1999) *Eco-labelling and Sustainable Fisheries*. Working Paper. Rome: FAO.

DEFRA (2005) *The Validity of Food Miles as an Indicator of Sustainable Development*. London: Department for Environment, Food and Rural Affairs.

Dolan, C. and Humphrey, J. (2000) 'Governance and Trade in Fresh Vegetables: The Impact of UK Supermarkets on the African Horticulture Industry', *Journal of Development Studies* 37 (2): 147-76.

Edwards-Jones, G.; Milà i Canals, L.; Hounsome, N.; Truninger, M.; Koerber, G.; Hounsome, B.; Cross, P. A.; York, E. H.; Hospida, A.; Plassmann, K.; Harris, I. M.; Edwards, R. T.; Day, G. A. S.; Tomos, A. D.; Cowell, S. J. and Jones, D. L. (2008) 'Testing the Assertion that "Local Food is Best": The Challenges of an Evidence Based Approach', *Trends in Food Science and Technology* 19: 265-74.

Edwards-Jones, G.; Plassmann, K.; York, E. H.; Hounsome, B.; Jones, D. L. and Milà i Canals, L. (2009) 'Vulnerability of Exporting Nations to the Development of a Carbon Label in the United Kingdom', *Environmental Science and Policy* (in press).

Fogelberg, C. L. and Carlsson-Kanyama, A. (2006) 'Environmental Assessment of Foods: An LCA Inspired Approach' in C. Fuentes and A. Carlsson-Kanyama (eds), *Environmental Information in the Food Supply System*. Stockholm: FOI, Swedish Defence Research Agency.

Gibbon, P. (2003) 'Value-chain Governance, Public Regulation and Entry Barriers in the Global Fresh Fruit and Vegetable Chain into the EU'. *Development Policy Review* 21 (5-6): 615-25.

Gibbon, P. and Bolvig, S. (2007) 'The Economic Impact of a Ban on Imports of Air Freighted Organic Products to the UK'. Consultancy report submitted to the International Trade Centre, Geneva.

Graffham, A., Karehu, E. and MacGregor, J. (2006) *Impact of EurepGAP on small-scale vegetable growers in Kenya*. Fresh Insights No. 6. Chatham: Natural Resources Institute and London: International Institute for Environment and Development and Department for International Development.

Graffham, A. and MacGregor, J. (2006) *Impact of EurepGAP on small-scale vegetable growers in Zambia*. Fresh Insights No. 4. Chatham: Natural Resources Institute and London: International Institute for Environment and Development, and Department for International Development.

Hendrickson, C. T.; Horvath, A.; Joshi, S. and Lave, L. B. (1998) 'Economic Input-output Models for Environmental Lifecycle Assessment', *Environmental Science and Technology* 32 (7): 184A-191A.

IPCC (2007) *Climate Change 2007: The Physical Science Basis*. Cambridge: Cambridge University Press.

IPCC (2001) *Climate Change 2001: The Scientific Basis*. Cambridge: Cambridge University Press.

IPCC (1995) *Climate Change 1995: The Science of Climate Change*. Cambridge: Cambridge University Press.

Jones, A. (2006) *A Life Cycle Analysis of UK Supermarket Imported Green Beans from Kenya.* Fresh Insights Paper 4. London: IIED.

Kramer, K. J., Moll, H. C. and Nonhebel, S. (1999) 'Greenhouse Gas Emissions Related to Dutch Food Consumption', *Energy Policy* 27 (4): 203-16.

Leontief, W. and Ford, D. (1970) 'Environmental Repercussions and the Economic Structure: An Input-output Approach', *Review of Economics and Statistics* 52 (3): 262-71.

Lillywhite, R.; Chandler, D.; Grant, W.; Lewis, K.; Firth, C.; Schmutz, U. and Halpin, D. (2007) 'Environmental Footprint and Sustainability of Horticulture (Including Potatoes): A Comparison with Other Agricultural Sectors'. Warwick: University of Warwick.

Market New Zealand (2008) 'French Retailers Plan to Double Eco-friendly Products within Three Years', 1 May (www.marketnewzealand.com/MNZ/news/story/14401/19033.aspx).

Milà i Canals, L.; Cowell, S. J.; Sim, S. and Basson, L. (2007a) 'Comparing Local Versus Imported Apples: A Focus on Energy Use', *Environmental Science and Pollution Research* 14: 276-82.

Milà i Canals, L.; Hospido, A.; Clift, R.; Truninger, M.; Hounsome, B. and Edwards-Jones, G. (2007b) 'Environmental Effects and Consumer Considerations of Consuming Lettuce in the UK Winter' in *LCA in Foods,* proceedings of the 5th International Conference, 25-26 April, Gothenburg, Sweden.

Ministère de l'Ecologie, du Développement et de l'Aménagement durables and FCD (2008) *Convention sur les Engagements pris par les Entreprises du Commerce et de la Distribution dans le Cadre du Grenelle de l'Environnement.* Paris: MEDA and Fédération des Entreprises du Commerce et de la Distribution.

Minx, J., Wiedmann, T.; Barrett, J. and Suh, S. (2007) 'Methods Review to Support the PAS Process for the Calculation of the Greenhouse Gas Emissions Embodied in Goods and Services'. Report to DEFRA by Stockholm Environment Institute at the University of York and the Department for Bio-based Products at the University of Minnesota.

Roelandt, C., Van Wesemael, B., and Rounsevell, M. (2005) 'Estimating Annual N_2O Emissions from Agricultural Soils in Temperate Climates', *Global Change Biology,* 11: 1701-11.

Saunders, C., Barber, A. and Taylor, G. (2006) *Food Miles: Comparative Energy/Emissions Performance of New Zealand's Agriculture Industry.* AERU Research Report No. 285. Lincoln, New Zealand: Lincoln University.

Schlich, E. H. and Fleissner, U. (2005) 'The Ecology of Scale: Assessment of Regional Energy Turnover and Comparison with Global Food', *International Journal of Life Cycle Analysis* 10 (3): 219-23.

Sim, S.; Barry, M.; Clift, R. and Cowell, S. (2007) 'The Relative Importance of Transport in Determining an Appropriate Sustainability Strategy for Food Sourcing: A Case Study of Fresh Produce Supply Chains', *International Journal of Life Cycle Assessment* 12: 422-31.

Smith, W. N.; Desjardins, R. L.; Grant, B.; Li, C.; Lemke, R.; Rochette, P.; Corre, M. D. and Pennock, D. (2002) 'Testing the DNDC Model Using N_2O Emissions at

Two Experimental Sites in Canada', *Canadian Journal of Soil Science* 82 (3): 365-74.

Soil Association (2008) *Air Freight Consultation: Recommendations for Standards.* Bristol: Soil Association.

Wallén A., Brandt, N. and Wennersten, R. (2004) 'Does the Swedish Consumer's Choice of Food Influence Greenhouse Gas Emissions?', *Environmental Science & Policy* 7: 525-35.

Wangler, Z. L. (2006) *Sub-Saharan African Horticultural Exports to the UK and Climate Change: A Literature Review.* Fresh Insights No. 2. London: IIED, funded by UK DFID.

Williams, A. (2007) 'Comparative Study of Cut Roses for the British Market Produced in Kenya and the Netherlands'. Report for World Flowers, November.

Appendix 1: Carbon terminology

Carbon	Shorthand for all greenhouse gases. Refers more directly to carbon dioxide which is the most common GHG.
Carbon emissions	Emissions of all GHGs
CO_2e	Carbon dioxide equivalent, measurement unit that translates the effect of all GHGs into carbon dioxide
Carbon footprint	Carbon emission caused by an activity
Carbon accounting	Measurement of carbon footprints
Carbon labelling	Display of the measurement of carbon footprints on a product. Also used to refer more broadly to the use of carbon accounting information
Carbon efficiency	Ability to have minimum GHG emissions
Carbon tax	Tax on emission of GHGs
Carbon hotspot	GHG-intensive activity in the supply chain
Carbon competitiveness	Ability to compete in terms of low GHG emissions
Life cycle analysis	Analysis of, in this context, GHG emissions throughout the various segments of a supply chain from primary production to end use and waste disposal. A comprehensive analysis takes into account emissions related to changes in land use.

Appendix 2: Carbon-labelling initiatives

Initiative	Aim	Context	Measurement methodology	Display methodology
Tesco (UK)	Long-term aim to carbon label all 70,000 products	Part of broader company goal to become more environmentally sustainable	Co-operate with the Carbon Trust. Preliminary use of air freight as proxy for climate change impact	Co-operate with the Carbon Trust. Preliminary label air-freighted products with airplane symbol
Casino (France)	To carbon label 3,000 of own-brand food products	Part of broader company goal to become more environmentally sustainable	Developed and BIS endorsed by French Environment and Energy Management Agency	Use a colour code denoting amount of CO_2 emitted in manufacturing, packaging and transporting product, amount of packaging to be recycled
Migros (Switzerland)	To identify best performers in product range	Company goal to reduce climate impact	LCA developed by Climatop in collaboration with Ecological Centre	Labels products with least carbon footprints as 'CO_2 champions'
Coop (Switzerland)	To reduce air-freight	Company goal to reduce climate impact	Simple indication of whether product was air-freighted	Air-freighted products labelled with airplane sticker
Carbon Trust (UK)	To promote labelling as part of general climate-change mitigation strategy	UK government goal to facilitate carbon labelling	Carbon Trust Pilot Methodology	Label products with grams of CO_2e and with downward pointing arrow indicating commitment to reduce emissions
BSI-Carbon Trust-DEFRA (UK)	Develop a potential, internationally applicable, measurement standard	UK government goal to facilitate carbon labelling	Develop fast-track standard for embodied carbon footprint measurement based on Carbon Trust pilot methodology	Not part of measurement methodology
Soil Association (UK)	Include climate change considerations in organic labelling	Desire to broaden understanding of organic agriculture to include climate-change considerations	Use air freight as proxy for climate change impact	Suggested to deny organic certification to air-freighted products
Wal-Mart (US)	To develop 'carbon scorecards' (indicators of carbon emissions of suppliers)	Drive towards ethical profile/large carbon footprint reduction goal	Own designed	No plans to display information to consumers. Presumed use of information as performance benchmark of suppliers

Patagonia (US)	To display environmental information on flagship products to the consumer	Part of company strategy to be environmentally sustainable	Own-designed simplified LCA	Display of information on individual product. Use of website to provide in-depth information
Timberland (US)	Long-term to display environmental information on all products to the consumer	Part of company strategy to be environmentally sustainable	Own-designed simplified LCA	Uses 'green index tags' on scale of 0-10
General Motors	To start a process of awareness about carbon emissions	Operates in a market where environmental awareness is on the rise	Unknown	Internal use of information, transfer of knowledge and technology
Carbon Disclosure Project	Set up Supply Chain Leadership Collaboration to create a standard to measure and manage emissions through supply chain	A not-for-profit organisation aiming to be largest repository of corporate carbon emission data in the world	Own-designed simplified LCA	Not designed for display but for supply chain management use
Reckitt Benckiser	To measure embodied carbon footprints so as to make reduction goals credible	Part of company commitment to reduce carbon emissions (embodied carbon footprint) by 20% by 2020	Own-designed simplified LCA to be measured by independent experts and verified by third parties	Not designed for display but for recording of embodied carbon emissions savings
Home Depot	To label products with sustainability information including carbon emissions	Part of company strategy to demonstrate environmental awareness	Unknown	Individual product labelling with range of sustainability indicators including carbon emission data
KRAV	To develop a label that may be used to carbon label both conventional and organic food	Joint industry and KRAV desire to avoid multiple climate labels	Defines climate-friendly production practices and labels accordingly rather than measure exact emission level	Not decided
Dell Computers	To commit suppliers to measure carbon emissions and to reduce them	Part of company strategy to demonstrate climate-change awareness	Unknown	Not for labelling individual products, but individual suppliers have to disclose emission data to the public
EU biofuel regulation	To define what constitutes a biofuel in order to facilitate compliance with forthcoming EU regulation	Introduced binding requirements for renewable energy use incl. biofuel use. Required definition of what constitutes a biofuel	Based on LCA taking complex issues like land-use changes into account	Not for display but to prove compliance with regulation

Lightning Source UK Ltd.
Milton Keynes UK
UKOW05n1034270814

237655UK00001B/1/P